Literati Modern

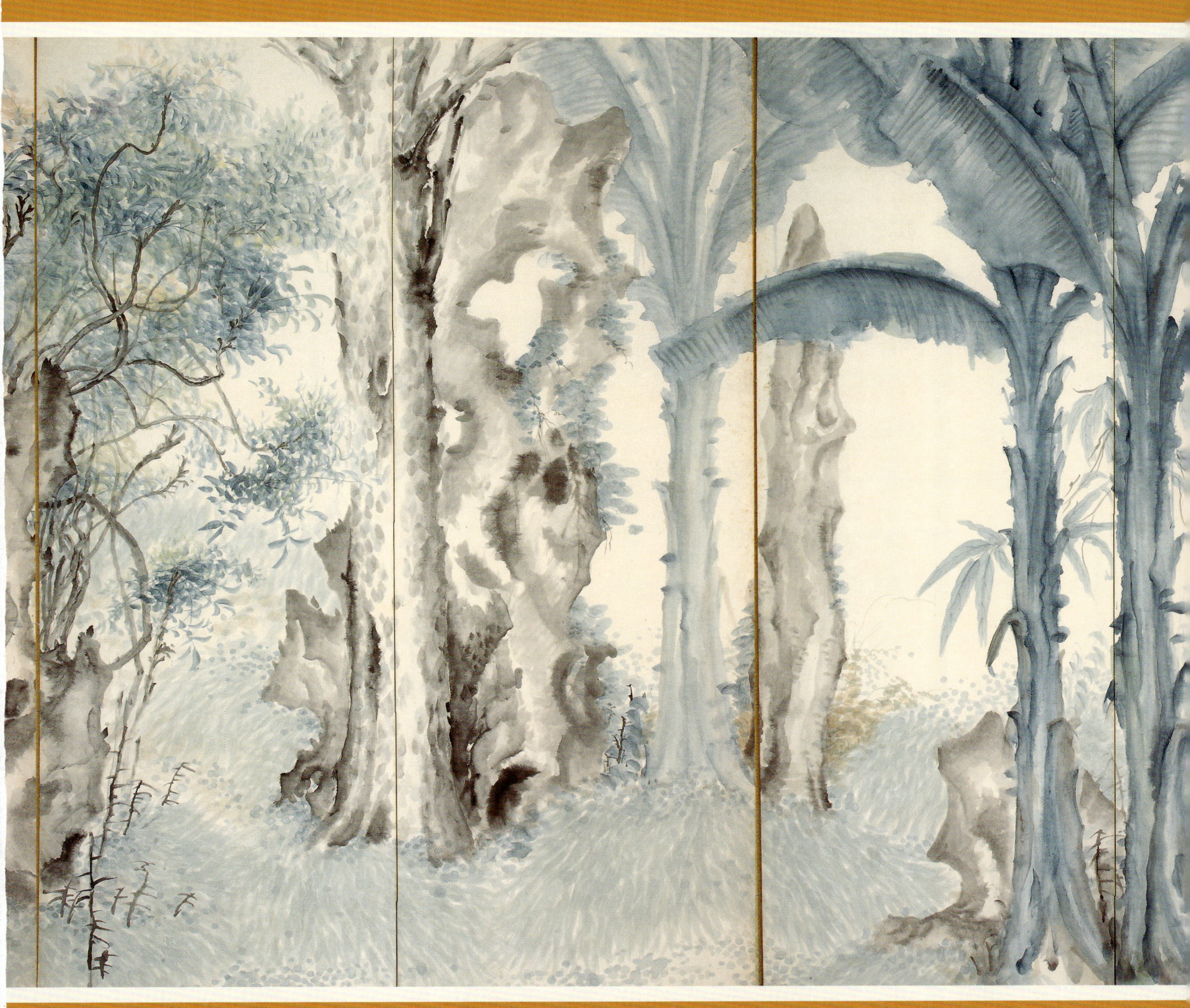

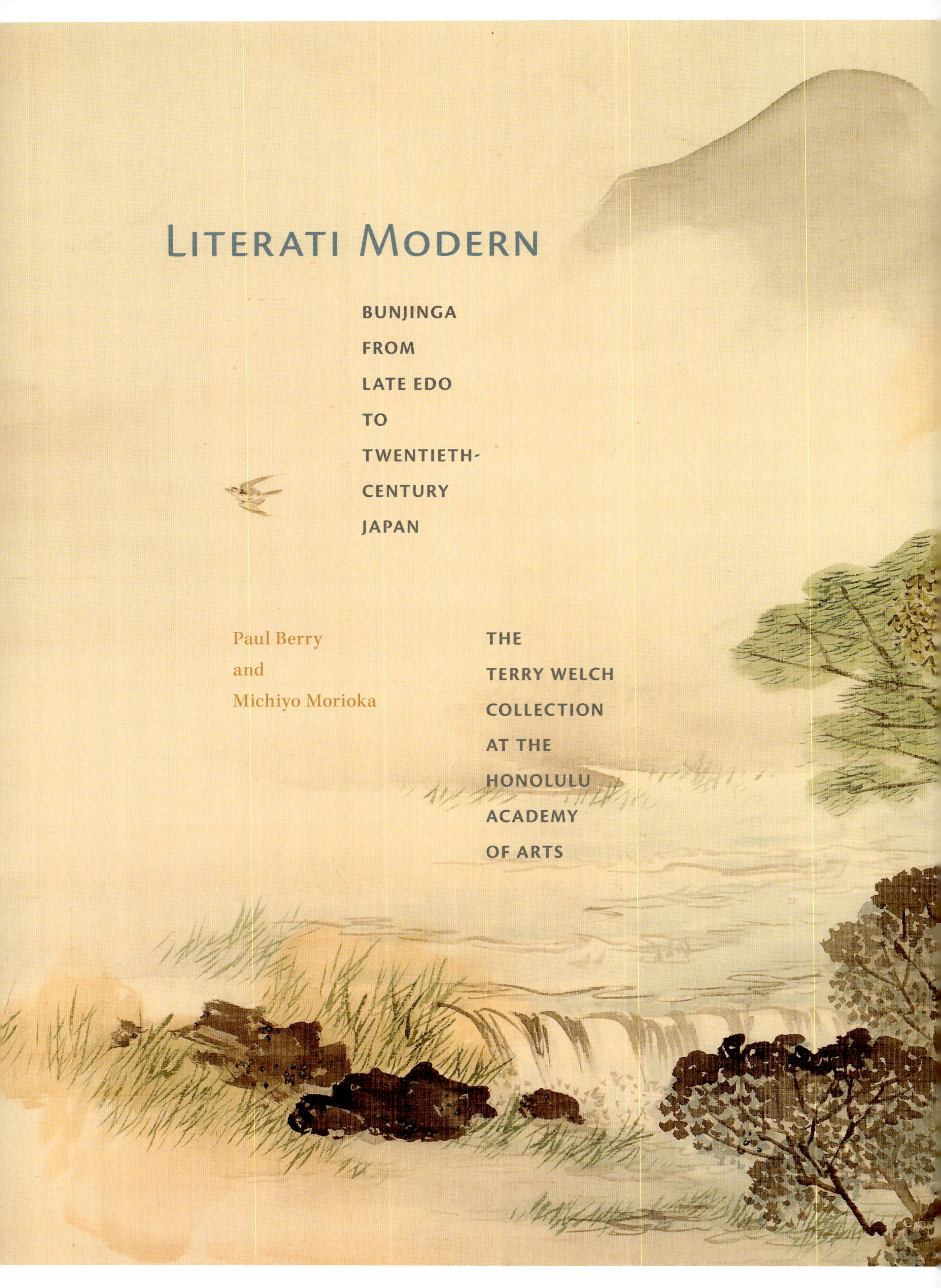

Literati Modern

Bunjinga from Late Edo to Twentieth-Century Japan

Paul Berry
and
Michiyo Morioka

The Terry Welch Collection at the Honolulu Academy of Arts

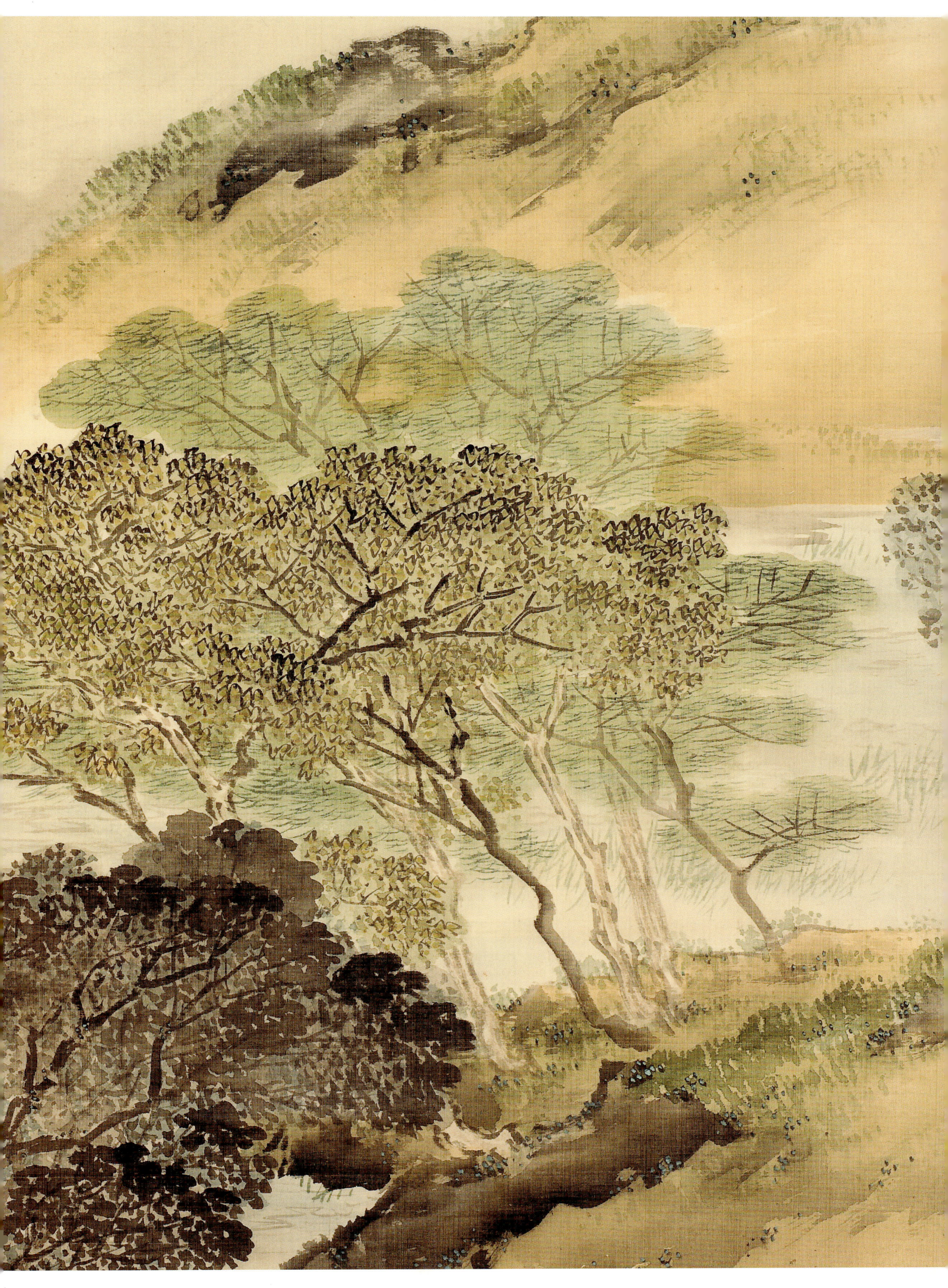

Literati Modern: Bunjinga from Late Edo to Twentieth-Century Japan
is supported in part by the Blakemore Foundation

NOTES TO THE READER

Throughout the text, Japanese names appear in the traditional manner, with family name first, followed by the given name or artist name. For individuals who reside outside Japan, names are presented in the Western manner, with the given name first.

In the painting captions, the letter "T" following the title signifies that the painting has an accompanying box (*tomobako*) inscribed by the artist. The letter "A" indicates a box with an authenticating inscription by either a member of the artist's family or a pupil, friend, or connoisseur.

Translations of Japanese texts are by the authors unless otherwise indicated. Painting titles have been transliterated where appropriate. Illegible or undeciphered characters transcribed from the paintings are represented by a box character (□).

Macrons are used to indicate long vowels in Japanese words and names, with the exception of commonly known place names (e.g., Tokyo, Kobe, Kyoto, Honshu, etc.).

The months and days prior to the 1873 conversion to the solar calendar are given according to the traditional lunar calendar. In the lunar system, the year begins roughly a month later than in the Western calendar. For artists who were active before or during the early Meiji period, birth/death dates are given based on the traditional East Asian lunar calendar.

Details

Page 1: Dōmoto Inshō 堂本印象, *Chinese Garden*, 1923 (right screen, cat. no. 75); pages 2–3: Okamoto Sukehiko 岡本亮彦 (1823–1883), *Summer Landscape with Hototogisu*. Hanging scroll: ink and color on silk, 46.4 × 88 cm. Purchase, 2005. 13196.1 (not in exhibition); page 7: Kondō Kōichiro 近藤浩一路, *Rocky Seashore*, late 1930s (cat. no. 52); page 9: Fujimoto Tesseki 藤本鐵石, leaf 8 of *Pleasures of the Literati Life*, 1856 (cat. no. 76); page 13: Takakura Kangai 高倉観崖, leaf 7 of *Album of Chinese Landscapes and Figures*, 1920 (cat. no. 82); page 29: Ogawa Sen'yō 小川千甕, *Fish-basket Kannon*, 1920s (cat. no. 83); pages 40–41: Yokoi Kinkoku 横井金谷, *Drawing Pure Spring Water to Compare Tea*, early 1800s (cat. no. 4); pages 74–75: Uragami Shunkin 浦上春琴, *Laughter on Spring Wind*, 1827 (cat. no. 24); pages 182–83: Suzuki Shōnen 鈴木松年, *Old Pine*, 1900 (cat. no. 69); pages 222–23: Suzuki Hyakunen 鈴木百年, *Spring and Autumn Landscapes*, 1866 (cat. no. 41)

This book is published in conjunction with the exhibition *Literati Modern: Bunjinga from Late Edo to Twentieth-Century Japan*, organized by the Honolulu Academy of Arts and presented at the museum from September 11 to November 16, 2008.

Published by Honolulu Academy of Arts

Distributed by University of Washington Press
PO Box 50096
Seattle, WA 98145-5096
www.washington.edu/uwpress

Library of Congress Cataloging-in-Publication Data
Berry, Paul.
Literati modern, bunjinga from late Edo to twentieth-century Japan : the Terry Welch collection at the Honolulu Academy of Arts / Paul Berry and Michiyo Morioka.
p. cm.
Published in conjunction with the exhibition held at the Honolulu Academy of Arts, Sept. 11–Nov. 16, 2008.
Includes bibliographical references and index.
ISBN 978-0-937426-84-5 (hardcover : alk. paper)
1. Painting, Japanese—19th century—Exhibitions. 2. Welch, Terry—Art collections—Exhibitions. I. Morioka, Michiyo, 1949–. II. Title.
ND1054.B47 2008
759.95209'034—dc22 2008028572

The paper used in this publication meets the minimum requirements of the American National Standard for Information Sciences—Permanence of Paper for Printed Library Materials, ANSI Z39.48-1992.

Principal photography by Tim Siegert, with cat. nos. 15, 21, and 46 by Paul Macapia. Signature and seal photography by Jeff Engelstad.
Designed by John Hubbard with assistance by Tina Kim
Edited by Suzanne Kotz
Typeset by Marie Weiler in Kepler, Cronos Pro, and Kozuka Gothic Pro
Proofread by Laura Iwasaki
Indexed by Candace Hyatt
Color management by iocolor, Seattle
Produced by Marquand Books, Inc., Seattle
www.marquand.com
Printed and bound by CS Graphics Pte., Ltd., Singapore

Contents

Foreword

To visit Terry Welch at his garden estate in rural Washington State is to be transported to a magical realm of water, trees, sky, and stone. One can feel the vital energy coursing through the surrounding hills, and it is not surprising to learn that this was a site sacred to Native Americans. Experiencing this environment helps one appreciate Terry's subtle and profound understanding of Japanese painting.

The Honolulu Academy of Arts acquired the Terry Welch Collection of Japanese paintings in 2005. Here I would like to give credit to Julia White, the Academy's former Curator of Asian Art who spearheaded this extraordinary acquisition and first introduced me to Terry Welch. I am also deeply grateful to the Academy's Board of Trustees, who unanimously supported acquisition of the collection.

Comprising more than eighty examples of eighteenth- through early twentieth-century painting, the Welch collection was formed over the span of three decades (the first work was bought in 1975). The collection includes folding screens, hanging scrolls, handscrolls, and albums. With the Academy's 1994 purchase of the Patricia Salmon Collection of Meiji (1868–1912), Taishō (1912–1926), and early Shōwa (1926–1945) figure paintings, our combined holdings may be unique among American museum collections of early twentieth-century Japanese painting. The Welch collection's greatest strengths are paintings created between 1868 and 1940, mainly the Meiji, Taishō, and early Shōwa eras.

The Edo period (1615–1868) is represented by many towering giants, especially of the *nanga* school, including Tani Bunchō, Kameda Bōsai, Yokoi Kinkoku, Nakabayashi Chikutō, Uragami Shunkin, Nukina Kaioku, Okada Hankō, Yamamoto Baiitsu, Haruki Nanmei, and Suzuki Hyakunen. Artworks of the Meiji, Taishō, and early Shōwa periods, which are now beginning to be widely appreciated in the United States, are represented by many equally eminent masters (especially *nihonga* painters), among them Shiokawa Bunrin, Suzuki Shōnen, Tanomura Chokunyū, Kōno Bairei, Kondō Kōichiro, Fukuda Kodōjin, Tsuji Kakō, Hashimoto Kansetsu, Dōmoto Inshō, Hirai Baisen, Ogawa Sen'yō, and Fusen Tetsu.

Among the finest masterpieces in the collection is one of six amazing works by Hirai Baisen, an almost photographic depiction of an imaginary place: Mount Hōrai (Ch., Penglaishan), the Daoist paradise island in the sea off China's eastern coast, rising from the mist as two cranes soar under its jagged peaks (cat. no. 57). Other astonishing works are a lush pair of six-panel screens with Chinese spirit stones and birds in a garden by Dōmoto Inshō, painted in 1923 at the height of the Taishō period (cat. no. 75), and a rare album of monochrome ink paintings with idyllic views of Micronesia, painted during World War II by Fusen Tetsu (cat. no. 60). The collection also includes several superb calligraphic works and ceramics. Among the latter is a beautifully inscribed sake cup made by the gifted Buddhist nun Ōtakagi Rengetsu (cat. no. 6).

On behalf of the Academy, I would like to express my deep gratitude to guest curator Michiyo Morioka and to Paul Berry, the catalogue coauthor. I would also like to thank Terry Welch and Uchiyama Takeo for their fine contributions. In early May 2005, Michiyo Morioka, Uchiyama Takeo, and Terry Welch visited the Honolulu Academy of Arts for a preliminary exhibition meeting and to discuss catalogue development. Subsequently, in 2006 and 2007, Michiyo and Paul made several trips to Honolulu to examine and select the final works. In addition, I would like to recognize the staff of the Asian Art Department, who oversaw the realization of this exhibition: Curator of Asian Art Dr. Shawn Eichman, Asian Art Department Manager Sati Benes, and Asian Art Collections Managers Megan Callan and Celeste Ohta.

I am also deeply grateful to the Blakemore Foundation, whose support has made this special exhibition and catalogue possible. Finally, on behalf of the Honolulu Academy of Arts, I would like to thank Terry Welch for his generosity, both in making his collection available to us for acquisition and for the many thoughtful gifts that are included as part of this acquisition.

Stephen Little, Director
Honolulu Academy of Arts

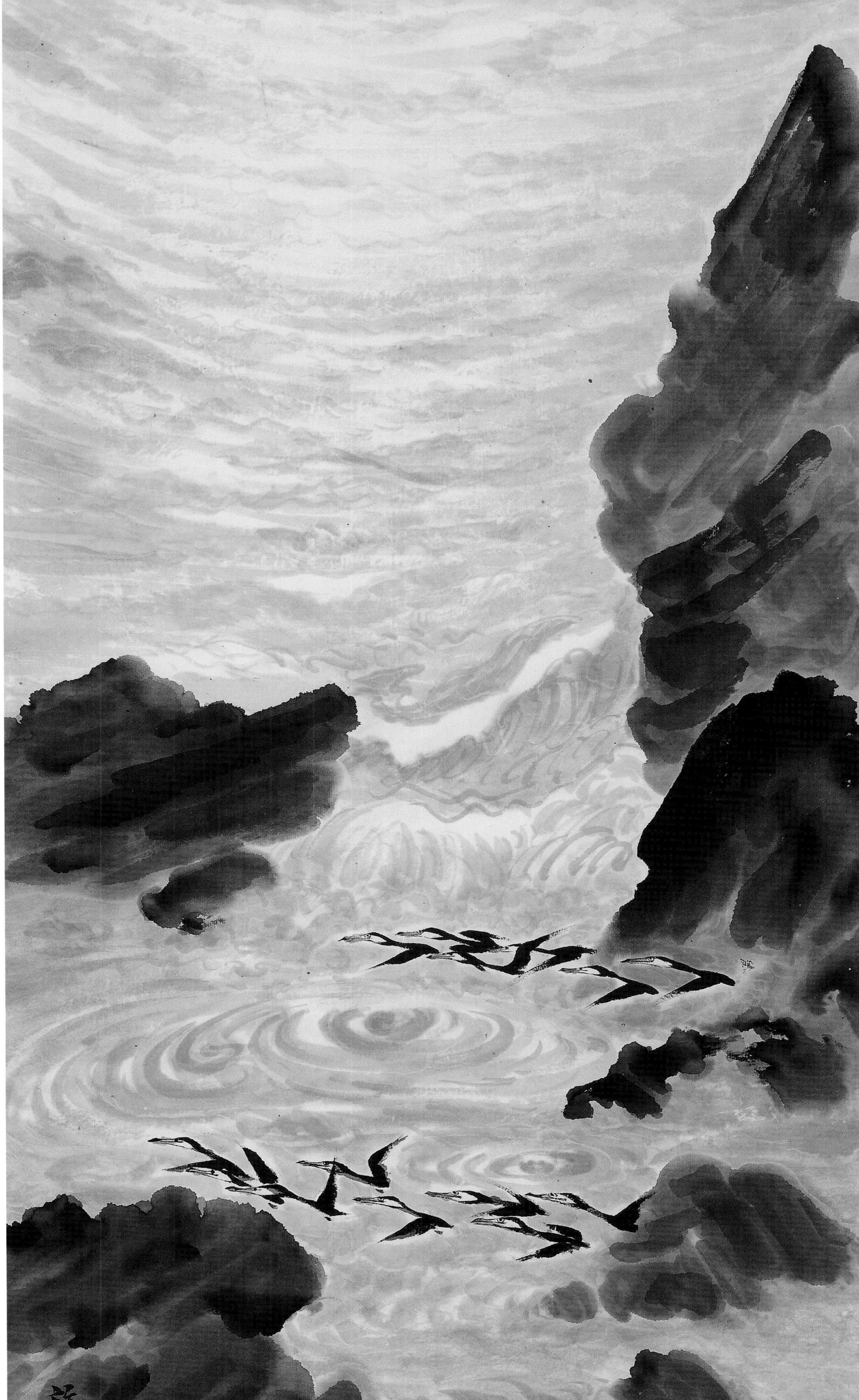

Thoughts on the Terry Welch Collection

Encompassing the late eighteenth to the early half of the twentieth century, the Terry Welch Collection consists of literati paintings as well as literati-influenced works by Maruyama- and Shijō-school artists. At the time Terry Welch began assembling the collection during the 1970s, Edo-period literati painting attracted little interest in Japan. There was, however, considerable enthusiasm for *shin nanga* 新南画, or new literati paintings of the early twentieth century. *Nanga,* a term deriving from *nanshūga* 南宗画 (Southern school painting), has been used interchangeably with the word *bunjinga* and refers to a Japanese tradition founded upon the freedom of expression and spirit associated with Chinese literati painting. In the latter half of the twentieth century, Japanese collectors sought *shin nanga* works but largely ignored nineteenth-century literati paintings. That an American collector had such an appreciative eye for late Edo-period literati painting is a surprise and a benefit to scholars and the art-loving public alike.

In late Ming China, professional painters active at the imperial court lost their creative spirit. Dong Qichang 董其昌 (1555–1636), a calligrapher-painter, criticized the imperial academic tradition, classifying it as "Northern school painting" (*hokushūga* 北宗画) while praising the literati tradition as "Southern school painting" (*nanshūga*) in emulation of the north-south division of Chan (Zen) Buddhism. Specifically, Dong admired the literati emphasis on subjective expression and the elegant aesthetics achieved through the use of free brushwork and restrained color. By the time *nanshūga* was introduced from China to Japan in the eighteenth century, the Kanō school, the official painting school of the Tokugawa government, had lost its vitality and come to rely on long-established painting models. Chinese literati ideals infused fresh creative energy into Japanese painting and gave rise to *bunjinga/nanga.* In the following century, however, *nanga* painters also began to fall into the repetition of old patterns.

During the transition from the final years of Tokugawa rule to the Meiji Restoration, drastic political and social changes dissolved the feudalistic system led by the samurai class. As a consequence, various schools of Japanese painting, including Kanō, suffered a loss of patronage. But oil painting (*yōga*) and literati painting continued to flourish. Oil painting had been studied in Japan since the late Edo period, and it found wide acceptance among the Japanese for its association with Western realism and rationality. In contrast to the traditional Japanese painting schools, literati painting gained momentum with the support of the new government leaders, formerly low-ranking samurai in the service of local fiefdoms whose educations had included basic Chinese studies. Their taste and bravado in facing the challenges of the new era affected the general public, and the popularity of literati painting spread. But the opinion of one American scholar, as described below, would cause the acceptance of literati painting to decline rapidly toward the end of the nineteenth century.

As Japanese society began to stabilize after the Meiji Restoration, traditional painting schools gradually regained their footing. The unexpected success and popularity of Japanese arts and crafts at the 1873 Vienna World Exposition led to their reemergence, and the Meiji government decided to protect and develop traditional Japanese arts within a general policy of promoting industries. To this end, in 1879 government bureaucrats and others founded the Dragon Pond Society (Ryūchikai 龍池会), one of whose aims was to reinvigorate older art forms. Painting schools began to revive with this support, but there was no move toward a new type of painting for the modern era until Ernest Fenollosa (1853–1908), an American scholar, arrived in Japan in 1878.

Fenollosa, who taught politics, economy, and philosophy at the Imperial University (now Tokyo University), became intensely interested in Japanese art. In 1882 he gave a pivotal lecture at the Dragon Pond Society in which he proclaimed the superiority of Japanese art over Western-introduced oil painting. Fenollosa defended traditional Japanese painting and criticized *bunjinga,* then at the height of its popularity. According to Fenollosa, literati painting had some merit in that it did not simply attempt to copy nature, as did oil

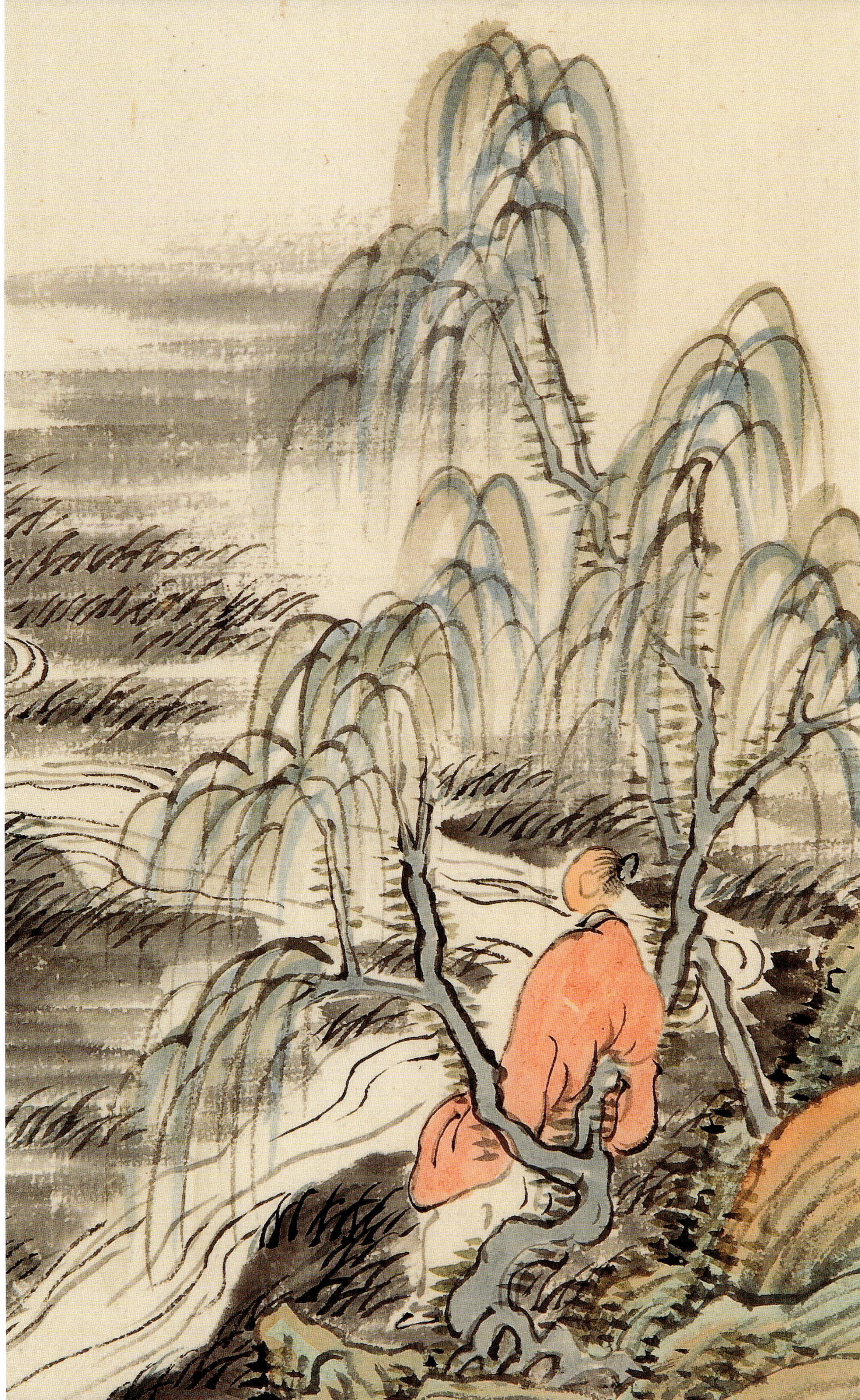

painting. He argued, however, that one could not consider *bunjinga* to be true painting because it represented ideas inspired by literary rather than pictorial values.

The effect of Fenollosa's lecture was far-reaching. The first Domestic Painting Competition (*Naikoku kaiga kyōshinkai* 内国絵画共進会), held in 1882, excluded oil painting. Furthermore, the publication of Fenollosa's speech as "The True Theory of Art" (Bijutsu shinsetsu 美術真説) during the competition encouraged artists working in various traditional styles but disheartened literati painters. By the time of the second Domestic Painting Competition in 1884, the submission of literati works decreased dramatically. Fenollosa sought to restore and revive Japanese art, using the Kanō school as its basis, and in this context his rejection of literati painting is understandable. But he went a step farther and denounced even the spirit of self-expression that was fundamental to literati painting. After Fenollosa left Japan in 1890, Okakura Tenshin 岡倉天心 (1863–1913) continued Fenollosa's goal of stimulating a new type of Japanese painting. He encouraged his students to preserve Japanese aesthetics while incorporating useful features of Western painting.

Meanwhile, *bunjinga/nanga* painters did not blindly adhere to old painting methods and formulaic brushwork. Rather than merely representing ideal landscapes of the imagination, artists began to portray actual scenes sketched from life (*shasei* 写生) and even experimented with the Western principles of perspective and three-dimensionality. With these approaches, some literati painters achieved success at the 1907 Bunten 文展, the first national exhibition sponsored by the government. But the large-scale paintings required by modern exhibition halls and the social recognition acquired through exhibitions directly contradicted the core literati concepts of self-expression and detachment from worldly activity. Clearly, the literati painting tradition was at a crossroads.

Shin nanga appeared after 1910 in Japan, around the time when Japanese painters and sculptors returning from Europe introduced new artistic trends. Convinced of an affinity between impressionism or postimpressionism and literati painting, Japanese artists began incorporating literati-inspired compositions and brush modes in their works.

In Tokyo, Imamura Shikō 今村紫紅 (1880–1916), his colleague Hayami Gyoshū 速水御舟 (1894–1935), who was influenced by Shikō, and Hirafuku Hyakusui 平福百穂 (1877–1933), originally a Maruyama-Shijō artist, began working in a *nanga*-influenced style in the mid-1910s. Oil painters such as Morita Tsunetomo 森田恒友 (1881–1933) and Yorozu Tetsugorō 萬鉄五郎 (1885–1927) also recognized the commonality between the Western expressionistic style and the literati principle of self-expression. Particularly noteworthy is the fact that the Japan Art Institute (Nihon Bijutsuin 日本美術院), which had initially rejected literati painting, began to accept it after the institute was revived in 1914. The restored institute recognized the significant role of literati painting in artists' efforts to create a modern Japanese style and welcomed as its members such contemporary literati painters as Tomita Keisen 冨田溪仙 (1879–1936) and Ogawa Usen 小川芋銭 (1868–1938).

In Kyoto, Tsuchida Bakusen 土田麦僊 (1887–1936) and Ono Chikkyō 小野竹喬 (1889–1979), both influenced by postimpressionism, found a corresponding sense of substance and structure in Cézanne's landscapes and the powerfully brushed works of Tomioka Tessai 富岡鉄斎 (1836–1924), the ultimate literati painter of modern Japan. They also associated the literati emphasis on amateurism with the naïveté of Henri Rousseau's art. Tomita Keisen studied Shijō techniques but was dissatisfied with its *shasei*-based approach. He found inspiration in the subjectivity of literati painting, which he related to Western expressionism. Hashimoto Kansetsu 橋本関雪 (1883–1945), the son of a Confucian scholar, explored a unique literati style.

Most of the artists in Tokyo and Kyoto who discovered a new direction for their art in literati painting died before the end of World War II. Chikkyō continued to work after the war, but his style became more color oriented. For the most part, the movement to incorporate aspects of literati painting into new *nihonga* possibilities ended with the war.

The Welch collection, with works by Keisen and Kansetsu, reminds us of the importance of the literati painting tradition within the modern *nihonga* world.

The Welch collection includes not only literati painting but also works of Shijō lineage or by Shijō-influenced artists. Yosa Buson 与謝蕪村 (1761–1783), who, with Ike Taiga, marks the peak of the Japanese literati tradition, achieved his manner of literati painting after studying various styles. A haiku poet, he also created unique *haiga* 俳画 paintings. Matsumura Gekkei 松村月渓, or Goshun 呉春 (1752–1811), studied the literati painting and haiku of Buson's last years and the *shasei*-based style of Maruyama Ōkyo 円山応挙 (1733–1795), and he eventually established the Shijō school. Although the Maruyama and Shijō schools are often considered to represent a "realistic" style, they were intimately connected with the world of haiku. Many modern-period painters, such as Takeuchi Seihō 竹内栖鳳 (1964–1942), Tsuji Kakō 都路華香 (1970–1931), and Ono Chikkyō, created haiku. Literati painting developed in close connection with Chinese literature and poetry, and in Japan the tradition integrated various painting styles in addition to Southern school and haiku aesthetics. The Welch collection offers a view of the complexity of the Japanese literati painting tradition.

From the end of the Edo period through the early years of the modern era, literati painting spread throughout Japan. Even after World War II, the tradition retained its popularity among prominent families in various regions. In recent years, however, it has virtually disappeared. From time to time, Japanese experts have reevaluated literati painting and discussed the significance of its modern revival, and exhibitions have reexamined examples of *bunjinga/nanga* in the modern-period lineage. However, *nihonga* painters in postwar Japan have increasingly focused on the immediate appeal of strong color, producing paintings that resemble *yōga*. Japanese connoisseurs and collectors have followed this trend. Terry Welch's profound love of Japan led him to an appreciation of Japanese attitudes toward the world and nature, which are distinct from those represented in the Chinese literati tradition or Western painting. For the Japanese viewer accustomed to Western ways of looking, the Welch collection might induce a sense of bewilderment but also unexpected discovery. For scholars and connoisseurs of Japanese art, it opens a window to fresh perspectives on the complexity of the Japanese literati tradition.

Uchiyama Takeo, Former Director
The National Museum of Modern Art, Kyoto

Collector's View | East of the Moon

Terry Welch

My first experience of Japan was in the fall of 1971, when I was twenty-three and catching my breath between advanced undergraduate studies and entering law school at the University of Washington. With the naïveté that only youth can exploit, I followed two suggestions from a friend: I lived in Kyushu, because it would be warmer in the winter, and I looked up the famous *ryokan* Yōyōkaku, in the town of Karatsu near Fukuoka. Within a few days of meeting innkeepers Ōkōchi Akihiko and Harumi, I was teaching English to their friends, whose lessons paid for my room and board. Can you imagine the effect of becoming acquainted with Japan while living and working in a *ryokan,* the premier setting for unlocking Japan's traditions and spirit? The love of nature is at the core of Japanese culture, and every aspect of an inn is a realization of the concept that we are not meant to be separate from the natural world. From the very construction of the inn, which relies on native materials, to the composition and presentation of meals (mostly local foods in season, often metaphorically linked to myth, literary traditions, or nature), the overriding experience of the *ryokan* is an appreciation of beauty in nature. In the experience of the thoughtfully designed garden, usually visually and physically integrated with the room, in the ritual significance of bathing in the *ofuro,* and in the sacredness of objects presented in the tokonoma, one is never far from the celebration of being alive and fully conscious.

In early 1972 I left the inn to stay in Tokyo with Whitney and Dorothy Howland. Whit was the Boeing Company's representative in Japan, and his wife, Dorothy, wrote a travel column for the *Mainichi Daily Newspaper.* It wasn't long before I fell under Dorothy's spell. We traveled around Japan together, and she implored me not to return to Seattle and law school. She claimed I was an artist and needed to find a way to express myself. She helped me sell my rare violin in Tokyo, and with the proceeds I bought a number of contemporary woodblock prints by artists represented by her friend Frances Blakemore. Frances and I hatched a plot whereby I would start a gallery in Honolulu called East of the Moon. In April I flew to Honolulu with my "art collection," and after researching the local scene, in July I opened my gallery in a mall off Kapiolani Boulevard. It lasted eleven days. Dejected, with the paltry profit from my few sales, I flew home to Seattle. Having been inspired by the many Japanese gardens I had seen and remembering Dorothy Howland's prophetic observation about my artistic nature, I abandoned the idea of law school and launched a landscape design company.

Thanks to my parents, I received a classical education emphasizing the liberal arts, languages, and music. I've always been impressed by the literati ideal and inspired by Confucian principles that celebrate the sage, a figure held to impeccable standards of incorruptible character and high ideals who dedicates himself to learning and the transformation of the self as an example to others. Embedded in this lifestyle was the concept of nature as an expression of the inner landscape of the artist's heart and mind. These scholars highlighted their individualism in the imaginative ways they painted the natural world, brushed calligraphy, and celebrated their friendships with kindred spirits. Their paintings—tranquil, expressionistic, and evocative—spoke to my taste and work as a landscape artist.

Besides my interest in Japanese paintings, during the 1970s I became intrigued by the mystical paintings of Northwest artists Mark Tobey, Morris Graves, and, especially, Guy Anderson. Their artwork had been a passion of Richard E. Fuller, the founder of the Seattle Art Museum, who patronized these artists in the early stages of their careers. All these men were interested in Asian mysticism; as a young man, Tobey had studied calligraphy and spent time in a Japanese Zen monastery. Influenced by the Asian painting tradition, these artists preferred ink and water-based pigments, and favored paper over canvas. Zen Buddhism influenced Graves. His depictions of rocks, birds, and trees express a life force not unlike that seen in Japanese paintings. They have a mysterious transparency, as if their subjects were engaged in a form of spiritual transformation. But it was Anderson who captivated me the most. His grand abstract images, executed in huge calligraphic brushstrokes, often feature circles that might signify a seed, the moon, or *enso* (cosmic unity). At times this cell-like structure reflected

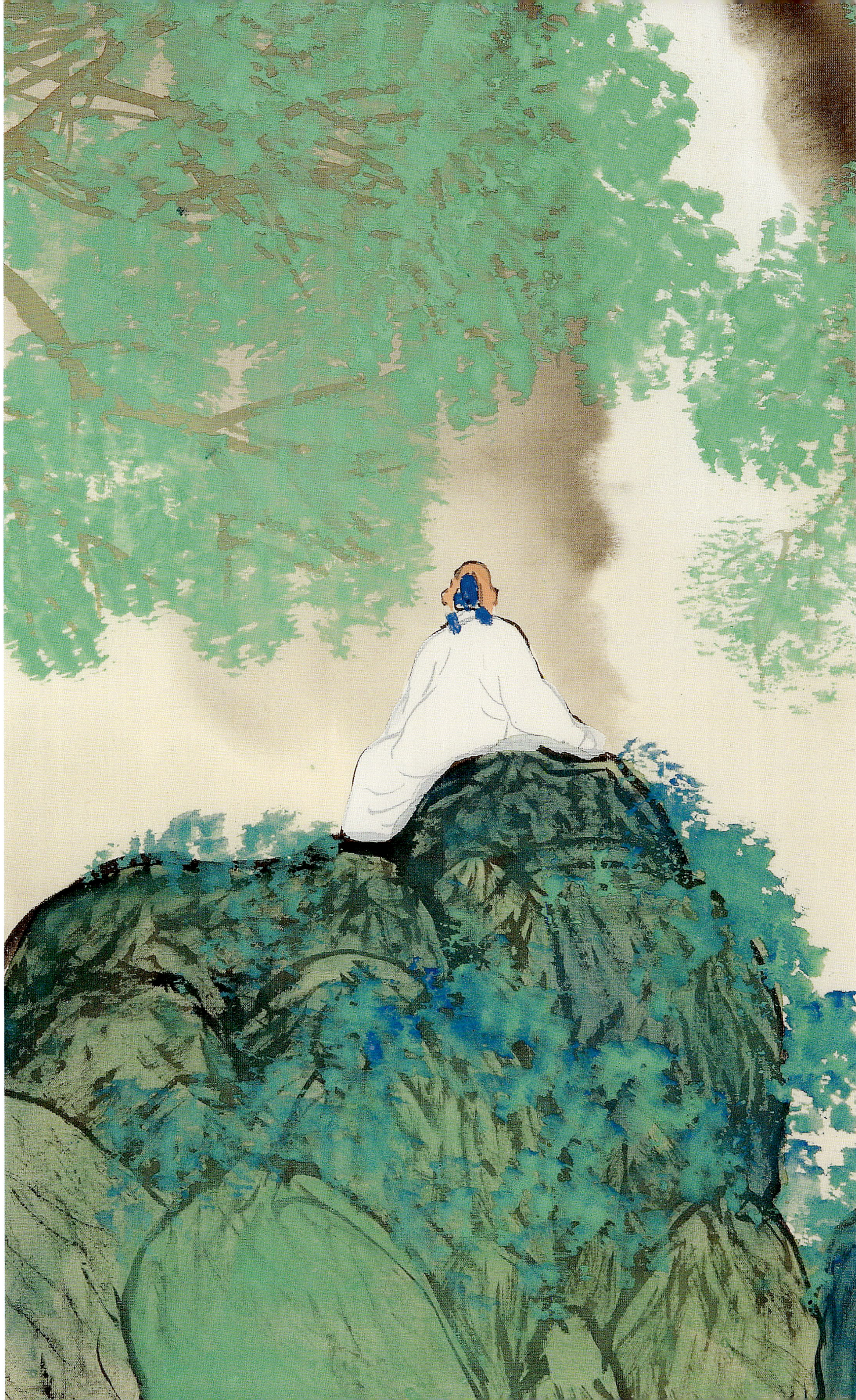

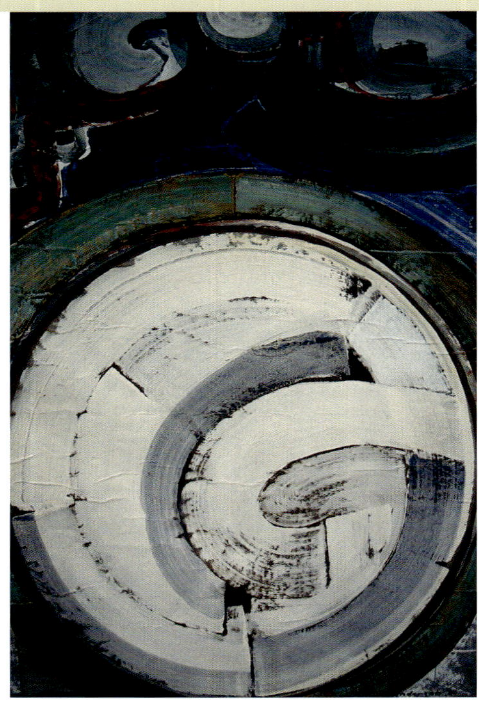

Guy Anderson (American, 1906–1998), *Triumph of the Egg*, 1980, oil on paper on board. Collection of Terry Welch.

the forms found in Northwest Coast Native art. The titles of Anderson's paintings reveal his passions: *Birth of Prometheus, Burial in Winter, Man Reading While in Flight, Umbilical, Triumph of the Egg.* His paintings have been well received in Japan.

Fortunately, by the late 1970s, I had early encouragement and mentoring from William Jay Rathbun, curator of Asian art at the Seattle Art Museum. Then I fell under the influence of Paul Berry at the University of Washington, followed by the infectious enthusiasm of Griffith and Patricia Way, who share an intense interest in tracing the evolution of Shijō painting from the late Edo period into the twentieth century. All these influences converged into my desire to show the transformation of *bunjinga*—literati painting—from the early 1800s to the mid-1900s. I was drawn to the same archetypal imagery found in the work of the Northwest mystical painters. Besides the grand themes detailed in Shunkin's handscroll *Laughter on Spring Wind* (cat. no. 24), Baisen's *Mount Hōrai* (cat. no. 57), Sen'yō's *Eight Views of Ōmi* (cat. no. 58), Shōnen's *Old Pine* (cat. no. 69), and Kaiseki's *Nachi Waterfall* (cat. no. 20), I gravitated toward the transcendental portrayal of plants as found in the quartet of paintings by Kaioku (cat. no. 64). How can one escape the power of Baiitsu's plum (cat. no. 63), Bunchō's expressive bamboo (cat. no. 61), Baisen's exuberant lotus (cat. no. 73), or Inshō's Chinese garden (cat. no. 75)? Even animals seem to be infused with a spiritual essence as evidenced in Bunrin's fox (cat. no. 66), Kakō's cranes (cat. no. 70), and Kyōson's mother dog (cat. no. 72). But it is the dramatic screen by Kinkoku (cat. no. 4) that captures the essence of the literatus's life: celebrating the wonder of nature, in nature among friends.

I am indebted to the American dealers Cheney Cowles and Howard Rogers as well as the Kyoto establishments of Mizutani Ishinosuke, Yamazoe Tenkōdō, Tessaidō, and Hoshino. I have benefited from and been inspired by many years of deep friendship with Paul Berry and Michiyo Morioka, the writers of this extraordinary catalogue. It was Julia White, former curator of Asian art at the Honolulu Academy of Arts, who first understood the significance of the collection. Subsequent support from Director Stephen Little and the trustees of the Academy delivered it to the Hawaiian Islands. Shawn Eichman, the new curator of Asian art, has proved to be an energetic and passionate advocate for this exhibition. I wish to thank the Blakemore Foundation for its considerable contribution to the production of this elegant book, brilliantly produced by Marquand Books. In this way, I have ended up with a gallery in Honolulu after all.

Artists in the Exhibition

Numbers refer to catalogue entries

Doi Gōga 土井贅牙 78
Dōmoto Inshō 堂本印象 75
Fujimoto Tesseki 藤本鉄石 65, 76
Fukuda Kodōjin 福田古道人 49, 50
Fusen Tetsu 不染鉄 60
Gotō Shūgai 後藤秋涯 53
Hagura Katei 羽倉可亭 9
Haruki Nanmei 春木南溟 35
Hashimoto Kansetsu 橋本関雪 13
Hazama Seigai 硼西涯 77
Hine Taizan 日根対山 33, 34
Hirai Baisen 平井楳仙 54–57, 73, 74
Hirose Taizan 広瀬臺山 17
Hoashi Kyōu 帆足杏雨 38
Honkō Fūgai 本高風外 27
Ichikawa Beian* 市河米菴 3
Ike Gyokuran 池玉瀾 14
Imao Keinen* 今尾景年 11
Kameda Bōsai 亀田鵬斎 2, 3, 19
Kawahigashi Hekigotō 河東碧梧桐 12
Kikuchi Gozan* 菊池五山 3
Kinoshita Itsuun 木下逸雲 32
Kobayashi Shunshō 小林春樵 47
Kondō Kōichiro 近藤浩一路 51, 52
Kōno Bairei 幸野楳嶺 68
Kubo Shunman* 窪俊満 3
Kuwagata Keisai* 鍬形蕙斎 3
Kushiro Unsen 釧雲泉 16
Kuwayama Gyokushū 桑山玉州 15
Maeda Mokuhō 前田黙鳳 45
Masuyama Sessai 増山雪斎 18
Mizuta Chikuho 水田竹圃 71
Nakabayashi Chikutō 中林竹洞 28, 62
Nakai Keigi* 中井敬義 3
Nakajima Kahō 中島華鳳 81
Noro Kaiseki 野呂介石 20
Nukina Kaioku 貫名海屋 5, 29–31, 64
Ogawa Sen'yō 小川千甕 58, 83
Okada Hankō 岡田半江 25, 26
Okamoto Toyohiko 岡本豊彦 23
Okuhara Seiko 奥原晴湖 44
Ōkubo Shibutsu* 大窪詩佛 3
Ōtagaki Rengetsu 大田垣蓮月 6, 7
Sakai Hōitsu* 酒井抱一 3
Shiokawa Bunrin 塩川文麟 66
Shirakura Jihō 白倉二峰 59
Sō Geppō 僧月峯 22
Suzuki Fuyō 鈴木芙蓉 1
Suzuki Hyakunen 鈴木百年 41
Suzuki Shōnen 鈴木松年 69
Tajika Chikuson* 田近竹邨 11
Takakura Kangai 高倉観崖 82
Tani Bunchō 谷文晁 3, 61
Tani Bun'ichi* 谷文一 3
Tanomura Chikuden 田能村竹田 21
Tanomura Chokunyū 田能村直入 42, 43, 79
Tomioka Tessai 富岡鉄斎 11, 46
Tomita Keisen 冨田溪仙 48, 80
Tsuji Kakō 都路華香 70
Uragami Shunkin 浦上春琴 24
Yamamoto Baiitsu 山本梅逸 63
Yamamoto Chikuun 山本竹雲 10
Yamanaka Shinten'ō 山中信天翁 8, 39, 40, 67
Yano Kyōson 矢野橋村 72
Yasuda Rōzan 安田老山 36, 37
Yokoi Kinkoku 横井金谷 4

*represented by a collaborative work

The Meeting of Chinese and Japanese Literati

Hu Gongshou, Yasuda Rōzan, and the Controversy over National Style

Paul Berry

From its origins in antiquity, the history of Japanese painting has been intertwined with international influences, especially those from China, India (in relation to Buddhist painting), and Korea. The connection with China is especially strong: Tang-dynasty painting influenced the development of *yamatoe* landscapes in the Heian period, Southern Song and Yuan painting played out in early Muromachi landscapes, and Ming-period Zhe-school painting affected the development of Kanō painting. Yet the most complex interaction occurred with the development of literati painting in eighteenth-century Japan. Even more eclectic than its Chinese predecessors, the Japanese form of literati painting accommodated the broadest range of Chinese and Japanese styles within an idealistic rubric that invested painting with levels of meaning far beyond the decorative and iconic functions that had predominated in earlier trends.[1]

Japanese literati painters venerated their Chinese counterparts, yet their social and artistic positions within their respective cultures were so different that a simple transplantation of the Chinese movement was impossible. To some degree Japanese literati were aware of the cultural differences with China, but their understanding was limited by the shogunate's restrictions on international travel. A remarkable transition occurred when a direct connection between Chinese and Japanese literati painters was finally established in the latter half of the nineteenth century, after the travel ban was dropped. A thorough examination of this long-delayed interaction between artistic movements has yet to be undertaken, yet the relationship between a prominent Shanghai painter, Hu Gongshou 胡公寿 (1823–1886, also known as Hu Yuan 胡遠), and his top Japanese disciple, Yasuda Rōzan 安田老山 (1830–1882; see fig. 1), illuminates some of the key features of the mixed reception of this interchange.

The development of literati painting in Japan from its beginning was deeply connected with the city of Nagasaki, the main port for the importation of foreign culture and goods during the Edo period. The introduction of Ōbaku Zen (the third sect of Zen to come to Japan) in the mid-seventeenth century brought with it a large number of Chinese priests along with new styles of calligraphy, portrait painting, seal carving, and tea drinking. In addition, these Chinese priests brought collections of paintings and calligraphy which Japanese painters gradually came to study. An increase in trade in the eighteenth century brought Chinese merchants, some of whom created paintings and calligraphy as an avocation, as well as a few professional painters. The works of these transient visitors had a great impact on the Japanese painters who met and studied with them in Nagasaki. Beyond these personal contacts, huge quantities of Chinese paintings, calligraphies, classic texts on Chinese painting, and painting manuals streamed into Japan. Over time these materials spread throughout the country and shaped the interests of painters and their patrons, especially in Edo and the Kyoto and Osaka areas. Although access to these imported materials grew over time, Nagasaki remained a focal point for artists who wished to dramatically improve their understanding of Chinese paintings, prompting painters from throughout Japan to spend periods of time in the city to meet with visiting Chinese and to study the large concentration of artworks.

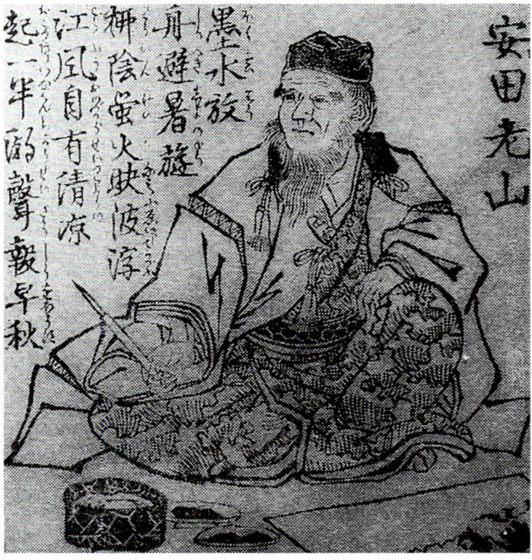

Figure 1. Yasuda Rōzan 安田老山. From Yasui Otsuyū 安井乙熊, ed. *Meiji eimei hyakunin shu* 明治英名百人首 (Tokyo: Tōkyō Shorin 東京書林, 1881).

Of the many painters in Nagasaki, the majority made brightly colored bird-and-flower works in Chinese-influenced styles. Literati painters were also numerous, and by the late Edo period, three painters were recognized as the most popular in the Nagasaki literati world; Hidaka Tetsuō 日高鐵翁 (1791–1871), Kinoshita Itsuun 木下逸雲 (1799–1866), and Miura Gomon 三浦梧門 (1809–1860). Of these, Itsuun and Tetsuō (fig. 2) were the most influential, both having studied with Jiang Jiapu 江稼圃 (b. c. 1745, act. in Japan from 1804), the most skilled of the resident Chinese painters.[2] Tanomura Chikuden 田能村竹田 (1777–1835) was much impressed by both of these younger artists during his second and longest stay in Nagasaki in 1826–27. Itsuun and Tetsuō, sought after as teachers until the ends of their lives, influenced a generation of Japanese painters. Itsuun's career, however, was cut short in 1866 when the boat in which he was traveling to Nagasaki from Edo capsized in a storm.

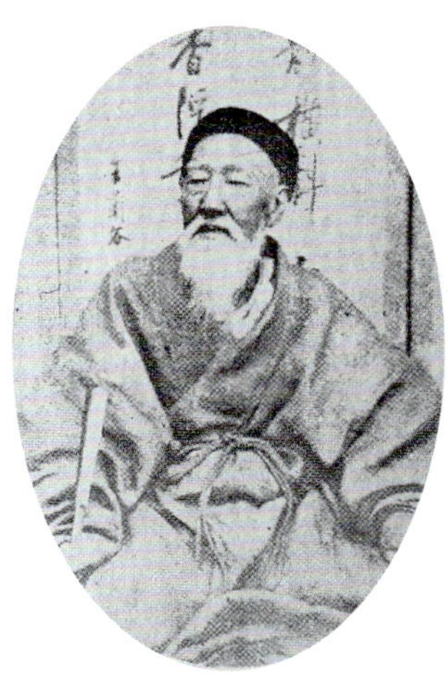

Figure 2. Hidaka Tetsuō 日高鐵翁, 1863. From Shimizu Hiroshi 清水博, *Gajin nagai unpei* 画人長井雲坪 (Nagano: Shinno Kyōikukai Shuppanbu 信濃教育会出版部, 1981).

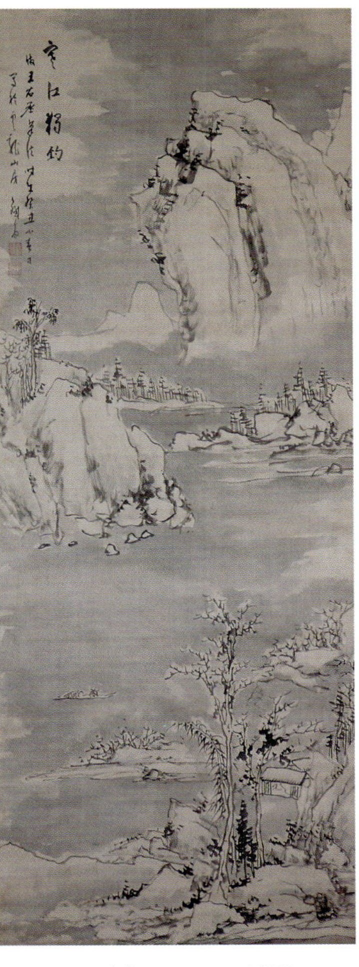

Figure 3. Hidaka Tetsuō 日高鐵翁, *Winter Landscape* 冬山水圖 (To sansui zu), 1853. Hanging scroll: ink on satin, 130.2 × 50.5 cm. Hakutakuan collection, Kyoto.

The head priest of the Nagasaki Rinzai Zen temple Shuntokuji 春徳寺, Tetsuō was best known for his many winter landscapes (see fig. 3) and his dramatic ink paintings of orchids. He was close friends with many of the Chinese staying in Nagasaki, including the painter Xu Yuting 徐雨亭 (b. 1824).[3] Tetsuō's decades-long association with the Chinese literati at Nagasaki so increased his interest in the contemporary painting world in China that he began to urge some of his students to travel to Shanghai to further their knowledge of literati painting.

Among the many literati artists who studied in Nagasaki with Tetsuō in the mid-nineteenth century was Yasuda Rōzan. His father held the hereditary position of doctor for the Takasu *han* 高須藩 near the town of Kaizu 海津 in Gifu prefecture. Both his first name Yō 養 and his artist's name Rōzan 老山 (Old Mountain) were taken from the nearby Yōrōzan 養老山. The mountain is famous for the Yōrō waterfall, its name, meaning "nourishing the old," deriving from ancient legends concerning the therapeutic properties of its water.

Rōzan loved painting in his youth and eventually moved to Nagasaki to study Chinese literati painting. The date of his arrival is unclear, but he is said to have studied with Xu Yuting 徐雨亭 (b. 1824) in addition to Tetsuō. The very active literati painting circles in Kyoto, Osaka, and Tokyo would have been the most obvious locations for an aspiring artist, and it must have been Rōzan's strong desire to learn from Chinese painting styles as directly as possible that led him to travel so far for his studies. In Nagasaki, he could be assured of seeing the most recently imported Chinese paintings as well as meeting immigrant Chinese painters, who, if not famous in their own country, at least offered an unmediated connection to Chinese culture and art.

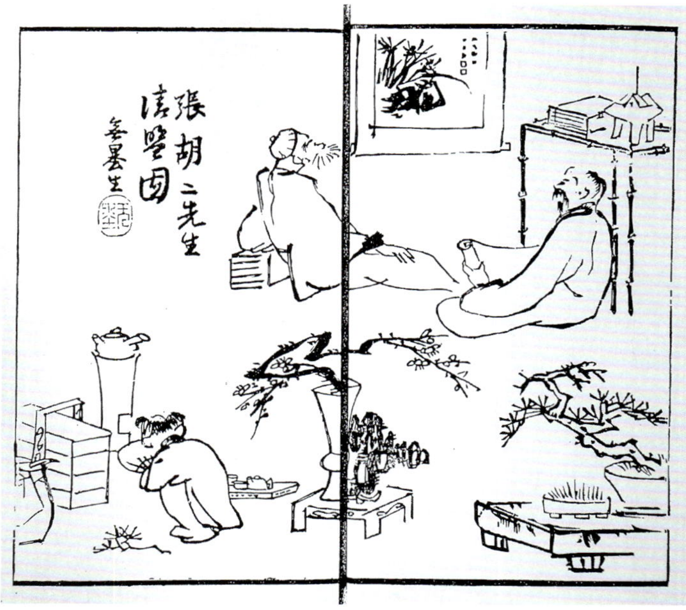

Figure 4. Nagao Muboku 長尾無墨, Hu Gongshou 胡公壽 (bearded figure on left). From *Chō Shishō Ko Kōju ryō sensei gafu* 張子祥胡公壽両先生画譜 (Tokyo: Takagi Kazusuke 高木和助, 1881).

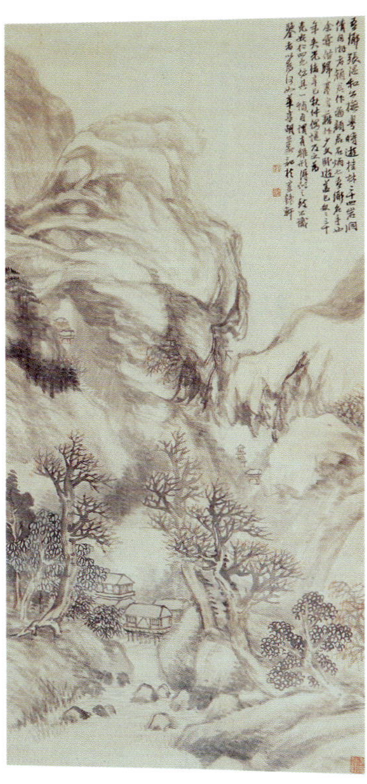

Figure 5. Hu Gongshou 胡公壽, *Grotto in Cliff—Impression of Autumn* (Yandong qiuyi tu 岩洞秋意圖), 1881. Hanging scroll: ink and color on paper, 126.2 × 60.7 cm. Shi Yunwen 石允文 collection.

Foreign missionaries had begun to arrive in Nagasaki during the late Edo period. Forbidden to propagate their religion, they often were employed as English instructors. One of the first was the Dutch-born Guido Verbeck (1830–1898), of the Dutch Reformed Church of America, who came to Nagasaki late in 1859.[4] From the beginning, Verbeck avoided the foreign compound at Deshima, choosing to live in a Japanese house in the city. Over time he attracted many students who later became famous, including the patriot-turned-rebel Saigō Takamori 西郷隆盛 (1827–1877) and the politician Itō Hirobumi 伊藤博文 (1841–1909). Verbeck received his supplies of Western goods from Shanghai and occasionally made the three-day boat trip there himself. It was through Verbeck's travel connections that Yasuda Rōzan and Ishikawa Kansen 石川潤泉 (1844–1917) disguised as Chinese, boarded a Chinese boat heading for Shanghai in early 1867.[5] Nagai Unpei 長井雲坪 (1833–1899) joined them a month later.[6] Initially the three men banded together and adopted new artist's names to mark their study in China: Gosui 呉水, Gozan 呉山, and Goko 呉湖, respectively.[7]

Their primary mentor was the noted Shanghai painter Hu Gongshou, then at the height of his career (see fig. 4). Tetsuō apparently had previously corresponded with Hu, probably having been introduced by others in the Chinese community in Nagasaki who maintained contact with Shanghai via the regular boat trade between the cities. Hu's appreciation of Tetsuō's painting is evidenced by a landscape that was taken to Shanghai and returned to Japan with an inscription by Hu praising Tetsuō's work.[8] Hu, although raised to be a scholar, had failed the central examinations and subsequently trained in painting with Shen Zhuo 沈焯 (d. 1901), a follower of the skillful but conservative style of Xi Gang 奚岡 (1746–1803).[9] Hu was one of a number of painters who moved to Shanghai in 1861 to avoid the chaos of the Taiping Rebellion (1850–64).[10] Among the other prominent painters then in Shanghai were Ren Xiong 任熊 (1823–1857), a great talent who died in his thirties, and Xu Gu 虚谷 (1824–1896), famous for paintings of fish done in a simplified yet distinctively dramatic and colorful style. Although Hu was one of the

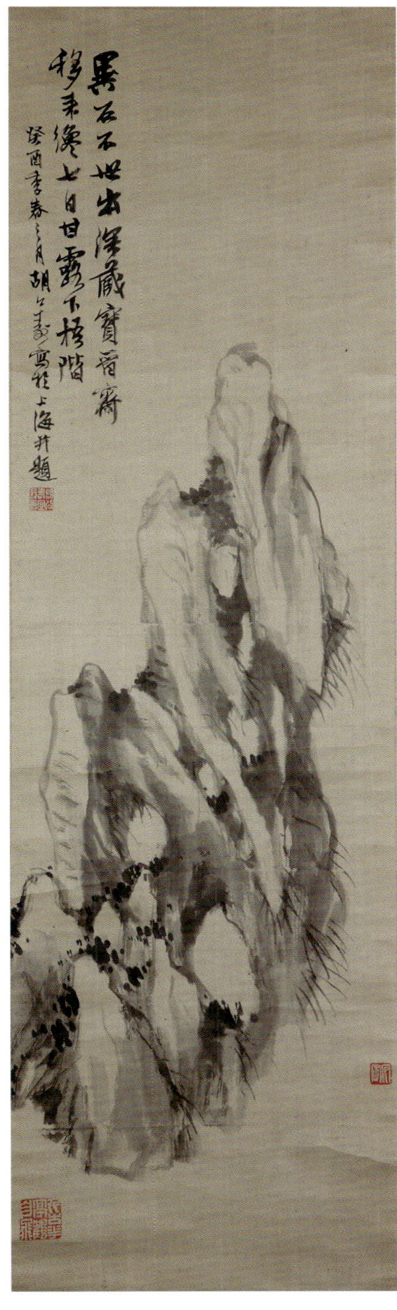

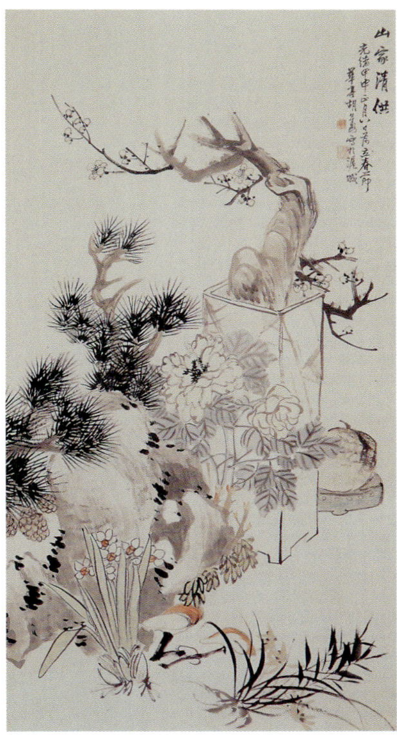

Figure 6. Hu Gongshou 胡公壽, *Taihu Stone* (Taihu shi tu 太湖石圖), 1873. Hanging scroll: ink on satin, 131.5 × 40.4 cm. Hakutakuan collection, Kyoto.

Figure 7. Hu Gongshou, 胡公壽, *Pure Offerings of a Mountain Home* (Shanjia qinggong tu 山家清供), 1884. Hanging scroll: ink and color on paper, 147.8 × 80.7 cm. Shi Yunwen 石允文 collection.

preeminent painters in Shanghai during his lifetime, the importance of his career was later overshadowed by the popularity of these several contemporaries and his most famous disciple, Ren Bonian 任伯年 (1840–1896).

Hu Gongshou was best known for his many ink landscapes, which often included light color accents in pink, blue, and green (fig. 5). In addition, Hu frequently painted *taihu* 太湖 stones (see fig. 6), dramatic trees, and compositions of flowers and miscellaneous desk ornaments (fig. 7). He created his paintings with wide outlines often achieved with the side of the brush tip, a technique that violated the standard Chinese emphasis on center-tip strokes made with the brush held vertically over the painting surface. The bold, casual quality of his paintings was quite different from the meticulous, reserved brushwork typical of many late Qing literati paintings such as those by Xi Gang 奚岡 (1746–1803). Hu usually wrote his distinctive calligraphy in a vigorous, slightly angular, cursive script derived from the style of the popular Tang calligrapher Yan Zhenqing 顏真卿 (709–785).

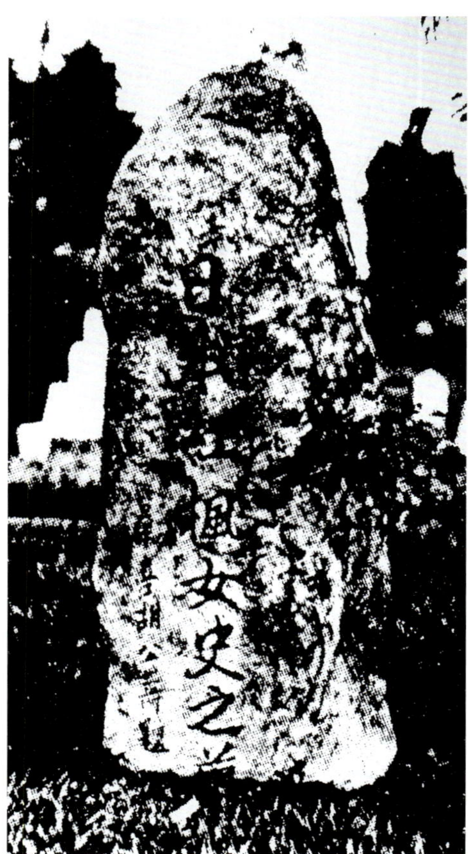

Figure 8. Ihara Kōfu 井原紅楓 gravestone with inscription by Hu Gongshou, re-erected in the Japanese cemetery in Shanghai, c. 1913. From Yoshizawa Hideo 米沢秀夫, *Shanhai shiwa* 上海史話 (Tokyo: Bōbō Shobō 畝傍書房, 1942).

Of the three early Japanese visitors to China, Unpei was the first to leave Shanghai. Guided by Chinese friends he had known in Nagasaki, Xu Yuting and Wang Kesan 王克三 (act. c. 1862–),[11] Unpei visited the nearby cities of Suzhou and Hangzhou and the famous Tientai Mountains 天台山. He returned to Nagasaki in the third month of 1868 during the turmoil that attended the establishment of the Meiji political order.[12] Bearing the latest news from China and eager to visit the new capital, three months later Unpei proceeded to Tokyo. There he contacted the painters Murata Kōkoku 村田香谷 (1831–1912) and Okuhara Seiko 奥原晴湖 (1837–1913), and for the next several years he immersed himself in the Kantō literati world. He traveled around Japan for a time before settling in the small town of Togakushi, north of Nagano, in 1879. Thereafter, Unpei became a well-known literati painter in northern Japan.

Kansen, now known as Gozan, traveled around China before going back to Japan in 1870.[13] He eventually returned to his hometown of Toyama in Ishikawa prefecture, where he continued to paint, although his sales suffered after news spread of his 1884 conversion to Christianity.

Unlike his compatriots, who had soon left Shanghai to travel about the country, Rōzan committed himself to his studies with Hu Gongshou. In 1869 Rōzan's wife, the painter Ihara Kōfū 井原紅楓 (1847–1872, also known as Teisha 停車), joined him in China. Skilled in painting bamboo and orchids, Kōfū had studied with the noted female literatus Chō Kōran 張紅蘭 (1804–1879), presumably in the Gifu area, before she and Rōzan had set out for Nagasaki. Kōfū died of illness just outside Shanghai, in Wusong 呉淞, in 1872. Rōzan erected a stone monument with a memorial inscription by Hu Gongshou at her grave beside the nine-story pagoda of Lunghuasi 龍華寺 temple in Shanghai (fig. 8).[14]

Rōzan's activities during his six years of study in Shanghai are still largely unclear, yet some aspects can be understood through the few paintings that survive from this period. He signed his works Banriō 萬里翁 (Old Man of Ten Thousand Miles) or Nihon no Banriō (Banriō of Japan) and often used that name on his seals. It is a reference to Dong Qichang's 董其昌 (1555–1636) famous advice for painters, "read one thousand books, travel ten thousand miles" 萬讀巻書萬里路読, a singularly appropriate expression for an artist who had traveled to China for the sake of his art. During his residence in Shanghai, Rōzan developed a distinctive approach to painting. The extent of his Chinese patronage is unknown, but he did develop contacts with visiting Japanese to whom he dedicated paintings.[15] It may have been the increasing popularity of his works among Japanese in China that encouraged his move to Tokyo in 1873. He had trouble receiving approval to reenter the country from Japanese authorities, who likely looked with suspicion upon his continued stay in China after the Meiji Restoration and his closeness with the Chinese artistic community. In any event, Rōzan first went to Taiwan in 1873 and drew a map of the island, which he submitted to the Japanese government. At this critical juncture in Japanese-Taiwanese relations,[16] it helped gain his readmittance to Japan.

Not long after appearing in Tokyo, Rōzan greatly impressed the prominent calligraphers Iwaya Ichiroku 巌谷一六 (1834–1905) and Kusakabe Meikaku 日下部鳴鶴 (1838–1922) at a literati gathering by creating an impromptu painting of a large rock.[17] Meikaku in particular had a keen appreciation of contemporary Chinese styles of painting and calligraphy. With their support Rōzan was able to rent a studio to train painters and to establish a patronage group of ten members from government circles. Rōzan's popularity grew so quickly that in 1876 he was among various artists called to paint in front of the Meiji emperor.[18] Within a few years he was living in a large house and hosting literati gatherings of his own.

This period marked the high point of enthusiasm for quickly painted, bold compositions in the Chinese styles new to Japan. Rōzan's submission of an ink landscape to the First National Industrial Exhibition (*Dai ikkai kokunai kangyō hakurankai* 第一回国内博覧会) in 1877 received the Phoenix Award (鳳紋賞). Although Rōzan did not submit a painting to the First National Painting Competition (*Dai ikkai naikoku kaiga kyōshinkai*), six painters who did were identified as belonging to the Rōzan school (Rōzanha 老山派).[19] Rōzan's work became so popular in Tokyo that he and Okuhara Seiko 奥原晴湖 (1837–1913) were generally considered the two most important literati painters of the early Meiji period.[20] Although she never traveled to China, Seiko developed a loose, expressive style of painting and calligraphy based on the study of Zheng Xie's 鄭燮 (1693–1765) works.

Rōzan's early work in Japan is well represented by an 1875 handscroll of bamboo, orchids, chrysanthemums, and plum flowers, *The Four Gentlemen* (Shikunshi 四君子, figs. 9, 10). Although the handscroll is a rare format for Rōzan, the striking compositions, strong brushwork, and skillful use of mid-range ink tonalities typify his style. In some of the signatures and seals on this work he occasionally used the "Banriō" name, although he shortly would drop it altogether in favor of "Rōzan." Throughout his career Rōzan frequently painted impressive *taihu* stones (fig. 11), plantains (fig. 12), and miscellaneous other plants. His paintings of potted plants on stands (fig. 13) matched similar themes popular in Shanghai.

Landscapes, usually in ink, were Rōzan's main interest. On rare occasions, as in the 1881 *Spring Landscape* (cat. no. 37), he accented slight areas with pale colors. Most rare were fully colored works such as an 1877 blue-and-green landscape (fig. 14). Rōzan handled colors skillfully, yet his real forte and a chief attraction of his work was a subtle use of ink tonalities. Generally speaking, most of Rōzan's landscapes are painted either with dry, angular brushwork that suggests layers of rocky surfaces (see cat. no. 36) or, more commonly, wetter brushwork with a curvilinear emphasis to the major forms (see cat. no. 37). In most works, regardless of theme, his distinctive strokes made with the side of the brush are a prominent feature, this characteristic brushwork forming the strongest link to the style of his teacher Hu Gongshou. Rōzan also seemed to develop his calligraphy after Hu's style, itself based on the cursive style of Yan Zhenqing 顔真卿 (709–785). Rōzan's calligraphy, however, was even more angular and irregular in composition than that of his teacher.

At the height of his popularity, in 1882, Rōzan unexpectedly fell ill and died.[21] The potential of his legacy or influence

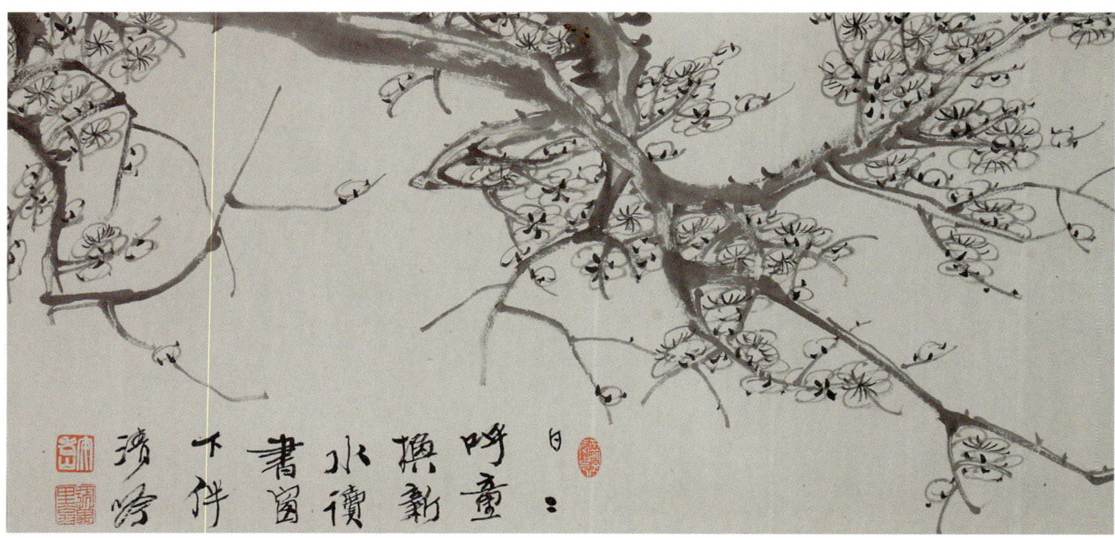

Figure 9. Yasuda Rōzan 安田老山, detail of plum flowers from *Four Gentlemen* (Shikunshi zu 四君子圖), 1875. Handscroll: ink on paper, 31.7 × 525.3 cm. Hakutakuan collection, Kyoto.

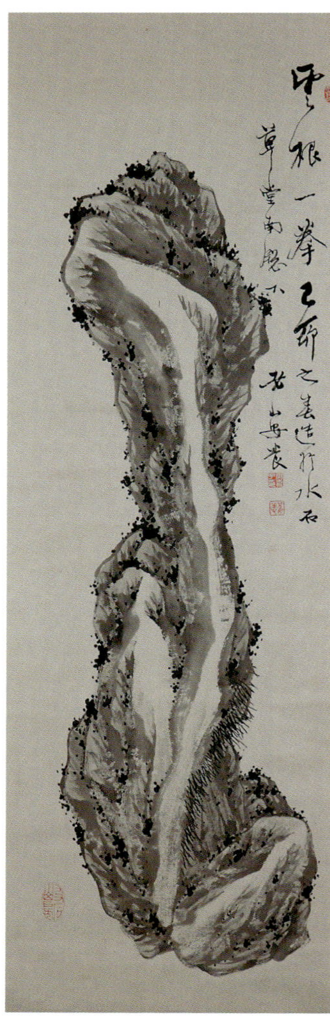

Figure 11. Yasuda Rōzan 安田老山, *Taihu Stone* (Taiko seki zu 太湖石圖), 1979. Hanging scroll: ink on paper, 134.8 × 40.4 cm. Hakutakuan collection, Kyoto.

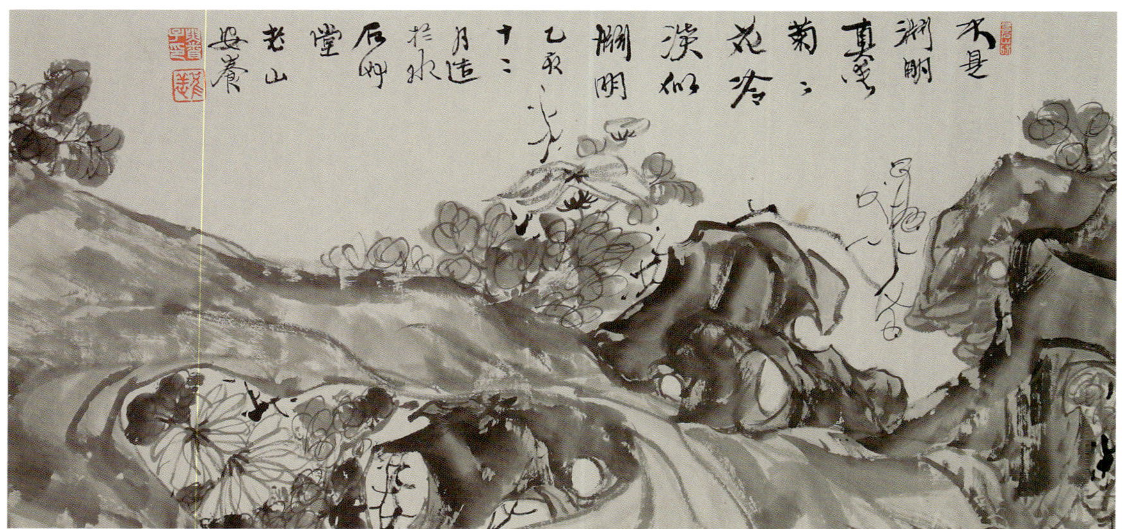

Figure 10. Yasuda Rōzan 安田老山, detail of chrysanthemums from *Four Gentlemen* (Shikunshi zu 四君子圖), 1875. Handscroll: ink on paper, 31.7 × 525.3 cm. Hakutakuan collection, Kyoto.

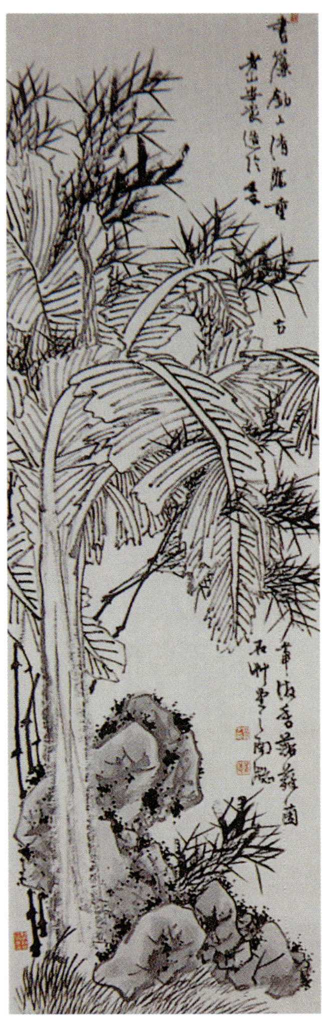

Figure 12. Yasuda Rōzan 安田老山, *Plantains and Bamboo* (Bashō chiku zu 芭蕉竹圖). Hanging scroll: ink on paper. Private collection, Japan.

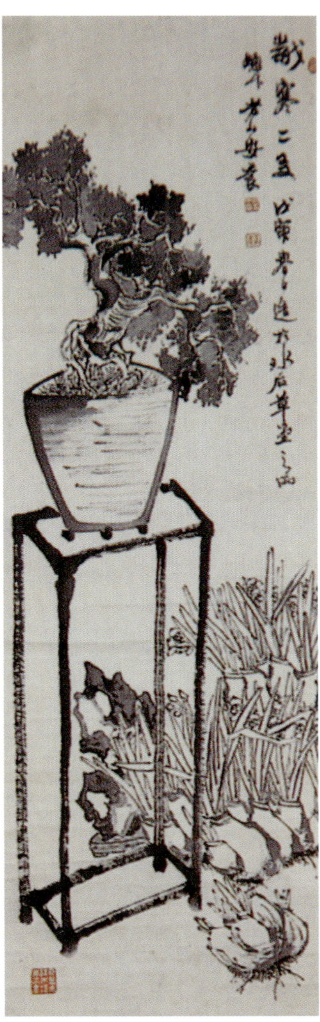

Figure 13. Yasuda Rōzan 安田老山, *Two Friends of Winter* (Saikan niyū zu 歲寒二友圖), 1878. Hanging scroll: ink on paper. Private collection, Japan.

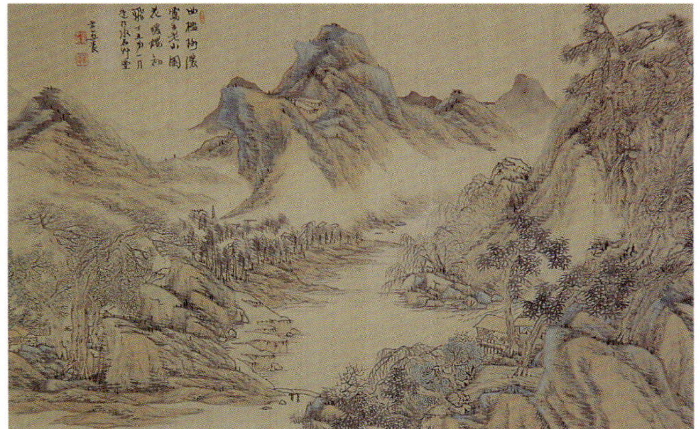

Figure 14. Yasuda Rōzan 安田老山, *Blue-and-Green Landscape* (Seiroku sansui zu 青緑山水圖), 1877. Hanging scroll: ink and color on silk, 69 × 21.2 cm. Private collection, Japan.

on his students would not be fully realized. By the 1890s the trend in Japanese literati painting had shifted from the bold expressiveness typical of the paintings of Rōzan, Seiko, Yamanaka Shinten'ō, and others to carefully constructed, complex, and colorful landscapes. Only those with an interest in contemporary Shanghai-school painting maintained a concern for Rōzan's work.

By the Taishō period, the standard evaluation of Rōzan's career had fully transformed from admiration to a critique of his originality and national identity. In writing the classic history of Japanese literati painting in 1919, Umezawa Seiichi 梅澤精一 (1871–1929) described Rōzan as faithful to Hu and in possession of a style rare in Japan, but he saw Rōzan as merely copying Hu and without a style of his own.[22] Umezawa criticized Rōzan for his careless approach to painting, saying he had not attained real depth and characterizing his current standing as extremely low. To support his position that Rōzan's work was imitative, Umezawa compared two album leaves by Hu with a small album painting by Rōzan of a single rock. The similarity between the broad, side-tip (*sokuhitsu* 側筆) brushwork is clear, but all the major distinctions of their styles are concealed in this odd juxtaposition of minor works. Umezawa did not stop with a critique of Rōzan's painting but narrated an anecdote that has often been repeated. According to Umezawa, Rōzan once

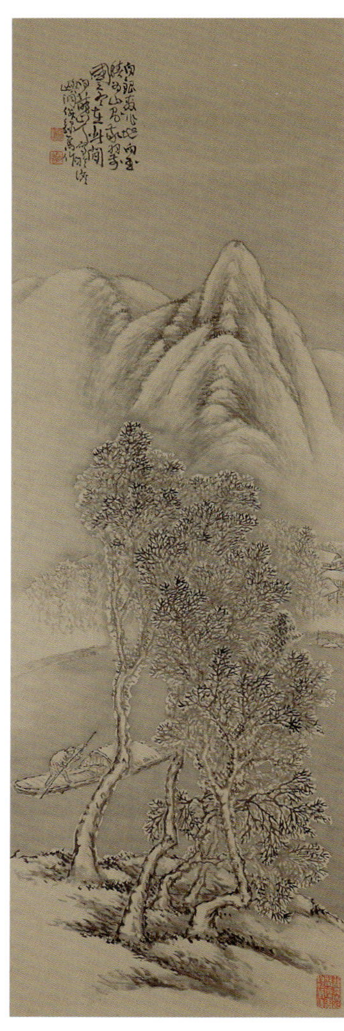

Figure 15. Sugawara Hakuryū 菅原白龍, *Boating on Wintry River* (Setchū kawabune zu 雪中河舟圖). Hanging scroll: ink and color on satin, 141 × 49 cm. Hakutakuan collection, Kyoto.

evaluated a painting by the literati artist Sugawara Hakuryū 菅原白龍 (1833–1898) by saying it "smells of Japan" (*wa kusai* 和臭い). Hakuryū replied that he was born a true Japanese in the Okitama county of Uzen 羽前置賜郡,[23] and therefore he naturally smelled of Japan. Hakuryū then asked Rōzan, "What country were you born in?" Rōzan was said to have been red-faced and speechless.[24]

This story, and its many repetitions and elaborations,[25] reveals a nationalistic attitude in an unusual setting. Not only has Japanese painting from its inception been influenced by Chinese painting, but this connection is especially complex in literati painting. Comparison of Rōzan's landscapes to those by Hakuryū (fig. 15) does highlight Rōzan's Shanghai-school emphasis on side-tip brushwork. Yet, setting aside that Ike Taiga 池大雅 (1723–1776) and his followers in the eighteenth century had used this same technique, Hakuryū's composition and brushwork were also developed from Chinese sources. In the nationalistic assertion of Japanese character that was such a prominent feature of twentieth-century Japan, a questioning of Rōzan's national identity, initially visible in the difficulty he had in repatriating himself from Shanghai, would have been well received in many quarters. Yet, whether this critique was motivated by simple nationalistic sentiments is open to question.

It is important to consider the work of Hu Gongshou's other Japanese students. Many artists studied with Hu in Shanghai, including Nagao Muboku 長尾無墨 (1832–1893), Kawamura Ukoku 河村雨谷 (1838–1906), Ōkura Uson 大倉雨村 (1845–1899), Taketomi Seishō 竹富清嘯 (1833–1899), Murata Kōkoku 村田香谷 (1831–1912), and Amano Hōko 天野方壷 (1824–1894). Although it is not possible in this essay to compare the paintings of all these artists to Hu's style, it must be noted that many landscapes by Seishō, Kōkoku, and Hōko bear considerable resemblance to works by Hu. Many of Hōko's paintings, in particular, share the dramatic side-tip brushwork that is so often mentioned in critiques of Rōzan's work.[26] Hōko had a significant career in Meiji-period Kyoto, Seishō was well regarded in his home prefecture of Kumamoto, and Murata Kōkoku acquired a significant national reputation, yet none of them received the public criticism to which Rōzan was subjected, despite equally visible connections to their studies with Hu Gongshou. That Rōzan was singled out for reproach may have been due to his prominence rather than the qualities of his painting.

Accounts of literati painting—even the most judgmental—always link Rōzan and Okuhara Seiko as the dominant artistic figures in Tokyo during the early Meiji period. Among those who felt their paintings were being ignored in favor of the roughly vigorous styles introduced from China, it may have rankled that Rōzan, a previously unknown artist who catapulted to fame and wealth upon his return from Shanghai,[27] and Seiko, an assertive country woman who dressed and acted much like a man and possessed a bold style based on the study of Zheng Xie (one of the eccentrics of Yangzhou),[28] would be more acclaimed than other artists of the day. Rōzan's abrupt death negated his ongoing influence. Later in life Seiko unexpectedly dropped the expressive style that had made her famous and retired to the country to paint highly controlled works with minute, careful brushwork, a decision that Umezawa refers to as a kind of revelation (*satori* 悟) of the faults of her early work.[29]

Implicit in the critique of Rōzan's style was an assessment of the Shanghai school itself as being nothing but a holdover of the unorthodox techniques of the eighteenth-century Yangzhou eccentrics. Conservative literati painters in China leveled the same reproach at Shanghai artists, and the use of this criticism against Rōzan while simultaneously charging him with being too Chinese seems willfully naïve.

Not everyone joined in this widespread denial of Rōzan's significance. Asakura Fumio 朝倉文夫 (1883–1964), the noted Western-style bronze sculptor from Chikuden's hometown of Taketa, was an avid collector of Rōzan's works, and several dozen of his paintings are still preserved in the Asakura Chōsokan Museum in Tokyo.[30] Asakura maintained patronage relations with a number of important Chinese painters in the first few decades of the twentieth century, and he admired Rōzan for introducing a new approach to painting in Japan. The Tokyo National Museum occasionally exhibits its 1874 Rōzan ink landscape, perhaps his largest known painting.[31]

Although the appraisal of Rōzan as being too Chinese is ironic in several respects, it reveals a larger, and ongoing, matter of national identity in Japanese painting. This issue concerns not only Japanese painters in regard to Chinese traditions and style but also the relationship of Japanese oil painters to Western styles and traditions. Given the unique reception and transformation of foreign influences within Japanese culture, these concerns are fundamentally invalid, yet cultural insecurity and its manipulation for various ends are continuing issues. It is significant that Rōzan's greatest popularity occurred at a time when Japan was most open to foreign influences and while its society was transformed through the study of Western models of government, education, and business. Rōzan's approach was original: he incorporated certain aspects of Hu Gongshou's style but in new compositions with dramatic brushwork that retain their freshness even today. As all art involves the reformation of various influences, the ultimate question is, What has been achieved? The accomplishments of Rōzan demonstrate the success of his pursuit of art, which led him to Shanghai and back.

NOTES

1. For a discussion of the differences between Japanese and Chinese literati painting, see Paul Berry, "The Relation of Japanese Literati Painting to *Nihonga*," in Michiyo Morioka and Paul Berry, *Modern Masters of Kyoto: The Transformation of Japanese Painting Traditions* (Seattle: Seattle Art Museum, 1999), esp. 35 and 36.

2. The most famous of Jiang's many extant works is the long handscroll depicting the Tientai 天台 mountain range. See illustrations of the original handscroll and the full-size woodblock-printed copy in *Edo jidai zushi* 江戸時代図誌, vol. 25, *Nagasaki-Yokohama* 長崎・横浜 (Tokyo: Chikuma Shobō 筑摩書房, 1976), plates 137 and 138.

3. See the essay on Xu's career in Tsuruta Takeyoshi 鶴田武良, "Ō Kokusan to Jo Utei" 王克三と徐雨亭 *Kokka* 国華 (1989): 20–31.

4. An early biography of Verbeck describes many of his activities in Japan and is illustrated with period photographs; see William Griffis, *Verbeck of Japan: A Citizen of No Country* (1900; reprint, Whitefish, MT: Kessinger Publishing, 2007).

5. Although some sources give the date of their trip to Shanghai as 1864, the correct date is 1867; see Yanagi Ryō 柳亮, *Kindai kaiga to bunjinga no chisei* 近代絵画と文人画の知性 (Yokohama: Kotobuki garō Tōkyō Bijutsu Shuppan Dezain Sentaa コトブキ画廊 東京美術出版デザインセンター, 1974), 61. A detailed account of their travel to Shanghai is in Shimizu Hiroshi 清水博, *Gajin Nagai Unpei* 画人長井雲坪 (Nagano: Shinano Kyōiku Shuppansha 信濃教育出版社, 1976), 74ff.

6. The son of a tofu dealer in Nuttari 沼垂, a suburb of Niigata city, Unpei had gone to Nagasaki in 1848. Still in his mid-teens, he was accepted as a student by Tetsuō. Through Tetsuō's introduction, Unpei met other artists active in Nagasaki, eventually becoming a disciple of Itsuun's. His long connection with Itsuun was recognized by the receipt of the name Unpei from his teacher on New Year's Day, 1864. He continued his studies with Itsuun until his teacher's untimely death at sea in 1866. See Yanagi, *Kindai kaiga to bunjinga no chisei*, 61. The details of Unpei's life presented here are largely from this source and from Shimizu, *Gajin Nagai Unpei*.

7. According to a letter from Unpei to a seal carver friend in Nagasaki, the three artists were lodging together soon after their arrival in Shanghai; see Shimizu, *Gajin Nagai Unpei*, 75–76.

8. Hu praised Tetsuō's talent in employing Ni Zan's 倪瓚 (1301–1374) style in his inscription on the painting dated to the spring of 1875, four years after Tetsuō's death. Hu notes that the painting was brought to him by a certain Zuigan 瑞岩. Although Nagai Unpei later used this same name,

this reference is clearly to another Japanese visitor, the antique dealer Sano Zuigan 佐野瑞岩, who is often mentioned in association with Chinese artists in Shanghai in the early Meiji period; see the discussion of Sano Zuigan in Lai Yu-chih, "Surreptitious Appropriation: Ren Bonian (1840–1895) and Japanese Culture in Shanghai, 1842–1895" (PhD diss., Yale University, 2005), 207–18. Tani Shin'ichi 谷信一 published a short discussion of the importance of this painting in *Nihon rekishi* 日本歴史, no. 223 (December 1966). The painting has been in the collection of the University of Michigan Museum of Art since the 1980s. The same Zuigan had taken a painting by Kinoshita Itsuun to Wang Kesan in 1872 for an inscription; see Tsuruta Takeyoshi 鶴田武良, "Ō Kokusan to Jo Utei" 王克三と徐雨亭, *Kokka* 国華, no. 1070 (1989): 22.

9. For more on Shen's work, see Stephen Little et al., *New Songs on Ancient Tunes: 19th–20th Century Paintings and Calligraphy from the Richard Fabian Collection* (Honolulu: Honolulu Academy of Arts, 2007), entry 33.

10. The date of Hu's arrival in Shanghai is given in Shimizu, *Gajin Nagai Unpei*, 77.

11. Wang Kesan was another of the prominent figures in the Chinese painting community in Nagasaki. He was best known for his ink plum paintings and calligraphy, although he also created landscapes. A map of Unpei's travels in China in provided in ibid., 74.

12. Different months in 1868 have been suggested for Unpei's return to Japan, but dated calligraphies by Chinese literati made for Unpei to mark his homecoming point to the third month; see ibid., 84–87.

13. Less is known about the activities of Kansen (Gozan) in China. His return to Japan is mentioned in ibid., 118. His involvement with Christianity is described in "Meiji no Kiristokyō senkaku Ishikawa Kumatarō to sono kazoku" 明治のキリスト教先覚石川熊太郎とその家族, *Toyama shidan* 富山史壇, no. 66.

14. See the entry in Araki Nori 荒木矩, ed., *Dai Nihon shoga meika taikan* 大日本書画名家大鑑 (1934; reprint, Tokyo: Daiichi Shobō 第一書房, 1975), 1451. The grave was later moved to the Japanese cemetery in Shanghai. The inscription by Hu on the front of Kōfū's grave reads: "Grave of the Japanese female scholar Kōfū, titled by Hu Gongshou of Huating" 日本紅楓女史之墓　華亭胡公壽題. One of the best sources for information on Kōfū is Yonezawa Hideo 米沢秀雄, *Shanhai shiwa* 上海史話 (Tokyo: Bōbō Shobō 畝傍書房, 1942), 159–61, 165–67. This work was reprinted in Yamashita Takeshi 山下武 and Takazaki Rikuji 高崎陸治, eds., *Shanhai sōsho* 上海叢書, vol. 1 (Tokyo: Ōsorasha 大空社, 2002). I would like to thank Joshua Fogel for sharing with me an early draft of his essay "Prostitutes and Painters: Early Japanese Migrants to Shanghai," from which I learned about Yonezawa's work. The finished version of Fogel's article, "Lust for Still Life: Chinese Painters in Japan and Japanese Painters in China in the 1860s and 1870s," appears in Elizabeth Lillehoj, ed., *Acquisitions: Art and Ownership in Edo-Period Japan* (Warren, CT: Floating World Editions, 2007), 149–68.

15. A large plum painting on paper dated to 1873 in the Hakutakuan collection states that it was made in Shanghai for a Mr. Nanba.

16. The early 1870s saw great tension between Taiwan and Japan over the beheading of shipwrecked Japanese sailors in 1871.

17. See Nakanishi Keiji 中西慶爾, *Kusakabe Meikaku den* 日下部鳴鶴伝 (Tokyo: Mokujisha 木耳社, 1984), 140.

18. There is a record of Rōzan creating impromptu paintings alongside other artists, including Meikaku, before the Meiji emperor at a gathering in the fourth month of 1876; see ibid., 182.

19. Iida Makoto 飯田真, "Yasuda Rōzan no kaiga" 安田老山の絵画, *Gifushi Rekishi Hakubutsukan kenkyū kiyō* 岐阜市歴史博物館研究紀要, no. 4 (March 1990): 92–94.

20. Umezawa Seiichi begins his discussion of literati painting in Tokyo during the Meiji period by stating that the representative painters were Okuhara Seiko and Yasuda Rōzan; see Umezawa, *Nihon nanga shi*, 933–34.

21. Rōzan left a considerable estate, but his second wife is said to have lost it through mismanagement within years of his death; see Nakanishi, *Kusakabe Meikaku den*, 140.

22. Umezawa Seiichi 梅沢精一, *Nihon nanga shi* 日本南画史 (Tokyo: Nanyōdō, 1919), 940–43.

23. Uzen is a mountainous region in the inner part of Yamagata prefecture in northern Japan.

24. In his later discussion of Hakuryū in the same volume, Umezawa gave a variation on this encounter. This time Rōzan is viewing a plum by Hakuryū when he makes the same complaint. Hakuryū's reply asserts that the "Japan smell" is not due to his being clumsy but to being Japanese and expressing himself and, furthermore, that to copy others is only to be a slave. The word "slave" (*dorei* 奴隷) is accented for emphasis in the original. Once again, Rōzan is said to be speechless; see Umezawa, *Nihon nanga shi*, 971. The time and place of the original incident are never clearly specified, and the details vary considerably from one account to another, casting some doubt on its historicity and the degree to what extent these versions accurately reflect the actual circumstances.

25. Some version of this incident is included in most biographical treatments of each artist. One of the more recent instances is the entry on Sugawara Hakuryū in Kawakita Michiaki 河北倫明, ed., *Kindai Nihon bijutsu jiten* 近代日本美術辞典 (Tokyo: Kōdansha 講談社, 1989), 191.

26. Although Hōko's works are only occasionally illustrated, the Ehime-ken Bijutsukan 愛媛県美術館 has a group of twenty-one major works by him in its collection in Matsuyama.

27. One measure of Rōzan's popularity is the large number of forgeries of his work; perhaps three out of ten works that survive today are questionable. Study of the seals on the forgeries reveals myriad differences that indicate they were created by many different hands with varying levels of skill.

28. See the doctoral dissertation on Seiko by Martha McClintock, "Okuhara Seiko (1837–1913): The Life and Arts of a Meiji Period Literati Artist" (PhD diss., University of Michigan, 1991).

29. Umezawa, *Nihon nanga shi*, 937–38. Seiko left Tokyo for Kumagaya 熊谷 in 1890 and about that time shifted her painting away from her renowned Zheng Xie style; see Kawashima Junji 川島恂二, *Gasan kara mita Okuhara Seiko* 画賛から見る奥原晴湖 (Tokyo: Rin Shobō りん書房, 1991), 992–93.

30. Illustrations of Rōzan's paintings are found in *Genshoku gendai nihon no bijutsu* 原色現代日本の美術, vol. 1 (Tokyo: Shōgakkan 小学館, 1980), plate 72, illus. 115–18 (this set of four seasonal landscapes by Rōzan is here mislabeled as the work of Okuhara Seiko 奥原晴湖), and ibid., vol. 4, illus. 3. In addition, see the pamphlet published for *Yasuda Rōzan ten* 安田老山展 at the Asakura Chōsokan 朝倉彫塑館 in 1989, and the leaflet with twenty-five illustrations of his work for *Yasuda Rōzan ten* 安田老山展 in Gifu prefecture at Kaizuchō Rekishi Minzoku Shiryōkan, 1997.

31. The Tokyo National Museum Rōzan landscape (*Landscape after a Wang Wei Poem*, ink on paper, 219 × 120.1 cm) is illustrated in Sakamoto Mitsuru 坂本満, *Kindai no taidō* 近代の胎動, Genshoku gendai Nihon bijutsu 原色現代日本美術, vol. 1 (Tokyo: Shōgakkan 小学館, 1980), plate 72.

The Transformation of Japanese Literati Painting in the Twentieth Century

Michiyo Morioka

Japanese literati painting, known as *bunjinga* 文人画 (literati painting) or *nanga* 南画 (southern painting), represents a well-established field of scholarly interest, its historical development and individual artists having been studied in great depth. The Chinese-derived literati tradition conjures up an image of an idealized landscape in vertical format with a non-Western spatial expression, portrayed with superb ink brushwork and inscribed with sophisticated Chinese-style poems (*kanshi* 漢詩). After its introduction in the early eighteenth century, the literati tradition would flourish in Japan for nearly two centuries. But in the twentieth century, known under the umbrella term *shin nanga* 新南画 (new *nanga*), literati painting would broaden its stylistic boundaries, defying easy generalization. Only in recent years have Japanese scholars begun to examine the significance and development of literati painting in modern Japan.[1] The diversity of their approaches and thematic focuses reveals the complexity and breadth of the topic, starting with the ambiguous meanings of the terms *bunjinga* and *nanga*. This short essay introduces some of the major issues in the transformation of literati painting in the twentieth century and provides a framework for understanding the modern-period artists and works included in this catalogue.

Literati Painting during the Meiji Period

During the 1860s and 1870s, in the transition from the late Edo to early Meiji period, literati painting continued to flourish with the strong patronage of new government leaders and a cultured elite well versed in the study of Chinese classics. Among those who established successful careers during this time were Hine Taizan 日根対山 (1813–1869), Haruki Nanmei 春木南溟 (1795–1878), Hoashi Kyōu 帆足杏雨 (1810–1884), Tanomura Chokunyū 田能村直入 (1814–1907), Yamanaka Shinten'ō 山中信天翁 (1822–1885), Yasuda Rōzan 安田老山 (1830–1882), and Okuhara Seiko 奥原晴湖 (1837–1912). Some artists, such as Rōzan, went to China to study painting; others, including Seiko, found fresh influences in books and paintings newly imported from the continent. Reflecting the dynamic political and social changes occurring during the transition from the feudal system to a modern monarchy, dramatic landscape compositions executed in flamboyant brushwork came into vogue. The widespread popularity of this style, however, exacerbated a proliferation of low-quality work with coarse brushwork, and critics began to complain, most famously in an 1882 newspaper review that ridiculed literati landscapes for depicting "mountains like yam potatoes and pine trees like wooden pestles" (*tsukuneimo no yama, surikogi no matsu*). Earlier in the same year, the influential American art historian Ernest Fenollosa (1858–1908) made his well-known denouncement of literati painting in a public lecture in Tokyo.[2]

To respond to these criticisms and to elevate their standing within the emerging art establishment of modern Japan, literati painters began to form formal associations and organizations. In 1897 Tanomura Chokunyū energized the Kyoto literati community with the founding of the Japan Nanga Association (Nihon Nanga Kyōkai 日本南画協会).[3] In Tokyo, leading artists Inose Tōnei 猪瀬東寧 (1839–1910), Kawamura Ukoku 川村雨谷 (1838–1906), and Takamori Saigan 高森砕巌 (1847–1917) organized the Japan Nanga Group (Nihon Nangakai 日本南画会) in 1898, and a similar organization also appeared in Osaka. The term *nanga* came into common usage around that time to emphasize the preeminence of painting, as opposed to the equal importance accorded painting, poetry, and calligraphy by the term *nanshūga* 南宗画 (Southern school painting) or *bunjinga*.[4] At the third Domestic Industrial Exposition in 1890, the new term *kaiga* 絵画 (painting) had replaced the traditionally used designation *shoga* 書画 (calligraphy and painting), signaling the importance of painting as an independent modern art form. The decision to employ the term *nanga* to name the new organizations reflected the artists' eagerness to advance literati painting in modern Japan. After the turn of the century, the literati movement gained momentum when Kyoto's Japan Nanga Association established branch offices in other cities; by 1904 its members numbered three thousand.[5] Tokyo's Japan Nanga Group was restructured in 1914, and it quickly became a leading literati group of national stature.

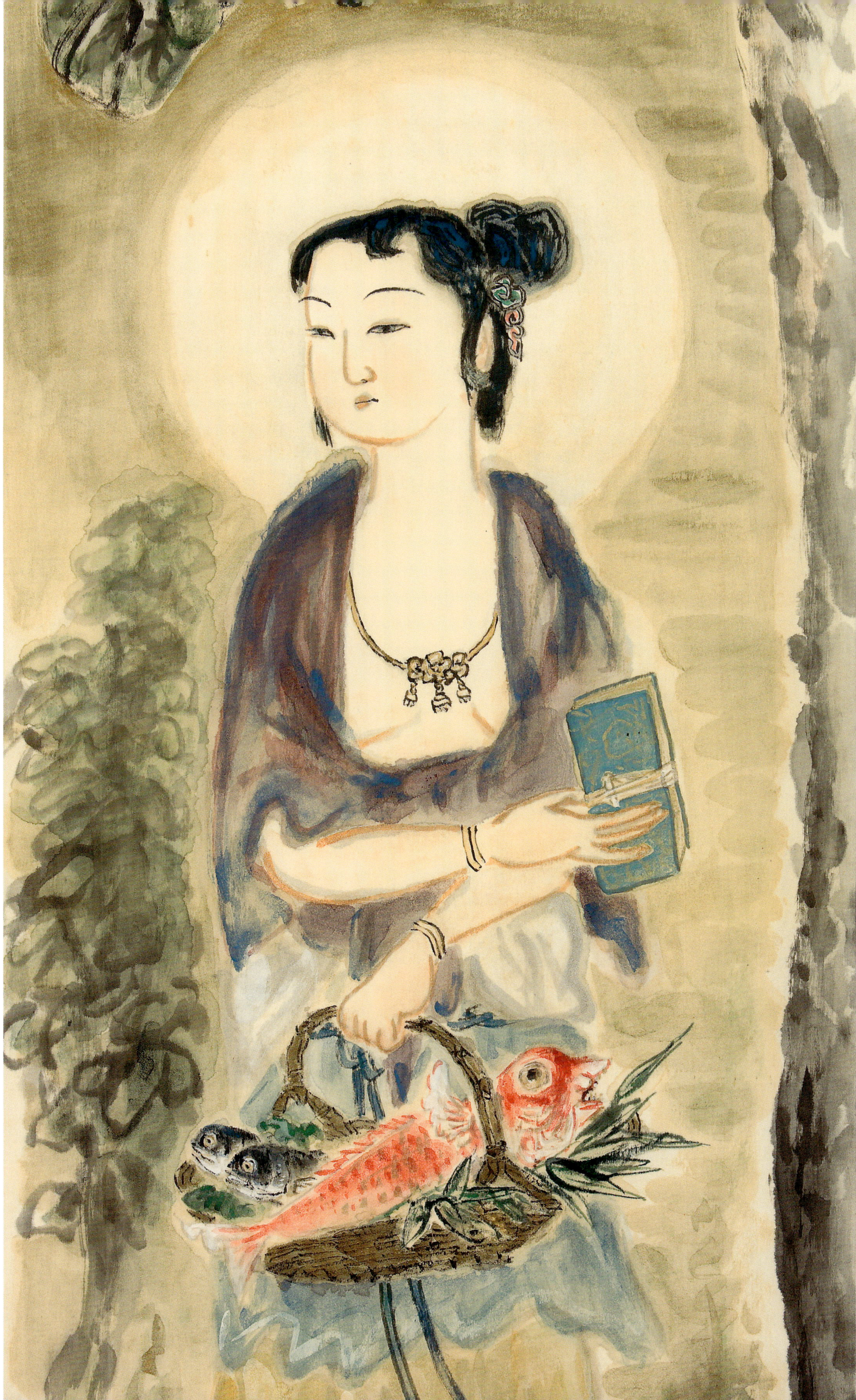

Throughout this period, literati painting was strongly appreciated on a popular level, but among modern-minded art insiders it faced the stigma of being considered outdated. At the annual Bunten, the government-sponsored exhibition first established in 1907, artists of various schools were competing with innovative, new styles influenced by Western art or various Japanese painting traditions, and Chinese-derived literati painting increasingly was viewed as old-fashioned. When literati painters tried to instill a sense of modernity by incorporating a new realism in their works, critics saw only a tired reliance on established formulas.[6] Moreover, at modern exhibitions, rows and rows of large paintings vied for the jurors' attention, and literati works began to take on a monumental and at times overtly decorative appearance. One critic asserted that most contemporary literati painters were "artisans" who were "affected by showmanship."[7] Recognizing that the public, professional nature of exhibitions contradicted the literati principle of art as intimate and personal, some voiced the opinion that the modern exhibition format was actually detrimental to literati painting.[8]

Others saw a fundamental lack of preparation as adversely affecting literati practice. In 1911 Mashizu Shunnan 益頭俊南 (1851–1916), a prominent literati painter, deplored the lack of classical learning among younger artists: their titles were often too elementary, and their signature inscriptions were poor.[9] Another protested that critics and scholars influenced by Western aesthetics and ways of thinking could not properly evaluate or appreciate literati painting.[10] As Japanese society changed under the influence of Western culture, literati painting itself was becoming too arcane and inaccessible to both the artists and viewers of the Meiji generation (although many superb paintings in the orthodox mode continued to be produced through the Taishō period). It was from these circumstances that *shin nanga,* or new literati painting, emerged.

The Shin Nanga Movement

Shin nanga is best understood as a broad movement rather than a stylistic designation. First appearing around 1917, the term encompassed a wide spectrum of paintings, all of which represented the new trend. In its rejection of the established Chinese-derived literati mode, *shin nanga* mirrored the general state of the Japanese art world, which witnessed an escalating schism between old school (*kyūha* 旧派) and new school (*shinpa* 新派). This conflict was most clearly manifested at the 1912 government exhibition in the separation of the *nihonga* (Japanese-style painting) division into conservative and progressive sections.

Soon after the turn of the century, a renewed interest in literati painting surfaced in both in *nihonga* and *yōga* (Western-style painting) circles under a new wave of Western influences. The notion of subjectivity, introduced with postimpressionism, triggered Japanese artists to reconsider literati painting and its principle of self-expression.[11] For *nihonga* painters searching for innovative forms of expression, literati painting was part of a wider exploration of past Japanese styles. Yokoyama Taikan 横山大観 (1868–1958), Imamura Shikō 今村紫紅 (1880–1916), and Tomita Keisen 冨田溪仙 (1879–1936) were among the earliest to experiment with the expressive brushwork of Japanese literati masters such as Ike Taiga 池大雅 (1723–1776), Yosa Buson 与謝蕪村 (1716–1783), and Tomioka Tessai 富岡鉄斎 (1836–1924).[12] *Yōga* painters were quick to find a parallel in the subjectivity of postimpressionism and literati painting. As early as 1911, Fujishima Takeji 藤島武二 (1867–1943), an esteemed *yōga* artist, pointed out the "psychological" similarity between Gauguin, Van Gogh, and Cézanne and Japanese masters such as Taiga and Buson.[13] Another *yōga* painter, Saitō Yori 齋藤與里 (1885–1959), asserted that the strength of literati painting was in the stylistic freedom with which artists individually interpreted nature.[14] Art historians would soon provide theoretical links by discussing the principles of literati painting in terms of modern European expressionism (*hyōgen shugi* 表現主義).[15] Filtered through the newly introduced Western concepts of subjectivity and individualism, which became prevalent in the Taishō art world, literati painting gained new significance, leading to a broader investigation of its traditions.[16]

It was in this context that two prominent art journals published special issues devoted to literati painting: *Kaiga seidan* 繪畫清談 in 1916, and *Chūō bijutsu* 中央美術 in 1917. The more conservative editorial in *Kaiga seidan* expressed the dilemma felt by many established literati painters. It defended traditional *bunjinga* as the lofty, Chinese-originated activity of cultured gentlemen but questioned how one could "paint about China without being born in China and having visited China," and stressed the need to transform the tradition to meet the demands of contemporary life.[17] *Chūō bijutsu* was more liberal in outlook, with essays contributed by both *yōga* and *nihonga* painters. Its editorial titled "The Emergence of *Shin Nanga*" (*Shin nanga no kiun ugoku* 新南畫の機運動く) possibly marked the first appearance of the term. It distinguished *shin nanga* from conservative literati painting, asserting that *shin nanga* was created not by professionally trained literati but by those outside the literati circle. It listed as representatives of this new movement not only *nihonga* painters (the late Imamura Shikō, Yokoyama Taikan, Terazaki Kōgyō, Yūki Somei, Hirafuku Hyakusui, Hashimoto Kansetsu, Tomita Keisen, Yasuda Yukihiko, Kobayashi Kokei) but also *yōga* painters (Kosugi Misei, Mitsutani Kunishirō, Morita Tsunetomo).[18] Propelled by the premise of self-expression and unconfined by established rules, *shin nanga* artists freely incorporated Western influences, Japanese traditions, and elements from newly introduced paintings from China.[19] A lack of training in traditional literati practice was regarded a positive factor in creating *shin nanga* because it freed the artist from preconceived ideas and moribund methods.

Although the terms *bunjinga* and *nanga* were used interchangeably to refer to literati painting in general, by the early twentieth century, *nanga* had come to signify painting by professional literati artists. To reinforce the ideal of literati art as the playful self-expression of amateur-scholars, several academics revived the term *bunjinga*.[20] This emphasis on nonspecialist practitioners further validated the pursuit of literati painting by other artists such as *yōga* painters, while disseminating the idea of "amateur painting" (*shirōtoga* 素人画) or "art as hobby" (*yogi geijutsu* 余技芸術). During the mid-Taishō period exhibitions of art by famous authors, poets, military leaders, and actors could be viewed. In particular, the literati-style paintings of the novelist Natsume Sōseki 夏目漱石 (1867–1916) were widely admired as the epitome of modern *bunjin* expression.[21] It may have been this trend that compelled Matsubayashi Keigetsu (1876–1963) to proclaim that he was a *nanga* painter, not an amateur who painted *bunjinga* as a hobby.[22]

With interest mounting in literati painting and *shin nanga,* literati artists trained in orthodox techniques launched the Japan Nanga Institute in 1921 to revitalize their field. Uniting the Kyoto, Tokyo, and Osaka literati circles, it counted among its members older artists, such as Tajika Chikuson 田近竹邨 (1864–1922), Yamada Kaidō 山田介堂 (1870–1924), and Komuro Suiun 小室翠雲 (1874–1945), and younger painters including Mizuta Chikuho 水田竹圃 (1883–1958), Yano Kyōson 矢野橋村 (1890–1965), and Shirakura Jihō 白倉二峰 (1896–1974). Suiun gradually emerged as the institute's leader.

Despite the general perception within the Taishō art world of the conservatism of traditional literati painting, the Japan Nanga Institute held a progressive outlook that mirrored the underlying philosophy of the *shin nanga* movement. Asserting the importance of the artist's expression of character over stylistic features, the group broadened the criteria by which literati painting was evaluated to include an understanding of nature based on observation, an absence of formulaic approaches, and the acceptance of "any work that shows literati spirit, including *ukiyoe* style."[23] Eager to advance literati painting nationwide, many institute artists actively competed at the government exhibitions while participating in their own annual exhibitions. For the next fifteen years, the group offered an important national venue for modern literati artists and welcomed as its members even those working in radically new, *yōga*-influenced styles, such as Mizukoshi Shōnan and Ogawa Sen'yō.[24]

Thus, in the early twentieth century, the precept of literati painting became less restrictive. What had become a relatively codified traditional practice took on an unprecedented diversity that encompassed multiple modes of expression. Some artists remained grounded in longstanding literati methods yet searched for more personal representations; some who were trained in literati techniques experimented with unorthodox styles; others applied Western technique to Chinese and Japanese themes; and still others worked independently from the usual artistic affiliations in highly individualistic methods. In the following brief discussion, I will characterize some of the individuals working in these diverse literati modes.

The Japan Nanga Institute Artists

The artists of the Japan Nanga Institute, represented by Komuro Suiun, Yano Kyōson, Mizuta Chikuho, and Shirakura Jihō, had received solid training in traditional literati painting and achieved reputations as the leading literati of the Taishō period. Seeking more personal, "realistic" representations—distinct from the stylized literati landscape of old—they visited China to experience its famous sites firsthand. Moreover, with their orthodox training as a foundation, they explored widely in search of new forms of expression. One of Kyōson's early works, *Nature Is Timeless*, dated 1920 (fig. 1), exemplifies this experimental approach. Just as in classic literati practice, the painting represents a Chinese landscape and refers to a Chinese poem, in this case by the Tang-dynasty poet Li Bo. But instead of the traditional emphasis on brushwork, Kyōson built his landscape by layering the eccentric geometric forms of the mountains and hills. In contrast, in *Red Cliff*, 1921 (fig. 2), a quintessential literati theme based on the prose-poems of the Chinese poet Su Shi, Jihō's brushwork and strong color accents are vigorously executed with a near total disregard of spatial constructs. The use of lively brushwork as a unifying element over the structure of the painting recalls Jihō's *Viewing Plum Blossoms*, 1922 (cat. no. 59). Over time, both Kyōson and Jihō widened their search for innovative styles, often employing Western perspective or contemporary themes, as in Kyōson's *Mother's Breast*, 1939 (cat. no. 72).

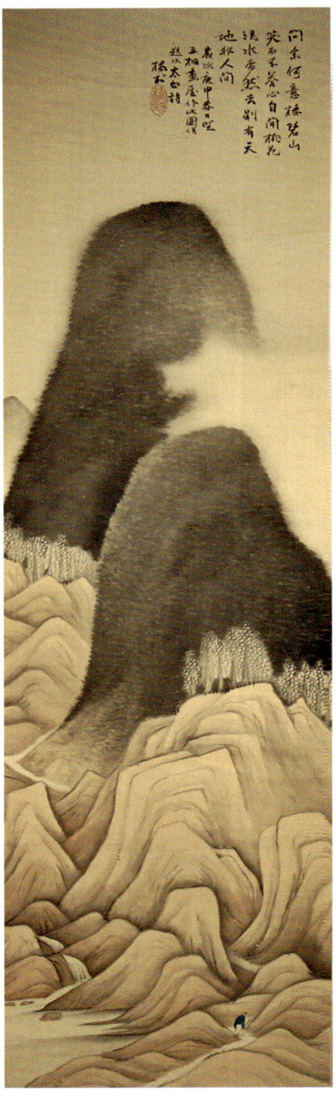

Figure 1. Yano Kyōson 矢野橋村, *Nature Is Timeless* 山中無暦図 (Sanchū Mureki zu), 1920. Hanging scroll: ink and color on silk, 137 × 42 cm. Private collection.

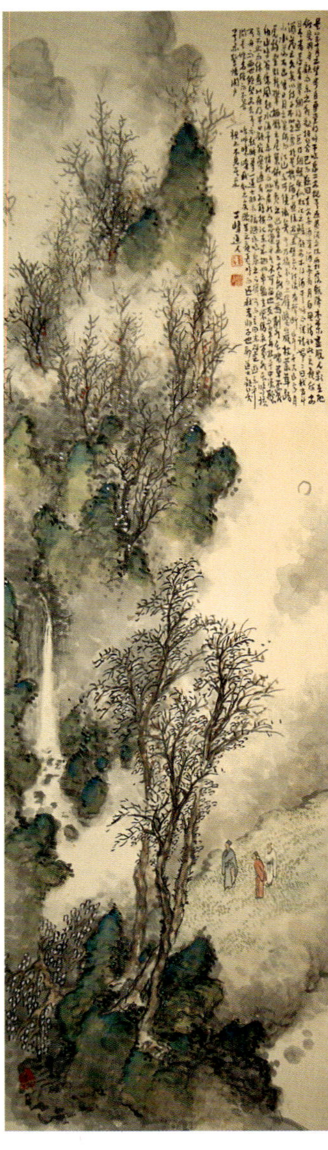

Figure 2. Shirakura Jihō 白倉二峰, *Red Cliff* 赤壁図 (Sekiheki zu), 1921. Hanging scroll: ink and color on paper, 144 × 42.5 cm. Private collection.

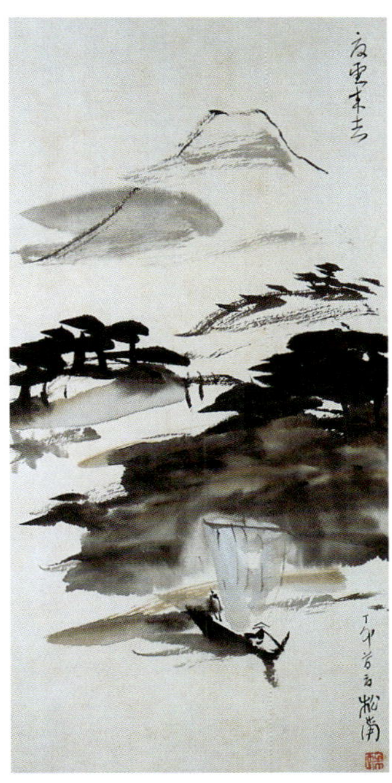

Figure 3. Mizukoshi Shōnan 水越松南, *Scattered Clouds Coming and Going* 散雲來去 (San'un raikyo), 1927. Album leaf: ink and light color on paper, 30.2 × 15.1 cm. Hakutakuan collection, Kyoto.

With its broad-minded standards, the Japan Nanga Institute accepted as members unique artists such as Yamaguchi Hachikushi 山口八九子 (1890–1933) and Mizukoshi Shōnan 水越松南 (1888–1985).[25] Hachikushi's lyrical style evoked the aesthetic of *haiga* (haiku painting), while Shōnan earned acclaim for his wildly brushed paintings of unconventional subjects such as the modern mailman portrayed in his 1927 *Village's Old Angel*, 1927.[26] One critic described his style as a mixture of elements from the Zen painter Sengai and Europe's Fauves (or "wild beasts"); another called his work "leftist" for its radical quality.[27] The small album leaf by Shōnan (fig. 3) included here is a traditional landscape subject, but the boldness of its wet brushwork gives a glimpse into his uninhibited style.

The institute's liberal attitude led one critic to comment, "I do not take a narrow view of literati painting. However, I question the validity of including paintings with unconventional intention or unusual expression just because they are new in the literati painting category. . . . Would it not actually lead to the destruction of literati painting rather than its development?"[28] The widely varied stylistic and thematic approaches taken by members of the Japan Nanga Institute demonstrate the institute's progressive outlook as well as the ever-broadening scope of literati painting in the early twentieth century.

Kyoto Nihonga Artists

Many Meiji-period Kyoto artists had studied literati tradition as transmitted by Matsumura Goshun, the founder of the Shijō school.[29] Later artists such as Tomita Keisen, Hashimoto Kansetsu, Dōmoto Inshō 堂本印象 (1889–1975), and Hirai Baisen 平井楳仙 (1889–1969) took inspiration more directly from the literati masters Buson and Tessai. During the Taishō period Keisen's loose brushwork in ink and color and seeming disregard for technical refinement became widely recognized as the quintessence of the new literati painting,[30] as exemplified by his *Su Dongpo* (cat. no. 80) and *A Boat Crossing a Large River* (cat. no. 48). Inshō and Baisen, both known for their exploratory attitudes, painted a variety of subjects in diverse styles. For Inshō, the concentration of his literati-mode works during the 1920s, such as *Chinese Garden*, 1923 (cat. no. 75), marked an important foray in his long, prolific career. Baisen's eclecticism was so pronounced that he often integrated various stylistic elements in one work. The pointillism that he derived from postimpressionism and literati brush technique, however, as seen in *Autumn*, 1920s (fig. 4), was a consistent presence in many of his early twentieth-century paintings (cat. nos. 54, 55, 73). Of the Kyoto painters, Kansetsu, the son of a Confucian scholar, was a true *bunjin* who easily integrated his knowledge of Chinese poetry and his excellent calligraphy into a pure literati expression (see cat. no. 13). Many of his Taishō examples, however, reveal a lighthearted playfulness, as in *Summer in a Waterside Village*, c. 1920 (fig. 5).

Despite their successful careers, all the artists mentioned above remained outside the mainstream Kyoto *nihonga* community. Keisen, known as an eccentric for his

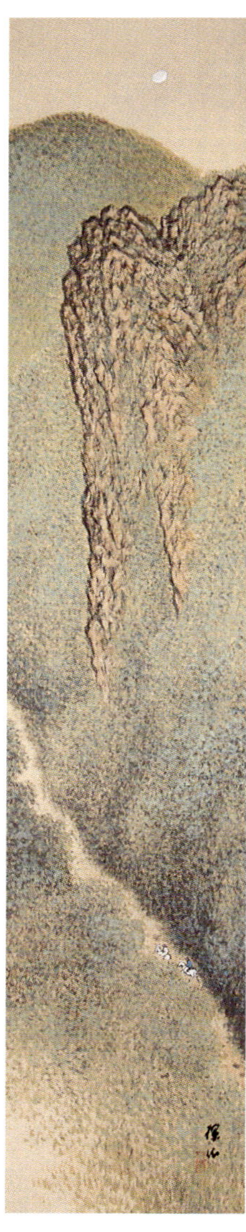

Figure 4. Hirai Baisen 平井楳仙, *Autumn* 秋之図 (Aki no zu), 1920s. Hanging scroll: color on silk, 130.6 × 27.6 cm. Collection of Terry Welch.

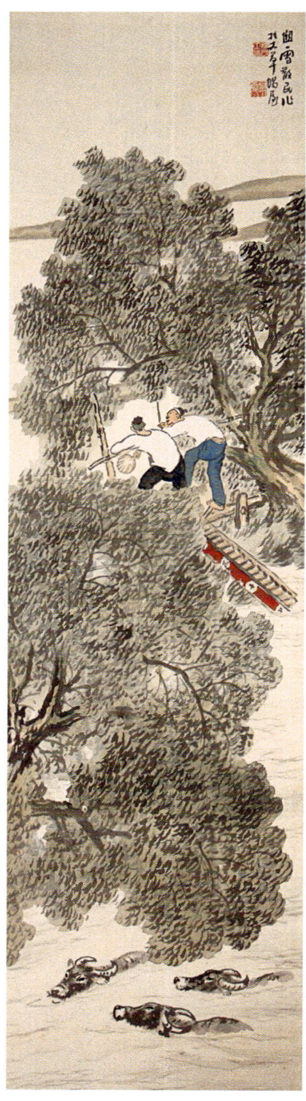

Figure 5. Hashimoto Kansetsu 橋本関雪, *Summer in a Waterside Village* 水邨夏日図 (Suison kajitsu zu), c. 1920. Hanging scroll: color on silk, 132 × 36.5 cm. Collection of Terry Welch.

frankness, was one of the few Kyoto artists who chose to center his activities at the Tokyo-based Japan Art Institute (Nihon Bijutsuin 日本美術院). Inshō's creative passion made him an unusually restless painter whose constant stylistic changes went beyond the standards of the Kyoto *nihonga* circle. The continuous evolution of his art would culminate most dramatically in the pure abstraction of his postwar work. Baisen defied the common practice of entering an established master painter's studio and instead independently advanced his career in the national arena. Outspoken and proud of his *bunjin* pedigree, Kansetsu was a controversial figure and feuded with his own teacher. Nonconformist and provocative, these painters evoked the independence and individualism that were associated with old masters such as Taiga and Buson.

Yōga-Nihonga Artists

Yōga, or Western-style, painters had ventured into *nihonga* even before the Taishō period. Asai Chū 浅井忠 (1856–1907) painted *nihonga* in Kyoto during his final years. Nakamura Fusetsu 中村不折 (1866–1943) and Shimomura Izan 下村為山 (1865–1949) produced ink-and-brush illustration and *haiga* as a result of their contact with the poet Masaoka Shiki in the 1890s and remained engaged with Japanese-style painting throughout their careers.

Crucial in the *shin nanga* movement were members of the Coral Group (Sangokai 珊瑚会), *yōga*-trained artists working in the *nihonga* tradition. Established in 1915, the group included Ogawa Usen 小川芋銭 (1868–1938), Hirafuku Hyakusui, Morita Tsunetomo, Kondō Kōichiro 近藤浩一路 (1884–1962), and Ogawa Sen'yō 小川千甕 (1882–1971), all of whom had worked as cartoonists and/or illustrators and shared a love of *haiga.* Attesting to their aggressive experimentation, each artist developed a highly individualistic *shin nanga* style. Kōichiro pioneered new brush techniques in ink and eventually established himself as a premier modern ink painter, as exemplified by *Rocky Seashore,* late 1930s (cat. no. 52). His colleague Sen'yō often combined vivid coloring with lively brush modes in paintings of almost childlike exuberance, such as in *Fish-basket Kannon,* 1920s (cat.

no. 83), and *Eight Views of Ōmi,* c. 1933 (cat. no. 58). Tsunetomo introduced a far more casual "amateurism" in his paintings. A graduate of the *yōga* department of the Tokyo Art School, Tsunetomo showed oil paintings at the Japan Art Institute exhibits but at the same time made ink-on-paper works.[31] *Under the Trees,* c. 1920 (fig. 6), exemplifies his lighthearted approach and the unassuming, unorthodox brush style of his country scenes.

Having little formal training in *nihonga* liberated these artists from the traditional rules. They freely depicted fresh Japanese themes in expressive, hybrid styles that resonated with modern sensibilities. One observer proclaimed that because *yōga* artists relied on internal feelings rather than superficial technique, their *nihonga* paintings could be superior in quality.[32] Some critics even argued that the *nihonga* by *yōga* painters were better suited for traditional display in tokonomas because they were not burdened by thick layers of pigment (as were many contemporary professional *nihonga*), which made it difficult to roll up hanging scrolls for storage.[33]

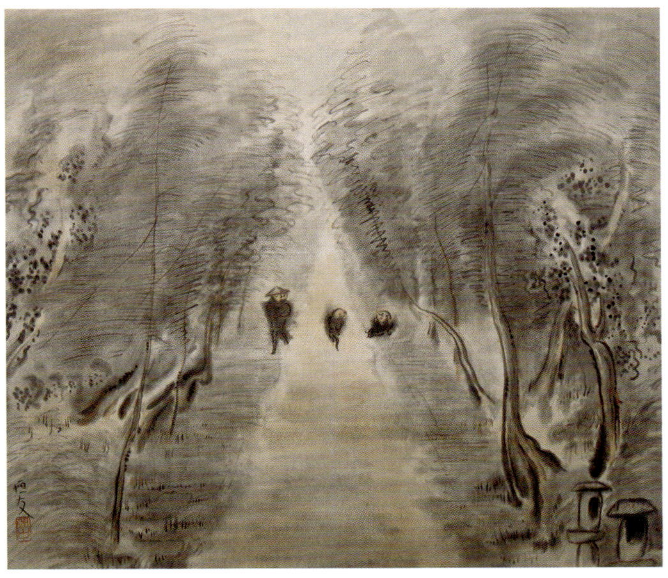

Figure 6. Morita Tsunetomo 森田恒友, *Under the Trees* 樹下 (Juka), c. 1920. Hanging scroll: ink and light color on paper, 49 × 58.2 cm. Collection of Terry Welch.

Independents

Numerous Japanese artists, or "outsider-individualists,"[34] refrained from participating in either large exhibitions or art organizations. Instead, they pursued their careers through small private shows and with the support of wealthy patrons. In general, they focused on creating intimate paintings intended for the traditional tokonoma setting. Tomioka Tessai, who never considered himself a professional painter and did not show at major exhibitions, can be considered their forerunner in some respects, although he remained an active member of Kyoto's art community. Moreover, Tessai occupied an important position in *shin nanga* in that his powerfully individualistic painting style directly inspired many younger artists in both *nihonga* and *yōga*.

Maeda Mokuhō 前田黙鳳 (1853–1918) and Fukuda Kodōjin 福田古道人 (1865–1944) represented the literati ideal of amateur painting and enjoyed the admiration of collectors. For example, in 1915, after traveling to Hokkaidō, Mokuhō stopped in a small harbor town in Aomori, where he was

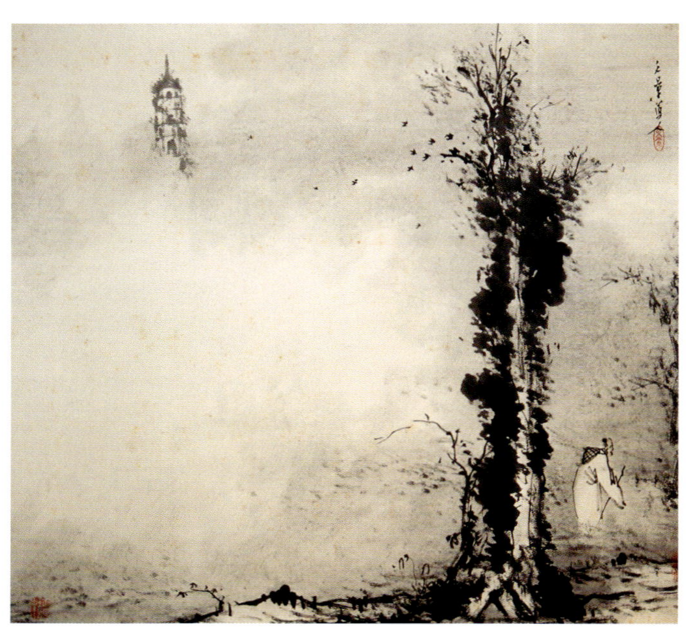

Figure 7. Hijiya Bunkei 泥谷文景, *Crows in the Evening* 暮鴉之図 (Boa no zu), c. 1935. Hanging scroll: ink on paper, 54 × 60 cm. Private collection.

besieged by requests for his painting.[35] Kodōjin's patronage group, established in 1928, included high-ranking government officials and prominent Japanese businessmen. Mokuhō spent many years in China studying early Chinese calligraphers, and he became renowned for a calligraphy style that would influence his unconventional landscape paintings (cat. no. 45). Like Mokuhō, Kodōjin asserted his individuality with the expressive power of his brushwork (see cat. nos. 49, 50), untutored and unhampered by technical concerns.

Other modern-period literati painters who worked independently include Irie Shikai 入江之介 (1862–after 1940), Kusunoki Keishū 楠瓊州 (1892–1973), and Hijiya Bunkei 泥谷文景 (1899–1951).[36] Bunkei studied with the Osaka literati artist Himejima Chikugai 姫島竹外 (1840–1928) for more than a decade but eventually found artistic stimuli through trips to Korea and China and in the works of early Qing individualists. His *Crows in the Evening*, c. 1935 (fig. 7), displays an eccentric composition reminiscent of Zhu Da 朱耷 (1624–1705). Although the figure and distant pagoda are depicted with relative care, the treatment of the prominent tree shows no standardized form and none of the recognizable, predetermined brushstrokes of traditional literati painting. Bunkei died virtually unknown except by a circle of passionate collectors and supporters.

Gotō Shūgai 後藤秋涯 (1886–1979) is an anomaly among this group of independent artists for his adherence to the conservative Chinese literati style. Superbly executed in fine brushwork, Shūgai's orthodox portrayals of Chinese landscapes such as *Idle Pleasures*, 1920s (cat. no. 53), found avid supporters among elite business leaders and art connoisseurs during his lifetime.

Takakura Kangai 高倉観崖 (1884–1957?), Murakami Kagaku 村上華岳 (1888–1939), and Fusen Tetsu 不染鉄 (1891–1976), all of whom trained initially as *nihonga* painters in Kyoto, may also be included among the independents. After establishing themselves at various exhibitions, each of these men withdrew from the main art scene. Kangai developed a fresh, colorful style inspired by a trip to the continent and influenced by Tessai and Kansetsu, as demonstrated by *Album of Chinese Landscapes and Figures,* 1920 (cat. no. 82). The highly personalized brush idioms of Kagaku and Tetsu, in contrast, depict internalized visions of an idealized world. Both lived as virtual recluses in their later years. An original member of the Association for the Creation of National Painting (Kokuga Sōsaku Kyōkai 国画創作協会, 1918–28), a progressive *nihonga* group in Taishō-period Kyoto, Kagaku severed his ties with the art world after the group disbanded in 1928. The haunting, abstract brushwork in *Land of the Immortals in the Northern Mountains,* 1939 (fig. 8), represents Kagaku's signature style from his last decade, when he devoted himself to painting Buddhist images and mountain landscapes.[37] Tetsu's *Village by the Sea,* 1940s (fig. 9), is but one of numerous examples in which he memorialized his beloved Izu Ōshima Island 伊豆大島; its maritime theme and ink brush style relate to an unusual handscroll included in this catalogue (cat. no. 60).

Except for Kagaku and Tetsu, who became known at major exhibitions early in their careers, many of the outsider-individualists who were self-taught and/or shunned established organizations were seldom discussed by Japanese critics during their lifetimes. Their activities and widely varied approaches, however, represent a significant facet of twentieth-century literati painting.

Conclusion

Reflecting on the place of literati painting in early Shōwa Japan, one scholar concluded that the orthodox literati style expressive of an unworldly Daoist philosophy was no longer tenable, just as immortal recluses could not exist in the Westernized modern world.[38] But instead of declining or disappearing, the literati painting tradition reinvented itself as the *shin nanga* movement, which emerged under the confluence of influences and changes affecting the Japanese art world in the early twentieth century. Multifarious and complex, the movement encompassed artists of different schools and regions, transcending even the *nihonga* and *yōga* divisions.

Figure 8. Murakami Kagaku 村上華岳, *Land of the Immortals in the Northern Mountains* 北山仙境 (Hokuzan senkyō), 1939. Hanging scroll: ink and light color on paper, 56.4 × 22 cm. Private collection.

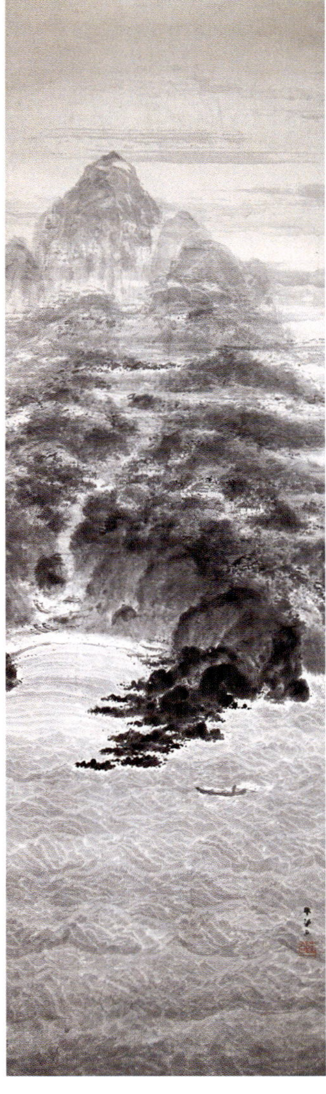

Figure 9. Fusen Tetsu 不染鉄, *Village by the Sea* 海村図 (Kaison zu), 1940s. Hanging scroll: ink on paper, 127.6 × 38.8 cm. Private collection.

The driving force behind *shin nanga* was the revival of the literati notion of self-expression as the modern concept of subjective art. With the emphasis on self, artists pursued literati painting on individual terms that echoed the eclectic practices of earlier masters but went far beyond the traditionally formulated boundaries and premises. Rather than celebrating an idealized China, twentieth-century artists more freely searched for new utopias in their immediate environments or in their internal visions. In the eighteenth century, Edo-period painters had been energized by exposure to newly imported Chinese *bunjinga.* The *shin nanga* movement invigorated twentieth-century Japanese painters by once again offering new possibilities for novel expressions and thereby transformed the classical literati ideal into viable modern tradition.

NOTES

1. Sakai Tetsurō 酒井哲朗, "Taishōki ni okeru nanga no saihyōka ni tsuite—Shin nanga o megutte" 大正期における南画の再評価について—新南画をめぐって, *Miyagiken bijutsukan kenkyū kiyō* 宮城県美術館研究紀要 3 (1988): 1–20; Miyagiken Bijutsukan宮城県美術館, *Kindai no bunjinga* 近代の文人画, exh. cat. (Sendai, 1993); Yamatane Bijutsukan 山種美術館, *Kindai no nanga—yūshin no sekai: Hyakusui・ Hōan・Kōyu・Kōichiro* 近代の南画—遊心の世界：百穂・放菴・恒友・浩一路, exh. cat. (Tokyo, 1993); Ibaraki Kenritsu Kindai Bijutsukan 茨城県立近代美術館, Tochigi Kenritsu Bijutsukan 栃木県立近代美術館, and Gunma Kenritsu Kindai Bijutsukan 群馬県立近代美術館, *Kita Kantō no bunjinga* 北関東の文人画 (Mito, Utsunomiya, and Takasaki, 1995); Gunma Kenritsu Kindai Bijutsukan, *Shizen ni asobi shizen ni utau—Kindai nanga ten* 自然に遊び、自然に謳う—近代南画展, exh. cat. (Takasaki, 1999); Hirabayashi Akira 平林彰, *Noguchi Shōhin to kindai nanga : Meiji no kyūtei gaka* 野口小蘋: 明治の宮廷画家 (Kōfu: Yamanashi Kenritsu Bijutsukan 山梨県立美術館, 2005).

2. From *Tokyo nichinichi shinbun* 東京日日新聞, October 9, 1882, cited by Hosono Masanobu 細野正信, "Nanga—Edo kara kindai e" 南画—江戸から近代へ, in Gunma Kenritsu Kindai Bijutsukan, *Shizen ni asobi shizen ni utau—Kindai nanga ten,* 8. For Fenollosa's opinion, see Kawakita Michiaki 河北倫明 and Takashina Shūji 高階秀爾, *Kindai Nihon kaigashi* 近代日本絵画史 (Tokyo: Chūō Kōronsha 中央公論社, 1978): 87–92. For Fenollosa's biography, see Lawrence W. Chilsom, *Fenollosa: The Far East and American Culture* (New Haven: Yale University Press, 1963).

3. Chokunyū was the first principal of the Kyoto Prefecture Painting School, which was founded in 1880 with literati painting as one of its four divisions. He established a private school about 1892 to teach literati painting and organized an exhibition of his own collection of paintings and calligraphies in 1897; see "Nanshū gaka no funpatsu" 南宗畫家の奮發, *Kaiga sōshi* 繪畫叢誌 62 (May 1892): 3, and "Chokunyū ō shoga no bakuryō" 直入翁書畫の曝凉, *Kaiga sōshi* 128 (September 1897): 2.

4. Suggested by Ōkuma Toshiyuki 大熊敏之 in his discussion of the origin of this term in "Kindai nangashi kō" 近代南画史考, in Gunma Kenritsu Bijutsukan, *Shizen ni asobi shizen ni utau—Kindai nanga ten,* 10–12.

5. "Nihon Nanga Kyōkai" 日本南畫協會, *Kaiga sōshi* 210 (September 1904): 3.

6. For example, see comments by Araki Jippo 荒木十畝 in "Tsukaretaru yonjūyonen no gakai" 疲れたる四十四年の畫界, *Bijutsu no Nihon* 美術之日本 4, no. 1 (January 1912): 5, and "Bunten sakuhin no

shikibetsu" 文展作品の色別, *Kaiga seidan* 繪畫清談 2, no. 11 (December 1914): 22.

7. Fukano Tatsu 深野達, "Nanga no shinzui towa nanzo" 南畫の眞髄とは何ぞ, *Kaiga seidan* 7 (August 1913): 51–52.

8. Taki Seiichi 瀧精一, "Nanga shokan" 南畫所感, *Chūō bijutsu* 中央美術 3, no. 6 (June 1917): 40.

9. Mashizu Shunnan 益頭峻南, "Gadai to rakkan" 書題と落款, *Kensei gashi* 研精畫誌 54 (October 1911): 21–22.

10. Matsubayashi Keigetsu 松林桂月, "Nangaka no shuchō" 南畫家の主張, *Bijutsu no Nihon* 美術之日本 2, no. 1 (January 1910): 14, and Sakai Hisayoshi 阪井久良岐, "Kyūha no zento" 旧派の前途, *Bijutsu no Nihon* 3, no. 5 (June 1911): 5.

11. Sakai Tetsurō, "Taishōki ni okeru nanga no saihyōka ni tsuite—Shin nanga o megutte," 3.

12. This is indicated by Taikan's *Mountain Path* 山路 (Yamaji), 1911; Shikō's *Eight Views of Ōmi* 近江八景 (Ōmi hakkei), 1912; and Keisen's *Cormorant Fishing Boats* 鵜船 (Ubune), 1912. Taikan's *Mountain Path* was praised as a "synthesis of Impressionist technique and literati brushwork" in a comment quoted in Nittenshi Hensan Iinkai 日展史編纂委員会, *Nittenshi 2, Buntenhen* 文展編 2 (Tokyo: Nitten, 1980), 273.

13. Fujishima Takeji, "Kontei to shinpo" 根底と進歩, *Bijutsu shinpō* 美術新報 10, no. 11 (September 1911): 341.

14. Saitō Yori 齋藤與里, "Shizen to nanga" 自然と南畫, *Bijutsu shinpō* 2, no. 15 (December 1915): 81.

15. First expressed by Taki Seiichi 瀧精一, in "Bunjinga no hongi" 文人畫の本義, *Shoga kottō zasshi* 書畫骨董雜誌 108 (June 1917): 5. For later essays, see Umezawa Waken 梅澤和軒, "Hyōgen shugi no ryūkō to bunjinga no fukkō" 表現主義の流行と文人畫の復興, *Waseda bungaku* 早稲田文学 186 (May 1921): 23–31; Taki Seiichi, "Bunjinga to hyōgen shugi" 文人畫と表現主義, *Kokka* 国華 390 (November 1922): 160–65.

16. The most notable example is Umezawa Seiichi 梅澤精一, *Nihon nanga shi* 日本南畫史 (Tokyo: Nanyōdō 南陽堂, 1919).

17. "Nanga taikan ni dai su" 南畫大観に題す, *Kaiga seidan* 4, no. 2 (February 1916): 2.

18. "Shin nanga no kiun ugoku" 新南畫の機運動く, *Chūō bijutsu* 3, no. 7 (July 1917): 2–3.

19. For example, Kosugi Misei discusses his excitement over finding the book on Jin Nong 金農 (1687–c. 1764) and Qian Du 錢杜 (1763–1844) in "Nanga to ginmi" 南畫と吟味 *Chūō bijutsu* 3, no. 7 (July 1917): 42.

20. Ōnishi Seigai 大西西崖, *Bunjinga no fukkō* 文人畫の復興 (Tokyo: Kōgeisha 巧藝社, 1921); see also note 15.

21. See "Shirōto shoga tenrankai" 素人書畫展覧会, *Kaiga seidan* 5, no. 3 (March 1917): 73, and Hirafuku Hyakusui 平福百穂, "Shirōto e no shumi" 素人繪の趣味, *Bijutsu no Nihon* 9, no. 1 (Jan. 1917): 7–9. For a comprehensive discussion of Sōseki's art, see Haga Tōru 芳賀徹, *Kaiga no ryōbun* 絵画の領分 (Tokyo: Asahi Shinbunsha 朝日新聞社, 1990.

22. Matsubayashi Keigetsu, "Nanga to bunjinga no betsu o akiraka ni seyo" 南畫と文人畫の別を明にせよ, *Kaiga seidan* 4, no. 2 (February 1916): 49–52.

23. Komuro Suiun, "Nangain no risō to shutchin sakuhin" 南畫院の理想と出陳作品, *Bi no kuni* 美之国 3, no. 8 (October 1927): 106, and Umezawa Waken, "Nangain shoken" 南畫院所見, *Atorie* アトリエ 3, no. 10 (October 1926): 76.

24. The Japan Nanga Institute remained active until 1936, after which many of its painters—at Nanga Renmei 南畫聯盟 (est. 1937) and Daitō Nansōin 大東南宗院 (est. 1941)—gathered under the leadership of Suiun in prewar Japan.

25. For the biography and works by Mizukoshi Shōnan and Yamaguchi Hachikushi, see Kyōto Kokuritsu Kindai Bijutsukan 京都国立近代美術館, *Ishoku no suiboku gaka: Mizukoshi Shōnan, Yamaguchi Hachikushi, Kusunoki Keishū* 異色の水墨画家：水越松南・山口八九子・楠瓊州, exh. cat. (Kyoto, 1976). For Shōnan, also see Himeji Shiritsu Bijutsukan 姫路市立美術館, *Mizukoshi Shōnan ten: Botsugo 20 nen* 水越松南展：没後20年, exh. cat. (Himeji: Himeji Shiritsu Bijutsukan Tomonokai 姫路市立美術館友の会, 2005).

26. For good color reproduction, see Kawakita Michiaki 河北倫明 and Horie Tomohiko 堀江知彦, *Genshoku gendai Nihon no bijutsu* 原色日本の美術 12: *Bunjinga to sho* 文人画と書 (Tokyo: Shōgakukan 小学館, 1979), plate 16.

27. Kawaji Ryūkō 川路柳虹, "Nangain no sakusha" 南畫院の作者, *Atorie* 12, no. 6 (June 1935): 45, and Okuse Eizō 奥瀬英三, "Nangain bekken ki" 南畫院瞥見記, *Bijutsu shinron* 美術新論 4, no. 10 (October 1929): 78.

28. Takeuchi Umematsu 竹内梅松, "Nangaten o miru" 南畫展を観る, *Bi no kuni* 3, no. 8 (October 1927): 82.

29. See a discussion by Paul Berry, "The Relation of Japanese Literati Painting to Nihonga," in Michiyo Morioka and Paul Berry, *Modern Masters of Kyoto: The Transformation of Japanese Painting Traditions, Nihonga from the Griffith and Patricia Way Collection* (Seattle: Seattle Art Museum, 1999), 32–34.

30. See an early comment by Saitō Yori, "Tomita Keisen ron" 冨田溪仙論, *Chūō bijutsu* 3, no. 8 (August 1917): 28–30.

31. For Tsunetomo's life and art, see Yamatane Bijutsukan, *Kindai no nanga—yūshin no sekai: Hyakusui・Hōan・Kōyu・Kōichiro*, 40–49, 78–83.

32. Tobari Kogan 戸張孤雁, "Kaiga to shizen" 繪畫と自然, *Bijutsu no Nihon* 4, no. 5 (May 1912): 7.

33. Ishi Hakutei 石井柏亭, "Yōgaka no nihonga" 洋畫家の日本畫, *Shinbi* 審美 5, no. 6 (June 1916): 23.

34. Term used by Paul Berry in his discussion of Fukuda Kodōjin, in Morioka and Berry, *Modern Masters of Kyoto*, 217.

35. See "Chihō zasshin" 地方雑信, *Kaiga sōshi* 340 (January 1916): 13. The members of the Kodōjinkai patronage group established in 1928 included high-ranking government officials and prominent leaders of the Japanese business world.

36. For Irie Shikai's biography and work, see Ōtsu Shiritsu Rekishi Hakubutsukan 大津市立歴史博物館, *Unexplored Avenues of Japanese Painting*, exh. cat. (Ōtsu, 2001), 188–89, plate 61. For Kusunoki Keishū, see Takiya Yuki 滝谷由亀, *Kusunoki Keishū gashū* 楠瓊州画集 (Tokyo: Sansaisha 三彩社, 1970), and Atsumi Kuniyasu 渥美国泰, *Kokō no nangaka Kusunoki Keishū: Sono seijaku no sekai* 孤高の南画家楠瓊州：その静寂の世界 (Tokyo: Geijutsu Shinbunsha 芸術新聞社, 1996). For Hijiya Bunkei, see Kyōto Kokuritsu Kindai Bijutsukan 京都国立近代美術館, *Ishoku no suibokugaka: Nozawa Joyō, Hijiya Bunkei, Ogawa Sen'yō* 異色の水墨画家：野沢如洋・泥谷文景・小川千甕, exh. cat. (Kyoto, 1975), no pagination, and Yamaguchi Genshu 山口玄珠, "Hijiya Bunkei sono ga" 泥谷文景その畫, *Nihon bijutsu* 2, no. 4 (April 1943): 89.

37. For Kagaku, see Kyōto Kokuritsu Kindai Bijutsukan 京都国立近代美術館, *Murakami Kagaku* 村上華岳 (Kyoto: Nihon Keizai Shinbun 日本経済新聞 and Kyōto Kokuritsu Kindai Bijutsukan, 2005), esp. plate 262.

38. Harada Bizan 原田尾山, "Gendai to nanga" 現代と南畫, *Nanga kanshō* 南畫鑑賞 9, no. 1 (January 1940): 23.

Literati Pursuits

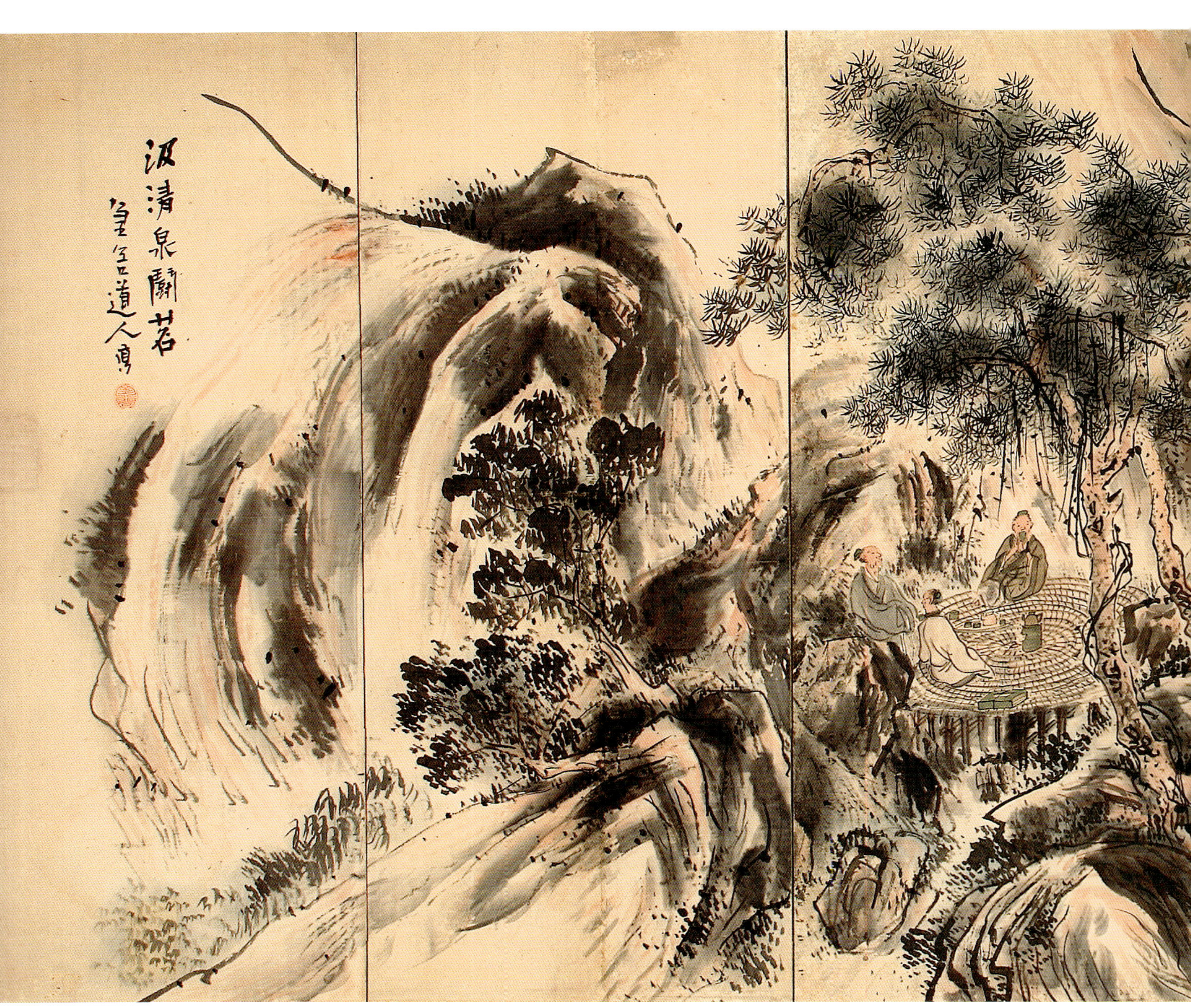

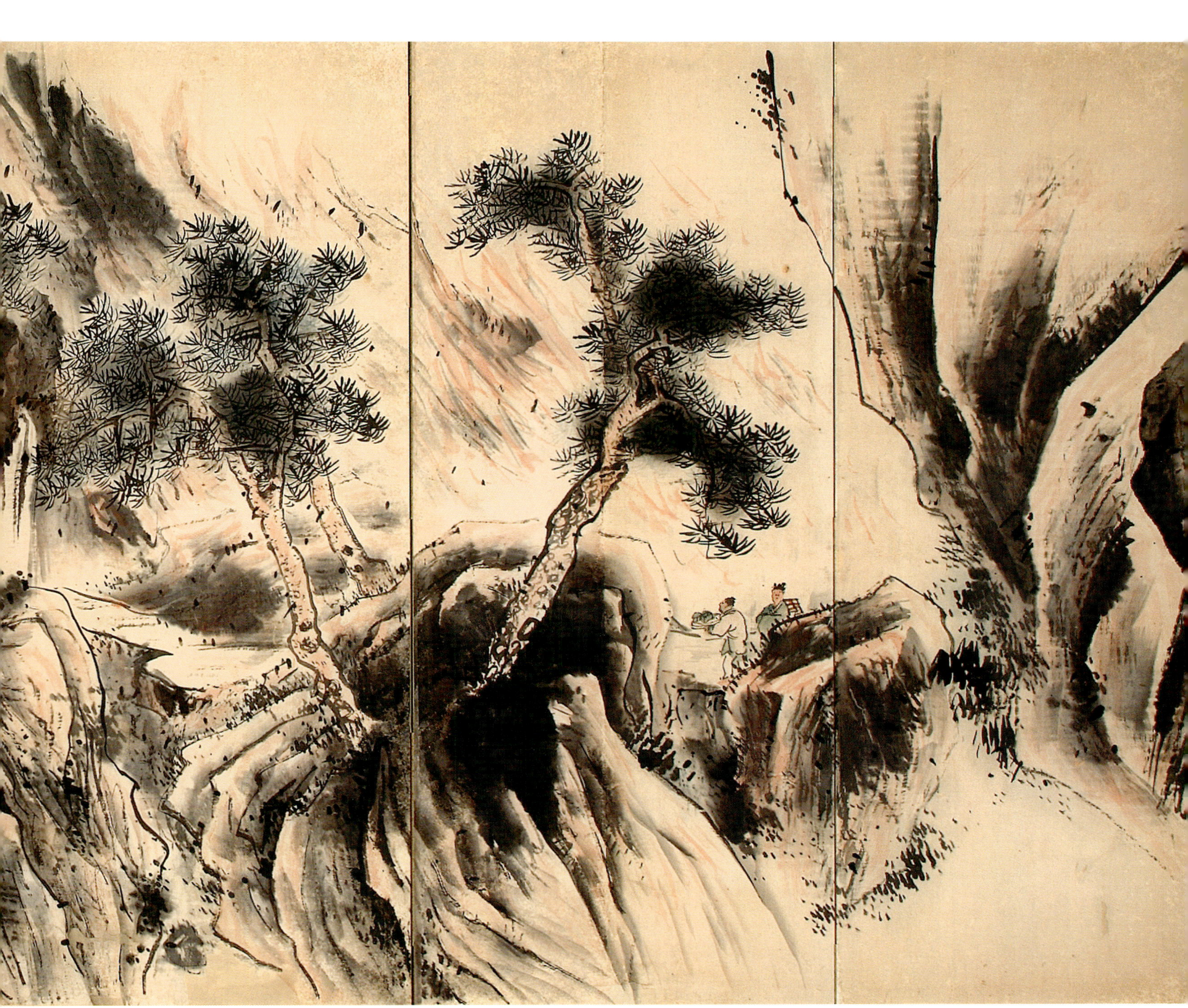

Suzuki Fuyō 鈴木芙蓉

1749–1816

The Gathering at the Orchid Pavilion, or Lanting 蘭亭, is the most popular of several noted themes depicting the gathering of scholars. It is based on the Eastern Jin-period (317–420) text *Lanting jixu* 蘭亭序集, written by Wang Xizhi 王羲之 (c. 307–c. 365), one of the truly famous calligraphers of East Asia. This brief account is the preface to thirty-seven poems written by some of the forty-one scholars attending the Spring Purification Ceremony at the Lanting outside the present-day city of Shaoxing 紹興 on the third day of the third month of 353. At this gathering, cups of wine were floated on lotus leaves along a meandering garden stream; when cups stopped near a scholar, he was obliged to drink the wine and compose a poem. The original text by Wang Xizhi became the most famous semicursive calligraphy in Chinese history, passed down through many copies and engravings long after the original was lost. The occasion itself became the ultimate paradigm for a literati gathering, generating similar meetings in China, Korea, and Japan that persist even today. A tradition of painted renditions of the party resulted in a wide variety of compositions that were transmitted to Japan in the form of Ming-period ink rubbings, which were copies of older handscrolls, and numerous vertical compositions in hanging scrolls in many styles.[1]

Fuyō repeatedly painted the Lanting theme, and differences among these compositions may reflect his exposure to a variety of Chinese Lanting paintings.[2] Certainly Tani Bunchō (see cat. no. 61) and his disciples painted the theme frequently, and during his repeated sojourns in Edo, Fuyō likely had access to their paintings and the Chinese works upon which they were based. Yet the similarity in motifs and compositions was the result of Fuyō studying the same Chinese sources. Even though it has often been suggested that Fuyō was Bunchō's student, this is contradicted by extant dated landscapes that show the older Fuyō had already established his style by the time he met Bunchō near the start of the latter's career. Fuyō and Bunchō were both drawing upon professional Chinese paintings and Ming-period landscapes of the Zhe school, styles that the Chinese literati had rejected yet that were easily accommodated by the eclecticism of the Japanese *bunjin*. The distinctive stiff and angular brushwork seen in the mountains and tree branches of Fuyō's work is reminiscent of similar treatments in the landscapes of Tang Yin 唐寅 (1470–1524).[3]

Fuyō's composition begins beyond an open viewing pavilion with a waterfall descending from distant hills and flowing into a garden in the middle ground, where boys place cups of wine on lotus leaves floating on the water. Just below them, four scholars listen to their compatriot read a newly composed poem as an attendant uses a pole to retrieve a wine cup from the stream. The next group consists of six literati musing on poetry or busy writing on the papers lying beside them. Wang Xizhi is shown composing his preface on a red lacquer table inside the prominently placed pavilion. One attendant grinds his ink, while Wang, his brush held in mid-air, follows the gaze of another attendant who watches geese floating in the stream. This iconography is a reminder that Wang was said to have taken inspiration for his elegant cursive calligraphy from the movements of swimming geese. At the bottom of the composition, two boys bearing food cross a stone bridge toward the pavilion. A subtle touch is the weir, necessary for trapping any stray cups of wine, that stretches across the river below the bridge. This gently zigzagging landscape with its distinctive brushwork demonstrates Fuyō's individuality and the need to bring his work out of the shadow of Bunchō's reputation to be considered in its own right.

PB

1. *Meandering Stream at Lanting* 蘭亭曲水之図 (Rantei kyokusui no zu)

1806
Hanging scroll: ink and color on silk
102 × 35 cm

SIGNATURE: *hei in boshun sha Fuyō Kiyō* 丙寅暮春寫 芙蓉木雍
Painted by Fuyō Kiyō in the third month of the *heiin* year [1806]

SEALS: *Kiyō no in* 木雍之印 (upper)
Bunki shi 文熙氏 (lower)

Purchase, 2005
13167.1

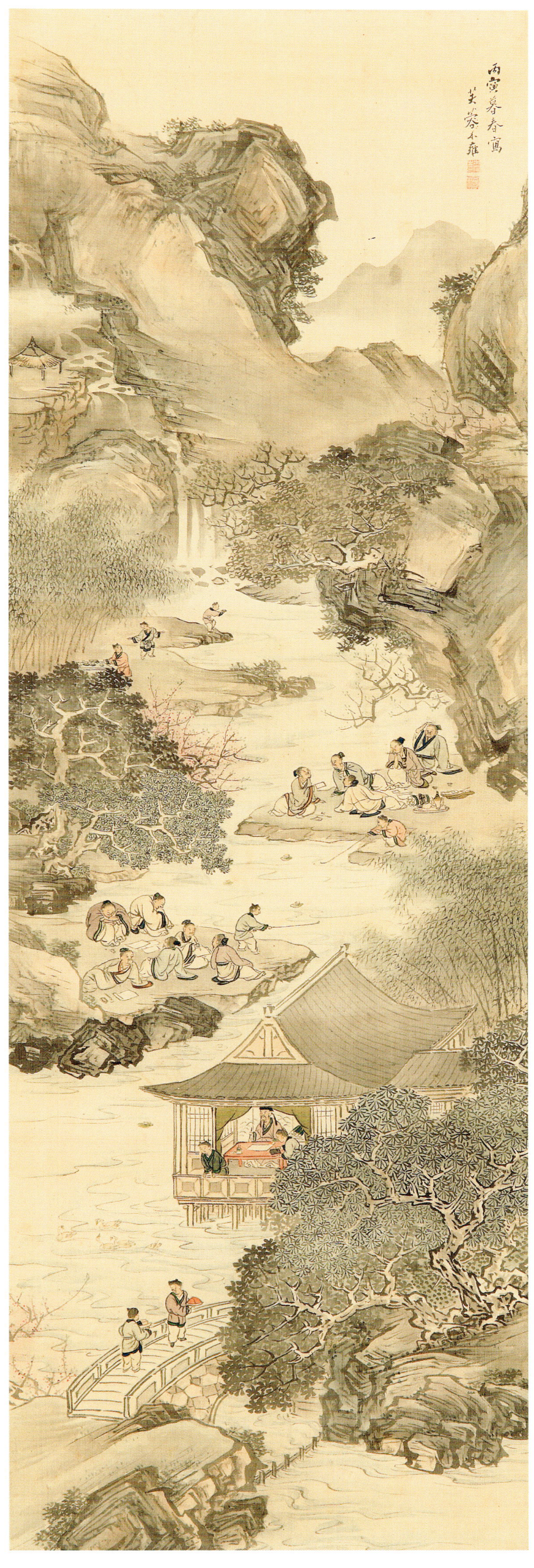

NOTES

1. See Marshall Wu's treatment of the Chinese painting tradition of this theme in *The Orchid Pavilion Gathering: Chinese Painting in the University of Michigan Museum of Art* (Seattle: University of Washington Press, 2000), vol. 1, 102–9, and vol. 2, 43–46. The full text of Wang's preface is translated in vol. 2, pp. 44–45, n. 15.

2. Compare with plate 44 in Tokushima Shiritsu Tokushimajo Hakubutsukan, *Wasurerareta bujin gaka Suzuki Fuyō to sono shuhen* (2004).

3. Refer to the examples illustrated in Anne De Coursey Clapp's *The Painting of T'ang Yin* (Chicago: University of Chicago Press, 1991). Even though authentic works by this noted Ming painter were rare in Japan at this time, copies, forgeries, and works in his style by minor painters were widely available.

Kameda Bōsai 亀田鵬斎

1752–1826

A Life of Drinking Sake is one of five quatrains that Bōsai composed in 1801 and collectively titled *Written on Returning to the Country When Becoming Fifty.*[1] Each verse presents an aspect of Bōsai's outlook on life and ends with the same final line.[2] Bōsai urged people to look beyond ideas of failure and success, and he celebrated the benefits of drinking wine:

不学仙兮不学佛 Not studying the Immortals, not studying the Buddhas,
無所見又無所述 Nothing to look at and nothing to say.
一生飲酒終無銭 A life of drinking sake ends with no money,
半生五十人事畢 Half a life, fifty years, knowing human affairs.

In his own life, Bōsai was renowned for drinking and even took part in advertised drinking bouts modeled after sumo tournaments.[3] Although he composed the verse in 1801, it is likely that he repeatedly chose it as a theme for calligraphy, and this striking example of his dramatic cursive script probably dates from around 1820. To those untutored in cursive script, the twisting forms of Bōsai's characters seem unintelligible but lively in their expressive brushwork. Yet far from writing any which way, Bōsai carefully followed the correct forms for cursive characters, making them not so difficult to read. He was celebrated as a calligrapher for the distinctive exuberance of his style.

The great bulk of Bōsai's calligraphies are undated, and the origins of his cursive style are obscured by the lack of early examples. Among the few works dated to his late thirties and early forties, regular and semicursive scripts predominate. It has traditionally been said that Bōsai's cursive style matured after he met the noted Zen priest Ryōkan 良寛 (1758–1851) in 1809 and 1810 during his travels in northern Japan. The hermetic Ryōkan is the most celebrated cursive-style calligrapher of the Edo period, and there is a resemblance between his works and those of Bōsai. Yet some examples from 1805 and 1807 demonstrate that Bōsai's cursive style was fully formed before he met Ryōkan. Their similar approach likely contributed to the deep friendship they swiftly formed.[4]

Both Bōsai and Ryōkan adopted as a model the so-called wild cursive (*kyōsho* 狂書) of the calligrapher most famous for the script, the Tang-dynasty Buddhist monk Huaisu 懐素 (c. 725–c. 785). Various works attributed to Huaisu became celebrated throughout East Asia through the popularity of copy books (*hōjō* 法帖) based on older ink rubbings. Even though Bōsai and Ryōkan had studied the works of the same calligrapher, their cursive calligraphies are discernibly distinct when closely examined. The differences have been attributed to the choice of model made by each man. Ryōkan chose Huaisu's *Autobiography* (Zixutie 自叙帖) for his study of cursive script,[5] and his script style reveals how deeply he had absorbed not only the form of individual characters but the overall irregular, expansive rhythm seen in the *Autobiography.*[6] Bōsai, however, looked at copy books based on the *Thousand-Character Classic* (Qianziwen 千字文) attributed to Huaisu. Although the cursive styles of Huaisu's texts are related, each character of the *Thousand-Character Classic* was conceived as fitting into the same-sized space, with less connection from one character to another and less of the irregularity of line and character size that typifies Ryōkan's work.

Bōsai gained high regard for his regular and semicursive scripts as well as his unusual formal regular script, which he employed for the many stele inscriptions he created. Yet it was the dancing quality of his wild cursive script as seen in *A Life of Drinking Sake* that was most acclaimed. PB

2. *A Life of Drinking Sake*
一生飲酒 (Isshō inshu)

c. 1820
Hanging scroll: ink on paper
106.3 × 28.1 cm

SIGNATURE: 鵬斎老人書

SEALS: *zenshin* 善身 (top right)
Chōkō no ki 長興之記 (sig. upper)
Bōsai 鵬斎 (sig. lower)

Purchase, 2005
13169.1

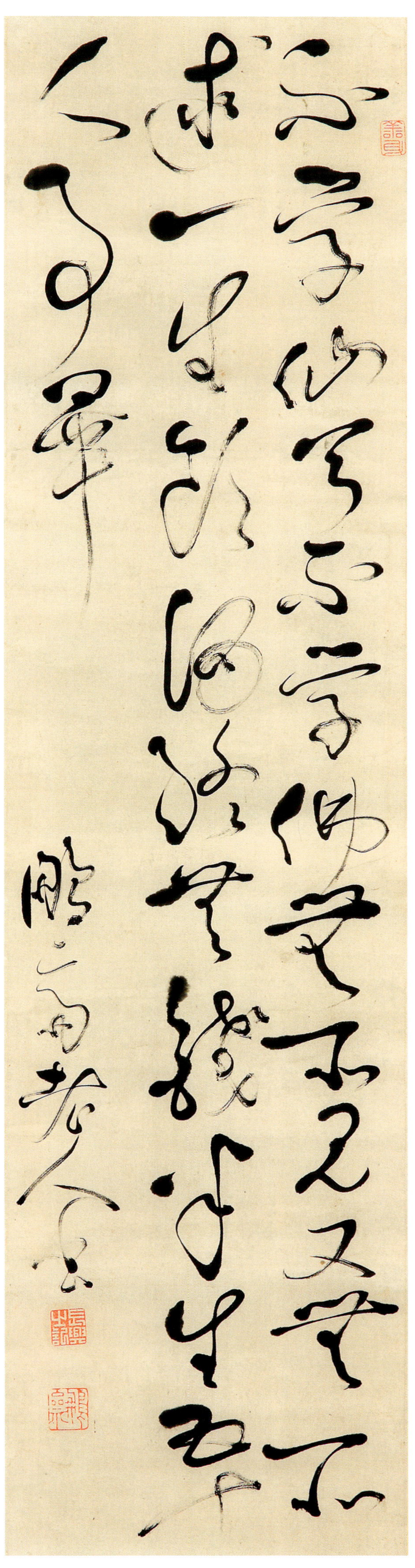

NOTES

1. Bōsai published these poems in the 1822 *Bōsai sensei shishō*, vol. 2, 18–19, reprinted in Sugimoto Eiji, ed., *Kameda Bōsai shibun shoga shu* (Tokyo: Miki Shobō, 1982), 126–27.

2. Another of these five quatrains is published with commentary in Tokuda Takeshi, ed., *Edo kanshi sen* (Tokyo: Iwanami Shoten, 1996), 1: 32–33.

3. See the 1816 *bantzuke* 番付 broadside for a drinking contest in which Bōsai participated in Sugimura Eiji, *Kameda Bōsai* (Tokyo: Kinsei Fūzoku Kenkyūkai Kan, 1978), 213.

4. See plates 87 and 93 in *Kameda Bōsai Sōshu* (Ojiyashi: Ojiyashi Kameda Bōsai-ten Jikkō Iinkai Kan, 2007).

5. Sugimura, *Kameda Bōsai*, 189–90.

6. The fullest treatment in English of Huaisu's career and the controversy surrounding the National Palace Museum version of the *Autobiography* is Adele Schlombs, *Huai-su and the Beginnings of Wild Cursive Script in Chinese Calligraphy* (Stuttgart: Steiner, 1998). Recently a detailed argument in favor of the authenticity of the Palace Museum version has been presented in Fu Shen 博申, *Shufa jianding jian Huaisu "Zixiutie" linchuang zhenduan* 書法鑑定懐素「自叙帖」臨床診斷 (Taipei: Diancang Yishu Jiating Chupanshe 典藏藝術家庭出版社, 2006).

Sakai Hōitsu, Tani Bunchō, and others

3. *Collaborative Work by Edo Literati Artists*
江戸文人合作 (Edo bunjin gassaku)

mid-1810s
Hanging scroll: ink and color on silk
93.4 × 32.5 cm
Purchase, 2005
13166.1

Moon
Sakai Hōitsu 酒井抱一 1761–1828
SIGNATURE: *Hōitsu hitsu* 抱一筆
SEAL: *Bunsen* 文詮

Plum
Kuwagata Keisai 鍬形蕙斎 1764–1824
SIGNATURE: *Shōshin* (or *Tsuguzane*) *hitsu* 紹眞筆
SEAL: *Shōshin* 紹眞

Plants
Kubo Shunman 窪俊満 1757–1820
SIGNATURE: *Shunman* 俊満
SEAL: *Shunman* 俊満

Bat
Tani Bunchō 谷文晁 1763–1840
SIGNATURE: *Bunchō* 文晁
SEAL: *Sen* (?) 仙 (?)

Oil lamp
Tani Bun'ichi 谷文一 1787–1818
SIGNATURE: *Bun'ichi hitsu* 文一筆
SEAL: *Bun'ichi* 文一

The *gassaku,* a collaborative work by two or more artists, represents one of the favorite activities among members of the *bunjin* circle. In format, the work could be a hanging scroll, album, handscroll, or even a screen. Any informal gathering might inspire artists to spontaneously create a joint work to celebrate their friendship and to exchange artistic ideas. A more formal collaboration might occur on special occasions such as a New Year party or a commemorative event. Furthermore, a connoisseur could commission specific artists to produce *gassaku,* and many examples came about when the patron himself went to each artist individually and requested that he contribute a painting or calligraphy. Regardless of the occasion and objective, the underlying premise of *gassaku* was art produced for pleasure in a playful spirit. The practice was not limited to literati artists: many Maruyama- and Shijō-school examples remain, and the tradition survived into the early twentieth century.

Five painters and five calligraphers participated in the making of this hanging scroll. Hōitsu is widely known as the founder of the Rinpa-school lineage in Edo. The younger brother of the lord of the Himeji fief, he received an elite samurai education, which included martial training and study of the tea ceremony and poetry. A man of urbane, refined sensibilities, Hōitsu retired early, which allowed him to delve into painting, haiku, and *kyōka* 狂歌 (a comedic form of the thirty-one-syllable *waka* poem). The Bunka-Bunsei era (1804–1830) witnessed Hōitsu's emergence as the central figure of the Edo cultural circle. The Rain Flower Hermitage (Ugean 雨華庵), his home on the outskirts of Edo, functioned as a lively salon for artists and intellectuals regardless of their social and economic differences.

Hōitsu's friend Tani Bunchō, the most established literati painter of his time, was famous for his highly eclectic approach. He was in service to Matsudaira Sadanobu (1758–1829), a powerful shogunate administrator, and Bunchō's status as a quasi-official artist deviated from the *bunjin* precept of freedom and independence. Bunchō enjoyed social prestige and wealth, however, and his tutelage

INSCRIPTIONS

UPPER RIGHT:
Ichikawa Beian 市河米菴 1779–1858
SIGNATURE: *Beian* 米菴
SEALS: *Kawa* 河 (upper)
Mitsui 三亥 (lower)

UPPER CENTER:
Ōkubo Shibutsu 大窪詩佛 1767–1837
SIGNATURE: *Shibutsu* 詩佛
SEAL: illegible

UPPER LEFT:
Kameda Bōsai 亀田鵬斎 1752–1826
SIGNATURE: *Bōsai suisho* 鵬斎酔書
SEAL: *Chōkō* 長興

MIDDLE RIGHT:
Kikuchi Gozan 菊池五山 1769–1849
SIGNATURE: *Gozan* 五山
SEAL: *Ichijigo-an* 一字娯庵 Hermitage of one-word amusement

LOWER RIGHT:
Nakai Keigi 中井敬義 1758–1824
SIGNATURE: *Tōdō* 董堂
SEAL: 席上走筆愈不工也敬義 Writing at a gathering makes one's work less labored, Keigi

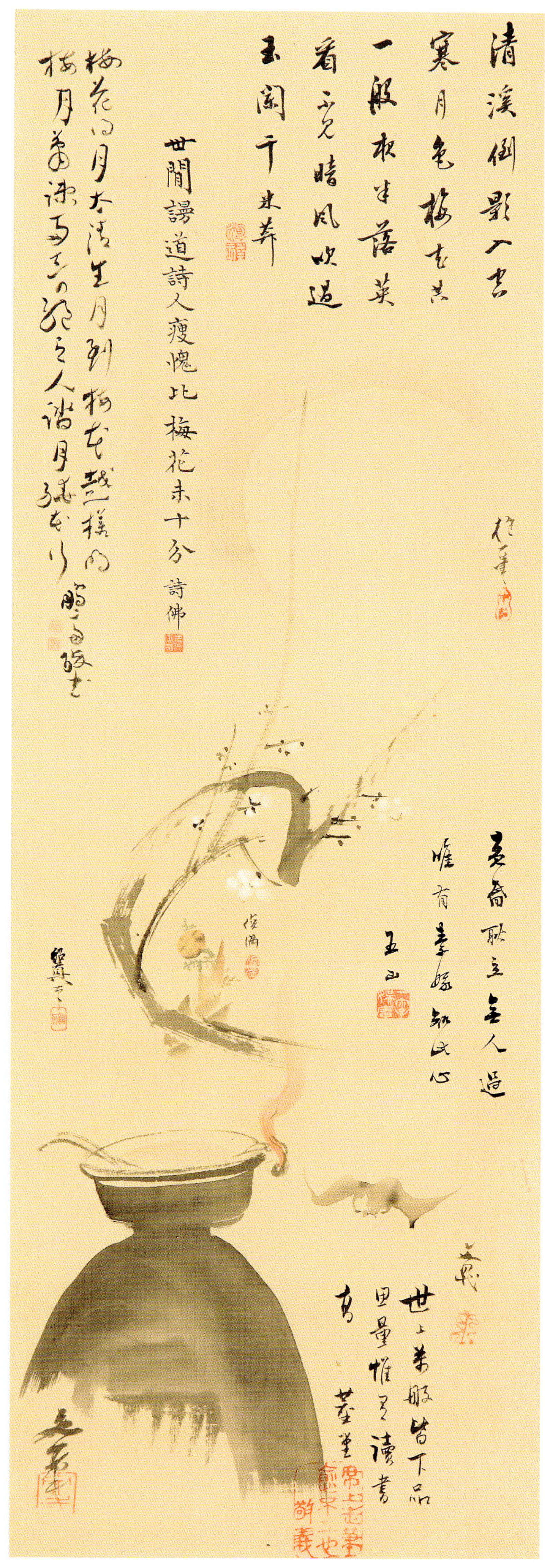

nurtured the next generation of important artists, including Watanabe Kazan 渡辺崋山 (1793–1841). Tani Bun'ichi trained under Bunchō and demonstrated great artistic promise. He married Bunchō's daughter and took the Tani family name but died prematurely at the age of thirty-one. Kubo Shunman was an *ukiyoe* print artist and painter who apprenticed under Kitao Shigemasa 北尾重政 (1739–1820). He was also a talented *kyōka* poet and playwright. Like Shunman, Kuwagata Keisai studied with Shigemasa and enjoyed a successful career as an *ukiyoe* artist under the name Kitao Masayoshi 政美. Upon becoming an official painter of the Tsuyama fief in 1794, he changed his name to Kuwagata Keisai and thereafter achieved popularity for simple line figure drawings and panoramic bird's-eye illustrations of Edo.[1]

Of the calligraphers, Ichikawa Beian was the son and student of Ichikawa Kansai 市河寛斎 (1749–1802), a respected Confucian scholar who taught Chinese-style poetry at his private academy. Beian himself achieved renown as a poet and scholar of Chinese studies. A connoisseur and avid collector of art as well, Beian was known as one of the three best calligraphers of his time. Kazan, the aforementioned literati painter, immortalized Beian in his famous Western-influenced portrait of 1837. Kikuchi Gozan, the son of a Confucian scholar in service to the Takamatsu fief in Shikoku, moved to Edo and studied poetry at Kansai's academy. Ōkubo Shibutsu, a doctor's son, was also a student at Kansai's school and later stood with Gozan as one of Edo's top poets.

Kameda Bōsai, born into a merchant family in Edo, exhibited an impressive scholastic aptitude while young and at the age of twenty-two opened a private Confucian academy that advocated an eclectic approach in interpreting ancient Confucian texts. A government edict of 1790 prohibiting the teaching of unauthorized Confucian doctrine eventually forced him to close his school. After a period of hardship, he gained fame as a calligrapher-poet-painter. Nakai Keigi was a respected Edo calligrapher who was also adept at composing haiku and *kyōka.*

The artists of this *gassaku* represent the top echelon of the Edo literati circle during the Bunka-Bunsei era, which marked the flowering of urban popular culture in Japan. Of the ten artists, all the painters except Shunman and all five calligraphers appeared in the 1817 *Great Ranking List of Literati Painters and Calligraphers* (Bunjin bokkaku ōmitate 文人墨客大見立).[2] Within the lively *bunjin* network, Hōitsu, Bunchō, and Bōsai in particular formed a strong friendship. As early as 1802, the three men are known to have traveled to a temple in Jōshū 常州, in Ibaraki prefecture, to examine a painting of Su Dongpo by a Muromachi-period ink painter.[3] In the next two decades they maintained an intimate relationship, attending drinking parties, creating joint works, and frequenting Hōitsu's Rain Flower Hermitage.[4]

A congenial exercise on the established literati theme of plum and moon, this *gassaku* is an elegant work with a harmonious, well-balanced composition. The prominent position of Beian's graceful inscription and its content suggest that he proposed the theme. Directly below appears Hōitsu's evocative moon, its silhouette delineated by a simple but skillful application of the subtlest wash. In contrast, Keisai's roughly brushed plum in the center bends dramatically and shoots out its branches, reaching to the moon. The one-line inscription by Shibutsu and two-line inscription by Bōsai echo the vertical stretch of the longest branch, while their distinct calligraphic styles make for a delightful comparison. At the bottom of the plum, Shunman reinforced the seasonality of the theme by adding two early spring plants, *fukujusō* and *fukinotō.*[5] Gozan's inscription is framed perfectly by a branch above and by Bunchō's superbly drawn bat below. Lastly, the layered broad ink strokes of Bun'ichi's oil lamp and Keigi's inscription anchor the whole composition. Touches of color in the painting and the red seals that follow the artists' signatures give welcome accents.

The individual inscriptions may be read and translated as follows:

Beian (upper right)

清渓倒影入窓寒	By the pure stream, shadows that enter the window are chilly.
月色梅花共一般	Moonlight and plum blossoms become all the same.
夜半落英看不見	At night, falling flowers are not seen by anyone.
春風吹過玉闌干	Spring wind passes by the jade railing.

Shibutsu (upper middle)

世間謾道詩人痩	Generally speaking, we poets remain thin in the world.
愧比梅花未十分	It is embarrassing, but compared to plum blossoms, we are not thin enough.

Bōsai (upper left)

梅花得月太清生	Plum blossoms under the moon increase their purity;
月到梅花越様明	The moon reaching the plums extends its brightness.
梅月蕭竦多奇龍	Plums under the moon quietly emerge as if magnificent dragons;
有人踏月残花行	Someone walks in the moonlight among fallen blossoms.

Gozan (center right)

黄昏耿立無人過	In the brightness of twilight no one passes by.
唯有素梅知此心	There is only white plum that knows my heart.

Tōdō (lower right)

世上萬般皆下品	Many things in this world are inferior.
思量惟有讀書高	Considering this, only reading is superior.

MM

NOTES

1. Asahi Shinbunsha, *Nihon rekishi jinbutsu jiten* (Tokyo, 1994), 524.

2. See the chart reproduced in Atsumi Kuniyasu, *Kameda Bōsai to Edo Kaseiki no bunjin tachi* (Tokyo: Geijutsu Shinbunsha, 1997), 101.

3. Ibid., 106.

4. See a detailed discussion by Atsumi in ibid., 104–47.

5. The yellow flower is *fukujusō* and the other probably *fukinotō*, an edible wild plant.

Yokoi Kinkoku　横井金谷

1761–1832

4. *Drawing Pure Spring Water to Compare Tea*
汲清泉闘茗

Early 1800s
Six-panel screen, originally four *fusuma* panels: ink and color on paper
129.8 × 332 cm

SIGNATURE: *Kinkoku Dōjin sha* 金谷道人寫

SEAL: *Kinkoku* 金谷

INSCRIPTION:
汲清泉闘茗
Drawing pure spring water to compare tea

Purchase, 2005
13144.1

In this idyllic gathering for drinking tea on a platform set over a mountain stream, three men chat together as they sit on a circular mat covered with tea utensils. A younger attendant draws water from a nearby stream, and several others approach, carrying what are likely more varieties of tea and snacks along with a bundle of books. As early as the Kamakura and Muromachi periods, Japanese gathered to compare different kinds of tea. The earlier occasions employed *matcha* 抹茶, powdered tea whipped to a froth with a bamboo whisk, but here the teas being compared are *sencha* 煎茶, slightly roasted tea leaves that are steeped in hot water. After its introduction in the late seventeenth century, *sencha* became the standard tea among literati painters and calligraphers.[1] Regardless of the type of tea, a requisite for any such gathering was the finest quality water, and mountain spring water drew the highest esteem. Behind the seated group a waterfall feeds the stream running under their platform, and the attendant with his back to us is likely drawing the water for tea. Having an occasion like this in the mountains was largely a daydream, yet such a splendid depiction would have created a delightful atmosphere in a room with tatami mats where one could have tea while embraced by this fantastic landscape.

Careful study of this six-panel screen reveals that it was originally painted on four large squares of paper, each of which has a rectangle of replaced and repainted paper to mask areas that once contained *hikite,* the inset metal handholds used for sliding *fusuma* panels. Kinkoku painted numbers of such four-panel *fusuma* sets during his career.[2] Such panels are normally a permanent feature of a room and over many decades they are likely to became abraded and scratched as well as faded by sunlight. This work was likely altered into a folding screen format to better preserve it after its condition had weakened. Although fainter than they once were, several colors are visible in the figures and tea utensils, and the pink washes that Kinkoku typically applied to mountains are clearly evident.

Kinkoku is best known for the roughly painted landscapes of his final years. He began his artistic career in his early thirties with the study of Yosa Buson's 与謝蕪村 (1716–1783) paintings, a practice that seems to have continued for the rest of his life. In the first years of the nineteenth century, he achieved a remarkable ability to capture the finer qualities of the lyrical, colored style of Buson's later landscapes. Over the next few decades, however, he more commonly practiced a bolder style and dramatic brushwork. The evidence provided by this screen throws new light on the origins of Kinkoku's later style.

The composition of the panel containing the figures seated over the stream is based on the early Buson painting *Sencha under the Pines,* which has been attributed to the 1760s (fig. 1).[3] Kinkoku frequently employed this Buson model in hanging scrolls and folding screens, including an 1805 scroll (fig. 2) from early in his career that follows the composition of *Drawing Spring Water to Compare Tea.*[4] Those that are titled all bear the same inscription as this screen, although Buson's original has only the artist's signature. A quick look at the impulsive brushwork of *Drawing Pure Spring Water to Compare Tea* would suggest that it might be a late work by the artist, yet the evidence of the signature and seal demonstrates the early date of the screen.[5] In following the technique of Buson's roughly painted early work, Kinkoku had found a precedent that was more dramatic yet less lyrical than the master's later paintings. This screen demonstrates that Kinkoku's famously wild brushwork may have been first suggested by his study of early Buson landscapes.[6]

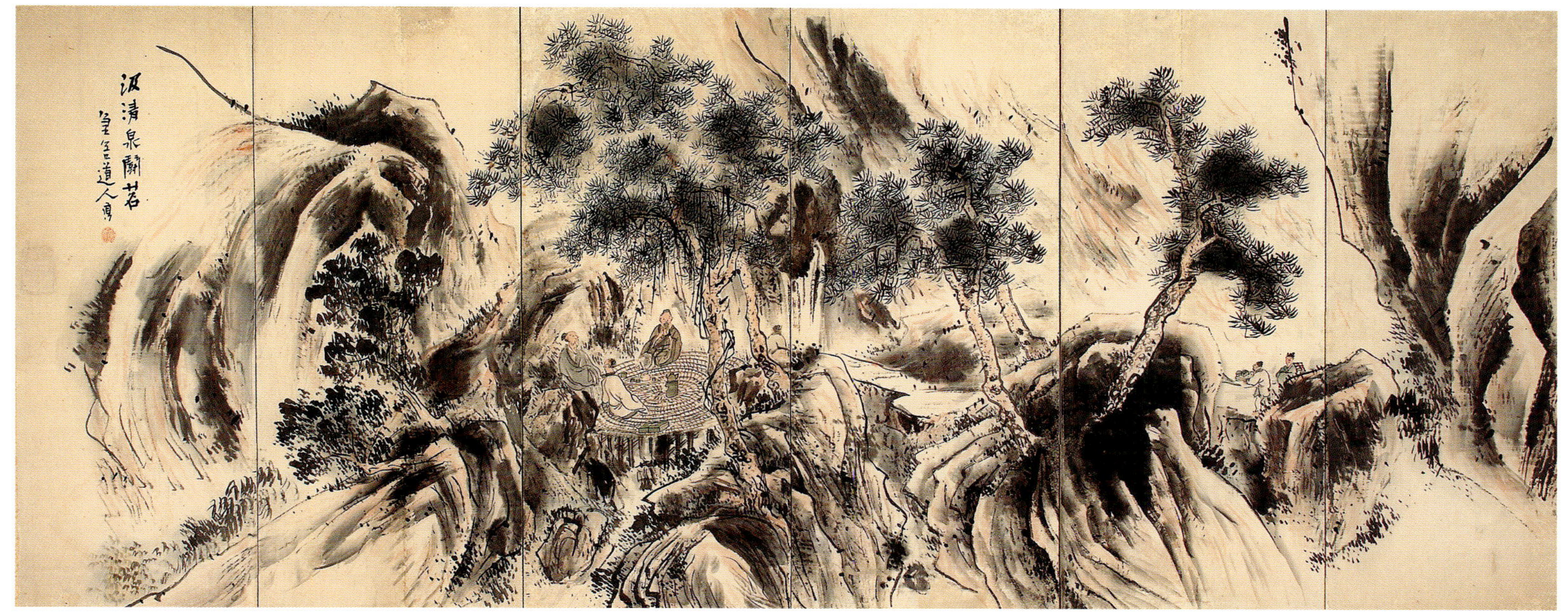

Drawing Pure Spring Water to Compare Tea illustrates the ease with which Kinkoku could expand the inspiration of a specific Buson scroll painting into a complex composition many times larger. The figures drinking tea remain the focus, yet the surrounding mountains with their dramatic combination of brushwork and washes establish the overall tone. The self-taught Kinkoku repeatedly turned to Buson's work for inspiration, but the ultimate expression is distinctly his own.

PB

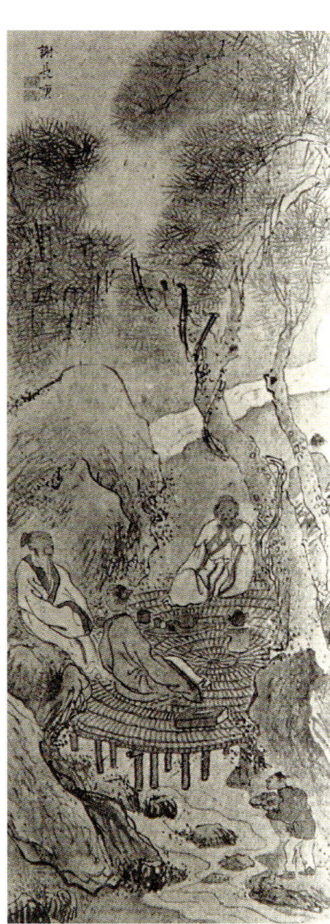

Figure 1. Yosa Buson, *Sencha under the Pines*, 1760s. Hanging scroll: ink and color on silk, 93 × 35.5 cm. Ex-Kataoka collection.

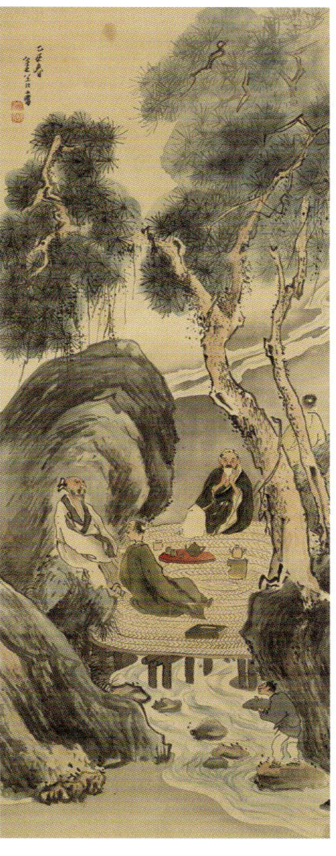

Figure 2. Yokoi Kinkoku, *Sencha under the Pines*, dated 1805, ink and color on silk, 108.7 × 43.9 cm. Private collection.

NOTES

1. For a survey of *sencha* practice in Japan, consult Patricia Graham, *Tea of the Sages* (Honolulu: University of Hawaii Press, 1998).

2. See four such sets at the Yukawa Jinja, illustrated in Rittō Rekishi Minzoku Hakubutsukan, *Ōmi Kotō-Konan no gajintachi* (Rittō, 1999), plate 26: 1–4.

3. A prewar photograph of this painting appears in volume 6 of Ogata Tsutomu et al., *Buson zenshū* (Tokyo: Kōdansha, 1992–), plate 123, where it is placed with works from 1758 to 1771.

4. This screen is in the collection of the Shiga Kenritsu Kindai Bijutsukan. The actual drawing style and signature type are quite different from the present work. Thanks to Patricia Fister for sharing a number of photos of related works from her archive of Kinkoku materials.

5. The calligraphy of the signature, especially the distinctive form of the second character, *koku*, is typical of that found on many dated works by Kinkoku from early in the 1800s. The impression of this seal, the most frequently used of his seals, is much more complete than usual, with the outermost line that surrounds the seal almost intact; in most impressions, two-thirds or more of that line has worn away. Taken together, these two aspects confirm the early date for this work.

6. There are other early Kinkoku paintings that have strikingly rough brushwork, such as the 1809 *Snowy Landscape* in Rittō Rekishi Minzoku Hakubutsukan, *Ōmi Kotō-Konan no gajintachi*, plate 31.

Nukina Kaioku　貫名海屋

1778–1863

Kaioku attained popularity as a painter, yet the greatest acclaim was reserved for his superb skill in calligraphy, and he became one of the most noted calligraphers in western Japan during the late Edo period. Kaioku first learned calligraphy in his hometown of Tokushima, where he studied the famous style of Mi Fu 米芾 (1051–1107) from Nishi Noriyuki 西宣行 (1764–1826), who had trained in Kyoto.[1] Kaioku continued to focus on Chinese-style (*karayō* 唐様) calligraphy throughout his career. Although he eventually knew many of the top calligraphers of his time, he was more influenced by his study of the copy books (*hōjō* 法帖) of famous Chinese calligraphers, including the works of Chu Suiliang 褚遂良 (597–658), Yan Zhenqing 顔真卿 (709–785), and Huaisu 懷素 (c. 725–c. 785).[2] Additionally, he studied the ancient Chinese-style works by Heian calligraphers such as Kūkai 空海 (774–835), the founder of Shingonshū 真言宗 Buddhism. Kaioku's deep study of these works appears to have given his own calligraphy a bold assertiveness that is lacking in the works of many of his contemporaries, who were still focused on the elegant tradition based on the styles of Wang Xizhi 王羲之 (303–361) and his son, Wang Xianzhi 王獻之 (344–386).

Throughout his career Kaioku displayed his great knowledge of Chinese calligraphy through the creation of excellent formal works in various styles. In the first month of 1849 he adopted the new name Tekisūō 摘菘翁, or "Cabbage-picking Old Man," and started signing his works Sūō.[3] He used this name on his works for the rest of his life, and his calligraphies from this time reveal a distinct change in style. In this last stage of his life, Kaioku rose above his models and combined a new freedom of brushwork with the extraordinary skill he had developed over decades of dedicated practice. Especially in the last several years before his death, Kaioku's cursive script took on an exceptional vitality, as can been seen in *Quatrain on Mountain Springs*.[4] The irregular yet vigorously composed characters that dramatically vary in size, coupled with the rough quality of line that runs from wet to dry, are classic features of this final style. The "Mountain Springs" 山泉 quatrain reads:

世薦元不到雲林	Sacrificing the world requires great denial to attain the clouds and trees.
孰測山霊蕩滌心	How to fathom the mountain's spirit to cleanse the mind?
己灑松風披不壁	I perceive the lofty pine winds unfurl without obstacle
也甑瀼雪策千尋	And, as the snow piles on the cauldron, plan an endless quest.

As each calligraphy is always a unique work, great calligraphers, when delighted with one of their creations, will calmly make corrections or insert forgotten characters rather than start over to create a "perfect" version. In this case Kaioku forgot the important characters for "clouds and trees" 雲林 in the first line on the right. After completing the work, he simply inserted the missing characters in a smaller size, following examples by noted Chinese calligraphers of the past.

Kaioku's achievements were carefully studied by the prominent Meiji calligrapher Kusakabe Meikaku 日下部鳴鶴 (1838–1922), and through Meikaku's many students, Kaioku's achievements helped form a basis for new developments in calligraphy at the end of the nineteenth century. PB

5. *Quatrain on Mountain Springs* 山泉七言絶句 (Sansen shichigon zekku)

c. 1860
Hanging scroll: ink on paper
180.6 × 65.4 cm

SIGNATURE: *Sūō* 菘翁
Cabbage [picking] Old Man

SEALS: 朝朝染翰 Every day dye the brush [in ink][5] (top right)
Kunmo 君茂 (sig. upper)
世味老来薄似紗 As years advance, the world's flavor becomes thin like gauze[6] (sig. lower)

Purchase, 2005
13181.1

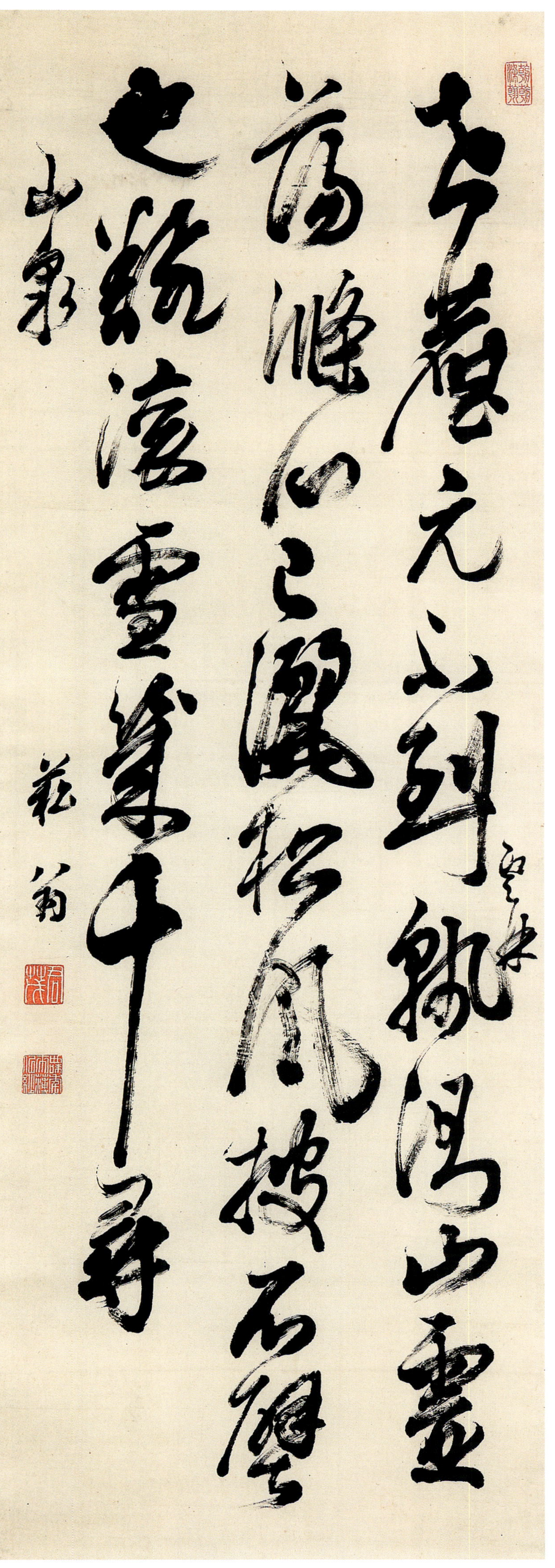

NOTES

1. Tanaka Sōkaku, "Awa no Sūō," *Shoron*, no. 17 (fall 1980): 101–2.

2. See Nakata Yūjirō's essay "Ichikawa Beian to Nukina Kaioku," in *Shodō zenshū* (Tokyo: Heibonsha, 1958), 23: 17–19.

3. See the chronology of his life in Hashimoto Yoshifumi, "Sūō nenpu," *Shoron*, no. 17 (fall 1980): 121–22.

4. See Nakata's comments on his final cursive style in "Ichikawa Beian to Nukina Kaioku," 19.

5. This is the first part of the last line in the verse *Early Audience at the Palace of Radiance* 早朝大明宮, by the Tang poet Jia Zhi 賈至 (718–772).

6. This is the first line of the noted Song poet Lu You's 陸游 (1125–1210) verse, *Clearing after Spring Rain in Lin'an* 臨安春雨初霽.

Ōtagaki Rengetsu 大田垣蓮月

1791–1875

Among Rengetsu's achievements—painting, poetry, calligraphy, and pottery—many consider calligraphy to be her strongest.[1] Rengetsu left numerous calligraphic works on paper (such as *tanzaku* and *shikishi*), sometimes combined with painting. She also created many pottery pieces incised or inscribed with her poetry.[2] This exquisite sake cup is a superb inscribed example in which her calligraphy retains the elegant quality of her ink pieces.

This hand-built cup with a slightly flaring lip is covered with a milky glaze textured with fine crackling. The dainty foot, left unglazed, reveals the warm reddish color of the clay. On the concave surface, the artist wrote with iron pigment a complete *waka* verse of 5-7-5-7-7 syllables and her signature. Responding to the circular space, however, Rengetsu scattered her poem freely to fill the entire surface in an irregular 5-9-6-7-4 arrangement. Echoing the shape of the cup, the round *no* の letter appears four times. Every letter and character enjoys balance and ample space, making the inscription expansive and airy. Following the rhythmic flow of her calligraphic lines, one can easily imagine the fluid movement of Rengetsu's hand as she moved from one letter to the next.

The poem reads:

山里の	*Yamazato no*
	A tree at the eaves of a house
軒の一木の	*Noki no hitoki no*
	in a mountain village
初し本二	*Hatsushiho ni*
	is beginning to change color.
秋の日か須そ	*Aki no hikazu zo*
	I can count the number of days
か曽へられ介る	*Kazoerarekeru*
	into the autumn season.[3]

An unpretentious masterpiece created by an untrained *bunjin* potter and adorned with her unique inscription, such a cup would have had tremendous appeal to scholars and well-educated members of the merchant class. By 1860 Rengetsu's pieces were so popular even outside the *bunjin* circle that fake Rengetsu ware began to appear.[4]

The calligraphy on this cup illustrates Rengetsu's mature style. As a samurai's daughter, she received substantial instruction in calligraphy before reaching adulthood. It is generally accepted that Rengetsu's individualistic writing style did not emerge until after her forties, when she moved to Okazaki after the death of her stepfather and began making a living as a poet-calligrapher-potter. The exact sources of her writing style are difficult to discern. It was common for a poet to learn both poetry and calligraphy styles from a single mentor. But Rengetsu studied with multiple teachers, including Kagawa Kageki 香川景樹 (1768–1843) and Mutobe Yoshika 六人部是香 (1806–1863), and she was deeply influenced by Kageki's teacher, Ozawa Roan 小沢芦庵 (1723–1801), making it difficult to pinpoint a single source. Rengetsu apparently did not follow the current vogue, either. Many early Meiji *waka* poets admired the poetry of Katō Chikage 加藤千蔭 (1735–1808) and studied his calligraphy style, but Rengetsu's work shows no influence of the Chikage school. Furthermore, despite friendly exchanges with Nukina Kaioku 貫名海屋 (1778–1863), a *bunjin* known as one of the three best calligraphers of the late Edo period, his Chinese-inspired style did not affect her.[5] It seems most plausible that she began to formulate her distinctive calligraphic style as she steadily fulfilled the increasing number of requests for her ceramic pieces, calligraphy, and painting.[6] In particular, the technical requirements for incising pottery are believed to have led her to favor a simpler style and form. To avoid complex characters and excessive linking, she wrote each letter broadly and clearly.[7] Thus Rengetsu developed her writing style independently, guided by the demands of her art and her particular aesthetic taste.[8] MM

6. *Sake cup* 杯 (Hai) A

1860s
Glazed earthenware
H. 3 cm, DIAM. 6.7 cm

SIGNATURE: *Rengetsu* 蓮月

Purchase, 2005
13224.1a

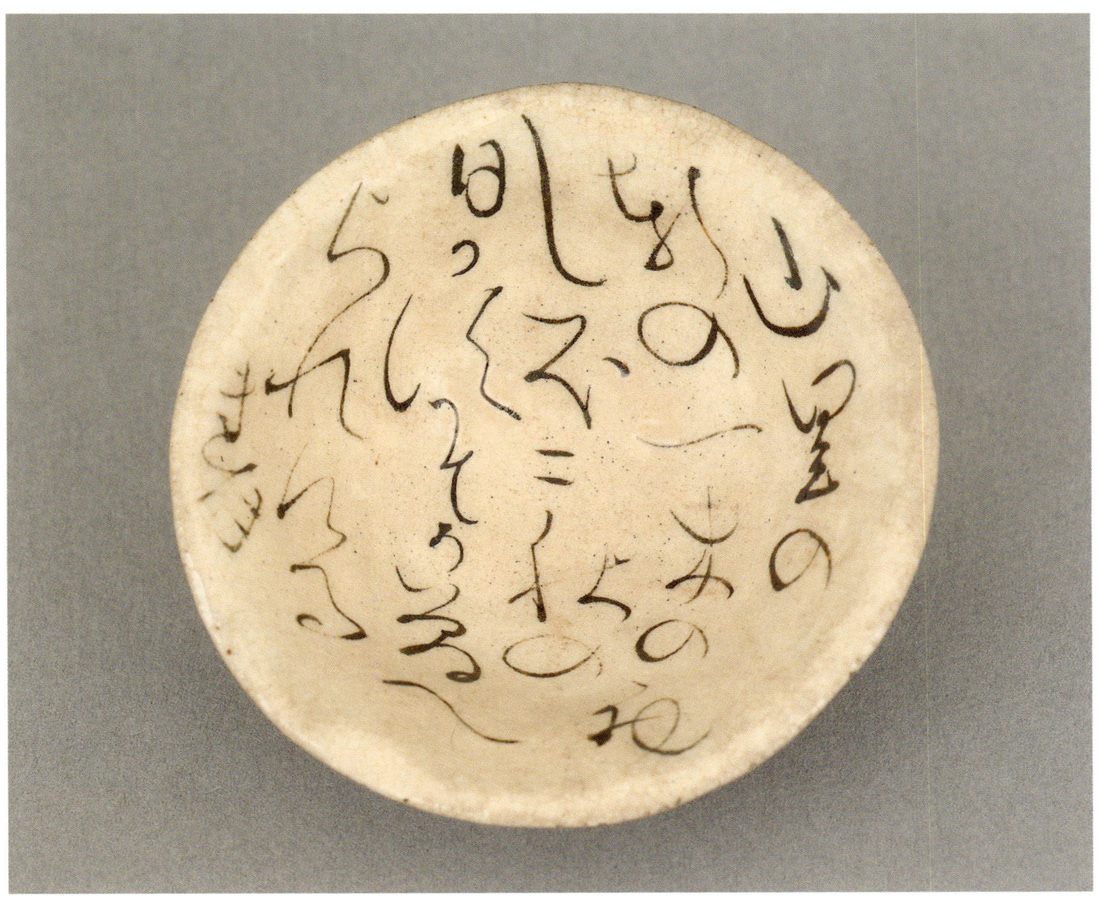

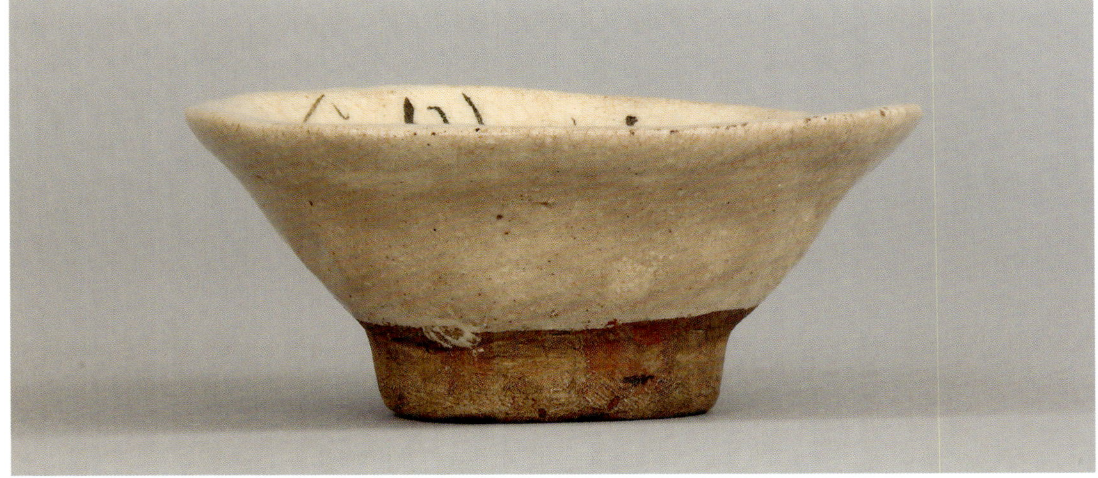

NOTES

1. Sayama Sei, "Ōtagaki Rengetsu no uta," in *Joryū bungaku hyōronshū: Chūsei kinseihen*, ed. Imai Kuniko (Nagano: Meikō Shobō, 1948), 121.

2. Incised examples outnumber inscribed pieces.

3. Published in Murakami Sodō, ed., *Rengetsuni zenshū, jō* (Kyoto: Rengetsuni Zenshū Hanpukai, 1927), "Shūi: akibu" section, 43.

4. Maeda Toshiko, *Bunjin shofu 11: Rengetsu* (Kyoto: Tankōsha, 1979), chronology section, no pagination.

5. In a letter to Tessai, Rengetsu mentioned that she had once displayed in her room a calligraphic work by Kaioku; see Murakami Sodō, ed., *Rengetsuni zenshū, ge* (Kyoto: Rengetsuni Zenshū Hanpukai, 1927), 80.

6. Maeda, *Bunjin shofu 11*, 99.

7. See the discussion by Tokuda Kōen, "Rengetsuryū no shotai kansei eno ayumi," *Sumi*, no. 44 (September 1983): 41–49.

8. For an excellent discussion of Rengetsu, see Pat Fister, *Japanese Women Artists, 1600–1900*, exh. cat. (Lawrence: Spencer Museum of Art, 1988), 157.

Ōtagaki Rengetsu 大田垣蓮月

1791–1875

Upon the loss of her second husband in 1823, Rengetsu became a nun and moved to Makuzuan 真葛庵 in the Chion'in compound with her stepfather, who also took Buddhist vows. She began to make pottery as a hobby. When her stepfather died a decade later, she settled in the Okazaki area and turned to pottery making to support herself. To lighten the physical burden on the nun, the young Tomioka Tessai 富岡鉄斎 (1836–1924) became her live-in helper around 1850, bringing clay to Rengetsu and transporting finished pieces to the Awata 粟田 kiln in eastern Kyoto.

Rengetsu hand-built her pieces at a small wooden stand with simple tools. The style of her pottery did not vary a great deal. She primarily produced *sencha* 煎茶 utensils for a Chinese-style steeped-tea ceremony, which had gained popularity in Japan since the eighteenth century. She also made wares for serving food and sake as well as those used for the older *chanoyu* 茶の湯 tea ceremony, which involved the whisking of powdered green tea.

Judging from its small size, this tea caddy would have been used to keep the powdered tea for *chanoyu.* The slightly misshapen form sets it apart from the perfection and polish of professional potters' work and evokes the *wabi* and *sabi* aesthetics of unaffected beauty and imperfection cherished by *chanoyu* practitioners. On the uneven surface of the container, one can easily recognize the impressions left by Rengetsu's fingers as she worked to build and mold the shape, define the mouth, and smooth the surface. The plain, off-white glaze reveals even more clearly the irregular tactile quality, enhancing its unpretentious charm, while the fine crackling gives a sense of delicacy. The only decoration is the verse that wraps around the surface. Using a sharp bamboo tool, Rengetsu incised the first three lines of her poem in the upper area of the container and continued the flow of the inscription down and around until its conclusion with her signature. The composition not only creates a rhythmic movement from right to left but also achieves a pleasant balance between the carved area and the plain ground.

Rengetsu's poem reads:

志らきくの	*Shiragiku no*
	White chrysanthemum
枕二ちかく	*Makura ni chikaku*
	Spread fragrance near my pillow.
可をるよハ	*Kaoru yo wa*
	On such a night
いめもいくよの	*Ime mo ikuyo no*
	I dream of many autumns
秋かへぬらん[1]	*Aki kaenuran*
	That have come and gone.

Rengetsu is believed to have studied with and been influenced by a handful of poets during her development as a *waka* poet. Many suggest, however, that she ultimately formulated her unique poetic style independently, driven by her personality,[2] as in her pottery and calligraphy. By the early Meiji period, Rengetsu had firmly established her reputation as the foremost female *waka* poet in Kyoto. In 1868 *Compilation of Waka by Two Women, Rengetsu and Shikibu* (Rengetsu Shikibu nijo waka shū 蓮月式部二女和歌集) was published, introducing her poems and those by her friend Takabatake Shikibu 高畠式部 (1785–1881). *A Diver's Harvest of Seaweed* (Ama no karumo 海人の刈藻), which followed two years later, was dedicated solely to Rengetsu's work and contained more than three hundred verses. Rengetsu herself was nonchalant about the publication and wrote to Tessai, "Other people are involved in this; I am not concerned."[3] The number of Rengetsu's extant *waka* is thought to be about nine hundred.[4]

This exceptionally beautiful tea caddy comes in a wooden box inscribed by Issui 一水, the resident priest of Jinkōin, where Rengetsu lived during the last ten years of her life.

MM

7. *Tea caddy* 茶入れ (Chaire) A

1860s
Glazed earthenware
H. 4.5 cm, DIAM. 6.5 cm

SIGNATURE: *Rengetsu* 蓮月

Purchase, 2005
13225.1a & 1b

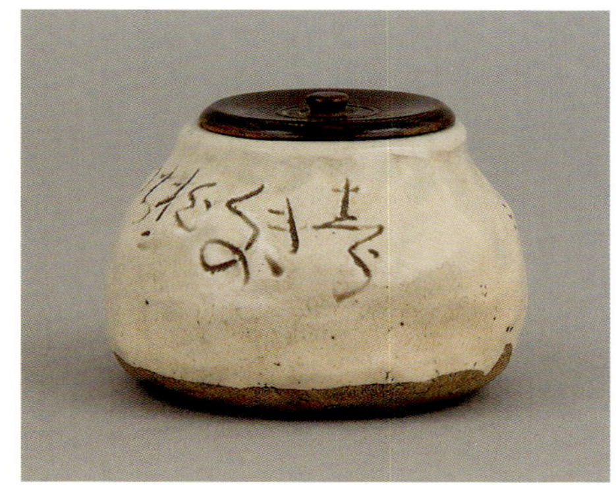

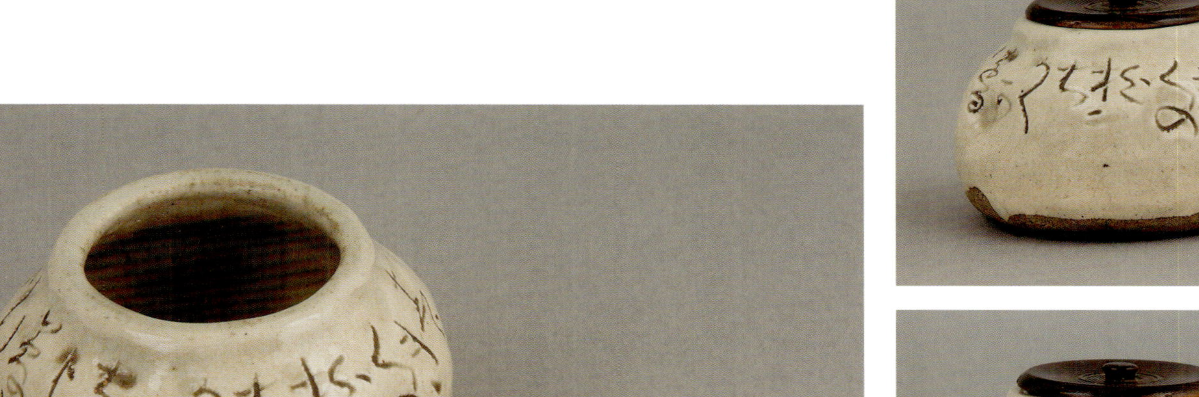

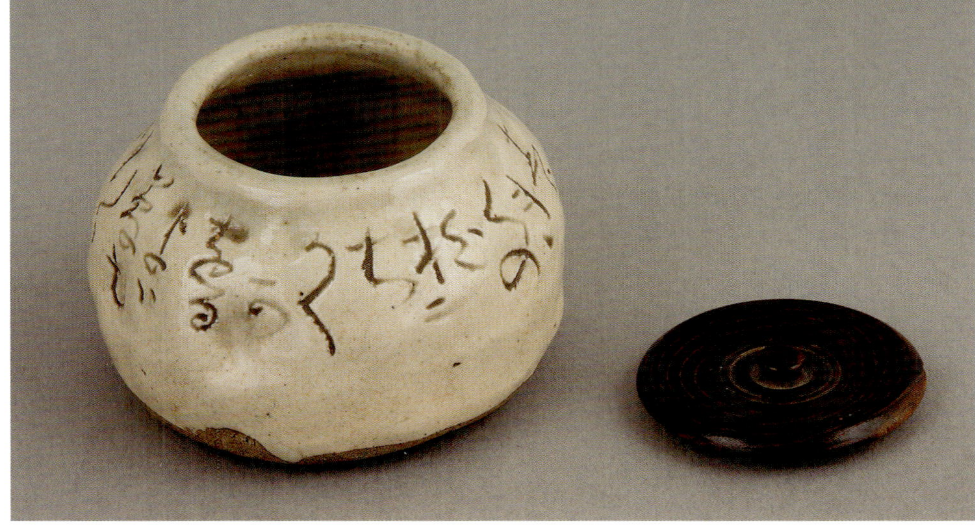

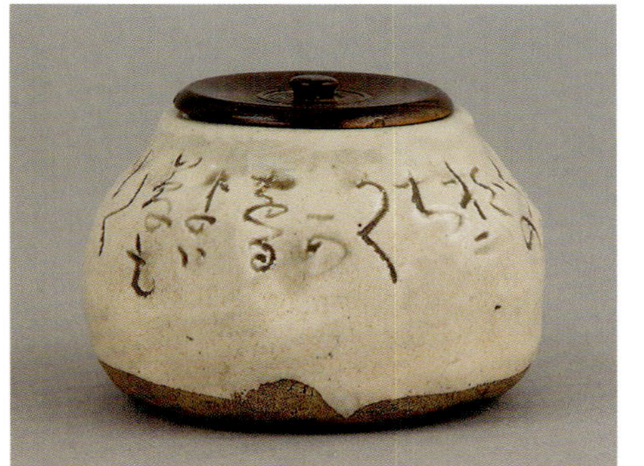

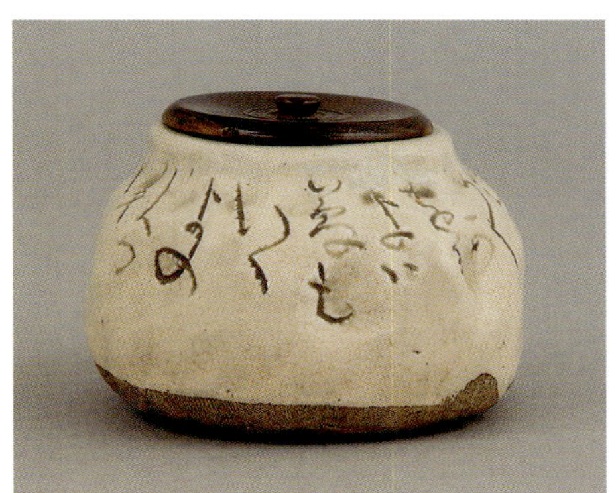

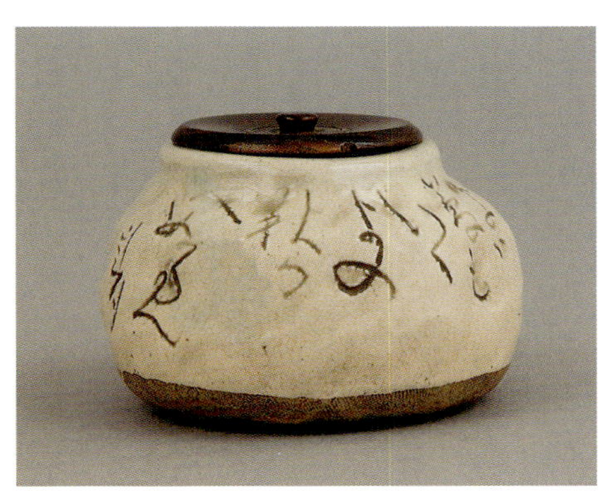

NOTES

1. Published in Murakami Sodō, ed., *Rengetsuni zenshū, jō* (Kyoto: Rengetsuni Zenshū Hanpukai, 1927), "Ama no karumo" section, 29.

2. Kimura Sekiryū, "Rengetsu o omou," *Daimai bijutsu* 4, no. 6 (June 1925): 31–33; Kono Miki, "Rengetsuni no uta," *Daimai bijutsu* 5, no. 10 (October 1926): 12; and Maeda Toshiko, *Bunjin shofu II: Rengetsu* (Kyoto: Tankōsha, 1979), 87.

3. Maeda, *Bunjin shofu II*, 84.

4. Ibid., 85.

Yamanaka Shinten'ō 山中信天翁

1822–1885

In some respects, Shinten'ō's painting is grounded in the distinctive brushwork of his noted calligraphy. This pair of scrolls allows an easy comparison between his cursive calligraphy and his unusual approach to painting bamboo. Although Shinten'ō had first studied calligraphy with Shinozaki Shōchiku 篠崎小竹 (1781–1851) and Saitō Setsudō 斉藤拙堂 (1791–1865), his own style was based on his careful examination of the *Zhengzuowei tie* 争座位帖 ink rubbing by the famous Tang calligrapher Yan Zhenqing 顔真卿 (709–785).[1] Although Yan is renowned for the monumental qualities of his formal regular script, he achieved equal prominence for his cursive style. Most calligraphies that are inscribed on stone steles are carefully composed to display the highest virtues of the calligrapher's style. The *Zhengzuowei tie* is unusual for being a rough draft of a personal letter from 764 composed in mixed cursive and semicursive script. Complete with crossed-out sections, this draft employs irregularly sized characters and curving strokes in which the hairs of the brush spread apart, achieving a bold expressiveness. Although the resemblance between his style and Yan's is striking, Shinten'ō was also influenced by the variety of individualistic cursive styles found in recently imported examples of Chinese calligraphy from the seventeenth century.

The twisting quality of line in Shinten'ō's calligraphy is also visible in the brushwork of many of his paintings. As bamboo leaves are fairly stiff, they are often individually drawn in a fairly straight manner, but the leaves in Shinten'ō's bamboo frequently bend and turn in contrary positions. In addition, most painters arrange bamboo leaves in clearly defined groups that radiate outward from a central point, yet Shinten'ō placed leaves at odd angles to one another, defying the expectation of elegantly composed clusters. This unusual manner creates an internal tension similar to that found in Shinten'ō's cursive calligraphy.

Irregularly brushed washes darken the area around the bamboo plants and give an impression of piled snow in mid-winter. The small, bent-over culms at the bottom of the composition suggest the weight of the sticky, moist snow. Although paintings of spring and autumn scenes were often displayed during the season they depict, winter and summer scenes were sometimes hung during the opposite season to provide a warming or cooling effect through visual suggestion. It is easy to imagine the fresh, crisp feeling this pair of scrolls might produce when hung during the hot summer months in Japan.

PB

NOTES

1. The similarity of Shinten'ō's calligraphy to that in the *Zhengzuowei tie* rubbing is clear upon comparison, and Tomioka Tessai recalled that Shinten'ō told him that it was the original source of his style; see Shintenkai, *Kokkō yohō* 国香餘芳 section, *Shinten'ō* (Nagoya, 1915), 2.

2. Getsukyō indicates the famous Togetsukyō 渡月橋 bridge over the Katsura River in Arashiyama, near where Shinten'ō's villa once stood.

3. Referring to ink pooled on an inkstone, this text is frequently engraved on Chinese *yūin* 遊印 seals.

4. The six forms of calligraphy are an old division of ancient calligraphy into archaic styles, including seal script, clerical script, and bird- and insect-shaped scripts. The poem is an oblique description and praise of bamboo in snow as shown in the painting.

8. *Quatrain in Cursive Calligraphy / Bamboo in Snow*
七言絶句草書/雪中竹図
(Shichigon zekku sōsho / Setchūchiku zu)

1884
Pair of hanging scrolls: ink on paper
135.3 × 34 cm each

Right scroll:
SIGNATURE: *Shinten'ō* 信天翁

SEALS: *shizen* 自然 naturalness (upper right)
Getsu kyō 月橋 Moonbridge[2] (sig. upper)
seiitsu 静逸 quiet relaxation (sig. lower)
bokuchi seikō 墨池清興 pool of ink is pure delight[3] (bottom left)

INSCRIPTION:
曉下天花作會同
青鸞粒黙白玲瓏
發頭直有凍雲宿
摘灑香延六書公
甲申二月詩畫於嵐山之麓以為
節堂詞兄属

Under the dawn sky flowers produce dew drops;
Bright green with shining white dots.
Emerging tops are straight—embedded in frozen clouds;
Plucked they disperse fragrance—like the six forms of calligraphy[4]

Poem and painting created in the second month of the *kōshin* year [1884], at the foot of Arashiyama, at the request of my elder brother in poetry, Setsudō

Left scroll:
SIGNATURE: *Shinten'ō* 信天翁

SEALS: 蝶鹿 butterfly deer (top right)
seiitsu 静逸 quiet relaxation (sig. upper)
侶鳳道人 (sig. lower)

INSCRIPTION:
日日相看咲不休
青 鸞 舞在水之流
新篁也是仍高爵
萬斛清風瀟灑蔵

Viewing things day-by-day produces laughter without rest;
Green phoenix dances in the flowing water.
New bamboo has its usual high refinement;
Vast pure wind is full of ethereal spirit.

Purchase, 2005
13200.1 & 2

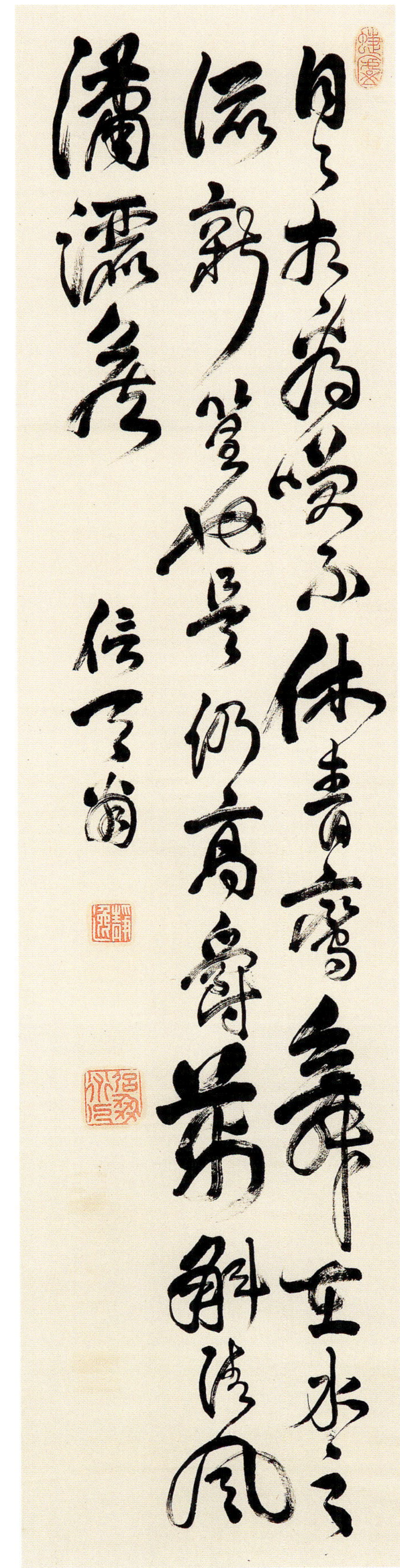

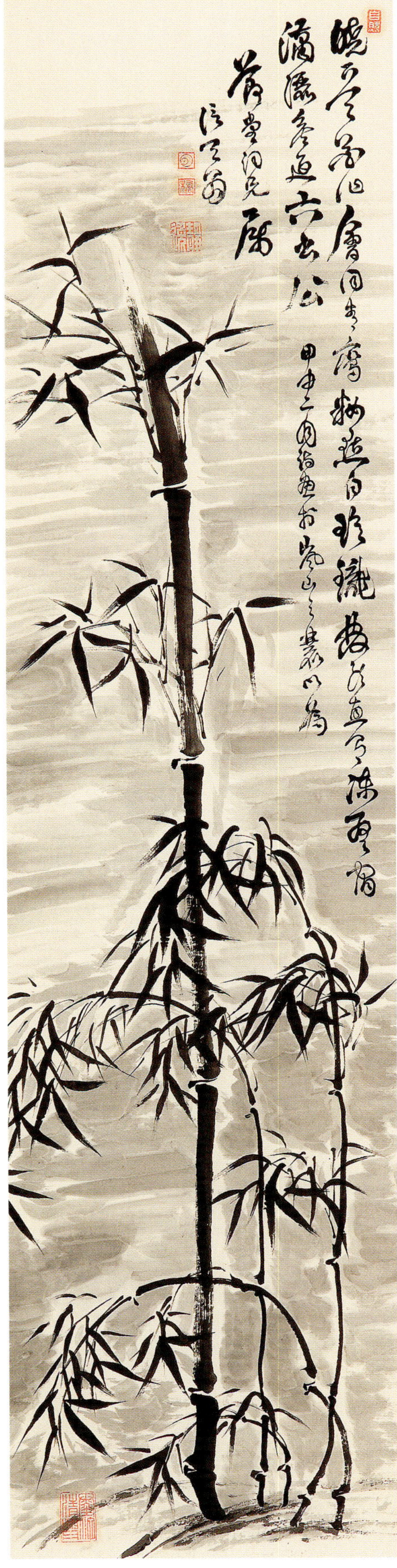

Hagura Katei　羽倉可亭

1799–1887

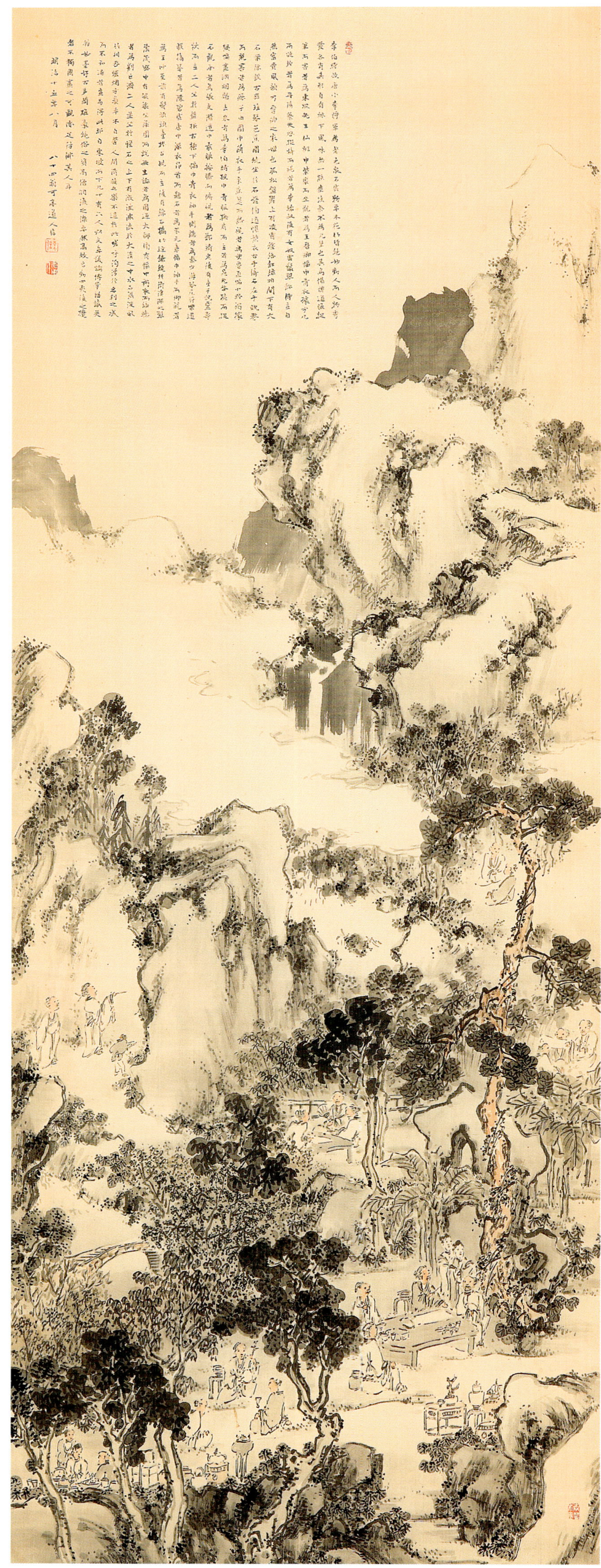

9. *Elegant Gathering in the Western Garden* (西園雅集 Seien gashū)

1882
Hanging scroll: ink and light color on silk
142.4 × 55 cm

SIGNATURE: *hachijūyon o Katei Dōjin Nobu*
八十四翁 可亭道人 信

SEALS: *mata ka* 亦可 (top right)
Yoshinobu 良信 (sig. upper)
Muyōjin 無用人 a useless person (sig. lower)
seigo 清娯 pure pleasure (bottom right)

Purchase, 2005
13193.1

INSCRIPTION:
李伯時效唐小李将軍為著筆法其設色泉石,雲物草木花竹皆絶妙動人,而人物秀發,各肖其形,自有林下風味,無一點塵埃気,不為凡筆也其烏帽黄道服捉筆而書者,為東坡先生仙桃巾紫裘而坐觀者,為王晋卿:幅巾青衣,據方几機而凝竚者,為丹陽蔡天啓捉椅而視者,為李端叔後有女奴雲鬟翠飾侍立,自然富貴風韻,乃晋卿之家姫也.孤松盤欝,上有凌霄纒格,紅緑相間,下有大石案陳設古器瑤琴,芭蕉圍繞,坐於石盤傍,道帽紫衣,右手椅石,左手執巻而間觀書者,為蘇子由,團巾繭衣,手乗蕉箑而熟視者,為黄魯直,幅巾野褐,據横幅畫淵明帰去来者,為李伯時,披巾服,撫肩而立者,為晁无咎,跪而捉石觀画者,為張文潜.道巾素服,按膝而俯視者為鄭靖老.後有童子執靈壽杖而立.二人於盤根古檜下,幅巾青衣,袖手側聽者,為秦少游琴尾冠,紫道服,摘琴者,為陳碧虚.唐巾深衣,昂首而題石者,為米元章.幅巾袖手而仰觀者,為王仲至.前有髫頭頑童棒古硯而立,後錦石橋,竹逕繚繞於清渓深処,翠陰茂密.中有袈裟坐蒲團而説無生論者,為圓通大師.傍有幅巾褐衣而諦聽者,為劉巨濟.二人並坐於怪石之上,下有激湍流於大渓之中,水石潺湲,風竹相吞,爐烟方裊,草木自馨,人間清曠之樂,不過於此嗟呼詢湧於名利之域而不知退者,豈易得此那,自東坡而下,凡十有六人,以文章議論,博學辨識英辭妙墨好古多聞,雄豪絶俗之資,卓然高僧羽流之傑卓然高致,名動四夷後之攬者,不獨圓画之可觀,亦足仿佛見其人耳

Li Gonglin [d. 1106] made a landscape in colors representing water, rocks, clouds, grass, trees, flowers, and bamboo, which was really impressive and wonderfully done after the style of Li Zhaodao [c. 670–730]. The figures were charmingly rendered and all with striking likenesses; they had the air of enjoying themselves among the trees as if they were quite free from the dust of the world. It was indeed a most interesting painting.

The man with a black cap and a yellow Daoist robe, holding a brush in the act of writing, was master Su Dongpo [Shi, 1036–1101]; the one with a peach-colored turban and a purple garment, who sat looking on, was Wang Jinqing [Shen, 1036–1089]; the man in dark blue clothes, who stood upright holding a square instrument, was Cai Tianqi [Zhao, fl. c. 1090] from Tanyang; and the man who grasped his chair and stood looking on was Li Duanshu [Zhiyi, fl. c. 1073]. Behind him stood a female servant whose hair was done up with jade trinkets and who had a rich and noble appearance; she was one of Wang Jinqing's courtesans. Under a large shady pine, on which some creeping plants with purplish flowers were entangled, stood a stone table with some antique objects and a lute with jade mounts. Close by was Su Ziyu [Che, 1039–1112], seated by a stone under a banana plant with a Daoist cap on his head, wearing a purple garment, supporting himself with his right hand on the stone and holding in his left a scroll he was reading. The man in a garment of coarse silk with a turban on his head, holding a palm-leaf fan in his hand and looking on very attentively, was Huang Luzhi [Tingqian, 1045–1105]; and the man with a strangely shaped cap of coarse cloth on his head, holding before him a scroll on which he was illustrating Tao Yuanming's [365–442] "Homecoming" [Guei chu lai 帰去来], was Li Gonglin [Longmien, c. 1040–1106]. Standing at his side, holding a hand on his shoulder, was Chao Wujiu [Buzhi, 1053–1110] in a blue robe with a loose cap on his head, while Zhang Wenqian [Lei, 1054–1113] knelt at his side with a stone in his hand, looking at the picture, and Zheng Jinglao [n.d.] in a Daoist cap and a white robe stood with his hands on his knees looking on. Behind him stood a boy holding a staff of immortality in his hand. Two men were seated on the coiling roots of an old juniper tree; the one with the cap on his head and his hands in the sleeves of his blue garment was Qin Shaoyu [Guan, 1049–1100]; he was listening attentively to Chen Bixu [Qingyuan, n.d.], who, wearing a high hat in the shape of a lute-tail and purple-colored Daoist garments, was playing a lute. But Mi Yuanzhang [Fu, 1051–1107], wearing a cap and a dark garment of Tang fashion, was standing with raised head writing on a stone tablet. At his side, looking on, with raised head and his hand in his sleeves, was Wang Zhongzhi [Qinzhen, n.d.]. In front of him stood a boy with short hair, holding an inkstone, and behind them could be seen an ornamented stone bridge. Bamboo growing along a clear stream formed a cool and shady place of luxuriant verdure. Here a Buddhist priest was seated on a straw cushion discussing the Discourse on Nonexistence [Wu sheng lun]. This was the great scholar Yuan Tong [d. 1090]. At his side was a man in a robe of coarse cloth, listening attentively; that was Liu Zhiji [Jing, c. 1043–1100]. The two men sat on strangely shaped stones, and below their feet was a rushing torrent, which flowed into a bigger stream. The water was murmuring among the stones, and the sound of the wind could be heard in the bamboo. A light smoke was curling in the air, and the plants and the trees exhaled sweet fragrance. The peaceful solitude of this scene could not be surpassed. Alas, those who covet fame and wealth do not know how to withdraw from the world. How could they ever reach this state of contentment?

Including Dongpo, there were sixteen men in all, experts in literature, poetry, calligraphy, painting, and antiquities, real heroes of their kind, besides great Buddhist and Daoist priests. They all stood high above the common level, and their fame has even reached foreign countries all over the world. People of future generations may find it worthwhile not only to look at this painting but also to imitate these men.[1]

The Elegant Gathering in the Western Garden, one of the famous themes of later Chinese painting, was widely known in eighteenth-century Japan and remained popular into the twentieth century. It assembles many of the famous literati of the Northern Song period into a wondrous garden landscape that seems too good to be true. The text at the upper left has been ascribed to the writer and painter Mi Fu (1051–1107) since at least the Ming period and appeared as part of his collected works in the seventeenth century, but the date of its original compilation remains unclear. Paintings of gatherings of literati in garden settings have been common since the Southern Song period, and this composition seems to have grown from that trend.[2] Its earliest antecedent is Wang Xizhi's 王羲之 (307–365) *Preface to the Lanting Pavilion* 蘭亭序, which describes a gathering alongside a meandering stream where figures write poems as they imbibe wine from floating cups. The Lanting Pavilion theme resonated throughout East Asia for many centuries, yet the much later Elegant Gathering in the Western Garden eventually rivaled it in popularity as a painting theme.

Paintings of the Elegant Gathering in the Western Garden usually employ a set iconography that was developed from the textual description of a party held in 1087 at the imperial son-in-law and noted painter Wang Shen's Western Garden in Kaifeng.[3] Sixteen key figures plus their attendants are usually distributed in four primary groups and supplemented with several pairs of isolated figures. The landscape setting shows small mountains, a stone bridge over a stream that courses through the middle of the composition, and a tall pine tree. Figures cluster around two stone tables; one group watches Su Dongpo writing calligraphy (identifiable by the female attendants mentioned in the text), and another views Li Gonglin painting. Other figures observe Mi Fu writing calligraphy on the vertical face of a large boulder. A group gathers around to listen to Chen Jingyuan play the *pipa* lute. Yuantong Dashi[4] and Liu Jing discuss Buddhism in a small bamboo grove, and Su Ziyu reads a scroll while Huang Luzhi looks on. These basic groups are all found in Katei's painting, yet the number of attendants, clothing, and details of the landscape all vary from work to work.

To judge from extant works, Katei's landscape painting style went from a more detailed treatment of figures and small objects to a bolder, looser approach in the Meiji period.[5] Artists most often painted the Elegant Gathering theme with heavy colors in the "blue and green" style, yet Katei employed subtle ink washes typical of many of his landscapes. This treatment is remarkable for being one of his more carefully painted and complex compositions from the Meiji period. Katei repeatedly took up classical painting themes; for example, he completed a pair of scrolls in a similar but more detailed style, *First and Second Outings to the Red Cliff,* in 1852. On these earlier paintings, Katei wrote out the full length of Su Shi's texts in a formal clerical script in very small characters.[6] The minute precision that Katei employed in writing the text on *Elegant Gathering in the Western Garden* is especially remarkable considering that he was well into his eighties. It is as though he were trying to emulate the great painter and calligrapher Wen Zhengming 文徵明 (1470–1559), who in old age became famous for his tiny regular script. Although Katei never had the ambition to challenge such illustrious predecessors, he, like other Japanese literati artists, was greatly inspired by their reputations. The emphatic outlines of the trees, rocks, and mountains may reflect his early study with Geppō. This complex composition, with its clusters of figures, impressive rocks and trees, and background of mountains and mist created by subtle layers of ink wash, is one of his finest creations.

PB

NOTES

1. This translation is adapted from that found in Osvald Siren, *A History of Early Chinese Painting*, vol. 2 (London: Medici Society, 1933), 53–54. The Chinese text is given here as Katei wrote it. The many versions of this text in circulation show slight differences among them: transposed characters, words replaced by synonyms, and so on. Katei's text is quite close to that in circulation in Japan. Chinese punctuation has been inserted into the text, although it too can vary slightly depending on the version.

2. The Southern Song painting theme Composing Poetry on a Spring Outing has sometimes been thought to be an early version of Elegant Gathering in the Western Garden, but it is more likely a precursor; see Mark Wilson's entry in Ho Wai-kam et al., *Eight Dynasties of Chinese Painting*, exh. cat. (Cleveland: Cleveland Museum of Art, 1980), entry 51, 66–69, and Itakura Seitetsu's "Ba En 'Seien gashū zukan' (Neruson Atokinsu Bijutsukan) no shiteki tachii," *Bijutsushi ronso* 16 (1999): 49–78.

3. Ellen Laing's "Real or Ideal: The Problem of the 'Elegant Gathering in the Western Garden' in Chinese Historical and Art Historical Records," *Journal of the American Oriental Society* 88, no. 3 (July/September 1968): 419–35, outlines the historical development of the theme and its improbable mixture of historical figures. More recent research in Japan speculates on the possibility that some kind of actual gathering might have included many of these individuals and attempts to interpret the iconography of the theme; see Fukunaga Masaichi, "Seien gashū o megutte," *Gakuso* 12 (1990): 73–86, part 2: 13 (1991): 81–95, and Itakura Seitetsu's "Ba En 'Seien gashū zukan' (Neruson Atokinsu Bijutsukan) no shiteki ichiókyozo toshite Seiengashu to sono kaigaka o megutte."

4. Yuantong Dashi 圓通大師 was often identified in Japan as Entsū Daishi, the Buddhist name given to Ōe no Sadamoto 大江定基 (d. 1035) during his long stay in China. Even though Sadamoto was dead before most of the other figures were born, this identification was very popular in Japan, and Katei's younger friend Tomioka Tessai was much taken with the idea of a Japanese monk associating with the top literati of the Song period.

5. This comparison is based on the paintings shown at the small 1999 exhibition of Katei's work at the Fushimi Inari shrine in Kyoto.

6. Hakutakuan collection, Kyoto.

Yamamoto Chikuun 山本竹雲

1820–1888

Unusual landscapes with bizarrely formed mountains were a periodic feature of the Chinese landscape painting tradition. Hine Taizan 日根対山 (1813–1869), Fujimoto Tesseki 藤本鐵石 (1817–1863), Yamanaka Shinten'ō 山中信天翁 (1822–1885), and Tomioka Tessai 富岡鐵斎 (1835–1924) were among the late Edo- and Meiji-period painters who shared this attraction for otherworldly scenes. Chikuun, an accomplished seal carver and connoisseur, was skilled at creating such fantastic landscapes, yet few of his works attain the whimsy of this composition. The waterside boardwalk in the lower right weaves around rocky outcrops until it finally reaches a pavilion set on pilings over the water. The gate visible at the bottom of the painting precedes a few buildings and a small village, glimpsed over the edge of a ridge topped by two pine trees. These signs of human habitation are dwarfed by the stony pinnacle that soars over the landscape, yet the focus of the painting is the tiny figure in the pavilion gazing over the water. Chikuun designed the prominent diagonal path to draw attention to the brightly colored structure silhouetted against the water.

The rocks and boulders of this landscape are accented with minature plateaus whose flat tops and rectangular angles protrude unexpectedly. The brushwork is freely rendered, with playful, irregular outlines to the architecture. The casual brushwork and transparent colors are reminiscent of landscapes by Aoki Mokubei 青木木米 (1767–1833) and Hosokawa Rinkoku 細川林谷 (1779–1843), both, like Chikuun, prominent in *sencha* circles. As Chikuun had studied seal carving with Rinkoku and would have been familiar with Mokubei's noted paintings, it is possible there was a direct influence.

PB

10. *Floating Mists over Green Forest*
浮嵐曖翠図 (Furan aisui zu)

1882
Hanging scroll: ink and color on satin
139 × 40.6 cm

SIGNATURE: *Chikuun sanho sei a* (?)
竹雲山苞生阿□

SEALS: *mei* 明西□人 (upper right)
□□外□□ (sig. upper)
tekisha 紗箋 (sig. lower)
天趣横生 (bottom right)

INSCRIPTION:
壬午秋暮寫博聴山建翁伯雅粲正之
Playfully painted in the ninth month of the *jingo* year [1882] for Chozan Ken-o's elegant correction

Purchase, 2005
13195.1

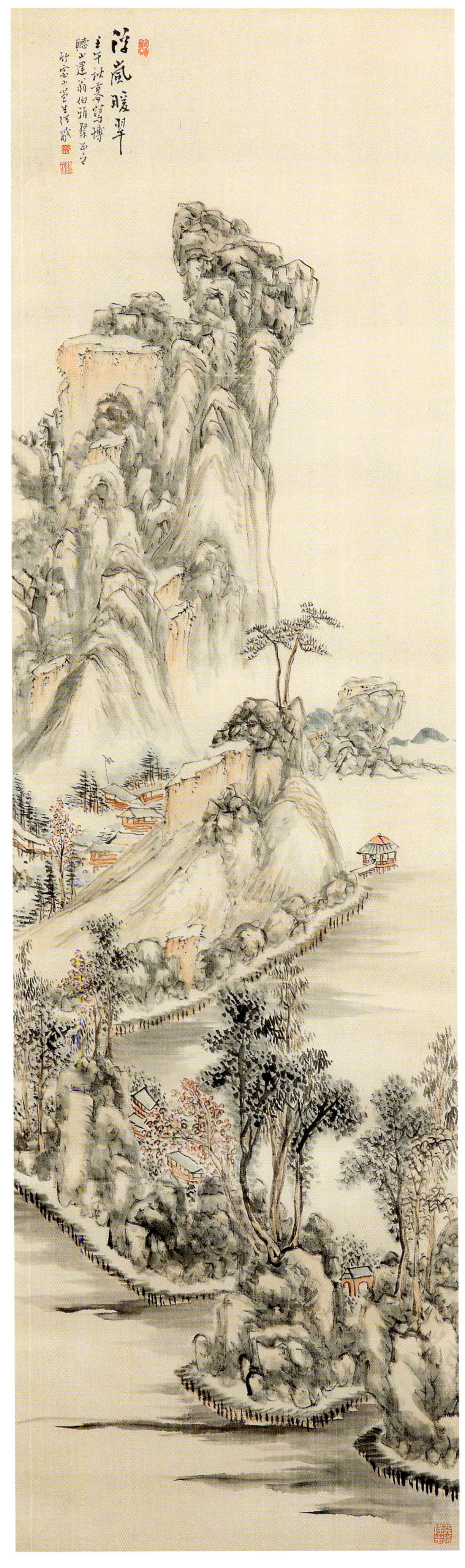

11. *Set of five blue-and-white* sencha *cups* 染付煎茶碗 (Sometsuke senchawan)

1911–12
Porcelain decorated in underglaze blue
H. 5 cm, DIAM. 7 cm each
Potter's seal: *Tōsen* 東洗
Purchase, 2005
13226.1–5

Tomioka Tessai 富岡鉄斎
1836–1924

Pine
SIGNATURE: *Nanajūroku ō Tetsu dōjin* 七十六翁鐵道人
INSCRIPTION:
窠風水月
Wind through pine,
moon on water

Bamboo
SIGNATURE: *Tessai gaishi* 鐵齋外史
INSCRIPTION:
入吾室者但有清風
Only pure wind enters
my room[1]

Imao Keinen 今尾景年
1845–1924

Angler
SIGNATURE: *Keinen ga* 景年畫
INSCRIPTION:
Ayutsuri ni 鮎鉤に
Dereba kinagashi 出連ハ気長し
Otoko kana 男かな
Trout fishing
Brings out patience
In a man

Fireflies
SIGNATURE: *Keinen ga* 景年畫
INSCRIPTION:
Furiyamishi 降やみし
Ame no michi yuku 雨の路(?)行
Hotaru kana 蛍かな
After the rain
Appear on a street (?)
Fireflies

Tajika Chikuson 田近竹邨
1864–1922

Reishi and Rock
SIGNATURE: *Shingai shūjitsu Chikuson sōsha* 辛亥秋日竹邨桑者 Chikuson, mulberry collector, autumn day of the *shingai* year [1911]
INSCRIPTION:
在年其壽
In years exists longevity

At the beginning of the 1910s, the three Kyoto artists who decorated these *sencha* cups were near the pinnacle of their careers. Tomioka Tessai was about to reach a level of creativity that would attract much interest from younger painters. Imao Keinen, who had trained under Suzuki Hyakunen 鈴木百年, was one of Kyoto's most prominent artists, and between 1907 and 1912 he sat on the prestigious jury for the government exhibition.[2] Although younger by several decades, the third artist, Tajika Chikuson, was known nationally as a new advocate of literati painting.[3] After moving from Kyūshū to Kyoto to apprentice under Tanomura Chokunyū 田能村直入 (1814–1907), Chikuson established a flourishing career, earning recognition every year between 1908 and 1914 at the government exhibition. Respected as one of the leading orthodox literati painters in the early Taishō era, he would play a central role in the founding of the Japan Nanga Institute (Nihon Nangain 日本南画院) in 1921.

The five *sencha* cups represent a type of collaborative work in which each artist painted designs on cups created by a potter who stamped his seal, Tōsen, on the bottom. Kyoto painters historically maintained close ties with the traditional craft industries. Like many of his colleagues, Keinen painted designs for *yūzen* textiles, and Tessai decorated tea utensils including cups, bowls, teapots, and plates.[4] Although Tessai did not consider himself to be a professional painter, he actively participated in the Kyoto art scene and developed friendships with other painters, including Chokunyū and Keinen.[5]

The delight in viewing a set such as this comes from the variety of creative solutions presented by the artists. Tessai carried over his powerful painting and calligraphy style even to this small format. On one cup, pine branches with sharp needles spread over the surface and reach out to frame a Chinese-style four-character line. The pine's light tone provides a perfect backdrop for the prominent inscription in darker blue. In another example, Tessai juxtaposed an eight-character inscription with a bamboo-and-rock motif. The assertiveness of his calligraphy is echoed by the vigorously brushed bamboo stalks and leaves, which reach over the rim of the cup. Typical of Tessai, his designs burst with energy and a childlike spontaneity.

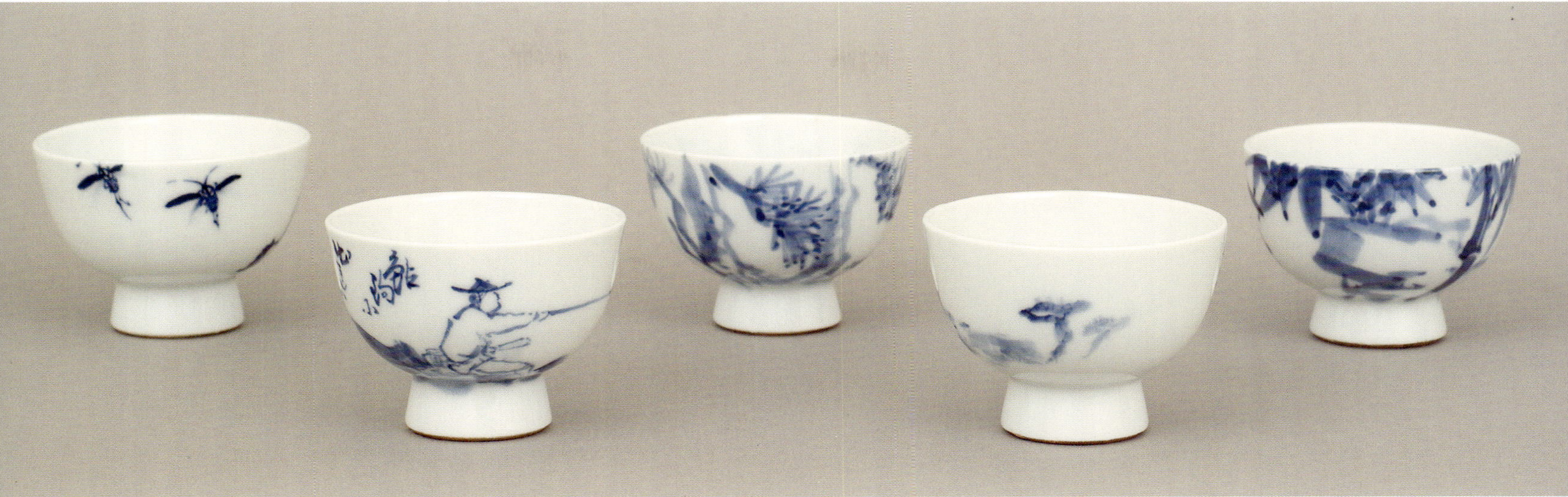

Left to right: Keinan *Fireflies*, Keinen *Angler*, Tessai *Pine*, Chikuson *Reishi and Rock*, Tessai *Bamboo*

In striking contrast, Keinen offers elegance and wit in his compositions and brushwork. In each of his decorations, Keinen added a haiku whose fluent calligraphic style matches his refined drawing. One of his cups represents an angler seated on a rocky bank, a fishing pole in his hand. He captured the complex human form with economical brush lines while defining the ground with broad, flat strokes. The placement of his humorous inscription rhythmically follows the silhouette of the rock outcrop behind the figure. On another cup, Keinen wrapped his calligraphy around one side of the cup and portrayed two fireflies on the other; they appear in flight, with the path of one taking it over the upper edge of the cup. Against the white background, the crisp depiction of the tiny insects is particularly effective.

Compared to the cups of the elder artists, Chikuson's depiction of *reishi* 霊芝 and rock is markedly modest but equally pleasing. Brushed with great sensitivity, his composition is almost abstract, particularly in a rock whose feather-shaped strokes are accented with dark dots. The rhythm of Chikuson's brushwork continues with the horizontal spread of the four-character inscription to the left. Although Chikuson, like Tessai, chose a literati subject and a Chinese-style inscription, his expression is restrained and clearly distinct from Tessai's dramatic style.

The *shingai* year (1911) inscribed by Chikuson is confirmed by Tessai's signature, which on the cup with a pine tree includes his age. The inscription on the box containing the set dates the work as 1912, suggesting the year when the firing process was completed. MM

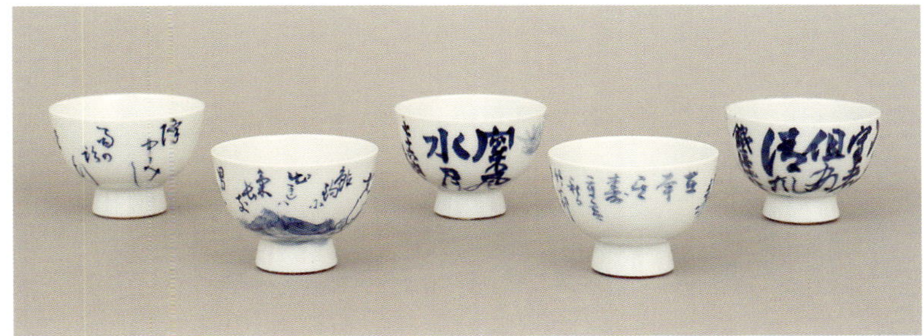

Potter's seal

NOTES

1. From a verse by Xie Hui of the Liang dynasty (502–556); see Morohashi Tetsuiji, *Daikanwa jiten*, vol. 2 (1959; reprint, Tokyo: Daishūkan Shoten, 1976), 507.

2. See the biography of Imao Keinen and the discussion of his work by Tamaki Maeda in Michiyo Morioka and Paul Berry, *Modern Masters of Kyoto: The Transformation of Japanese Painting Traditions, Nihonga from the Griffith and Patricia Way Collection* (Seattle: Seattle Art Museum, 1999), 122–25.

3. For Chikuson's biography, see Yui Kazuto, *20 seiki bukko nihongaka jiten* (Tokyo: Bijutsu Nenkansha, 1998), 239, and "Tajika Chikusonshi iku," *Kaiga seidan* 10, no. 4 (April 1922): 12–13.

4. Examples are illustrated in Kyōtoshi Bijutsukan, *Seitan 150-nen kinen: Tomioka Tessai ten*, exh. cat. (Kyoto: Kyōtoshi Bijutsukan and Kyōto Shinbunsha, 1985), 284–93.

5. A discussion of Tessai's relationship with Chokunyū appears in Kyōto Furitsu Sōgō Shiryōkan, *Tanomura Chokunyū to Tomioka Tessai: Sono gagyō to nanga no kiseki*, exh. cat. (Kyoto, 1985), no pagination.

Kawahigashi Hekigotō 河東碧梧桐

1873–1937

More than 14,000 of Hekigotō's published verse have been collected, yet he was so prolific that it is not uncommon to find calligraphies of haiku, such as this one, that were never published.[1] Translations by their very nature are interpretations into another language and culture, yet the translation of haiku is among the most difficult as their extreme brevity causes nuances to shift with even the smallest of changes. One reading of this haiku is:

盆梅の前	*Bonbai no mae*
	In front of the potted plum
正月の	*shōgatsu no*
	New Year's ennui
草臥るを座る	*kutabireru o suwaru*
	sits.

In the case of the translation offered above, simply ordering the images in a more typical English syntax would yield: "Sitting in New Year's exhaustion before a potted plum." Not only does this translation become prose, it places the person sitting as the subject of the text. In haiku the meaning is determined as much by the sequence of associations set by the order of the imagery as by the grammatical structure.

Considering the procession of elements in their original order, the potted plum, or *bonbai,* is a bonsai of a plum tree that is especially admired for its blossoms. Potted plums of early-blooming or forced varieties have traditionally been sold around the New Year, an association that telegraphs the season even before it is determined by the word for the New Year, *shōgatsu.* In the original order the subject continually shifts, creating tension as to the effect that subsequent images may have on the reader's associations. Hekigotō may be describing himself or someone else. Although a reference to this person appears in the last line, he or she is not the center of the poem any more than the miniature plum tree; the real focus is "New Year's ennui." This combination of specific elements and a specific moment is a classic feature of a haiku, but the decentered quality wherein all parts affect the whole produces a measure of ambiguity that is new. Without a reference to flowers, the haiku gives no hint whether the person sitting on the grass is looking at the bonsai or staring abstractedly into space while seated on a veranda or even by a tokonoma, where the bonsai might be temporarily displayed.

Hekigotō's development of a radically new style of calligraphy was triggered in 1907 by a gift of ink rubbings from Nakamura Fusetsu 中村不折 (1866–1943). They had been taken from ancient steles, the *Cuanbaozi* (爨宝子, J., Sanbōshi) of 405 from the Eastern Jin period and the *Zhongyue songgao lingmiao* (中嶽嵩高霊廟, J., Chūgaku Sūkō reibyō) of 456 from the Wei dynasty. Both steles were inscribed in variant styles of clerical script (*reisho*), and Hekigotō seems to have adopted the squared-off straight lines from the *Cuanbaozi* and the bold, irregular character compositions from the *Zhongyue songgao lingmiao.*[2]

Intoxicated by the excitement of creating a completely unanticipated style of calligraphy for haiku, Hekigotō plunged into the study of ancient Chinese calligraphy. His next major source of inspiration came with the publication of the Han-period script written with brushes on strips of wood and called *mujian* (木簡, J., *mokukan*). Edited by the noted scholars Luo Zhenyu 羅振玉 (1866–1940) and Wang Guowei 王國維 (1877–1927), the 1914 *Liushazhuijian* (流沙墜簡, J., Ryūsa tsuikan) reproduced hundreds of *mujian* from the Han dynasty and later periods that had been discovered

12. *Potted Plum Haiku* 盆梅俳句 (Bonbai haiku)

1930s
Hanging scroll: ink on paper
128.2 × 33 cm
SIGNATURE: *Heki* 碧
SEAL: *Hekigotō* 碧梧桐
Purchase, 2005
13208.1

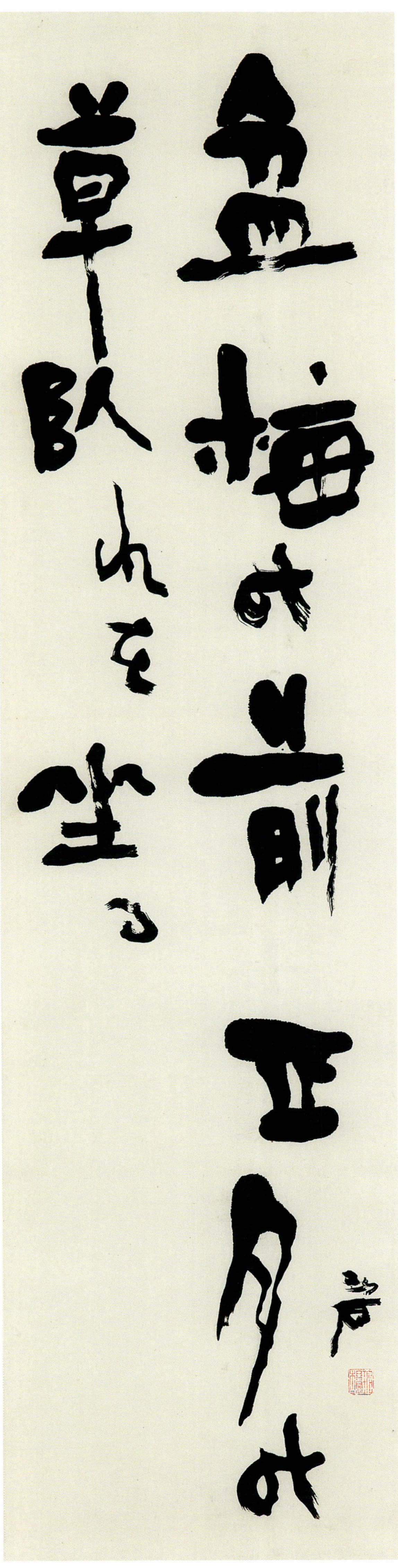

during Aurel Stein's second archaeological expedition (1906–8) to the desert areas of western China. Study of these early examples of brush-written script prompted Hekigotō to soften the quality of his line while providing even more examples of dramatic, irregular character compositions. Hekigotō continued experimenting with various styles until he achieved a creative synthesis in his last works.

Even though undated, the current work is in a style representative of those Hekigotō wrote in the last decade of his life. The prominent horizontal strokes are remnants of his study of the *Cuanbaozi* stele inscription, yet the swelling roundness of the strokes and the occasional thickening and thinning of the line, as seen in the second-to-last character of the right line (*gatsu* 月), are aspects that appear especially in his late calligraphies. The unusual asymmetrical compositions of characters and their overall placement on the paper reveal Hekigotō's interest in pushing standard forms to the limit. Most calligraphers would have placed their signature and seal in the large blank space at the end of the poem in the second line, but Hekigotō placed them in the small space to the right of the verse. He usually signed his work, as he does here, with the single character *Heki*, yet he writes this character in so many ways that his signatures are rarely identical. Although extremely well learned in calligraphy, Hekigotō preferred to write characters that seem rough and naive. So different from the enchanting ephemeral elegance of the usual calligraphy employed for haiku, his bold approach gives a sense of monumentality similar to the ancient steles that first captured his attention.

PB

NOTES

1. Kurita Yasushi, ed., *Hekigotō zenkushū* (Tokyo: Kagyūsha, 1992).
2. Refer to the biography of Hekigotō in this volume. For more information on these stele inscriptions, consult Iijima Shunkei, *Sōgō shodō daijiten* (Tokyo: Tōkyōdō Shuppan, 1982), and Fushimi Chūkei, *Hokugi Chūgaku sūkō reibyō hi, Shoseki meihin sōkan*, vol. 70 (Tokyo: Nigensha, 1970).

Hashimoto Kansetsu　橋本関雪

1883–1945

13. *Sound of the Wind in the Pines / Seven-Character-Line Calligraphy*
松濤満地図並七古書
(Shōtō manchi zu hei shichi ko sho)　T
1918
Pair of hanging scrolls: ink and light color on paper
181.8 × 52.6 cm each

Right scroll:
SIGNATURE: 白沙邨者録近作 Recent work recorded by the resident of White Sand Village
SEALS: *Sōkai iju* 滄海遺珠 Pearl left in the depth of the ocean (top right)
Hashi-shi Shidō 橋氏士道 (sig. upper)
Kansetsu 関雪 (sig. lower)

Left scroll:
SIGNATURE: 関雪散客自写意境以遣懐歳在戊午十一月十三日 I, Kansetsu the recluse, paint my fantasy world for self-amusement, on the thirteenth day of the eleventh month of the *bogo* year [1918]
SEALS: *Hashi-shi Shidō* 橋氏士道 (sig. upper)
Kansetsu 関雪 (sig. lower)
Tōkai takusen 東海謫仙 Banished immortal of the Eastern Sea (bottom right)
Meigetsu kinkai 明月襟懐 Bright moon in heart (bottom left)

Purchase, 2005
13214.1 & 2

The son of a Confucian scholar, Hashimoto Kansetsu grew up with an abundant knowledge of Chinese classical literature. As he gained fame as a Kyoto *nihonga* painter, he maintained his self-identity as a *bunjin,* traveling to China almost annually to explore the sources of literati painting. While many of Kansetsu's exhibition pieces represented Chinese subjects, he revealed his literati predisposition more strongly outside the arena of national competitions. For example, his 1916 *Paintings by Kansetsu, a Wanderer* (Kansetsu sanmin gashū 関雪散民画集) illustrated sixty-four early paintings in diverse styles, many of which were accompanied by his original *kanshi* 漢詩 inscriptions.[1] A decade later, in 1924, Kansetsu proclaimed himself a literati painter in *Path to Literati Painting* (Nanga e no dōtei 南画への道程) and covered topics varying from theoretical and historical aspects of literati painting to practical guides on box inscriptions (*hakogaki* 箱書き) and the proper handling of ink and brush.[2]

This diptych attests to Kansetsu's position as *bunjin* extraordinaire of his generation. His application of brusque, dry strokes in an expressive, semicursive calligraphy creates a dynamic visual rhythm, with characters and brush lines varying in size and thickness. True to the literati spirit of spontaneity, Kansetsu ran out of space as he proceeded from right to left, forcing him to compress the characters on the left half to complete the poem. The inscription can be translated as follows:

昆山之仙玉作骨	The immortal of Mount Kunlun,[3] his bone is made of jade;
朝起汲泉飲明月	Rising in the morning, he draws water from the spring and drinks to the still bright moon.
鹿車西赴瑤池宴	He rides to the west on a deer-drawn carriage for a party at Yaochi Pond,[4]
王母臺榭辞金闕	And leaves the Queen Mother of the West's pavilion through the golden gate.
乗鶴時游渤海東	Riding on a crane to roam east of the Bohai Sea,[5]

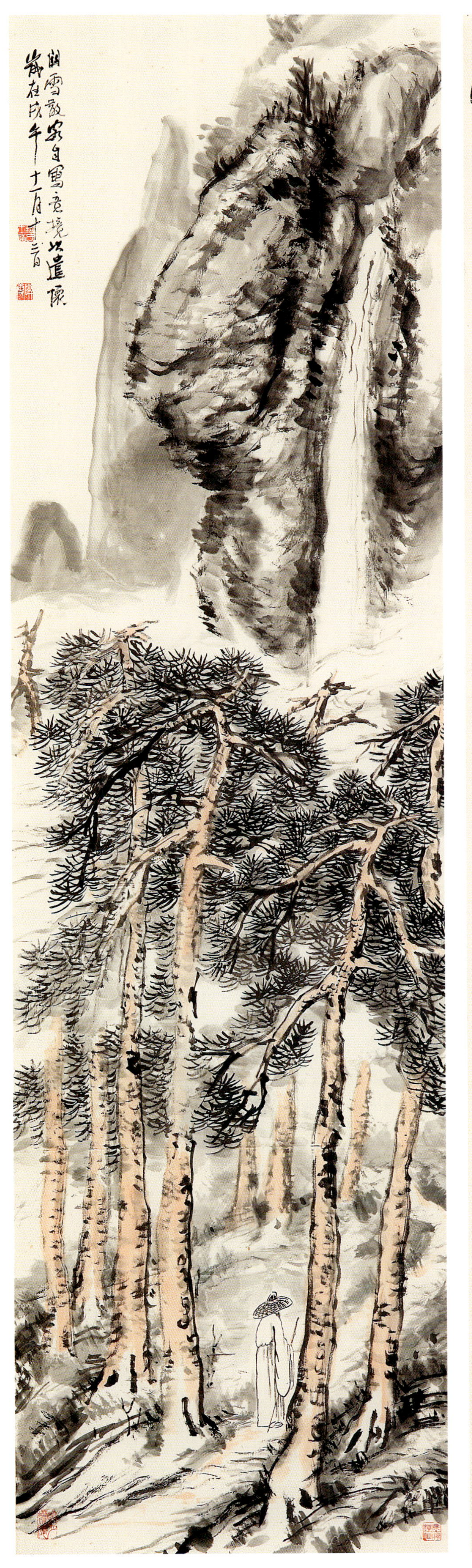

蓬莱紫極攀白雪	At Penglai Palace,[6] he climbs up on the white snow.
失脚驚天落人間	He slips and surprises himself, falling to the human realm;
回首塵寰路茫然	Looking around in the dusty world, his path is lost.
神符丹砂渾不随	Magical protection and substance, he forgot to bring with him.
平生志懐在山林	All his life, he wanted to stay in the mountains and forests
烟雲跌宕胸此蕩	Where clouds and mists float freely, making his mind expand.
葛衣烏帽青玉杖	He wears humble clothes and a black cap, carrying a bamboo cane,
文章題獻聖天子	And dedicates his writing to the emperor.
一到城市一俯仰	Upon arriving in the city, he looks up and down.
玉笏金冕未必軽	Jade tablet and golden headdress[7] are not to be taken lightly;
飛詔忽降九重城	In response to an urgent decree, he immediately goes to the emperor's palace.
松風吹送千山影	Pine breeze brings the image of a thousand mountains;
散髪振衣入帝京	He shakes out his hair, dusts off his garment, and enters the imperial capital.

On the left, the painting depicts a gentleman walking through a pine forest representing the ideal world where "clouds and mists float freely" and the immortal-recluses let their minds "expand." With loose, dry brushwork, Kansetsu created the perfect counterpart for his calligraphy. In spite of the overall sophistication of his ink brush, the slightly awkward figure, the wavering outlines of the pine trees, the roughly depicted mountains and waterfall, and a spatial ambiguity all contribute to the artlessness so valued in literati painting. To describe the essence he cherished, Kansetsu used the phrase "childlike feeling" 稚拙感 (*chisetsukan*) for an innate quality that could not be forced.[8] Also crucial to literati painting, in Kansetsu's view, was the beauty of "antirealism" (hishajitsu 非寫実), which he felt was being rejected by modern trends.[9] His artistic beliefs mirrored the literati ideal, which prized amateurish lack of skill over technical refinement and the artist's inner world over external reality. Thus, Qing artists such as Daoji 道濟 (1642–1707) and Jin Nong 金農 (1687–c. 1764), known for their individualistic styles and unorthodox brushwork, were among the literati masters Kansetsu admired.[10]

The date of this diptych, 1918, was a triumphant year when Kansetsu for the third time won the highest award at the government exhibition with a pair of screens, *Mokuran* 木蘭, representing a famous Chinese heroine.[11] The painting combined Shijō naturalism and the traditional *nihonga* technique of *urahaku* (gold leaf applied to the back of silk) with the Western realism of chiaroscuro. On the national stage, Kansetsu's intent was to please and impress viewers with his consummate execution of an ambitious painting. Nothing can be more distant from *Mokuran* than this diptych. Kansetsu reserved such authentic expressions of his literati aspirations for private exhibitions, where he was unburdened by the pressures of competition. MM

NOTES

1. Miyazaki Ichisada, "Hashimoto Kansetsu to kangaku," *Miyazaki Ichisada zenshū* 22 (Tokyo: Iwanami Shoten, 1992), 371. For a list of books of Kansetsu's paintings published during his lifetime, see Asahi Shinbunsha, *Botsugo gojūnen kinen: Hashimoto Kansetsu ten*, exh. cat. (Nagoya, 1994), 141.

2. Hashimoto Kansetsu, *Nanga e no dōtei* (Tokyo: Chūō Bijutsusha, 1924).

3. Mount Kunlun refers to the western mountain paradise, where the Queen Mother of the West has her mythical abode. This important Daoist deity grows the peaches of immortality and rules over other female deities and immortals.

4. Yaochi Pond, or Jade Pond, is believed to be at Mount Kunlun.

5. Bohai Sea refers to the gulf enclosed by the Liandong and Shandong Peninsulas on the coast of northeastern China.

6. Penglai refers to the legendary mountain of the immortals, supposedly located on an island at the eastern edge of the Bohai Sea.

7. The jade tablet and golden headdress are associated with the emperor and important officials.

8. Hakusasonjin, "Nigacha hiyameshi," *Daimai bijutsu* 5, no. 10 (October 5, 1926): 30.

9. Hashimoto Kansetsu, "Shinpen zakki," *Bi no kuni* 2, no. 10 (October 1926): 12 and 14.

10. Kansetsu regarded Jin Nong's work as "close to amateur painting" and admired his "happy-go-lucky" personality; see Hashimoto Kansetsu, "Kin Tōshin to iu otoko," *Atorie* 11, no. 3 (March 1934): 14–15.

11. Mokuran (Ch., Mulan) was a legendary woman-warrior who went to war in her father's place. Walt Disney Pictures released an animated film, *Mulan*, in 1998, introducing her story to the United States. A color illustration of Kansetsu's painting is in Asahi Shinbunsha, *Botsugo gojūnen kinen*, 54–55.

Landscapes

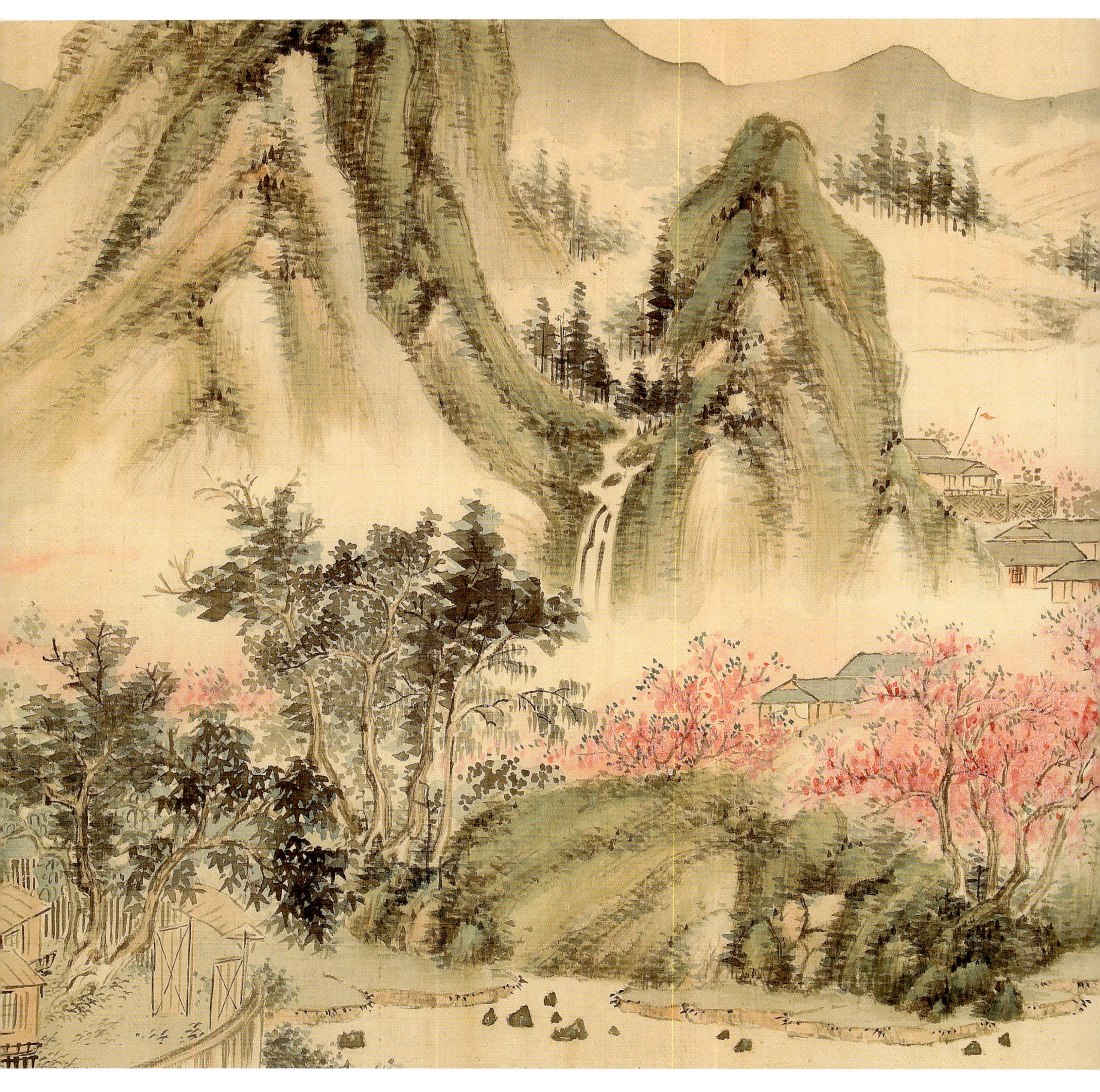

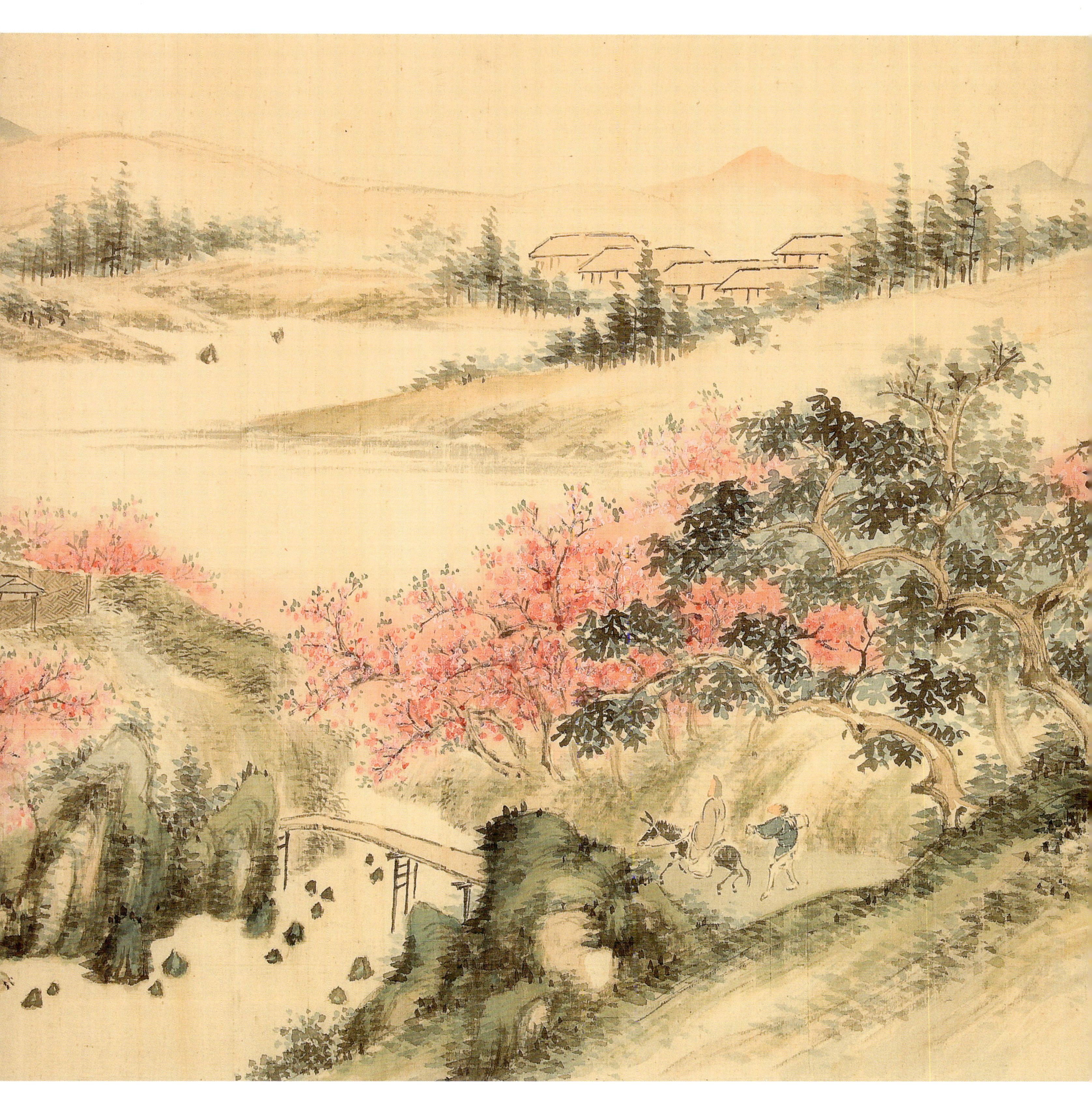

Ike Gyokuran 池玉瀾 (TRADITIONAL ATTRIBUTION)

1727/8–1784

A descendant of gifted women poet-calligraphers and wife of the celebrated literati painter Ike Taiga 池大雅 (1723–1776), Ike Gyokuran was herself an accomplished artist who often added original poetic inscriptions to her paintings.[1] The couple lived in a small house in Kyoto, unconcerned with material wealth and immersed in painting and calligraphy activities. Their unorthodox, art-centered lifestyle was widely admired in the *bunjin* community.

Gyokuran received early painting lessons from the noted literati artist Yanagisawa Kien 柳沢淇園 (1706–1758). After her marriage, Taiga became her teacher. Working with models given by Taiga and copying his paintings, she developed a brush technique influenced by his distinct, expressive style. In turn, Gyokuran introduced Taiga to the world of Japanese classical poetry, and they began studying *waka* with a prominent courtier-poet, Reizei Tamemura 冷泉為村 (1712–1774), in the mid-1760s.[2] Gyokuran's paintings are more playful than those of her husband, and her individuality is unmistakable both in her eccentric brush touch and in the idiosyncratic forms of her compositions. Although she created many large paintings, Gyokuran's intimately sized works are more plentiful, including her imaginative, original compositions in the fan format.

Willows on the Riverbank features a series of embankments surrounded by water washed in pale blue. A scholar is quietly seated in a boat, enjoying the spring scene. The willow trees depicted with curving brush lines seem to dance in the breeze, with one center tree towering over the rest. The whimsy of this composition is characteristic of Gyokuran's landscapes. The flowing inscription echoes the form and direction of the top embankment and refers to the scene:

川きし能	*Kawagishi no*
	Along the riverbanks
柳乃みきわ	*Yanagi no miki wa*
	Branches of willow trees
うちなひき	*Uchinabiki*
	Lean and sway gently
波のよるへと	*Nami no yoru he to*
	Over the rippling of water.
かすむ春風	*Kasumu harukaze*
	The spring wind casts haze.

The *Shōfū* seal used in the lower left of this painting means "pine wind" and can be also read as *matsukaze.* It is believed that Gyokuran used this seal to honor the memory of her family tea house, Matsuya.[3] A *Gyokuran* seal consisting of two separate seals and an oval-shaped *Shōfū* seal appears in the artist's work from the early 1760s through the late 1770s.[4] But close examination of the two seals used in this work suggests that they are variants of documented examples, and thus this painting was likely done after Gyokuran.[5] Blending Japanese-style poems and Chinese-derived literati painting, Gyokuran achieved a distinct, personal expression that ultimately transcended Taiga's influence. The existence of numerous later paintings in Gyokuran's style demonstrates her enduring popularity as one of the most renowned female artists of Edo-period Japan.

MM

14. *Willows on the Riverbank* 柳蔭山水図 (Ryūin sansui zu)

Hanging scroll: ink and light color on paper
72.6 × 17.6 cm

SIGNATURE: *Gyokuran* 玉瀾

SEALS: *Gyokuran* 玉瀾
Shōfū 松風 pine wind (bottom left)

Purchase, 2005
13160.1

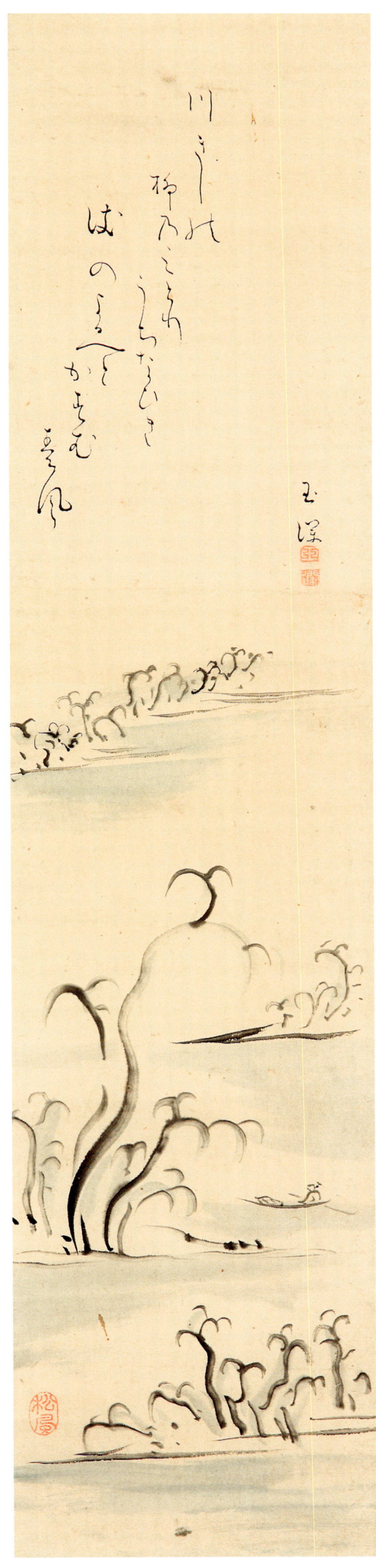

NOTES

1. Gyokuran may have continued to use her surname, Tokuyama 徳山, after her marriage to Taiga; see Kyoko Kinoshita, "The Life and Art of Tokuyama Gyokuran," in Felice Fischer et al., *Ike Taiga and Tokuyama Gyokuran: Japanese Masters of the Brush*, exh. cat. (Philadelphia: Philadelphia Museum of Art, 2007), 33.

2. Ibid., 41.

3. Hitomi Shōka, "Gyokuran," *Nanga kenkyū* 2, no. 9 (September 1958): 11.

4. Kinoshita, "The Life and Art of Tokuyama Gyokuran," 48–49.

5. Typically Gyokuran defined forms by employing forceful dark outlines, giving her painting a dramatic flair. The depiction of the willows in this painting varies from those in Gyokuran's documented works. Compare with examples in Felice Fischer et al., *Ike Taiga and Tokuyama Gyokuran*, fig. 23, plates 113, 122, 147, 160, and 162.

Kuwayama Gyokushū 桑山玉洲

1746–1799

Traditionally Gyokushū has been considered one of the key disciples of Ike Taiga 池大雅 (1723–1776), yet unlike other of Taiga's followers, Gyokushū does not show obvious stylistic influence from the older master. Recent investigations of his early career have revealed an unexpectedly diverse background, one that matches Gyokushū's often overlooked personal statement on his development as a painter. In the draft manuscript *Gyokushū gashu* 玉洲畫趣, written in 1790, Gyokushū stated that he never had a painting teacher, but having met painters in Edo, and later knowing Taiga and Kimura Kenkadō 木村蒹葭堂 (1736–1802), he decided to directly study various works rather than follow the direction of any particular artist.[1] A long period of gradual exploration of many styles preceded his development of a unique approach to landscape painting during the last decade of his life. This unusual style emphasized forms boldly outlined with an even, rounded line coupled with layered washes of color. In his last years Gyokushū painted many works in this new manner, including striking nighttime winter scenes with falling snow.

Spring Landscape is an excellent example of this final stage of Gyokushū's evolving personal style. The theme of a staff-holding scholar on his way to visit an isolated country retreat, accompanied by an attendant bearing a *qin,* is often repeated in literati painting, but the visionary quality of the landscape being traversed is Gyokushū's own creation. In the lower right, the attendant appears between the dramatic, leaning forms of four large trees whose trunks consist of distinct washes bound by thick outlines. The scholar pauses on a bridge while regarding a distant waterfall. The path, marked by horizontal strokes against a green ground, rises swiftly to a closed gate that stands in front of a courtyard with an open pavilion. The red lacquer table inside the pavilion is set with cups, awaiting the scholar's visit. The trees and rocks in the middle-ground prominence have vertical, wriggling outlines, their colored washes adding a light, whimsical quality to the scene. A wall of mist silhouettes the foreground features and separates them from the towering peaks and waterfall in the distance. The bright green foliage is punctuated by scattered pink and white dots representing spring flowers. This manner of colorfully abstracting the landscape represents Gyokushū's lasting contribution to literati painting of the late eighteenth century. PB

15. *Spring Landscape* 春景山水図 (Shunkei sansui zu)

c. 1797
Hanging scroll: ink and color on silk
101 × 36.4 cm

SIGNATURE: *Gyokushū Kuwa Shisan sha* 玉洲桑嗣燦寫

SEALS: *Kuwa San* 桑燦 (sig. upper) *Meifu* 明夫 (sig. lower)

Private collection

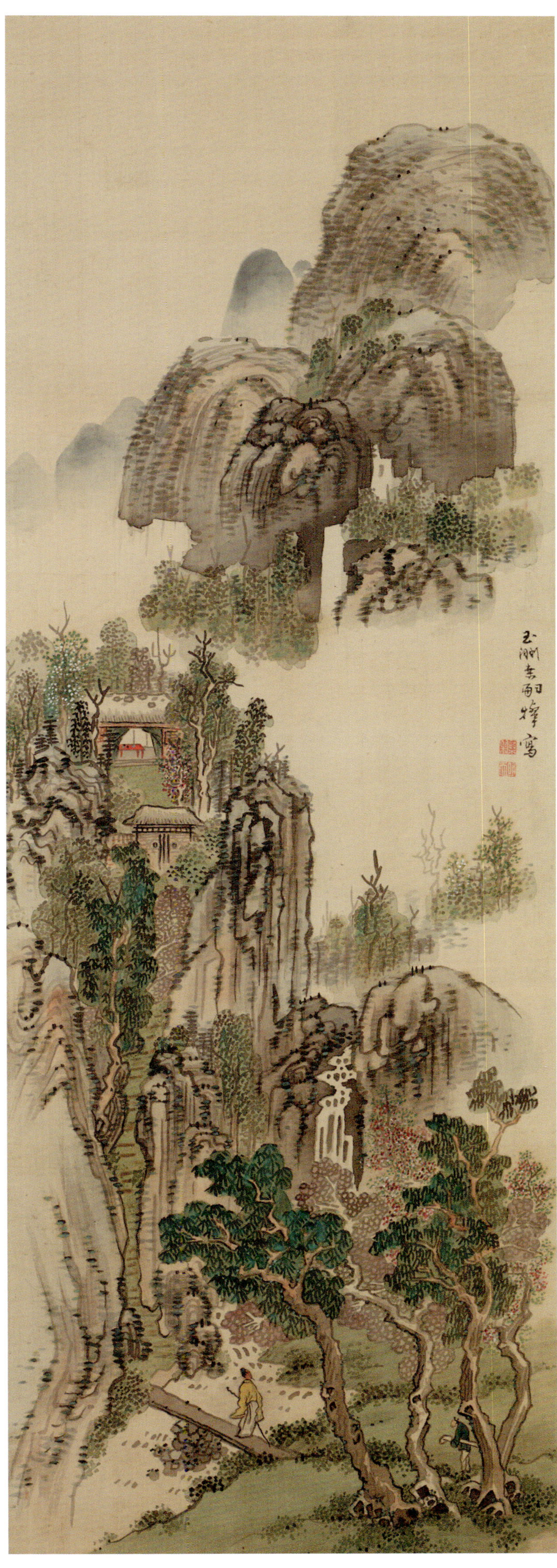

NOTE

1. The reevaluation of Gyokushū's career has been led by scholars working in Wakayama; consult Kondō Takashi, ed., *Tokubetsu ten—Kuwayama Gyokushū* (Wakayama: Shiritsu Hakubutsukan, 2006). Gyokushū's comments on his own career are discussed on pp. 86–87.

Kushiro Unsen 釧雲泉

1759–1811

An often-stated ideal of the literati life was to travel ten thousand miles, a goal most *bunjin* fulfilled by taking occasional trips. Unsen, however, spent his whole career in a decades-long journey from the Nagasaki area to the village of Izumozaki 出雲崎 in Niigata prefecture, with long periods in Okayama, Osaka, and Edo. During these years of travel, Unsen became acquainted with prominent literati artists, including Tanomura Chikuden 田能村竹田 (1814–1907), Uragami Gyokudō 浦上玉堂 (1745–1820), Tani Bunchō 谷文晁 (1763–1840), and Kameda Bōsai 亀田鵬斎 (1752–1826), yet his approach to painting remained unaffected. Few works are extant from the first decades of Unsen's career, and paintings from his time in Okayama, from 1791 to 1793, form the basis for understanding his early style.[1] It seems that Unsen was largely self-taught, developing his approach with the help of the many Chinese paintings he saw during his early years in Nagasaki. By the time he arrived in Okayama, his interest in fully formed landscape compositions with prominent mountain slopes filling the background was already established. His choice in Chinese examples—not the styles of Japanese literati painters—influenced these rather full compositions.[2] In this respect Unsen was similar to Hirose Taizan 広瀬臺山 (1751–1813) and his focus on the study of Chinese paintings, yet Unsen preserved a certain soft, free feeling in his brushwork compared to the more controlled, precise manner of Taizan.

This freedom of brushwork is a prominent feature of *Visiting a Friend—Discussing Antiquity.* The comparatively wet strokes of ink combined with the casual construction of architecture, trees, and mountain slopes imbue the work with a whimsy that matches the friendly energy of the two men engaged in animated conversation by the second-story window of the house. Light tones of ocher and green add warmth to the pale ink tonalities. Unsen's unique approach won the appreciation of Chikuden, and Kameda Bōsai was so moved by Unsen's work that he composed a biographical text for a large stele that was eventually erected in Izumosaki.[3] PB

16. *Visiting a Friend—Discussing Antiquity*
訪友論古図 (Hōyū ronko zu)

1793
Hanging scroll: ink and color on silk
141.6 × 45.8 cm

SIGNATURE: *Saihi Taishū* 西肥岱就
Taishū of Saihi [area near Nagasaki]

SEAL: *Taishū* 岱就

INSCRIPTION:
癸丑三月望後一日寫於東備之寓居
Painted in the *kichū* year [1793], third month, sixteenth day, while staying in Tōbi [Bizen area in Okayama prefecture]

Purchase, 2005
13162.1

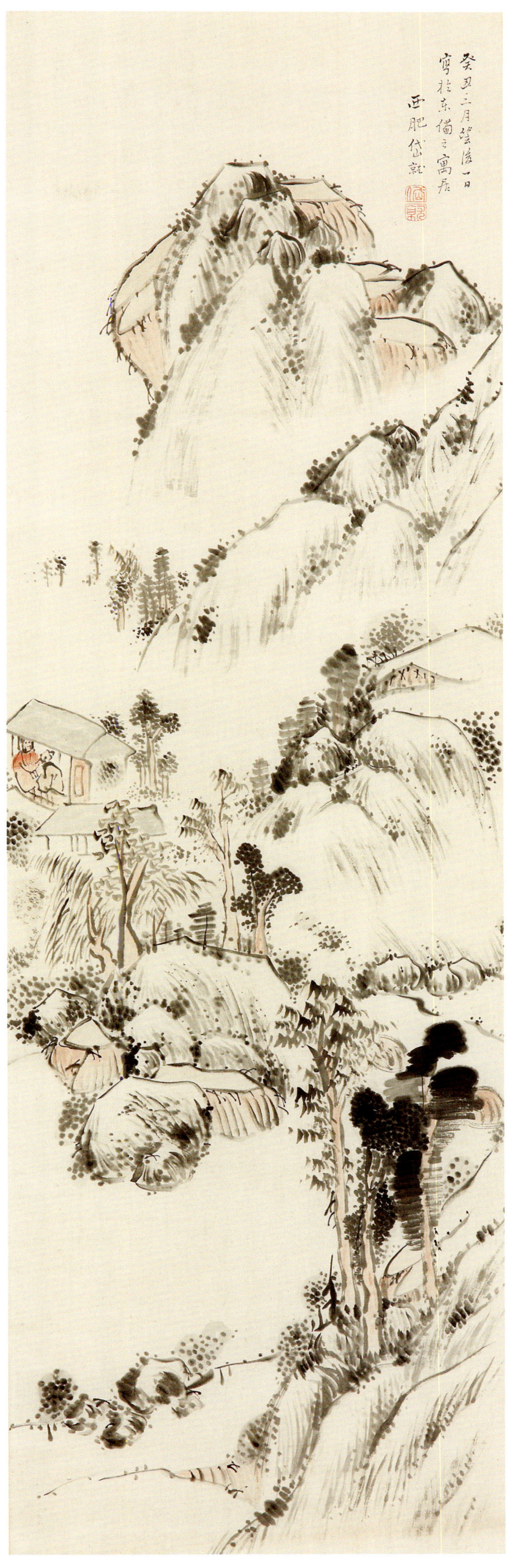

NOTES

1. Although it is often stated that Unsen was in Okayama prefecture from 1792 to 1793, an inscription on a painting in the University of Michigan Museum of Art dated to the seventh month of 1791 demonstrates that he had arrived by the previous year. Refer to entry 19 on Unsen in Celeste Adams and Paul Berry, *Heart Mountains and Human Ways* (Houston: Museum of Fine Arts, 1983), 64–65.

2. The best survey of Unsen's work remains the more than fifty paintings reproduced in Ōmura Seigai, ed., *Unsen ibokushū* (Osaka: Hōko Shoin, 1923).

3. See Sugimoto Eiji, *Kameda Bōsai no sekai* (Tokyo: Miki Shobō, 1985), 73–74.

Hirose Taizan 広瀬臺山

1751–1813

The unassuming beauty of the plum blossom and its ability to flourish in winter made it a beloved subject of literati painters and poets. Taizan's *Plum Blossom Studio* represents a gentleman in his cottage surrounded by flowering white plum in a rustic setting. It is the ideal world of the scholar-recluse, communing with nature away from the mundane affairs of the world. For Taizan, who performed his official samurai duties loyally for much of his life despite his desire to pursue the *bunjin* lifestyle, the subject must have been particularly meaningful.

Noro Kaiseki 野呂介石 (1747–1828), a literati artist and contemporary of Taizan's, proclaimed in his painting treatise:

> All paintings of plum blossoms should be night scenes. The ancients, too, wrote many poems about plum blossoms and the moon. Therefore the Plum Blossom Studio always has lanterns displayed so as to represent a night scene.[1]

The association of flowering plum and the moon in literati tradition is both aesthetic and symbolic. The beauty of plum blossoms opening in a frost-covered environment led one Chinese poet to describe the effect as if "moonlight [were] hanging from the trees" on a cold night. The pristine radiance of the blossom stood for purity, distinguishing both the plum and the moon from everything else in nature.[2]

Taizan's *Plum Blossom Studio* indeed depicts a night scene in which the sparkling white of blossoms is matched only by the brilliance of the moon. A scholar-recluse seated in his modest cottage gazes at the moon through an open window, his back rounded as if to guard against the winter cold. The old plum trees gently extend their craggy branches to frame the figure. One imagines the blossoms permeating the air with their subtle fragrance. Although not luxurious, the architecture mirrors the refined taste of its resident in its unpretentious stone fence and simple gate. Moreover, prominently situated by the entrance is a natural rock of bizarre shape, one of the prized objects in the garden of a cultured gentleman. A stream originating in the mountains in the background winds around the house to add spatial depth. Its icy surface evokes the feeling of the chilly air.

A respected literati painter of his time, Taizan often created complex landscapes with orthodox brushwork and attention to proper details. This painting, an excellent example of Taizan's intimate-scale work, shows a more relaxed approach. His brushwork, which Tanomura Chikuden 田能村竹田 (1777–1835) once praised as "filled with vitality" and "[intentionally] clumsy,"[3] here demonstrates an unaffected ease and naturalness. The strong brush lines of the gnarled, twisted plum trees contrast with the soft, broad washes of the mountains. Color is applied sparingly but effectively. The faint blue wash that bathes the moon intensifies its luminosity. Scattered green dots of vegetation animate the scene without being intrusive. Through a careful composition and confident brushwork, Taizan portrayed a quiet corner of the ideal *bunjin* world, its sense of intimacy enhanced by the painting's small size.

One literati painter characterized Taizan as "a man of few wants; amidst worldly confusion he was otherworldly" and observed that he "never responded by over-reacting; in his deportment he was upright and cautious."[4] These traits are confirmed by an 1811 portrait of Taizan painted by his close *bunjin* friend Katagiri Ranseki 片桐蘭石 (1744/59–1807/19). Taizan appears in the portrait as an elegant elderly gentleman with a placid expression and dignified pose; he has a long beard and wears a black cap,[5] just like the figure depicted in *Plum Blossom Studio*. MM

17. *Plum Blossom Studio*
梅華書屋図 (Baika shooku zu)

c. 1800
Hanging scroll: ink and color on silk
30 × 19 cm (116 × 37 cm overall)

SIGNATURE: *Taizan* 臺山

SEALS: *Seifū* 清風
Un 雲 (?) (bottom right)

Purchase, 2005
13163.1

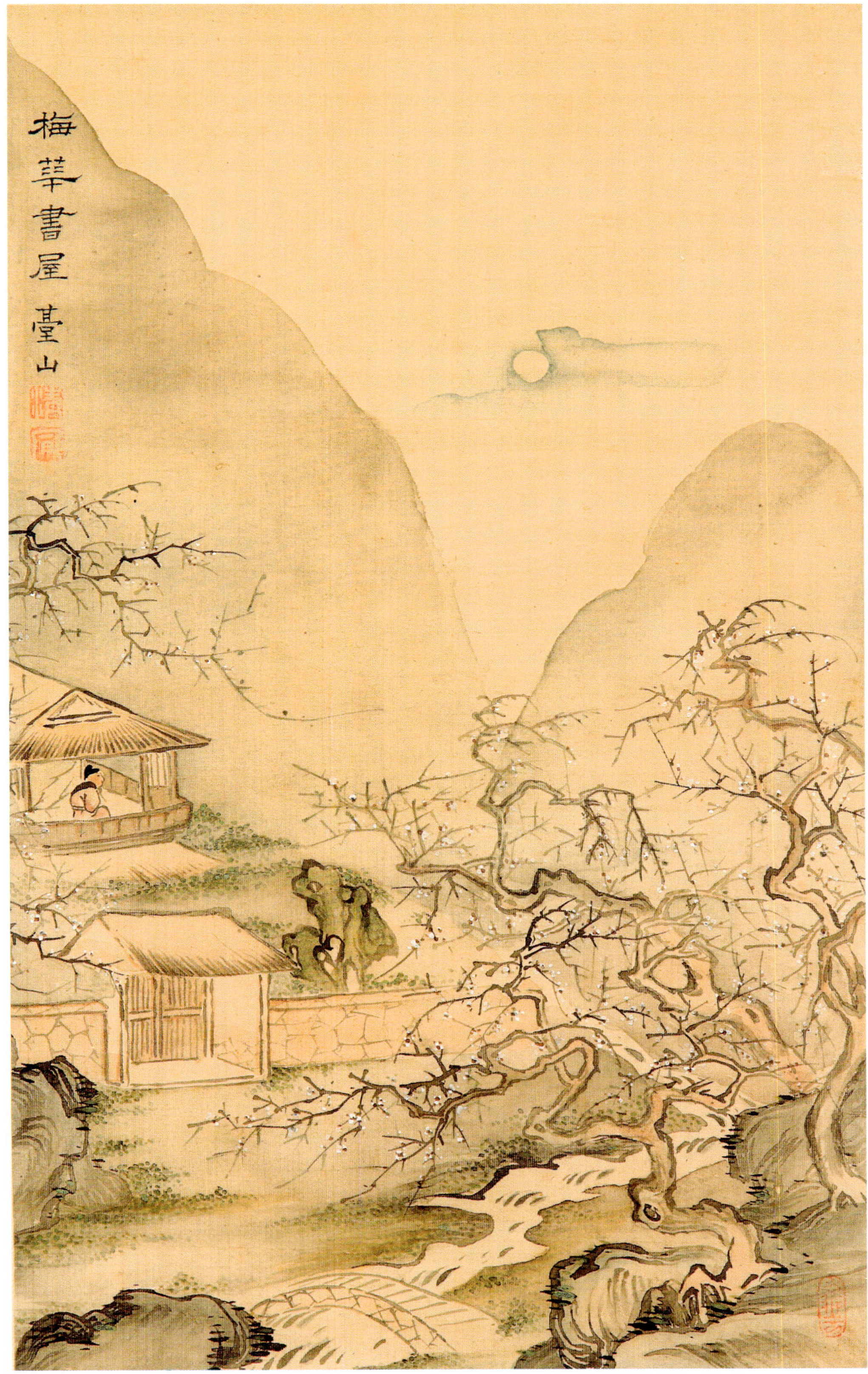

NOTES

1. From Kaiseki's *Shihekisai gawa* (Shihekisai's talks on painting); translation by Hugh Wylie in "Nanga Painting Treatises of Nineteenth-Century Japan: Translations, Commentary, and Analysis" (PhD diss., University of Kansas, 1991), 21.

2. See Maggie Bickford, *Ink Plum: The Making of a Chinese Scholar-Painting Genre* (Cambridge and New York: Cambridge University Press, 1996), 50–52.

3. From Chikuden's *Sanchūjin jōzetsu* (The prattling of a mountain hermit); translation by Wylie in "Nanga Painting Treatises," 107. "Clumsy" 拙 is a term of praise that signals the literati ideal of amateur painting, free from excessive professionalism.

4. Kanai Ujū (1796–1857), in his *Musei shiwa* (Talks on "Silent Poetry"); translation by Wylie, "Nanga Painting Treatises," 167–68.

5. See the illustration in Kurihara Naoshi, *Hirose Taizan* (Tokyo: Miki Shobō, 1991), on the first page after the cover.

Masuyama Sessai 増山雪斎

1754–1820

18. *Pure Conversation among Green Mountains*
青山中清談図 (Seizan chū seidan zu)

c. 1816[1]
Hanging scroll: ink and color on paper
183 × 94 cm

SIGNATURE: *Sekiten Dōjin* 石顛道人
Stone-crazy Daoist

SEAL: *Sessai* 雪斎

Purchase, 2005
13164.1

As the eldest son of the daimyo of the Ise Nagashima *han* 伊勢長島藩, and eventually a daimyo himself, Sessai was in the unusual position of being both a wealthy patron of the arts and a skilled painter and calligrapher. He spent much of his life interacting with the cultured literati circles in the capital city of Edo, but he also encouraged the arts in the *han* domain and visited the noted painters of Osaka. The range of his connections with artists and collectors made him well aware of the diverse trends in painting, and from among these he chose two quite different styles when creating his own works. When painting birds and flowers, Sessai usually employed flamboyant colors, minute details, and dramatic birds, especially peacocks. His landscapes, though impressive in scale, were comparatively mild in tone and brushwork, approaching the *pingtan* 平淡 aesthetic of "blandness" favored by the Chinese literati. That the skillful flourishes of fine detail and showy color of his bird-and-flower paintings are entirely absent in his landscapes reveals how clearly Sessai perceived the divisions among different modes of painting.

Sessai's output seems to have increased after his 1801 retirement as daimyo. The style of *Pure Conversation among Green Mountains* is similar to a number of Sessai's landscapes from the last two decades of his life, which were most often bucolic views of distant green mountains painted with light, casual brushwork. One of his largest extant works, this painting was intended to be viewed from a distance while displayed in a very large tokonoma. Seen this way, the spatial relationship between the foreground trees, the buildings beyond them, and the massive range of hills is especially effective. At the base of the cliffs runs a line of houses elevated on pilings above the wide expanse of water. Through the open window of one house, three scholarly figures engage in conversation around a red lacquer table. Such tables, almost unknown in Japan, were a common feature of wealthy households in China, and Japanese artists added these attractive red accents to their works, having seen them so often in paintings imported from the mainland. The rear mountain peaks are all triangular, with a waterfall, earthen tones, and clumps of vegetation providing satisfying accents to their gently inclined slopes. Sessai's passionate admiration for unusual stones is reflected by his adoption late in life of the alternate name Sekiten Dojin (Stone-crazy Daoist), which he used on this work.[2] PB

NOTES

1. The seal and signature on this work are very similar to those seen on the Mi-style landscape dated 1816 in Mie Kenritsu Bijutsukan, *Eao no fūryū saishi—Masuyama Sessai ten zuroku*, exh. cat. (Tsu, 1993), plate 30.

2. Ibid., 4.

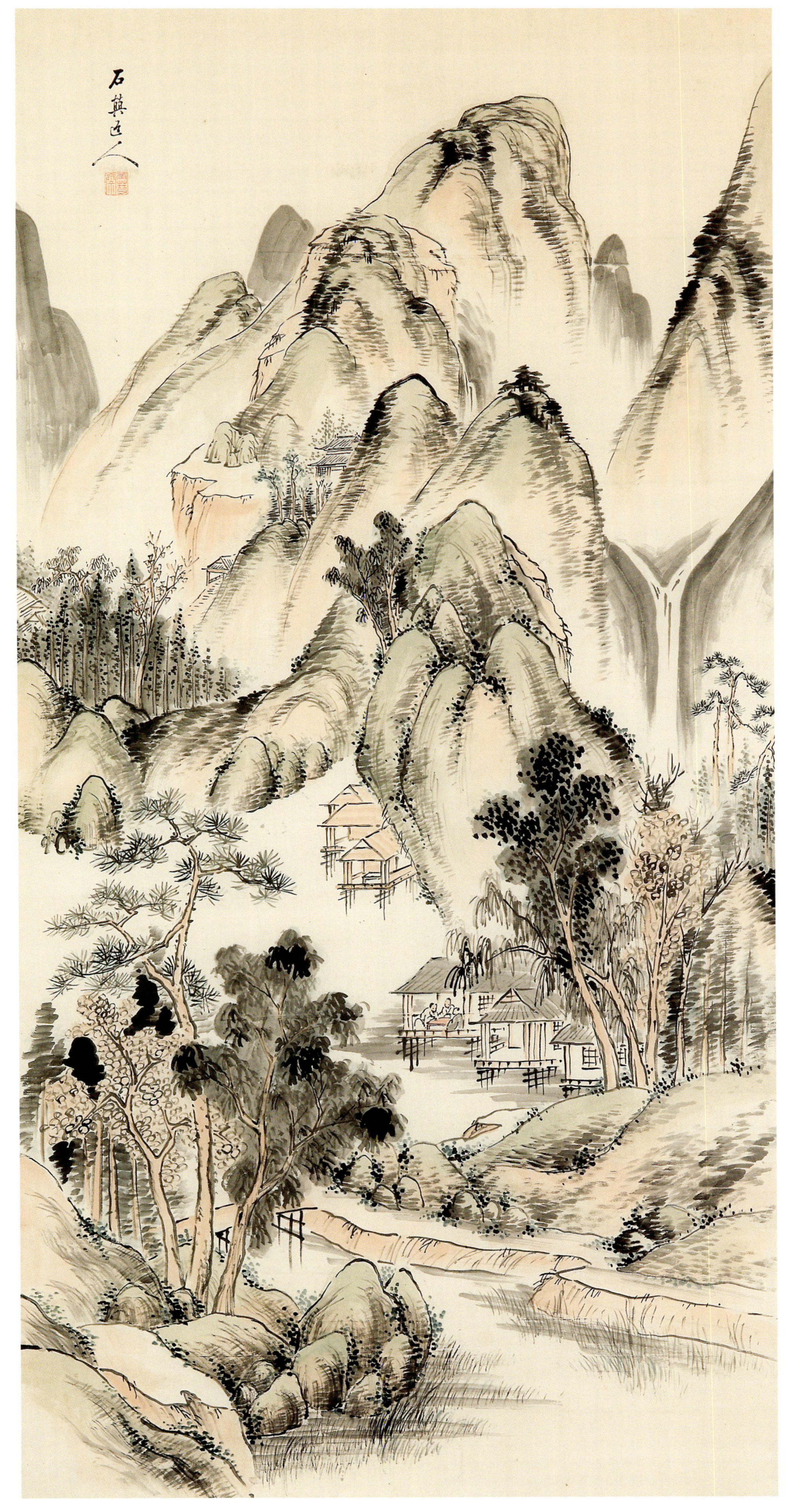

Kameda Bōsai 亀田鵬斎

1752–1826

Kameda Bōsai was most famous for his wild cursive script, yet he was also appreciated for the dramatic simplicity of his paintings. His work gained a larger audience when twenty-nine of his landscapes appeared in a woodblock-printed book (1816) called *Mountains of the Heart* (Kyōchūzan 胸中山).[1] Bōsai created the original works during a single day while he was drinking; the popularity of the colored illustrations made after the paintings led to many printings of the book during the Edo period.[2]

Whether working in a large or small format, Bōsai seems to have quickly laid out his compositions with bold, brushed outlines that he then filled in with ink and color washes. The late Ming period saw some Chinese literati painters create simplified landscapes with strong brushwork,[3] and merchant-artists like Yi Fujiu 伊孚九 (1698–1747) created concise versions of simple landscapes in the style of Ni Zan 倪瓚 (1301–1374) which influenced many Japanese painters. Although indebted to these precedents, Bōsai's reduction of scenery to its basic elements exceeded their abbreviations. Bōsai employed similar, rough lines for mountains, trees, and buildings, which he tinted with only a few color washes; he relied on the vigor of his brushwork to hold the interest of the viewer. Created in an impromptu fashion, Bōsai's works vary in quality and can tend toward sloppiness. The best examples, however, have a kind of monumentality that expresses the essence of the idealized literati landscape.

The dynamic contrast of energetic brushwork with an expansive, stable composition makes *Clearing after Rain, Clustered Peaks* one of Bōsai's finest landscapes. The man poling a boat in the center of the foreground river establishes a viewpoint for the entire work. An empty mid-ground pavilion lies below a plateau with a cluster of houses overshadowed by towering peaks. These mountains are depicted in a variety of shapes, colors, and ink washes, the most unusual being the central group of narrow spires pressed closely together. The overall effect is more complex and carefully balanced than most of Bōsai's work.

Bōsai is renowned for his cursive calligraphy, yet his regular and semicursive scripts were also quite accomplished. The high quality of the semicursive inscription on this painting is another of its charms. A close look at the strokes reveals fluid variations in line width and torsion within each character. The way Bōsai balanced angular and cursive elements may be indebted to his study of these traits in the work of the noted Tang-dynasty calligrapher Yan Zhenjing 顏真卿 (709–785), whose style he praised as an ideal model in his 1819 preface to the *Compendium of Semicursive Calligraphy* (Gyōsho ruisan 行書類纂) by Seki Kokumei 関克明 (1768–1835).[4] PB

NOTES

1. See the facsimile edition: Kameda Bōsai, *Mountains of the Heart* (New York: George Braziller, 2007).

2. See Roger Keyes's discussion of various editions in his *Ehon: The Artist and the Book in Japan* (New York: New York Public Library; Seattle: University of Washington Press, 2006), 196, 283–84.

3. Paintings by Zhang Ruitu 張瑞圖 (c. 1570–1641) and Ni Yuanlu 倪元璐 (1593–1644) were in Japan by this time, although the dramatic simplifications of Zhu Da 朱耷 (1626–1705) were still unknown.

4. See Stephen Addiss's translation of Bōsai's preface in *The World of Kameda Bōsai*, 118–19.

5. This term had a certain currency in the late eighteenth century. A noted seal carver, Sodani Gakusen 曽谷学川 (1738–1797), used the alternate name Seikyō Dōjin 醒狂道人.

19. *Clearing after Rain, Clustered Peaks*
雨霽群峯図 (Usei gunpō zu)

1807
Hanging scroll: ink and color on silk
113.2 × 50 cm

SIGNATURE: *Teibō haru Bōsai suisha* 丁夘春鵬斎酔冩 Bōsai intoxicatedly painted in the *teibō* year [1807], spring

SEALS: *seikyō* 醒狂 sober exhilaration (upper right)[5]
Bōsai Kanjin 鵬斎閒人 (sig. upper)
Chōkō shiin 長興私印 (sig. lower)
Taihei suimin 太平酔民 peaceful, drunken people (bottom right)

INSCRIPTION:
雨霽群峯蒼翠濃
湖山風景几間重
援毫何必求真似
漫冩讀書瀟灑胸
Clearing after rain, clustered peaks in deep verdure
Scenery of lakes and mountains with a plateau in its midst
Grasping the brush, I question the necessity to seek close resemblance
Freely painting, reading books with a light-hearted spirit

PUBLISHED: Stephen Addiss, *The World of Kameda Bōsai* (New Orleans: New Orleans Museum of Art; Lawrence: University Press of Kansas, 1984), plate 14; Atsumi Kuniyasu 渥美国泰, *Kameda Bōsai to Edo kaseiki no bunjintachi* 亀田鵬斎と江戸化政期の文人達 (Tokyo: Geijutsu Shinbunsha 芸術新聞社, 1995), plate 166.

Purchase, 2005
13168.1

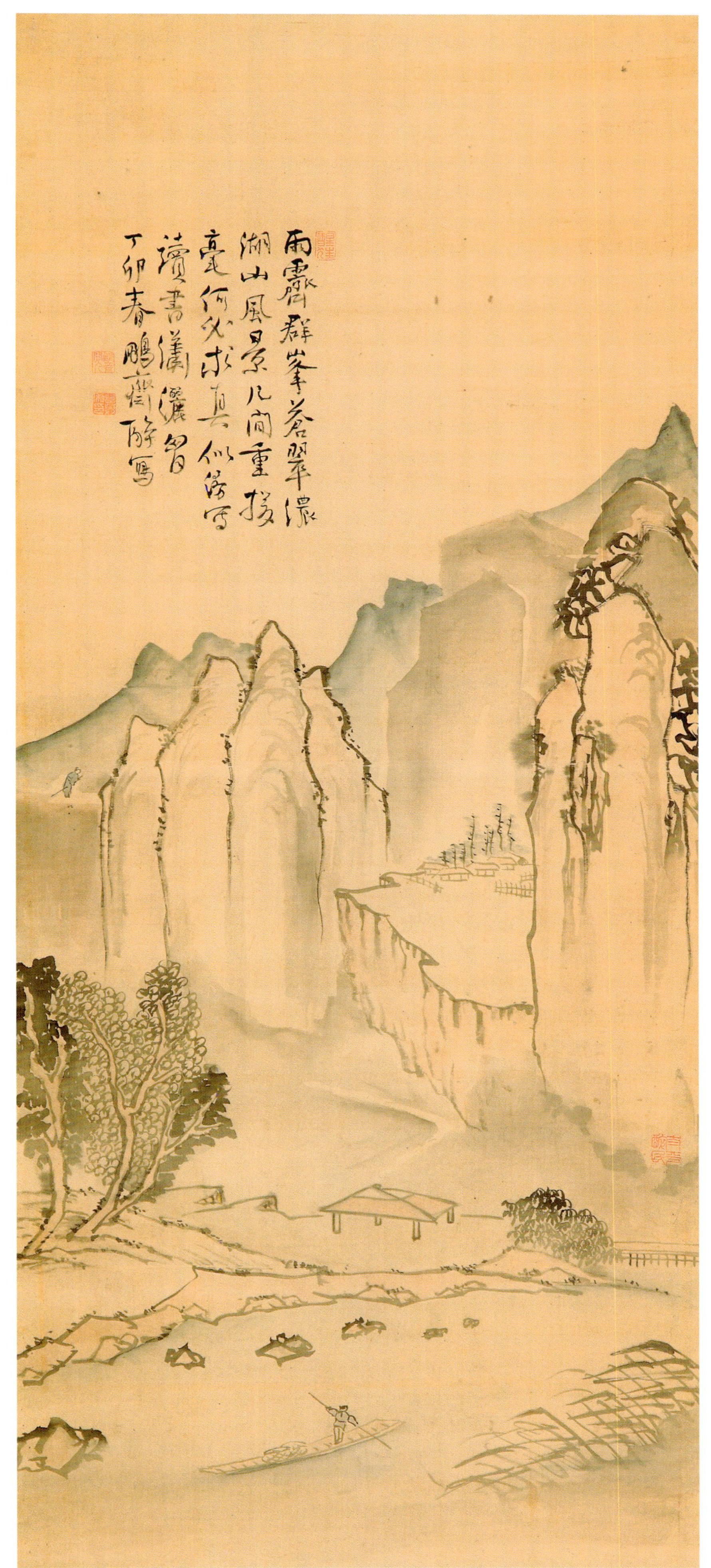

Noro Kaiseki 野呂介石

1747–1828

20. *Nachi Waterfall* 那智滝図 (Nachi taki zu)

1808
Hanging scroll: ink and color on silk
144 × 36.3 cm (183.5 × 52 cm overall)

SIGNATURE: *Boshin shūjitsu dai Kaiseki Ryū* 戊辰秋日題介石隆
Inscribed by Kaiseki Ryū in autumn of the *boshin* year [1808]

SEALS: *Daigaku shōsha* 臺岳樵者
Woodcutter of Mount Dai (right)
Dai goryū in 第五隆印 (left)

Gift of Terry Welch, in honor of Howard Rogers, 2005
13170.1

The Nachi waterfall is the most important site for nature worship in the Kumano 熊野 area of the southeastern Kii Peninsula 紀伊半島 (Wakayama prefecture). In the thickly forested mountains of Kumano, the Nachi River cascades over forty-eight waterfalls. At the largest, the Nachi waterfall, also known as The First Fall (Ichi-no-Taki 一の滝), water drops straight down 133 meters. The mystic powers of nature manifested at Kumano dovetailed with the syncretic religious beliefs of both Shinto and Buddhism.[1] Since the tenth century, Kumano has attracted many pilgrims ranging from imperial family members to common people.

Kaiseki visited the Nachi waterfall for the first time in 1789, shortly before he began serving the Kii domain, and began painting the site soon after. He made at least three more trips to the Kumano area in 1793, 1794, and 1807.[2] The strenuous and at times dangerous journey through the mountains required Kaiseki to carry not only food and cooking utensils but also climbing ropes.[3] On his first trip he was accompanied by ten people, including officials and laborers, and stayed for six nights in a temporary hut they built in the wilderness.[4] His firsthand experiences of the mountains and the waterfalls enabled him to depict the spectacular scenery with confidence, and he became known especially for his views of the Nachi waterfall. Kaiseki balanced his deeply instilled samurai ethic with a strong desire to pursue the literati lifestyle. The Nachi waterfall provided a perfect subject through which he could express his pride in the domain he served while fulfilling his yearning to paint.

The painting represents a particular compositional type known as Three Waterfalls in One View (Sanbaku ikkan no zu 三瀑一観之図), in which the first, second, and third falls are shown in one panoramic view.[5] Kaiseki carefully built his landscape with controlled, orthodox brushwork, including so-called alum heads in the texturing of the mountain, a Chinese landscape convention. From the foreground to the back, he layered the mountain forms one after another to represent the awe-inspiring grandeur of Kumano, with its precipitous cliffs and dense forest. Except for the upper left, where faintly silhouetted distant peaks appear, Kaiseki emphasized the soaring majesty of the mountains and the staggering height of the waterfalls. The breathtaking landscape solicits veneration for its manifestation of divine power but does not invite viewers to enter.

The artist's inscription conveys his intent to capture the spiritual essence of the waterfalls:

休費真景工	"Don't waste time painting a true view.
摸真還不似	You might copy the form yet not capture the spirit.
遥飛三瀑泉	As for the three waterfalls cascading in the distance,
誰言非那智	Who can say it is not Nachi?"
往年此君	In the past, a friend inscribed this
屈子所題鄙画也	on my humble painting.

屢探屢寫那智勝　Many times I visited, and many times I painted the view of Nachi.
三瀑奇絶最難寫　The magnificence of the three waterfalls is the most difficult to depict.
畫罷得否自不知　Even when the painting is finished, I do not know if I captured its spirit.
投筆嗒然問造化　I throw away the brush with a sigh and ask the creator [why it is so difficult].

Kaiseki refers to "true view" (*shinkei* 真景), the literati interest in the pictorial realism introduced from the West in the eighteenth century. In his treatise, *Shihekisai's Talks on Painting* (Shihekisai gawa 四碧斎画話), Kaiseki espoused the study of the brush methods of older masters while advocating the investigation of nature with one's own eyes. Yet his ultimate goal was to create a composition taken "from the true landscape within one's own mind."[6] Thus, Kaiseki's *Nachi Waterfall* is a quasi-realistic representation, which transmits his idealized vision of a mystic landscape based on his observation of the actual topography. MM

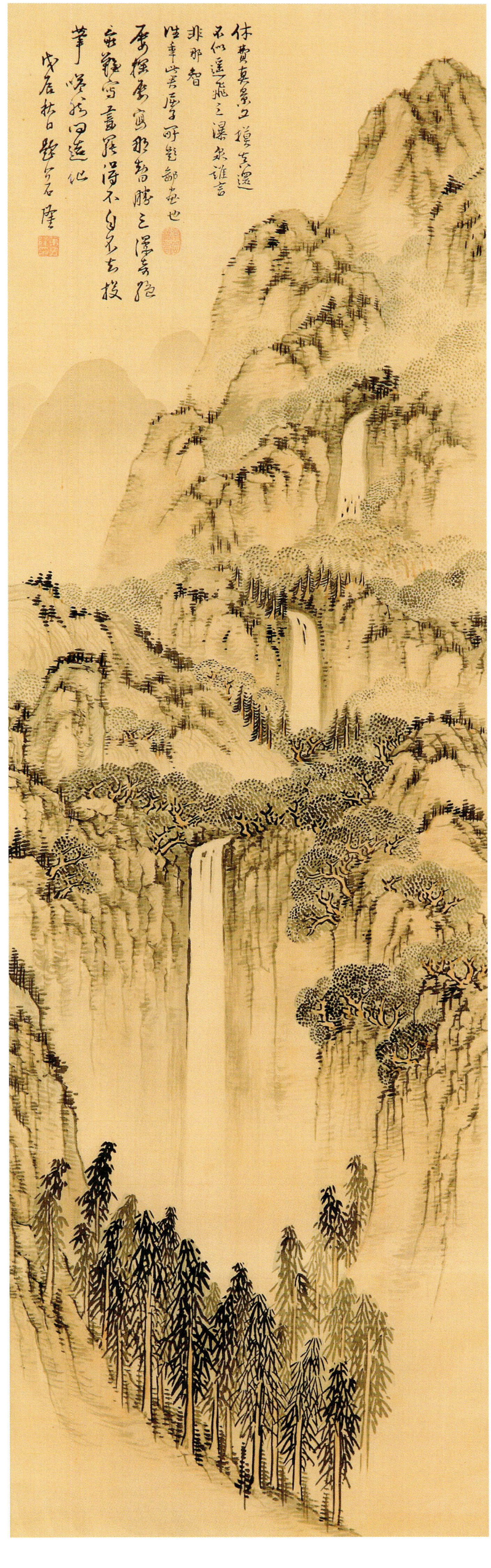

NOTES

1. For a detailed study of the significance of Kumano, see D. Max Moerman, *Localizing Paradise: Kumano Pilgrimage and the Religious Landscape of Premodern Japan* (Cambridge, MA: Harvard University Asia Center, 2005).

2. See the chronological record of Kaiseki's life in Wakayama Kenritsu Hakubutsukan, *Noro Kaiseki tokubetsuten*, exh. cat. (Wakayama, 1978), no pagination.

3. Furukawa Hokka, "Takaku Aigai to Noro Kaiseki, ge," *Nanga kanshō* 7, no. 12 (December 1938): 38.

4. Mori Senzō, "Noro Kaiseki," in *Mori Senzō chosakushū, dai sankan* (Tokyo: Chūō Kōronsha, 1988), 318.

5. For a well-known color version of this theme by Kaiseki, see Minamoto Toyomune, comp., and Sasaki Jōhei, ed., *Kyōto gadan no jūkyūseiki 2: Bunka Bunseiki* (Kyoto: Shibunkaku Shuppan, 1994), 107, and Wakayama Kenritsu Hakubutsukan, *Noro Kaiseki tokubetsuten*, plates 44 and 45.

6. Hugh Wylie, "Nanga Painting Treatises of Nineteenth-Century Japan: Translations, Commentary, and Analysis" (PhD diss., University of Kansas, 1991), 18.

Tanomura Chikuden　田能村竹田

1777–1835

21. *Crossing a River in Wind and Rain* 風雨渡江図 (Fūu tokō zu)　A

1829
Hanging scroll: ink and color on paper
181 × 47.8 cm

SIGNATURE: *Chikuden sei Ken* 竹田生憲

SEALS: *Ken in* 憲印 (sig. upper)
Chikuden 竹田 (sig. lower)

Private collection

INSCRIPTION:
嘗聞當局者迷傍觀者得予謂更有不當局不旁觀者安心打眠不知門前有風雨過者昔者寫風雨渡舟蘇人江芸閣題句云一間山閣亂雲中竹韻松濤面面通有箇山人間太甚坐觀雪浪臥聽風苡略得其意

今茲己丑寓大阪府醉古松良友索作此圖良友博窮理旁嗜書畫因揭蘇句及數語錄示兼博一粲時十月望日也

Although I have heard it said "The go player is unaware if he has lost his position, while it is quite clear for the onlooker," my experience is not that of the player or that of the onlooker, but of sleeping relaxedly, unaware whether there is a storm blowing outside or not. Once, when I was visiting Nagasaki, I made a painting, *Wind and Rain while Residing in a Valley*, and the man from Suzhou Jiang Yunge 江芸閣 [J., Kū Unkaku, in Nagasaki c. 1809–29][1] inscribed a poem on it:

> A small mountain pavilion in the midst of
> stormy clouds,
> The sound of the bamboo leaves, the voice of
> the wind in the pines could be heard from
> all directions.
> In its midst a man of the mountain relaxes,
> Sitting while watching the snow pile up on
> the hills, resting while listening to the
> wind.

This work is meant to express that feeling.

Now in 1829, while staying in Osaka, my good friend Matsumoto Suiko repeatedly requested this painting. Suiko, a person of wide learning who thoroughly studies things, has a strong passion for desirable calligraphy and painting. We shared a laugh while chatting over Jiang Yunge's poem. On the fifteenth day of the tenth month.

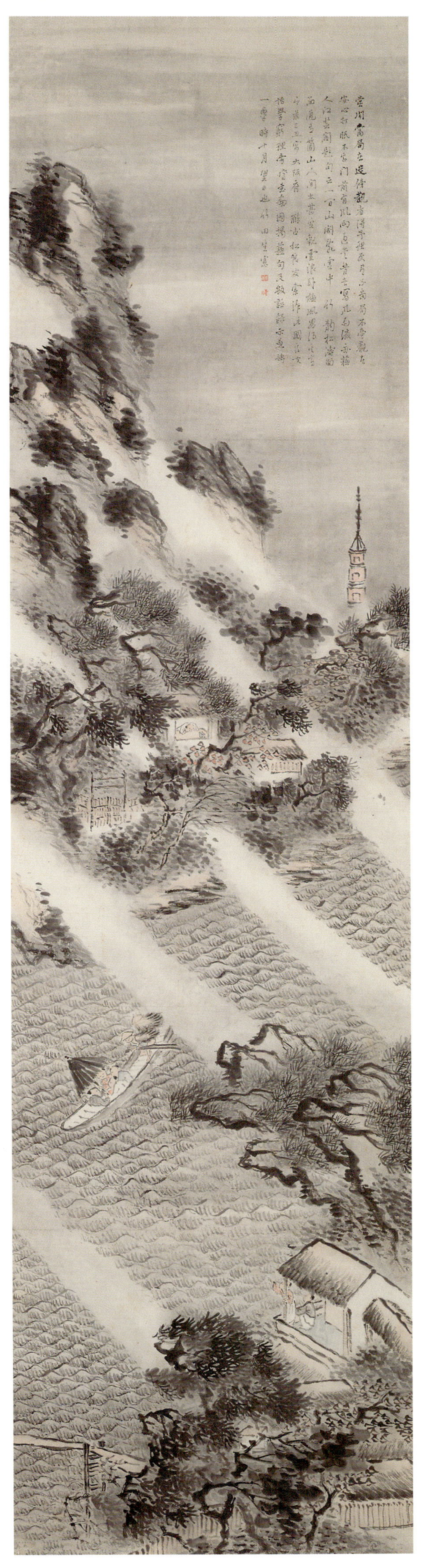

Crossing a River in Wind and Rain is one of the noted, long-"lost" works of Tanomura Chikuden, one of the finest literati painters of the Edo period.[2] Many of Chikuden's best works are of comparatively small size, but this painting is one of his largest. Due to the scale, the brushwork is bolder than usual, yet the extreme delicacy of the calligraphy is typical of the high style Chikuden achieved in his last years. The theme of crossing water during a rainstorm, so evocatively depicted here, became one of his most popular compositions during the last decade of his life.[3]

Chikuden seems to have initiated the theme with a work made in 1827 for his younger friend Kinoshita Itsuun 木下逸雲 (1799–1866) in Nagasaki.[4] Chikuden painted at least four related compositions in that year and made more later upon special request. *Crossing a River in Wind and Rain* is especially noteworthy among these for its dedication to Matsumoto Suiko 松本醉古, a doctor who lived in the Kitahama area of Osaka. Suiko had long been a friend and patron of Chikuden's; by 1826 he had given Chikuden a sophisticated Qing-period seal that he often used on his finest works.[5] Suiko had been the intended recipient of Chikuden's most renowned creation, the 1830 album *Yet Again, One More Pleasure* (Matamata ichirakujō 亦復一樂帖). Chikuden asked Rai San'yō 頼山陽 (1780–1832) to write a postscript to the album, but San'yō became entranced by its excellence and refused to return it, forcing Chikuden to create the *One Pleasure* (Ichirakujō 一樂帖) album for Suiko as a substitute.[6] *Crossing a River in Wind and Rain* maintains the high standard of these other works, which form the most impressive group of paintings that Chikuden created for a single patron.

Chikuden's fame rests on the combination of his remarkable, sensitive brushwork, which he developed from the close study of Qing-period paintings, and his sophisticated use of Chinese inscriptions. Most Japanese literati painters quoted famous Chinese poems or texts in their inscriptions, and the more advanced among them created their own quatrains, adding either short comments on the circumstances or dedications to patrons. Chikuden, however, often composed long inscriptions that rival those of the finest literati painters of China. He became skilled in *ci* 詞 (J., *shi*), one of the most difficult forms of Chinese verse. *Ci* are long poems based on the complex rhyme schemes of ancient Chinese songs and have lines of irregular length that are not parallel in structure like those of simpler quatrains. Even quatrains have rhyme schemes that necessitate knowing not only the sound but the tone of individual characters in Chinese. Although Japanese literati could read written Chinese, few knew the pronunciation, much less the correct tones, for the characters. As a result many Edo-period poems written in Chinese have the correct parallel line structure but do not rhyme properly when read aloud with Chinese pronunciation. As the structure of *ci* poetry is based entirely on sound and tone, most Japanese never attempted to write them. Chikuden, however, learned the correct tones from Chinese immigrants and became quite skilled in this arcane verse form.

Chikuden so prized his inscriptions that he started to collect them for publication in the last years of his life. Shortly after his death, his disciple Hoashi Kyōu 帆足杏雨 (1810–1884) expanded the artist's original 1829 selection into the 1839 five-volume *Inscriptions on My Paintings* (Jigadaigo 自画題語). The inscription on *Crossing a River in Wind and*

Rain, which appears as the sixteenth entry in the second volume, enables the viewer to interpret the painting.

Four figures huddle together under an umbrella in a vessel while two boatmen struggle to safely traverse the turbulent, wind-blown waves. The boaters are observed by two men, one excitedly pointing his hand at them from a window in the second floor of a house at the bottom of the composition. These two groups of figures—the boaters and the onlookers—correspond to the go player and the observer in Chikuden's inscription, while the figure seen dozing at his book-laden desk in the window of a middle-ground house represents Chikuden. This clever relationship between a complex inscription and an equally intricate painting well displays the high level of his achievement as a literati painter. PB

NOTES

1. Jiang Yunge was the younger brother of the prominent visiting Chinese painter Jiang Jiapu (J., K. Kaho, 1756–1815). Yunge is believed to have tutored Chikuden in poetry and calligraphy; a number of Chikuden's paintings have inscriptions by him.

2. The last record of this painting seems to be Tanomura Chokunyū's 1881 box inscription and the text on the satin wrapper for the scroll, in which Chokunyū recalls knowing Suiko during his childhood study in Osaka at the school of Ōshio Heihachirō (1793–1837).

3. Another version of a similar composition with the same title, made in the same year, is found in *Nihon no bunjinga: Nanga meisakuten* (Osaka: Nihon Keizai Shibunsha, 1971), plate 61. Although the inscription on this work is similar, it is not dedicated to Matsumoto.

4. See Paul Berry, "Tanomura Chikuden 1777–1835: Man Amidst the Mountains" (PhD diss., University of Michigan, 1985), 105–6, 205–6, and plates 37–40.

5. This seal, reading "One blossom—a thousand mountains of greenery" 一咲千山青, is of the same design as one with the same reading used by Tanaka Hakuin (1866–1934) on his title for Tanomura Chokunyū's handscroll *Great View of Rivers and Mountains* (cat. no. 43). In his self-published seal record, Chikuden mentions receiving the seal from Suiko; see the appendix to Iijima Isamu, *Tanomura Chikuden, Nihon no bijutsu,* no. 165 (Tokyo: Shibundō, 1980).

6. The *One Pleasure* album disappeared before World War II and was rediscovered only recently. It was shown at a 1997 exhibition on *sencha;* see Ōsaka Shiritsu Bijutsukan, *Sencha—bi to sono katachi* (Osaka, 1997).

Sō Geppō 僧月峰

1760–1839

Geppō's works are unusually free of Taiga's influence considering that Geppō devoted his life to preserving the belongings of the earlier painter and had lived in the noted Taigadō residence at Kyoto's Sōrinji temple. In many of Geppō's landscapes, the main motifs show prominent outlines, a technique that may have been popular in Kyoto in the early decades of the nineteenth century as other artists such as Azuma Tōyō 東東洋 (1755–1839) also employed it.[1] In *Moonlit Fishing Village* Geppō carefully modulated the outlines of the trees, houses, and hills to add variety to the brushwork. Atmospheric washes suggest late evening, with the moon rising over several boats moored in the bay and bands of mist extending across the distant hills. Five foreground trees dramatically frame the lower half of the composition; a view looking through trees is more commonly found in woodblock prints than in literati paintings of this period. A path meanders from the bottom edge through the trees to a cluster of village houses in the middle distance. The houses seem closed for the night, yet two men are out, conversing as they walk toward the village. The light touches of color on the figures and their warm, animated portrayal reflect the subtle influence of Buson's similar treatment of figures. This complex evocation of a quiet moonlit night reveals the talent of this little-studied artist whose companions included many of the celebrated painters of the day. PB

22. *Moonlit Fishing Village* 月下漁邨圖 (Gekka gyoson zu)

Hanging scroll: ink and color on silk
110.8 × 41 cm

SIGNATURE: *Geppō* 月峰

SEAL: *Shinryō* 辰亮

Purchase, 2005
13171.1

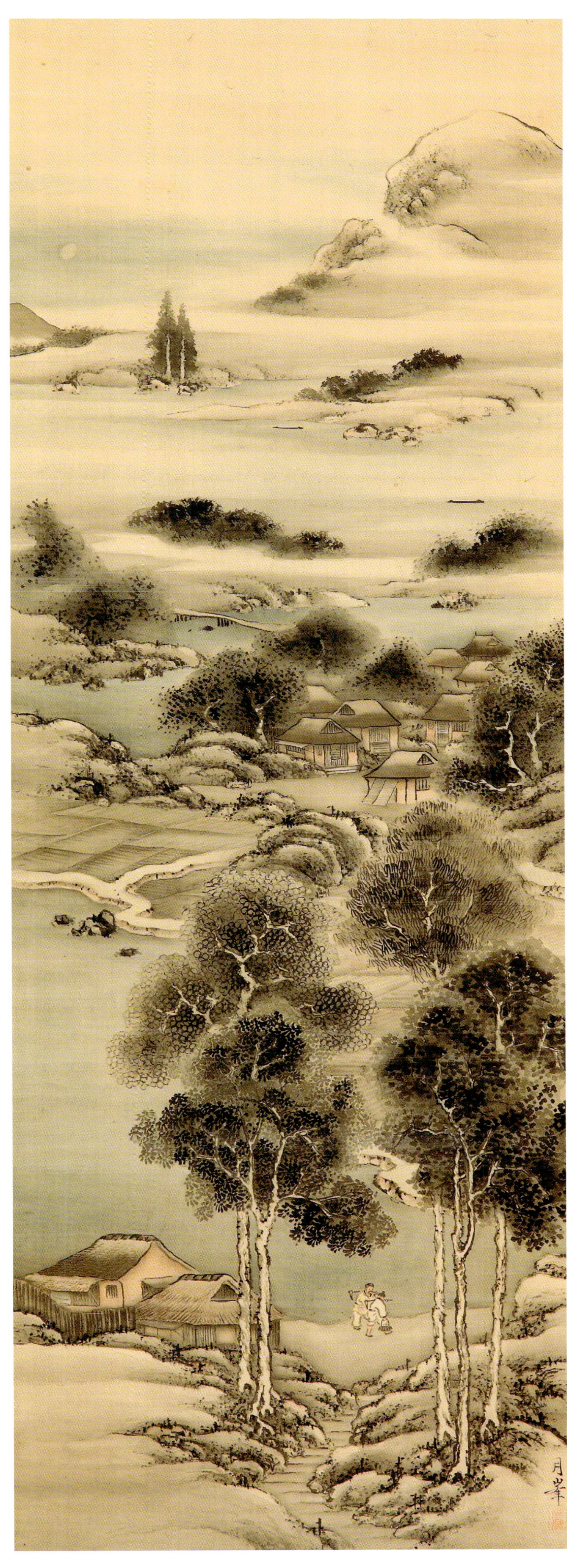

NOTE

1. Geppō could also paint in a softer mode that emphasized washes more than bold outlines, as demonstrated in a painting of a White-robed Kannon done in 1833 with his son Giryō; see Kyōto Bunka Hakubutsukan, *Miyako no eshi wa hyakka ryōran: "Heian jinbutsu shi" ni miru Edo jidai no Kyōto gadan* (Kyoto, 1999).

Okamoto Toyohiko 岡本豊彦

1773–1845

Okamoto Toyohiko built his career on the popularity of a style he based on the paintings of his teacher Matsumura Goshun 松村呉春 (1752–1811) which, in turn, were in the manner of the literati works of Yosa Buson 与謝蕪村 (1716–1783). In particular, Toyohiko adopted Goshun's lyrical combination of atmospheric ink washes with soft, fluid brushwork and transparent, warm colors. The resulting paintings express a bucolic view of the pleasures of country life.

Summer Mist reveals how Toyohiko abstracted and simplified these features from the works of Buson and Goshun. The most direct reference to Buson is the blue-robed figure looking out the window of his house, his gaze seeming to pass above the garden fence to meet the eyes of the viewer. Buson had adopted this striking figure who looks out from the painting from its occasional appearance in Chinese works; he used it so frequently that it became a well-known trait of his oeuvre. While Goshun's paintings often remain very close to those of his teacher Buson, Toyohiko here further simplified Goshun's approach, especially in an increased use of unpainted areas (*yohaku* 余白) to effectively suggest the misty atmosphere. The lush foliage of summer is depicted with a variety of patterned brushwork. The dots and short strokes are repetitious, yet minute variations among them prevent the painting from becoming hard and formulaic. The landscape is an idealized combination of hills, rural retreat, and several faintly colored expanses of water with rippling surfaces.

The darker or mysterious aspects of nature are never visible in Toyohiko's soothing rural scenes, whose quiet, relaxed quality is responsible for their enduring popularity. This sunny atmosphere was continued in works by his student Shiokawa Bunrin (see cat. no. 66) and, in turn, by Bunrin's students before finally appearing as one of the popular Shijō-school aspects found in the works of many twentieth-century *nihonga* painters based in the Kyoto area.

PB

23. *Summer Mist* 夏霞 (Natsu gasumi)

1820s
Hanging scroll: ink and color on silk
40.2 × 76.4 cm

SIGNATURE: *Oka Toyohiko* 岡豊彦

SEALS: *Toyohiko* 豊彦 (sig. upper)
Shigen 子彦 (sig. lower)

Purchase, 2005
13172.1

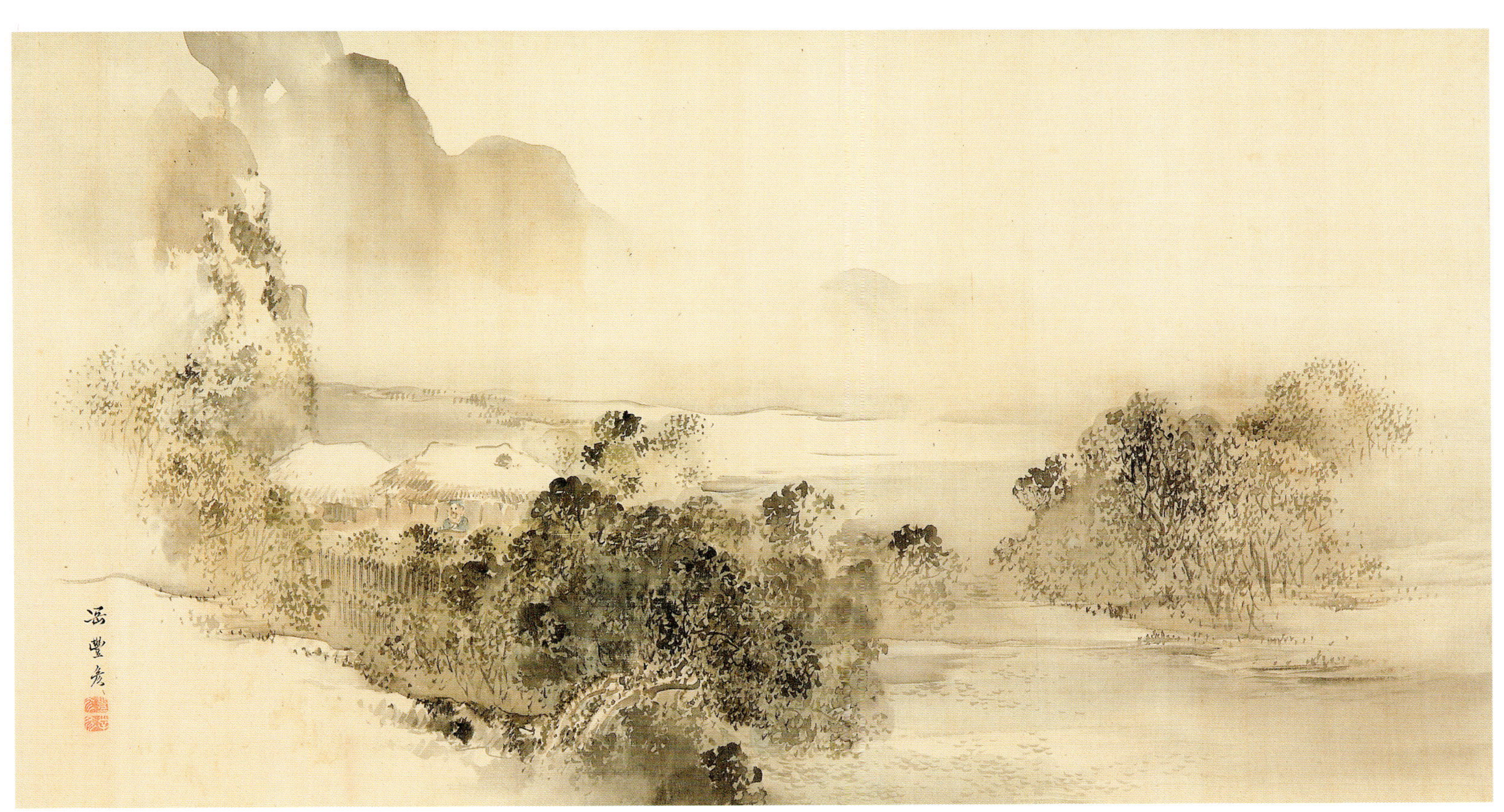

Uragami Shunkin 浦上春琴

1779–1846

24. *Laughter on Spring Wind*
笑春風図 (Shō shunfū zu) A

1827
Handscroll: ink and color on silk
40.5 × 209 cm
SIGNATURE: *Shunkin Rōjin sha* 春琴老人寫
SEAL: *Suian* 睡庵
Gift of Terry Welch, in honor of
William Jay Rathbun, 2005
13154.1

This handscroll represents a remarkable confluence of painters and calligraphers, Japanese and Chinese artists, and poetry and painting in the context of *sencha* tea practices. The inspiration for the handscroll was an appreciation of the horizontal calligraphy by Yi Fujiu 伊孚九 (J., Yi Fukyū) that serves as its title. Although a trader focused on importing items into Nagasaki from China, Yi Fujiu became so celebrated for his comparatively simple style of painting that he was regarded as the supreme literatus among the various artists who visited Japan from China. His approach directly influenced the work of Ike Taiga 池大雅 (1723–1776), Kan Tenju 韓天寿 (1727–1795), Noro Kaiseki 野呂介石 (1747–1828), and many others. The overall condition of this handscroll is excellent, but Yi Fujiu's calligraphy is worn and faded, and was likely so at the time it was selected for this piece. That it occupied a place of esteem despite its condition not only demonstrates the high regard accorded Yi Fujiu but also suggests that his works were rare; certainly only a few reliable examples remain today.[1]

The three brief characters for "Laughter in the Spring Wind" (*shō shunfū* 笑春風) were very famous in Japan for being the last three characters in a renowned Tang-dynasty verse, "At a Villa South of the Capital" 題都城南莊 by Cui Hu 崔護 (act. c. 796). This quatrain was so well known that it was continually cited in relation to peach blossoms and was adopted by the Zen community in Japan for its suggestion of the uncertainty of life:[2]

去年今日此門中	Last year on this day I was inside the gate;
人面桃花相暎紅	Her face and the peach blossoms both reflected pink.
人面不知何處在	Her countenance is not known—where could she be?
桃花依舊笑春風	Peach blossoms continue as before, laughing in the spring wind.

A striking encounter led the speaker to search a year later in spring for the same face, but only laughter in the spring wind remained. The character *shō* 笑, for laughter, is used as a substitute for the character *shō* 咲, for blooming, allowing a skillful fusion of the blossoming flowers and the laughter they had shared. The fame of this poem was such that the viewer of the painting was meant to recall it while reading the title, at once understanding that the theme would be peach blossoms with an undertone of transience.

Shunkin's painting begins with his own signature tucked into a blank space on a hillside,[3] suggesting that he had already planned for Kaioku to create the main inscription at the left end of the composition. A scholar riding on a donkey and accompanied by a footman carrying a *qin* emerges on a path that leads from the woods toward a bridge surrounded by blossoming peach trees. The path continues on to a rural village; a few more homes are seen in the distance across a bay. The village presses against the base of green mountains that are split by a large waterfall. A foreground compound whose front gate is wide open suggests that the three elderly men seen gesturing into the distance have just come out to greet someone. Although a man carrying a pair of buckets is approaching and a more distant boy is leading a water buffalo back to the village, the old men's excitement seems to be for a person who has yet to appear.

The classic composition of the handscroll takes the viewer on a journey through the countryside, from the original narrow path to the open vista over water to the magnificent mountain peaks. The display of the bucolic delights of the country coupled with arrays of peach blossoms is intended to recall the famous *Peach Blossom Spring* by Tao

Title by Yi Fujiu 伊孚九 (1698–1746)
Shō shunfū 笑春風
SIGNATURE: *Yi Fujiu* 伊孚九
SEALS: *Ichijtsu shunjū* 弌日春秋
One day in spring and autumn (top right)
illegible (sig. upper)
Fujiu 孚九 (sig. lower)[6]

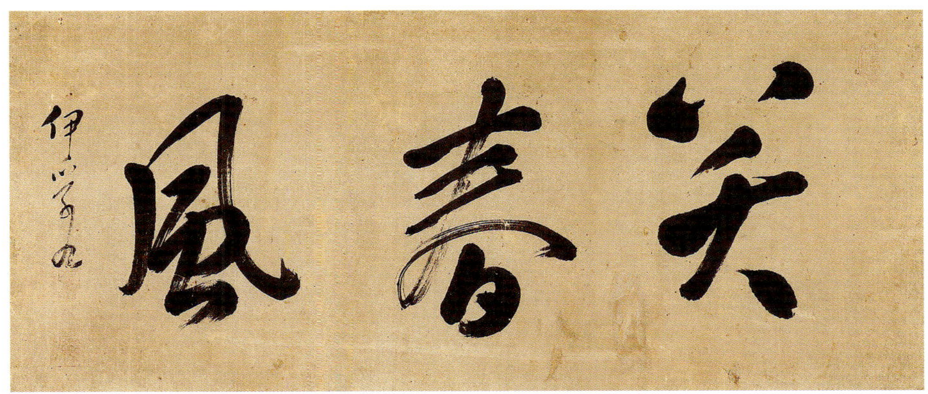

Yuanming 陶淵明 (365–427), a narration of the discovery of an agrarian utopia by a fisherman who had lost his way. Yet the iconography of the text and the painting tradition based upon it demand the presence of the fisherman, his boat, and a stream that passes through a cave. The omission of these standard features places the painting at a distance from *Peach Blossom Spring*, just as it is not a literal version of Cui Hu's poem. Instead, these allusions to the famous traditions connected to peach blossoms add depth to our appreciation of this unique vision of spring.

Only a few landscape handscrolls by Shunkin are known, and even more unusual here is his application of color. The layering of ink brushwork, washes, and heavy pigments is extremely rare among Shunkin's landscapes. This rich, coloristic effect suggests his awareness of quality works in the styles of literati painters employed by the imperial court in seventeenth-century China. Shunkin's effort to create an especially fine landscape handscroll, Kaioku's poetic inscription, and the much later postscript by the noted Osaka calligrapher Shinozaki Shōchiku 篠崎小竹 were all inspired by requests from their friend Tanaka Kakuō 田中鶴翁 (1782–1848). Kakuō maintained the Kagetsuan 花月庵 tea studio in Osaka for the propagation of *sencha* 煎茶, the steeped tea that had long been favored by Chinese and Japanese literati.[4] The Kagetsu style of *sencha*, with its claim that it maintained the tradition of *sencha*'s founding figure, Baisaō 賣茶翁 (1675–1763), became important to literati painters. A clerical-script inscription inside the box lid states that the scroll is a possession of the Kagetsuan studio.[5] Literati gatherings for drinking *sencha* involved the appreciation of utensils and art objects, and a handscroll like *Laughter on Spring Wind*, with its wealth of poetic allusions assembled around the venerated calligraphy of Yi Fujiu, would have been admired far more than a work by any single artist. Beyond being a superb example of Shunkin's talent as a painter, this handscroll demonstrates the aesthetic richness of *sencha* practices among the literati in the late Edo period.

PB

NOTES

1. Among the few apparently authentic works are the complexly constructed landscape triptych from the Hasegawa family of Matsuzaka in Mie prefecture and several works at the University of Kansas Museum of Art.

2. The last line of the poem is a common one-line text practiced by Zen priests which at times was also carved into wooden placards for hanging on temple buildings, such as the *hondō* at Unganji.

3. This is a rare position for a signature, yet it is occasionally seen in Chinese and Japanese landscape handscrolls.

4. See Patrica Graham's *Tea of the Sages: The Art of Sencha* (Honolulu: University of Hawaii Press, 1998), for the history of *sencha* in Japan, and pp. 148–55 for the career of Tanaka Kakuō.

5. Although not clearly signed or sealed, it is possible that the clerical-script box title and inscription are by Tanaka Kakuō. A small note by Shōchiku dated to 1843, the same year as his postscript, is squeezed into an open space on the inside of the box lid, indicating that the clerical-style inscription was created at an earlier date.

6. Problematic Yi Fujiu seals are legion, and I am unaware of any seals that precisely match these examples. The other seal is extremely hard to read due to fading.

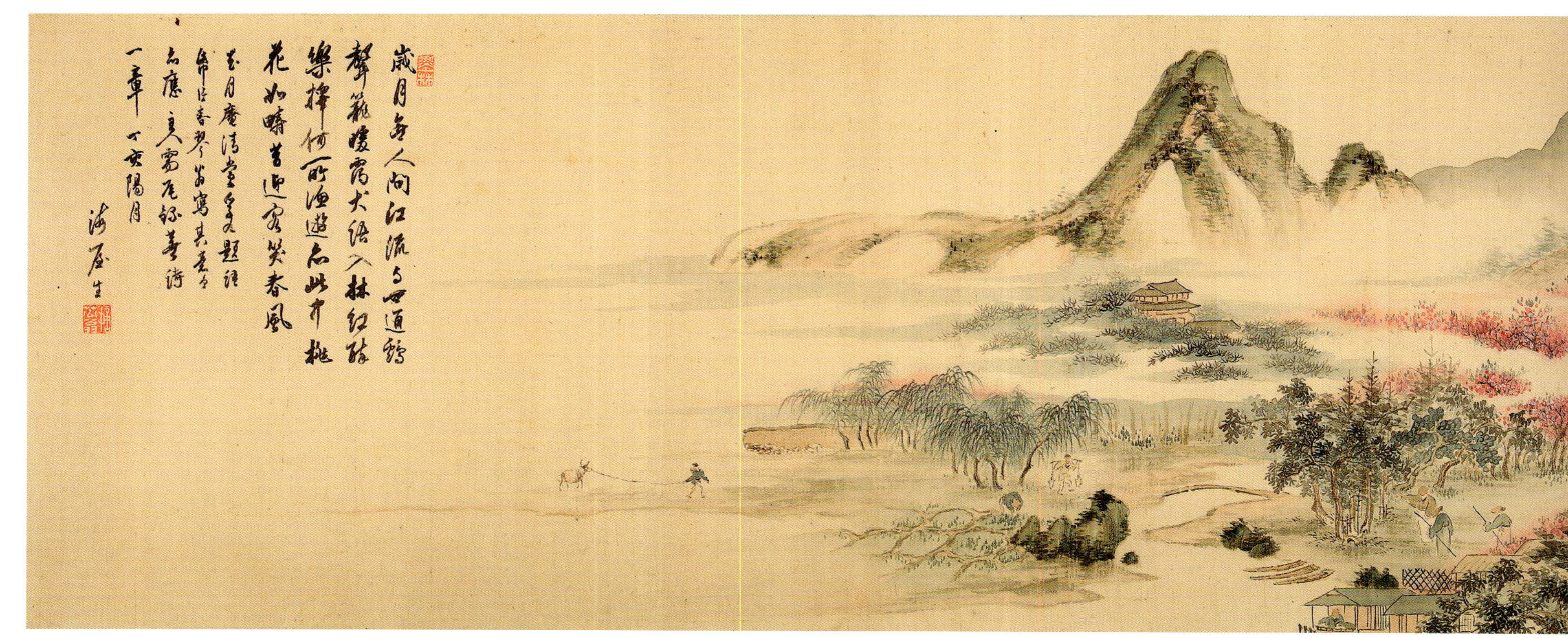

Inscription by Nukina Kaioku 貫名海屋 (1778–1863)
1827

SIGNATURE: *Kaioku sei* 海屋生

SEALS: *bokurin* 墨林 (upper right)
Tekisūō 摘菘翁 Cabbage-picking Old Man (sig.)

歳月每人問、江流与世通、鶏聲籠暖靄、犬語入林紅、
酔樂擇何所、漁遊亦此中、桃花如疇昔、迎客笑春風。
花月庵清賞孚九題語紙片春琴翁寫其意予亦應主人需尾録蕪詩一
章丁亥陽月

Always people ask about months and years,
The way they flow like rivers and generations.
Roosters crowing in their baskets in thick morning mist,
Dogs barking penetrates the pink trees.
Delightful intoxication to choose wherever
Fisherman go or even here [in this painting]—
Peach blossoms recall whose past,
Receiving a visitor laughing in the spring wind.

For Kagetsuan's pure appreciation, Old man Shunkin painted this after the idea of Yi Fujiu's title characters written on a fragment of paper while I, at the Master's [Kagetsuan] request, added this poem, in the tenth month of the *teigai* year [1827].

26. *Lofty Pine Expressing Longevity* 喬松供寿図 (Kyōshō kyōju zu)

1838
Hanging scroll: ink and light color on paper
137.2 × 45.4 cm

SIGNATURE: *Hankō Denshuku* 半江田粛

SEALS: *Denshuku* 田粛 (sig. upper)
Hankō 半江 (sig. middle)
Shōgai gahitsu reishi hitsu 生涯画筆隷詩筆 (sig. lower)[2]

INSCRIPTION:
喬松供壽図　寫祝
節富国手六旬栄壽
戊戌首夏

Lofty Pine Expressing Longevity painting

Drawn to celebrate Doctor Tokitomi's sixty years of splendid longevity. The *bojutsu* year [1838], fourth month

Purchase, 2005
13177.1

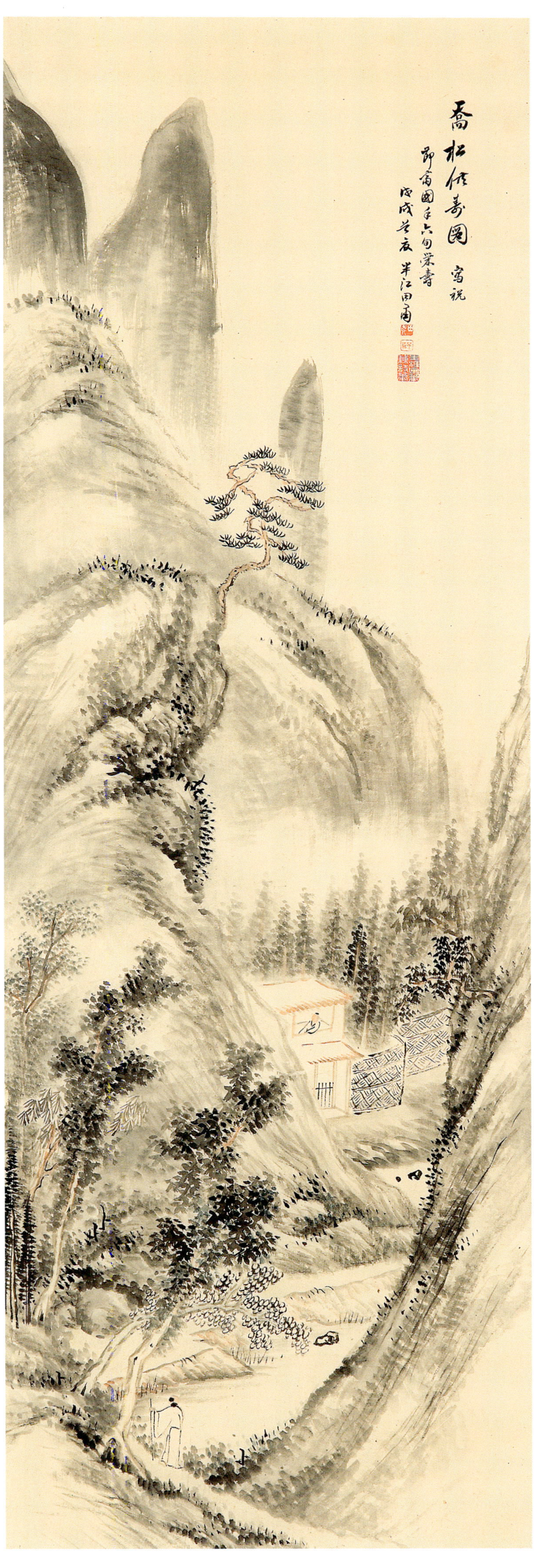

NOTES

1. For a quick comparison of the works of Beisanjin and Hankō, see Ōsaka Shiritsu Bijutsukan, *Beisanjin narabi ni Hankō zuroku,* exh. cat. (Kyoto: Benridō, 1941).

2. The three seals on this painting closely match the photographs of the seal impressions provided in the seal appendix of ibid.

Honkō Fūgai 本高風外 (TRADITIONAL ATTRIBUTION)

1779–1847

Honkō Fūgai's work allows appreciation from several viewpoints. He developed the general style of his painting and calligraphy from his study of the works of the noted literati painter Ike Taiga 池大雅 (1723–1776), and so Fūgai has been seen as a literati painter. This characterization is reinforced by the landscapes, Chinese-style figures, Daoist immortals, and other popular literati themes that make up the majority of his paintings. Another perspective emphasizes Fūgai's role as a Zen priest and appreciates his work as a kind of Zen painting (*zenga* 禅画). This comparatively recent category is defined variously as paintings of Zen themes, paintings and calligraphy created by a Zen priest regardless of style, or paintings of any theme imbued with a Zen aesthetic. Depending on the nature of the work, a particular painting might be included in several or all three of these categories. Fūgai's work may be regarded as *zenga* primarily due to his status as a Zen priest, yet a number of his paintings are of popular Zen topics such as Daruma. The category of Zen aesthetics is notoriously ambiguous,[1] yet the comparatively untutored quality of Fūgai's brushwork links it to the simple directness of most *zenga*, which can also be viewed as a kind of folk art created by Zen priests. In the West, Fūgai has been appreciated in both literati and *zenga* contexts, while in Japan his role as a Sōtō Zen priest gains more notice.[2]

The bulk of Fūgai's works are ink paintings, sometimes with faint color or blue-tinted ink (*seiboku* 青墨). More rarely he employed a full range of heavy pigments in landscapes for the blue-and-green style and for colorful figure paintings. Although Taiga's works frequently exhibit a humorous quality, Fūgai strengthened that tendency to the point that his paintings usually exude a light happy feeling, which is a common feature of many *zenga*. Occasionally, when depicting Daoist immortals, Fūgai created dreamlike visions of a fantasy world populated by richly dressed, laughing figures, as seen in a remarkable pair of strongly colored six-panel screens from 1832 in the collection of the Los Angeles County Museum of Art.[3]

Following his usual mode for landscape painting, in *Visiting a Mountain Valley* Fūgai loosely derived his brushwork from Taiga, especially the tendency toward an uneven inking of the brush (*katabokashi* 片暈かし), which generates tonal variety within the stroke. The composition is a classic theme of literati painting, in which an elderly figure, alone amid nature, goes to the mountains to view a waterfall from a well-placed pavilion. The cursive signature, Fūgai's distinctive trademark, gave rise to his nickname, Tako Fūgai 蛸風外, for its resemblance to an octopus (*tako*) with dangling legs.

Much like the popular *zenga* artist Sengai 仙厓 (1750–1837), Fūgai usually employed the same seal on his works, the Yuko seal seen here. As is the case with Sengai's noted seal, there are many versions of Fūgai's much-used seal. The seal impressed on this painting is a variant of the standard example, suggesting that this work was likely done after the artist.[4] Even though art historians in Japan have only recently started to understand the importance of *zenga*, the fact that so many high-quality older works were done in the manner of noted priests is testimony to the great popularity they enjoyed.

PB

27. *Visiting a Mountain Valley* 山溪入客圖 (Sankei nyūkyaku zu)

Ink and slight color on paper
125 × 31.2 cm

SIGNATURE: *Fūgai* 風外

SEAL: *kōyū* 好幽 Liking dark elegance

Purchase, 2005
13173.1

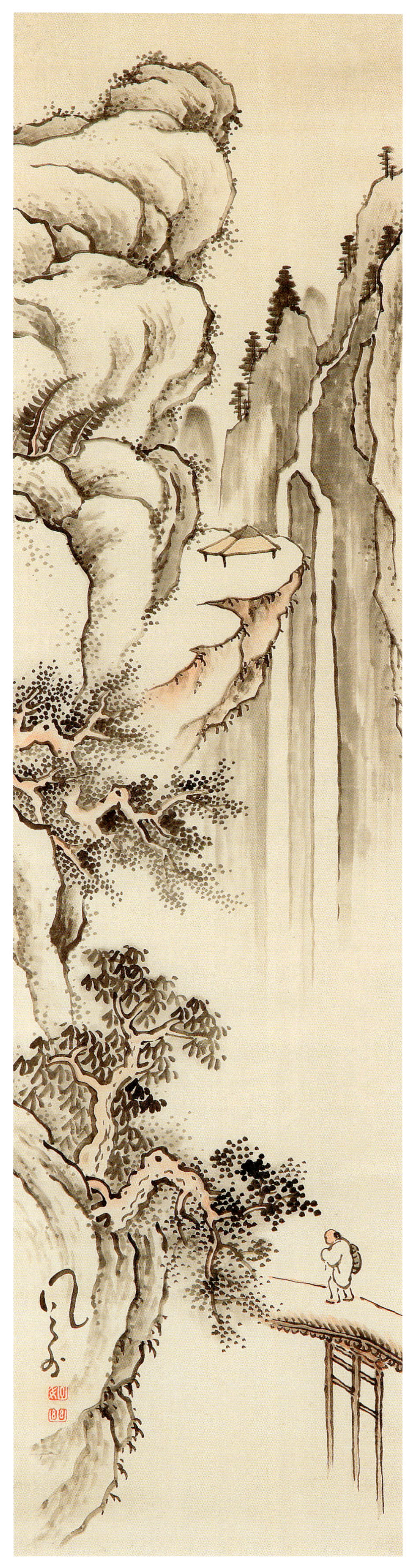

NOTES

1. Hisamatsu Shin'ichi's *Zen and the Fine Arts* (Tokyo and Palo Alto: Kodansha, 1971) is the most noted attempt to define Zen aesthetics.

2. This can be seen in the main works on the artist: Fujimoto Bokusen, *Fūgai* (Nagoya: Fūgai Hakkan Inkai, 1987), and Endō Tomohiko, ed., *Ushakurō kōkan roku* (Tokyo: Kokusho Kankōkai, 2004).

3. For an illustration, see Tsuji Nobuo et al., eds. *Bunjinga—shoha. Zaigai Nihon no shihō,* vol. 6 (Tokyo: Mainichi Shinbunsha, 1980), plates 116–19.

4. Compare the seal on this work with the comparison seal from Fujimoto, *Fūgai,* as seen in the seal appendix in this volume.

Nakabayashi Chikutō 中林竹洞

1776–1853

A staunch advocate of the Chinese ideal of the amateur scholar-painter, Nakabayashi Chikutō was part of the conservative trend in Japanese literati painting in the early nineteenth century. Since the beginning of his artistic training under Yamada Kyūjō 山田宮常 (1747–1793) and Kamiya Ten'yū 神谷天遊 (1721–1801), he studied the works of Yuan and Ming masters, and eventually wrote numerous treatises and instructions on painting, setting forth the orthodox Southern School doctrines. One of the most important influences on him was the style of Huang Gongwang 黄公望 (1269–1354), a Yuan master, which Chikutō knew through copies, woodblock prints, and works by later artists. In Huang's landscapes, forms are built up with dark brushwork layered over lighter ink, and parallel texture strokes are applied to define mountains accented with plateaus and clustered rocks. Later Ming painters such as Dong Qichang 董其昌 (1555–1636) modified Huang's style, abstracting the rocks into more rectangular, geometric shapes. Chikutō's landscape painting often reveals the Huang Gongwang style as transmitted by Ming masters. In *Cranes and Pine Trees,* however, Chikutō completely transformed the master's idiom to create a deeply personal vocabulary.

Cranes and Pine Trees represents Chikutō's mature work, characterized by lighter forms and sensitive brushwork. Typical of his style, the rocks are square or rectangular in shape, and mountain surfaces show light, horizontal texture strokes. Here Chikutō wove the rock formations and jutting plateaus into a vibrant tapestry. Although the composition is dense with carefully rendered details, Chikutō's delicate brushwork imparts a sense of weightlessness.

Chikutō structured the painting carefully. The clustered trees on the foreground island are nearly centered, while the mountain behind them soars in an asymmetrical composition. Multiple waterfalls cascade like silk ribbons down the mountain face before merging with a stream below. Chikutō opened the upper left corner for a water vista with distant mountains silhouetted in blue. Although this compositional scheme had been common in the Chinese landscape tradition since the Ming period, Chikutō intensified the spatial tension by juxtaposing a solid mountain wall on one side to a deep spatial plunge on the other.

Although not specified by the artist, the painting has a clear reference to Hōraisan 蓬莱山, the island of the immortals in the East China Sea. Two graceful cranes perch on tall pine trees in the foreground, and others rest on a prominent pine branch that extends diagonally over the water, above which many more cranes fly, approaching the island. Elegant trees adorn the land, while dainty red and white flowers bloom along the contours of the cliff and at the feet of the trees and rocks. Chikutō's exquisite coloring and feathery brush style enhance the otherworldliness of the utopian scene, and the absence of mist brings out the ethereal beauty of the landscape with unnatural clarity.

Because Chikutō adhered to a fairly narrow range of styles, modern scholars tend to characterize him as uninventive or conventional in composition even as they praise his skillful brushwork and the decorative surface quality of his paintings.[1] In *Cranes and Pine Trees,* however, Chikutō not only wielded his brush with distinction but created imaginative composition with a masterful organization of pictorial space. By reworking the style of past masters, Chikutō eventually attained an unmistakably individual expression of his own aesthetic sensibility. MM

28. *Cranes and Pine Trees* 群鶴松泉図 (Gunkaku shōsen zu)

1830s
Hanging scroll: ink and color on silk
131.5 × 42.8 cm

SIGNATURE: *Chikutō sanjin sha* 竹洞山人寫 Sketched by Chikutō, a recluse

SEALS: *Seishō no in* 成昌之印 (sig. upper)
Azana Hakumei 字伯明 (sig. lower)

INSCRIPTION:
Gunkaku shōsen zu 群鶴松泉圖
Painting of cranes and pine trees

Purchase, 2005
13175.1

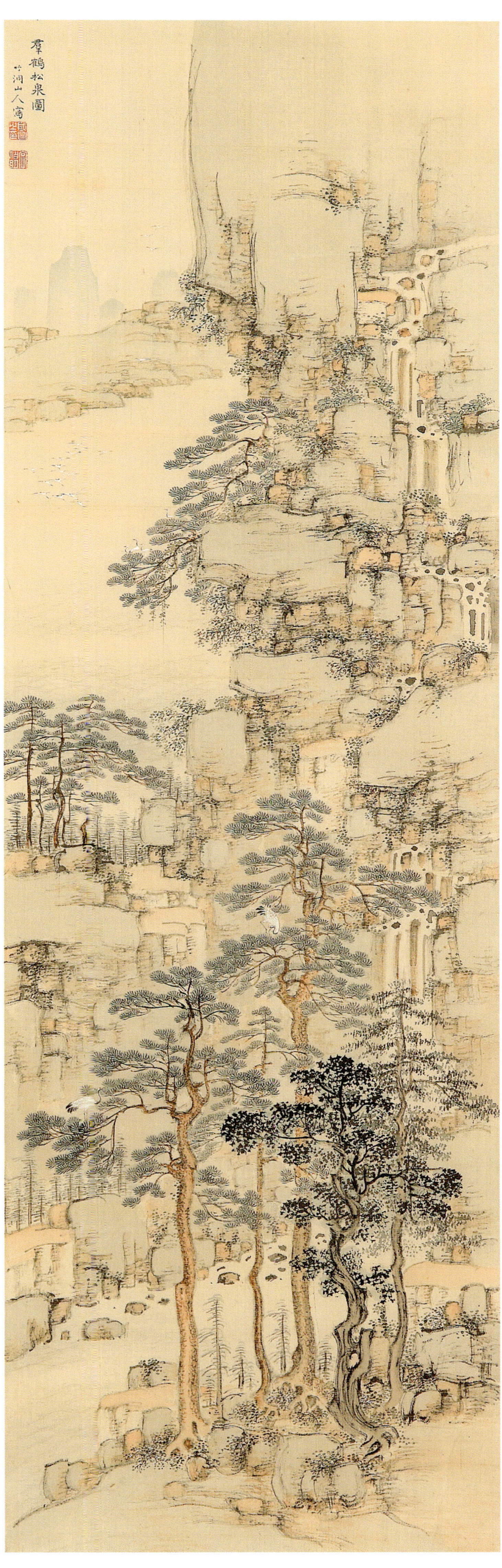

NOTE

1. See James Cahill, *Scholar Painters of Japan: The Nanga School*, exh. cat. (New York: The Asia Society, 1972), 120, and *Song of the Brush: Japanese Paintings from the Sansō Collection* (Seattle: Seattle Art Museum, 1979), entry for plate 52.

Nukina Kaioku 貫名海屋

1778–1863

The Unzen, or "cloudy springs," of the title refers to Narutaki 鳴滝, or Roaring Falls, deep in the hills of Tokushima prefecture near the center of Shikoku Island. In the sixth month of 1835, Kaioku left Kyoto for Nagasaki, taking a circuitous route through Shikoku. In the tenth month of that year, he visited Narutaki with his younger cousin Tadaaki 伊章.[1] Shortly thereafter, Kaioku made a twelve-leaf album, *Famous Places of the Provinces* (Shokoku meisho 諸国名所), for Kameyama Muken 亀山夢研 (1796–1863) of Onomichi, a noted patron who had been close to Rai San'yō 頼山陽 (1780–1832) and Tanomura Chikuden 田能村竹田 (1777–1835).[2] One leaf in this album, titled *Naruzen* 鳴泉, has a composition quite similar to *Unzen Waterfall in Autumn*, and Kaioku's description of the waterfall's location confirms that it is Narutaki.

Waterfalls have been a continually popular theme in East Asian painting since antiquity and usually appear among the mountains in landscape paintings. The vision of pure water descending from steep peaks generated an appreciation that mixed spiritual concerns with a sensitivity for nature. A waterfall is often such an exclusive focus that a few vertical brushstrokes on a blank stretch of paper are enough to evoke its presence. Japan, a mountainous country full of waterfalls, has a long tradition of paintings of famous falls, although the examples found in literati paintings are most often imaginary. But actual places also attracted attention as a theme. Beyond the many depictions of the falls at Nachi 那智, Yōrōzan 養老山, and Minō 箕面, lesser-known falls such as Narutaki were sometimes painted. When *Unzen Waterfall in Autumn* is compared to photographs of the falls today, there is a remarkable resemblance. The manner in which the water drops from one level to another over the layered surface of the 85-meter cliff face is well described in the painting. Although there was a widespread interest in "true-view paintings" (*shinkeizu* 真景圖) in the latter half of the Edo period,[3] this work is better placed in the older tradition of paintings of famous places (*meishoe* 名所絵), as suggested by the title of Kaioku's earlier album. The majority of waterfall paintings feature a single descent of splashing water, while Kaioku's treatment takes the individual character of Narutaki as the basis for an arresting composition that is accented by the separate stream of water falling over rocks on the left. The wavering, delicate brushwork of the trees with autumn foliage makes a vibrant contrast to the large wet strokes and ink washes of the rocky cliff.

In the Meiji and Taishō periods, *Unzen Waterfall in Autumn* was one of Kaioku's most well-regarded works. It had been in the collections of Itō Hirobumi 伊藤博文 (1841–1909) and Inoue Kaoru 井上馨 (1836–1915), two key political figures in their time. Originally the painting was kept in a box with inscriptions by the literati painters Murata Kōkoku 村田香谷 (1831–1912) and Egami Keizan 江上瓊山 (1863–1925), along with a meticulous full-scale copy by Yamamoto Chikuun 山本竹雲 (1820–1888).[4] Only the finest works among literati paintings were accorded this deluxe treatment.

PB

NOTES

1. See the account in *Honolulu Bijutsukan meihin ten: Nihon kaiga shūfuku kyōryoku kikaku: Heian–Edo no Nihon kaiga* (Shizuoka: Shizuoka Kenritsu Bijutsukan, 1995), plate 39.

2. This album is now in the Seikadō Bunko collection; see the entry on it in *Nihon no bunjinga I ten zuroku* (Tokyo: Seikadō Bunko Bijutsukan, 1995).

3. For a discussion of *shinkeizu* in the Edo period, see Melinda Takeuchi, *Taiga's True Views* (Palo Alto: Stanford University Press, 1994).

4. Although this box and Chikuun's copy have since disappeared, a record of them and a photograph of Chikuun's work can be found in Sasaki Jōhei and Sasaki Masako, eds., *Koga sōran, Bunjinkei*, vol. 1 (Tokyo: Kokusho Kankōkai, 2006), 545, plates 2553-1 and 2553-2. This work was published in color in a 1933 sale catalogue of the Suzuki family collection; see *Suzuki-ke zōhin nyūsatsu* (Tokyo: Tōkyō Bijutsu Kurakubu, 1933), plate 1. It sold for the impressive amount of 14,830 yen. The painting was first reproduced as a full-page illustration in *Kokka bijutsuka hō shū*, n.d.

29. *Unzen Waterfall in Autumn* 雲泉秋景圖 (Unzen shūkei zu) A

1837, eleventh month
Hanging scroll: ink and color on paper
133 × 63.2 cm

SIGNATURE: *Kaioku sei* 海屋生苞

SEALS: *Nukina Hō in* 貫名苞印 (sig.)
Kaikyaku ikkyō 海客逸興 Kaikyaku's special interest (bottom right)

INSCRIPTION:
雲泉在阿波府西南十許里乙未十月余在郷与
従弟伊章同探得詩及圖
繡葉蒼嵒霜色深
雖無涓滴欲留心
此中嚄瀉千尋雪
不省跳珠混袖襟
歳丁酉之暢月為力山雅契賞鑒

Unzen is near Tokyori in the Awa district. I went to that area in the tenth month of the *otsubi* year [1835] with my younger cousin Tadaaki, and it resulted in this poem and painting.

Embroidered leaves, a green cliff deep with frosty color
Even without the smallest drop of water to pay attention to
Amidst this thundering water—snow from a great height
Unable to focus on the flying pearls that soak my sleeves

In the second month of the *teiyū* year [1837], dedicated to the elegant Rikizan's appreciation

PUBLISHED: *Kokka bijutsuka hō shū* 国華美術家寶集, [pre-1926]; *Suzuki-ke zōhin nyūsatsu* 鈴木家蔵品入札 (Tōkyō Bijutsu Kurakubu 東京美術倶樂部, 1933), plate 1; Shimada Shūjirō 島田修二郎, ed., *Zaigai hihō* 在外秘宝. *Shōheiga, rinpa, bunjinga* 障屏画琳派文人画 (Tokyo: Gakushū Kenkyūsha 学習研究社, 1969), plate 96; Tsuji Nobuo 辻惟雄, et al., eds., *Bunjinga—shoha* 文人画・諸派. *Zaigai Nihon no shihō* 在外日本の至宝, vol. 6 (Tokyo: Mainichi Shinbunsha, 1980), plate 32. *Honolulu Bijutsukan meihin ten: Nihon kaiga shūfuku kyōryoku kikaku: Heian—Edo no Nihon kaiga* ホノルル美術館名品展：日本絵画修復協力企画：平安〜江戸の日本絵画 (Shizuoka Kenritsu Bijutsukan 静岡県立美術館, 1995), plate 39; Sasaki Jōhei 佐々木丞平 and Sasaki Masako 佐々木正子, eds., *Koga sōran* 古畫総覧. *Bunjinkei* 文人系, vol. 1 (Tokyo: Kokusho Kankōkai 国書刊行会, 2006), 545, plates 2553-1, 2553-2.

Gift of Mrs. Robert P. Griffing Jr., 1967
3495.1

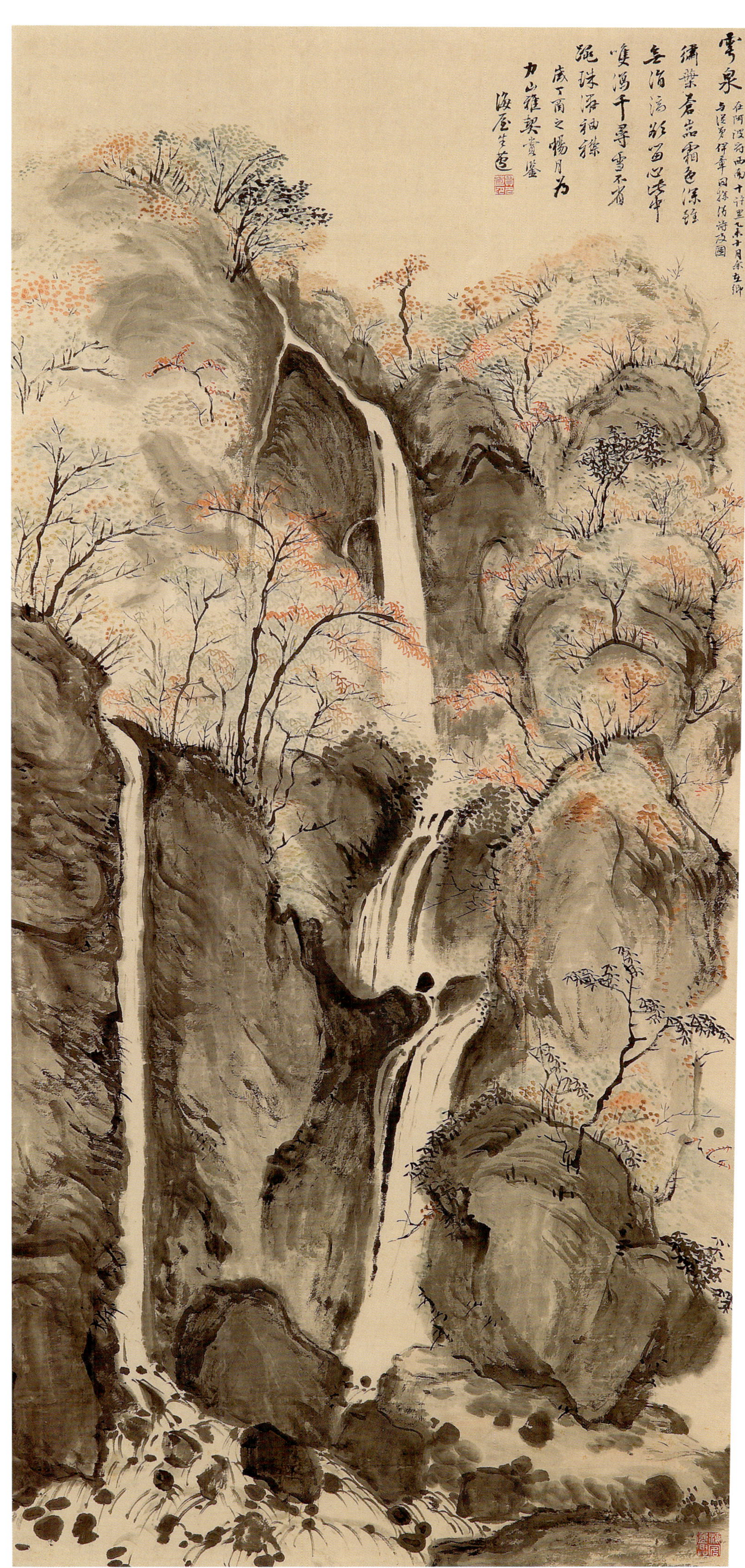

Nukina Kaioku 貫名海屋

1778–1863

Viewing Plum Flowers in Snow is one of the most dramatic creations among the many landscapes painted by Kaioku. Most of his paintings have comparatively soft, unobtrusive brushwork, yet in this work the strokes have a bravura quality accentuated by strong tonal contrasts, which emphasize a sense of depth between the foreground figure and the distant mountain peaks. This composition and brushwork suggest that Kaioku was inspired by the kind of professional Chinese landscape paintings especially popular in the circle of Tani Bunchō 谷文晁 (1763–1840) in Edo.

A man on a donkey proceeds along a path leading to a mountain valley on the right. His destination, however, may be the house perched over a stream in a narrow ravine on the left. The pink walls of the house are surrounded by branches that may represent the plum trees of the title. The dramatic focus of the composition begins with the foreground cluster of bare trees. These would have been painted first, with the diagonal path and rocks protruding from the bay carefully placed around the extended tree limbs. Kaioku cleverly suggested a patch of mist at the base of the mountains, thereby silhouetting the top of the largest tree. The prominence of these trees is extended by the complex angles and colorful accents of the massive mountain spire directly behind them. The ink washes in the sky and water allow areas of blank silk to appear as if covered in snow, an impression reinforced by slight touches of white *gofun* 胡粉, a coating made of ground shell. Unusual for a winter landscape, an application of ground malachite green pigment intensifies the remarkable atmosphere of the work.

Like the 1837 *Unzen Waterfall in Autumn* (see cat. no. 29), *Viewing Plum Flowers in Snow* was a prized famous landscape in the first decades of the twentieth century. It was among the treasured objects in the renowned collection of Kanō Jihei 嘉納治兵衛 (1862–1951), published in 1907 in a large-format folio.[1] In 1934 Kanō, the seventh-generation owner of the Hakutsuru sake brewing company, opened one of the most important private art museums in Japan, the Hakutsuru Bijutsukan 白鶴美術館, to exhibit his large collection of Chinese and Japanese art.[2]

Famous paintings tended to accumulate multiple comments from the major artists who viewed them, and the satin wrapper for *Viewing Plum Flowers in Snow* has inscriptions by the following prominent literati: Tomioka Tessai 富岡鐵斎 (1836–1924), Tani Tesshin 谷鐵臣 (1822–1905, dtd. 1898), Ishikawa Kōsai 石川鴻齋 (1833–1918), Yoshitsugu Haizan 吉嗣拝山 (1846–1915, dtd. 1899), and Iwaya Ichiroku 巌谷一六 (1834–1905, dtd. 1899). Such comments may be perfunctory, but those on important works are more elaborate. In this case the scholarly Tessai was reminded of a statement by the Southern Song Confucian Lu Zuqian 呂祖謙 (1137–1181), while the others wrote extended remarks in their varied calligraphy styles. *Viewing Plum Flowers in Snow* and the other paintings by Kaioku in this catalogue (see cat. nos. 5, 29, 31, 64) represent the finest group of his work outside Japan. PB

NOTES

1. Kanō Kakudō, ed., *Hakutsuru jō*, vol. 1 (Kyoto: Unsōdō, 1907), plate 54. A receipt kept with the documents in the scroll box reveals that Kanō bought the painting from dealers in Osaka in 1903 for 1,800 yen, an extremely large amount at that time.

2. According to the Hakutsuru Bijutsukan records, this work was never acessioned by the museum. The family retained possession of many art objects, and this painting was among works that left the family collection at some point.

3. This "Kaikyaku" signature appears on a variety of Kaioku's works in the 1830s and 1840s.

4. Judging from several inscriptions on paintings from the sixth and seventh months of 1841, it is clear that Kaioku spent some weeks in Ueno 上野, yet whether this is the Ueno area of Edo or the Iga Ueno 伊賀上野 area of Mie prefecture or elsewhere is not clear. See Nakata Yūjirō's chronology in Ueda Sōkaku and Nakata Yūjirō, *Nukina Sūō* (Tokyo: Nigensha, 1962), 15.

30. *Viewing Plum Flowers in Snow*
雪中見楳図 (Setchū kenbai zu) A

1841
Hanging scroll: ink and color on silk
140.2 × 56.8 cm

SIGNATURE: *Kaikyaku* 海客[3]

SEALS: *Rinraku* 林樂 enjoyment of the woods (upper right)
Kan wa haku un bō 閒和白雲芒 peaceful space between white clouds and pampas grasses (sig. upper)
我愛其静 I love this quietude (sig. lower)

INSCRIPTION:
雪晨興忽動
驢上涉阪陀
溪景己無限
遙梅喜奈何
辛丑之遯月作於上野之寓所

Snow at dawn begins, suddenly start to move
On donkey back, passing through the valley.
The river scenery—myself—limitless
Distant plum flowers—how to express the joy?

Made this while staying at Ueno in the sixth month of the *shinchū* year [1841][4]

PUBLISHED: Tajima Shiichi 田島志一, ed., *Nanshū meigaen* 両宗名畫苑, folio 21 (Tokyo: Shinbi Shoin 審美書院, 1904–10), plate 9; Kanō Kakudō 嘉納鶴堂, ed., *Hakutsuru jō* 白鶴帖, vol. 1 (Kyoto: Unsōdō 芸艸堂, 1907), plate 54.

Purchase, 2005
13180.1

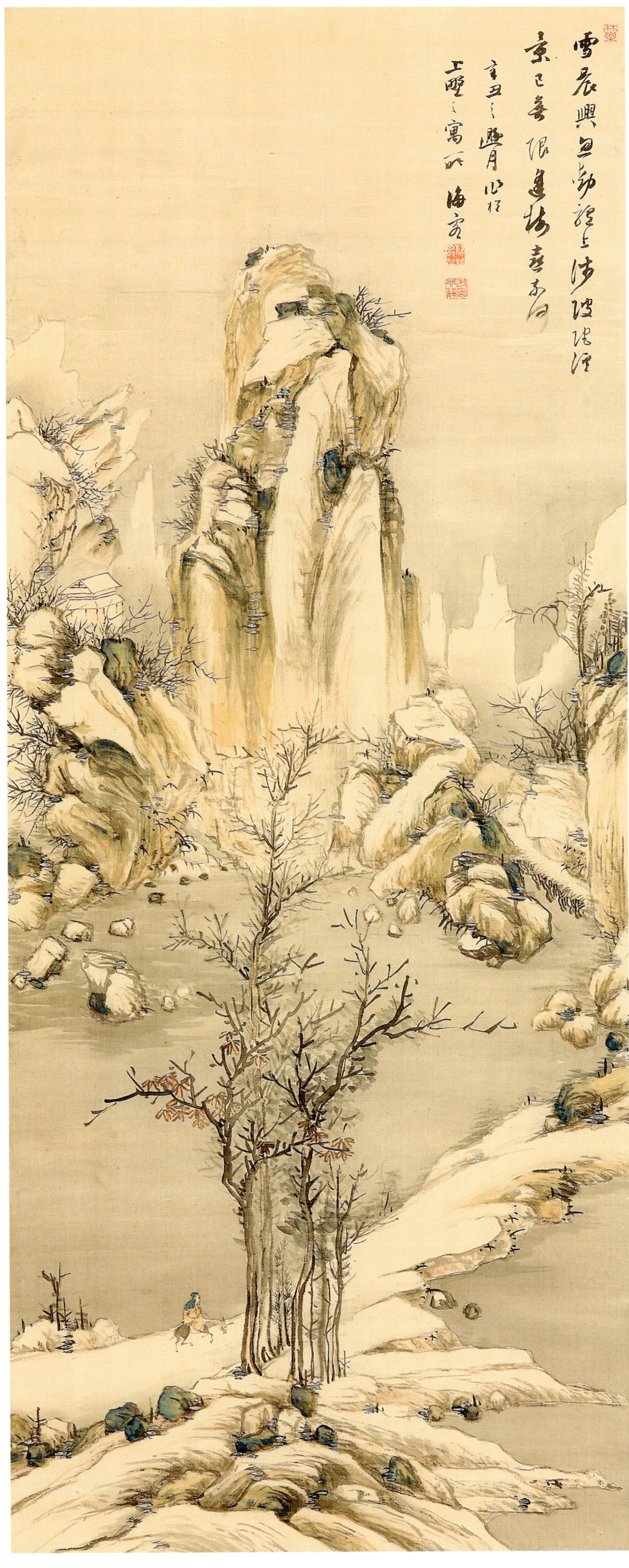

Nukina Kaioku 貫名海屋

1778–1863

Nukina Kaioku studied Chinese paintings ranging from the Yuan and Ming to Qing periods. On a visit to Nagasaki in 1836, he met Kinoshita Itsuun (see cat. no. 32), one of the principal artists of the city's literati circle, and received instruction from Hidaka Tetsuō 日高鉄翁 (1791–1871), a Zen monk-painter renowned for his knowledge of newly imported Chinese paintings. Kaioku's own collection included numerous paintings from the continent. Indicative of his study of a large number of Chinese works, Kaioku's landscapes vary in composition and style.

The orthodox, idealized approach of *Landscape with Bamboo Grove in Light Red Wash* stands in contrast to the immediacy of the artist's firsthand experience of the actual site of his earlier *Unzen Waterfall in Autumn* 雲泉秋景図 (cat. no. 29). Here, Kaioku carefully constructed a composition that smoothly zigzags from the foreground to the back. Myriad bamboos grow along the riverbank, their gradual change in size and tonality giving spatial depth to an enclave of scholarly residences. A waterfall streams from the tall central mountain and creates a thick mist below. Kaioku's sophisticated ink brushwork varies from a sensitive linear treatment of the bamboo to an intricate layering of modulating strokes and horizontal dots on the earthen banks and mountains. Applied broadly to the landmasses, the transparent wash of reddish color, accented by pale green, injects the landscape with a fresh, lyrical beauty. The scholar reclining on an armrest in his house is in perfect harmony with his natural surroundings. A red lacquer desk in the adjacent room draws the viewer's attention.

Kaioku's poem alludes to the tea-drinking practice popular among *bunjin* and evokes the spirit of enjoyment central to literati ideals:

乍聴涼雨入疎櫺	Suddenly listening to the cool rain enter the latticed window,
亭畔蕭々萬竹青	By my hut are ten thousand green bamboo making a sound.
掃葉呼童燃石鼎	I sweep the leaves and call a boy to heat my stone pot;
開函随地品茶経	I open the box, sit down, and refer to *The Classic of Tea.*[1]
霊芽次第浮雲液	The young tea leaves gradually float up in the misty hot water;
玉乳更番注瓦瓶	Again and again, I pour pure water into my ceramic teapot.
笑殺盧仝徒七碗	I laugh at that Lu Tong who drank only seven cups;[2]
風回几簟夢初醒	Wind circulating around the armrest and mat, I now wake up from a dream.
丁未之歳秋七月 寫并録周千秋詩	In autumn, seventh month of the *teibi* year [1847], painted and recorded Zhou Qianqiu's poem

The painting is contained in a double box. The eminent Meiji-Taishō calligrapher Kusakabe Meikaku 日下部鳴鶴 (1838–1922), who admired and studied Kaioku's calligraphy, inscribed the lid of the inner box "Landscape with bamboo grove in light red wash by Kaioku" 海屋翁浅絳竹林山水畫幅. On the back are two inscriptions by Meikaku (dated 1910) and Noguchi Shōhin 野口小蘋 (1847–1917). The latter was a distinguished female literati painter whose artistic lineage can be traced back to Kaioku, as her teacher Hine Taizan 日根対山 (1813–1869) had studied with him. MM

31. *Landscape with Bamboo Grove in Light Red Wash* 浅絳竹林山水図 (Senkō chikurin sansui zu) A

1847
Hanging scroll: ink and color on silk
117.5 × 50.7 cm

SIGNATURE: *Kaioku sei hō* 海屋生芭

SEALS: 隱己 recluse (upper right)
Kunmo shi 君茂氏 (sig. upper)
Hōchikujōsha 方竹杖者 Person of the Square Bamboo Cane[3] (sig. lower)

PUBLISHED: *Hagiwara Chōkichi shi shozōhin nyūsatsu uritate* 萩原長吉氏所蔵品入札売立 (Tokyo: Tōkyō Bijutsu Club 東京美術倶楽部, March 3, 1913); Sasaki Jōei 佐々木丞平 and Sasaki Masako 正子, eds., *Koga sōran: Dai niki bunjingaha ikkan* 古画総覧第二期文人画派一巻 (Tokyo: Kokusho Kankōkai 国書刊行会, 2006), plate 1289.

Purchase, 2005
13182.1

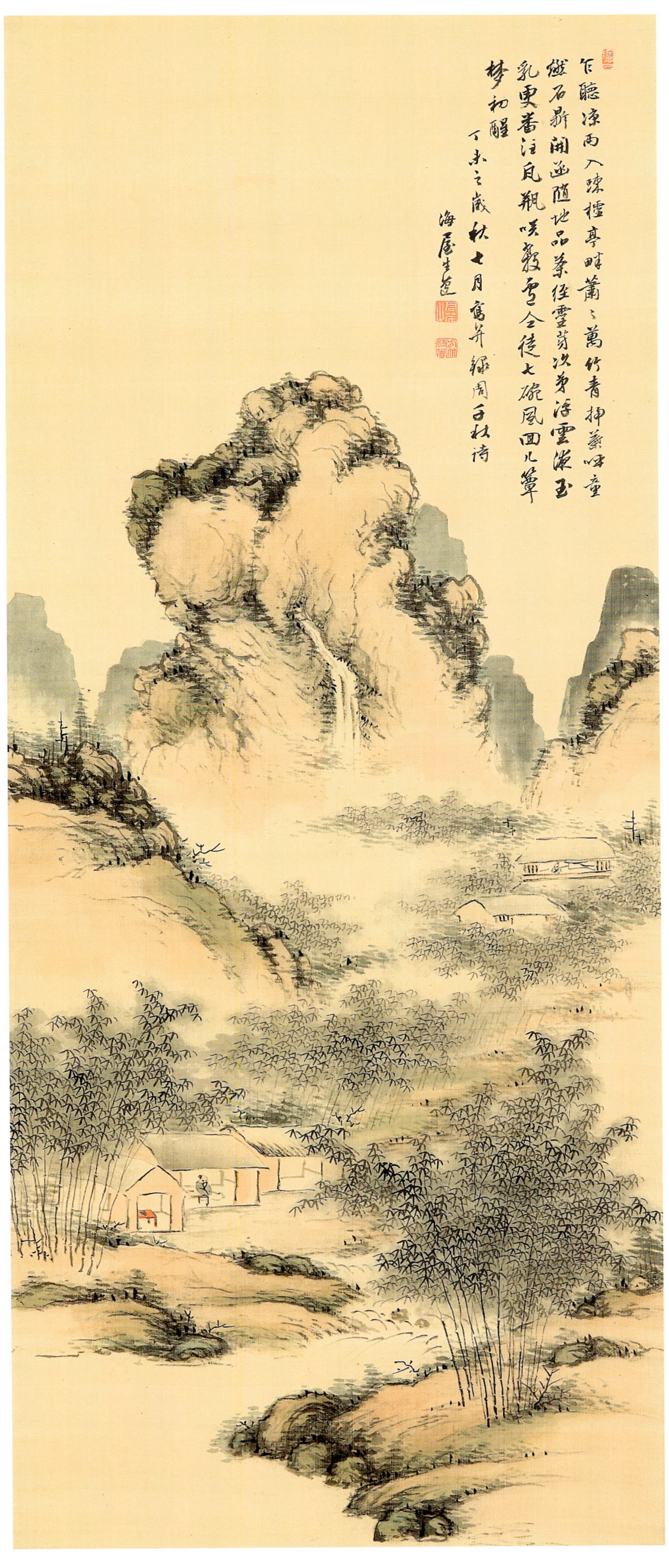

NOTES

1. *The Classic of Tea* 茶経 (Ch., *Chajing*, J., *Chakyō*), written by Lu Yu 陸羽 (733–804), was the first comprehensive work on the history, cultivation, and making of tea.

2. Lu Tong (790–835) was a poet known for his lifelong study of tea culture and his love of tea. He wrote a famous poem about drinking seven cups of tea.

3. The bamboo type *hōchiku* (Ch., *fang zhu*) was used to make walking canes for scholars in China and Japan and by association symbolized uprightness. Kaioku grew *hōchiku* in his garden and named his studio after it. This seal also can be read as *Hōchikushisha* 方竹枝者 (Person of the Square Bamboo Branch); see John M. Rosenfield and Fumiko E. Cranston, *Extraordinary Persons: Works by Eccentric, Nonconformist Japanese Artists of the Early Modern Era (1580–1868) in the Collection of Kimiko and John Powers*, vol. 2, ed. Naomi Noble Richard (Cambridge, MA: Harvard University Art Museums, 1999), 208.

Kinoshita Itsuun 木下逸雲

1799–1866

Living in the port of Nagasaki, Itsuun had the opportunity to see large numbers of recently imported Chinese paintings, to study with the city's few resident Chinese artists, and to meet with literati painters from all over Japan who traveled to this pivotal area to advance their art. This deep study of Chinese models allowed Itsuun to create landscapes and bird-and-flower paintings in a variety of styles. His works generally can be divided into those painted with considerable attention to fine detail and those more loosely composed with comparatively free brushwork.

Although twenty-two years younger than Tanomura Chikuden 田能村竹田 (1777–1835), Itsuun became a good friend of the senior painter during Chikuden's second visit to Nagasaki in 1826. Boats crossing streams or bays became one of Chikuden's favored topics during his sojourn in this city filled with small vessels taking people around its irregular coastline (see cat. no. 21). The two artists shared a common interest in this ancient theme of Chinese and Japanese painting. *Boat Returning in Autumn Mountains* presents a more relaxed approach than the layered subtleties Chikuden constructed. Itsuun's achievement is seen in the tremulous brushwork that extends from the calligraphy to the mountain forms and overhanging trees. Only in the fisherman and boat does his skill in careful depiction become clear, with close attention given to the wicker fish baskets inside the craft and to the man using a single oar to propel his boat. Itsuun applied transparent color washes over the mountains, rocks, and foliage but accented the ink dots in the mountain peaks and slopes with touches of bright green malachite. The painting closely reflects the content of the seven-character-line quatrain in the inscription:

老樹懸崖葉半秋	Old trees hanging from a cliff with mid-autumn leaves
草亭三面枕寒流	Thatched hut with three sides, a poor scholar's pillow
釣船帰去斜陽盡	Fishing boat returns as dusk settles
惟有青山對白鷗	Thoughts of white gulls against green mountains
甲辰臘月寫 於養竹山房西軒	The *kōshin* year [1844], twelfth month, painted this under the western eaves of Cultivating Bamboo Mountain Studio [Yōchikuzanbō]

Itsuun engaged in many of the activities of a rich literati lifestyle, including painting blue-and-white Kameyama 亀山 porcelain ware, raising lotus imported from West Lake China, attending *sencha* gatherings, writing poetry and calligraphy, and painting. Among this diversity, painting was his greatest accomplishment, and the enjoyment of the idealized view of living in nature is well portrayed in the atmospheric qualities and poetic sensibility of *Boat Returning in Autumn Mountains*. PB

32. *Boat Returning in Autumn Mountains*

秋山帰船図 (Shūzan kisen zu)

1844
Hanging scroll: ink and color on silk
123.6 × 42 cm

SIGNATURE: *Itsuun* 逸雲

SEALS: *Kinoshita Shōsai* 木下相宰
(sig. upper)
Itsuun 逸雲 (sig. lower)

Purchase, 2005
13183.1

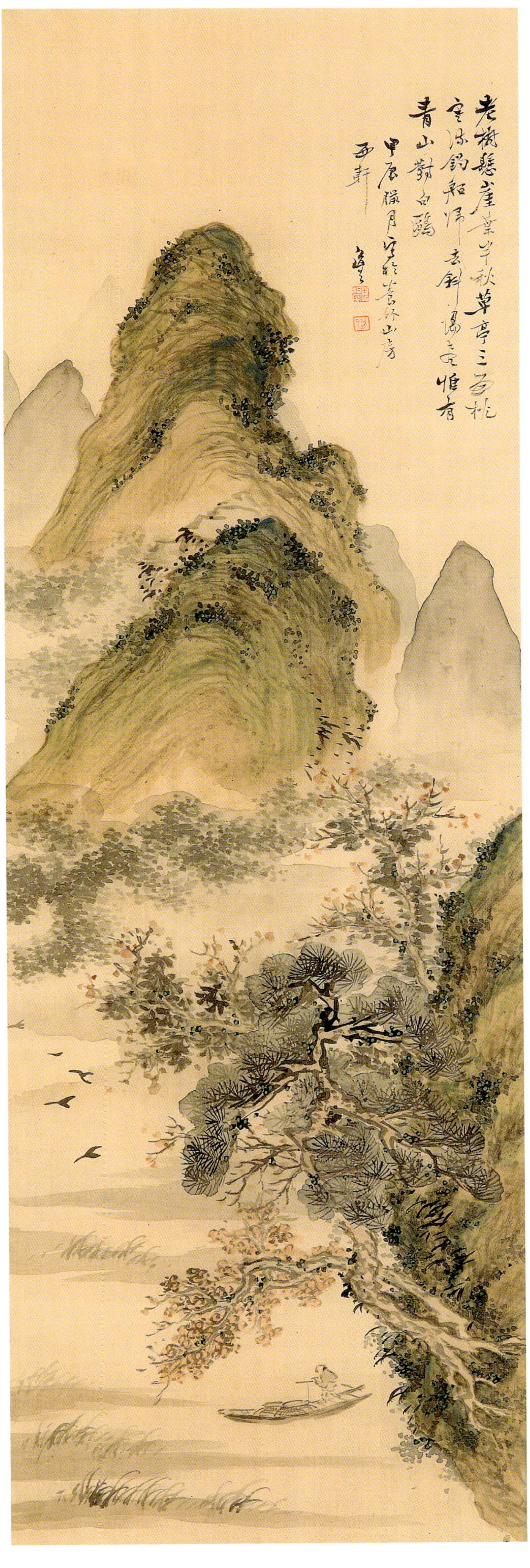

Hine Taizan　日根対山

1813–1869

Originally from Osaka, Hine Taizan settled in Kyoto in 1846 and moved several times within the city before his death. Upon his second move in 1854, he began calling his studio Taizanrō (Taizan Pavilion), a name that thereafter appeared in his inscriptions, as on *Rain Passing over the Spring Forest*. By 1857, the year he completed this work, Taizan was among the most successful Kyoto literati artists and commanded top prices for his paintings.

Taizan's prolific output as a professional artist was attested by one of his pupils, Inose Tōnei 猪瀬東寧 (1838–1917), who compiled reduced-size copies of his teacher's paintings into a three-volume book titled *Record of Eye Encounter* (Gūganroku 遇眼録). Of the 1,300 works Tōnei copied in 1860 and 1861, many were dated, and it is possible to tally Taizan's production as between 300 and 400 paintings per year.[1] The sheer volume may have resulted in some carelessly executed paintings, a criticism leveled by Hidaka Tetsuō 日高鉄翁 (1791–1871) years earlier.[2] But Taizan created many masterpieces that fully demonstrate his expert brush technique, understanding of Chinese precedents, and appreciation of *bunjin* values and aesthetics.

Taizan painted all subjects, including birds and flowers and female subjects, and even superb portraits, but he was best known for his landscapes. *Rain Passing over the Spring Forest* is an excellent example of his lyrical style. The scenery is meant to be Chinese, but instead of depicting soaring peaks of grandeur, Taizan created a gentle landscape with rounded mountains softly enveloped with moisture. A modest thatched-roof residence is glimpsed to the right of the foreground cluster of trees, and a bridge on its left leads to a path into the mountains. A small but elegant pavilion strategically perched on the hillside in the middle ground faces a cascading waterfall, the source of the stream in the foreground. A figure with a tattered umbrella hurries down the path, bringing a human intimacy to the landscape. Taizan's brushwork is relaxed and assured, with ink tonality and wet brush perfectly controlled. He defined the mountains by layering gray washes and fibrous textured strokes. The foliage of the foreground trees is carefully distinguished, displaying the range of his brush technique. The refreshing feeling of spring rain is enhanced by the glossy surface of the satin ground.

The painting is accompanied by a box with an authenticating inscription dated 1923 by Hirao Chikka 平尾竹霞 (1856–1939), a Kyoto literati artist who studied under Tanomura Chokunyū 田能村直入 (1814–1907). MM

33. *Rain Passing over the Spring Forest*
春林過雨図 (Shunrin kau zu) A

1857
Hanging scroll: ink on satin
134 × 51 cm

SIGNATURE: *Hi Shōnen* 日小年

SEALS: *Hi Chō* 日長 (sig. upper)
Shōnen fu 小年父 (sig. lower)

INSCRIPTION:
春林過雨丁巳□夏日寫於對山楼
Rain Passing over the Spring Forest, painted at Taizanrō in the summer of the *teishi* year [1857]

Purchase, 2005
13189.1

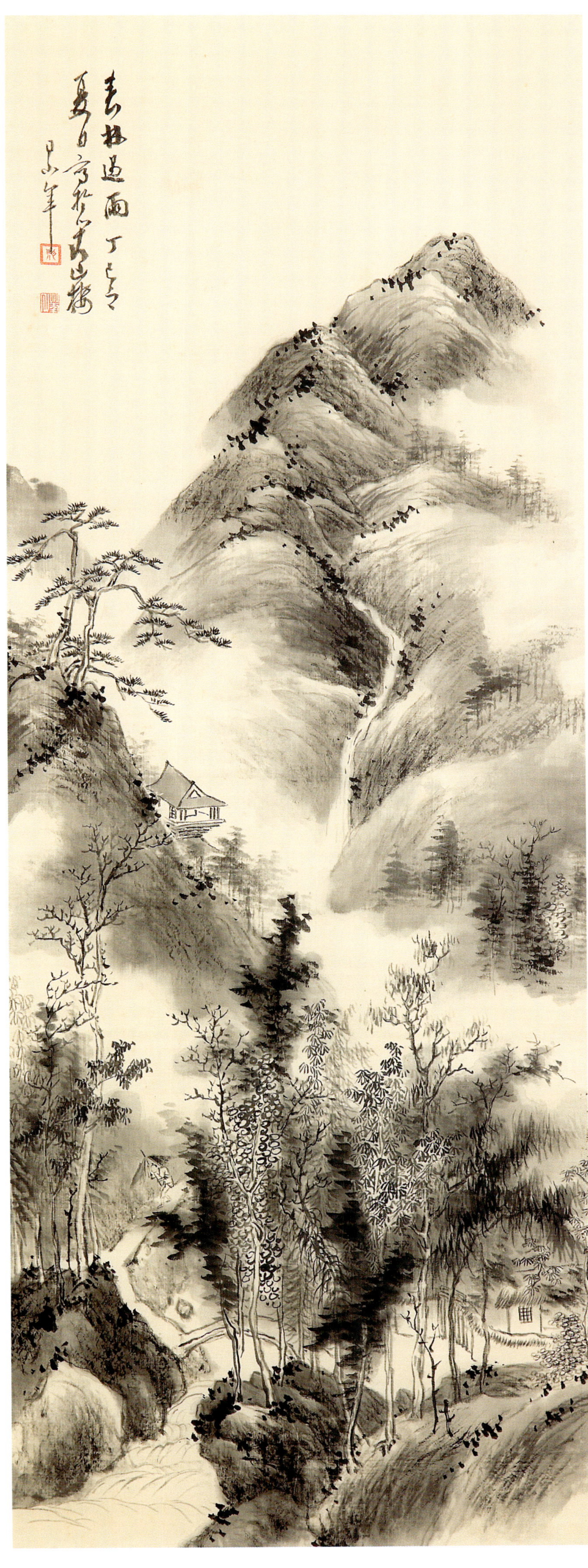

NOTES

1. Nagata Yasuhiro, "Hine Taizan no sakuhin," in Izumisano Shishi Hensan Iinkai, *Izumisano shishi shiryō dai nishū: Hine Taizan sakuhinshū* (Izumisano, Osaka, 2001), 5.

2. For Tetsuō's comment, see Umezawa Seiichi, *Nihon nangashi* (Tokyo: Nan'yōdō, 1919), 952–53, and Kanmuri Toyoichi, "Hine Taizan no gafū to sakuhin," in Izumisanoshi Kyōiku Iinkai, *Hine Taizan*, exh. cat. (Izumisano, Osaka, 1970), 48.

Hine Taizan　日根対山

1813–1869

Fujioka Tōho 藤岡東圃 (1870–1910), author of *The History of Early Modern Painting* (Kinsei kaigashi), placed Taizan "first among the Kyoto *bunjin* painters" of the late Edo period and described his brushwork as "powerful yet flavored with the refinement of Kyoto."[1] Requests for paintings poured in during the final ten years of Taizan's career. At the same time, his most successful students entered his studio: Inose Tōnei 猪瀬東寧 (1838–1917), Noguchi Shōhin 野口小蘋 (1847–1917), and Atomi Kakei 跡見花蹊 (1840–1926).

The last decade of Taizan's life coincided with the political and social turmoil that brought the feudalistic Tokugawa regime to an end after nearly 250 years of unbroken leadership. Faced with pressure from the West and economic crises, shogunal officials bickered to no end, while assassinations and shifting political alliances among government leaders, aristocrats, and various fiefs mirrored the deteriorating situation. In 1864 much of Kyoto was razed as the result of civil war. Taizan lost many friends and supporters, some to political struggle and others to illnesses. Rai Mikisaburō 頼三樹三郎 (1825–1859) was executed for plotting against the shogunate in 1859 in the Ansei Purge 安政の大獄, and Fujimoto Tesseki 藤本鉄石 (1782–1863), active as an imperial loyalist, was killed in 1863 during the civil war. In the same year, Taizan's teacher, Nukina Kaioku 貫名海屋 (1778–1863), died of illness, and his lifelong patron Satoi Fukyū 里井浮丘 (1799–1866) followed three years later. Taizan's own health began to fail due to many years of heavy drinking. Even so, in 1867 he was busy again fulfilling many painting commissions.[2]

Dated three years before Taizan's death, *Reminiscing about the Past under a Tree* is poignant in its serenity. Seemingly unaffected by the growing turmoil around him or his own fragile health, Taizan persisted in representing the classical ideal. In the painting, two Chinese scholars are engaged in conversation under a group of tall pine trees. One tree gracefully leans over as if to provide a canopy for the figures. In the background stands a mountain of vivid green, crowned precariously by square-topped rocks. Distant peaks silhouetted in light blue wash give fresh accents. A waterfall flows from the side of the mountain, reaching the stream below, which encircles the small peninsula in the foreground where the figures are seated. Taizan's brushwork is unlabored and the composition uncomplicated, giving the image an improvisatory air, although he painted a number of similar scenes. His inscription refers to Wang Meng 王蒙 (1301–1385), one of the four Yuan masters, but this tranquil work shows little connection with the Chinese painter's style of extreme texturing and tumultuous compositions. Rather, Taizan created here a personal statement of a time-honored literati vision: at rest in nature, embraced by the sound of water and the surrounding mountains, the scholars are lost in deep conversation about the past. The painting evokes traditional values cherished by generations of *bunjin:* the harmony of man and nature, respect for antiquity, and the importance of friendship. MM

34. *Reminiscing about the Past under a Tree* 林下話舊図 (Rinka wakyū zu)

1866
Hanging scroll: ink and color on silk
136 × 49.4 cm
(194 × 73.4 cm overall)

SIGNATURE: *Taizan Hi Shōnen*
対山日小年

SEALS: 小橋流水 Small bridge, flowing water (upper right)
山静似太古 Mountain is quiet as if great antiquity (sig. upper)
日長如小年 The length of a day resembles a year[3] (sig. lower)
萬事無如在杯手 Nothing like having a cup in one's hand (bottom left)

INSCRIPTION:
林下話舊丙寅嘉平月仿王叔明畫法
Reminiscing about the past under a tree, in the manner of painting by Wang Shuming, the twelfth month of the *heiin* year [1866]

Purchase, 2005
13190.1

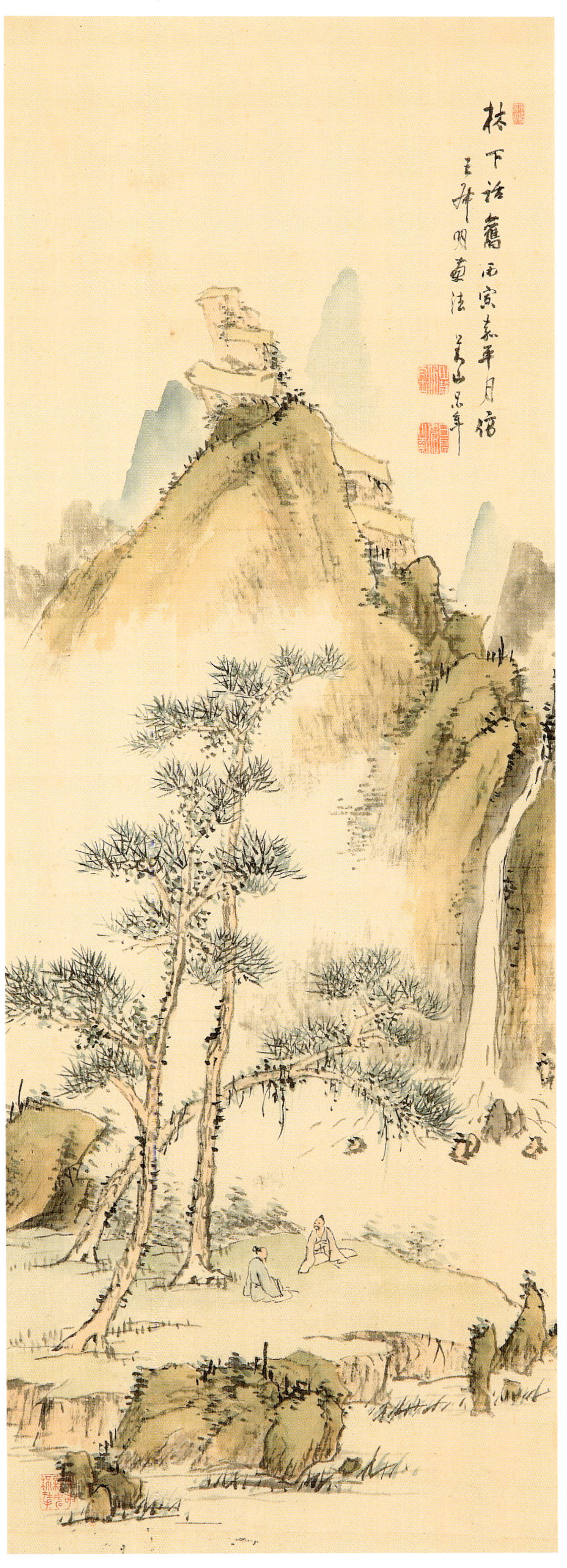

NOTES

1. Kanmuri Toyoichi agrees with Tanaka Toyozō's interpretation that Tōho was referring to Kyoto literati painters of the *bakumatsu* period and not the entire history of literati painting; see Kanmuri Toyoichi, "Hine Taizan no gafū to sakuhin," in Izumisanoshi Kyōiku Iinkai, *Hine Taizan* (Izumisano, Osaka, 1970), 49.
2. Kanmuri Toyoichi, *Meiji no nangaka: Kōin sagen 4* (Osaka: Kinki Shuppan Insatsu, 1990), 186.
3. From a five-character, eight-line poem by the Sung poet Tang Geng; see Nagata Yasuhiro, "Hine Taizan—Zenhanki no geijutsu," in Rekishikan Izumisano, *Kyōdo ga unda gajin, sono 2: Hine Taizan,* exh. cat. (Izumisano, Osaka, 2001), 5.

Haruki Nanmei 春木南溟

1795–1878

Haruki Nanmei came from an illustrious family lineage. His father, Haruki Nanko 南湖 (1759–1839), was a distinguished Edo painter who vied for popularity with Tani Bunchō 谷文晁 (1763–1840) as one of the leading literati artists of his time. Nanmei received instruction from his father as well as from Bunchō,[1] and he studied Chinese predecessors, becoming proficient not only in landscape painting but also at bird-and-flower subjects.[2] Eventually he achieved techniques superior to those of his father and worked in diverse styles, much like Bunchō. In particular, Nanmei's paintings were said to outshine his father's in their expression of "refinement and elegance" (*ryūrei* 流麗).[3] Toward the end of the Edo period, Nanmei enjoyed the patronage of many high-ranking samurai, including Yamauchi Yōdō 山内容堂 (1827–1872), who built a house for Nanmei next to his own villa.[4] The political and social upheaval of the early Meiji era had little effect on Nanmei's successful career. His samurai patrons became the officials of the new government and continued to support him.

Immortal's Pavilion in Spring Daybreak is impressive for its virtuoso composition. Recalling the familiar literati theme of a mythical realm away from the vulgar world, Nanmei enhanced a lofty Chinese-derived landscape with a striking color combination in the blue-and-green tradition. Picturesque mountain formations arise from the mist, echoed by the faint silhouettes of faraway peaks, while the cliffs and hills of the middle ground and foreground are crowned by carefully portrayed trees of various types. Palatial architecture graces the central mountain peak, and more buildings are hidden in the wooded area below. The focal point is the drama of the foreground, where a stream courses through a tunnel-like opening and cascades over a series of rock benches. Just above, along the diagonal sweep of land, two visitors are seen. Nanmei's sensitive rendering of the figures brings warmth and tenderness to this idealized landscape of perfection. The pink blossoms that surround the figures, likely peach, may refer to the utopian hideaway celebrated in *Peach Blossom Spring* by Tao Yuanming 陶淵明 (365–427). Throughout the composition, Nanmei's brushwork remains subtle and precise, and his sophisticated layering of ink and color washes is exemplary. A landscape of compelling beauty, *Immortal's Pavilion in Spring Daybreak* symbolizes the *bunjin* yearning to retire from public life and to live in idyllic contentment in nature. A painting such as this would have been enormously appealing to the cultured members of the samurai class entangled in the political turmoil of the final years of the Tokugawa regime. MM

35. *Immortal's Pavilion in Spring Daybreak* 僊閣春曙図 (Senkaku shunsho zu)

1853
Hanging scroll: ink and color on silk
121.3 × 36.3 cm

SIGNATURE: *Kōun gaishi* 耕雲外史

SEAL: *Nanmei* 南溟

INSCRIPTION:
僊閣春曙
癸丑仲秋為臥雲雅兄清囑

Immortal's Pavilion in Spring Daybreak

Respectfully painted at the request of my elegant friend Gaun in the eighth month of the *kichū* year [1853]

Purchase, 2005
13185.1

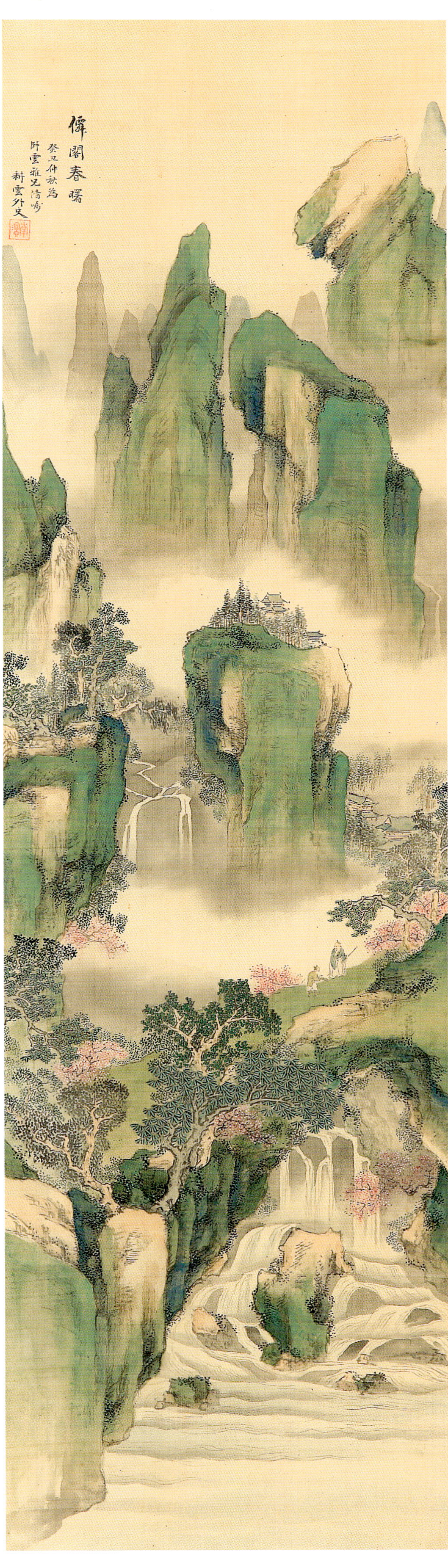

NOTES

1. Umezawa Seiichi, *Nihon nangashi* (Tokyo: Nan'yōdō, 1919), 508.
2. See his painting titled *One Hundred Cranes* (Hyakkaka zu) in Atsumi Kuniyasu, *Kameda Bōsai to Edo Kaseiki no bunjin tachi* (Tokyo: Geijutsu Shinbunsha, 1995), 248.
3. Umezawa, *Nihon nangashi*, 508.
4. Araki Nori, ed., *Dai Nihon shoga meika taikan, denki gehen* (1934; reprint, Tokyo: Daiichi Shobō, 1975), 1348.

Yasuda Rōzan 安田老山

1830–1882

During his seven years of study with the noted painter Hu Gongshou 胡公壽 (1823–1886) in Shanghai, Rōzan developed two main approaches to painting landscapes. The basic features of his landscape styles are well illustrated by the differences in the two paintings by Rōzan in this catalogue (see also cat. no. 37). *Autumn Landscape* is constructed with especially dry brushwork that produced a vigorous, yet slightly crumbly line. Rōzan employed this brushstroke to build up his landforms with angular horizontal lines, which are repeated at a slight incline throughout the composition. The hard, almost architectural surface of the land contrasts effectively with the many vertically twisting evergreen pine trees, whose presence in such numbers is unusual in an autumn scene. The season is symbolized by the foreground leafless tree, starkly silhouetted against the white paper representing the bay. Other bare branches appear among the cluster of large trees, but it is the tree inclining over the water that represents the approach of winter.

At first glance it is easy to overlook signs of habitation, yet behind the trees on the right are a few houses, and below the main peak a gate and several roofs are visible. The solitary angler in a boat gives a certain lonely melancholy to the scene. The drunkenness during the Double-nine Festival 重陽節, which Rōzan alludes to in the inscribed verse, adds an unexpected dimension to the serenity of this autumnal view:

門外時々列錦屏	The view beyond the gate is sometimes arrayed like a brocade screen;
千林非復藉時青	A thousand trees do not repeat the time of greenery.
一從澆羅重陽酒	From being poured through gauze—Chōyō wine;[1]
醉殺秋山便不醒	Dead drunk in the autumn mountains—still not sober.

Rōzan enjoyed the Chinese custom of making large paintings even though the mountings sometimes had to be truncated to accommodate the limitations of Japanese tokonoma. Most of the original mountings of Rōzan's paintings are in a Chinese style that is complete down to the round, rather than flat, cord used for hanging the work. Rōzan's popularity in early Meiji Japan was due in part to the sense of contemporary China that his works effectively conveyed.

PB

36. *Autumn Landscape*
秋景山水図 (Shūkei sansui zu)

1878
Hanging scroll: ink on paper
167.5 × 66.2 cm

SIGNATURE: *Rōzan An Yō* 老山安養

SEALS: *han sō meigetsu* 半窓明月
half window, bright moon
(upper right)
yubin shi in 臾聞子印 (sig. upper)
rōyō 老養 (sig. lower)
tekken masen 銕硯磨穿
(bottom left)

INSCRIPTION:
戊寅春日造於水石艸堂為
池本雅君清玩
Made on a spring day in the *boin* year [1878] at the Suiseki Sōdō for the elegant Mr. Ikemoto's pure delight

Purchase, 2005
13201.1

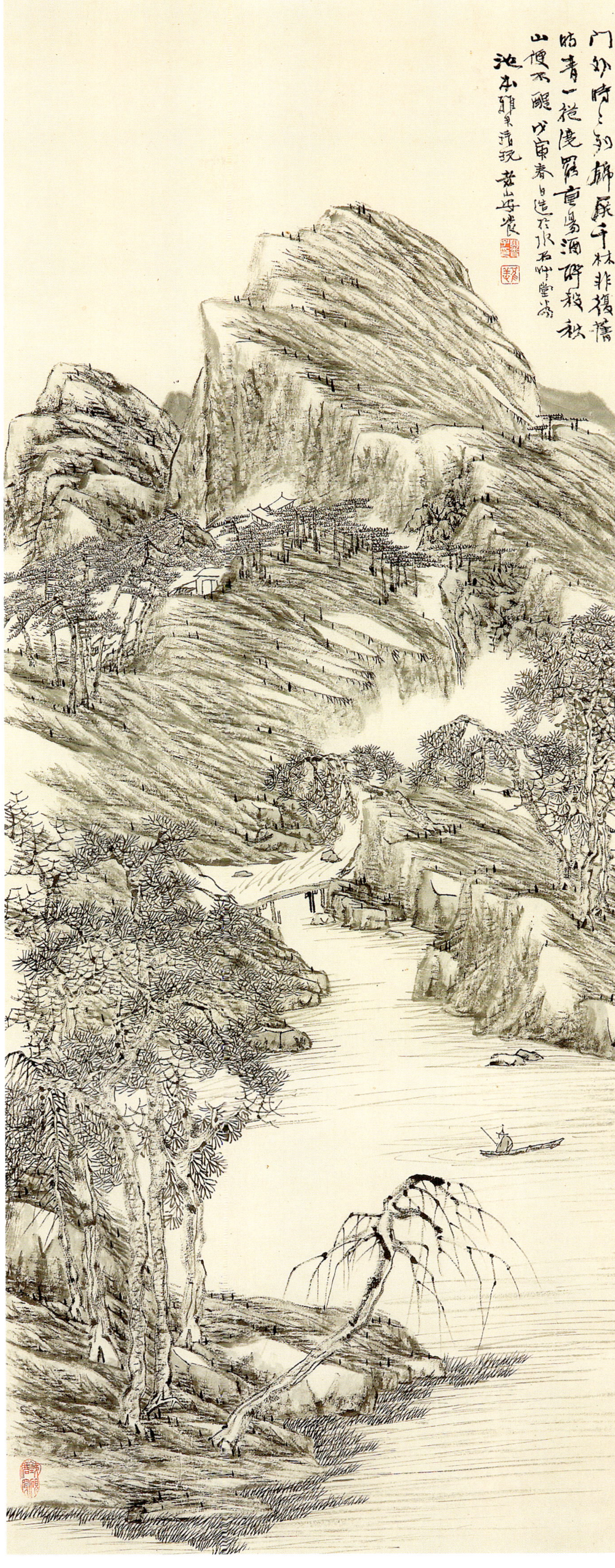

NOTE
1. Chōyō wine is the chrysanthemum wine drunk during the Double-nine Festival held in East Asia on the ninth day of the ninth month of the lunar calendar.

Yasuda Rōzan 安田老山

1830–1882

Rōzan's driving passion to be a literati painter led him at an early age to leave his home outside Nagoya for Nagasaki and then for Shanghai, where he studied with one of the top painters of the city, Hu Gongshou 胡公壽 (1823–1886). After seven years in China, he returned to Japan and achieved great acclaim in Tokyo before dying unexpectedly from a sudden illness. His career in Japan lasted a scant twelve years, but he created many paintings. Primarily a landscapist, Rōzan also painted dramatic images of rocks, plantains, plum flowers, bamboo, and other favorite literati themes. Rarely employing color, he focused on generating interest through his brushwork and a skillful application of ink tonalities.

Spring Landscape typifies Rōzan's classic way of mixing fluid curving brushwork with restrained ink washes. He accented the pale tonalities of the hills and tree branches with patches of dark leaves and intense "moss" dots scattered over the rocks and hills. Most unusual for him is the rare application of color to the foreground figure and several flowering trees; the sparse use of color accents the varied tones of ink. Even though Rōzan usually included a few houses in his landscapes, here hidden behind foreground trees, the solitary figures he draws often produce a feeling of loneliness.

Rōzan's inscription of the well-known poem "Visiting Hu Yin" 尋胡隱君 by Gao Qi 高啓 (1336–1374) adds another dimension to the work:

渡水復渡水　Crossing water and again crossing water,
看花還看花　Seeing flowers and again seeing flowers.
春風江上路　Spring breezes along the canal,
不覺到君家　Can't remember reaching your home.

Gao, whose works were popular in Japan during the Edo and Meiji periods, lived in Suzhou, a city full of the canals and bridges that appear in the poem. Crossing water repeatedly is a necessary experience when walking the streets of Suzhou, and here the reverie of being swept away by the blossoms and spring wind has been transposed from the city to this rural scene.

PB

37. *Spring Landscape* 春景山水図 (Shunkei sansui zu)

1881
Hanging scroll: ink and light color on paper
153.9 × 48.3 cm

SIGNATURE: *Rōzan An Yō* 老山安養

SEALS: *yūseki sanbō* 友石山房
Friend of Stones Mountain-studio (upper right)
yubin shi in 臾聞子印 (sig. upper)
rōyō 老養 nourishing old age (sig. lower)

INSCRIPTION:
辛巳夏日造於舎雪樓雨窓
Created on a summer day in the *shinshi* year [1881] by the rain window of the Shasetsurō Pavilion

Purchase, 2005
13202.1

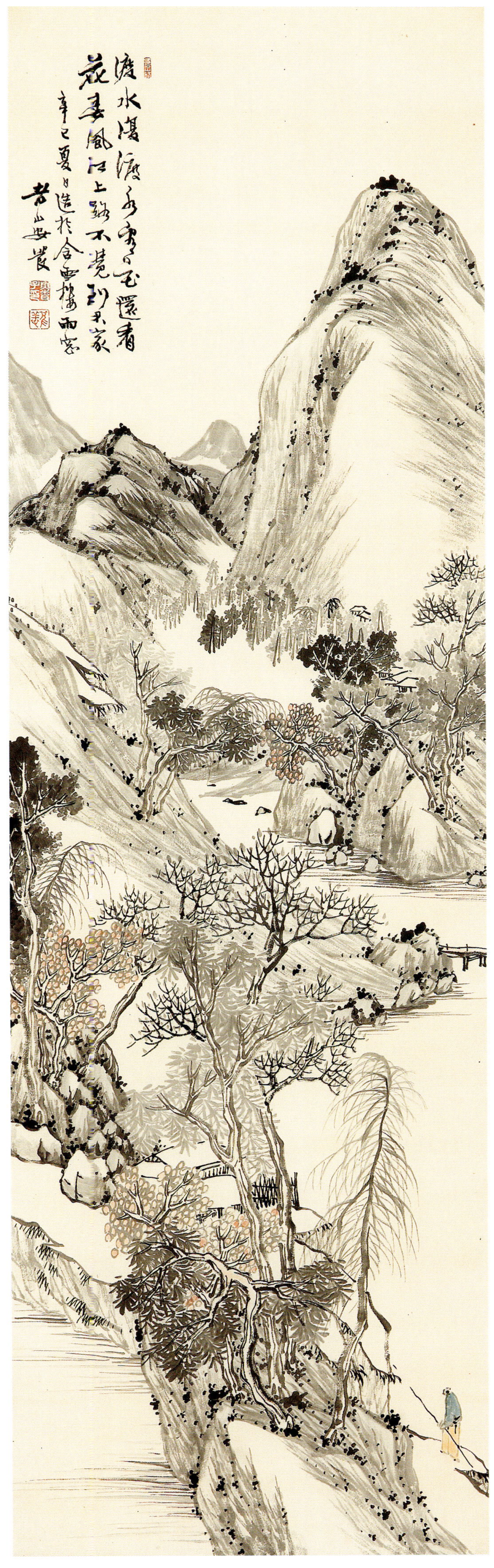

Hoashi Kyōu 帆足杏雨 (TRADITIONAL ATTRIBUTION)

1810–1884

Hoashi Kyōu's long, prolific career spanned the turbulent years of transition from the late Edo to the early Meiji era. The son of a wealthy farmer in Ōita, Kyushu, Kyōu became a pupil of Tanomura Chikuden 田能村竹田, with whom he traveled through Kyushu, Osaka, Kyoto, and western Honshu. Kyōu eventually settled down in Ōita to the literati life: painting, composing poems, and visiting other *bunjin* to nurture friendships. During the late 1840s Kyōu's mature style, characterized by carefully executed, sensitive brushwork and occasional additions of light color, began to emerge.[1] Mirroring the conservatism of late-Edo literati painting, his works generally adhere to orthodox principles. Although known mostly for his landscapes, Kyōu was an accomplished painter of birds and flowers as well.

In *Landscape in Snow* the convoluted forms of diagonal landmasses dynamically thrust upward, culminating in the tall, central snow-covered peak. Pale ink washes evoke the chilly atmosphere, while soft, twisting brushstrokes are layered to shape the mountains and rocks accented by darker dots. Wooden bridges cross over the river, and a path ascends the side of the mountain. Desiccated craggy trees dominate the foreground, dwarfing the three travelers riding on horseback. Partially hidden by the mountain in the middle ground, the rustic house on a flat plateau by the river is clearly their destination. The bright colors of their garments give a cheerful air to the visitors, who blithely converse under their umbrellas. Despite their nonchalance, the inscription refers to the difficulty of the snow-covered path to Shu (Sichuan province):

蜀道之難兮	As for the hardship of the road to Shu,
難於上青天	It is more difficult than going up to the clear heaven.
矧加之積雪萬丈	With ten thousand feet of snow in addition,
其難如何	Imagine how much harder it is.
故雪棧苦於涉世者	Therefore I paint the snow-covered path,
作此	Which causes more suffering than living in this world.

The influences of Chinese literati painters such as Wu Zhen 吳鎮 (1280–1354), Shen Zhou 沈周 (1427–1509), Wen Zhengming 文徵明 (1470–1559), and Wang Hui 王翬 (1632–1717) are often ascribed to Kyōu's paintings after the 1860s,[2] but in fact Kyōu, like many artists of his time, based his understanding of them on eighteenth- and early-nineteenth-century Chinese works that only loosely emulated the earlier masters. In this snow landscape, the depiction of winter trees with branches spreading like fingers recalls Wang Hui's style, and the figures strongly reflect those of Chikuden.

The combination on this painting of two seals below the signature (*Hen'en no in, Kyōu shiga*) appears on many of Kyōu's works. But the seals used here differ from the well-documented, standard examples. Thus, the painting is likely a later work created after the artist. During the early Meiji period, Kyōu held considerable artistic stature and influence in his home province of Ōita, despite the fact that he did not have many formal pupils. The Meiji government commissioned Kyōu to create a painting for the 1873 Vienna Exposition, and people vied to own his work after the mid-1870s, compelling the artist to paint ten works a day to fulfill requests.[3] The excellent quality of this landscape attests to the popularity and respect Kyōu enjoyed in his later years.

MM

38. *Landscape in Snow* 雪景山水図 (Sekkei sansui zu)

Hanging scroll: ink and color on silk
127.8 × 50.2 cm

SIGNATURE: *Kyōu en son nō*
杏雨遠邨農

SEALS: *Kyōu fui* 杏雨布衣 Kyōu, commoner (upper right)
Han'en no in 驅遠之印 Han'en's seal (sig. upper)
Kyōu shiga 杏雨詩画 painting and poem by Kyōu (sig. lower)
家在杏華春雨邨 Residence in the village of apricot blossom and spring rain (bottom left)

Purchase, 2005
13186.1

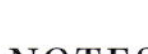

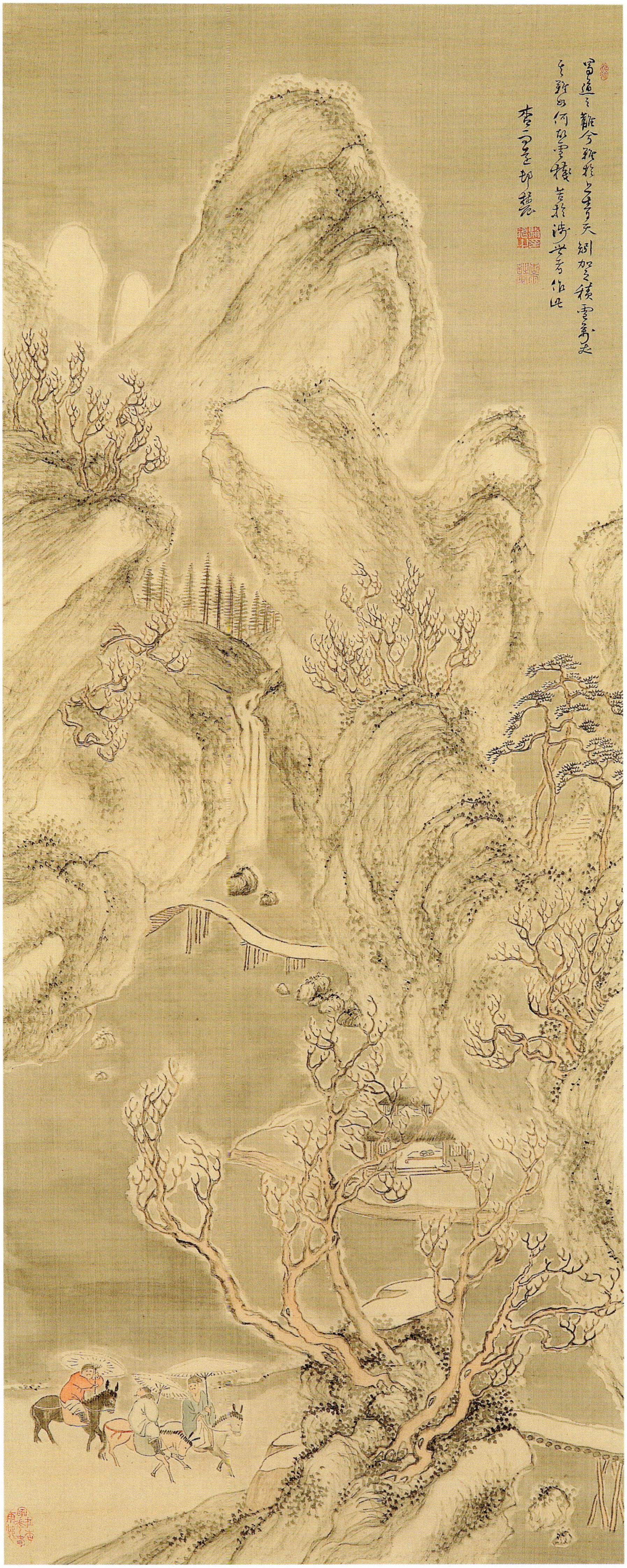

NOTES

1. Munakata Ken'ichi, "Nanga no ryūseiki kara suitaiki made o ikita nangaka Hoashi Kyōu no sakuga," in Ōita Kenritsu Geijutsu Kaikan, *Hoashi Kyōu ten zuroku*, exh. cat. (Ōita, 1984), 42.
2. Ibid., 42–44.
3. Ibid., 150.

Yamanaka Shinten'ō 山中信天翁

1822–1885

Yamanaka Shinten'ō painted rocks, pine trees, butterflies, birds, and flowers but was best known for his many landscapes.[1] Rarely employing color, his landscapes are appreciated for their bold ink brushwork and dramatic compositions of towering mountains with knotty protrusions of rocks. Shinten'ō was a senior friend of Tomioka Tessai 富岡鐵斎 (1836–1924), and it is thought that Tessai's early attraction to simple, expressive brushwork was fostered by his admiration for Shinten'ō's works.

Deep in the Woods, A Thatched Hut has many of the classic features of Shinten'ō's landscapes, including dominating peaks and a hut under trees. This painting's connection to the poem inscribed on it is unusually close:

絶澗深林著草廬	Cut off by a mountain torrent deep in the woods, living in a thatched hut,
期吾異日下同居	I hope someday to share the same residence.
山人睡覺踞危石	A man of the hills sleeping by dangerous rocks
老緑陰中讀道書	Old man in green shade reading Daoist books

The thatched hut cut off by a mountain torrent is identical to that in the verse. The fantastic stone tower behind the house and trees depicts the dangerous rocks mentioned in the inscription. Such poetic sentiments are common features of many literati landscapes and could be applied equally to quiet, conservatively brushed scenery. But Shinten'ō's dark, expressive outlines inject a sense of turbulence to his already twisting manner of depicting rocks and tree trunks. He used gray tonalities effectively in areas of water and mist, yet the overall graphic power of the painting is created by the strong contrast of dark ink against white paper.

This interest in the forceful portrayal of simplified landscape forms was shared by many literati painters of the early Meiji period, including Yasuda Rōzan 安田老山 (1830–1882), Okuhara Seiko 奥原晴湖 (1837–1912), Hine Taizan 日根對山 (1813–1869), and Nakanishi Kōseki 中西耕石 (1807–1884). Even though there are many exceptions, approaches to painting in the nineteenth and twentieth centuries often seem to parallel changes in society at large. In this case, one can see the turmoil of the early Meiji period reflected in the rough assertiveness that appeared in literati painting, marking a reversal of the refined sensibilities and subtle brushwork found in the earlier generation of artists such as Tanomura Chikuden 田能村竹田 (1777–1835), Nakabayashi Chikutō 中林竹洞 (1776–1853), Okada Hankō 岡田半江 (1782–1846), and others. At the same time, imported Chinese literati paintings of the seventeenth century with the same assertive brushwork were increasingly available. As a connoisseur of Chinese paintings, Shinten'ō wrote many box inscriptions, some of which are noted in prewar sale catalogues of Chinese painting. Thus, the style exhibited in *Deep in the Woods, A Thatched Hut* was the result of a complex intersection of social changes and a corresponding evolution of literati aesthetics. PB

39. *Deep in the Woods, A Thatched Hut*
深林草廬之図 (Shinrin sōro no zu)

c. 1875
Hanging scroll: ink on paper
136.3 × 47.3 cm

SIGNATURE: *Shinten sei Ken sha hei dai*
信天生獻寫并題

SEALS: 會經我眼即戊有 (upper right)
Yamanaka Ken in 山中獻印 (sig. upper)
Mō i yō sei 蒙以養正 Nurturing uprightness while young (sig. lower)
Seiitsu 静逸 (bottom left)

Purchase, 2005
13198.1

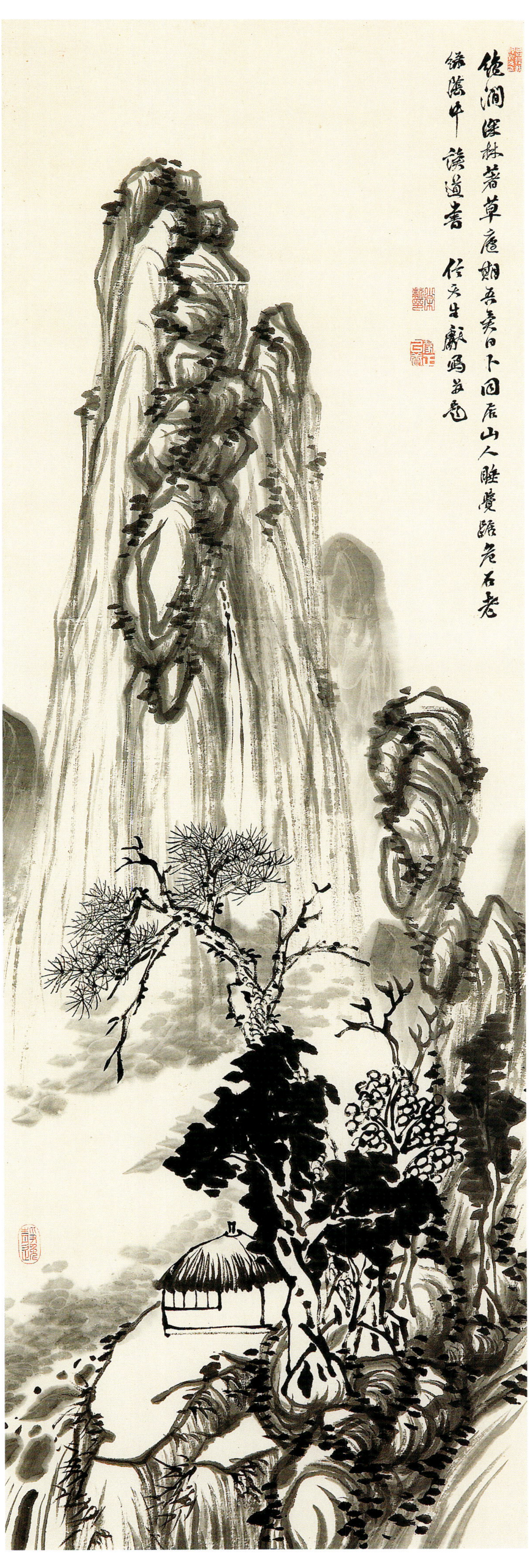

NOTE

1. The variety of Shinten'ō's themes is well displayed in the seventeen compositions found in Paul Berry and Yokoya Kenichirō, *Unexplored Avenues of Japanese Painting: The Hakutakuan Collection* (Ōtsushi: Rekishi Hakubutsukan; Seattle: University of Washington Press, 2001), plates 10, 11, 59, and 64 and the figures on pp. 136–37.

Yamanaka Shinten'ō 山中信天翁

1822–1885

Originally from Owari province (Aichi prefecture), the scholar-poet Yamanaka Seiitsu, popularly known as Shinten'ō, moved to Kyoto during the 1850s and became a supporter of imperial loyalists in the political conflict that brought an end to the shogunate. After the Meiji regime was established, Shinten'ō received a series of official posts in recognition of his contributions. In 1873 he retired from service, living out the last decade of his life as one of the leading figures of the Kyoto literati community at his elegant villa in Arashiyama, Kyoto. A famed calligrapher, Shinten'ō was primarily self-taught in painting. The untutored quality that manifests in his powerful brushwork and daring compositional distortions reflects the literati concept of amateurism which distinguishes his work from the refined style of the professional painter.

A pair of narrow, elongated hanging scrolls, these landscapes exemplify Shinten'ō's mature style. One marvels at the artist's ingenuity in creating a landscape scene in such a severely constricted format. The viewer easily identifies with the scholar in the foreground on the right, crossing a bridge under large willow trees. Although the figure is simply drawn, Shinten'ō carefully defined the details of his hat and staff. More willow trees are seen on the embankment in the middle ground, and several sailboats dot the water leading to the distant hills. Shinten'ō is known for his bold, expressive brushwork, and the fluid rendering of the willow trees displays another facet of his brush style.

Shinten'ō juxtaposed the quiet composition on the right with a more dramatic treatment on the left. Traversing the water in the foreground, a raised walkway originates from the corner, where Shinten'ō created a point of visual interest by grouping roughly drawn rocks, an awkwardly shaped tree, and a cluster of bamboo depicted with unexpected delicacy. The winding path partially reenters at the center left, and above it a cliff surface with clinging trees suddenly rises. Represented with nearly an equal ink value as the foreground rock, this protruding cliff has an ambiguous spatial position. Moreover, its rounded form is denied solidity by the empty space above it, where Shinten'ō's calligraphy asserts the two-dimensional reality of pictorial space. A rejection of the principles of Western perspective and an insistence on East Asian spatial conventions, which energize the composition with tension and instability, are among the prevalent features of Shinten'ō's mature landscapes. The houses elevated on pilings above the water toward the background, where a lone figure is shown, are also a recurring motif in his work.[1]

Shinten'ō inscribed his poems in his typical calligraphic style that emphasizes the curvature of lines, achieved by the twisting movement of his brush:

Right:

一橋復一橋	I cross a bridge one after another;
垂柳重垂柳	Weeping willows layer one after another.
遥訪美人行	From afar I travel to visit a friend;
流鶯也呼友	Bush warblers in the tree call each other.

Left:

繪事吾所快	Painting is what I enjoy;
文章理本同	Writing is essentially the same.
於山質韓子	About mountains, one asks Hanzi;
水乃問氾公	About water, one asks Fangong.[2]

MM

40. *Visiting a Friend through Weeping Willows*
垂柳訪友図 (Suiryū hōyū zu)

1870s and later
Pair of hanging scrolls: ink on satin
149.2 × 16 cm

Right scroll:
SIGNATURE: *Shinten'ō* 信天翁

SEALS:
Shishin 師心 Following one's heart (upper right)
Seiitsu 静逸 (sig. upper)
忘毀誉可以清心 To be oblivious of slander or praise makes a pure heart (sig. lower)
清如中□□ (bottom right)

Left scroll:
SIGNATURE: *Shinten'ō heidai* 信天翁併題

SEALS:
Senshin 洗心 To cleanse the heart (upper right)
Seiitsu 静逸 (sig. upper)
Mō i yō sei 蒙以養正 Nurturing uprightness while young (sig. lower)
修得到某華 By pursuing one's path, one attains plum blossom (bottom right)

Purchase, 2005
13199.1 & 2

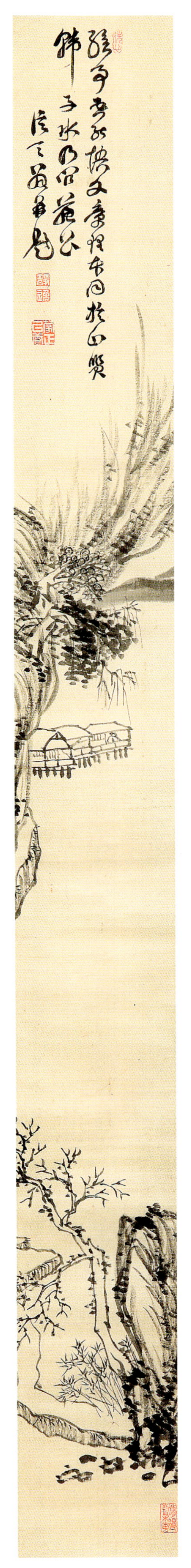

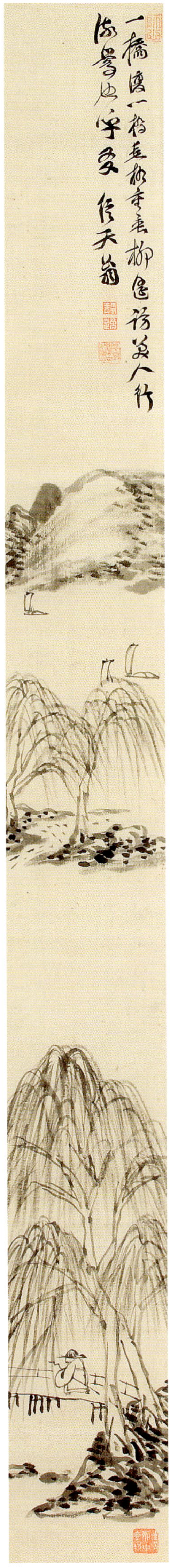

NOTES

1. See examples in Katō Ruiko and Shimada Yasuhiro, eds., *Bunjinga no kindai: Tessai to sono shiyū tachi* (Kyoto: Kyōto Kokuritsu Kindai Bijutsukan, 1997), 146, 147, 149, 151. The landscape on p. 146 shows a composition similar, although reversed, to the left painting of the Honolulu pair.

2. Fangong is likely the Song-dynasty landscape master Fan Kuan. "Hanzi" in the previous line has not been identified.

Suzuki Hyakunen　鈴木百年

1825–1891

41. *Spring and Autumn Landscapes* 春秋山水図 (Shunjū sansui zu)

1866
Pair of six-panel screens: ink and color on paper
157.5 × 336 cm each

SIGNATURE (both screens): *Hyakunen* 百年

SEALS (both screens): *Gasendō shu* 画仙堂主
Gasendō master (sig. upper)
Seiju no in 世壽之印 Seiju's seal (sig. lower)

INSCRIPTIONS:
慶應丙寅小春寫於摘星楼
Painted at the Tekisei Pavilion in the tenth month of the *heiin* year of Keiō [1866] (right screen)
丙寅小春寫
Painted in the tenth month of the *heiin* year (left screen)

Gift of Terry Welch, in honor of Julia White, 2005
13146.1 & 2

Suzuki Hyakunen, the founder of the Suzuki school, employed patience and humility to cultivate his position in mid-nineteenth-century Kyoto, a city already crowded with professional painting studios both old and new.[1] His eclectic style, derived from the Maruyama and Shijō lineages and the Kanō, Tosa, and literati masters, found a decisively positive reception from Kyoto residents. Despite his success, Hyakunen called himself an "amateur" while urging Shōnen, his son and successor, to achieve true professionalism and carry on the family legacy.[2] The well-educated son of an astronomer and Daoist diviner, Hyakunen maintained literati interests throughout his career and enjoyed friendships among the Kyoto *bunjin* circle.

Spring and Autumn Landscapes exemplifies Hyakunen's incorporation of Shijō-school naturalism, tempered with literati-flavored brushwork, and reflects his reserved artistic temperament. First popularized by the Shijō artists at the end of the Edo period, paintings portraying ordinary human activities in the seasonal cycle of nature remained popular in Kyoto into the following Meiji era. Younger Kyoto artists

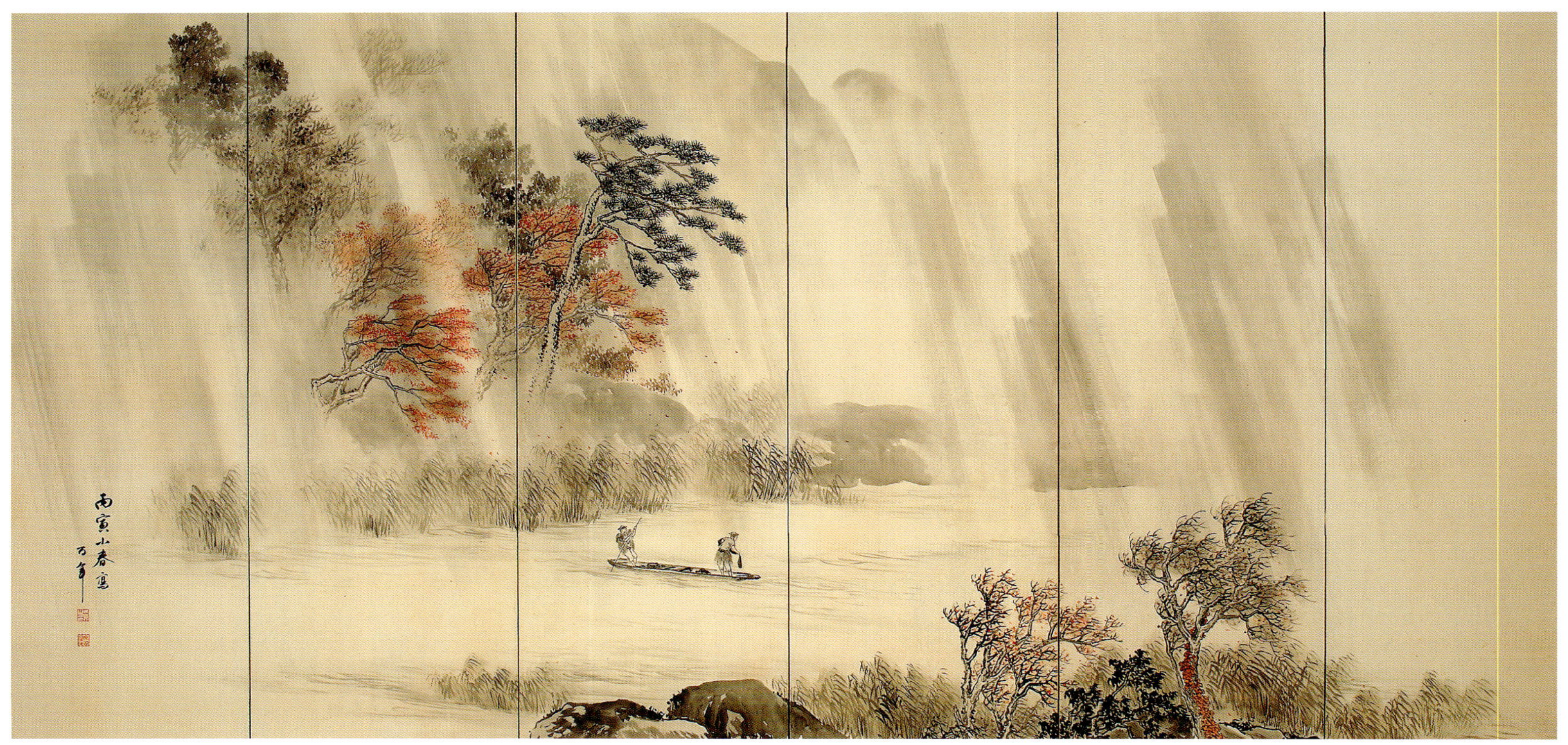

would revitalize the tradition in the early twentieth century by depicting contemporary rural scenes with a greater sense of realism. Hyakunen here juxtaposed two seasonal scenes of contrasting mood. In spring, on the right, a farmer prepares a field in an open landscape gently brightened by red and white plum blossoms. Several paths lead to distant mountains, whose bases are shrouded in mist. Employing the realist technique transmitted by the Maruyama and Shijō schools, Hyakunen kept a low viewpoint to indicate a deep spatial recess. On the left screen, in an autumn scene enlivened by vivid orange foliage, two fishermen are busy at work. Diagonal, swift washes applied with a wide brush indicate rainy weather. Blown by the wind, tree branches lean and reeds bend, while red leaves dance in the air. In both screens Hyakunen achieved the lyricism associated with the Shijō school. His brushwork, however, is more relaxed and literati influenced than the tightly structured techniques of the naturalist tradition.

By the time Hyakunen painted this work in 1866, his school was well on its way to becoming one of the most prosperous ateliers of his time. When Kyoto artists formed the Cloudlike Society (Jounsha 如雲社) in 1868 to hold inter-school gatherings and exhibitions, Hyakunen did not participate. Already enjoying economic security and bright prospects for his new school, he may have found it unnecessary to take part in such a group,[3] or he may have refrained from joining due to his rivalry with Shiokawa Bunrin 塩川文麟 (1808–1877), a leading Shijō painter and a key figure in the Cloudlike Society. Behind Hyakunen's professed humble amateurism lay a fiercely competitive artist who navigated the changing Kyoto art world with talent, self-discipline, and social astuteness. MM

NOTES

1. Harada Heisaku, *Bakumatsu Meiji Kyōraku no gajin tachi* (Kyoto: Kyōto Shinbunsha, 1985), 82–83. Among those active in Kyoto were painters of the Tosa, Kanō, Mochizuki, Maruyama, Shijō, Kishi, and Hara lineages as well as independent literati artists.

2. "Suzuki Hyakunen den," *Kyōto bijutsu kyōkai zasshi*, no. 89 (November 1899): 13.

3. Kanzaki Ken'ichi, *Kyōto ni okeru nihongashi* (Kyoto: Kyōto Seihan Insatsusha, 1929), 38.

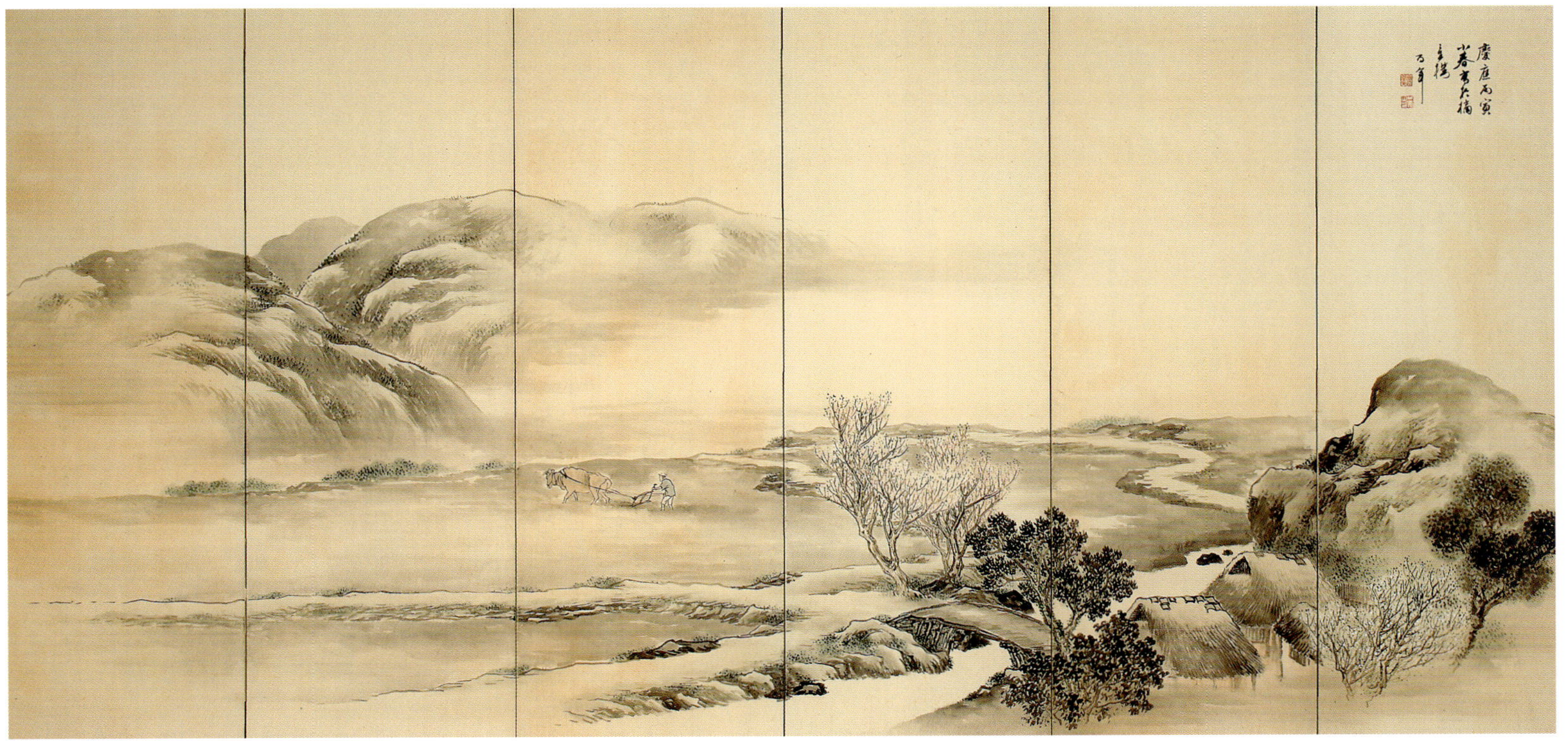

Tanomura Chokunyū 田能村直入

1814–1907

A child prodigy in painting, Chokunyū originally modeled himself after the style of the famous Tanomura Chikuden 田能村竹田 (1777–1835), who had adopted him at the age of eight. After Chikuden's death in 1835, Chokunyū took up an intense study of imported Chinese paintings, and until the end of the Edo period his painting style varied widely, depending on the source he was following. Only in the first decade of the Meiji period did his own manner become established. Even though stylistically diverse, Chokunyū's Edo-period paintings, mostly signed and sealed Shōko,[1] are still characterized by his preferences for strong color, minute brushwork, and complex compositions.

Throughout the Edo period, Japanese literati painters often referred in their inscriptions to the Four Masters of the Yuan period, Huang Gongwang 黃公望 (1269–1354), Wu Zhen 吳鎮 (1280–1354), Ni Zan 倪瓚 (1301–1374), and Wang Meng 王蒙 (c. 1308–1385). In doing so, they were following the precedent of Ming and Qing painters whose works they had studied through copies, as there were no genuine works by these four Yuan painters in Japan. Yet the paintings of Wang Meng were apparently not available even as later copies, and his approach was transmitted only by works done vaguely in his style by painters who lived hundreds of years after his time. The diverse paintings attributed to Wang's style in Japan are typified by complex compositions and fine, dense brushwork.

Landscape in the Style of Wang Meng depicts a narrow mountain valley with a sequence of waterfalls that leads to a spreading pond at the bottom of the composition, where a scholar and an attendant carrying a *qin*, the ideal instrument of the literati, cross a bridge under spreading pine boughs. Folded ridges are repeatedly duplicated within the mountains. The extraordinary number of pine trees conveys the idea of immortality, while the colored leaves on the few other trees suggest that the season may be autumn. Several temple compounds tucked into grottoes alongside the watercourse add to the atmosphere of a spiritual retreat. The mannered repetition of pines and mountain ridges indicates that Chokunyū was influenced by an eighteenth-century Chinese painting intended to vaguely suggest some aspect of the Wang Meng tradition. That Japanese literati painters often imperfectly understood some of the famous styles of Chinese painting can be seen as a limitation, yet it may have also freed their imaginations and helped them create new styles that were not trapped in the past. PB

42. *Landscape in the Style of Wang Meng*
摹黄鶴山樵之圖意 (Mō Ōkaku Sanshō no zui)

c. 1850
Hanging scroll: ink and color on silk
134.7 × 34 cm

SIGNATURE: *Den Shōko* 田小虎

SEAL: *Shōko* 小虎[2]

INSCRIPTION:
mo Ōkaku Sanshō no zui
摹黄鶴山樵之圖意
After the idea of a painting by Yellow Crane Mountain Woodcutter [Wang Meng]

Purchase, 2005
13204.1

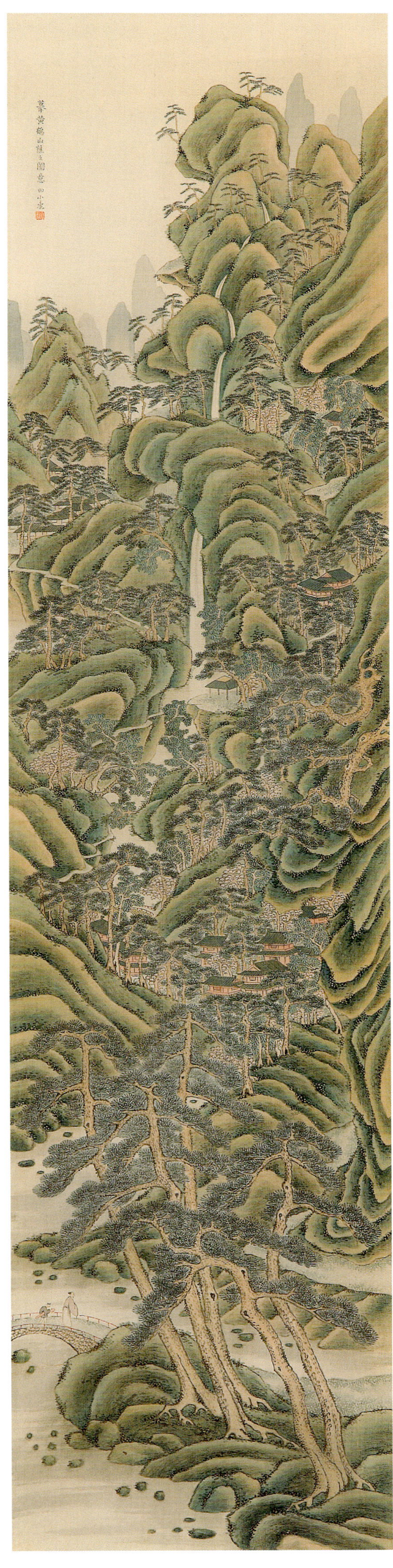

NOTES

1. Chikuden gave Chokunyū the name Shōko (Small Tiger) in 1831. It was a reference to the famous painter Gu Kaizhi's 顧愷之 (c. 344–c. 405) alternate name of Hutou 虎頭 (Tiger Head), suggesting that Chokunyū was a "small" Gu.

2. Well over three hundred seals used by Chokunyū were still extant at the time of his death, yet only a few of them are found on his Edo-period works. It seems that many of his earliest seals had been lost or given away. The seal and signature style of this work can still not be confirmed by the few published examples. It would take a new survey of his many early works to clearly establish the features of the first half of his career.

Tanomura Chokunyū 田能村直入

1814–1907

Tanomura Chokunyū was one of the most prolific and long-lived literati painters in Japanese history. Even the productive Tomioka Tessai 富岡鐵斎 (1836–1924) did not match his output. Among the tens of thousands of paintings Chokunyū created, the great majority are hanging scrolls; the rest are mostly fans, albums, and screens. Landscape handscrolls were a common format in China, yet they never attained the same degree of popularity among Japanese literati painters, and Chokunyū rarely painted handscrolls such as *Great View of Rivers and Mountains.*

The painting is of moderate length for a handscroll, allowing a full view of a broad river flowing through a mountain valley. In the lower right corner, a stooped figure stands between several houses whose roofs emerge from a bamboo grove that lies at the base of a cliff. Above, to the left, are several buildings where a solitary person gazes into the distance at sailboats moving down the river. At the center of the composition, two pine trees extend over an open-air pavilion where another figure, barely visible behind a post, contemplates the autumn colors scattered across the countryside. An elderly man with a staff and a boy attendant holding a *qin* appear to be headed for the pavilion. To the left, patches of mist hover over a forest of bamboo penetrated by a stream with a neighboring footpath. The composition concludes with a rising hillside where two people greet each other in front of the gate to an elaborate house. In the background, a waterfall pours down a tall cliff. These detailed features of an idealized natural world, accented with light colors and delicate brushwork, typify Chokunyū's mature landscape style, which dominated the final decades of his long life.

Twenty-eight years after the work was completed for a Mr. Shima 嶋, it was remounted. The original owner requested that Tanaka Hakuin 田中伯陰 (1866–1934) add a title in large characters and a postscript, as was the custom for Chinese landscape handscrolls. Originally from Shizuoka, Hakuin had come to Kyoto when he was seventeen and soon began to study with Chokunyū, becoming one of the most noted of his numerous disciples by the late Meiji period. Prominent followers were often asked to authenticate and inscribe the works of their teachers, and Hakuin's postscript suggests that he was honored to have his calligraphy bracket a fine painting by the artist who had so influenced his own career. PB

43. *Great View of Rivers and Mountains*
江山大観図 (Kōzan taikan zu)

1896
Handscroll: ink and color on silk
36 × 130.2 cm

SIGNATURE: *Chokunyū Dōjin Denchi* 直入道人田癡

SEALS: *shōyō* 逍遥 sauntering (upper right)
Chi 癡 (sig. upper)
Shōko 小虎 (sig. lower)
shizen tennen 自然天然 nature—natural (bottom left)

Purchase, 2005
13155.1

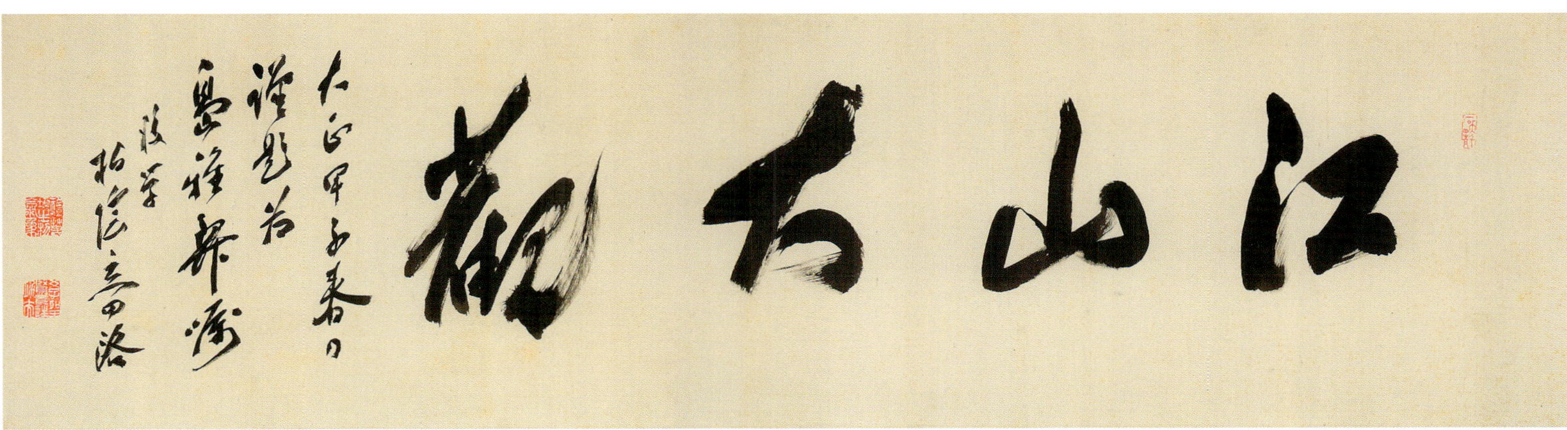

Title by Tanaka Hakuin 田中伯陰 (1866–1934)
江山大観
大正甲子春日謹題為嶌雅弊嘱
Great view of rivers and mountains, respectfully titled in the *kōshi* year [1924], spring, for the elegant Mr. Shima

SIGNATURE: *Kōgaku Hakuin shujin Denraku* 後学伯陰主人田洛

SEALS: *isshō sen sansei* 一笑千山青 (upper right)

□□□主物 氣象 (sig. upper)
学聖賢□□□夫 (sig. lower)

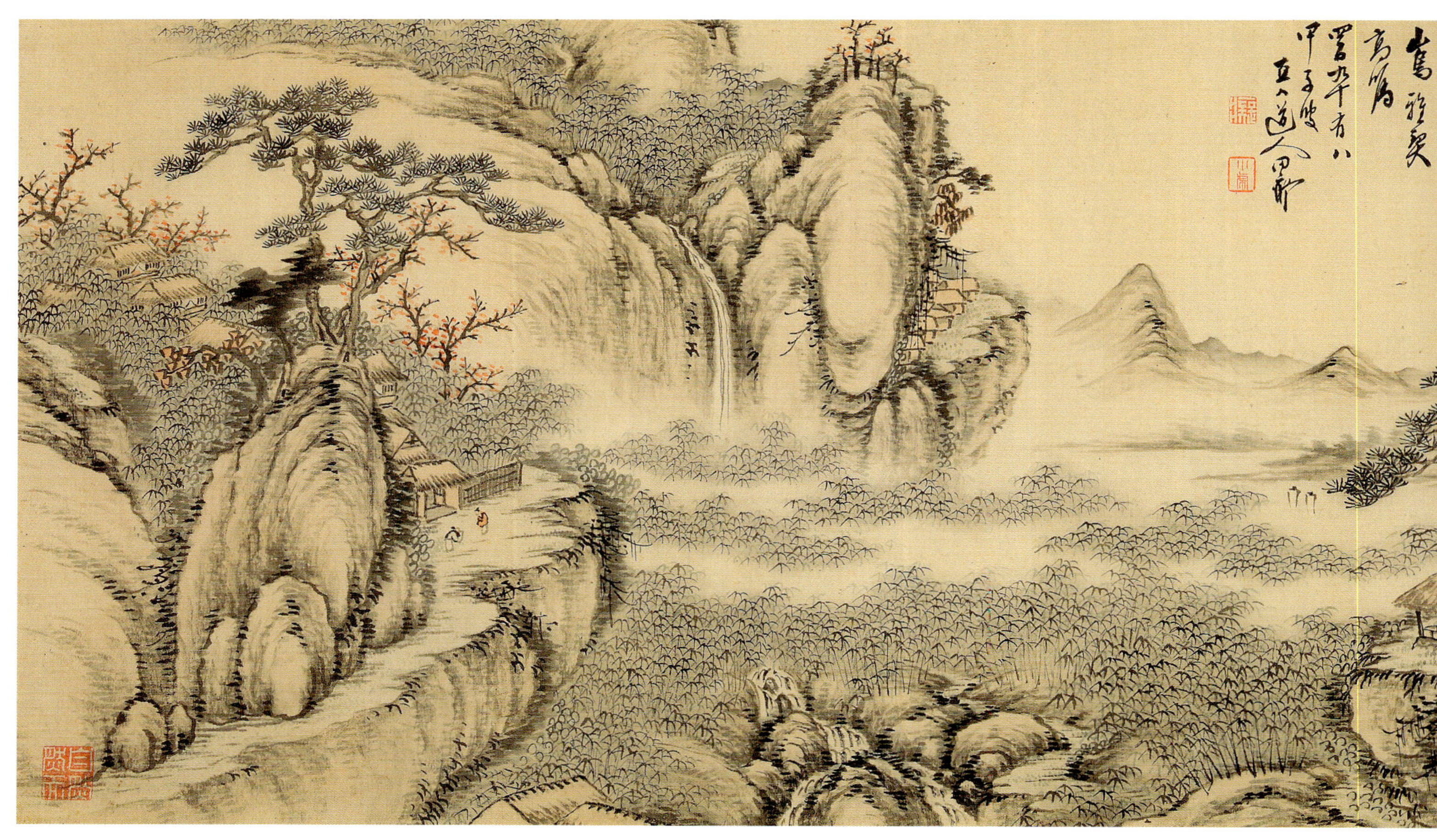

INSCRIPTION:

地僻人稀苔色青
山禽聲雜石泉聲
竹盡望岩閑讀古
唯覚清風南腋生
明治二十有九年丙申小春寫并題
於南宗畫学校為嶌雅契高囑
四百九十有八甲子叟

In the countryside people are few,
moss is colored green.
Varied sounds of mountain birds,
sound of a spring emerging from rocks.
Bamboo fills the view from the cliff, relaxing by reading of antiquity.
Who recalls the pure breeze from southern budding leaves?

Painted and titled in the tenth month of the *heishin* year [1896] at Nansōga Gakkō[1] at the elegant Mr. Shima's lofty request, by the 498 *kōshi* [daily cycles] Old Man[2]

NOTES

1. The name of Chokunyū's painting school is usually pronounced in this manner, although the term *nansōga* 南宗畫 can also be pronounced *nanshūga*.

2. "*Kōshi*" 甲子 refers to the sixty pairs of characters that were used in East Asia to specify years in the sixty-year cycle system that was initiated in China more than three millennia ago. This same set of sixty pairs of characters were also used to designate a sixty-day cycle in the traditional lunar calendar. The lunar calendar split the year into twelve thirty-day months, conveyed by six repetitions of this sixty-day cycle. Age could be represented as the number of daily cycles, obtained by multiplying one's age in years by this factor of six cycles of days that occurred every year. In 1896 Chokunyū was eighty-three years old (counting one year old at birth); multiplying 83 by 6 results in the number 498 seen in his inscription. Chokunyū, Tomioka Tessai (see cat. no. 46), and other literati occasionally used this calculation to indicate their age.

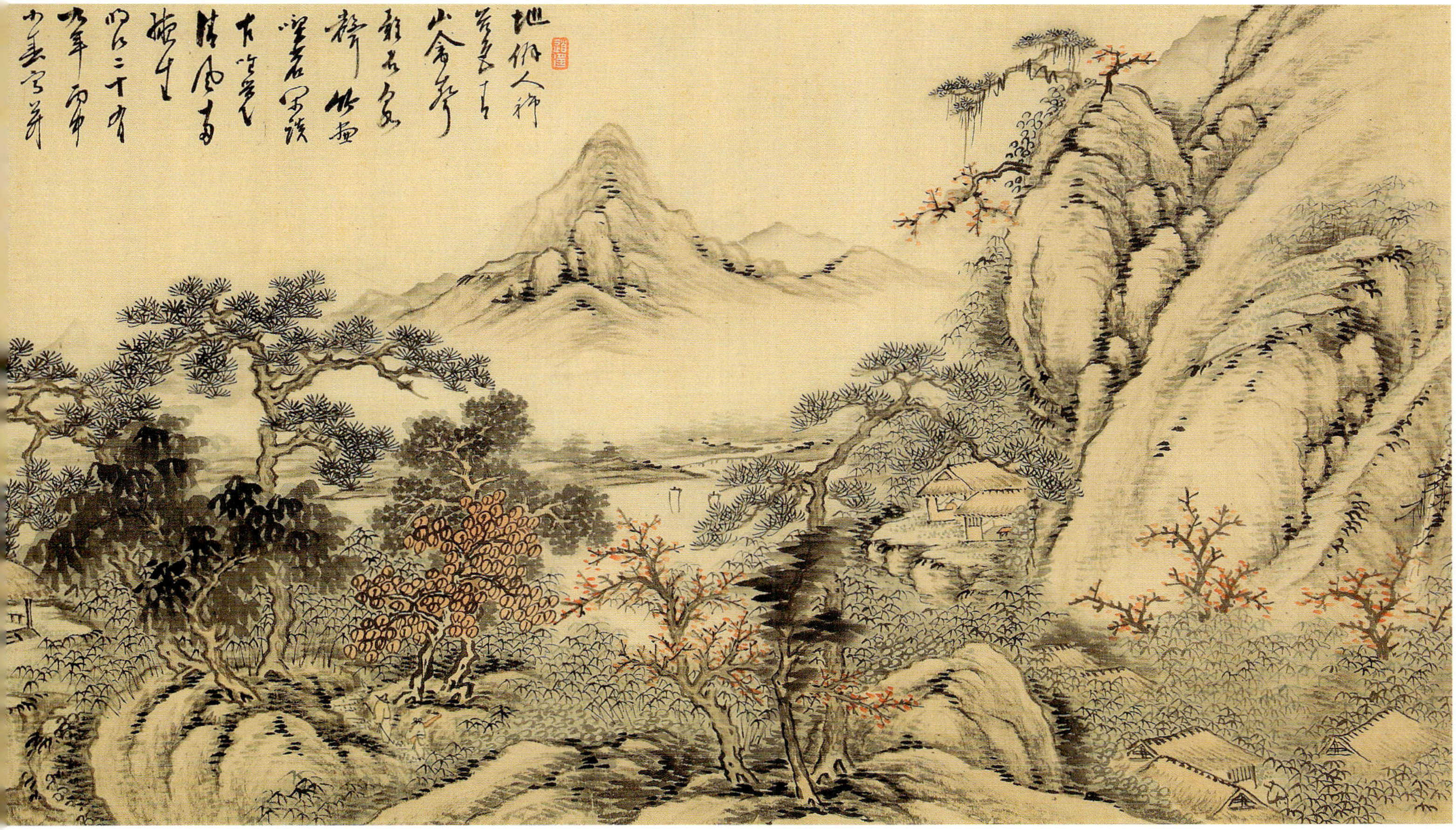

Postscript by Tanaka Hakuin

SIGNATURE: *Kōgaku Hakuin shujin Denraku* 後学伯陰主人田洛

SEALS: 任自然 (upper right)
Denkei no in 田啓之印 (sig. upper)
Hakuin 伯陰 (sig. lower)

INSCRIPTION:
此巻先師直入翁往年應嶋雅契尊甫君之嘱即畫近頃防裝□需余之題跋静處嶋雅弊亦有与□風雅之清交因不可辞然而物得其處其中道自存矣茲感　雅契尊甫君断愛物深愛護之孝志所然抱筆題四大字豈獨水長山高之意而已哉併謹記其由巻尾於畫禅室中干時大正十三年歳在甲子之暮春

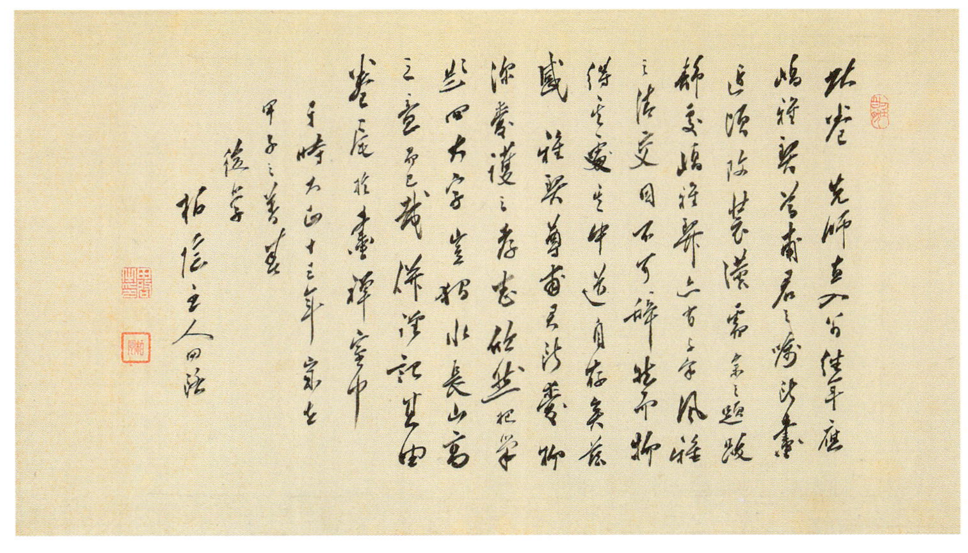

Okuhara Seiko 奥原晴湖

1837–1912

44. *Elegant Mood of Mountain Residence*
山荘幽韻図 (Sansō yūin zu)

Late 1860s
Hanging scroll: ink on paper
37 × 25.6 cm

SIGNATURE: *Seiko Okuhara Setsu* 晴湖奥原節

SEALS: *Shūsui shōyō* 秋水笑蓉 (upper right)
Seiko 晴湖 (sig. upper)
Tenshin 天真 (sig. lower)
Bokuto en'un 墨吐烟雲 (bottom right)

Purchase, 2005
13205.1

Elegant Mood of Mountain Residence, an exquisite painting from Okuhara Seiko's early period, is an amalgamation of the education she received in her hometown in the Koga domain 古河藩. Her teacher, Hirata Suiseki 枚田水石, was a cultivated samurai well acquainted with the Edo literati circle through his training with Tani Bunchō 谷文晁 (1763–1840). Under Suiseki's tutelage, Seiko voraciously studied Chinese painting manuals and made copies of Chinese and Japanese masters, including Muqi, Wu Zhen, Shen Zhou, Wen Zhengming, Shen Nanpin, Tani Bunchō, Watanabe Kazan, Tsubaki Chinzan, and Nakabayashi Chikutō. Among the more than 3,700 sketches and studies Seiko left, more than 250 are copies of the works of various masters duplicated in the original size.[1]

After Seiko moved to Edo in 1865, she began studying the works of Zheng Xie 鄭燮 (Zheng Banqiao 鄭板橋, 1693–1765). During the following decades she produced works influenced by Zheng's dramatic brush style. Seiko's new paintings and calligraphies, characterized by a daring, self-assured expression, appealed to the leaders of the newly established Meiji government, and she gained wide popularity in Tokyo.

Judging from the style of the inscription and signature, Seiko painted *Elegant Mood of Mountain Residence* soon after moving to Edo but before she developed her Zheng-influenced style. The small composition, representing a gentleman's modest retreat nestled among tall trees, displays the restraint of the "classical" Chinese mode in its well-structured composition and careful brushwork. A building occupies the center of the composition, but it is mostly hidden by trees and melds into the surrounding landscape. Two scholars conversing on a path in the lower right seem to invite the viewer into the painting. The large cluster of rocks in the foreground anchors the composition and balances the soaring trees overhead. Seiko carefully distinguished their species by portraying the distinct foliage of each tree. Spatial expression is subtle yet rational, as suggested through the succession of trees that diminish in size and lighten in tone. The brushwork is sensitive and controlled, but not rigid. By keeping the range of ink tonality narrow, Seiko avoided an ostentatious contrast of dark and light. The refined, sophisticated style thus achieved is in complete harmony with the unassuming yet elegant scholar's hermitage represented in the painting. Seiko's calligraphy, perfectly positioned in the upper left corner, echoes the painting in its unaffected dignity.

In her inscription Seiko indicated her knowledge of Chinese painting and expressed her admiration for Guan Tong 關仝, a tenth-century landscape painter, and Ju Rui 朱鋭, a twelfth-century court painter of the Southern Song. She also demonstrated her own scholarly virtue of humility:

山荘幽韻	The quiet mood of mountain residence—
關仝出之以豊潤	Guan Tong could express it with luxuriant feeling,
朱鋭出之以高簡	Ju Rui could express it with simple feeling,
並稱紳品	Their paintings are both of divine class.
余又偶然背摹大意	I also happen to copy from memory of their generous spirit,
其神妙之致	But as for their divine and wonderful results,
不得形似	I cannot even achieve the form-likeness.
深有偲干前賢也	I feel deeply humbled before the ancient masters.

MM

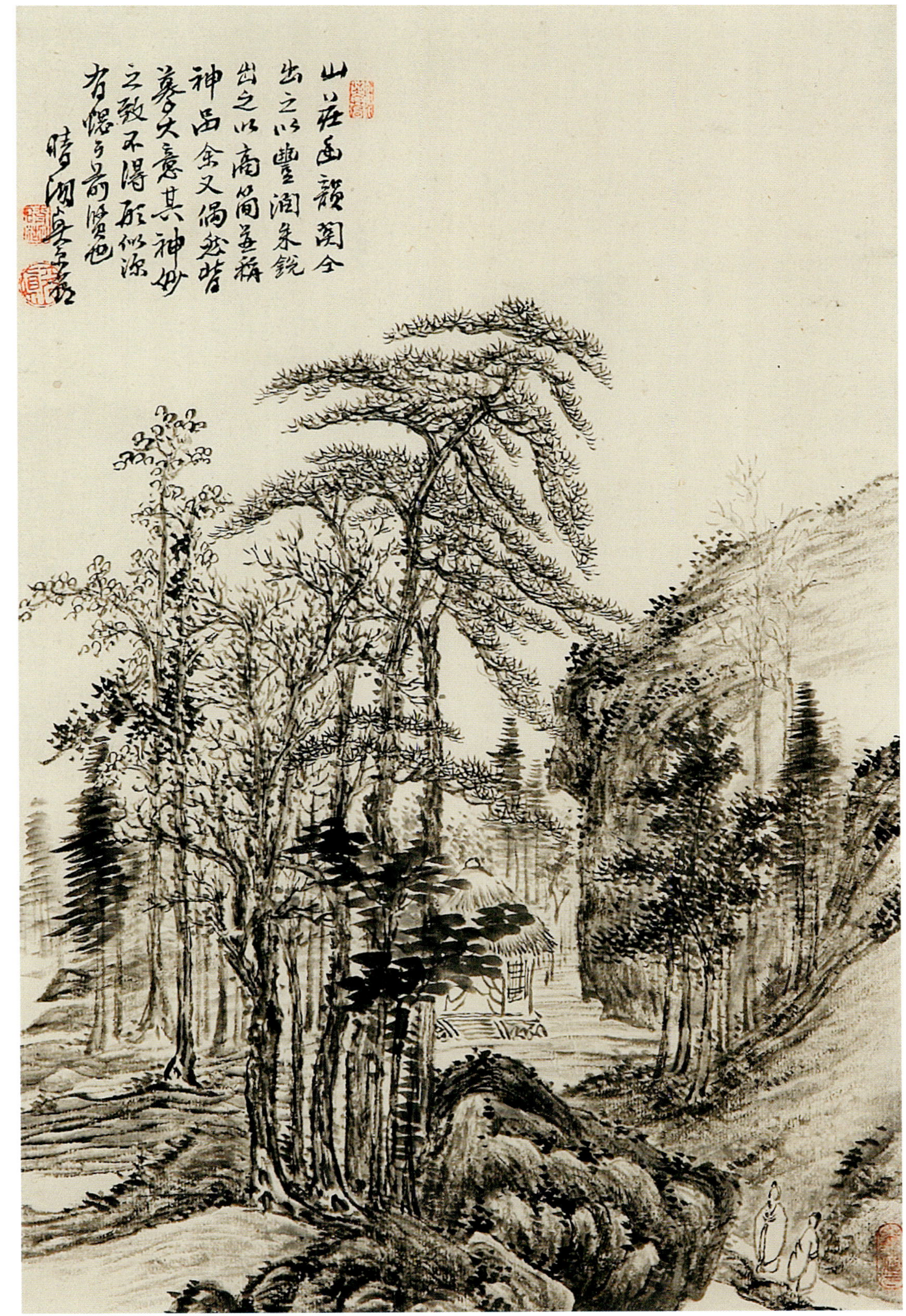

NOTE

1. Fujikake Shizuya, "Okuhara Seiko," *Okuhara Seiko gashū* (Tokyo: Kōgeisha, 1933), 3 and 5. An excellent record of Seiko's study of Chinese and Japanese paintings is found in Koga Rekishi Hakubutsukan, *Okuhara Seiko funpon shiryō mokuroku* (Koga, 2002). It lists 788 examples, giving painting titles and signatures of the works Seiko copied.

Maeda Mokuhō 前田默鳳

1853–1918

Maeda Mokuhō became most well known for his research into ancient Chinese styles of calligraphy as part of a broader epigraphy movement known as *kinsekigaku* 金石学, or the study of metal and stone, after the bronze vessels and stone stele that best preserve the writings of antiquity. These studies, based on ink rubbings of original inscriptions, first became popular in the Northern Song period, and after a modern enthusiasm developed in eighteenth- and nineteenth-century China, the movement spread to Japan in the late Meiji period. The research led to new antiquarian trends in calligraphy styles that affected painters as well as calligraphers. Mokuhō was a friend of Nakamura Fusetsu 中村不折 (1866–1943), founder of the Shodō Hakubutsukan 書道博物館,[1] the museum of calligraphy in Tokyo, and his interest led him to make repeated trips to China in search of rare stele inscriptions.

Mokuhō's research inspired his development of new calligraphy styles, which were influenced by the ancient examples he collected and also affected the brushwork and themes he used in painting. Eventually he presented his findings in a book that asserted the fundamental identity of calligraphy and painting.[2] Although best known as a calligrapher, Mokuhō made a wide variety of paintings in which he applied his theories. He created many paintings of ancient bronze vessels similar to those in fashion among contemporary Chinese painters in Shanghai. Yet his startling landscape compositions are his most dramatic works.[3]

For thousands of years, unusual mountain peaks and oddly shaped rocks have been prized in China as expressing the mysterious power of nature. This attitude encouraged painters to create fantastic vistas that sometimes exceed those found in reality. The strange prominences and vertical peaks of *Landscape Inspired by a Poem on Zhongshan* are reminiscent of exposed basaltic columns, although the stone arches add an unworldly, dreamlike atmosphere. Pines and other trees with autumnal colors enliven the otherwise stark expanse of massive rock walls and silhouetted distant spires. The bold, stiffly brushed outlines of the mountains and plants carry out Mokuhō's idea of using ink strokes from regular and clerical styles of calligraphy in his painting. The overall composition is expressive of a mental landscape rather than a literal view of nature.

The inscription consists of the first four couplets of five-character lines that form the first of five verses on Mount Zhongshan 鍾山 by the noted historian and poet Shen Yue 沈約 (441–513):[4]

霊山記地徳	Spirit Mountain records the virtue of the land;
險峭資嶽霊	Its severity enhances the spirit of the peak.
終南表秦観	Mount South End marked the place of the Qin tower;
少室邇王城	Mount Lesser Chamber was near the royal city.
翠鳳翔淮海	Emerald phoenix soars above the Qinhuai River and the sea;
衿帯繞神坰	Natural defenses surround this sacred land.
北阜何其峻	Northern summit—how severe,
林薄杳葱青	Woods a pale, indistinct green.[5]

Shen's poetry celebrates the ideal of reclusion in nature and has been compared to that by the even more famous Tao Yuanming 陶淵明 (365–427). Stele inscriptions from the Six Dynasties (220–589) were written in the calligraphic styles most admired by those studying epigraphy during Mokuhō's time, and it is natural that he would have selected a verse from this period. This pairing of poetry and dramatic mountain formations rising from water provides a complete expression of Mokuhō's vision of literati painting.

PB

45. *Landscape Inspired by a Poem on Zhongshan*
鍾山詩意山水図 (Shōzan shii sansui zu)

1913
Hanging scroll: ink and color on silk
152.5 × 42 cm

SIGNATURE: *Mokuhō Dōjin* 黙鳳道人
Silent Phoenix Daoist
大正癸丑之夏黙鳳道人寫併録鍾山詩
In the summer of the Taishō year of *kichū* [1913], Mokuhō Dōjin painted this and recorded the *Zhongshan* poem

SEALS: *Den shi* 田氏 (sig. upper)
Mokuhō 黙鳳 (sig. lower)

Purchase, 2005
13206.1

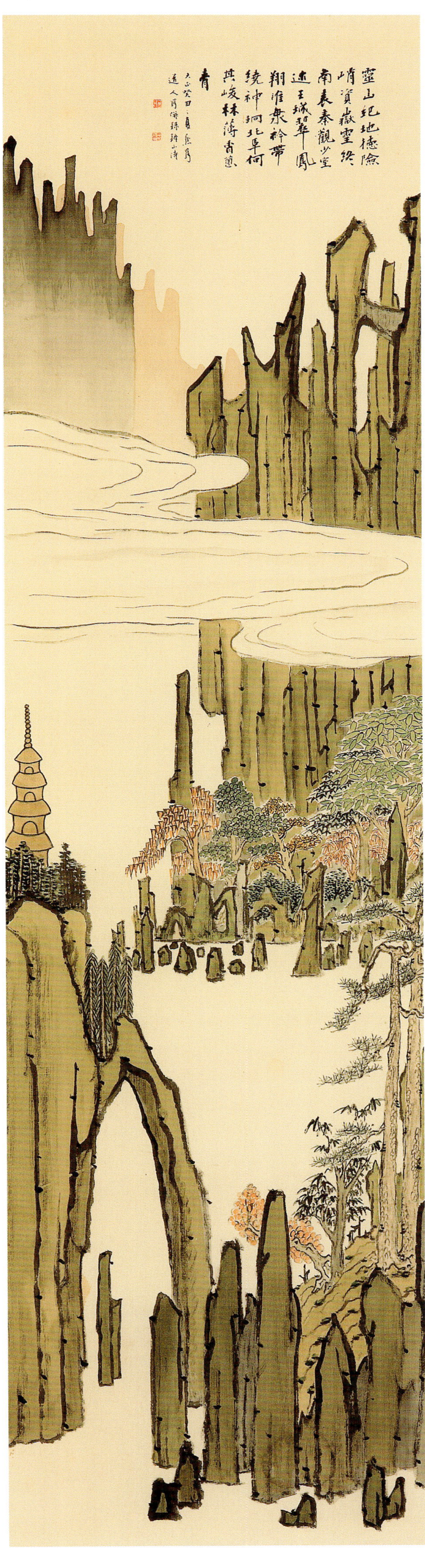

NOTES

1. Refer to cat. no. 12 on Kawahigashi Hekigotō in this catalogue for more information on the central role that Fusetsu played in Japanese studies of epigraphy.

2. *Shoga kenkyūhō*, 2 vols. (Tokyo: Kōkadō, 1910).

3. See the several examples introduced in Paul Berry and Yokoya Kenichirō, *Unexplored Avenues of Japanese Painting: The Hakutakuan Collection* (Ōtsushi: Ōtsushi Rekishi Hakubutsukan; Seattle: University of Washington Press, 2001), plate 58 and illus. on p. 137.

4. See Richard B. Mather, *Shen Yueh (441–513)*, vol. 1, *The Age of Eternal Brilliance*, Sinica Leidensia, 61 (Leiden: Brill, 2003).

5. This translation is adapted from those by Richard B. Mather, *Shen Yueh*, 5, and *The Poet Shen Yueh (441–513)* (Princeton, NJ: Princeton University Press, 1988), 16–17. Consult these works for notations on the geographical references in the poem.

Tomioka Tessai 富岡鉄斎

1836–1924

On the box for this painting, Tomioka Tessai states that he viewed this work and wrote its title on the lid after cleaning his studio on the auspicious day of the emperor's birthday in 1916. Despite the mundane circumstances in which he titled this work, *Sweeping Away the World's Dust* represents the lofty ideals cherished in the literati tradition. A superb example of Tessai's early Taishō work, the painting displays all the features associated with his mature landscape style, such as dynamic ink brushwork and a powerful vertical composition with little regard for spatial depth. Around the time Tessai produced this work, his paintings were the object of much attention and discussion among artists seeking to achieve modern, individual styles. In 1915 one critic bemusedly described Tessai as "an old painter who was new," commenting that the up-and-coming generation of painters who had been vociferously rejecting anything traditional had suddenly found the meaning of self-expression in Tessai's art.[1]

The characteristically dynamic composition of *Sweeping Away the World's Dust* displays a strong sense of structure. It extends vertically in a zigzag manner through repeated rocks and landmasses before ending at a mountain wall with a waterfall. The surging upward movement of the land is relieved by the open space of the river, along which small buildings with figures offer points of interest. Spirited but controlled, Tessai's brush execution matches the forceful, well-constructed composition. Rock forms are generously layered in wet and dry brushwork in a rich range of tones, with rugged strokes outlining the rock edges. Masses of trees follow the contour of the rock outcrops, becoming nearly fused to the active landscape. In late works, Tessai often employed concentrations of bright color to emphasize central motifs. The muted red and green of this painting, however, are harmoniously integrated into the whole and take on a supplementary role, enhancing the beauty of the ink.

At the various mountain retreats in this lively landscape, scholars are quietly engaged in their individual pursuits. For example, in the foreground, two men converse in a house built over the river on pilings, and another man seems to read or write in the building behind. Depicting the popular *bunjin* concept of withdrawing from the vulgar world to live in nature, Tessai reinforced his message in an inscription:

清泉白石與我周旋	Pure spring and white stones all around like friends,
可以樂而忘老	Allowing me to enjoy [life] and forget about growing old.
大正五年八月 四百八十三甲子叟 鐵齋外史	The eighth month of the fifth year of Taishō, Tessai, an old man of 483 *kōshi* [daily cycles][2]

Sweeping Away the World's Dust was once in the collection of the Adachi Museum 足立美術館. One of the best examples of his ink-on-paper landscapes from the early Taishō period, the painting attests to Tessai's brilliance at the height of his creativity: his self-expression and vision of a literati utopia achieve perfect equilibrium in a highly expressive yet loosely disciplined style. Tessai painted prolifically until his death at the age of eighty-eight. His proclivity for dramatic wet brushwork and disregard for spatial depth would increase toward his last years, often making his landscapes appear turbulent or on the verge of dissolving into black masses of ink. MM

46. *Sweeping Away the World's Dust*
掃蕩俗塵 (Sōtō zokujin) T

1916
Hanging scroll: ink and color on paper
149.2 × 39.4 cm

SIGNATURE: *Tessai gaishi* 鐵齋外史

SEALS: 戲之耳 merely amusement (upper right, impressed upside down)
Tessai 銕齋 (sig. upper)
Tomioka hyakuren 富岡百錬 (sig. lower)

PUBLISHED: Tessai Kenkyūsho 鉄斎研究所, *Tessai Kenkyū,* no. 23 (January 1976)

Private collection

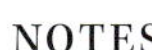

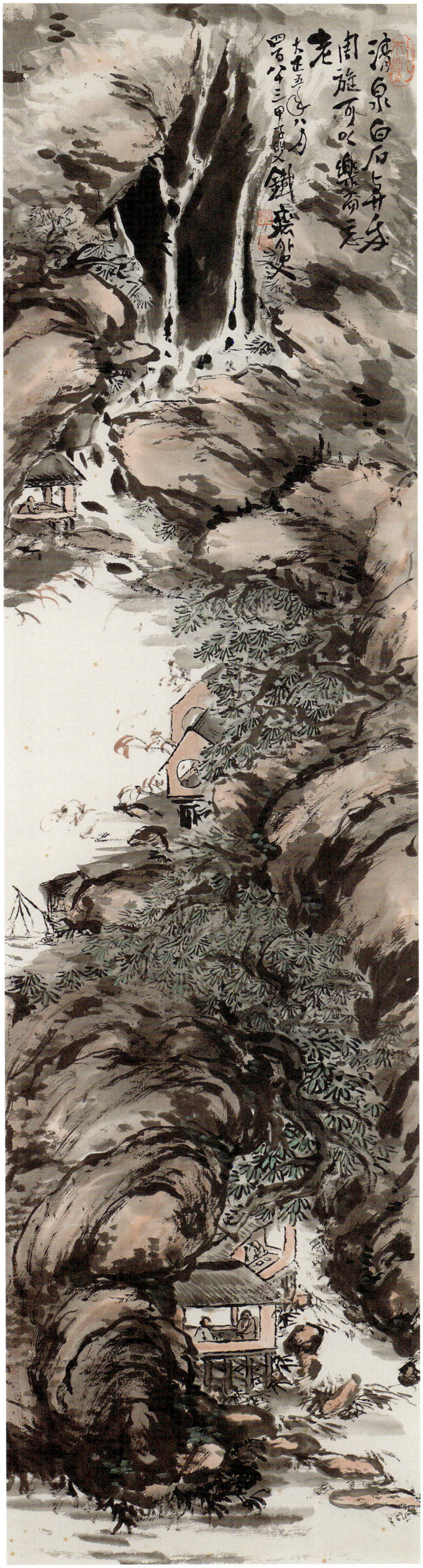

NOTES

1. Misawa Kyūkō, "Fukkatsu shita Tessaiō no seikatsu," *Kaiga seidan* 3, no. 8 (August 1915): 34.

2. Tessai indicated his age by referring to *kōshi,* the sixty pairs of characters used in the Chinese-originated system to specify years in a sixty-year cycle system. The same set of characters were also used to designate a sixty-day cycle in the traditional lunar calendar, resulting in one year consisting of six *kōshi* cycles. Thus 483 divided by 6 results in 80 years plus 180 days (three *kōshi* cycles), making Tessai 81 years old in 1916 (according to the traditional calculation of being one year old at birth). See also note 2 at cat. no. 43 in this volume.

Kobayashi Shunshō 小林春樵

1888–1929?

In this spectacular painting, Kobayashi Shunshō represents one of the most picturesque spots in the Tsukigase valley overlooking the Nabari River. Famous for its plum blossoms, Tsukigase, also referred to as Tsukinose or Tsukise, is located in a dramatic gorge in northeastern Nara prefecture. It was already known as a scenic site in the eighteenth century, when Saitō Setsudō 斉藤拙堂 (1797–1865), a respected scholar in Chinese studies, compiled *Record of the Tsukise Landscape* (Tsukise kishō 月瀬記勝, 1851) to extol its beauty and further spread its reputation during the mid-nineteenth century. Setsudō's two-volume book, which comprised essays and illustrations, was republished in a more portable format in 1884 and became a popular souvenir item in the shops of the Tsukigase area throughout the Meiji and Taishō periods.[1]

Because plum blossoms epitomized the virtues idealized by *bunjin* and the unusual landscape sparked their imaginative spirit, the Tsukigase valley in early spring became an important theme for literati artists. Tomioka Tessai, for example, once expressed his admiration for the valley in a long handscroll.[2] Shunshō's hanging scroll, painted during the Taishō period, reflects the resurgent interest in the literati painting tradition among *nihonga* artists at the time.

In his version, Shunshō transformed the celebrated literati subject into a vibrantly colored landscape of monumental scale. Surveyed from a high vantage point, the valley presents its lively topography in great detail. The near hillside is woven into an irregularly patterned tapestry of terraced fields varying in texture and color. Farmhouses and ramshackle outbuildings line the path that curves toward the river and reappears in a long ribbon across the rounded mountain forms on the opposite side. In the far distance, a clear blue mountain chain rises under an equally blue sky. The overall feeling of pastoral bliss is enhanced by clusters of blossoming white plums, which modestly accent the green-and-brown landscape. Shunshō deemphasized the use of traditional ink outline and employed color more freely, as if working in oil. Devoid of any ostentatious display of skill, his brushwork is unmannered and relaxed, echoing the literati aesthetic. The external world and the artist's internal sentiment coalesce perfectly through the unassuming rhythm of Shunshō's brush and the fusion of *yōga* with the literati mode.

Of the same generation as Hirai Baisen (see cat. nos. 54–57, 73, 75) and Dōmoto Inshō (see cat. no. 75), Shunshō with *Plum Trees in Tsukigase* demonstrated the experimental attitude that gripped young artists during the Taishō period. That Shunshō chose to inscribe the box that contains this work with green pigment instead of ink further indicates his penchant for the untraditional and unconventional.

MM

47. *Plum Trees in Tsukigase*
月ヶ瀬梅林之図
(Tsukigase bairin no zu) T

1910s
Hanging scroll: color on silk
175.5 × 69.2 cm

SIGNATURE: *Shunshō* 春樵

SEAL: (?) *Shunshō* □春樵

Purchase, 2005
13216.1

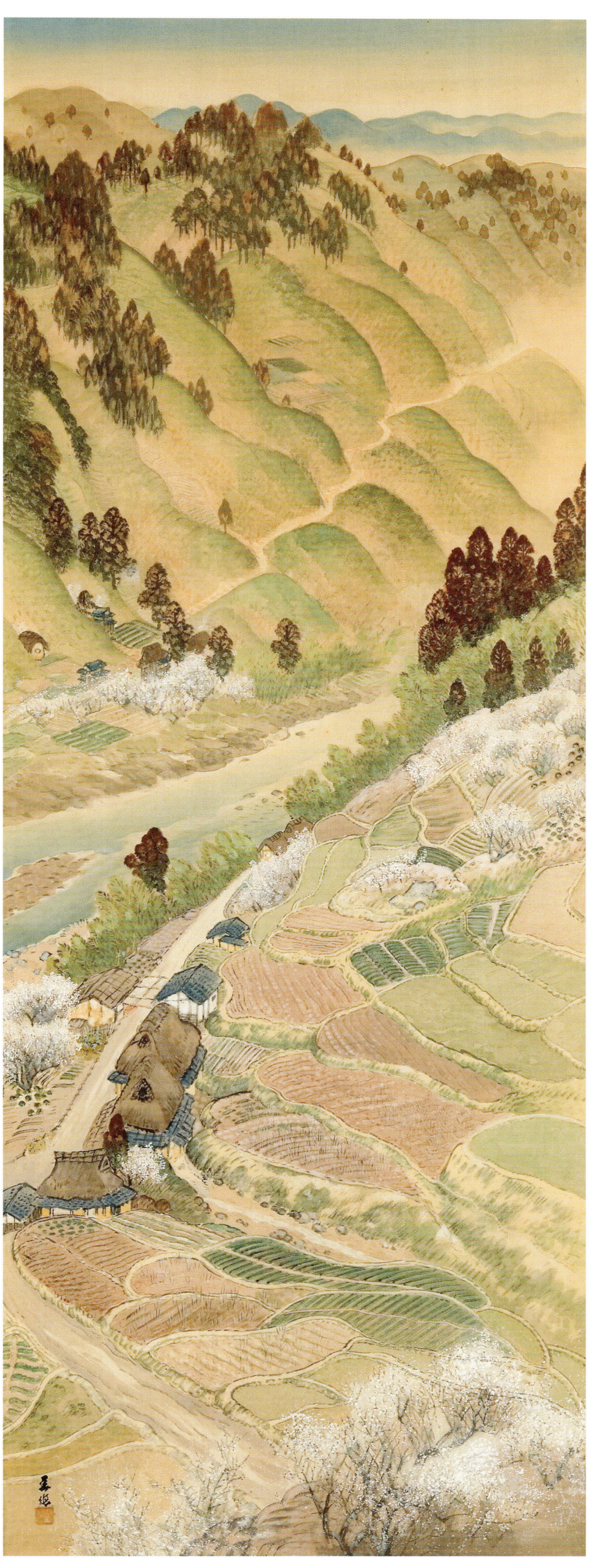

NOTES

1. Inaba Nagateru, *Rekishi sanpo: Tsukigase bairin* (Tokyo: Bunshindō, 1987); see http://jiten.search.biglobe.ne.jp/j/60/09/9f/4a811a2781ce2a93570abb1561348f96.htm (accessed February 2008).

2. Tessai's handscroll is illustrated in Kyōtoshi Bijutsukan, *Seitan 150-nen kinen: Tomioka Tessai ten*, exh. cat. (Kyoto: Kyōtoshi Bijutsukan and Kyōto Shinbunsha, 1985), plate 291.

Tomita Keisen 冨田溪仙

1879–1936

The lyrical beauty of this painting takes one's breath away. Set against layers of wet ink, vivid greens dash across the foliage and distant mountains. Touches of blue and red add further vibrancy. The forms in Keisen's landscape seem to dance and dissolve: the tall trees in the foreground lean precariously over a house, the hillside along the left liquefies in ink washes, and the farthest mountains appear as weightless as cloud and mist. Embraced in the freshness of late spring or early summer, a small boat carries passengers across the water.

The loose brushwork, vivid color, and casual compositional approach are salient features of Keisen's mature style. For his bold brush style, Keisen drew inspiration from Japanese literati masters such as Ike Taiga 池大雅 (1723–1776) and Tomioka Tessai (see cat. nos. 11, 46), while his use of bright color was influenced by *yamatoe* and the Rinpa tradition. Throughout his life Keisen also admired the childlike freedom of Sengai's 仙厓 (1750–1837) art, which he believed derived from the monk's unconstrained, enlightened state of mind.[1] The seeming lack of technical polish in this image was deliberate, for Keisen's early paintings show the mastery he acquired under the tutelage of Tsuji Kakō (see cat. no. 70). Only after years of artistic experiment and soul-searching did Keisen attain his individual style, in which, one critic proclaimed, his "suppression of technique" (*botsu gikō* 没技巧) in fact signified his consummate achievement.[2]

During the 1920s Keisen was a leading artist of Tokyo's Japan Art Institute (Nihon Bijutsuin 日本美術院), although he continued to reside in Kyoto. Both his unconventional painting style and character traits stimulated lively discussions among critics and fellow artists in journals such as *Daimai bijutsu* (November 1925) and *Atorie* (April 1929).[3] Behind the facade of flamboyance and eccentricity, however, Keisen was a sensitive man with a tender spot. This is manifested in *A Boat Crossing a Large River* in quiet details such as the individualized poses of the passengers in the boat, the tiny birds flying over the distant water, and the steps leading to a small structure on the opposite bank. Each of these delicate touches contributes to the painting's overall lyricism. MM

48. *A Boat Crossing a Large River*
泛舟横大江図 T

1926
Hanging scroll: ink and color on silk
133.4 × 51.4 cm

SIGNATURE: *Keisen* 溪仙

SEAL: *Ensōrōjin* 燕巣楼人 Man of Swallow's Nest Pavilion

Gift of Terry Welch, in honor of Griffith and Patricia Way, 2004
13009.1

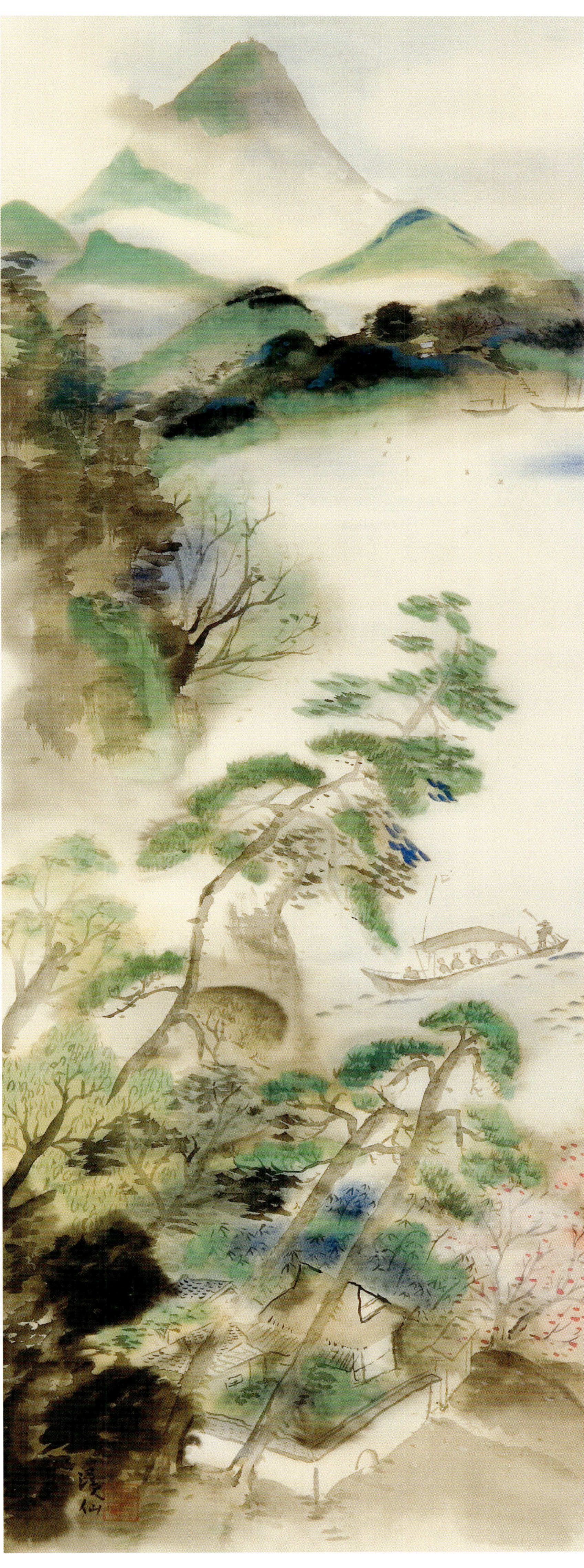

NOTES

1. Tomita Keisen, "Sengai oshō no koto," *Atorie* 8, no. 8 (August 1931): 37.
2. In the words of Tokubi Yō, "Keisen kun no hanmen," *Daimai bijutsu* 4, no. 11 (November 1925): 20.
3. Ibid. and Kotenrō-shujin, "Keisen to Hyakusui," *Daimai bijutsu* 4, no. 11 (November 1925): 18.

Fukuda Kodōjin 福田古道人

1865–1944

Self-taught in painting, the eccentric poet-painter Fukuda Kodōjin created landscapes in a variety of unusual styles. The combination of rough, angular brushwork in the mountains and trees with simple interior washes found in *Mountain Valley in Quiet Mood* is typical of his works from 1912.[1] The poem inscribed on the painting was first published in 1912 as one of four poems in Kodōjin's verse collection, *Seisho's Mountain Studio Collection* (Seisho Sanbō shū 静處山房集):

唯有白雲動	Only white clouds moving,
我心帰一閑	My spirit returns to a point of ease,
超然窮達外	Transcendent—beyond failure or success,
獨坐見空山	Sitting alone viewing the empty mountains.[2]

By the late 1930s, when the box accompanying the painting was inscribed, Kodōjin's style had become more complex and employed soft, curvilinear lines. Because the stylistic evidence for an early date is quite strong, it is likely that the painting was mounted several decades after its creation, and the box date refers to the time of mounting.

The attractiveness of Kodōjin's early style comes from the vigor of the brushstrokes and the rhythmicality of angular forms like those atop the highest peak. The composition of the painting well matches the verse: the abbreviated form below the pine tree is a figure sitting in isolation, watching the movements of white clouds. Kodōjin did not enter competitive painting exhibitions, and he was unconcerned with the technical flourishes necessary to impress selection committees. Ironically, his flouting of convention eventually won him the support of some of the major art patrons in Japan.[3]

PB

49. *Mountain Valley in Quiet Mood*
溪山幽趣図 (Keizan yūshu zu) T

c. 1912; box dated 1939, second month[4]
Hanging scroll: ink on silk
128.2 × 34.8 cm

SIGNATURE: *Kodōjin ga hei dai*
古道人畫并題

SEALS: *mushin* 无心 no mind (upper right)
Fukuda Sekō 福田世耕 (sig. upper)
Seisho 静處 (sig. lower)
Kodōjin 古道人 (bottom right)

Purchase, 2005
13221.1

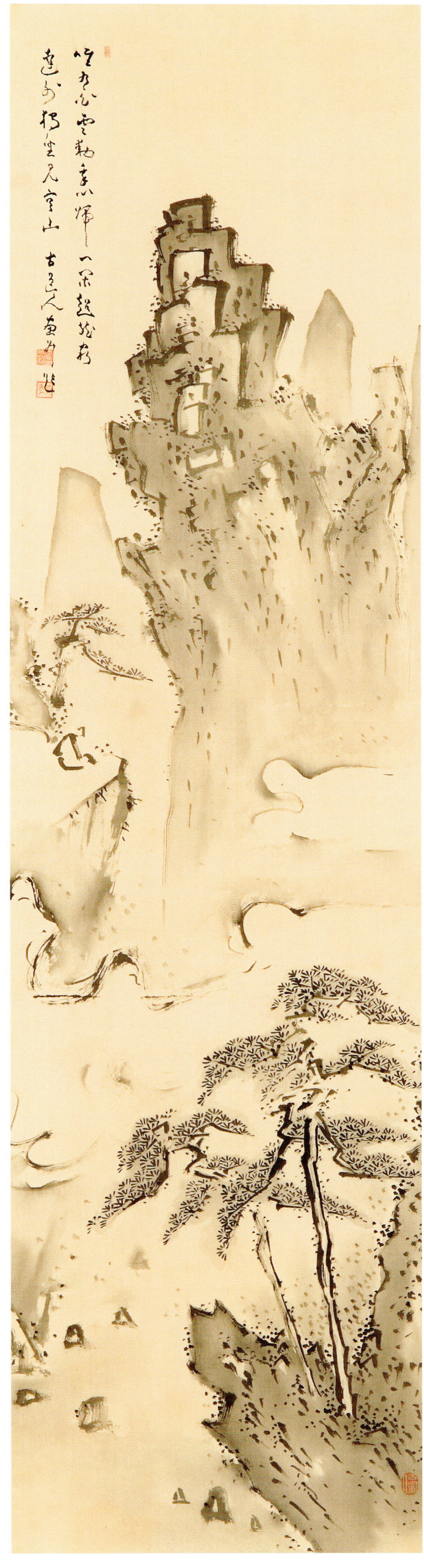

NOTES

1. See a landscape with similar brushwork from 1912 in Stephen Addiss and Jonathan Chaves, *Old Taoist: The Life, Art, and Poetry of Kodōjin (1865–1944)* (New York: Columbia University Press, 2000), color plate 1. Other landscapes with similar technique from 1912 are in private collections in Japan.

2. Refer to Jonathan Chaves's translation of this poem in ibid., 95.

3. See Paul Berry and Yokoya Kenichirō, *Unexplored Avenues of Japanese Painting* (Ōtsu: Shiritsu Rekishi Hakubutsukan; Seattle: University of Washington Press, 2001), 192–93.

4. The title and date are found in the artist's inscription on the box lid of the painting.

Fukuda Kodōjin 福田古道人

1865–1944

Originally noted more for his poetry than his painting, Kodōjin set the tone for his landscapes through his inscriptions. Because the relationship between Chinese verse and painting is one of the defining features of literati painting, Kodōjin's original poems, such as the one transcribed here, were a sophisticated touch much appreciated by his patrons:

蘿月松風夕	Moon seen through ivy, pine breeze in the evening,
秋高石上禪	At the height of autumn, *zazen* atop a stone.[1]
閒去制龍手	At leisure, yet controlling the dragon's claws,
無心獨澹然	With no mind, meditating on calmness.

The poem's references to meditation and controlling dragon claws hark back to "Visiting the Temple of Gathered Fragrance" 過香積寺, a famous poem by Wang Wei 王維 (701–761), a celebrated poet of the Tang dynasty who was traditionally regarded as the founder of literati painting.[2] In Wang's verse, a much quoted line, "Quiet meditation controls poisonous dragons" 安禅制毒龍, is often interpreted to mean that meditation restrains the disturbing passions of the mind. Kodōjin similarly presents meditation as controlling the sharp talons of the dragon's hand. Kodōjin's Chinese verse frequently makes such references to noted poems from the Six Dynasties and Tang periods.[3]

The dramatic vista of *Autumn Spirit—One Pavilion* begins with a boulder-strewn river overhung with pine trees, which are described with the most abbreviated combination of squiggly outlines and rubbed, dry brushwork, suggesting needles. Irregular, pine-covered, rocky precipices tower over the rushing waters in a profusion of twisting lines. A horizontal section of outlined clouds floats around the upper story of a pavilion, concealing all but the tiled ridgepole of a second building. More pines appear above the clouds, which are themselves surmounted by soaring, distant peaks. The brushwork throughout the painting is typical of Kodōjin's untutored approach, its naïveté conveying the appealing sincerity of his thought. PB

50. *Autumn Spirit—One Pavilion*
秋心一亭図 (Shūshin ittei zu) T

1933
Hanging scroll: ink on paper
134 × 28.8 cm

SIGNATURE: *Kodōjin* 古道人

SEALS: *muja* 無邪 not bad (upper right)
Fukuda Sekō 福田世耕 (sig. upper)
Seisho 静處 (sig. lower)

Purchase, 2005
13220.1

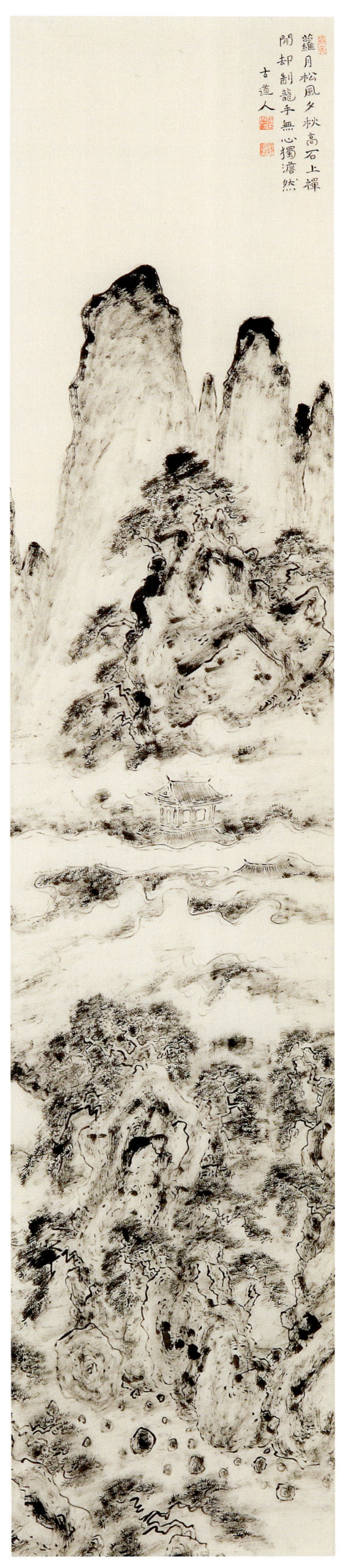

NOTES

1. *Zazen* refers to seated meditation as conducted in Zen Buddhism. Kodōjin's verses include multiple references to Zen.

2. See Pauline Yu, *The Poetry of Wang Wei* (Bloomington: Indiana University Press, 1988), 145.

3. See Jonathan Chaves's discussion of Kodōjin's Chinese verse in Stephen Addiss and Jonathan Chaves, *Old Taoist: The Life, Art, and Poetry of Kodōjin (1865–1944)* (New York: Columbia University Press, 2000).

Kondō Kōichiro 近藤浩一路

1884–1962

The years between 1918 and 1923 marked a turning point in Kondō Kōichiro's artistic career. Established as a successful cartoonist-illustrator in the mid-1910s, Kōichiro abandoned oil-painting practice and began working earnestly in the traditional Japanese medium of ink. Success came quickly. In 1919 the Japan Art Institute (Nihon Bijutsuin 日本美術院) accepted his three *nihonga* entries for its annual exhibition.[1] Two years later he became a member of this prestigious Tokyo art group. *Winter Mountain* is an invaluable example from Kōichiro's earliest *nihonga*. Only a handful of his works from this crucial time are known today.

During this transformative period, Kōichiro became active in the Red Jar Group (Sekiyōkai 赤甕会) and the Coral Group (Sangokai 珊瑚会). The members of these art organizations were primarily *yōga*-trained artists who were introducing new approaches to *nihonga*. The Red Jar Group exhibited *nihonga* paintings by *yōga* graduates of the Tokyo School of Fine Arts, including Kōichiro. One of the eight works Kōichiro showed at the seventh Red Jar exhibition, held in Tokyo in 1920, was titled *Winter Mountain* (Fuyu no yama 冬の山).[2] It is likely that the painting in the Honolulu Academy of Arts collection is related to this work or may be the same one.

While details of the Red Jar Group's activities await further research, recent scholarship has brought to light the contribution of the Coral Group to the Taishō art world.[3] By the time Kōichiro joined in 1918, the three-year-old group included Ogawa Usen 小川芋銭 (1868–1938), Hirafuku Hyakusui 平福百穂 (1877–1933), Morita Tsunetomo 森田恒友 (1881–1933), Ogawa Senyō 小川千甕 (1882–1971), and Kawabata Ryūshi 川端龍子 (1885–1966). Like Kōichiro, they had worked as cartoonists and/or illustrators, shared a love of haiku and *haiga* painting, and were bringing new sensibilities to *nihonga*. Reflecting this experimental attitude, Kōichiro's known works from this period display a wide stylistic range.[4] In the handscroll *Flowers in Rain along the Sumida Riverbank* (Bokutei kau 墨堤花雨, 1918), Kōichiro combined literati-inspired free brushwork in ink and color with incisive figural depictions reminiscent of cartooning. In the following year he sought to create a realistic sense of light in the landscape *Morning Sun* (Asa no hi 朝の日) by adopting the traditional *urahaku* 裏箔 technique of applying gold leaf to the back of silk. In turn, *Morning Twilight* (Reimei 黎明, c. 1920) displayed dazzling color with an extensive use of gold over vivid blues and greens. Several works from this time attest his admiration for the expressive dry-brush style of Uragami Gyokudō 浦上玉堂 (1745–1820).[5]

In subject and style, *Winter Mountain* relates to the aforementioned *Morning Sun,* one of the three paintings marking Kōichiro's impressive debut at the 1919 Japan Art Institute exhibition. In the quiet landscape, moisture-saturated white clouds hang heavily in the gloomy sky, and a single tree stands in the fallen snow on the mountain below. A bright blue band, most pronounced between the lowest ribbon of cloud and the mountain, can be read either as part of the sky or as water in the distance. With no clear indication of the scale of the tree or the mountain, the spatial expression and perspective remain ambiguous, as often happens on a snowy day. The amorphous image recalls *Hidakagawa* (日高川, 1919) by Murakami Kagaku 村上華岳 (1888–1939), in which *yamatoe*-inspired mountains are accented by a tree in the background. In *Winter Mountain,* however, Kōichiro employed a much looser technique, as if working in Western watercolor, layering ink and color in broad sweeps and applying only minimal linear definition.

As in *Morning Sun,* the true theme of this painting, deriving from the artist's earlier training in *yōga,* is the realistic depiction of light and atmosphere. The muted light filtering through the air and shimmering on the surface of the snowy landscape turns the ordinary scene into an utterly unworldly one. Kōichiro achieved this by enveloping the mountain in a translucent veil of *gofun* white and gold wash. *Winter Mountain* is a testament to Kōichiro's synthesis of *yōga* aesthetics with *nihonga* materials and techniques, an approach he continued later even when working almost exclusively in *sumi* ink.[6]

MM

51. *Winter Mountain* 冬乃山 (Fuyu no yama) T

c. 1920

Hanging scroll: color on paper

144 × 50 cm

SIGNATURE: *Kōichiro saku* 浩一路作
Painted by Kōichiro

SEAL: *Kōkōya* 浩浩乎(?)

Purchase, 2005

13222.1

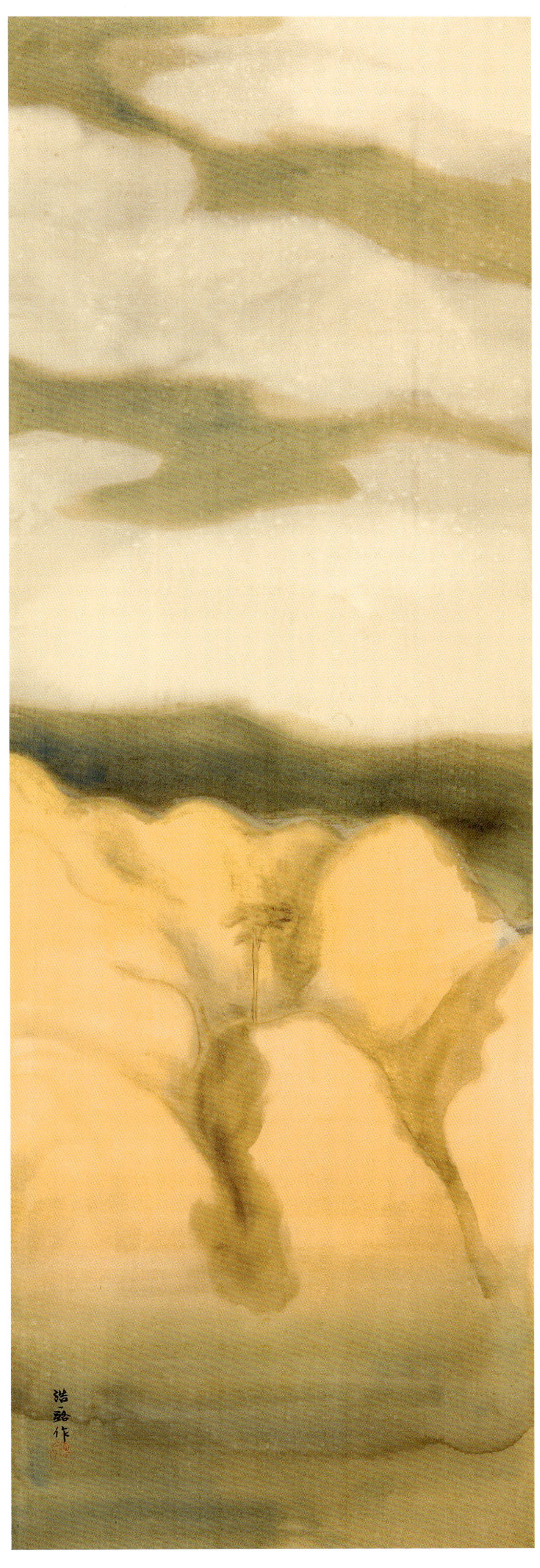

NOTES

1. The institute jury accepted only 8 out of 534 submissions that year; see Hirabayashi Akira, "Kondō Kōichiro no gagyō—Inten jidai o chūshin ni," in *Hikari no suibokuga: Kondō Kōichiro no zenbō*, ed. Noji Kōichirō and Hirabayashi Akira, exh. cat. (Tokyo: Yomiuri Shinbun Tōkyō Honsha and Bijutsukan Renraku Kyōgikai, 2006), 14.

2. Noji and Hirabayashi, *Hikari no suibokuga*, 186.

3. For a detailed discussion of the Coral Group, see Kikuya Yoshio, "Sangokai ronkō," *Bijutsu kenkyū*, no. 377 (February 2003): 30–58.

4. Kōichiro's early *nihonga* examples, including those mentioned here, are illustrated in Noji and Hirabayashi, *Hikari no suibokuga*, 14, 28–31, and 36–37.

5. Hirabayashi, "Kondō Kōichiro no gagyō," 14.

6. On Koichiro's continuing experiments with traditional material and techniques, see Ono Michitaka, "Kondō Kōichiro shōron," *Hōshun*, no. 286 (April 1979): 18–20.

Kondō Kōichiro　近藤浩一路

1884–1962

Kondō Kōichiro took up ink painting after working in black and white as a cartoonist during the mid-1910s. His interest in *sumi* ink, however, had emerged almost a decade earlier, while he was studying *yōga* at the Tokyo School of Fine Arts. Urged by a student in the *nihonga* division, Kōichiro bought his first Chinese brush for ink painting around 1907.[1] In 1911, one year after graduating, he organized a joint exhibition of ink painting in *hankiri* size (approx. 45 × 15 cm) 水墨画半切展 with his classmate Fujita Tsuguji 藤田嗣治 (1886–1968).

Although he continued to show oil paintings at various venues until 1913, Kōichiro eventually switched to *nihonga* and became a member of the Japan Art Institute (Nihon Bijutsuin 日本美術院) in 1921. During this period of transition, Koichiro experimented both in strong color and with ink. In *Amatsu in Awa Province* (Bōshū Amatsu 房州天津, 1918), he sketched a fishing village in a narrow (less than 18 cm) but long (5.4 m) handscroll, displaying brushwork so ebullient that the ink seems about to liquefy on the paper.[2] *Six Views of Cormorant Fishing* (Ugai rokudai 鵜飼六題), shown at the Japan Art Institute exhibition in 1923, is his best-known work. Featuring six large paintings in a horizontal handscroll format, it showcases the artist's novel handling of ink and unconventional compositions, successfully evoking the poetic mood of night fishing and the dramatic effect of its illumination.

One year after his success with *Six Views of Cormorant Fishing,* Kōichiro recorded his thoughts on *sumi* ink:

> For example, take piano in music. One can create an infinite number of harmonies and melodies by combining the notes between the extreme high and the extreme low key from its range. Likewise, ink also offers infinite variations of dark and light, or of modulation, before it reaches white. In fact, I regard black ink and the color white as part of ink's tonality; they represent the ultimate opposites. . . . Ink itself does not possess five colors. Only by interacting with white can it begin to create beautiful music and color.[3]

Rocky Shore fully demonstrates Kōichiro's words, displaying the full gradation of ink tones between black and white. He employed the darkest ink for rendering the rocks and birds while reserving the white of the paper and the faintest gray to represent the powerful rays of the sun and its reflection upon the water. The humorous depiction of cormorants hints at Kōichiro's background as a cartoonist-illustrator. Although Kōichiro portrayed the effect of light in countless paintings, works representing the sun itself are small in number. For the magnificent sun in *Rocky Seashore,* Kōichiro applied unconventional long brushstrokes, as if inspired by Van Gogh. In contrast, swirls and wavy lines, executed with playful freedom, convey the complex movement and rushing sound of water through jutting rocks. The animated, rhythmic brushwork and rich tonal range indeed correspond to Kōichiro's notion of creating "beautiful music and color" in ink. Furthermore, the artist achieved a perfect balance between the phenomena of the external world and his personal ink brush style. In later years Kōichiro would increasingly focus on the moment-by-moment shift of light and often would sacrifice expressive brushwork for a more objective approach.

The subject of the shore was clearly among his favorites. One of the paintings Kōichiro showed at the Japan Art Institute members' exhibition in Czechoslovakia in 1930 was titled *Rocky Seashore,*[4] and another painting of the same title was included at his solo exhibition in 1935.[5] In 1936, when Kōichiro withdrew from the Japan Art Institute, he moved to a town in northern Tokyo prefecture and named his home Earthen Brush Residence (Dohitsukyo 土筆居). The painting style and the signature "Kōichiro at the Earthen Brush Residence" on this work suggest its date as the later 1930s.[6]

MM

52. *Rocky Seashore* 荒磯 (Araiso) T

Late 1930s
Hanging scroll: ink on paper
129.6 × 29.4 cm

SIGNATURE: 於土筆居浩一路 Kōichiro at the Earthen Brush Residence

SEAL: *Gachūsai* 画虫斎 Studio of Painting Worm

Purchase, 2005
13223.1

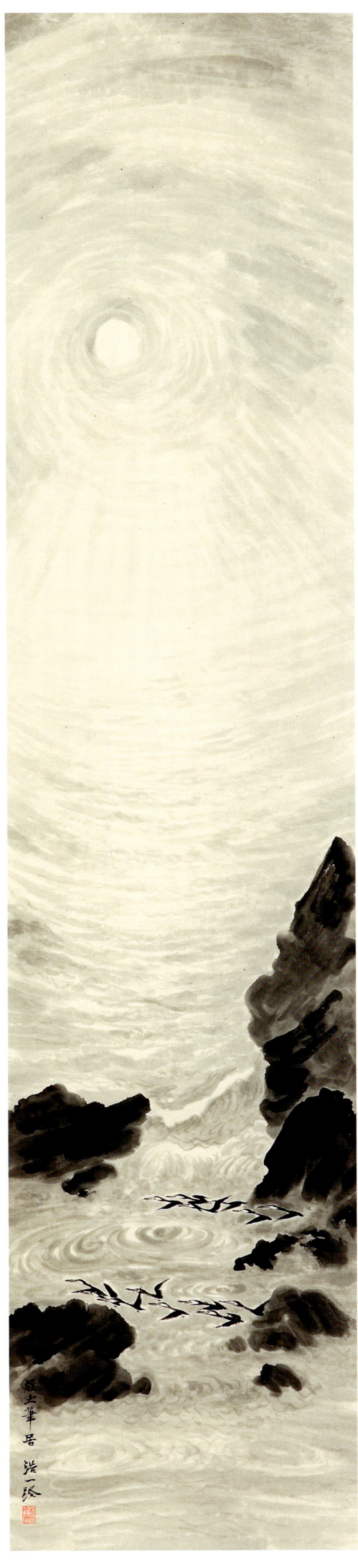

NOTES

1. Kawauchi Eriko, "Kondō Kōichiro—Sumi tono taiwa," in Sano Bijutsukan, *Bokusai no shijin: Kondō Kōichiro* (Mishima: Sano Bijutsukan, 2002), 88–89.

2. For a good reproduction of this painting and *Six Views of Cormorant Fishing*, see Noji Kōichiro and Hirabayashi Akira, eds., *Hikari no suibokuga: Kondō Kōichiro no zenbō*, exh. cat. (Tokyo: Yomiuri Shinbun Tōkyō Honsha and Bijutsukan Renraku Kyōgikai, 2006), 33–35, 74–77.

3. Kondō Kōichiro, "Bokuga ni tsuiteno kansō," *Chūō bijutsu* 10, no. 9 (September 1924), reprinted in Kanagawa Kenritsu Kindai Bijutsukan and Yamanashi Kenritsu Bijutsukan, *Kondō Kōichiro ten*, exh. cat. (Kōfu: Yamanashi Kenritsu Bijutsukan, 1979), no pagination.

4. Noji and Hirabayashi, *Hikari no suibokuga*, 187.

5. Saida Soshū, "Kondō Kōichiroshi koten," *Tōei* 12, no. 1 (January 1936): 52.

6. The *Gachūsai* seal on this painting derives from a comment made by a novelist friend, Shiga Naoya, around 1927 that Kōichiro was "a painting worm," as in "bookworm"; Noji and Hirabayashi, *Hikari no suibokuga*, 187.

Gotō Shūgai 後藤秋涯

1886–1979

53. *Idle Pleasures* 閒怡

1920s
Album of twelve leaves: ink and color on silk
27 × 17.8 cm each

SIGNATURES:
title page: *Shūgai dōjin sho* 秋涯道人書
leaves 1, 2, 4, 6–10, 12: *Shūgai dōjin sha* 秋涯道人寫
leaves 3, 5, 11: *Shūgai dōjin* 秋涯道人
postscript: *Nyoi sankyaku sho* 如意山客書

SEALS:
title page: *Rochūjin* 蘆中人 (upper right), *Han'un sansō* 半雲山荘 (sig. upper), *Shūgai* 秋涯 (sig. lower)
leaves 1–12: *Shūgai* 秋厓 (sig. upper), *Nin shizen* 任自然 Indulge in nature (sig. lower)
postscript: *Rochūjin* 蘆中人 (upper right), *Musoku* 無息 (sig. upper), *Shūgai* 秋厓 (sig. lower)

Purchase, 2005
13158.1

Gotō Shūgai's superb album *Idle Pleasures,* representing popular *bunjin* retreats and activities, shares the literati ideals that inspired Fujimoto Tesseki (see cat. no. 76) some seventy years earlier when he made a similarly themed album. Such albums follow the tradition established by *Ten Pleasures and Ten Conveniences* (Jūben jūgi jō 十便十宜帖), the celebrated works painted by two Edo-period literati masters, Ike Taiga 池大雅 (1723–1776) and Yosa Buson 与謝蕪村 (1716–1783). In Shūgai's album, "idle pleasures" not only refers to the various scenes portrayed but also hints at the joy he associated with the act of painting.

Twelve scenes in delightfully colorful, diverse compositions are introduced in a seasonal sequence, opening with the early-winter white plum set against a landscape. Typical of Shūgai's approach, a logical organization of space takes the viewer's eye from the foreground to the back of this leaf. In the second leaf, a willow tree with fresh leaves stands by the lakeshore, and in the third, a man admires blossoming trees from a stone bridge. The bright pigments seen in this leaf and many others in the album indicate Shūgai's indebtedness to the decorative *yamatoe* style. The transition to summer begins with the fourth leaf, in which two gentlemen drink tea and converse. In the next scene, a scholar crosses a rustic bridge into a mist-covered bamboo forest. In the sixth leaf, the only monochrome painting in the entire album, Shūgai represented a rainy landscape in elegant gray ink. The seventh leaf features a man admiring a cascading waterfall, the image of coolness in the summer. The shift to fall starts with the eighth scene, of a scholar seated on a bench by a lush plantain. The ninth leaf lyrically portrays a man on a boat playing a flute under the moon. The autumn season peaks in the next leaf, in which a vivid vermillion maple captivates viewers on a boat. The trees with withered brown leaves in the eleventh leaf signify the winter season. Unique within this album, the composition of this scene emphasizes the two-dimensional patterns created by the spreading tree branches. Bare trees appear in the final snow-covered landscape, in which a scholar is on his way to visit a friend. At this point, the viewer perhaps realizes that the act of looking through the album is itself an idle pleasure.

Shūgai traced his artistic lineage through his teacher Tajika Chikuson 田近竹邨 (1864–1922) and Chikuson's teacher Tanomura Chokunyū 田能村直入 (1814–1907) to the illustrious Edo-period literati master Tanomura Chikuden (see cat. no. 21), who was known for his orthodox style based on the study of Chinese paintings. In fact, Chikuden's *Yet Again, One More Pleasure* (Matamata ichirakujō 亦復一楽帖), another famous album on the theme of ideal *bunjin* enjoyment, included an image of a man playing the flute, although different in composition from Shūgai's work. As declared in his inscription on the thirteenth leaf, Shūgai did not adopt the dramatic brushwork and unconventional approaches favored by the dominant artistic current of the period. Rather, the restrained brushwork and well-structured composition of this album confirm his adherence to the conservative stylistic lineage.

Shūgai's work makes an interesting comparison with an album of similar thematic inspiration by his contemporary Takakura Kangai (see cat. no. 82). Although striking in their stylistic contrast, the albums demonstrate the continuing validity of the traditional literati theme into the twentieth century and the Taishō penchant for vivid color.

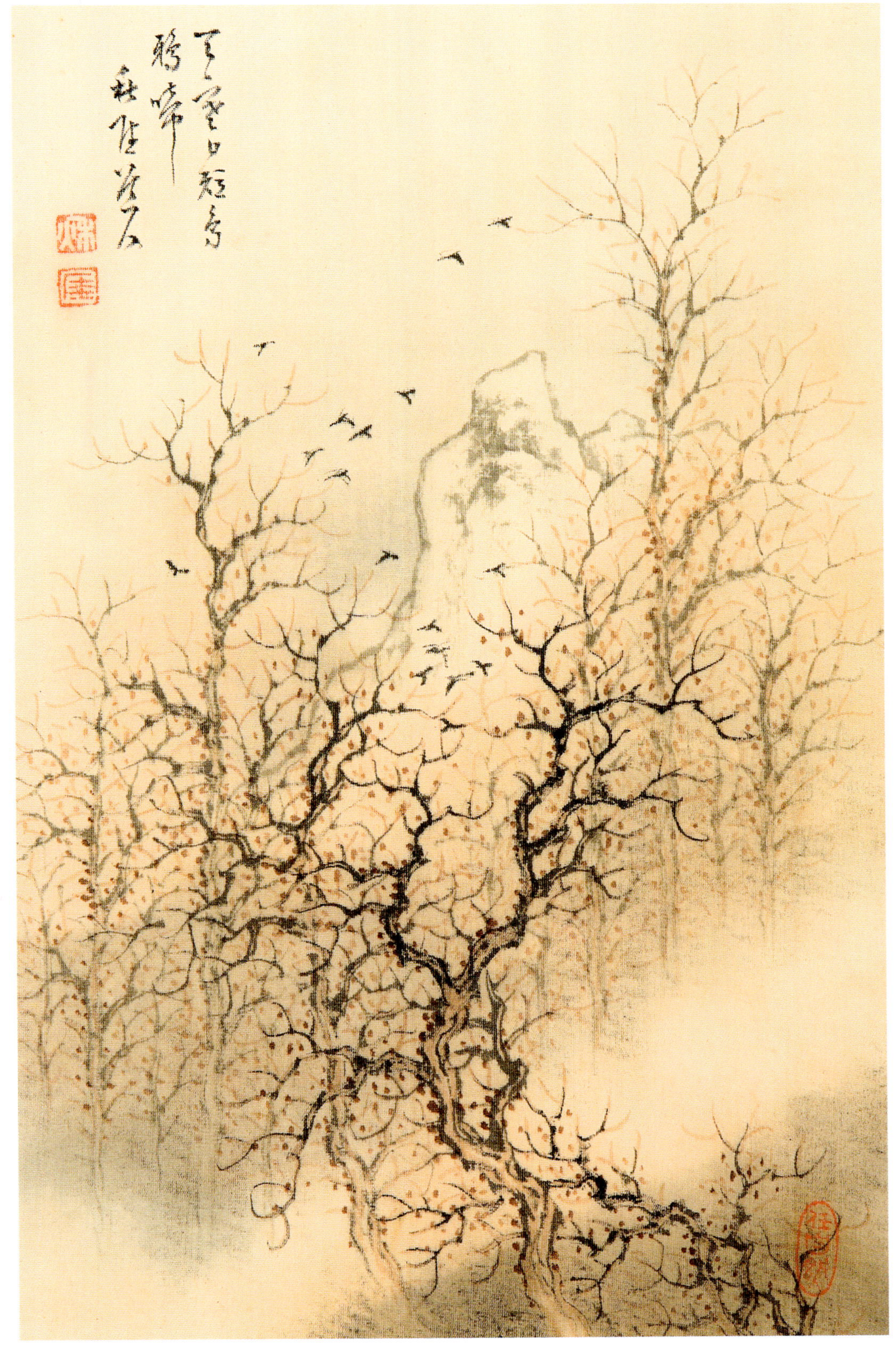

11

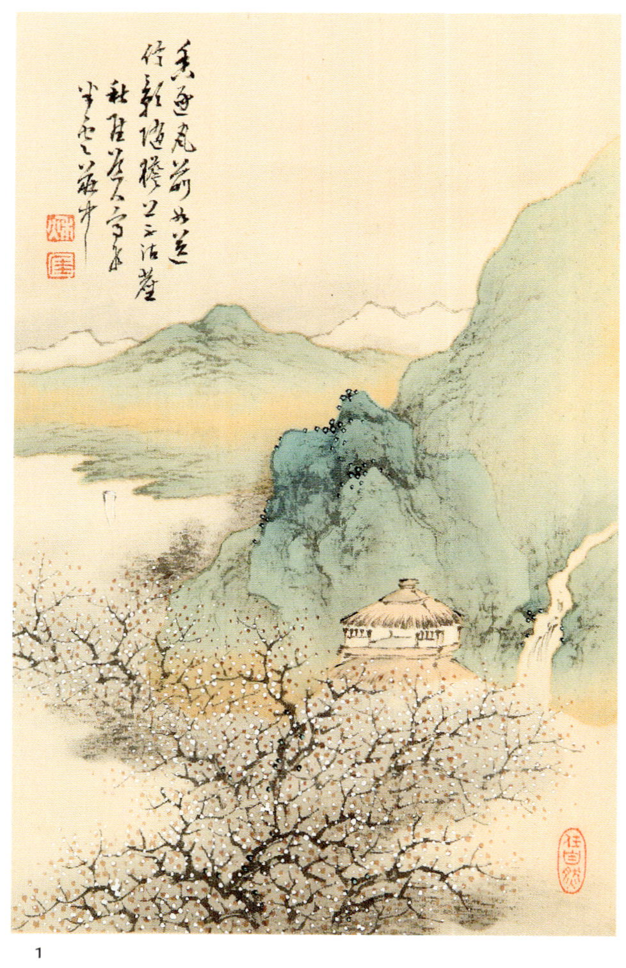

1

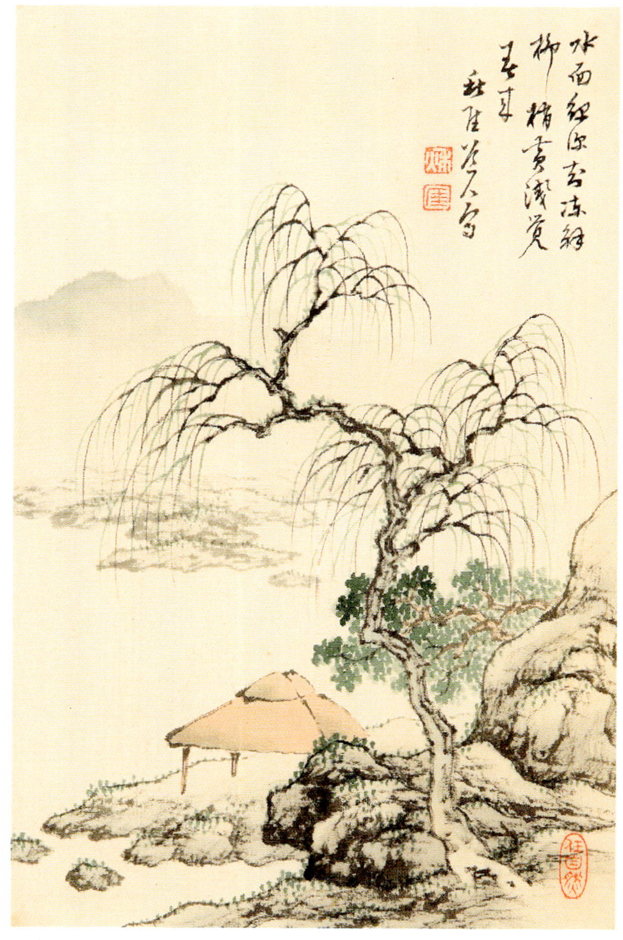

2

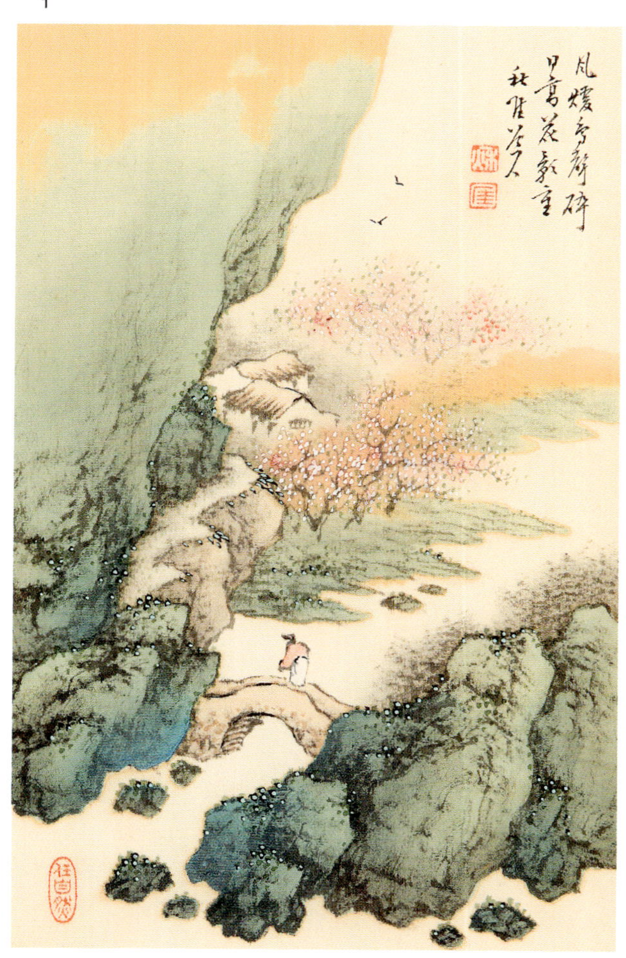

3

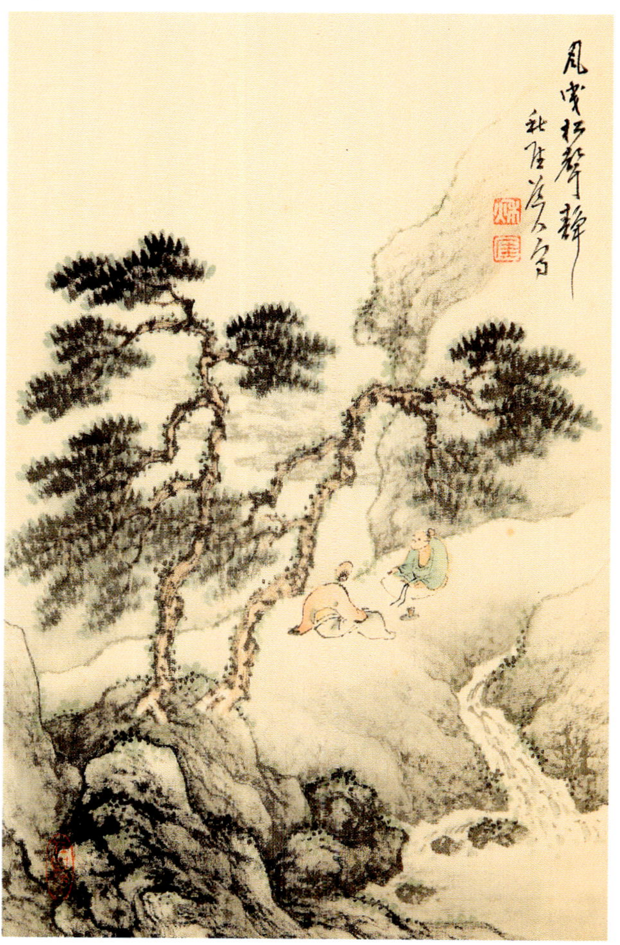

4

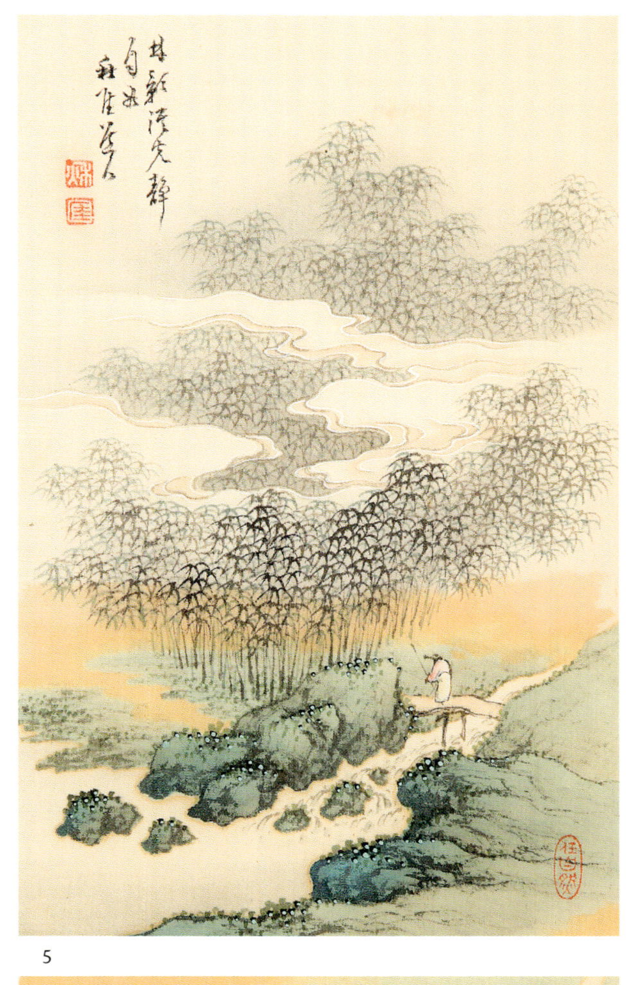

5

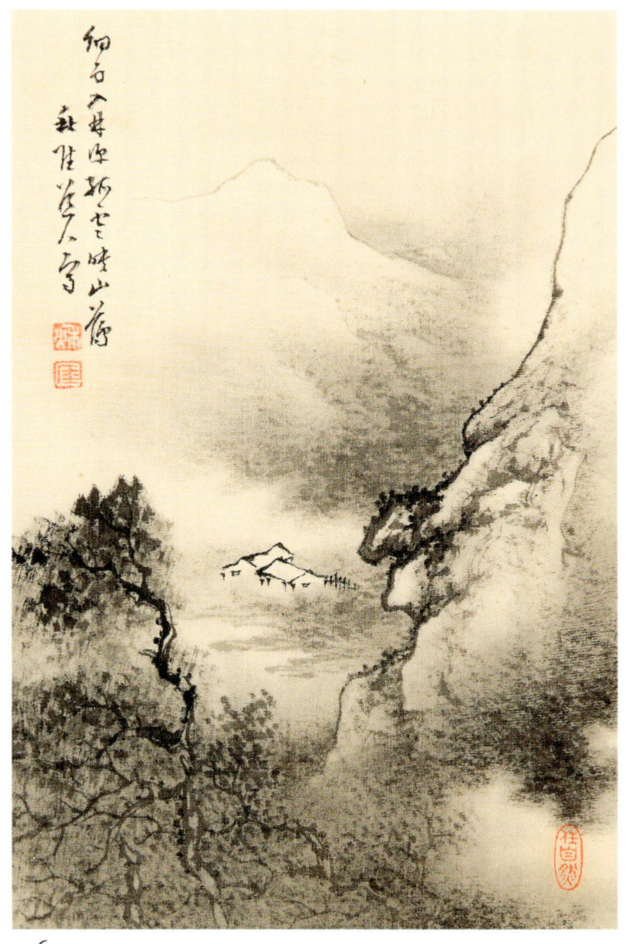

6

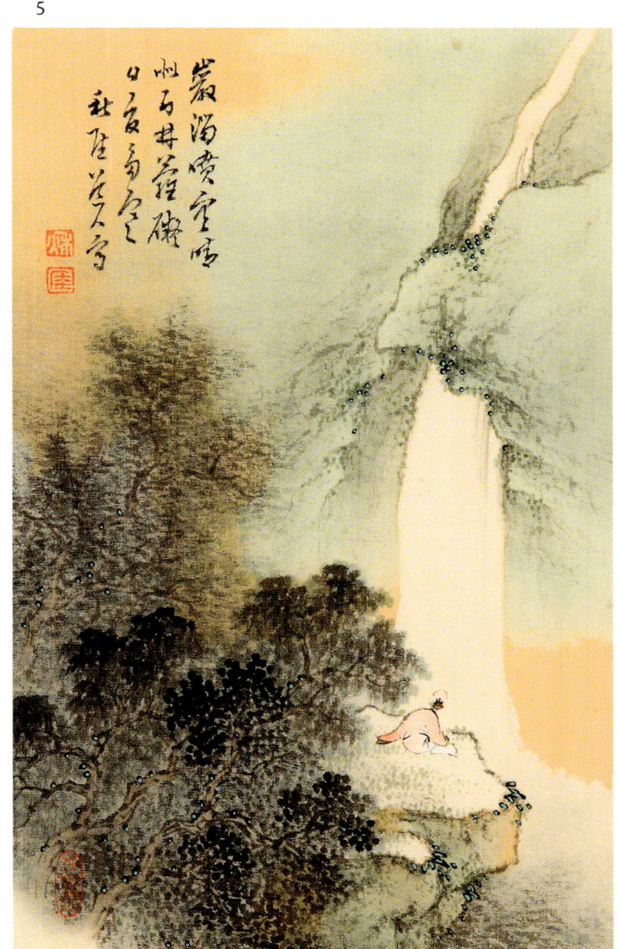

7

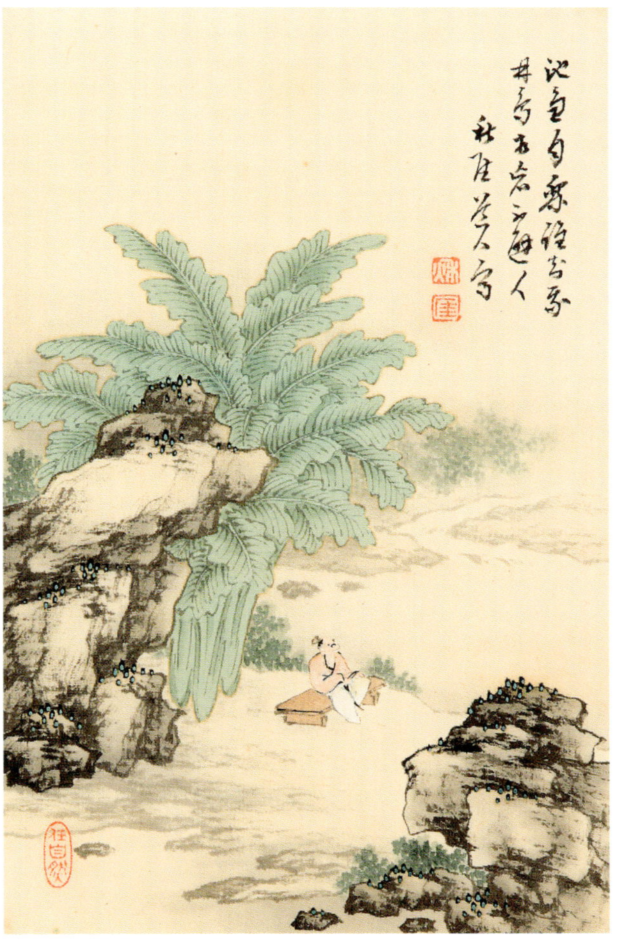

8

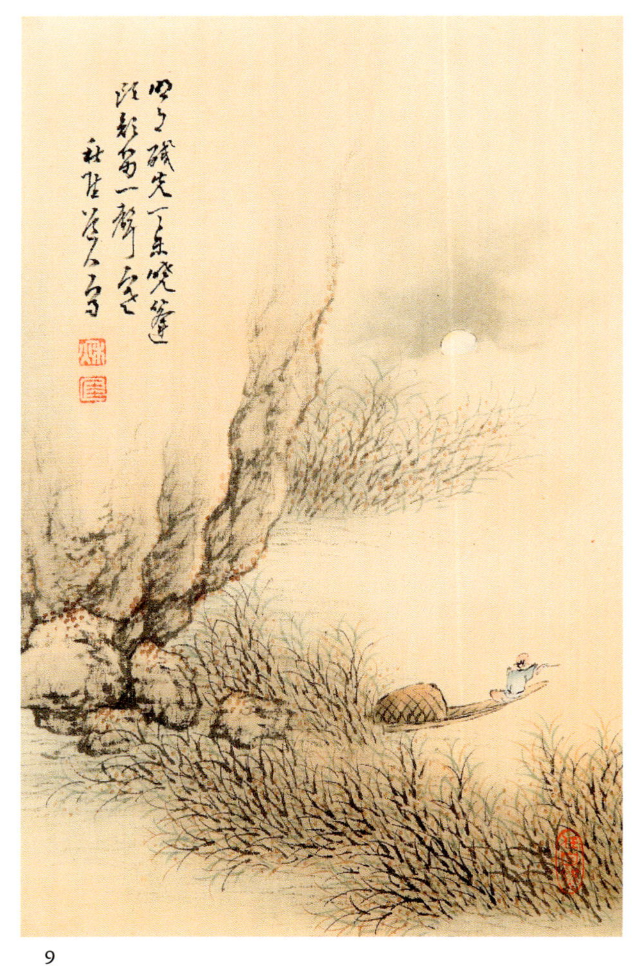

9

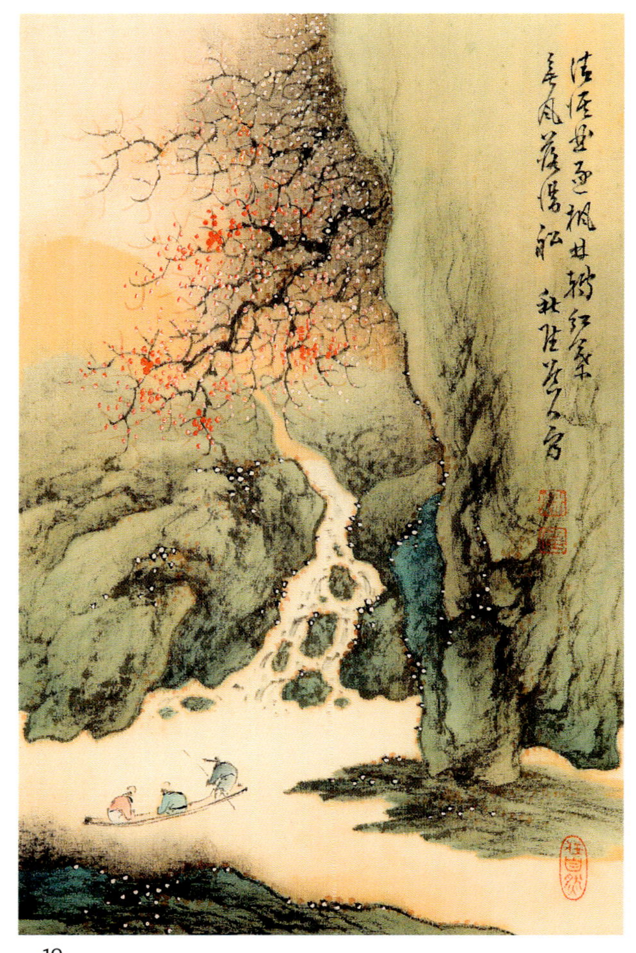

10

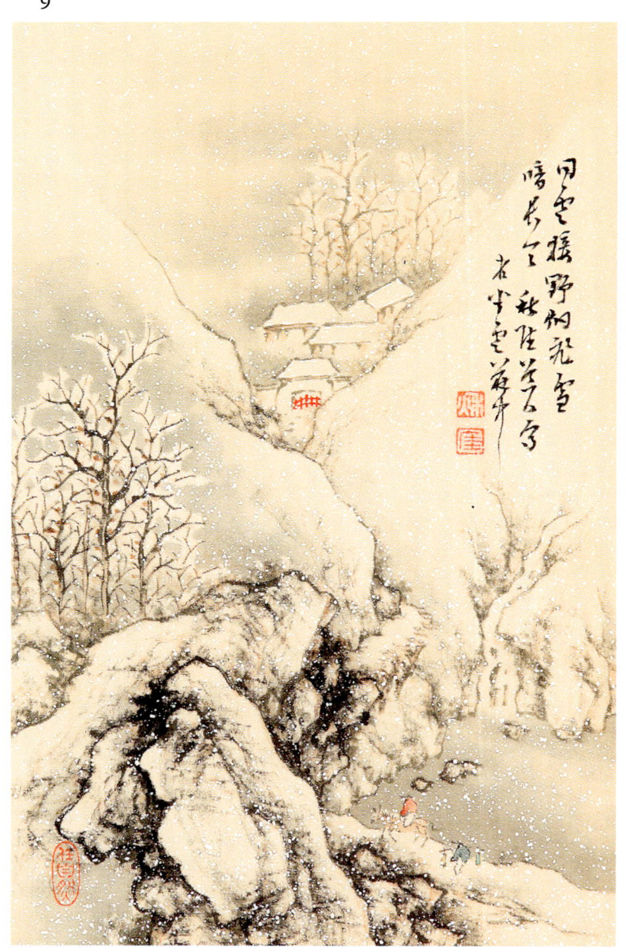

12

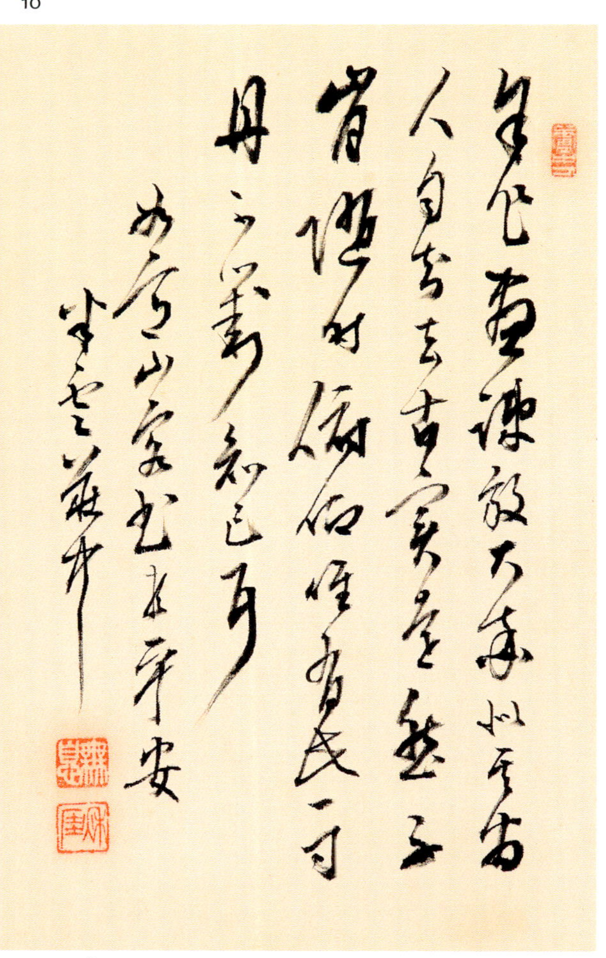

postscript

The inscriptions may be translated as follows:

1. 香逐風前如送竹 Fragrance follows the wind as if to accompany the bamboo;
   影随檐上不沾塵 Shadow [of the plums] follows above the eave, not touching the dust.

2. 水面緑深知凍解 Water is deep green, and we know its frozen surface will melt;
   柳梢黄浅覚春来 Tips of willow branches are light green, and we realize the spring has come.

3. 風煖鳥聲碎 Wind is warm, as the birds' sound scatters;
   日高花影重 Sun is high, as the flowers' shadows are layered.

4. 風曳松聲静 Wind trailing, the sound of pine becomes quiet.

5. 林影溪光静 Shadows of woods and the light of the stream are quiet as they should be.

6. 細雨入林深 Fine rain becomes deep entering the forest;
   孤雲映山薄 Lone cloud becomes thin reflecting on the mountain.

7. 巌溜噴空晴似雨 Waterfall splashes in the air as if rain on a fine day;
   林靄礙日夏多寒 Mist in the forest covers the sun as the summer increases in coolness.

8. 池魚自楽詎知我 Fish in the pond enjoying themselves; why would they care about me?
   林鳥相忘不避人 Birds in the forest, losing themselves, become oblivious of people.

9. 明月残光天未暁 Bright moon remaining, the dawn has not broken;
   篷頭韻笛一聲寒 Sitting in a boat, the sound of the flute is cold.

10. 清溪曲逐楓林轉 Pure stream winds and turns following the maple forest;
    紅葉無風落満船 Red leaves fall even without wind and fill our boat.

11. 天寒日短烏鴉啼 The sky is cold and the day short; the crows cry.

12. 日雲接野地 Sun and cloud touch the earth;
    飛雪暗長天 Flying snow darkens the sky.

Postscript

余作畫疎放
大素似其為人
自知去古実遠
然不肯隨時俯仰
唯有此一寸丹心
以對知己耳

I paint in a carefree manner, generally reflecting my character. I myself know that it is far from the ancients, but I do not wish to follow the fashionable trend of the time. There is only this—one inch of my red heart, with this I face my friends!

如意山客書
於平安半雲荘中

Inscribed by a Hermit Nyoi at Half-Cloud Villa in Kyoto

MM

Hirai Baisen 平井楳仙

1889–1969

Sudden rain was a subject that fascinated Hirai Baisen in the 1910s, when his fame began to spread at major *nihonga* competitions. At the 1914 Taishō Exposition (Taishō Hakurankai 大正博覧会), Baisen shared the top award with the respected female artist Uemura Shōen 上村松園 (1875–1949). One of his entries was titled *Shower Coming* (Shūu kitaru 驟雨来る). In the following year Baisen submitted to the Bunten a set of three paintings, which included *Shower* (Shūu 驟雨), and received the second-place award, the highest given that year. Of nine artists who received the honor, Baisen was the youngest. He had been successful at the Bunten since its inception in 1907, and this new achievement further elevated his standing in the Kyoto *nihonga* community. The Exhibition of New Works by Twelve Great Kyoto Painters, held at the Shirakiya Kimono Shop in Tokyo in 1917, presented Baisen alongside well-established older artists such as Kikuchi Hōbun 菊池芳文 (1862–1918), Takeuchi Seihō 竹内西鳳 (1864–1942), Tsuji Kakō 都路華香 (1870–1931), and Yamamoto Shunkyo 山元春挙 (1871–1933).[1]

Shower over a Mountain Village, dated 1916 by Baisen, comes from the most triumphant and creative period of his career. The work is significant as it closely relates to the 1915 Bunten piece, a depiction of night rain based on the artist's trip to Kinosaki 城崎, a site famous for hot springs in northern Hyōgo prefecture.[2] For the narrower format of this painting, Baisen adjusted the composition by cropping the left side of the earlier work.[3] The result is wonderfully asymmetrical and dramatic. Massive trees soar from the foreground, with the stretch of buildings along the path reinforcing their upward movement, leading the viewer's eye from the tiny kimono-clad figure to the brooding sky above. Faint diagonal ink lines on the surface of the painting indicate the wind and rain striking against trees and houses, introducing an almost auditory element. Baisen depicted most of the foliage by directly applying color dots, as if working in oil. The lively brushwork also recalls the loose brush style associated with the literati tradition. Daring in composition and unconventional in technique, *Shower over a Mountain Village* amply demonstrates the inventive approach that characterized Baisen's oeuvre during the 1910s.

MM

54. *Shower over a Mountain Village*
山市驟雨 (Sanshi shūu) T

1916
Hanging scroll: color on silk
127.2 × 42.4 cm

SIGNATURE: 丙辰春楳仙寫 Painted by Baisen in the spring of the *heishin* year [1916]

SEAL: *Baisen* 楳僊

Purchase, 2005
13210.1

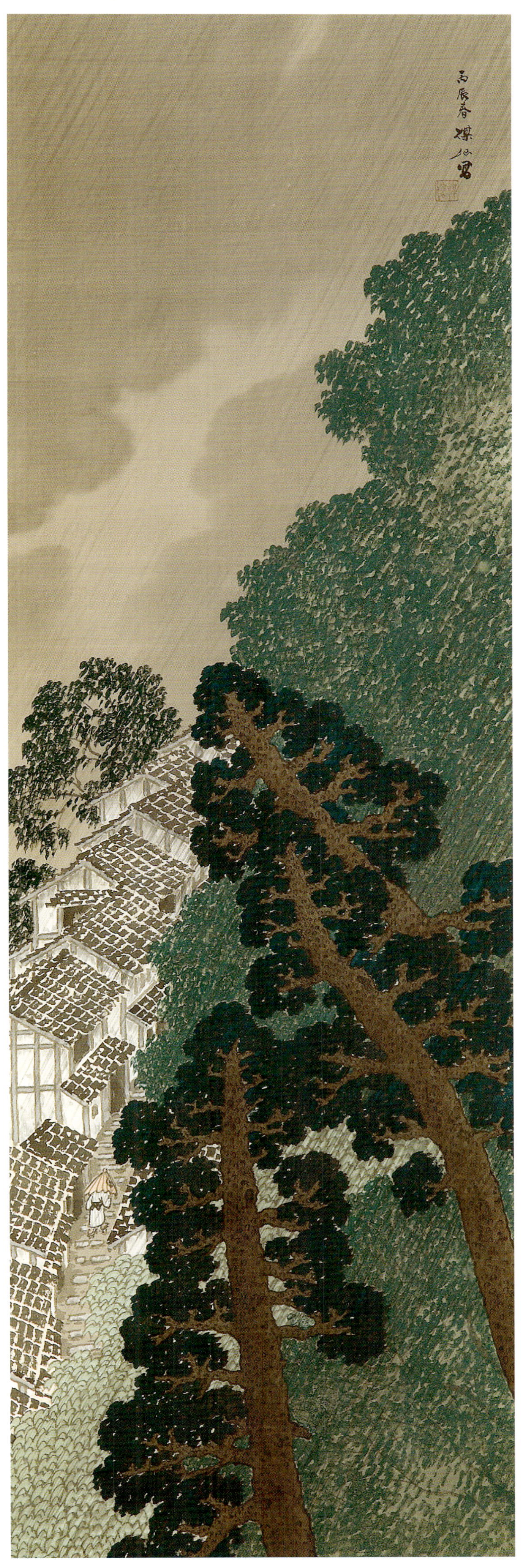

NOTES

1. Taguro Rin, "Banshun no sho tenrankai," *Bijutsu no Nippon* 9, no. 5 (May 1917): 22.

2. "Kinosaki to Kamogawa to ima hitotsu wa risōteki ni kaita," *Kaiga seidan* 3, no. 10 (November 1915): 68.

3. For Baisen's 1915 Bunten painting, see Nittenshi Hensan Iinkai, *Nittenshi 4, Buntenhen 4* (Tokyo: Nitten, 1981), 134.

Hirai Baisen 平井楳仙

1889–1969

The most extraordinary feature of *Cloud over Mount Hiei* is the heavily layered green brushwork of the tree foliage that covers nearly half the painting's surface. The direct application of color, adopted from oil painting and also inspired by the freedom of literati brushwork, was popular among *nihonga* artists at the time as they explored the innovative handling of a traditional medium. Baisen frequently experimented with this method, as seen in his *Shower over a Mountain Village* 山市驟雨 (cat. no. 54) and other paintings.[1] In this work, however, he pushed the technique to the extreme. Applying layer upon layer of wet strokes in varying shades of green, at times mixed with ink, he created a spontaneous pooling effect over the foreground trees. The loose fusing and blending of wet dots obliterated forms and instead created a strikingly textural and tactile surface. To prevent the trees from completely dissolving into the mass of green, Baisen strategically added bright blue pigment to highlight their silhouette.

The season in *Cloud over Mount Hiei* is high summer. The vertically swelling cloud of gigantic size is a formation popularly known as *nyūdōgumo* 入道雲, which typically appears during the hottest months in Japan. By repeating the bulbous shape of the trees in the cloud, Baisen achieved a surging upward movement. The overall application of an opaque yellowish wash is an unusual choice for the sky, but it demonstrates Baisen's desire to enhance the beauty of the greens and blues below. Moreover, the painter might have intended to signify the smothering heat of a Japanese summer, with the golden sky and its thick humidity, through the drenching brushwork of the foliage.

Overlooking the city of Kyoto, Mount Hiei is home to the Enryakuji 延暦寺 temple, which was founded by the Tendai-sect priest Saichō 最澄 (767–822). The stone torii gate that peeks from behind the dense foliage in Baisen's work still stands today, marking an entrance to a small shrine at the temple site. Unlike the bold treatment of the trees, Baisen carefully outlined the structure, without which the painting would have become a nearly abstract exercise in color.

MM

55. *Cloud over Mount Hiei*
比叡雲峰 (Hiei unpō) T

Late 1910s
Hanging scroll: color on silk
128.6 × 42 cm

SIGNATURE: *Baisen* 楳仙

SEAL: *Baisen* 楳僊

Purchase, 2005
13212.1

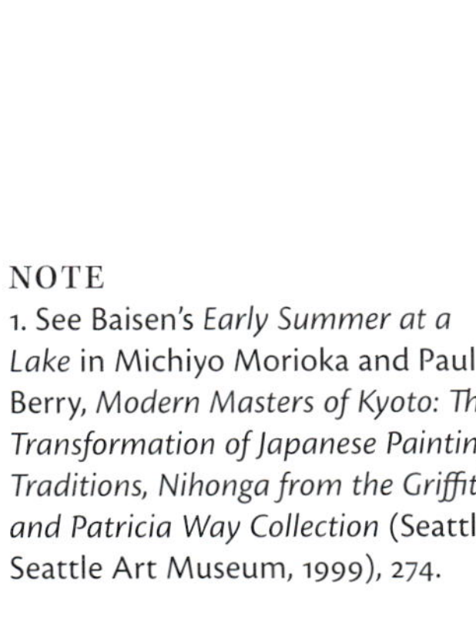

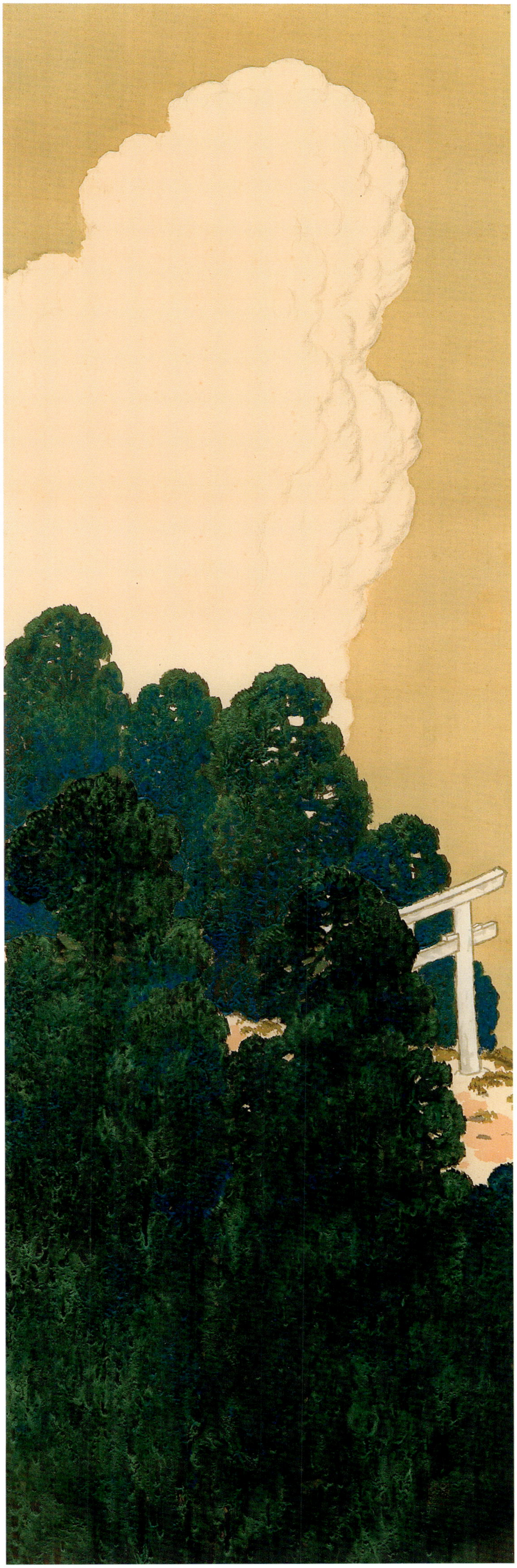

NOTE

1. See Baisen's *Early Summer at a Lake* in Michiyo Morioka and Paul Berry, *Modern Masters of Kyoto: The Transformation of Japanese Painting Traditions, Nihonga from the Griffith and Patricia Way Collection* (Seattle: Seattle Art Museum, 1999), 274.

Hirai Baisen 平井楳仙

1889–1969

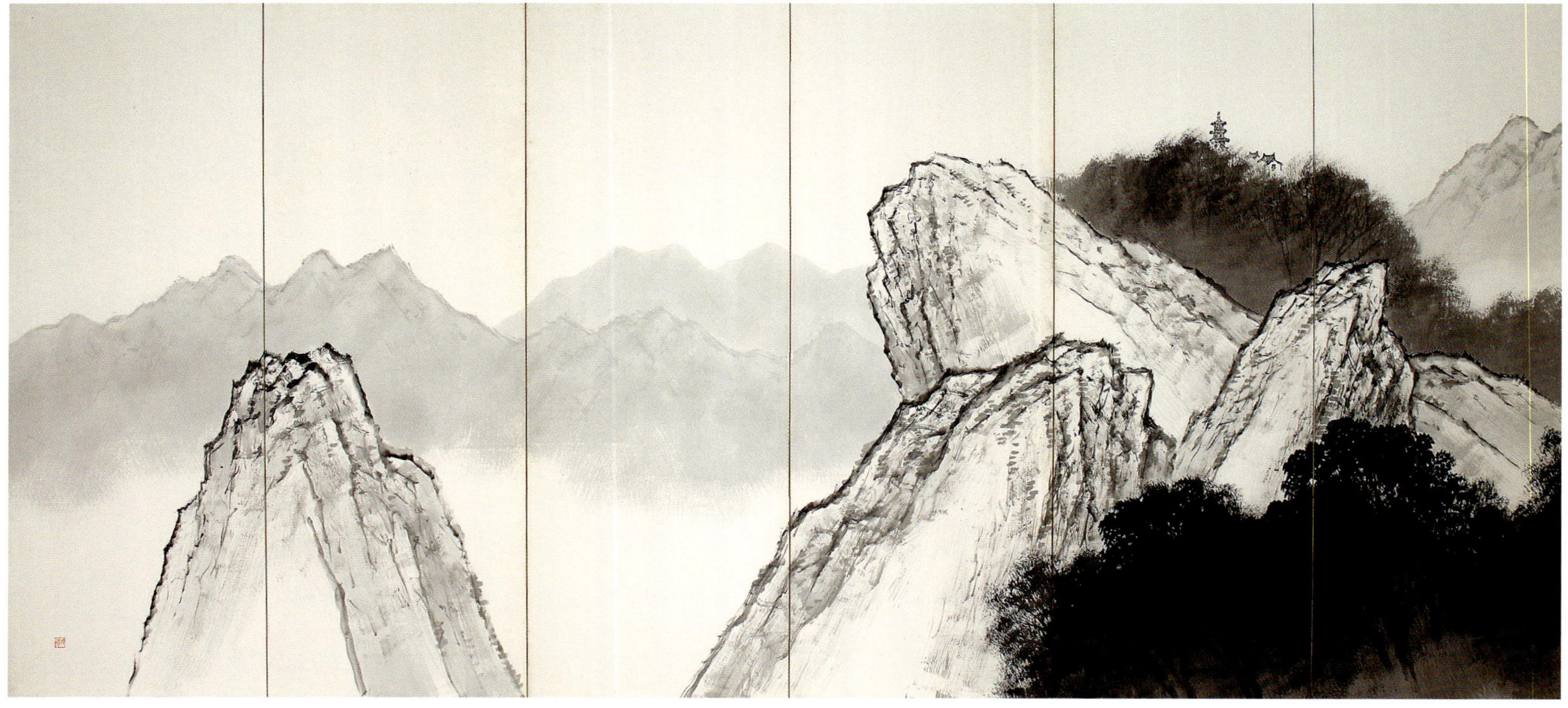

Although Hirai Baisen was known primarily as a bold colorist, he did not exclude monochrome from his experimental approach to painting. In fact, Baisen's awareness of ink technique and effect had emerged early in his career, as demonstrated by paintings from the 1910s such as *White Lotus* (cat. no. 73) and *Plum in Snow / Rising Sun* (cat. no. 74). At the end of the Taishō period, his interest in ink surged. He submitted a pair of literati-inspired hanging scrolls titled *Mountain Rain* (San'u 山雨) to the 1925 government exhibition and also produced at least several pairs of ink landscape screens.[1] *Mountains in China* is another example that confirms the artist's serious foray into ink around that time.

Baisen's dynamic composition of this painting maximizes the expressive potential of monochrome. To that end, the artist joined two screens in a continuous panorama of bare mountain peaks and verdant forests depicted with a distinct brush method. By alternating powerfully thrusting rocky peaks with thickly forested areas throughout the foreground, Baisen created not only a visual rhythm of light and dark but also the tactile contrast of solid and soft. The distant mountain chains, which emerge in light gray ink, provide a spatial depth that enhances the vastness of the unobstructed view. Baisen's handling of his brush has little reference to the established formula of the traditional Kyoto school. Rather, his individualistic approach mirrors the literati spirit. The craggy mountain forms are depicted in dark brittle lines and textured with traces of ink layered with a wide brush. Echoing this treatment, some of the faraway peaks are silhouetted in scratchy, rough outlines.

56. *Mountains in China* 中国山岳図 (Chūgoku sangaku zu)

Late 1920s
Pair of six-panel screens: ink on paper
166.5 × 372 cm each

SIGNATURE: *Baisen* 楳仙 (right screen)

SEAL: *Baisen* 楳僊 (both screens)

Purchase, 2005
13152.1 & 2

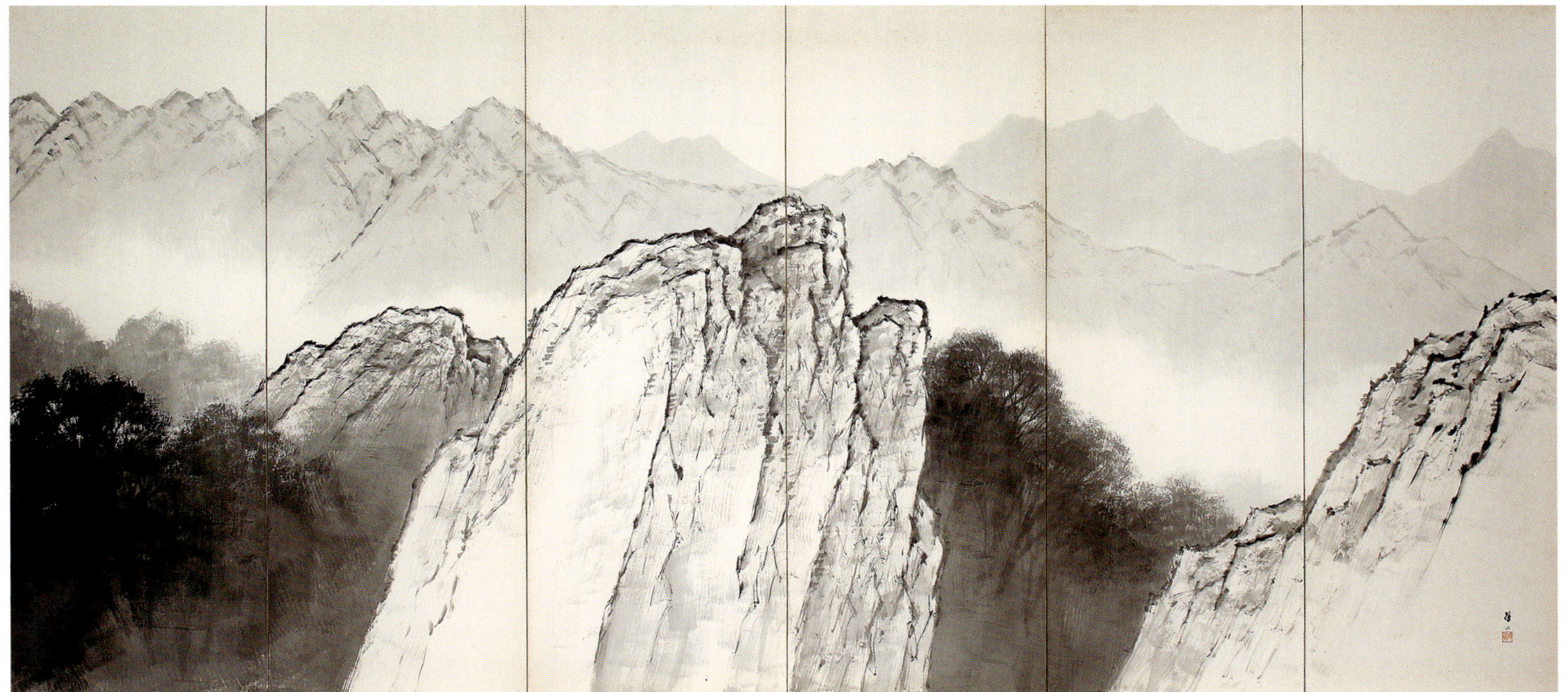

In contrast, a darker wet brushwork saturates the trees and foliage. The crumbled paper fibers that can be seen in the surface of the screens are a sign of the wetness of Baisen's brush.

The minuscule architecture in the left screen, including a Chinese-style pagoda, indicates the locale of this landscape. Baisen was less concerned with the attraction of exotic scenery than with discovering what fresh expression he might achieve in the traditional ink-on-paper medium. By the late 1920s Baisen had established himself as one of the most successful young artists in Kyoto, but the concentration of his ink experiments from this period suggests he was never complacent with his achievement. MM

NOTE

1. See another example of Baisen's ink landscape screens and a discussion by Paul Berry in Michiyo Morioka and Paul Berry, *Modern Masters of Kyoto: The Transformation of Japanese Painting Traditions, Nihonga from the Griffith and Patricia Way Collection* (Seattle: Seattle Art Museum, 1999), 272–73.

Hirai Baisen 平井楳仙

1889–1969

This dramatic painting by Hirai Baisen demonstrates how Japanese artists continued to invent new visions from ubiquitous traditional themes. Mount Hōrai (Ch., Penglaishan) is one of three mythical mountain-islands, along with Eishū 瀛州 (Ch., Yingzhou) and Hōjō 方丈 (Ch., Fangzhang), traditionally believed to exist in the East China Sea off the northeastern coast of China. This elusive paradise was inaccessible to ordinary humans, but the Daoist immortals reached it magically by airborne transport such as cranes. In Japanese painting, Hōrai symbolized longevity, and as an auspicious landscape it commonly incorporated other stock emblems of long life, such as the pine, crane, and tortoise. A well-known work by Nagasawa Rosetsu 長沢蘆雪 (1754–1799) portrays Hōrai as a fantastically shaped mountain-island, covered with pine trees, to which a procession of tortoises approaches from the sea and a line of cranes arrives from the sky.[1] Besides its potential for unusual landscape imagery, Mount Hōrai appealed to literati painters as an imaginary haven. *Cranes and Pine Trees* (cat. no. 28), an elegant composition by Nakabayashi Chikutō 中林竹洞, most likely refers to Mount Hōrai. Tomioka Tessai 富岡鉄斎 (1836–1924) also produced numerous paintings of this theme in his typically lavish ink and color style.

Baisen's Mount Hōrai is stunning in its austerity. The famous peak emerges from a foreboding darkness and soars upward like an impregnable fortress. Carefully shaded on its side, the mountain conveys its solidity in rectangular geological formations that are so sharp they might have been defined by an axe. The angularity of the rocks is a stylistic feature of Anhui painting that became popular in Japan in the early nineteenth century through paintings and woodblock books imported from China. Tanomura Chikuden 田能村竹田 (1777–1835) created a number of works with this style of rocks, as did other artists. Here, Baisen took the characteristic angularity even further. Miniature pine trees grow on the mountaintop and cling to its side, while cranes glide below, further emphasizing the staggering monumentality of the peak. In this stark landscape, the palace where the immortals find refuge is perched dangerously close to the deep fissure that bisects the mountain. Although tiny in scale, its jewel-like presence and carefully rendered green roof and red pillars signal the palace's singular importance.

Reducing the brushwork mostly to fine texture strokes and subtle outlines, Baisen represented the entire landscape in an unusual combination of ink and yellow-ocher with a most effective use of gold highlights. The edges of the bare cliffs and rock outcrops are brushed with gold, making the mountain shimmer in ethereal light. Baisen's Hōrai is one of the most novel representations of the popular theme. Dating to the early Shōwa period, the painting demonstrates the artist's undiminished originality despite the general critical perception that by then his creativity had waned.[2]

MM

57. *Mount Hōrai*
蓬莱山 (Hōraisan)　T

c. 1930
Hanging scroll: color on silk
127 × 41 cm

SIGNATURE: *Baisen* 楳仙

SEAL: *Daibutsu Baisen* 大佛某仙

Gift of Terry Welch, in honor of Stephen Shanaman, 2005
13211.1

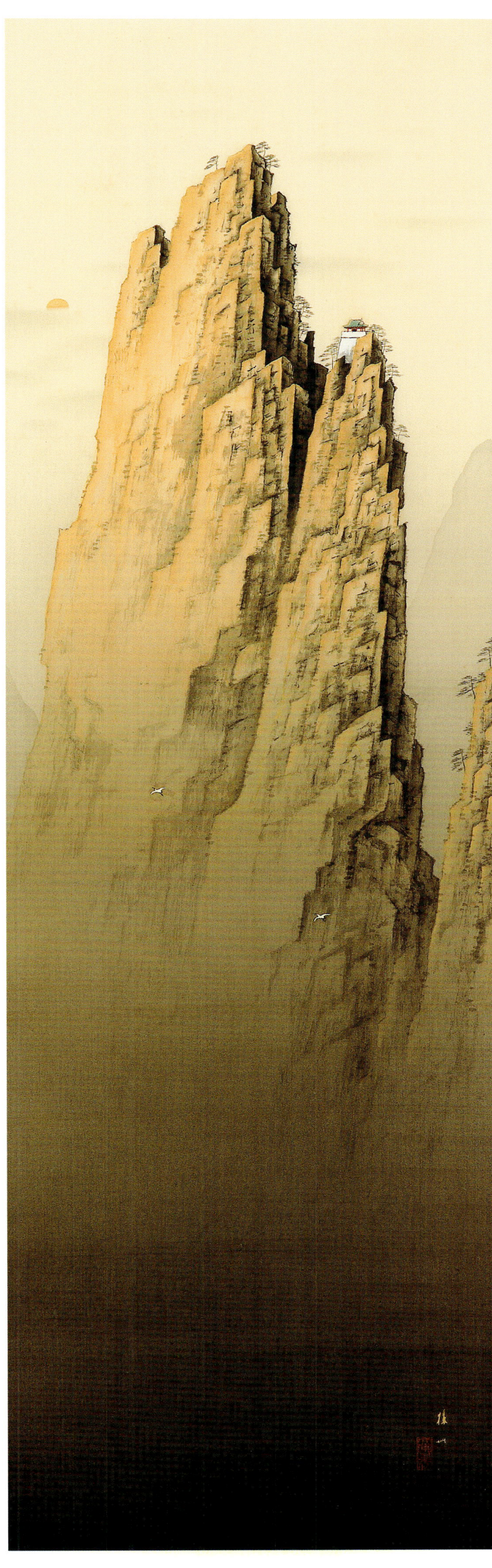

NOTES

1. Color illustration in Chibashi Bijutsukan and Wakayama Kenritsu Hakubutsukan, *Botsugo 200nen kinen: Nagasawa Rosetsu*, exh. cat. (Tokyo: Nihon Keizai Shinbunsha, 2000), 141.

2. See the biography of Hirai Baisen in this catalogue.

Ogawa Sen'yō 小川千甕

1882–1971

Eight Views of Ōmi represents an important theme in Japanese painting. It derives from the Eight Views of the Xiao and Xiang 瀟湘八景, which originated in Chinese literati circles in the eleventh century. After its introduction to Japan through Chinese ink paintings, artists gradually adopted the theme to various native localities, and within this expanded genre, Eight Views of Ōmi gained wide popularity for its illustrations of Lake Biwa 琵琶湖 in the province of Ōmi 近江 (Shiga prefecture). Each of the eight sites is distinguished for its scenic beauty, and some are historically significant: *Evening Snow on Mount Hira* (Hira no bosetsu 比良の暮雪), *Night Rain at Karasaki* (Karasaki no yau 唐崎の夜雨), *Autumn Moon at Ishiyama* (Ishiyama no shūgetsu 石山の秋月), *Evening Bell at Mii* (Mii no banshō 三井の晩鐘), *Boats Returning to Yabase* (Yabase no kihan 矢橋の帰帆), *Geese Descending at Katada* (Katada no rakugan 堅田の落雁), *Evening Glow at Seta* (Seta no sekishō 瀬田の夕照), and *Clearing Mist at Awazu* (Awazu no seiran 粟津の晴嵐).

Ogawa Sen'yō knew Lake Biwa well. While studying *yōga* painting under Asai Chū 浅井忠 (1856–1907) in Kyoto, Sen'yō made frequent sketching trips to the region.[1] More than two decades later, in 1933, he returned to Lake Biwa and went on a guided tour aboard a steamboat.[2] It was a memorable year in his career, for he had begun to participate in the Japan Nanga Institute (Nihon Nangain 日本南画院) exhibition with a resolve to pursue literati painting. *Eight Views of Ōmi* exemplifies Sen'yo's distinctive painting style from that crucial period. With only a token regard for scientific perspective, Sen'yō created a fanciful composition packed with details. The dazzling *yamatoe* color applied directly with a lively brush, combined with a sketchy ink line, infuses the painting with a childlike exuberance. The rickety architectural forms and humorous figures, reminiscent of his earlier involvement in *manga,* further contribute to the overall whimsy.

The compact screen includes all eight locations. The Ishiyamadera temple 石山寺 is depicted in the lower right. Founded in 749, the Shingon-sect temple was renowned for its association with Lady Murasaki. Sen'yō represented the temple's Moon Viewing Pavilion (Tsukimitei 月見亭), where Murasaki is said to have written part of the *Tale of Genji.*

In the center of the right screen is the Seta Bridge, which crosses the lake from the temple area to the village of Seta. To the left of the bridge rises Awazu Castle, known for the battle of the Genji clan in the twelfth century. In the center of the left screen, on the wooded hillside, Sen'yō represented Miidera temple 三井寺, the popular name for the Onjōji 園城寺, established in 746. The tower adjacent to the temple houses a large black bell, which according to a legend was once stolen and dragged up Mount Hiei by Benkei 弁慶, a twelfth-century warrior-monk. On the water, boats with white sails return to the shore of Yabase. The enormous pine supported by many wooden posts is the famous tree of Karasaki, a subject painted by numerous artists. Beyond the Karasaki pine on the western shore of Lake Biwa is Katada, the location of the Ukimidō Floating Temple 浮御堂. Finally, in the background of the left panel stands snow-covered Mount Hira.

In creating his version of the famous theme, Sen'yō ignored some components of its standardized iconography. For example, he omitted geese from the Katada scene, and no rain is shown at Karasaki. Instead, he organized the eight localities into a visually coherent panorama and incorporated four seasons, starting with spring at the Ishiyamadera temple and ending with winter at Mount Hira. Moreover, the screen is rich with amusing vignettes. Note a horse giving its groom a hard time on the Seta bridge, and the fisherman casting a net under the same bridge. Near Awazu Castle, a man walks with his ox-drawn cart along the pine-lined path, while a farmer tills the land, his chickens nearby. Farther to the left, two children are busy harvesting persimmons in the autumn season.

Sen'yō enjoyed excursions and travels from early in his career. During the 1930s his trips extended to Hokkaido and Karafuto 樺太 (Sakhalin Island) in the north, Okinawa to the south, and as far as China and Taiwan.[3] Even on a modest outing, he took great pleasure in observing local inhabitants and the surrounding scenery, recording his discoveries in great detail in often humorous travelogues.[4] The great affection with which Sen'yō portrayed common people in this screen reflects his deep sense of humanism. MM

58. *Eight Views of Ōmi* 近江八景図 (Ōmi hakkei zu)

c. 1933
Two-panel screen: ink and color on paper
63.4 × 162.8 cm

SIGNATURE: *Sen'yō ga* 千甕画

SEAL: illegible

Gift of Terry Welch, in honor of Michiyo Morioka, 2005
13153.1

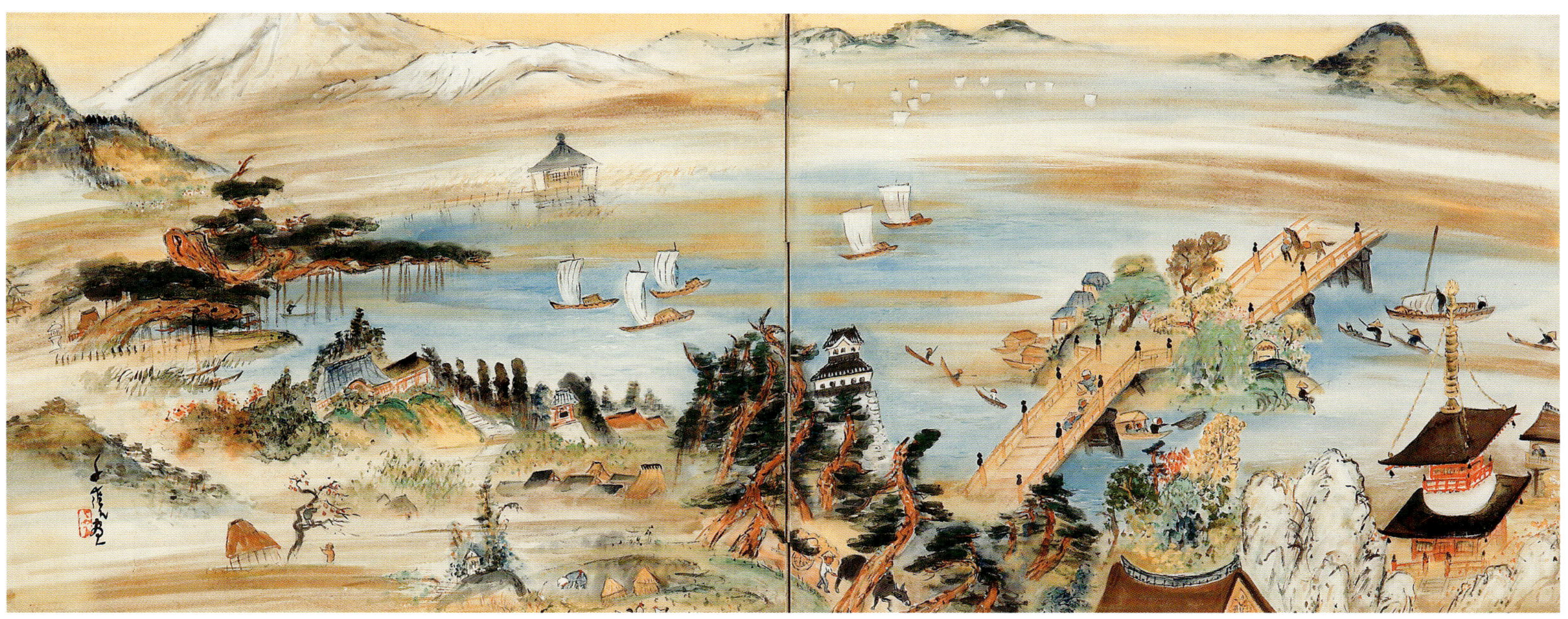

NOTES

1. See Ogawa Sen'yō, "Annai," *Bijutsu shinron* 8, no. 8 (August 1933): 28.

2. Ibid.

3. See "Sen'yō nenpu," in Ogawa Sen'yō, *Gashū: Ogawa Sen'yō* (Kyoto: Benridō, 1967), 17–19.

4. For example, "Manpo ki," *Atorie* 1, no. 4 (June 1924): 53–58; "Suigō isseki," *Bi no kuni* 5, no. 3 (March 1929): 136–37; "Waranji haite," *Bijutsu shinron* 5, no. 7 (July 1930): 47–49; and "Pekin kō," *Nanga kanshō* 11, no. 10 (October 1942): 7–10.

Shirakura Jihō 白倉二峰

1896–1974

The landscape in Shirakura Jihō's *Viewing Plum Blossoms* pulsates with energy. Curvilinear rocks and mountain forms fill the composition as if they were organic matter, brimming with life. A stream runs by a hermitage, and blossoming white plum trees dot the scenery, their craggy profiles mimicking the contours of the rock outcrops. The artist's near total disregard for rationally constructed space makes the land in the lower half of the painting appear as if it might tumble down. Perfectly at ease within this precarious environment, a scholar in a red robe calmly looks out the window of his humble abode. It is Jihō's exuberant brushwork that unifies the composition and holds everything in place. Layering and weaving his wet brushstrokes, Jihō vigorously defined the rock shapes, textured their surfaces, and delineated the plum trees. An array of rainbow colors in subtle washes and strokes lifts the image into a vision of fantasy more inviting than foreboding.

After apprenticing under a literati painter in his early teens, Jihō studied Western-style painting in Tokyo and achieved recognition as a *yōga* painter at the government exhibitions of 1914 and 1915. Soon after, however, he returned to his initial discipline and became a pupil of Tajika Chikuson 田近竹邨 (1864–1922), a noted Kyoto literati master who had trained under Tanomura Chokunyū 田能村直入 (1814–1907). In 1919 Jihō's landscape entry *Secluded Dwelling, Healing Worldliness* (Shindō izoku 深堂醫俗) was accepted to the *nihonga* section of the government exhibition.[1] Painted soon after his "debut" as a literati artist, *Viewing Plum Blossoms* exemplifies Jihō's early style and mirrors the 1919 piece in its vibrant brushwork and vertical landscape filled with rounded rock forms, winding path, and cascading stream. This painting is more spontaneous and direct in approach, however, and its immediacy and charm distinguish it from the more stately competition piece.

Viewing Plum Blossoms demonstrates how a modern artist could create an utterly new, exciting version of a centuries-old, traditional theme. Painted by generations of literati artists, the conventional subject presents the literati ideal of a scholar-recluse enjoying plum blossoms in his abode, away from the dust of the world. Jihō's work offers a telling contrast with the more classical version of the theme rendered by Hirose Taizan (see cat. no. 17) a hundred years earlier.

MM

59. *Viewing Plum Blossoms* 梅花書窓 (Baika shosō) T

1922

Hanging scroll: ink and color on silk

126.8 × 35.8 cm

SIGNATURE: 二峰作於鴨西高池居 Painted by Jihō at Kōchikyo studio on the west of the Kamo

SEALS: (?) (?) *sanjin* □□山人 (sig. upper) *Shirakura Jihō* 白倉二峰 (sig. lower)

Purchase, 2005

13217.1

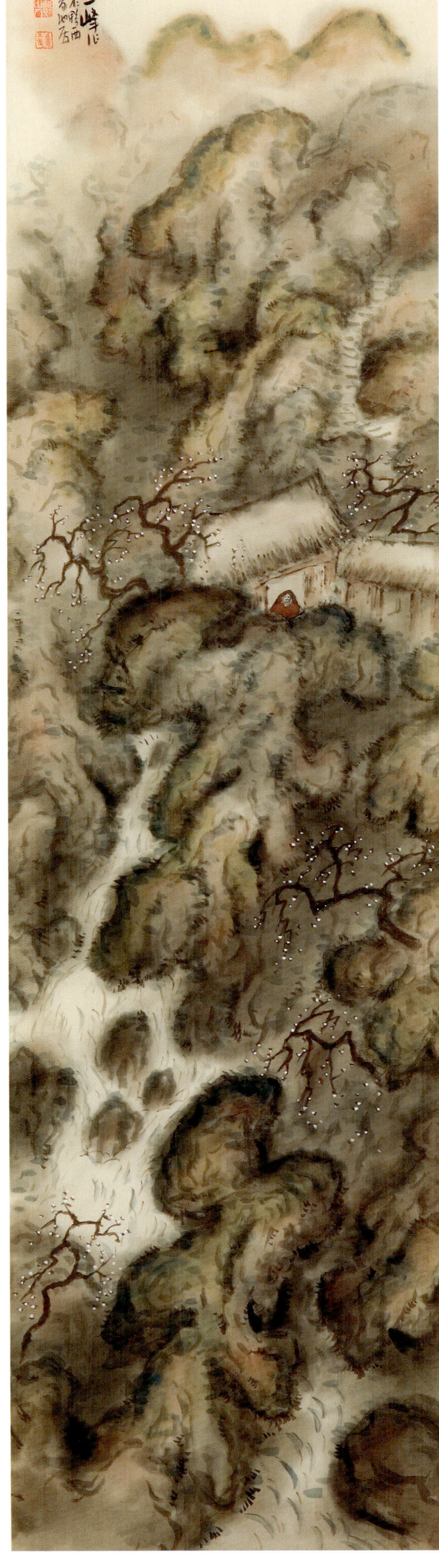

NOTE

1. For an illustration of this work, see Nittenshi Hensan Iinkai, *Nittenshi 6, Teitenhen 1* (Tokyo: Nitten, 1982), 96.

Fusen Tetsu 不染鉄

1891–1976

WITH INUI KATSUJI 乾勝二, ACTIVE 1940S AND AFTER

60. *Scenes of the South Sea Islands* 南洋の風景 (Nanyō no fūkei)

1944
Handscroll: ink and color on paper
26.6 × 35.6 cm each image

SIGNATURES: 昭和拾九年拾二月吉日風物不染鐵画
Landscape painted by Fusen Tetsu on an auspicious day in December 1944 (leaf 13, right)
人物乾勝二画 Figures painted by Inui Katsuji (leaf 13, left)

SEALS: *Fusen Tetsu ga* 不染鐵画 (leaves 1, 7)
Tetsu 鐵 (leaves 2–6, 8–10)
Katsuji 勝二 (leaves 2, 5, 7, 11–13)
Fusen Tetsji gain 不染銕二画印 (leaf 13)

Purchase, 2005
13156.1

The extraordinary *Scenes of the South Sea Islands* showcases Fusen Tetsu's breathtaking ink brushwork in twelve separate paintings.[1] The work stands out in his entire oeuvre for its unusual subject matter and collaborative production. Tetsu represented the lush island landscapes of the South Pacific, and Inui Katsuji depicted the figures. The captivating power of Tetsu's brush style is evident throughout but is particularly compelling in his portrayal of the jungle, as in leaf seven below. Unleashing his saturated ink brush, he layered loose wet strokes to convey the primordial force and thick humidity of the tropical forest. The presence of numerous lizards and the dark-skinned islander depicted

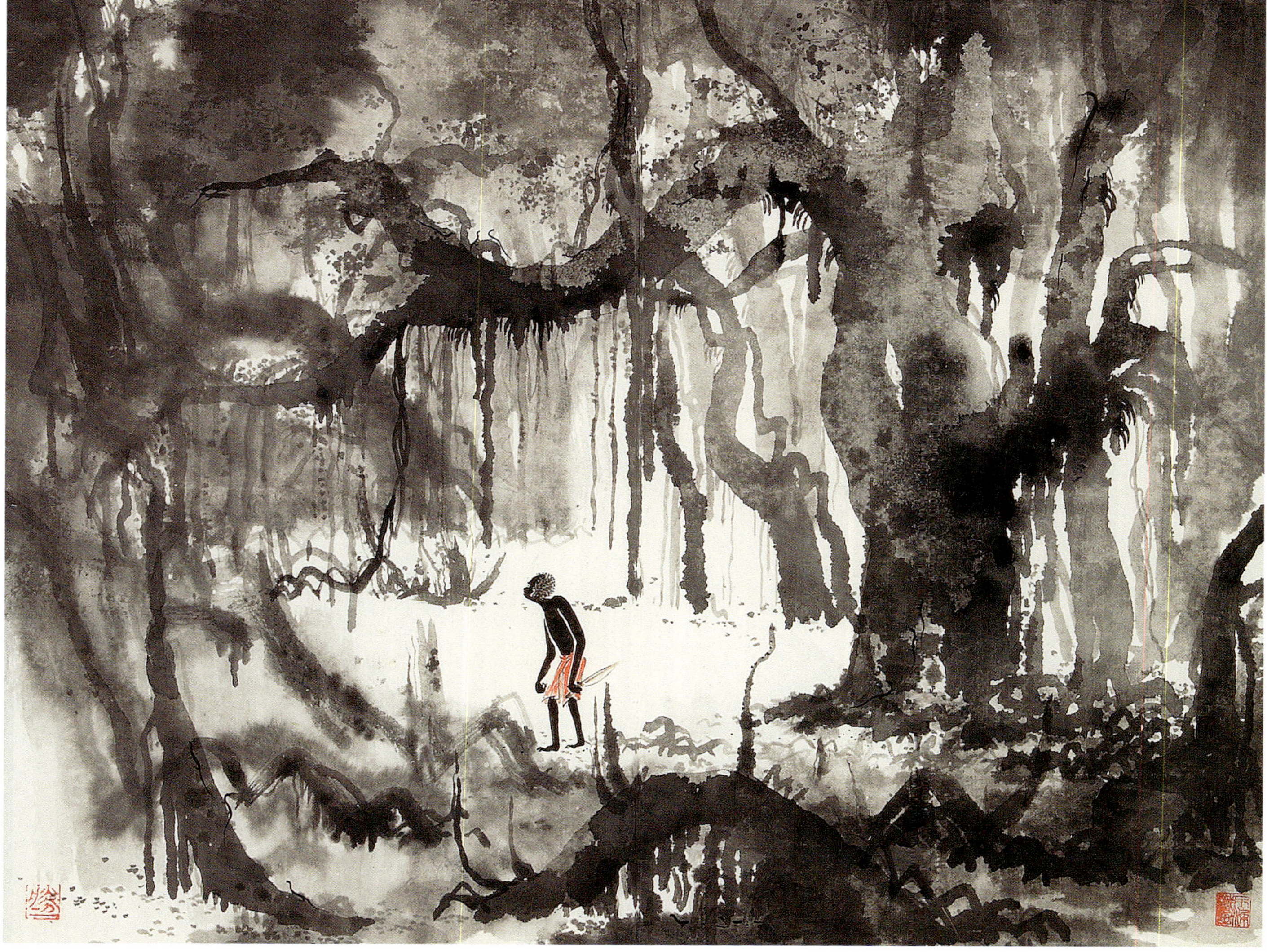

by Katsuji inject a sense of realism into the nearly abstract landscape.

During the 1920s and 1930s, Japanese artists began to turn to the South Pacific for exotic subjects and themes with which to revitalize their art. One of the early accounts of the region by a *nihonga* artist came from Kawabata Ryūshi 川端龍子 (1885–1966), who in 1934 traveled to the islands of Palau and Yap, which were under Japan's administrative control.[2] Ryūshi felt that the tropical landscape, in which "everything was brilliant under the glaring sun right on the equator," was better served by the medium of oil. The pedestrian character of the flowers and small birds deflated his high expectations of island natural life, but he found bananas and pineapples to be appealing subjects for still lifes. The "naked" appearance of the natives and the ubiquitous presence of lizards impressed him, but he was disinclined to depict the latter in painting. What most attracted Ryūshi were the dense forests of palm trees. He believed this subject, new to Japanese painting, would require a high degree of skill to be successfully portrayed in *nihonga*.

The motifs Ryūshi described all appear in *Scenes of the South Sea Islands*. In particular, the palm trees about which Ryūshi enthused are portrayed beautifully by Tetsu, and the lizards that caught his attention make frequent appearances. Tetsu's twelve scenes of island landscapes and lifestyle are intended to be enjoyed one by one, with the viewpoint changing dramatically from one scene to another. The opening view is a panorama, with the main island in the center and tall palm trees soaring from two small islands nearby; multiple boats are visible on the sea. Tetsu's brushwork is explosive in the second scene, a close-\up of palm trees and a figure collecting coconuts. Directly applying angular strokes of varying ink tonality, he defined the form but not the detail of the trees. In the third leaf, the viewpoint pulls back to show the tall conical hills along the beach from a low vantage point. In the fourth scene, a bird's-eye view, a cultivated field is enclosed by a luxuriant circle of palm trees with the ocean in the distance. To portray the peaceful lives of the islands' inhabitants, in harmony with nature, Tetsu took a more lyrical approach in gray tonalities here. Some scenes, such as the eleventh and twelfth leaves, highlight Katsuji's well-defined figure painting with Tetsu providing simple background motifs. In several instances, Tetsu's brushwork dissolves into pure abstraction. In leaf six, a scene of a rain shower, ink blotches signify plants and diagonal shafts of gray wash suggest rain, while figures and lizards anchor the image in reality.

Tetsu's collaborator, the Nara artist Katsuji, graduated from the Kyoto Municipal Special School of Painting (Kyōto Shiritsu Kaiga Senmon Gakkō 京都市立絵画専門学校) in 1941.[3] His figures with their clarity and accents of vivid color perfectly complement Tetsu's expressive ink style. Both painters signed their names with a surprisingly similar delicacy on the last page, a village scene done in evocative ink showing the artists at work inside two houses. The figure on the right represents Tetsu, whose signature and large red seal appear nearby, while the figure in the house to the left is Katsuji, as suggested by the proximity of his signature and seal.

By the time this painting was made, in December 1944, Japan had lost control of most of the islands in the South Pacific to the Allied powers. Tetsu's activities during the war are not known, and there is no record of a trip to the South Pacific. But plenty of photographic images and reports about the islands were available in Japan. Moreover, the themes of island, ocean, and fishing villages were deeply ingrained in Tetsu's psyche, owing to his experiences as a fisherman on the Izu islands during his youth. Tetsu immortalized the Izu seascapes in many of his ink paintings, some including the U-shaped cove with a sandy beach similar to the scene in leaf nine.[4]

Largely forgotten since his death, Tetsu's unique paintings have recently recaptured the interest of Japanese experts. *Scenes of the South Sea Islands* should further fuel their enthusiasm. MM

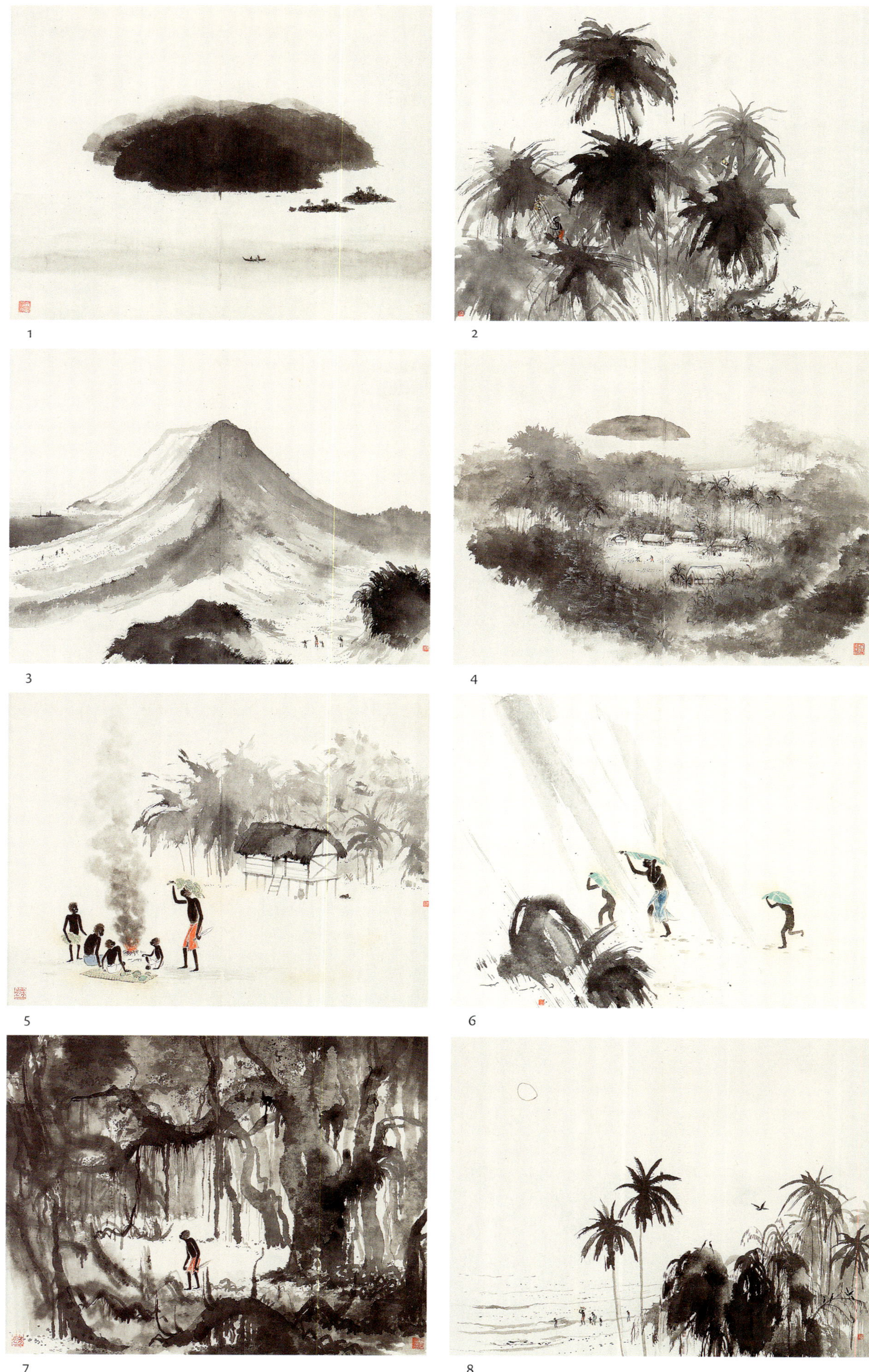

1 2 3 4 5 6 7 8

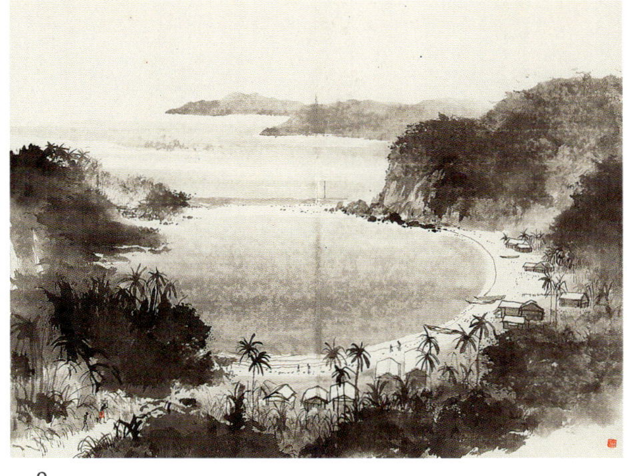

9

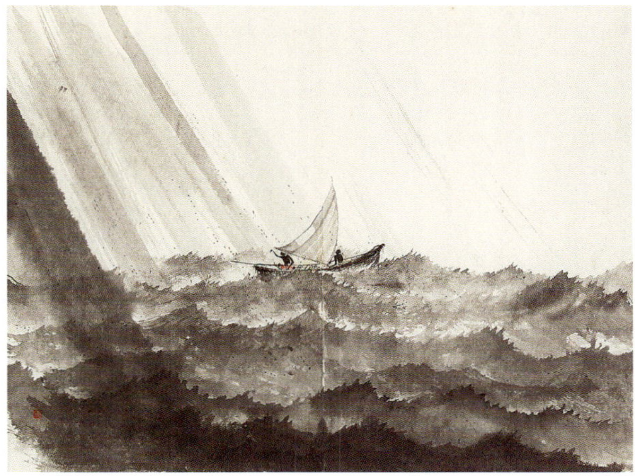

10

11

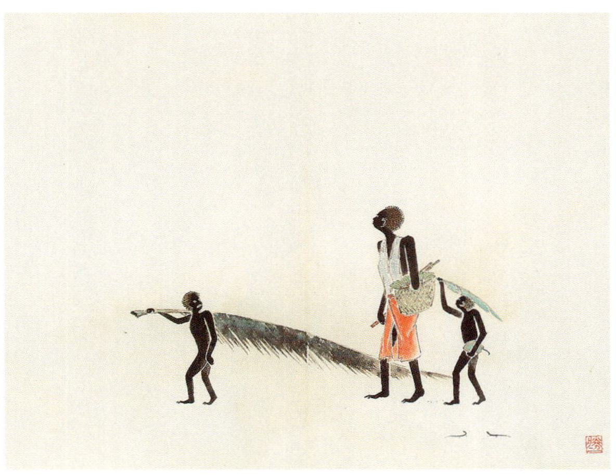

12

13

NOTES

1. Originally an album, the paintings were converted to a handscroll in 2004.

2. As a result of its contribution to the Allied cause during World War I, Japan received a South Pacific Mandate from the League of Nations in 1919. Under this mandate, Japan exercised administrative control over island territories in Micronesia—Caroline, Mariana, Marshall, and Palau—until World War II. For Ryūshi's account introduced in this paragraph, see Kawabata Ryūshi, "Nan'yō o kaku," *Tōei* 11, no. 6 (June 1935): 20–21.

Mano Noritarō 真野紀太郎 (1871–1958), a *yōga* artist, published an early account of Southeast Asia and the South Pacific in 1925. See his essay "Gaka no mita nan'yō," *Atorie* 2, no. 12 (December 1925): 80–92.

3. See *Gagakkō-Geidai 100 shūnen kinen dōsōsei meibo, 1880–1980* (Kyoto: Kyōto Shiritsu Geijutsu Daigaku Bijutsu Gakubu Dōsōkai, 1980), 93. It is known that Tetsu taught art at a middle school in Nara in the late 1920s. Katsuji may have been one of his pupils.

4. See Nara Kenritsu Bijutsukan, *Botsugo nijūnen kinen tokubetsu ten: Junjō no gaka, Fusen Tetsu ten*, exh. cat. (Nara, 1996), plates 28–30 and 33.

Plants and Animals

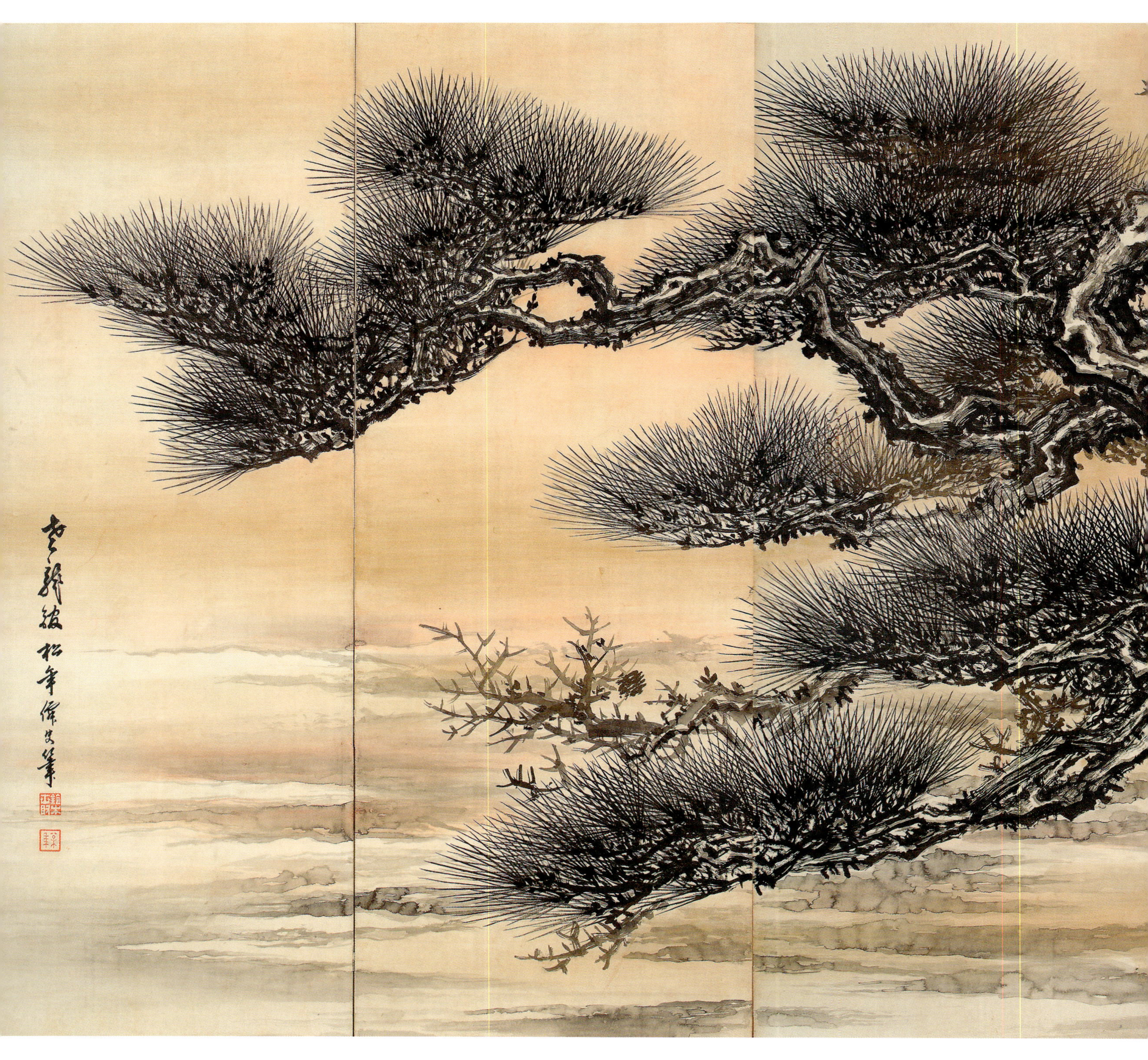

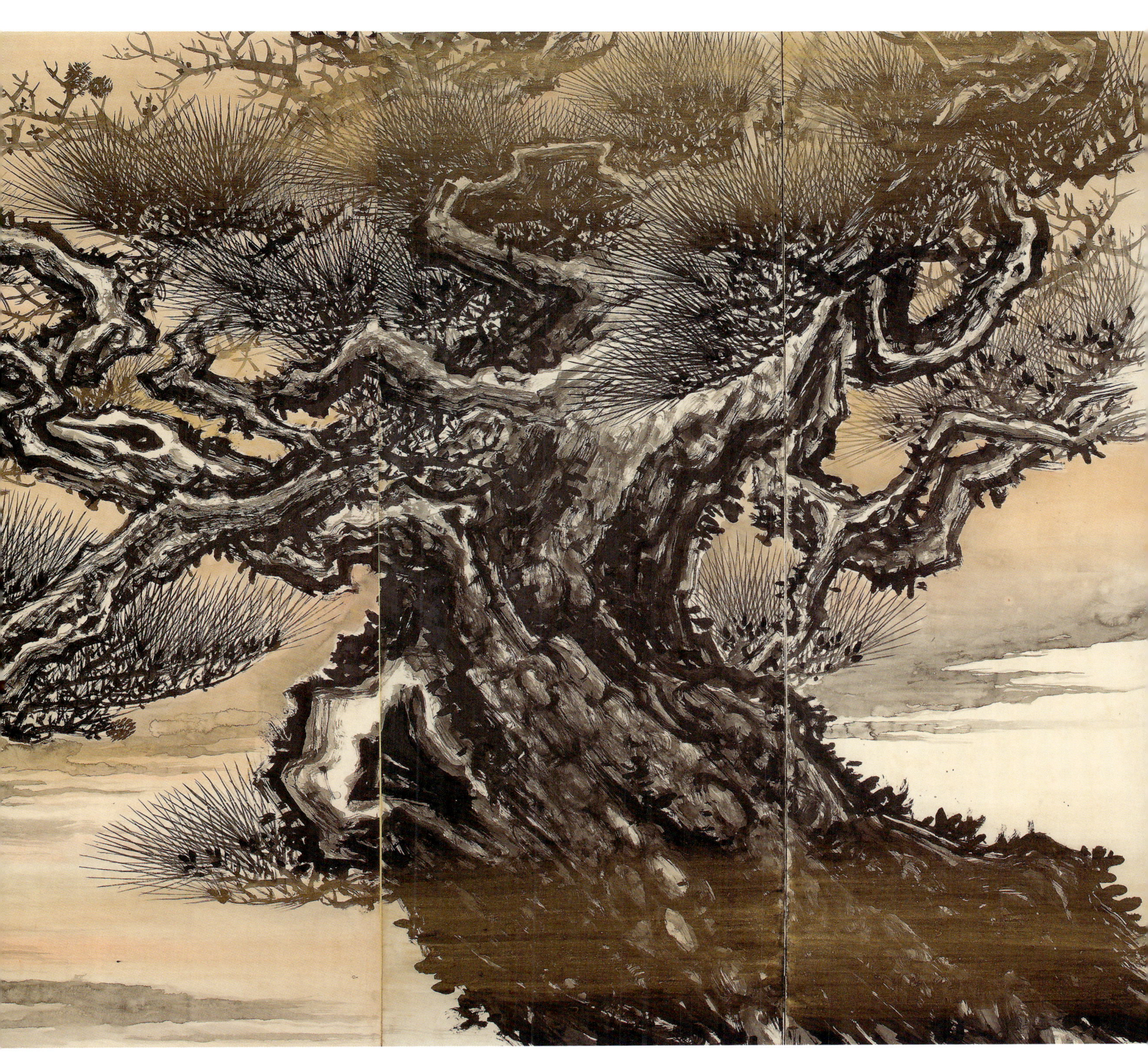

Tani Bunchō　谷文晁

1763–1840

61. *Landscape and Bamboo* 山水竹図 (Sansui chiku zu)

1804
Set of three hanging scrolls: ink and light color on paper
173 × 95.6 cm each

Right scroll:
SEALS: *Bunchō ga in* 文晁画印 (sig. upper)
illegible (sig. lower)

Middle scroll:
SIGNATURE: *Bunchō* 文晁

SEAL: *Bunchō* 文晁

INSCRIPTION:
Bunka kigen mōka sha 文化紀元孟夏寫
Painted in the fourth month of the first year of the Bunka period

Left scroll:
SIGNATURE: *Bunchō* 文晁

SEALS: illegible[1] (sig. upper)
Tani Bunchō sha (sig. lower)

INSCRIPTION:
甲子孟夏寫于水雲軒中
Painted in the fourth month of the *kōshi* year [1804] in Suiunken Studio

Purchase, 2005
13165.1–3

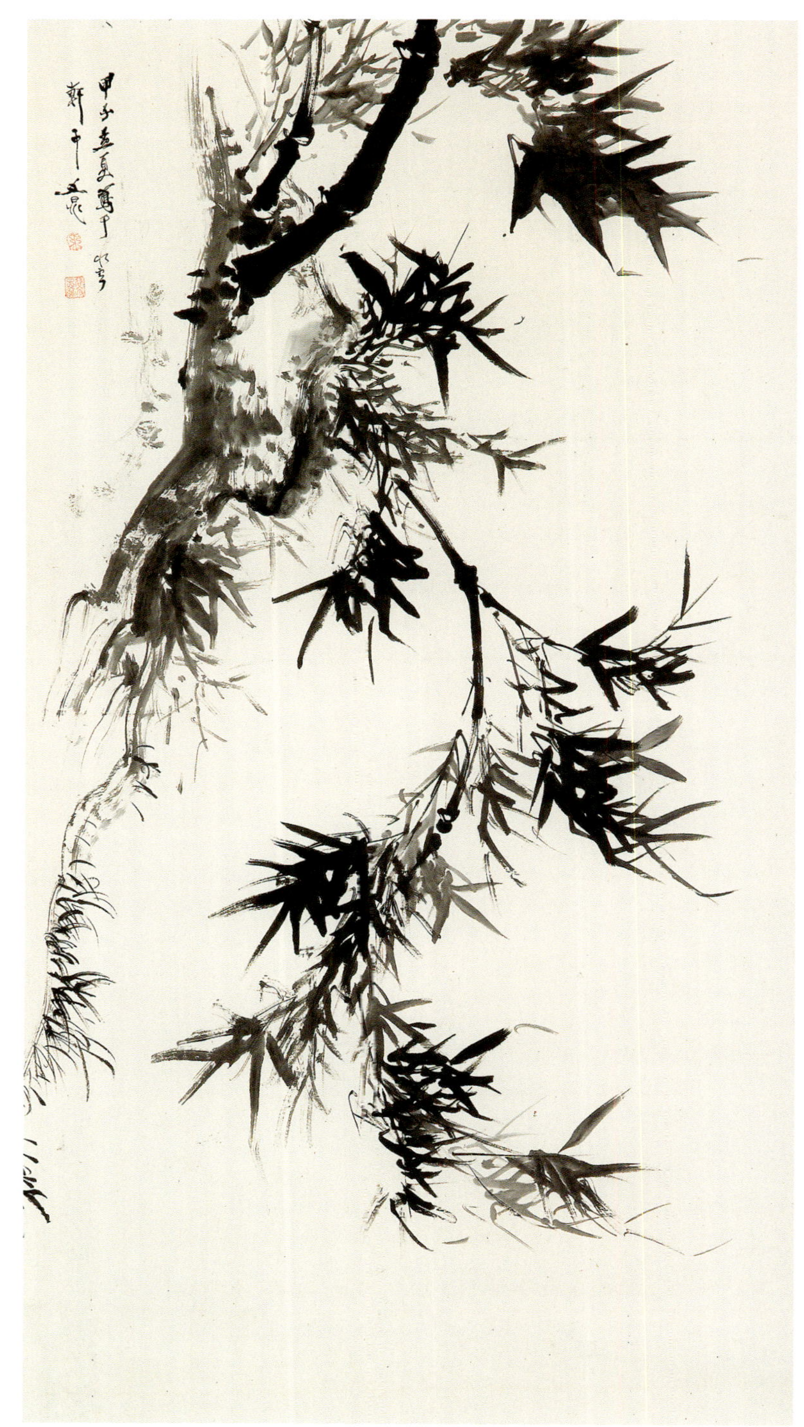

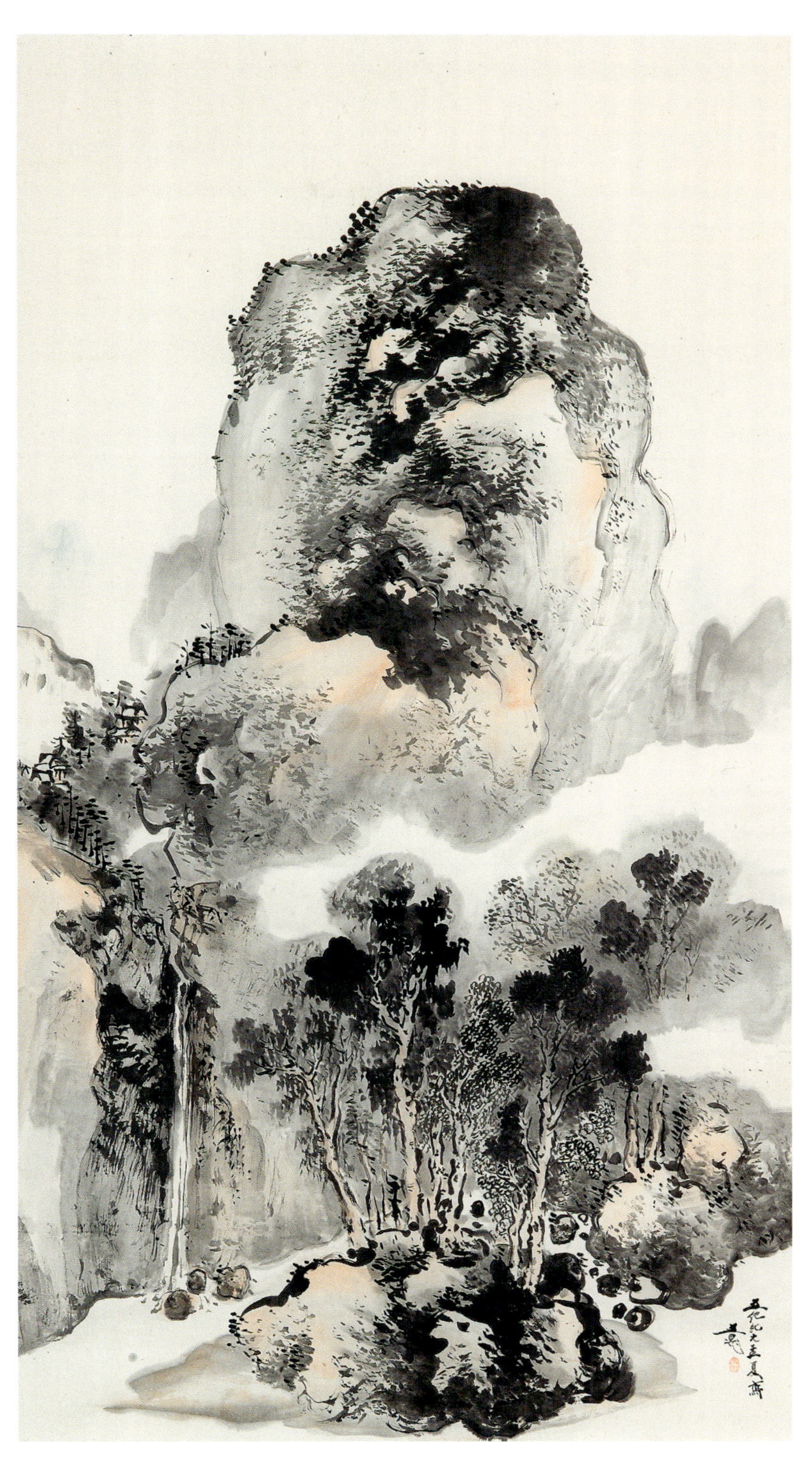

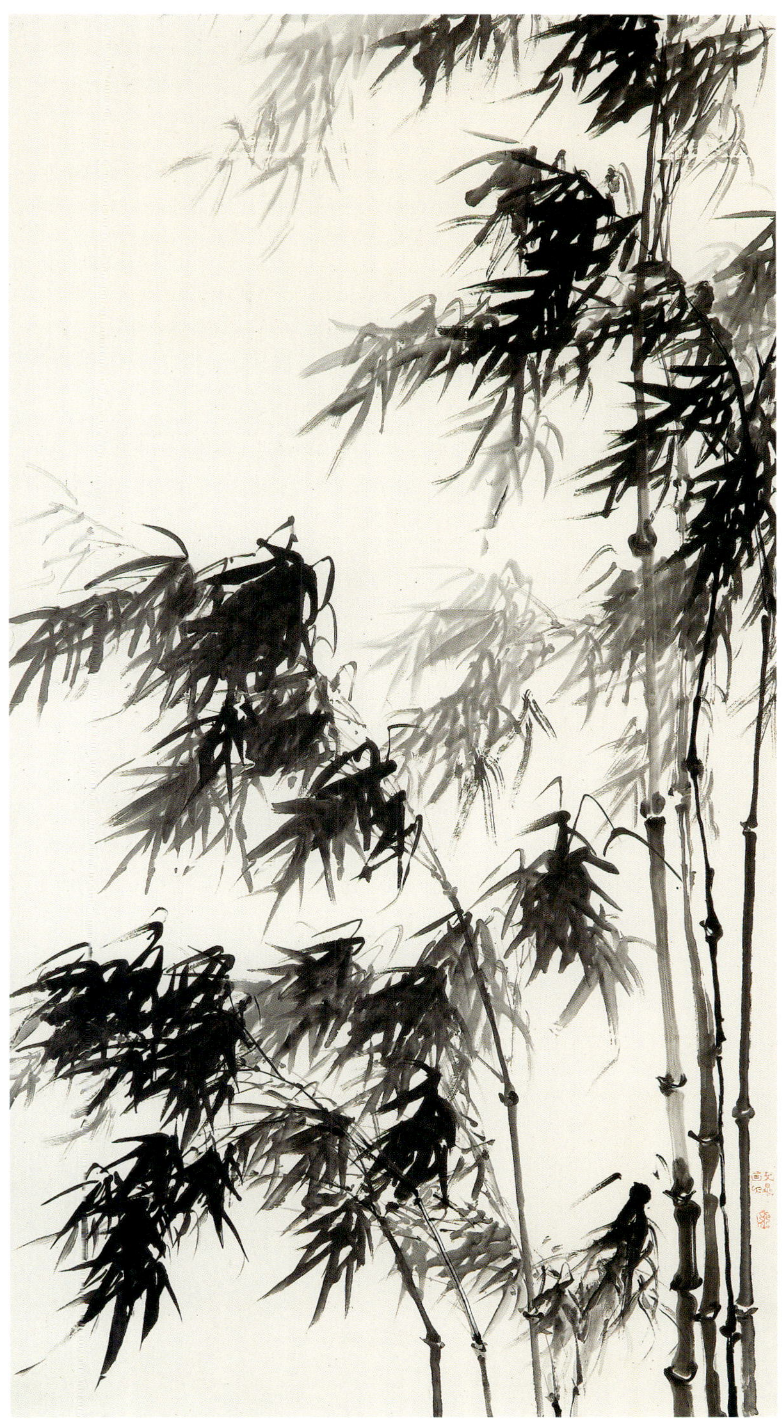

In the latter half of his life Tani Bunchō was one of the most celebrated painters in the city of Edo. His flamboyant personality and great skill in a variety of styles won support from numerous wealthy patrons for whom he produced many large paintings. The members of the ruling class often required sets of scrolls to fill the large tokonoma in their residences, and such triptychs were generally the purview of Kanō-school artists. But although he did not have an official position, Bunchō completed a number of diptychs and triptychs for similar patrons.

Unlike their Chinese precursors, Japanese literati painters were quite eclectic in their stylistic interests. Bunchō's approach to landscape was influenced more by professional painters on the edge of the Chinese literati world than by the major literati styles of the continent. His landscape composition with its central mountain mass and rough brushwork shows his knowledge of the imported works of artists such as Xie Shichen 謝時臣 (1487–c. 1560), well known in Japan by the late eighteenth century. Throughout his later career Bunchō employed similar mountain compositions in which only the character of the brushwork varied; the loosely brushed, watery quality of the ink in this landscape is typical of his works of the early Bunka period, as are the distinctive horizontal strokes of the signature.[2] The wet brushwork and ink washes reinforce the atmospheric quality of the mists rising behind the foreground group of trees. The massive mountain with a waterfall descending along its side completes this classic view of nature, which hints at the ancient landscape compositions of the Northern Song period (960–1127).

Although triptychs were often formed of consistent themes, it was also common for a central landscape or figure painting to be flanked by works on a different subject. In this case Bunchō chose to display his talent at painting the classic literati theme of bamboo. The powerful composition of the left scroll shows bamboo suspended from a cliffside, the upward arc of the bamboo tips countering the downward thrust of the main culm. Painted with a brush fully loaded with ink, the leaves tend to blend into one another. The right scroll presents a view of a bamboo grove swept by a wind strong enough only to twist the leaves in the same direction without bending the culms. Once again the brushwork is fully saturated, with ink flowing together in the major groupings of leaves. Yet, here and there, very dry strokes that split the hairs of the brush tip add effective accents. Both paintings have a casual air that belies the technical achievement of using such wet brushwork without losing control of the individual shapes while promoting an overall effect.[3]

PB

NOTES

1. In a recently discovered record of Bunchō's seals, it was noted that this seal was made of bronze and had been uncovered in the grounds of a Shinto shrine. It became one of Bunchō's most used seals.

2. This work is painted in a similar fashion to *Autumn Landscape* from 1808 at the Tokiwa Bijutuskan; see Tawarachō Hakubutsukan, *Botsugo hyakurokuju nen Tani Bunchō ten* (Tawarachō, 2000), plate 49. Bunchō's signature went through a number of well-defined changes during his career.

3. These works are similar in their skillful brushwork to the superb bamboo handscroll by Bunchō at the Spencer Museum at the University of Kansas.

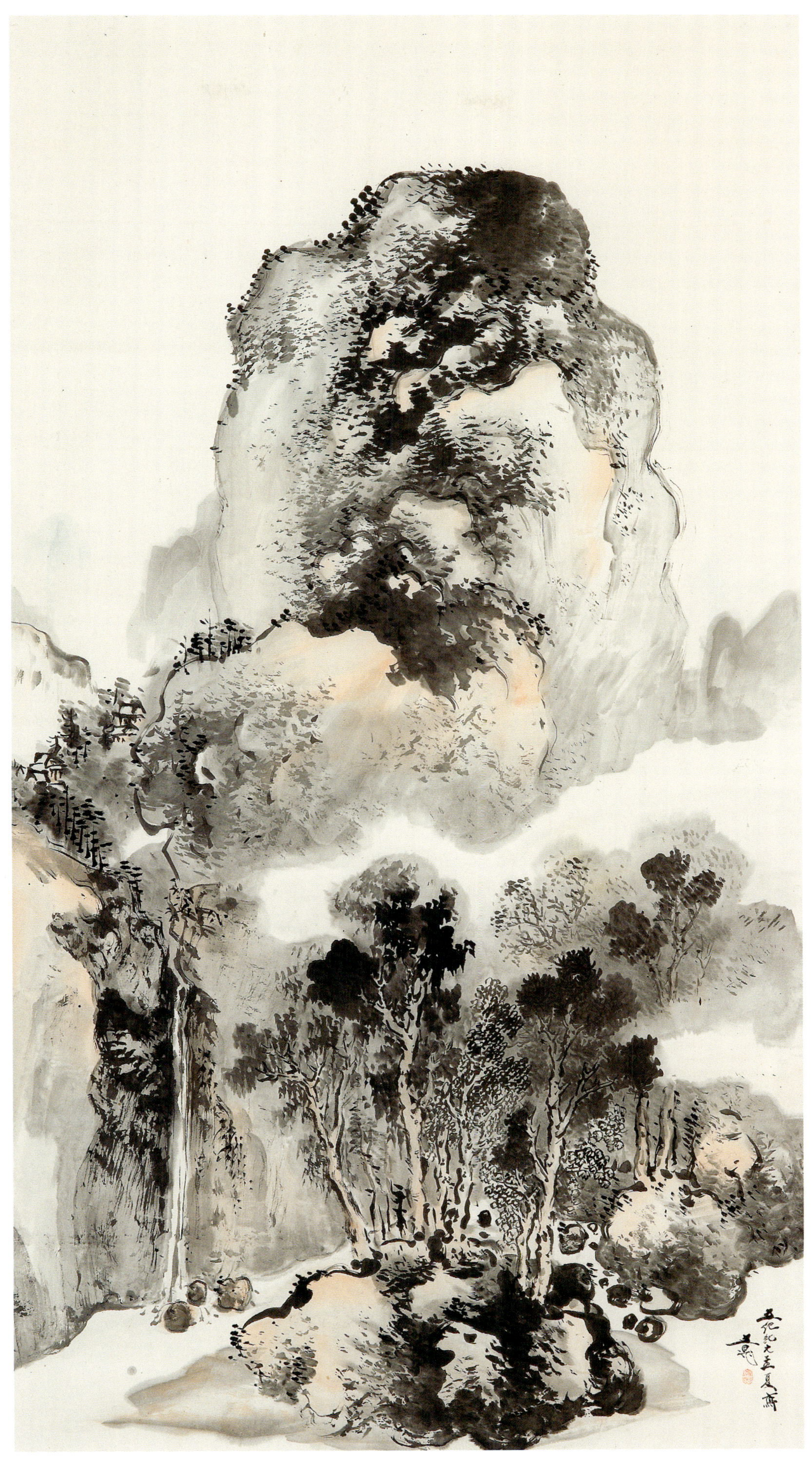

Nakabayashi Chikutō 中林竹洞

1776–1853

The Chinese orchid, bamboo, pine, and prunus are the plants most favored by East Asian scholars. Each carries symbolic value. Elegant and graceful in appearance and delicate in fragrance, the orchid came to stand for a highly principled gentleman who sought the pleasures of a quiet life removed from worldly affairs. For scholar-painters who shunned decorative beauty and excessive representational details, an orchid in monochromatic ink became an ideal vehicle for self-expression. Furthermore, the slender, supple lines of orchid leaves not only fulfilled a descriptive function but also corresponded to the brush techniques of calligraphic practice. The orchid offered amateur scholar-painters a subject they could paint with relative ease.

Elegant Orchids by Nakabayashi Chikutō is a work by a master literati painter. His skillful brushwork is evident in the fluid brush lines of the orchid leaves, accented by shorter strokes and dots that depict the blossoms. The composition is clear, with each leaf and blossom beautifully defined and their relationship to their neighbors carefully established. The rectangular-shaped rocks with flat tops, textured with horizontal strokes, are one of the hallmarks of Chikutō's landscape style. The outlines that delineate the rocks, however, are more robust than usual, emphasizing the angular forms and enhancing their symbolism of strength. The vigorous brushwork of the rocks contrasts with and augments the flowing lines of the orchid. Small *reishi* 霊芝 command the viewer's attention with their distinct curvilinear shape and strategic positioning. The fundamental concept of literati painting as a means of self-expression and communication among friends is signified by Chikutō's brushwork. In both the orchid and the rocks, the viewer is aware of the deft movements of the artist's hand and brush.

Chikutō's dignified yet relaxed calligraphy echoes the refined expression of his painting. The inscription includes a five-character, eight-line poem (*gogon risshi* 五言律詩) that reads:

幽蘭在空谷	Elegant orchid exists in a quiet valley,
自与凡花異	Distinguishing itself from ordinary flowers.
紫芝生石畔	Purple fungus grows at the foot of the rock,
嶷然饒古意	Lofty and full of ancient sentiments.
擧世逐繁華	The whole world pursues extravagant display,
群芳争艶麗	Multiple fragrances vying for the florid beauty.
貞堅獨自持	As for steadfastness and purity, orchid alone possesses them—
何人知此味	Who can understand this beauty?
閑居無事	In my leisurely life, with no special
借筆墨以發浩気	affairs, I borrow brush and ink to
漫寫蘭竹数紙	express my understanding. I sketch
適友生國宝至	orchid and bamboo on several papers;
因以此幅贈之	Just then comes my friend Kokuhō.
時丁亥重陽日	Therefore, I make a gift of this painting.
	Ninth day of the ninth month of the *teigai* year [1827]

The "Kokuhō" 國宝 mentioned in the inscription was Ōkura Ryūzan 大倉笠山 (1784–1850), Chikutō's devoted student. Chikutō addressed Ryūzan here as his friend by his nickname, revealing their close relationship. Tanomura Chikuden 田能村竹田 (1777–1835) once recorded that Chikutō shunned social gatherings after retirement but always took enormous pleasure in seeing Ryūzan.[1] The eldest son of a wealthy sake merchant in Kasagi 笠置, south of Kyoto, Ryūzan entrusted the family business to his younger brother so he could immerse himself in literati pursuits. His wife, Shūran 袖蘭, was also a *bunjin* and an accomplished seven-string *qin* player trained by Uragami Gyokudō 浦上玉堂 (1745–1820). Together, the couple were active members of the literati community in Kyoto.[2]

MM

62. *Elegant Orchid* 幽蘭図 (Yūran zu)

1827
Hanging scroll: ink on paper
134.4 × 56 cm

SIGNATURE: *Ōhara sanjin Seishō*
大原山人成昌

SEALS: *Shin* (?) *gen bi* 心□元微
(upper right)
Seishō no in 成昌之印 (sig. upper)
Azana Hakumei 字伯明 (sig. middle)
Chikutō 竹洞 (sig. lower)
冰清雪白 Pure like ice, white like snow
(bottom left)

Purchase, 2005
13174.1

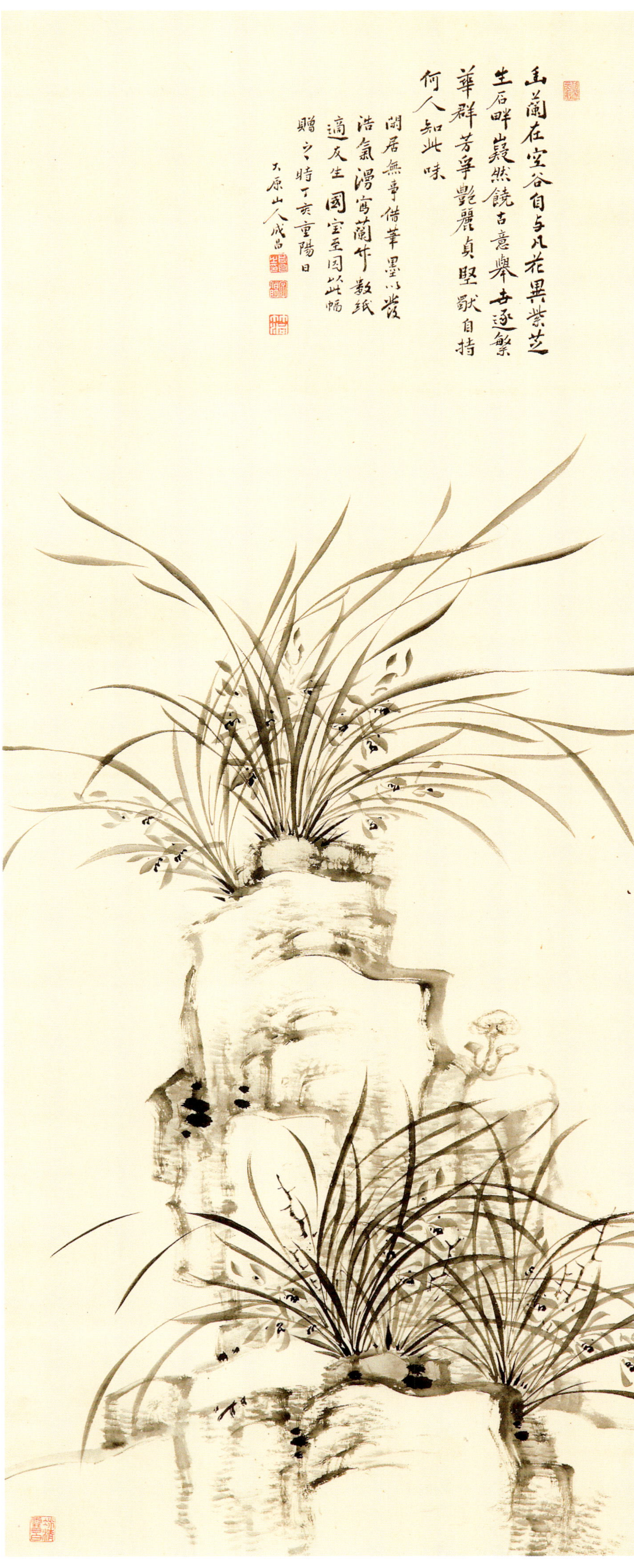

NOTES

1. From *Chikuden sō shiyū garoku* (1833), quoted by Murakami Yasushi, *Minami Yamashiro Kasagi shusshin no bunjin: Ōkura Ryūzan, sono tsuma Shūran no e to sho* (Kyōtanabe: Taibōan, 1998), 31.

2. For the art and biography of Ryūzan and Shūran, see ibid.

Yamamoto Baiitsu 山本梅逸

1783–1856

True to his name Baiitsu—meaning "Elegance of the Plum"—the artist often painted plum flowers. Yet only once in a great while did Baiitsu make such impressive, large works as this example.[1] Paintings of plum flowers have enjoyed great popularity in Japan for centuries, and many have been inspired by the compositions attributed to the noted Yuan-dynasty plum-flower painter Wang Mian 王冕 (1287–1359). Works attributed to Wang, or following his style, were imported in considerable numbers in the Muromachi period for the collections of Zen monasteries and their supporters. By the mid-Edo period, Wang's style was equally appreciated among literati painters.

Although Wang Mian was far from the only painter to do so, his compositions especially stressed boldly curving arcs of branches much like those seen in this work. Paintings of flowering plum boughs typically have vertical compositions with branches ascending or sweeping downward; more rarely the compositions are horizontal. Occasionally the plum hangs from a cliff, similar to the bamboo in the left scroll of the Tani Bunchō triptych (see cat. no. 61). Baiitsu added bamboo to this composition, cleverly outlining it to set its white culms and large leaves apart from the dense, black brushwork of the plum branches. The smooth, even brushstrokes of the bamboo contrast with the edges of the branches, whose irregularity effectively suggests the roughness of the bark. Baiitsu increased the sense of depth by painting a few rear limbs in lighter tones of ink. Sometimes he wrote in formal regular or clerical scripts, but here the cursive calligraphy of his brief inscription nicely contrasts with the more precise strokes used for the plants.

The artist's talent is best displayed by the complex overlapping of various elements of the plum and bamboo. Every time a branch, leaf, or flower overlapped, Baiitsu had to leave a gap to be filled in later with the intervening element. Many instances of this interweaving technique are visible among the bamboo culms and the plum limbs. The freely brushed blossoms, whether buds or fully open, are portrayed from every angle. The variation of ink tonalities throughout the painting is another excellent feature, with many "colors" of ink present in even a short stretch of branch. Among the literati, painting a variety of plants in ink was a preferred way of demonstrating skill with a brush, and the many subtleties achieved in this painting were intended to overpower the viewer with the artist's superb technique.

The great breadth of the scroll would have required a very large tokonoma for its display, suggesting that Baiitsu created it for a wealthy merchant or daimyo.[2] Although Baiitsu also made spectacular folding screens of birds and flowers, the austere elegance of his literati vision may be best expressed in the ink play seen here. PB

NOTES

1. The Cleveland Museum of Art has *White Prunus*, a large, complex plum painting by Baiitsu from 1854 in a vertical composition (inv. no. 1975.93: ink on paper, 172.4 × 79 cm). The single sheet of paper in the Honolulu painting is much larger than the standard size and slightly larger than that found in the Bunchō triptych (cat. no. 61).

2. The importance of the original commission is suggested by inscriptions discovered in the process of a recent remounting of this work. Identical inscriptions by the original mounter were found inside the *futai* strips hanging from the top edge and on the wooden pole inside the bottom of the mounting.

63. *Plum Blossoms and Bamboo* 梅竹図 (Baichiku zu)

1835
Ink on paper
97 × 176.6 cm

SIGNATURE: *Baiitsu Yamamoto Ryō* 梅逸山本亮

SEALS: *Yamamoto Ryō in* 山本亮印 (sig. upper)
Gyokuzen Koji 玉禅居士 (sig. lower)

INSCRIPTION:
乙未暑月戲墨於玉禅室中
The *otsubi* year [1835], sixth month—Playing with ink in the Gyokuzenshitsu studio

Purchase, 2005
13178.1

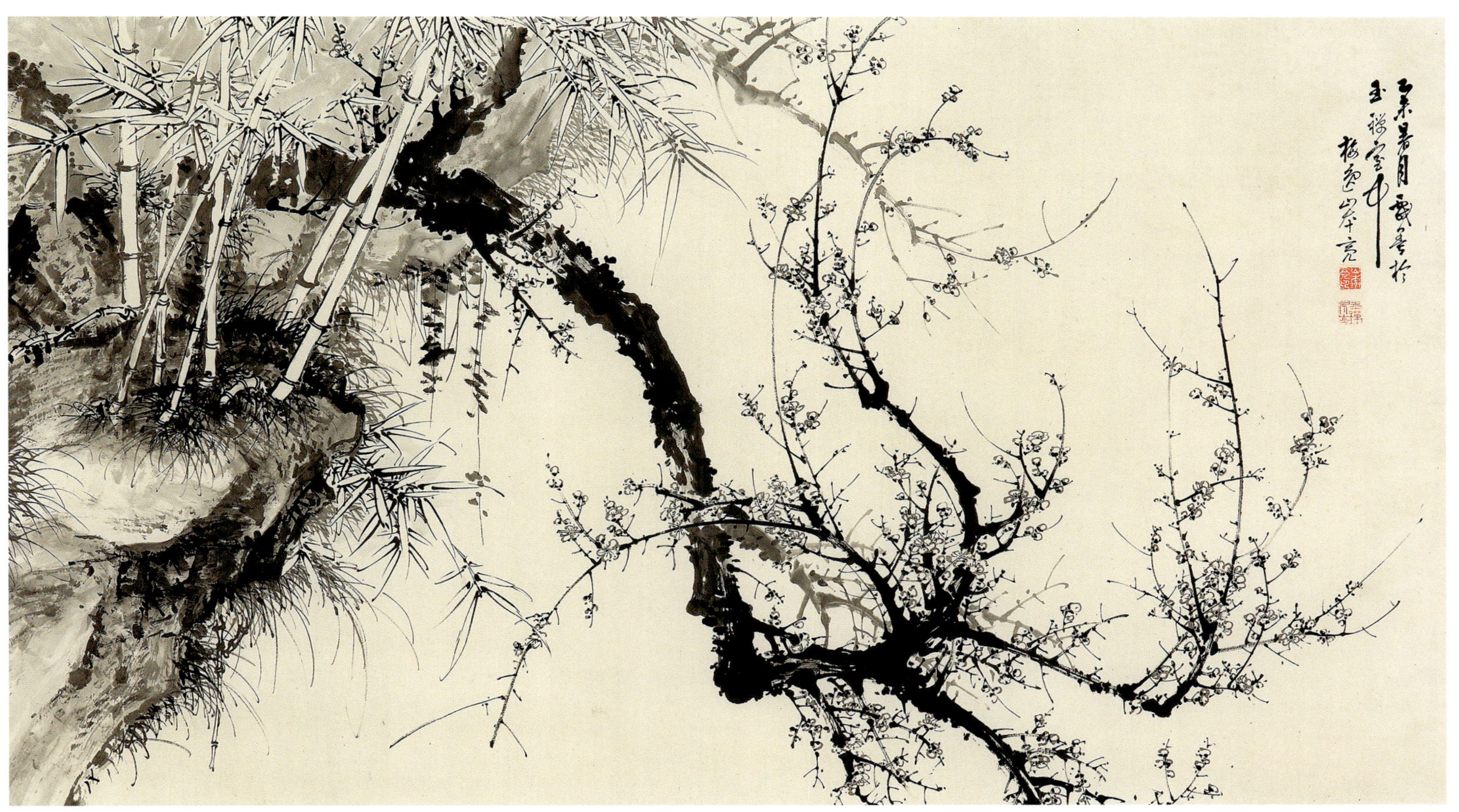

Nukina Kaioku 貫名海屋

1778–1863

64. *Plants of Four Seasons* 四時花卉図 (Shiji kaki zu) A

Late 1840s
Set of four hanging scrolls: ink and color on satin
140.7 × 49.7 cm each

SIGNATURES: *Kaisō shiga* 海叟詩畫 (spring)
Kaisō 海叟 (summer)
Kaisō heidai 海叟并題 (autumn)
Kaisō sha hei roku kyūsaku 海叟寫并録舊作 (winter)

SEALS (all four scrolls): *Jūsui* 拾翠 (upper right)
Kunmo shi 君茂氏 (sig. upper)
Hōchikujōsha 方竹杖者 Person of the Square Bamboo Cane[1] (sig. lower)

Purchase, 2005
13179.1–4

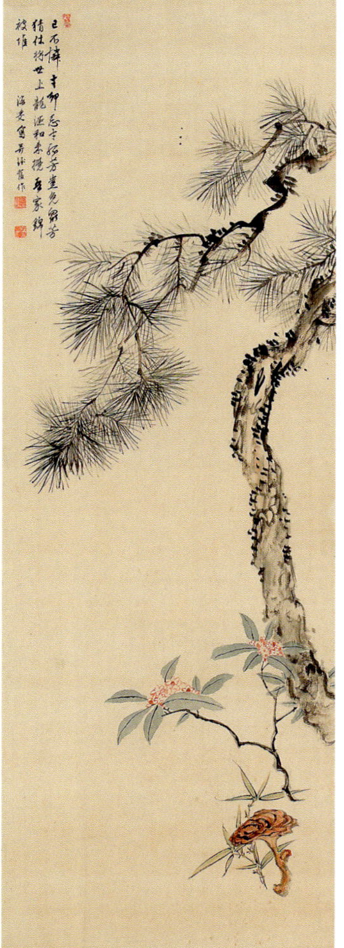
Winter

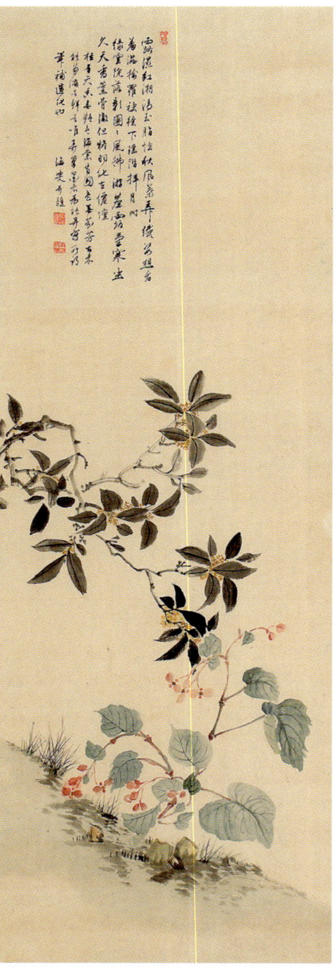
Autumn

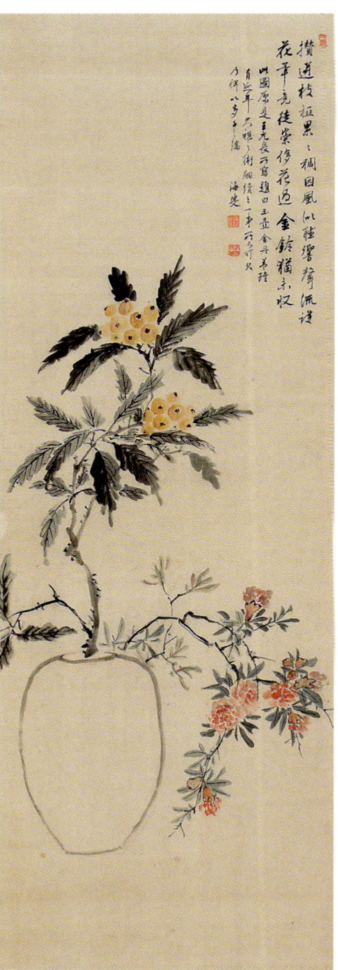
Summer

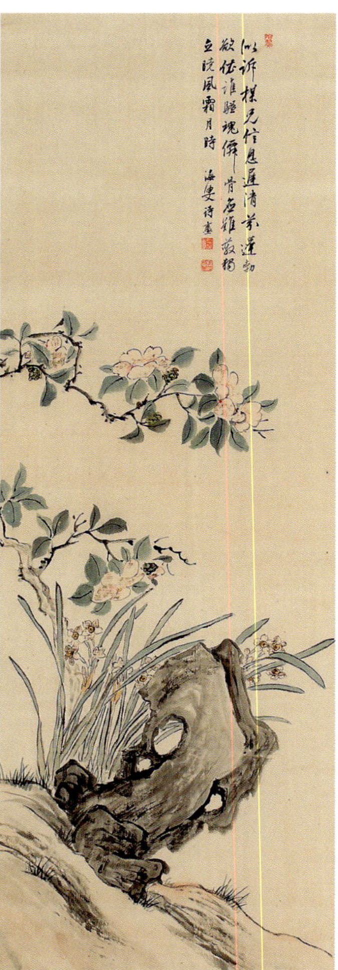
Spring

Nukina Kaioku enjoyed a great reputation as one of the best calligraphers at the end of the Edo period. A distinguished scholar of Chinese studies, he was also an accomplished painter known primarily for ink landscapes. *Plants of Four Seasons,* an ambitious set of hanging scrolls, brings to light Kaioku's excellent compositional skill and his proficient brush handling outside the landscape genre while demonstrating the importance of the birds-and-flowers theme to literati artists.

Early spring is represented by a white camellia and yellow narcissus juxtaposed to a convoluted rock. Narcissus, which blooms early in the season along with plum, is among the plant motifs favored by the *bunjin.* Kaioku's awkward outline of the narcissus leaves recalls the unorthodox brush style of Chinese artists such as Jin Nong 金農 (1786–1764), who produced numerous flower paintings.[2] The dramatic entrance of the camellia branch from the side of the composition was a device widely employed in the eighteenth century after it had first appeared in Yuan plum paintings. The dabs of brownish pigment on the petals of the camellia and narcissus indicate that the flowers are in the early stages of decay. As suggested by Kaioku's seven-character-line quatrain, they have passed their prime as they wait for the plum:

似訴楳兄信息遅	As if protesting the news of plum blossoming late,
清芬蓬勃欲依誰	On whom could the narcissus depend for a sudden burst of pure fragrance?
騒魂僊骨應難蔽	The spirit of the poet and the bone of the immortal should be difficult to hide.
獨立暁風霜月時	It stands alone all day in the wind of the dawn and in the frost of the moon.

In the summer painting, a white vase holds branches of loquat (*biwa* 枇杷) and flowering pomegranate (*zakuro* 石榴). Because it produces multiple fruits of golden color, loquat is symbolic of wealth, while pomegranate, with its numerous seeds, signifies wishes for posterity.[3] Kaioku sensitively and beautifully executed the pomegranate flowers, forming petals with a wet brush in thin color accentuated with darker hues. A similar technique applied to the loquat fruits gives them the appearance of roundness. Skillful variation of ink tone in the loquat leaves creates the illusion of depth. In some of the pomegranate blossoms and leaves, Kaioku subtly blended green and pink in the same stroke. In contrast to the luxuriant three-dimensionality of the plants, the white vase stands out in its severity as an abstract, flat shape defined by a broad, sketchy outline. In his inscription Kaioku stated that the painting was based on a work by one "Wang Yuanchang,"[4] but the "boneless" (Ch., *mogu,* J., *mokkotsu* 没骨) wash technique Kaioku utilized to define leaf and flower forms without outlines, here and in other scrolls, is generally associated with Shen Zhou 沈周 (1427–1509) and Chen Shun 陳淳 (1483–1544), painters admired by literati artists in the late Edo period. Kaioku's inscription can be translated as follows:

攢迸枝椏累々稠	Branches that gather and scatter are numerous and dense.
因風似聴響聲流	Wind causes us to hear the sound of water flowing.
護花畢竟徒崇侈	To protect flowers is but a luxury after all.
花過金鈴猶未収	Flowers have passed, but golden bells are not yet removed.

此圖原是王元長所寫 題曰玉壺金丹□隆 有延年久視之術 嗣續之一事所不可欠 乃裨以多子之瑞	This painting is based on the original by Wang Yuanchang titled *Jade Vase and Pill of Immortality.* Although there is the magic of prolonging your life, as for the affairs of posterity, you must have [pomegranate] because this benefits you with the happy sign of having many children.

Two plants represent autumn. *Mokusei* 木犀, also known as *keika* 桂花 (*Osmanthus fragrans*), with clusters of small, intensely fragrant yellow blossoms, is known as sweet osmanthus in the West. *Shūkaidō* 秋海棠 (*Begonia evansiana*) has lovely pink flowers hanging from its reddish stems. Again, Kaioku skillfully manipulated a wet brush dipped in color to portray leaves and flowers without outline, juxtaposing the delicate forms of *shūkaidō* to the sturdier *mokusei* above. The choice of these two plants is explained in the inscription in Kaioku's elegant semicursive (*gyōsho* 行書) style:

露濕紅潮濟玉脂	Dawn dampens the red mixed with a light jade color.
怯秋風葉弄纎姿	The leaves that are afraid of the autumn wind swing with delicate figures
想看羞澀掄羅袂	If you wish to see the shy forms of flowers, you must pull up your silk sleeves
徐下瑶階拝月時	And slowly descend the stairs of precious stone and pay respect to the moon.
緑雲院落影團々	Green cloud of trees in the courtyard casts shadows everywhere.
風拂游塵露気寒	Wind blows the dust, and dew makes the air chilly.
座久天香薫骨徹	If you linger there, the heavenly fragrance will penetrate your bones.
但疑羽化在僊壇	You wonder if you are becoming an immortal to live in their abode.

桂有天香無艶色 海棠有國色無芬芳 古来能兼備者鮮 是唯弄筆墨者為能并寫 所謂筆補造化也	*Keika* has heavenly fragrance but lacks luxurious color; *Kaidō* has beautiful color but lacks fragrance. Since ancient times, the plants that have both are rare. Only those who play with brush and ink can achieve what nature cannot. It means that the brush can supplement nature.

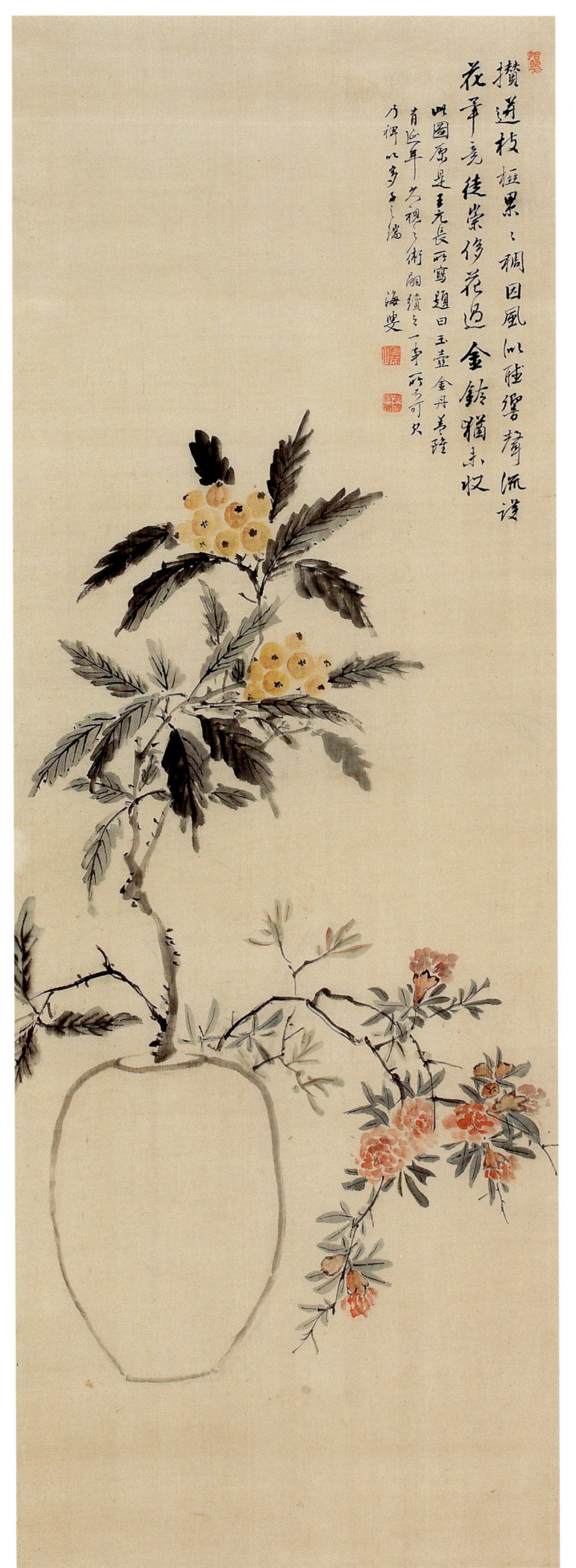

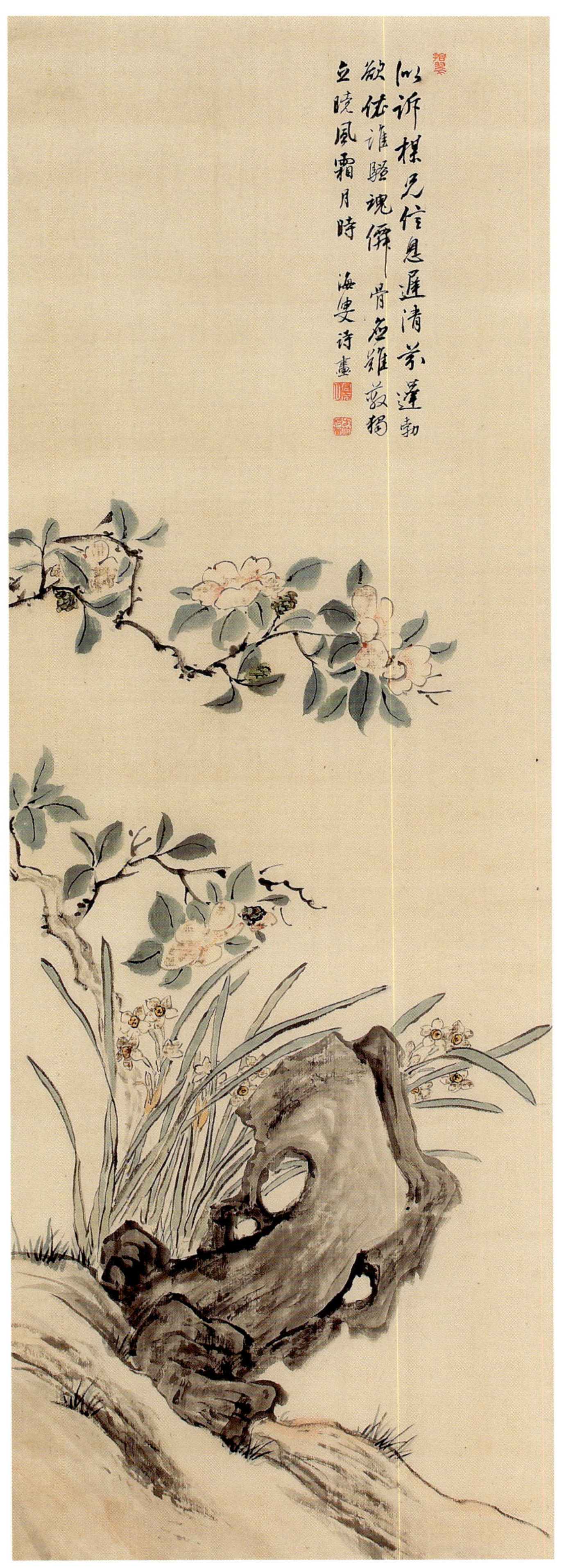

Unlike the spring and autumn paintings, which are set in natural environments, and the summer scroll, which has an arranged setting, the plants in the winter painting appear to exist in abstract space. A pine dominates the composition with its rough trunk and long overhanging branch, accompanied by *reishi* 霊芝, *sasa* 笹 or bamboo, and aromatic *jinchōge* 沈丁花, commonly known as daphne (*Daphne odora*). Without any depiction of the ground or setting, the spatial relationship of the plants is ambiguous. The *jinchōge* wraps two of its branches around the pine, while its stem overlaps unnaturally with the *sasa* leaf. Kaioku's poem seems to express the proud sentiment of the *jinchōge*, which finds itself in the distinguished company of auspicious plants:

已不憐才却忌才	You do not appreciate others' talents; not only that, you envy it.
孤芳豈免衆芳猜	As for the lonely fragrant flower, how can it escape the mistrust of all others?
休将世上龍涎和	Stop mixing your common fragrance
来攪吾家錦被堆	With my cluster of beautiful flowers.

Painted on a lustrous satin ground, *Plants of Four Seasons* has a monumental scale that suggests Kaioku produced the set for a special occasion. In a demonstration of their high esteem for the artist, Meiji-period *bunjin* extensively inscribed the box containing these scrolls in 1896. Ema Tenkō 江馬天江 (1825–1901) inscribed the title on the front of the box lid. On the back, Tenkō, Kaioku's calligraphy pupil Kōbayashi Takusai 小林卓斎 (1831–1916), and the *bunjin* Nakamura Kakudō 中村確堂 (dates unknown) each wrote a long inscription extolling the virtue of Kaioku's work.

MM

NOTES

1. See note 3 at cat. no. 31.

2. See similarly awkward outlines of day lilies by Jin Nong in Marshall P. S. Wu, *The Orchid Pavilion Gathering: Chinese Painting from the University of Michigan Museum of Art*, vol. 1 (Ann Arbor: University of Michigan, 2000), 240. The possible circumstances of his influence on Japanese artists during Kaioku's time remain to be ascertained.

3. See Tōkyō Kokuritsu Hakubutsukan, *Kisshō: Chūgoku bijutsu ni komerareta imi*, exh. cat. (Tokyo, 1998), 138, 184–86.

4. This artist has not been identified.

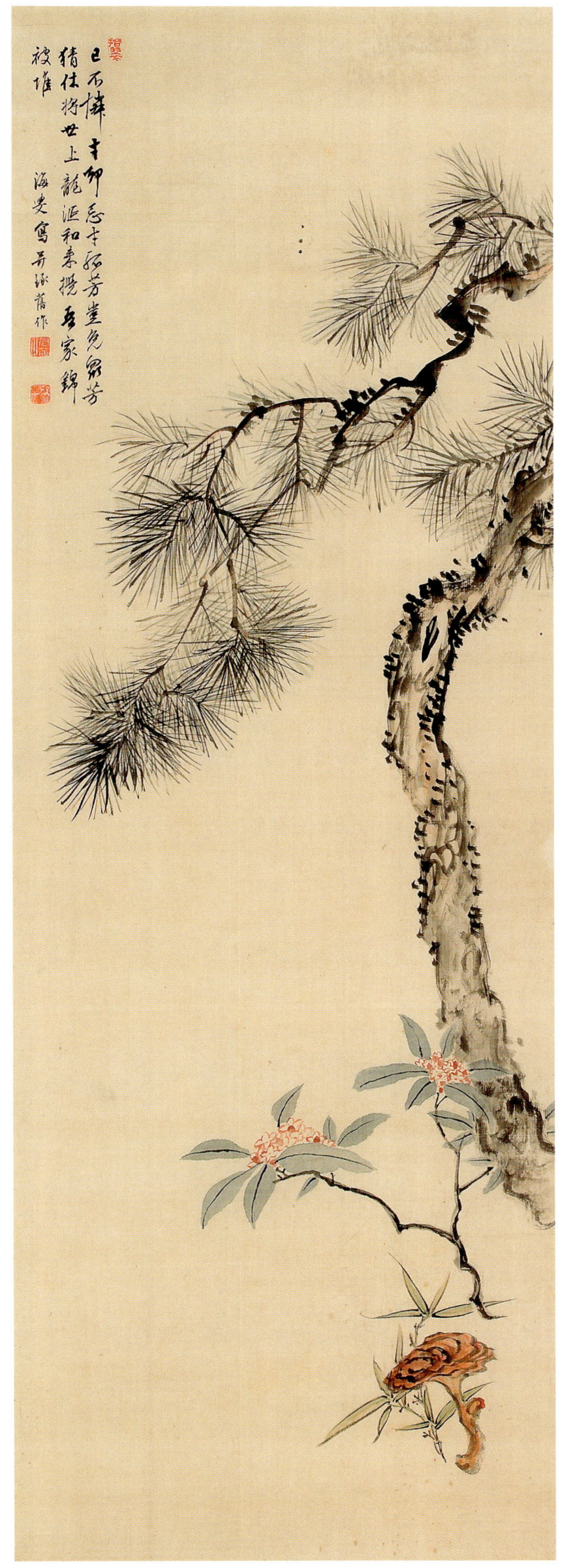

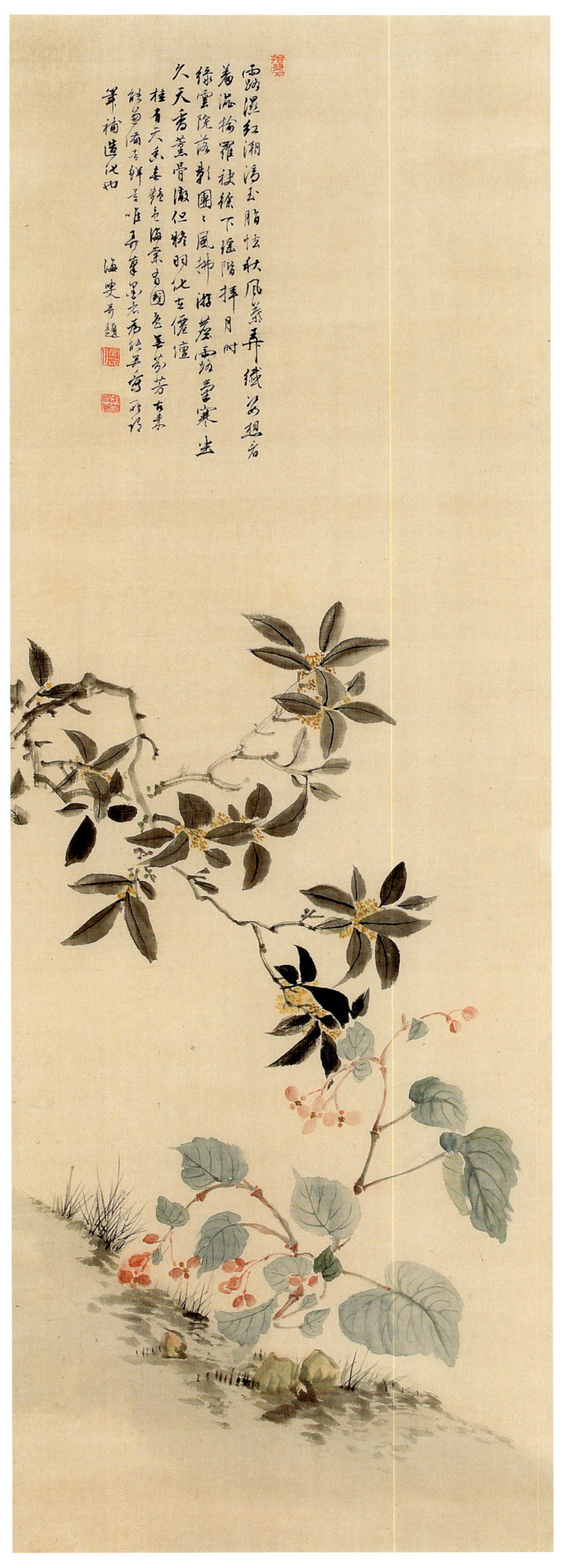

Fujimoto Tesseki 藤本鉄石

1817–1863

Pine trees are one of the most enduring painting themes in East Asian culture. Symbolizing endurance and longevity, they were represented in many ways, sometimes in association with cranes, tortoises, and other motifs of immortality. The composition of *Old Pine,* combining *reishi* 霊芝, rocks, and a pine tree, is sometimes known as Fungus of Immortals and Longevity (*Shisen ennen* 芝仙延年).[1] Although a popular theme for any occasion, such paintings were often given to celebrate the recipient's sixtieth birthday.

The late Edo and Meiji periods saw an explosive growth in the popularity of this theme among literati painters, with many examples by Tesseki, Yamanaka Shinten'ō 山中信天翁 (1822–1885), Nukina Kaioku 貫名海屋 (1778–1863), Tomioka Tessai 富岡鐵斎 (1836–1924), and others. Beyond their auspicious meaning, these paintings, often quite large, were displays of the bravura brushwork of the artists. By the mid-nineteenth century, many ink paintings on this theme by literati from the late Ming and early Qing periods had been imported to Japan. The pines by Tesseki and Shinten'ō, in particular, seem to have been strongly influenced by these examples, including the fashion of painting on satin to add a sheen to the ink tonalities.[2]

Tesseki created *Old Pine* with powerful brushwork that contrasts the prickly straight lines of the needles with the sensuous curving outlines of the mist coiling around the branches. He used essentially two tones of ink, a simplicity that adds to the graphic power of the whole composition. A profusion of fungi sprout from the trunk, while a prominent stone leans over the exposed roots of the pine. In an added touch of elegance, visible behind the tree base are the arching leaves and blooms of orchids, which were often employed to symbolize the virtues of a scholar living in isolation in the country. The strength of the brushwork and calligraphy are typical of the energetic expansiveness found in many of Tesseki's larger works. A certain irony surrounds Tesseki's celebrations of longevity, an aspiration he willingly sacrificed for his political beliefs but which resulted in the long-lasting esteem of his friends.[3] PB

65. *Old Pine* 老松図 (Oimatsu zu)

1859
Hanging scroll: ink on satin
158 × 51.6 cm

SIGNATURE: *Tessenshi* 鐵仙史

SEALS: *Fujimoto Shinkin* 藤本真金 (sig. upper)
Hitsu (?) *jingū* 筆□神遇 (sig. lower)
Fujimoto Shinkin 藤本真金, *Juraku* 壽樂, delight in longevity, *tomon baisai* 都門賣菜 Selling vegetables in the capital, *Kibi danshi* 吉備男子 Man of Kibi (bottom right)

INSCRIPTION:
挺龍雲畔松
訖木澗邊石
此際採恭芝
不尋黄与赤
鐵仙史作時己未中秋

A prominent dragon amid clouds—the bankside pine,
Reaching the tree and torrent beside the rock.
On this occasion picking the venerable fungus [of immortality],
Not seeking the Yellow and Red [of alchemy].

Created by Tessenshi in the eighth month of the *kibi* year [1859]

Purchase, 2005
13188.1

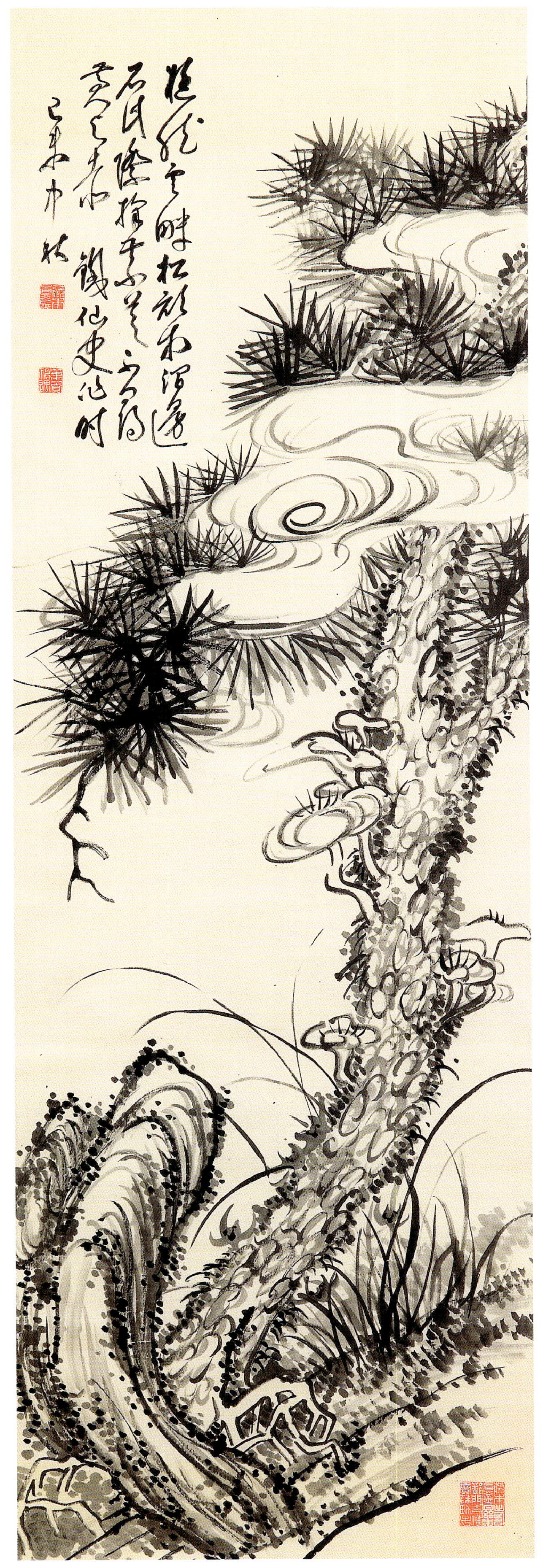

NOTES

1. Kanai Shiun, ed. *Tōyō gadai sōran* (Tokyo: Kokusho Kankōkai, 1997), 882.

2. Shinten'ō, Tessai, and others of their circle made many box inscriptions on such seventeenth-century Chinese paintings, although these have yet to be systematically studied.

3. Consult the biography section in this catalogue for the dramatic circumstances of his death, which caused him to be considered a martyr in the cause of imperial restoration.

Shiokawa Bunrin 塩川文麟

1808–1877

Bunrin usually followed the themes and Shijō-school approach of his teacher Okamoto Toyohiko 岡本豊彦 (1773–1845), yet late in his career he often made larger hanging-scroll paintings that reveal a Meiji-period preference for bold presentation. The long-standing literati interest in depictions of moonlit plum blossoms and evening landscapes was extended in the mid-nineteenth century by an ever-broadening variety of nighttime scenes. Bunrin, in particular, developed a reputation for the skillful ink tonalities with which he rendered images of fireflies and nighttime motifs.[1]

White Fox on a Moonlit Night conveys a dramatic nighttime atmosphere through a combination of ink washes and broad dark brushstrokes in the tree trunks, branches, and grasses. *Byakko,* the white fox connected with the Shinto worship of Inari 稲荷, was a common subject of paintings (see the related theme by Kōno Bairei, cat. no. 68);[2] when shown in forest settings, the fox is associated with *sugi* 杉 trees (cryptomeria or Japanese cedar). There was once a famous *sugi* tree on the grounds of Fushimi Inari called *Shirushi no sugi* 験杉, and trees figure in early legends of the shrine. Visitors to Fushimi Inari picked a twig from the sacred tree, and if it soon withered at home, they knew their wishes would not be granted.[3] Bunrin's *sugi* are ancient, old-growth trees that fill the right side of the composition in dramatic contrast to the half-moon emerging from dark clouds. The white hairs of the fox are meticulously drawn with *gofun* 胡粉, a traditional white pigment made from finely ground shell. The fox has a confident, even spritely expression that agrees with its positive role as the guardian of Inari, a deity of rice cultivation. The positioning of the brilliant white fox against its dark surroundings makes for a riveting image, as attractive as it is mysterious. Its graphic power shows Bunrin's individuality, which exceeded the more reserved nature of his immediate predecessors in the Shijō-school lineage. PB

66. *White Fox on a Moonlit Night*
月夜白狐図 (Getsuya byakko zu)

Hanging scroll: ink and color on silk
127.2 × 50.2 cm

SIGNATURE: *En Bunrin* 塩文麟

SEALS: *En Bunrin* 塩文麟印 (upper)
Shion shi 子温氏 (lower)

Purchase, 2005
13191.1

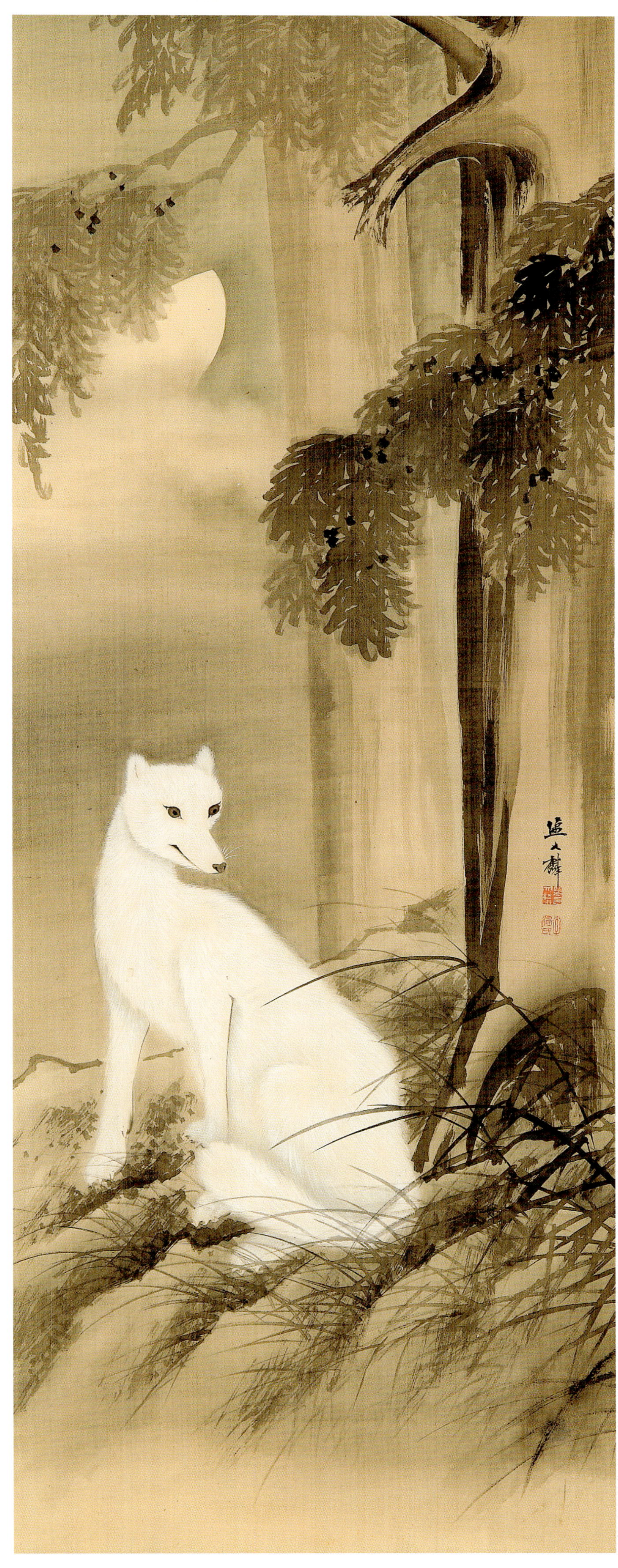

NOTES

1. Examples of Bunrin's dramatic treatment of fireflies include a hanging scroll at the British Museum and a six-panel screen at the Nelson-Atkins Museum of Art in Kansas City.

2. For a discussion of *byakko* in Shinto, see Karen Smyers, *The Fox and the Jewel: Shared and Private Meanings in Contemporary Japanese Inari Worship* (Honolulu: University of Hawaii Press, 1999). For a treatment of the fox in Japanese mythology, see M. W. de Visser's lengthy essay "The Fox and the Badger in Japanese Folklore," *Transactions of the Asiatic Society of Japan* 36, no. 3 (1908): 1–159, and Michael Bathgate, *The Fox's Craft in Japanese Religion and Culture* (London: Routledge, 2003).

3. See De Visser's comments on this tree based on an 1836 source and also his remarks on the importance of trees to Inari worship at Fushimi in "The Fox and the Badger in Japanese Folklore," 134–35, 144.

Yamanaka Shinten'ō 山中信天翁

1822–1885

Shinten'ō most commonly painted towering mountain landscapes, often of considerable size.[1] Beyond these, he painted all manner of themes, including birds and flowers, even butterflies. Rarely employing color, he focused on unusual compositions with strong brushwork and fine ink tonalities. In *One Hundred Things as You Wish,* Shinten'ō assembled various items in a basket as though they had just been collected on a trip to the country. His arrangement of persimmons and chrysanthemums with an unseasonal branch of flowering plum represents the pleasurable aspects of everyday life that even those without wealth may enjoy. The simplicity of the topic is given much greater depth through the long inscription, which presents a classic literati emphasis on the meaning and enjoyment of life:

> 是以音者形為畫題所謂畫苑韻
> 事無有百事如意者挟富貴
> 者不能為之別於佞耶然如無恒
> 産匹夫善以一心之正為無不百
> 事如意也昔作此図者必有所成
> 写之予亦喜仿此
> 戊寅九月九日并題於渡月橋西草堂

> This painting shows how we use sound to create form and use it as a theme for painting. It is what we call an elegant game in the painting world. Regarding not having the state of the "hundred things one wishes for," those who possess wealth cannot help but have everything they want. Being wealthy does not mean that one is mean or petty. Nevertheless, if a humble person, who lacks a constant means of livelihood, is good-hearted, he can have everything he desires through correctness of heart. In the past, those [without wealth] who created this kind of image certainly had achieved the state of having everything they wished for [through correctness of heart] and expressed it in their paintings. I, too, gladly follow this.
>
> Painted and inscribed on the ninth day of the ninth month in the *boin* year [1878] at the Western Studio by Togetsukyō bridge.[2]

The prominence of the text adds to the Chinese quality of the work, which is reinforced by the mounting design, whose uncomplicated format and fabric color follow the mode favored on the continent. Shinten'ō could write in a variety of scripts, and the twisting, cursive strokes seen in the inscription are an excellent example of his most famous style. Scrolls of moderate size with involved inscriptions were especially favored for the *sencha* gatherings that Shinten'ō frequently enjoyed with his friends. Although it depicts just a few items gathered in a basket, the written sentiments suggest that this painting was intended as a microcosm of the delights of the botanical world. PB

67. *One Hundred Things as You Wish*
百事如意図 (Hyakuji nyoi zu)

1878
Hanging scroll: ink on satin
120.5 × 33.2 cm

SIGNATURE: *Shinten'ō* 信天翁

SEALS: 蕩浮漚 (upper right)
Seiitsu 静逸 (sig. upper)
忘毀誉可以清心 To be oblivious of slander or praise makes a pure heart (sig. lower)
餘時作詩人 Spare time makes the poet (bottom left)

Purchase, 2005
13197.1

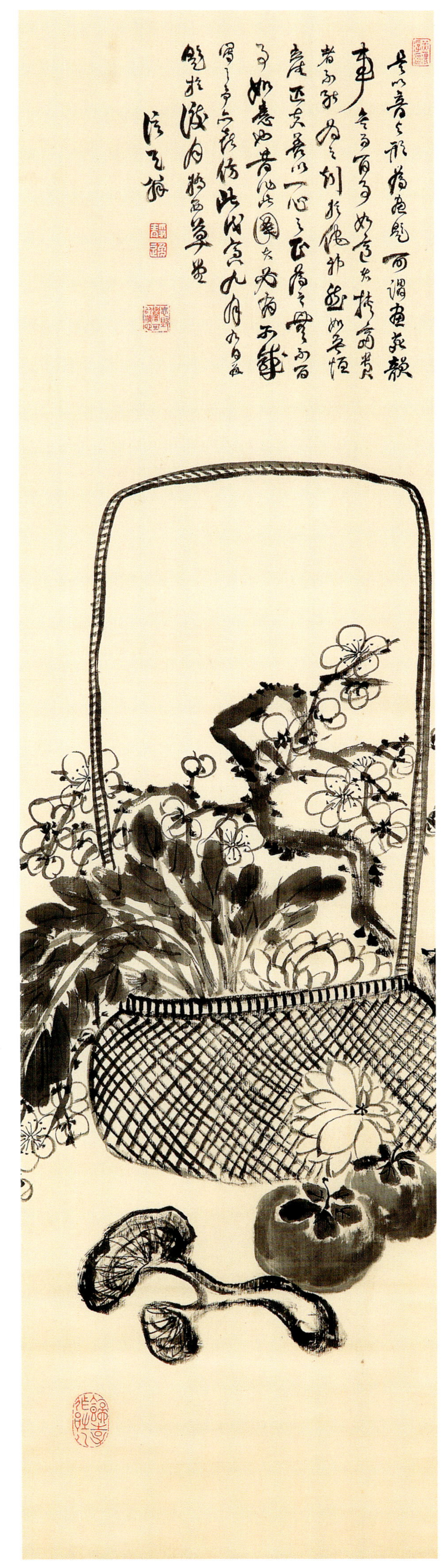

NOTES

1. See the dozens of examples, including screens, in Shintenkai, *Shinten'ō* (Nagoya, 1915), and Hekinanshi Bunkazai Senmon Iinkai, *Shinten'ō ibokushū* (Hekinanshi: Hekinanshi Kyōiku Iinkai, 1981).

2. Michiyo Morioka made the initial draft of this translation.

Kōno Bairei 幸野楳嶺

1844–1895

The viewer faced with this startling painting immediately questions its meaning. Many Kyoto *nihonga* painters, reflecting the popular Maruyama and Shijō traditions of naturalistic animal representation, tended to depict the fox as a wild creature in a lyrical landscape setting. Despite his descriptive brushwork, Kōno Bairei took a different approach with unusual imagery that references the animal's supernatural power.

The fox, considered to have magical abilities for purposes both malicious and benevolent, has been long associated with Inari 稲荷, the Shinto deity of rice.[1] Typically portrayed as a white fox, the animal is believed to be a sacred messenger of Inari or a manifestation of the deity itself. Legends and folk tales abound in Japan about a fox who possesses and torments humans with its shape-shifting ability, but the subject of a fox leaping over a torii gate appears only occasionally.[2] According to beliefs that date to the seventeenth century, at least all the foxes of Japan came as divine messengers of Inari to the deity's shrine in Kyoto, and they could jump over torii and haunt humans. Relying on their skill as tricksters, they obtained various ranks from Inari. A story from about 1700 tells of a man sitting before the Inari shrine when a fox comes out and jumps back and forth over the torii. The animal invites the astonished man to join him and, when he demurs, offers to help. Taking the man's kimono, the fox throws a long rope over the torii and pulls it back and forth over the gate, making the man feel as if he also were jumping.[3] When the man returns home after this encounter, the villagers chase him away. He realizes that he has turned into a fox, thus falling into the animal realm of Buddhist existence.

Although it is difficult to identify the specific source of Bairei's inspiration, the theme of his painting is clearly the divine aspect of the fox's association with Inari. The magnificent, beautiful fox jumps over the torii, his graceful form full of energy and tension, and his whiteness highlighted by the black and red of the gate. The robust cryptomeria (*sugi* or Japanese cedar) next to the gate is an important iconographic element that appears in the legend of the Inari shrine (see cat. no. 66). By concealing the bottom of the torii and the cryptomeria tree with mist, Bairei called attention to the height of the gate, further stressing the animal's extraordinary power. A convincing representation of a magical moment in a naturalistic style, the image successfully captures the dual nature of the fox as a living creature and an object of worship.

White Fox Jumping over a Torii Gate, dated 1875 in the box inscription by the artist, comes from the first decade of Bairei's career as a professional painter. In 1871 he began studying with Shiokawa Bunrin 塩川文麟 (1808–1877), a Shijō-school painter, with the permission of his first teacher, Nakajima Raishō 中島来章 (1796–1871). Bairei's work and Bunrin's *White Fox on a Moonlit Night* (see cat. no. 66) offer an attractive teacher-disciple comparison not only in their apparent contrasts but also in the similarities seen in the configuration of the cryptomeria tree and the layered brushstrokes of the tree trunk.

MM

68. *White Fox Jumping over a Torii Gate*
華表白狐図 (Kahyō byakko zu) T

1875
Hanging scroll: ink and color on silk
128.6 × 56.2 cm

SIGNATURE: *Bairei Toyo* 楳嶺豊

SEALS: *Kōno Naotoyo* 幸野直豊 (sig. upper)
Bairei 楳嶺 (sig. lower)

Purchase, 2005
13192.1

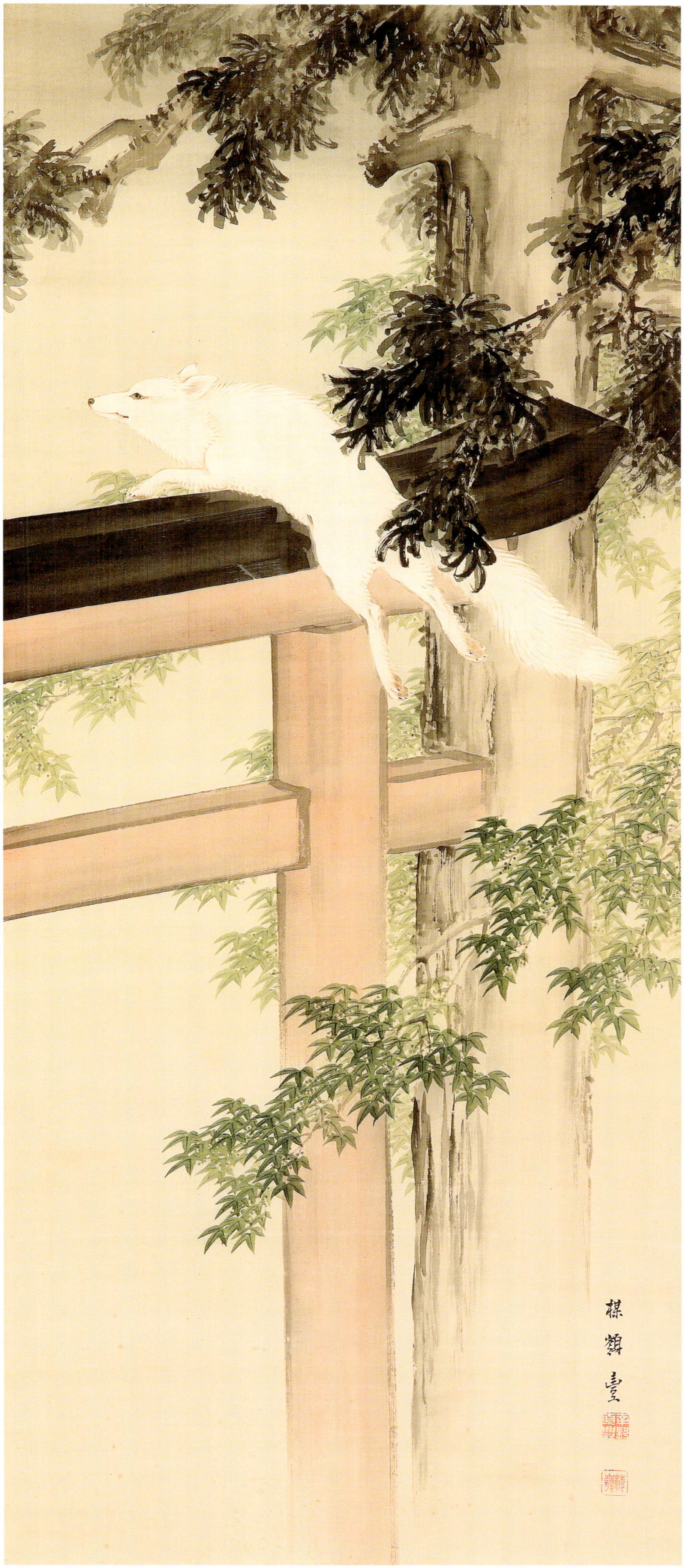

NOTES

1. A good English-language source for this topic is Karen Ann Smyers, *The Fox and the Jewel: Shared and Private Meanings in Contemporary Japanese Inari Worship* (Honolulu: University of Hawaii Press, 1999).

2. The two stories cited in this paragraph come from M. W. de Visser, "The Fox and the Badger in Japanese Folklore," *Transactions of the Asiatic Society of Japan* 36, no. 3 (1908): 62 and 99–100.

3. De Visser's account is vague as to exactly what the fox did with the man's coat—whether he wore it or tied it to the end of the rope, for example.

Suzuki Shōnen　鈴木松年

1848–1918

69. *Old Pine* 老松図 (Rōshō zu)

1900
Pair of six-panel screens: ink, color, and gold on paper
155 × 360 cm each

SIGNATURES: *Shōnen senshi hitsu* 松年遷史筆 (right screen)
Rōryūkan Shōnen senshi hitsu 老龍館松年遷史筆 (left screen)

SEALS: *Senshin* 洗心 (upper right, right screen only)
Suzuki Seken 鈴木世賢 (sig. upper)
Shōnen 松年 (sig. lower)

Gift of Terry Welch, in honor of Stephen Little, 2005
13147.1 & 2

INSCRIPTION:

北風吹群木　葉々飛作塵
獨有松樹在　蒼々顔色新
屹立深澗底　歳寒見精神
不敢遜霜雪　気勢老益振
飛鶴長結契　竹柏可卜隣
壽将踰萬歳　豈啻期千春
明治庚子穐日
造於老龍館

The north wind blows through trees,
Scattering leaves and raising dust.
　The pine exists in solitude,
Its dark green color appearing fresh.
　Soaring like a mountain by a deep river valley,
　It is in winter that we see its spirit emerge.
Not yielding to frost and snow,
　Its stature becomes more robust in old age.
Flying cranes always remain its friends,
　And bamboo and oak can be its neighbors.
Its life span is no mere one thousand springs,
　Certainly surpassing ten thousand years.

In autumn of the *kōshi* year of Meiji [1900]
Created at the Old Dragon Hall

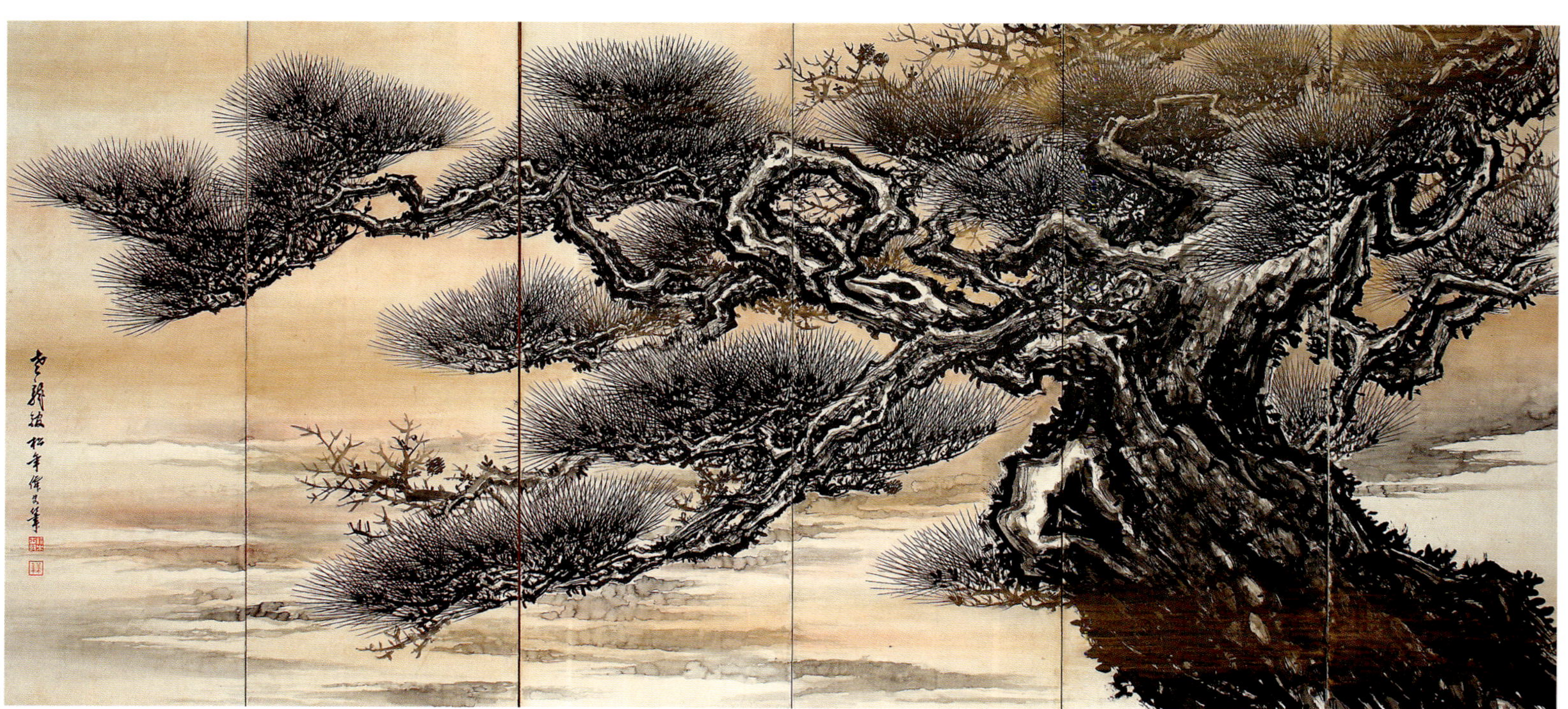

This spectacular painting represents Suzuki Shōnen's powerful artistic vision at its best. With its overwhelming monumentality and sheer dynamism, the painting expresses the aesthetic of the Meiji period, in which Shōnen flourished. In both screens, a thick trunk of pine extends from one corner, its form and movement resembling the body of a dragon covered with scales. By tightly cropping the top and bottom of the pines, Shōnen conveyed the massive size of the trees, which seemingly burst out of the pictorial space. In each screen, the craggy pine branches bend and twist through all six panels. The magnificent rising sun in the right screen enhances the auspicious symbolism of the pine, its warm glow reflected on the surface of the water in the background. The two screens do not create a single continuous composition. Rather, the images suggest two separate trees growing side by side, oriented in different directions. While viewing the screens together strengthens the impact, the fullness of each composition allows them to be shown separately.

Shōnen combined a bold brush technique, exemplified by the outlined forms of the tree trunks and branches, with a precise, sharp delineation of the pine needles. Despite the bizarre, fanciful appearance of the pines, the images are firmly based on a study of nature: the complex structure of the branches is clearly and carefully defined in three-dimensional space. In the depiction of the marshy background, Shōnen applied the faintest washes in ink and color, creating an unexpected lyricism. Washes of gold make the mist sparkle with the fresh feeling of early morning.

Shōnen received basic artistic training from his father, Hyakunen 百年 (1825–1891), and succeeded him at the Suzuki school Hyakunen established, but Shōnen cultivated his own more dramatic style. During the 1880s and 1890s, Shōnen, Kōno Bairei 幸野楳嶺 (1844–1895), and Kishi Chikudō 岸竹堂 (1826–1897) were considered Kyoto's foremost painters. The period was referred to as the era of *Shō chiku bai* 松竹梅, or pine, bamboo, and plum, taking the first character in each name—"pine" from Shōnen, "bamboo" from Chikudō, and "plum" from Bairei. Appropriately, Shōnen produced many pine paintings in his career. He enjoyed working on a monumental scale and is said to have kept nearly ten pairs of screens in his studio at any given time so that he could paint the moment inspiration struck.[1] Dated 1900, this pair from the peak of Shōnen's career is a superb example of the virile style on which he built his reputation. MM

NOTE

1. "Gendai meigaka den 5: Suzuki Shōnen," *Kaiga seidan* 5 (May 1913): 54.

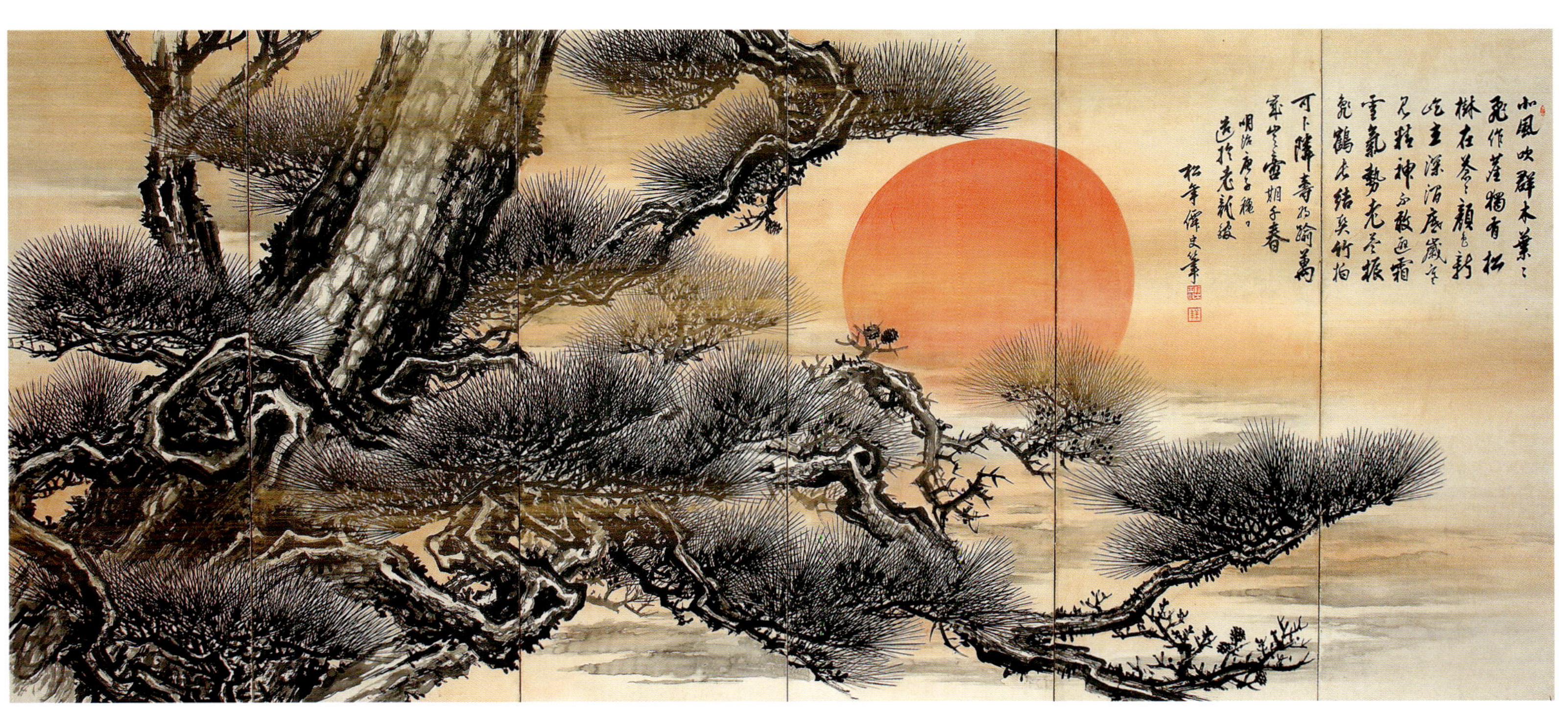

Tsuji Kakō 都路華香

1870–1931

Throughout his career Tsuji Kakō painted numerous species of birds, from the heroic eagle and graceful crane to the more commonplace rooster and crow. In documented examples of his oeuvre, however, paintings of cranes outnumber all others. In some, the crane is combined with pine as an auspicious symbol of longevity; many others portray the bird against a background of water, one of Kakō's favorite motifs. The most unusual example, a crane-shaped ceramic hand-warmer decorated by Kakō, was once in the collection of his fellow Kyoto painter Nishiyama Suishō 西山翠嶂 (1879–1958).[1] The crane was also the subject of Kakō's successful submission to the 1914 government exhibition, a pair of six-panel screens titled *Wild Cranes and Quiet Clouds* (Kan'un yakun 閑雲野鶴). A masterful representation of two cranes flying against a background of golden and silver clouds, this stunning combination of naturalism and decorative beauty won a second-place award that year.[2]

The relatively informal style of the screen in the Honolulu Academy of Arts collection suggests that Kakō painted it for a private commission or sale. This unpretentious representation of a traditional subject demonstrates Kakō's solid *shasei* (sketching from life) foundation. Unassuming and descriptive, the bold ink strokes describing the black tail feathers reveal Kakō's consummate brush skill. Most memorable, however, are the whimsical expressions of the cranes, which distinguish them from those painted by Kakō's contemporaries. One crane seems almost to smile and the other turns its curious button eyes toward the viewer; they recall the humor often seen in the animal paintings of Nagasawa Rosetsu 長沢蘆雪 (1754–1799). In the background, gray ink washes representing water subtly change their tonality to create a misty atmosphere, while the faint orange wash bathing the upper left evokes the light of the rising sun. The directionality of the cranes, the abrupt ending of the ground line at the left, and the hint of sunlight at the upper left raise the possibility that the screen originally might have been paired with another six-panel screen on its left. Viewed as a single screen, however, the composition is well-balanced and satisfying.

The last decade of the Meiji era, to which *Cranes* can be dated based on the signature style, marked a pivotal period in Kakō's career. Having emerged as one of the new leaders of the Kyoto painting world after the passing of its elders, including his teacher, Kōno Bairei 幸野楳嶺 (1844–1895), Kakō pursued his own modern expression by experimenting in diverse styles and studying the wave theme. Many of his works from the period favor dramatic compositions and unconventional brushwork. The quiet beauty of this screen introduces another facet of Kakō's oeuvre during this important period. MM

NOTES

1. See Tomita Keisen, ed., *Kakō bokushō* (Kyoto, 1932), 4 and plate 62.

2. Illustrated in Michiyo Morioka and Paul Berry, *Modern Masters of Kyoto: The Transformation of Japanese Painting Traditions, Nihonga from the Griffith and Patricia Way Collection* (Seattle: Seattle Art Museum, 1999), 48.

70. *Cranes* 鶴図 (Tsuru zu)

c. 1908
Six-panel screen: ink and color on paper
122.7 × 261.6 cm

SIGNATURE: *Kakō saku* 華香作

SEALS: *Miyako yoshikage in* 都良景印 (sig. upper)
Kakō 華香 (sig. lower)

Purchase, 2005
13149.1

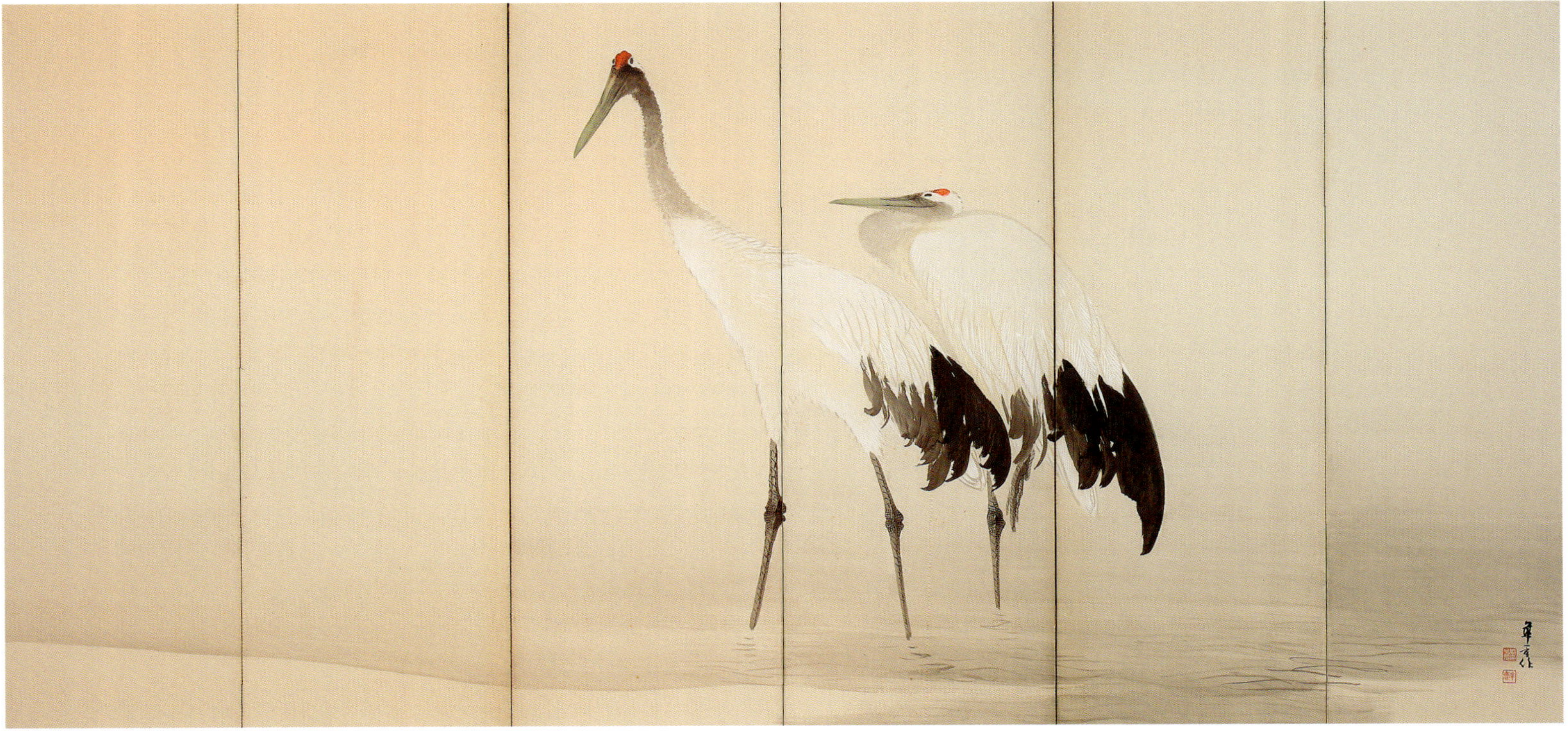

Mizuta Chikuho　水田竹圃

1883–1958

Mizuta Chikuho earned his reputation as an ink painter loyal to the orthodox literati mode. His paintings often incorporated light color but avoided the thick application of bright pigments even when it became a vogue in the Taishō art world. From early in his career Chikuho's admirers uniformly praised his brush technique as "classic" and his resulting ink expression as "dignified and upright."[1] At the government competitions, however, his ambitious large-scale landscapes drew criticism for lacking a strong emotional impact despite impeccable brushwork and elegant compositions.[2] In general, the public nature of competitive exhibitions compelled artists to submit paintings of impressive size and formality. It was through privately commissioned small works that artists exercised greater freedom and spontaneity. This hanging scroll exemplifies the latter category and comes from the period when Chikuho busied himself as a major literati painter at both the government-sponsored and Japan Nanga Institute (Nihon Nangain 日本南画院) exhibitions.

Gibbons Grasping at the Moon is lucid in its thematic message and rich in ink expression. Chikuho utilized the vertical, elongated format most effectively to create a masterful composition and displayed, within its small scale, a wide range of ink-brush technique varying in tonality, wetness, and stroke shapes. The juxtaposition of a cascading waterfall and a large dry branch in the middle of the scene forcefully directs the viewer's eye to the gibbons below. The two animals link arms to form a chain as they dangle from the branch, trying to reach the reflection of the moon on the water. The image represents a metaphor of the Zen teaching that all things in life are illusory. The playfulness of the image is matched by Chikuho's succinct inscription in a casual calligraphic style:

水中明月輪	As for the bright moon in the water,
可翫不可覓	It can be played with but cannot be found.
彌猴徒自狂	Gibbons merely become crazy,
触破寒潭碧	Touching and breaking the cold blue-green pond.

Gibbons and monkeys have been endearing subjects in the Japanese painting tradition. In particular, the eighteenth- and nineteenth-century artists of the Maruyama and Shijō schools in Kyoto popularized a new realist style based on the close observation of animals. Foremost among them is Mori Sosen 森狙仙 (1747–1821), whose lifelike portrayals of monkeys gained a large following in the Kyoto-Osaka area.[3] The lineage of the realist school was transmitted to the twentieth-century *nihonga* painters of Kyoto, among whom Takeuchi Seihō 竹内栖鳳 (1964–1942) and Hashimoto Kansetsu 橋本関雪 (1883–1945) became known for their superb depictions of animals, including monkeys and gibbons.

Chikuho's painting, however, references an even earlier tradition in Japan, which began with the introduction of Chinese ink painting. A famous triptych at Daitokuji in Kyoto by Mu Qi 牧谿, a thirteenth-century Chan monk-painter, included a scene of a long-armed gibbon clasping its baby. The work inspired many later Japanese artists, including Hasegawa Tōhaku 長谷川等伯 (1539–1610). During the Edo period, the compositional element of gibbons forming a vertical chain became associated predominantly with the Kanō 狩野 artists. Thus, Chikuho transformed a Kanō-school device with a Zen reference into a freely brushed literati expression.

MM

71. *Gibbons Grasping at the Moon*
猿猴捉月図 (Enkō sokugetsu zu) T

1930s
Hanging scroll: ink on silk
118 × 20.4 cm

SIGNATURE: 竹圃散人寫於蟻池庵
Painted by Chikuho at the Ant Pond Hermitage

SEALS: illegible (upper right)
Den Kei in 田敬印 (sig. upper)
Chikuho 竹圃 (sig. lower)

Purchase, 2005
13218.1

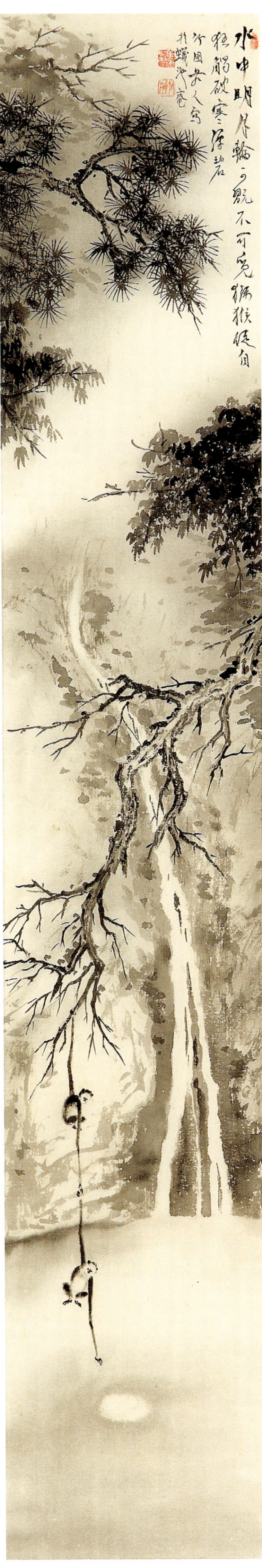

NOTES

1. See "Mizuta Chikuho shi sakuga tenrankai," *Kaiga seidan* 5, no. 8 (August 1917): 48, and Soeda Tatsurei, "Nangain dai gokai ten o miru," *Bi no kuni* 3, no. 2 (February 1927): 88.

2. See a comment on Chikuho's submission to the 1929 government exhibition in Nittenshi Hensan Iinkai, *Nittenshi 9, Teitenhen 4* (Tokyo: Nitten, 1983), 553.

3. The monkeys Sosen painted are Japanese macaques. Gibbons in Chikuho's painting are apes with long arms and no tail, found in China but not in Japan.

Yano Kyōson 矢野橋村

1890–1965

72. *Mother's Breast* 乳 (Chichi)

1939
Pair of two-panel screens: color on paper
189.2 × 72 cm each

SIGNATURE: *Kyōson usō sha* 橋村迂叟寫 Painted by Kyōson, an old man ignorant of worldly affairs

SEALS: *Kazutoshi* 一智 (sig. upper)
Kyōson 橋村 (sig. lower)

PUBLISHED: Hirakatashi Kyōiku Iinkai, *Yano Kyōson ten: Kindai suiboku no seisui* (Hirakata, 2002), 46

Purchase, 2005
13151.1 & 2

As a literati painter active in the early twentieth century, Yano Kyōson strove to fulfill both traditional ideals and modern artistic demand. He espoused the study of past Chinese and Japanese masters but not excessive preoccupation with old rules, advocated the observation of nature to grasp its essence rather than strict forms, and emphasized the importance of integrating modern sensibilities into one's art.[1] In his own work, he explored many styles and genres to break the monotony of the ink landscapes associated with *nanga*. For example, thirty new paintings shown at his one-person exhibition in 1931 included not only orthodox ink landscapes but also a full-color painting of a contemporary female subject, Ōtsue-inspired works, and Shijō-influenced landscapes.[2] Furthermore, throughout his career, Kyōson made a conscious effort to display monumental screens that would advance literati painting beyond the intimate scale of the tokonoma (*tokonoma geijutsu*) to the spacious public arena of modern exhibitions.

In 1939 Kyōson established the Heaven and Earth Society (Kenkonsha 乾坤社) to provide a new venue for *nanga* painters which would be free from the politics and restrictions that constrained other organizations.[3] *Mother's Breast* was shown at the society's first exhibition, held in Osaka and Tokyo in the fall of that year. At first glance, the painting represents a delightful scene of a mother dog watching over her mischievous puppies romping beneath *bashō* 芭蕉 plants.[4] This endearing subject showcases Kyōson's brush skills and his refined color scheme. The artist's careful portrayal of plants and animals reveals his close study of nature, including observation of his family pets. He depicted the mother dog's fur with fine brush lines and represented the red flowers, an object of interest to the playful puppies, in exquisite detail. With more relaxed brushwork but an equally objective approach, Kyōson drew the *bashō* plants with their tattered and withered leaves. The mother's vigilant pose and alert expression as well as the ragged appearance of the *bashō* impart a feeling of tension and unease, lifting the painting above the ordinary level of bird-and-flower subjects.

For Kyōson, the 1930s marked a time of prosperity as well as hardship. In the early part of the decade, he attained prominence in the art world as a jury member for the prestigious government exhibition and as a proponent of the Osaka literati movement at the Japan Nanga Institute (Nihon Nangain, 日本南画院). The Osaka Art School (Ōsaka Bijutsu Gakkō 大阪美術学校), which he had founded in 1924, continued to flourish in Hirakata 枚方 with a brand-new building and museum. To finance his educational activities, he also busied himself with numerous private exhibitions of his works.[5] During the late 1930s, however, the escalating Chinese-Japanese war began to cast a shadow over Kyōson's world. In 1937 he received the devastating news that one former Osaka Art School student had been injured and another killed at the front line.[6] On March 1, 1939, a blast at a military arsenal in the vicinity of his school caused heavy damage to the main school building. On that day Kyōson immediately evacuated his family but defied the military police by hurrying back to the school to prevent further damage.[7] With his typical fortitude, in the aftermath of the disaster Kyōson managed to repair and reopen the school within six months. It was later that year that Kyōson established Kenkonsha and organized its first exhibition.

Taking into account the events of 1939, one can find deeper meaning behind the innocuous facade of *Mother's Breast.* As embodied by the title and the dignified portrayal of the mother dog, the painting denotes the ideas of nurture and protection, signifying Kyōson's resolve to lead the Osaka art circle by overseeing the Heaven and Earth Society and his school. The unsettling portrayal of the *bashō* plants, full of broken and desiccated leaves with angular shapes and sharp points, may symbolize the uncertainty and perils of wartime Japan. Also ambiguous and disturbing are the discarded flowers on the ground, one of which has been torn apart, its petals scattered about. Kyōson was an optimist, however, who had steadily attained his goals by hard work and perseverance. *Mother's Breast* ultimately expresses his hope for the future, the puppies' growth ensured by their mother's watchfulness and guidance. Even the *bashō* plants exhibit promise, with young leaves poised to unfurl and reveal their elegant form.

MM

NOTES

1. Yano Kyōson, "Dai ichinin gabō zatsuwa," *Daimai bijutsu* 5, no. 2 (February 1926): 22–24, and the artist's "Seishū kanwa," *Daimai bijutsu* (October 1934), quoted by Takeda Toshiya, "Osaka Bijutsu Gakkō o sōsetsu shita kyōikusha Yano Kyōson," in Hirakatashi Kyōiku Iinkai, *Yano Kyōson ten: Kindai suiboku no seisui*, exh. cat. (Hirakata, 2002), 63.

2. See "Yano Kyōson shi koten," *Tōei* 7, no. 6 (July 1931): 20–21.

3. "Ken" denotes the first and "kon" the last of the eight diagrams in the *Book of Changes.* Together they stand for opposites such as "heaven and earth."

4. The image of a similar dog, perhaps her mate, appeared earlier in Kyōson's work. In 1933, at the twelfth exhibition of the Japan Nanga Institute, he showed a pair of six-panel screens titled *Spring Noise*, which depicted the artist's pet dog against the background of a bamboo grove. Illustrated in Hirakatashi Kyōiku Iinkai, *Yano Kyōson ten*, 42–43.

5. For example, see "Yano Kyōson shi koten," 20–21; "Tatehiko, Kyōson meishoe ten," *Tōei* 7, no. 9 (November 1931): 35; "Yano Kyōson shi shikishi ten," *Tōei* 8, no. 1 (January 1932): 51; "Yano Kyōson shi shinsakuga ten," *Tōei* 8, no. 9 (September 1932); and "Yano Kyōson shi koten," *Tōei* 11, no. 11 (November 1935).

6. Takeda, "Ōsaka Bijutsu Gakkō o sōsetsu shita kyōikusha Yano Kyōson," 64.

7. Ibid., 65.

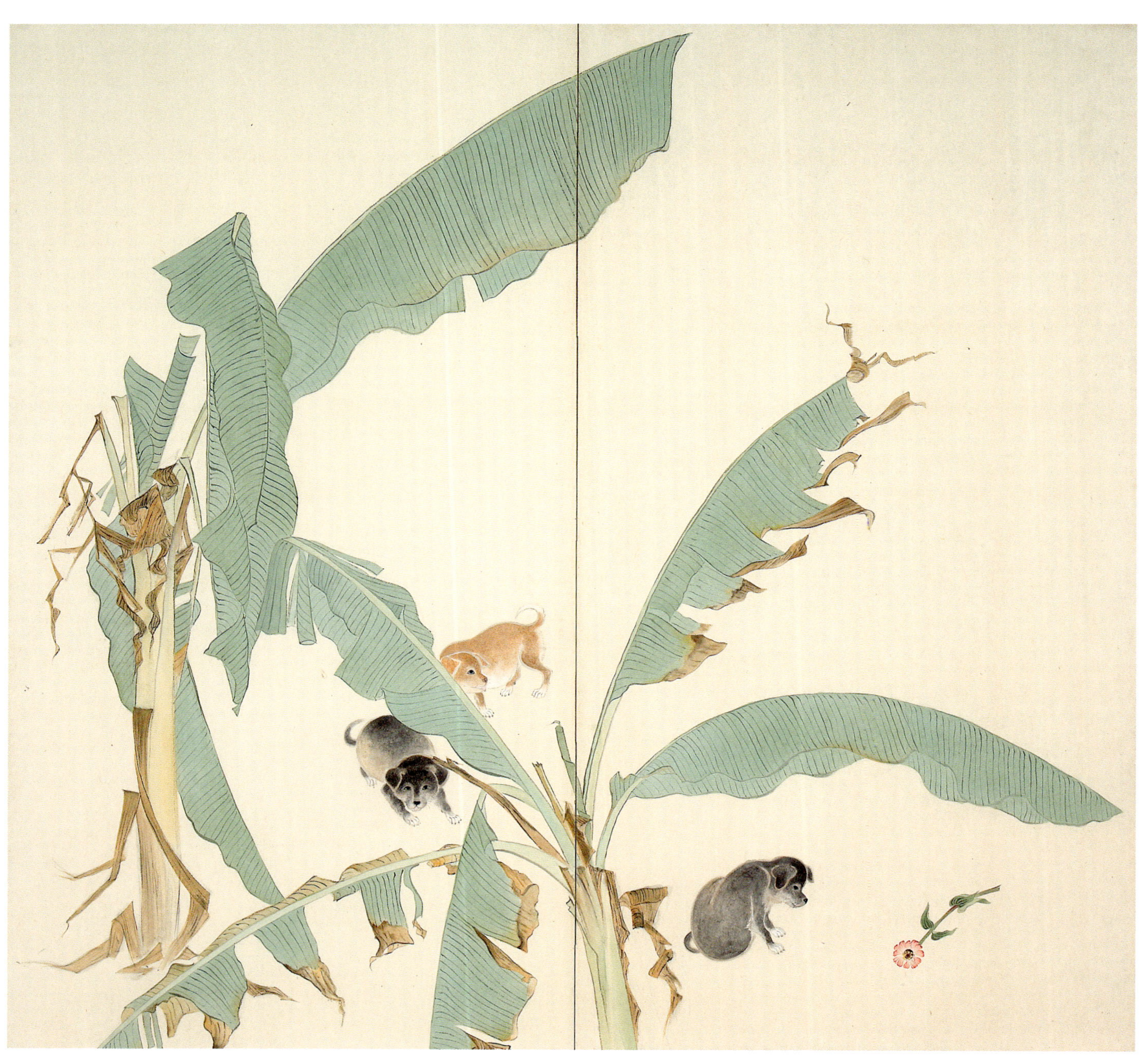

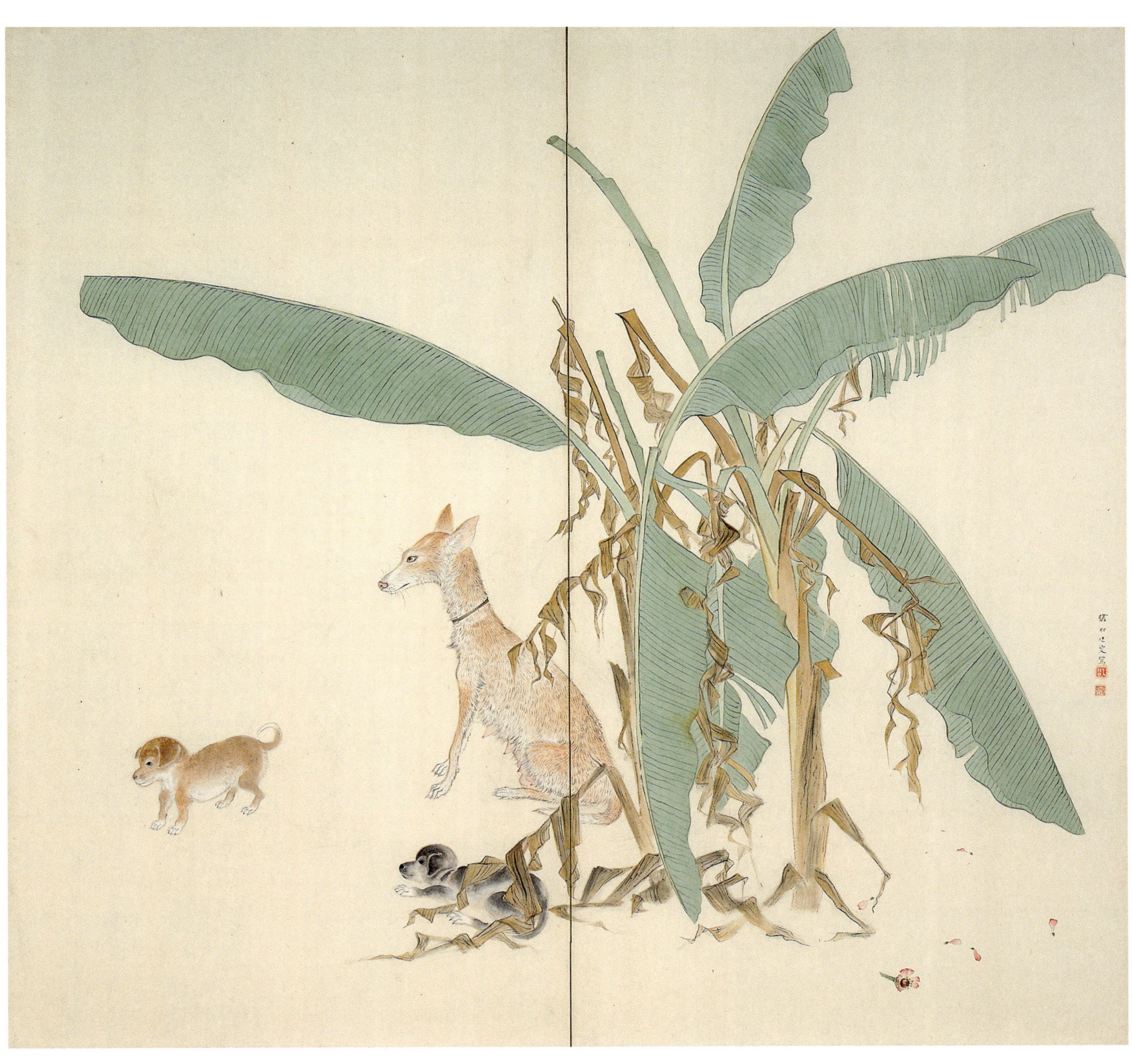

Hirai Baisen 平井楳仙

1889–1969

The beauty of *White Lotus* by Hirai Baisen immediately evokes the decorative aesthetic of the Rinpa school. Just as the Edo masters revitalized the native *yamatoe* tradition to achieve dynamic expressions indicative of their time, Baisen here created a twentieth-century counterpart reflecting his modern sensibilities. Large paintings of the lotus motif rose in popularity among *nihonga* artists during the Taishō period, but Baisen's version distinguishes itself from the others in its daring unconventionality.[1]

Of the many features that make this work striking, foremost is Baisen's color choice. An exquisite light gray ink, covering almost the entire surface of the painting, represents the large lotus leaves and stems. Its luminous tone imbues the image with an ethereal aura and contrasts most effectively with the vivid blue of the water and the pristine white of the flowers. Delicate touches of gold and silver in the flowers highlight their precious quality and further enhance the unworldly air of the plant. The lotus rises from the mud to bloom above the water, and inherent in this subject is the well-known Buddhist notion of the lotus as a signifier of spiritual perfection and enlightenment.

In depicting the leaves, Baisen used the technique commonly known as *sujimegaki* 筋目描き, or crease-line drawing, which takes advantage of the absorbent property of *gasenshi* 画仙紙, a paper of Chinese origin. When ink strokes are applied side by side to *gasenshi,* they spread rapidly but do not merge or blur. Itō Jakuchū 伊藤若冲 (1716–1800), an eccentric Edo-period Kyoto painter, used this technique masterfully to show the textured patterns of fish scales, bird feathers, and layered chrysanthemum petals.[2] Rather than applying ink washes to depict the flat plane of the lotus leaves, Baisen adopted the *sujimegaki* technique, adding pale ink meticulously, stroke by stroke, letting the edges of the strokes emerge to suggest the finely reticulated interior veins of the leaf. Baisen reserved the use of brush line for outlining the flowers and delineating the major veins of the leaves. The white of the flowers and dewdrops is the color of the paper itself. The white paper ground also appears unevenly around the perimeter of the leaves, providing more texture and suggesting the plant's organic quality.

Baisen carried his experimental practice even to the rendering of the water, for which he densely layered small blue dots. He explored this method in other paintings of this time. His entry to the 1915 government exhibition, a set of three paintings titled *Summer* (Natsu 夏), included a countryside scene of night rain which displayed a "pointillist" technique that one critic likened to postimpressionism and the manner of Ike Taiga 池大雅 (1723–1776).[3] *Shower over a Mountain Village,* 1916 (see cat. no. 54), shows Baisen's looser use of a similar method.

Baisen may have come to explore the pointillist technique independently, or he may have been inspired by Imamura Shikō 今村紫紅 (1880–1916), a Tokyo artist. *Eight Views of Ōmi* (Ōmi hakkei 近江八景), in which Shikō modernized the traditional subject through a combination of strong color and an extensive use of dots, received the second-place award at the 1912 government exhibition, but caused a controversy for its radical approach.[4]

Enticing in its dazzling composition and color, *White Lotus* strikes a perfect balance between nature and artifice, tradition and modernity. It attests to Baisen's fearless artistic vision during the early Taishō period, when he emerged as one of the most exciting young *nihonga* artists. MM

73. *White Lotus* 白蓮 (Byakuren) T

1915
Hanging scroll: ink and color on paper
137 × 42 cm

SIGNATURE: 乙卯初冬楳仙寫 Painted by Baisen in the early winter of the *otsubō* year [1915]

SEAL: *Baisen* 楳仙

Purchase, 2005
13209.1

NOTES

1. An early example is *Lotus*, the 1911 Bunten entry by Sakakibara Taizan (1890–1963); see Nittenshi Hensan Iinkai, *Nittenshi 2, Buntenhen 2* (Tokyo: Nitten, 1980), 240. For different approaches taken by various artists, see *Lotus*, c. 1922, by Tokuoka Shinsen (1896–1972), in Nangoyashi Bijutsukan and Chūnichi Shinbunsha, *Botsugo nijūnen, Tokuoka Shinsen ten*, exh. cat. (Nagoya, 1992), 36; *Ogura Pond*, 1924, by Uda Tekison (1896–1980), in Kyōto Kokuritsu Kindai Bijutsukan, *Kyōto no nihonga: 1910–1930*, exh. cat. (Kyoto, 1986), plate 124; and *Red Lotus and White Goose*, early 1920s, by Nishimura Goun (1877–1938), in Michiyo Morioka and Paul Berry, *Modern Masters of Kyoto: The Transformation of Japanese Painting Traditions, Nihonga from the Griffith and Patricia Way Collection* (Seattle: Seattle Art Museum, 1999), 200.

2. For Jakuchū's outstanding examples of *sujimegaki*, see Kyōto Kokuritsu Hakubutsukan, *Tokubetsu tenrankai: Botsugo 200 nen, Jakuchū*, exh. cat. (Kyoto, 2000), plates 86–88, 94, 95, 98, 99, and 102.

3. See the comment by Matsumoto Matatarō, "Bunten no nihonga o hyōsu," *Shinbi* 4, no. 11 (November 1915): 59–60.

4. Illustrated in Tōkyō Kokuritsu Hakubutsukan, *Nihon Bijutsuin sōritsu 100 shūnen kinen tokubetsu ten: Kindai Nihon bijutsu no kiseki*, exh. cat. (Tokyo: Tōkyō Kokuritsu Hakubutsukan and Shadan Hōjin Nihon Bijutsuin, 1998), 94–97. See also Nittenshi Hensan Iinkai, *Nittenshi 2, Buntenhen 2*, 473–74.

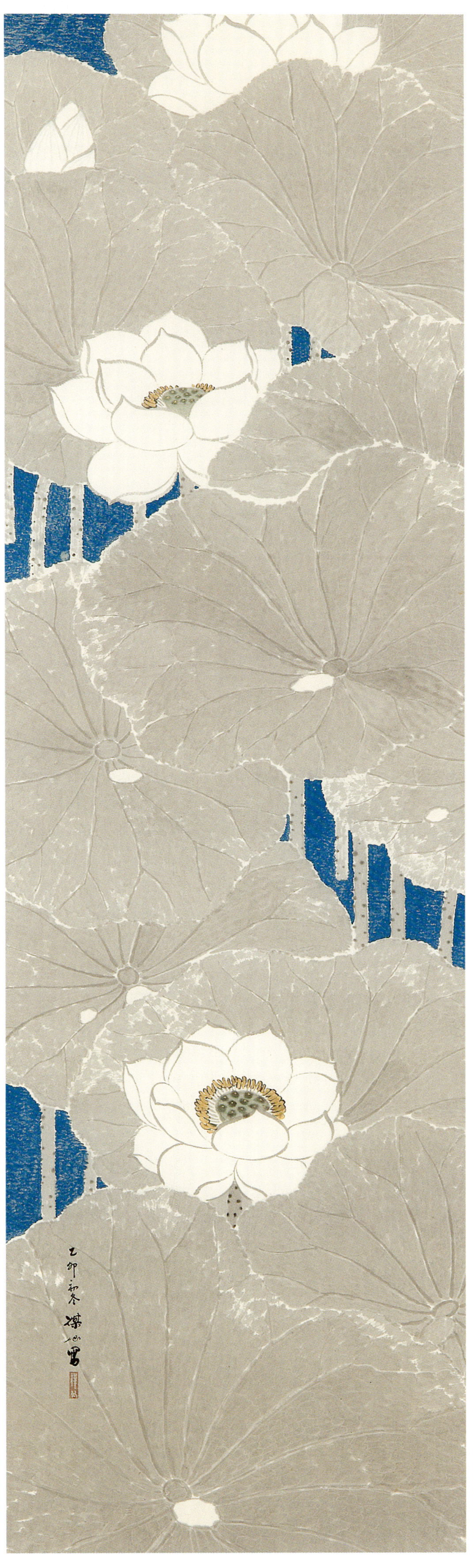

Hirai Baisen 平井楳仙

1889–1969

74. *Plum in Snow / Rising Sun* 梅と日の出図 (Ume to hinode zu)
Late 1910s
Set of three hanging scrolls: color on silk
140.6 × 50.2 cm each
SIGNATURE: *Baisen* 楳仙 (each scroll)
SEAL: *Baisen* 楳僊 (each scroll)
Purchase, 2005
13213.1–3

In this set of three paintings, Hirai Baisen imaginatively transformed a time-honored subject into a stunning image. The rising sun is one of the premier auspicious symbols in Japan, a painting of which graces the alcoves of traditional Japanese houses at the beginning of each New Year holiday. The plum has also carried strong symbolism in Asia, where scholar-painters have celebrated its virtues of quiet beauty and strength in expressive ink paintings. Instead of ink brushwork as a defining tool, however, Baisen dynamically combined form and color in an unorthodox composition to achieve a unique visual statement.

The two plum compositions contrast in their focus. The painting on the right represents the vitality of the plum, the lively growth of its young shoots featured in an elegant and largely two-dimensional pattern. Its counterpart on the left conveys the plum's rugged sturdiness, with thin branches and robust old trunks woven into a more unusual and complexly layered arrangement in three-dimensional space. In both, Baisen ignored the evocativeness of empty space and emphasized the earthy vigor of the plum by crowding its branches into the picture frame. In a sophisticated touch, he represented the snow-covered branches by leaving the silk ground unpainted and filling the background with a pale gray ink wash. The outlined forms of the branches reveal his layering of surprisingly intricate ink brushwork in a range of tones and stroke shapes. White blossoms peek from under the snow throughout both compositions, while white *gofun* 胡粉 in loose dots indicates falling snowflakes. A Japanese bush warbler (*uguisu* 鶯, *Cettia diphone*), its utmost delicacy in perfect contrast to the roughness of the plum, is perched on a twig in the upper left corner of the left painting.

Flanked by the active, near-monochromatic plum paintings, the rising sun stands out in its brightness and minimalism. Because the subject has always generated great demand, Japanese artists have vied to individualize their expressions of the rising sun (*hinode*) through ingenuity and inventiveness. Baisen's rendition is notable in both its bold simplicity and its subtlety. Perfectly balanced within the composition, the sun's silhouette is blurred, the lower portion enveloped in haze. The graded tonality of the background contributes a sense of atmosphere, making the whole painting shimmer with warm light.

A tantalizing contrast between cool and warm, complexity and austerity, and earth and sky, this set of paintings shows Baisen at the height of his creative power and originality. MM

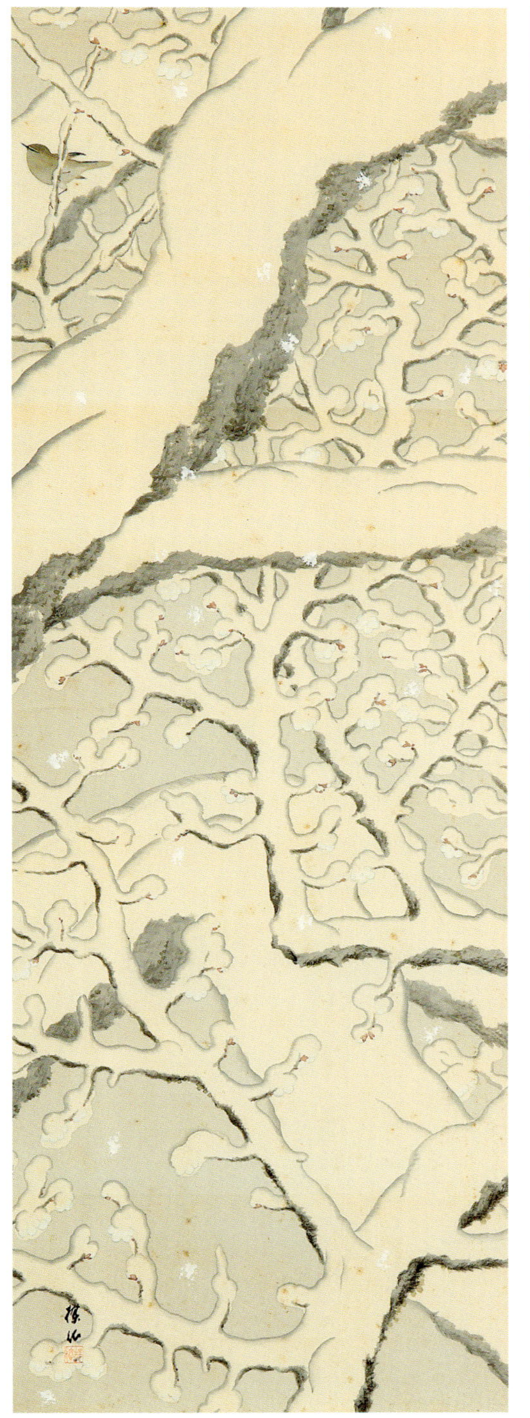

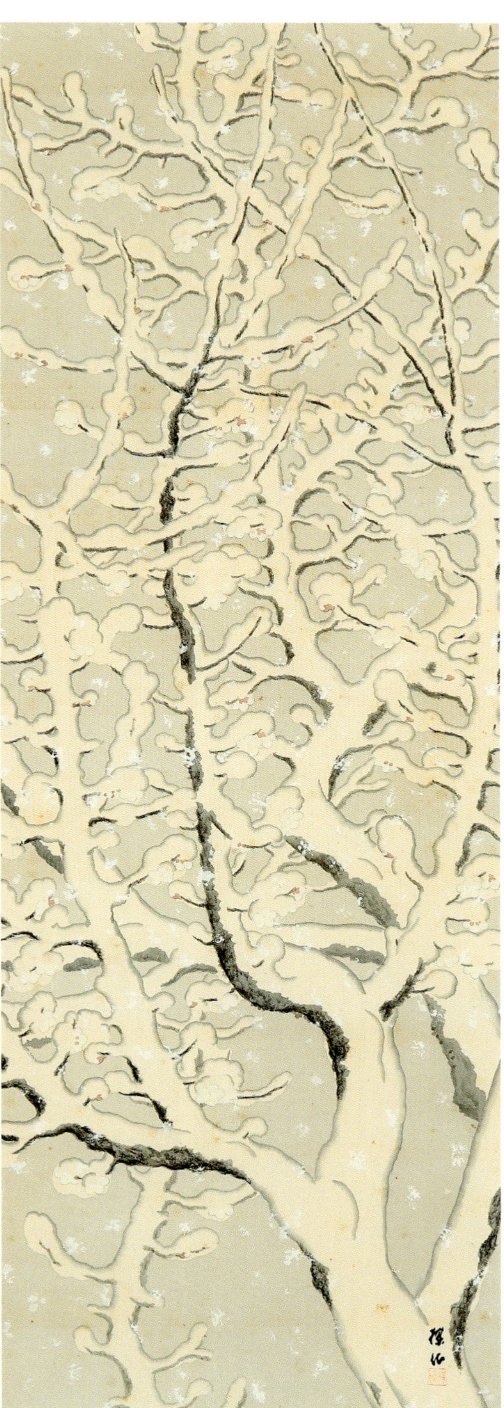

Dōmoto Inshō 堂本印象

1891–1975

75. *Chinese Garden* 中国庭園図 (Chūgoku teien zu)

1923
Pair of six-panel screens: ink and color on paper
171.6 × 377.8 cm each

SIGNATURES: *Inshō sei* 印象生 Created by Inshō (right)
Kigai kajitsu Inshō sei 癸亥夏日印象生 Created by Inshō, summer of the *kigai* year [1923] (left)

SEAL: *Inshō* 印象 (both)

Gift of Terry Welch, in honor of Richard Washburn Welch and Renee Clarisse Bonzon, 2005
13150.1 & 2

Dōmoto Inshō made his first trip to China in the spring of 1921, traveling to Shandong 山東 province on the eastern coast as well as to central and northern regions. In that fall, he submitted two paintings of Chinese subjects to the Teiten: *Playing with Ball* (Chōkiku zu 調鞠図) and *Bright Mountain in Snow* (Sōzan eisetsu 爽山映雪).[1] The former, a monumental figure painting portraying Chinese aristocrats engaged in a ball game, won the highest award that year and received nearly universal praise for its polished figural treatment and beautiful color.[2] Although overshadowed by the success of the other entry, the captivating *Bright Mountain in Snow* presents a Chinese temple in a dreamlike snowy landscape strongly influenced by *yōga*. Inshō returned to China in 1922 and 1923 in search of new inspiration. Even as Chinese subjects and literati painting energized him, he explored a wide variety of styles. An exhibition of new works shown at the Mitsukoshi department store in 1923 included many literati titles and eclectic stylistic experiments, some reminiscent of Hashimoto Kansetsu (see cat. no. 13) and others influenced by *shasei* realism or *ukiyoe.*[3]

Although virtually ignored in the postwar assessment of his career, literati painting occupied an important place in Inshō's oeuvre, particularly during the 1920s.[4] His rising popularity and star status in the late Taishō art world did not make him complacent. Rather, Inshō dressed humbly and lived in a rented house while dedicating himself to reading and researching in order to make himself a better painter.[5] He embraced the resurgent interest in literati tradition, which led young artists to "discover" Tomioka Tessai (see cat. nos. 11, 46) and to the 1921 establishment of the Japan Nanga Institute (Nihon Nangain 日本南画院) in Kyoto.

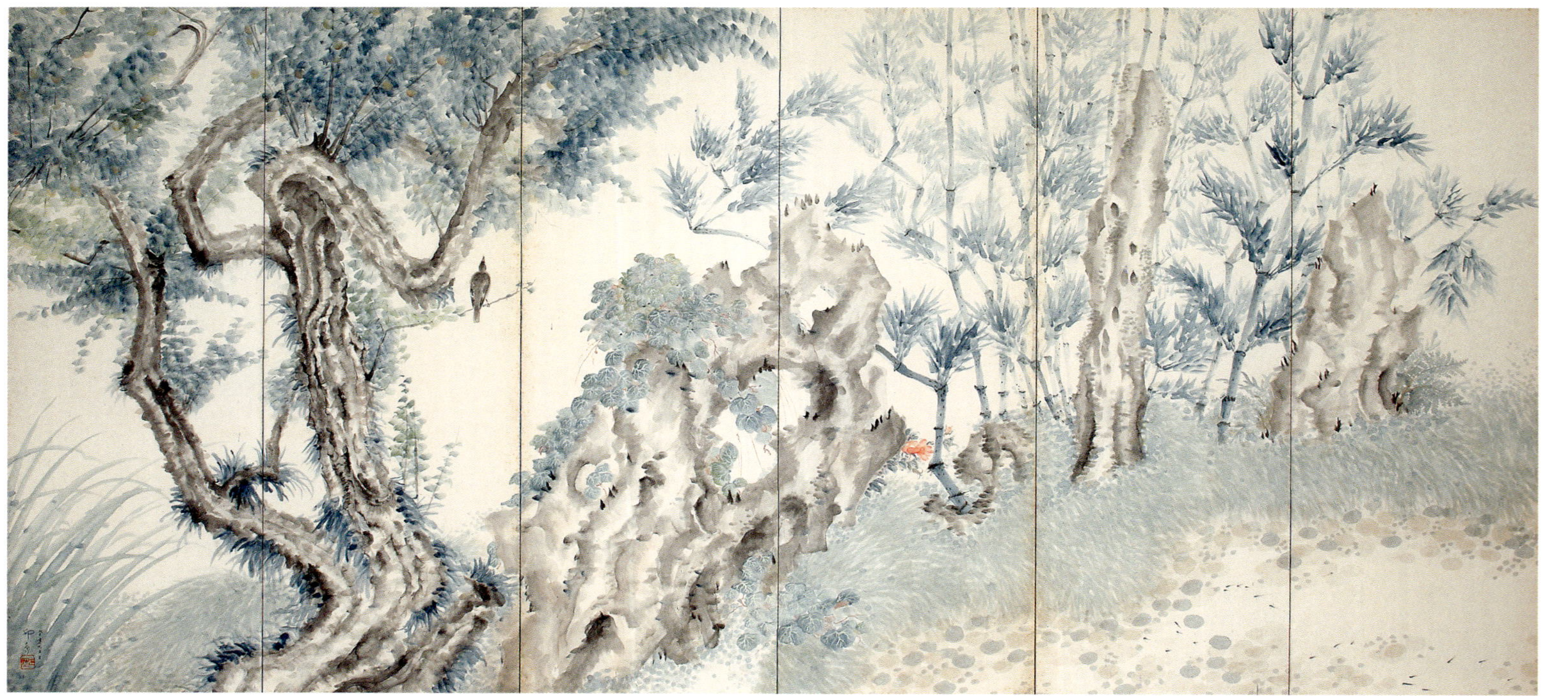

Chinese Garden, a pair of large screens executed with an ebullient wet brush, signals the profound influence of literati aesthetics on this multitalented artist. The itinerary of Inshō's 1922 trip to China included Suzhou 蘇州, famous for its picturesque stone bridges and beautiful gardens. The painting, likely based on what Inshō observed at one of those sites, represents a theme rarely seen in his screens. Fantastic rocks and trees enliven both screens, which are united by a central pond. Although the screens are virtually continuous in composition, each half can be appreciated by itself for its visually exciting forms and rich textural variety. The viewer is made to feel as if he or she is actually walking in a garden, with plants towering overhead, a sensation emphasized by the nearly lifesize format and Inshō's cropping of the treetops. The presence of birds and tiny fish provides a feeling of intimacy. Inshō's animated brush style keeps the painting vital and fresh, recalling the works of Tomita Keisen (see cat. nos. 48, 80). A similar approach elegantly combining gray ink and light blue with highlights in bright color also appears in Inshō's other literati examples from this period.[6]

MM

NOTES

1. For good color reproductions of these works, see Kyōto Furitsu Dōmoto Inshō Bijutsukan, *Dōmoto Inshō* (Kyoto: Kyōto Bunka Zaidan, 1992), 16–17.

2. See comments in Nittenshi Hensan Iinkai, *Nittenshi 6, Teitenhen 1* (Tokyo: Nitten, 1982), 538.

3. "Dōmoto Inshō shi shinsakuga ten," *Bijutsu no Nihon* 15, no. 2 (February 1923): 19–20.

4. See a discussion on this topic by Paul Berry, in Michiyo Morioka and Paul Berry, *Modern Masters of Kyoto: The Transformation of Japanese Painting Traditions, Nihonga from the Griffith and Patricia Way Collection* (Seattle: Seattle Art Museum, 1999), 284–85.

5. Katayama Naotake, "Mikiki no mama," *Daimai bijutsu* 5, no. 4 (April 1926): 11.

6. For example, *Gentleman Amusing Himself,* c. 1923, published in Morioka and Berry, *Modern Masters of Kyoto,* 285.

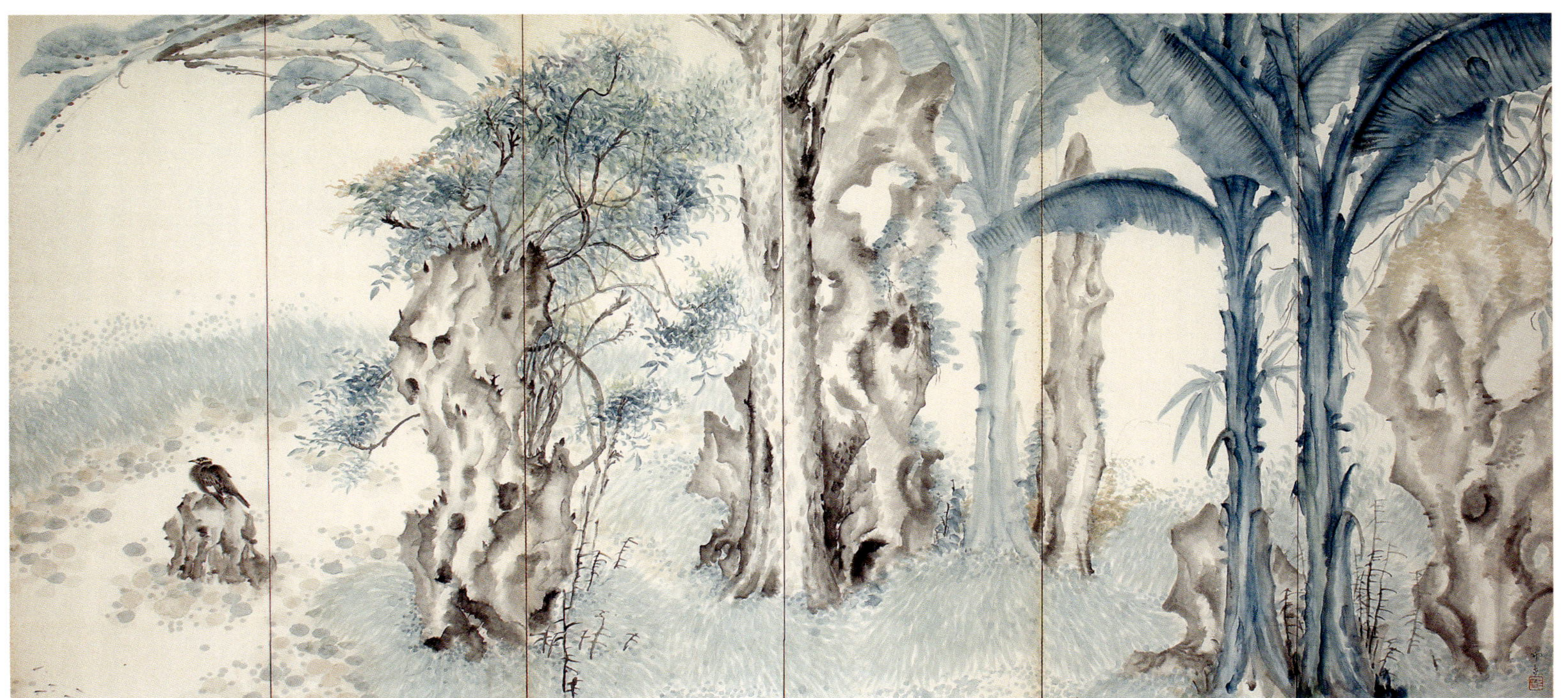

Figures

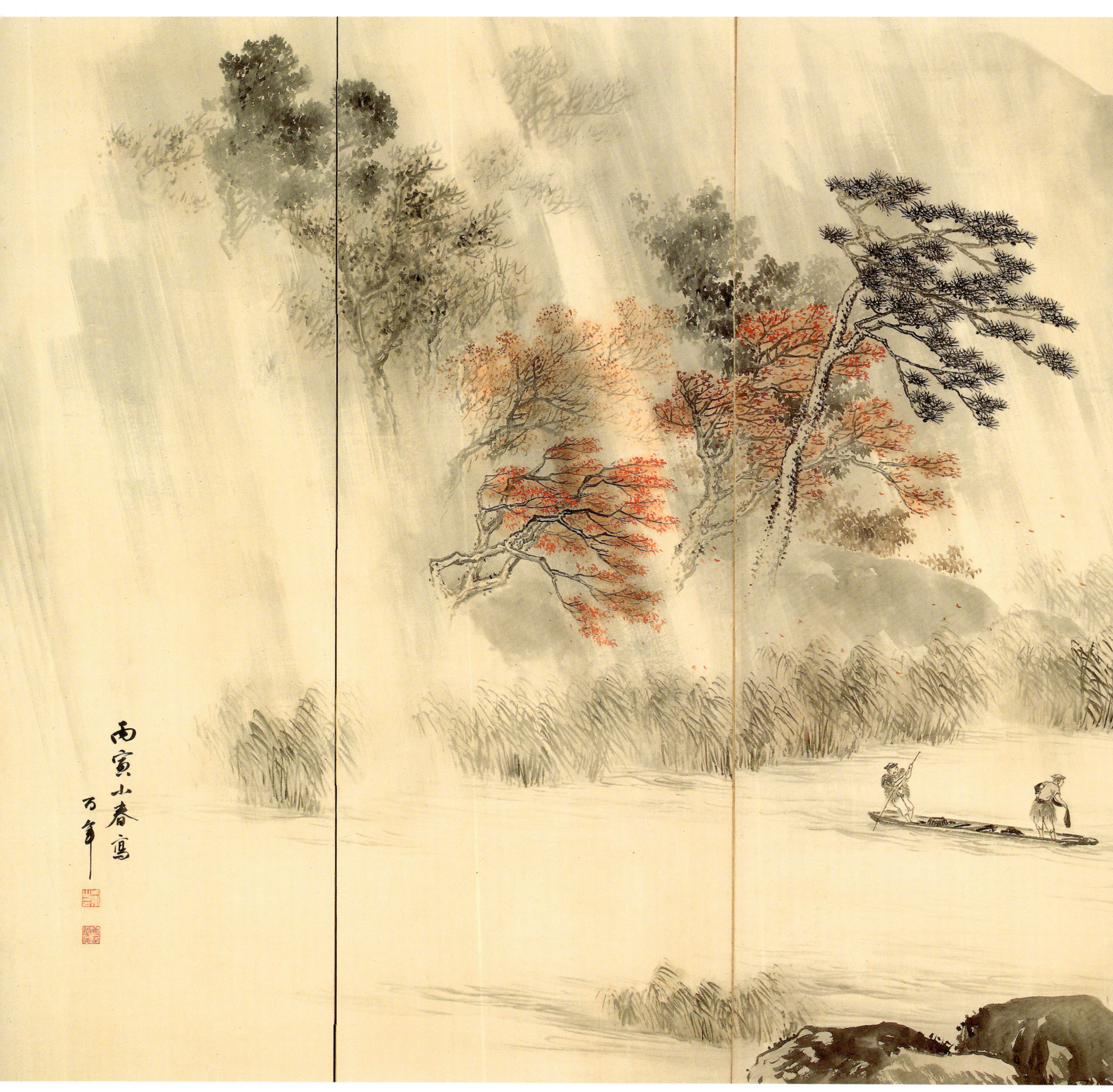

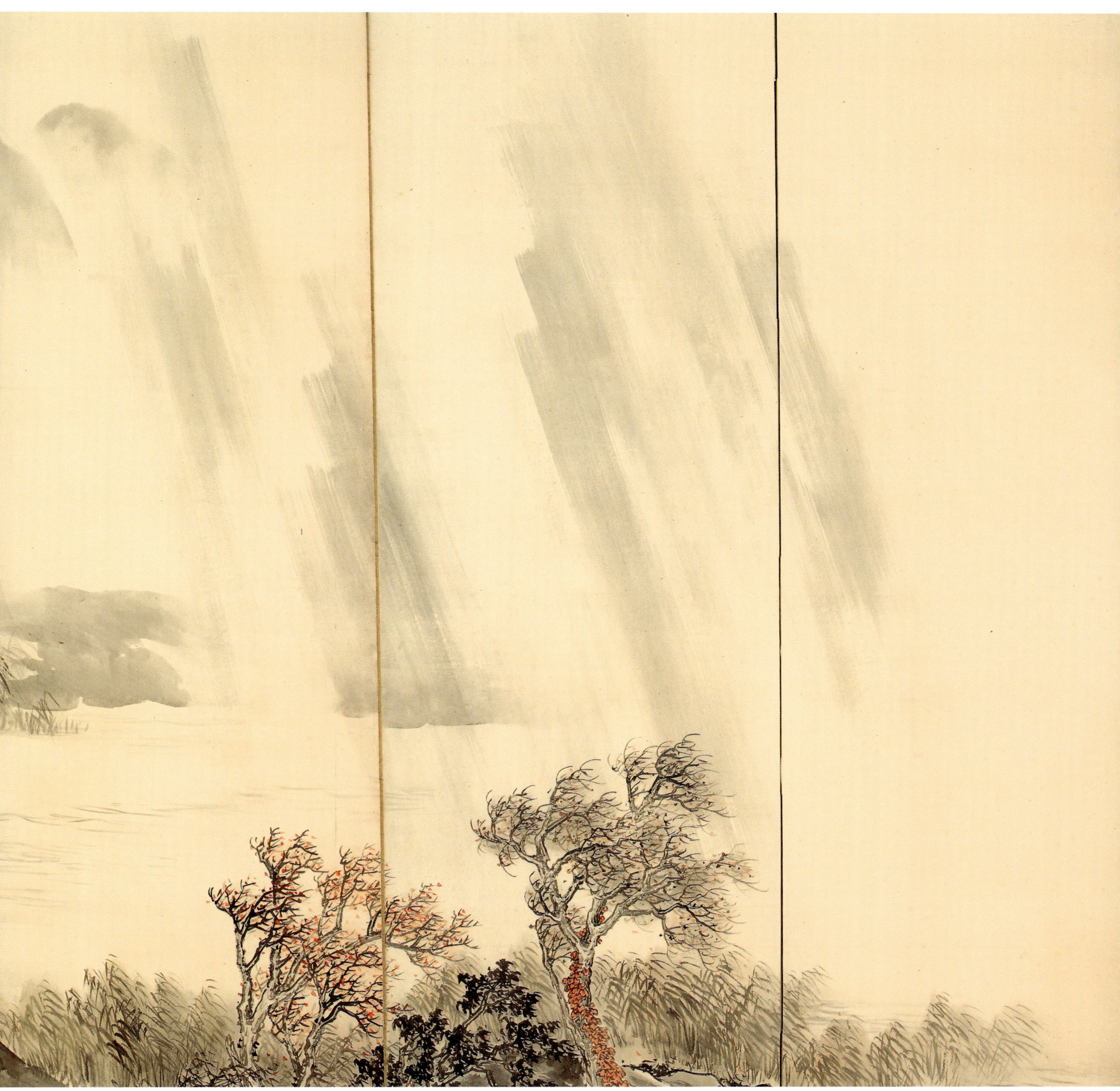

Fujimoto Tesseki 藤本鐵石

1817–1863

76. *Pleasures of the Literati Life* 人生一楽帖 (Jinsei ichiraku jō)

1856
Album of twelve leaves: ink and heavy color on paper
18.4 × 16 cm each leaf

SIGNATURE: *Tesseki Sanjin* 鐵石山人 (leaf 12)

SEALS (each leaf):
Shinkin 真金 (sig. upper)
Tesseki 銕石 (sig. lower)
(?) *dei* □泥 (leaf 12 only, bottom left)

Purchase, 2005
13157.1

As one of the leaders of the quixotic Tenchūgumi 天誅組, who futilely rebelled against the shogunate in 1863, Tesseki was glorified posthumously for his martyrdom for the imperial cause.[1] Given the political extremity that engendered the group's hopeless attacks on superior forces, it may come as a surprise that Tesseki's paintings are most noted for a lighthearted whimsy in spirit and execution. Most frequently he painted loosely structured landscapes with tremulous brushwork, often using only ink yet not infrequently adding bright pigments in a literati version of the Chinese tradition of blue-and-green landscapes. Aside from landscapes, he most commonly painted Rakan 羅漢, the imaginative figures representing the disciples of the historical Buddha, a popular theme among Japanese literati painters (see the example by Tanomura Chokunyū, cat. no. 79). The majority of his works are hanging scrolls, yet Tesseki also created a variety of albums, especially on the Rakan theme.

Pleasures of the Literati Life employs the ever popular theme of the enjoyable activities of the *bunjin.* While in no way copying their content or style, this album follows the spirit of the tradition established by the famous albums *Ten Pleasures and Ten Conveniences* (Jūben jūgi 十便十宜) by Ike Taiga 池大雅 (1723–1776) and Yosa Buson 与謝蕪村 (1716–1783) and Tanomura Chikuden's 田能村竹田 (1777–1835) *Yet Again, One More Pleasure* (Matamata ichirakujo 亦亦一樂帖). The power of Tesseki's idealized vision of literati life as seen in this album may have been linked to his desire to change the grim reality of Japanese politics, even at the cost of his life.

In the first leaf a man on a mountain peak looks down on a "sea" of clouds; in the second a man searches the sky for the return of his crane, a bird once cultivated as a pet in China. The third leaf shows a scholar on horseback with an attendant fording the Rang River in China's Szechuan province. The enjoyment of books is represented in the fourth leaf by a scholar reading in a garden under spreading plantain leaves. The delights of drinking are revealed in the fifth leaf by three figures who converse alongside a stream, an abandoned wine gourd and cup just visible to the side. In the sixth work a man soaks his feet in a stream, illustrating an escape from the constraints of mundane society, the so-called dusty road of the scene's title. An attendant washes the trunk of a *wutong* 梧桐 tree under the gaze of a scholar, illustrating the carefree amusements of the garden in the seventh leaf. In the eighth image, a man leaning against a willow gazes at the wind-ruffled streamside grasses in the fading light before moonrise. A scholar peers at trees bending over a stream after being awakened by the call of the *hototogisu* bird in the ninth leaf. The tenth scene shows two figures playing go below a cliff, the title suggesting that they are enjoying their outdoor game barefoot. Three scholars share *sencha* tea by a stream in a bamboo grove in the eleventh leaf, aptly titled "A magical place." The final image has a more meditative tone, with a solitary traveler visible in the window of a boat rocking in the waves.

Tesseki seems to have developed his painting style by directly studying the works of his Chinese and Japanese literati precursors. The works of Japanese *bunjin* often seem lighter or more playful than many of the paintings by their Chinese compatriots, yet the brushwork and themes of Tesseki's creations stand out as whimsical even in the Japanese context. His humor is well demonstrated by the clever relationship of the titles to the images in this album, as in leaves six and ten. Although his style was much admired, its influence is seen mostly in the paintings of two younger artists, Murayama Hanboku 村山半牧 (1825–1868) and Tomioka Tessai 富岡鐵齋 (1836–1924), in his early work. PB

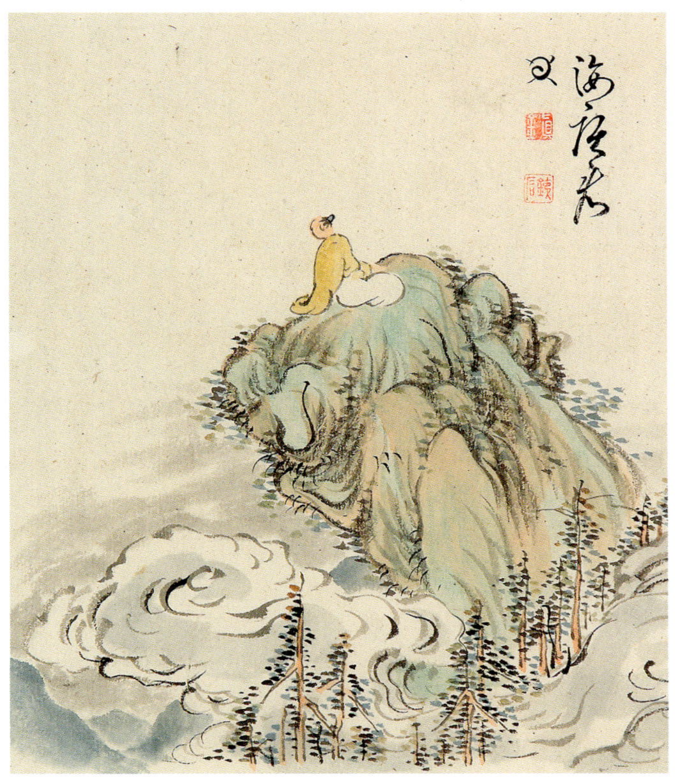

1 海底看日 Viewing the sun in the depths of the sea

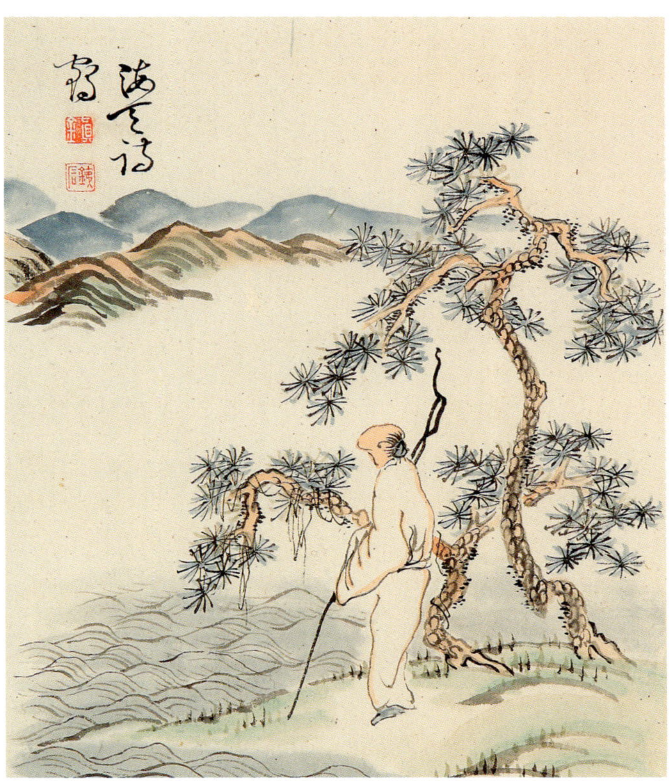

2 海天待鶴 Heavenly sea—awaiting a crane

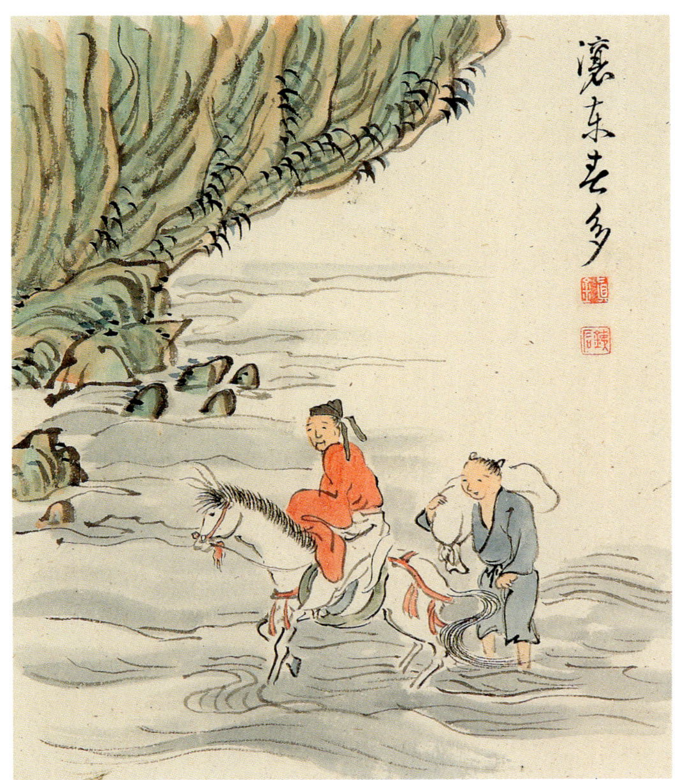

3 □東春多 East of the Rang River—many Springs

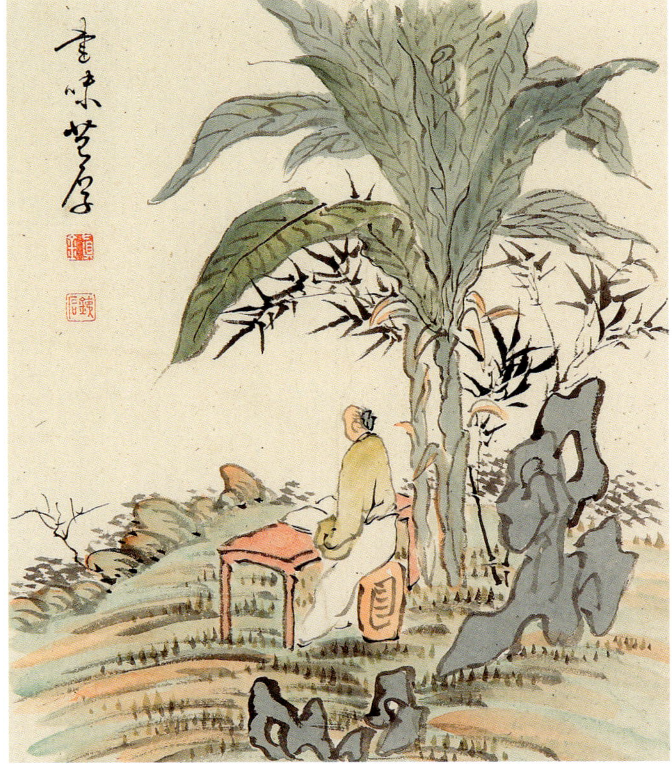

4 書味芭厚 Savoring books—luxuriant plantains

NOTE

1. Refer to the biographical section for more about the circumstances of his dramatic death.

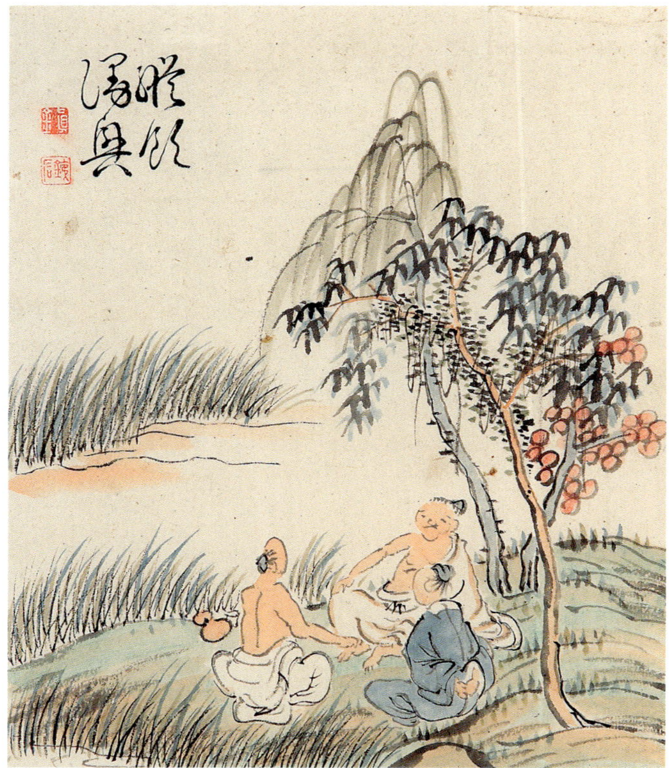

5 縱飲漫興 Indulging in drink—full of exhilaration

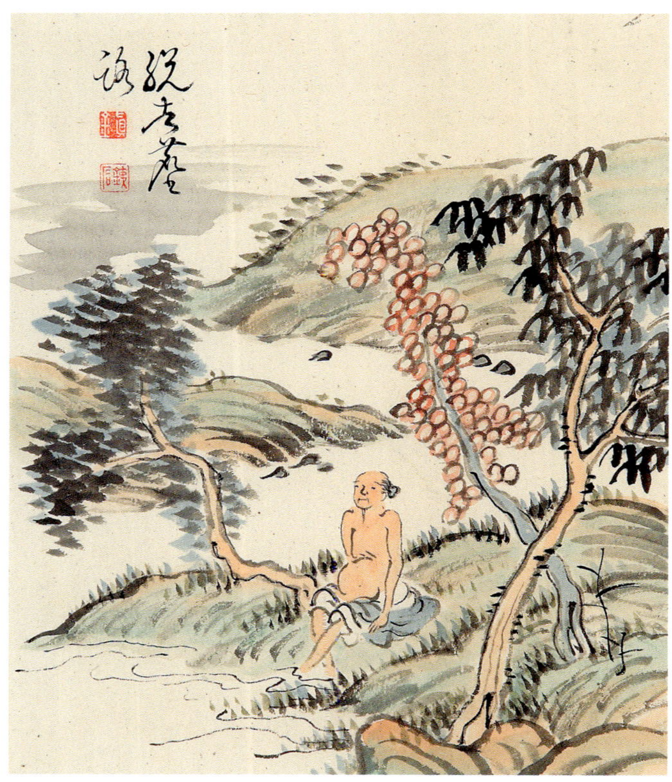

6 脱走塵路 Escaping from the dusty road

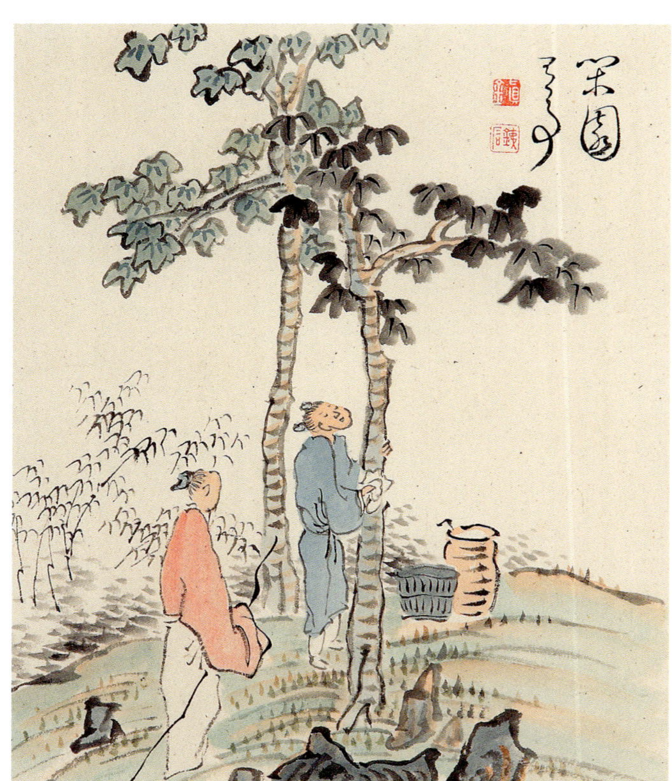

7 閑園不事 Relaxing in a garden free of cares

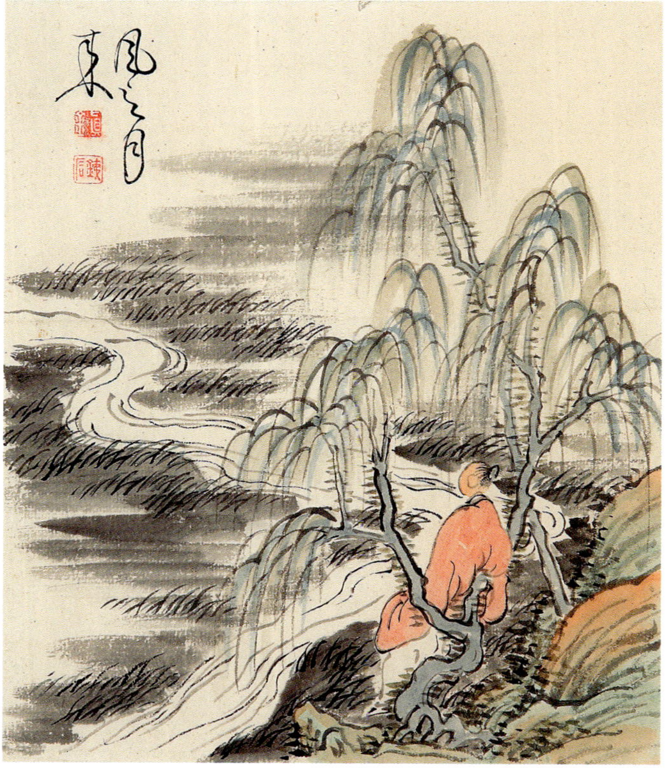

8 風与月来 Wind and moon arrive

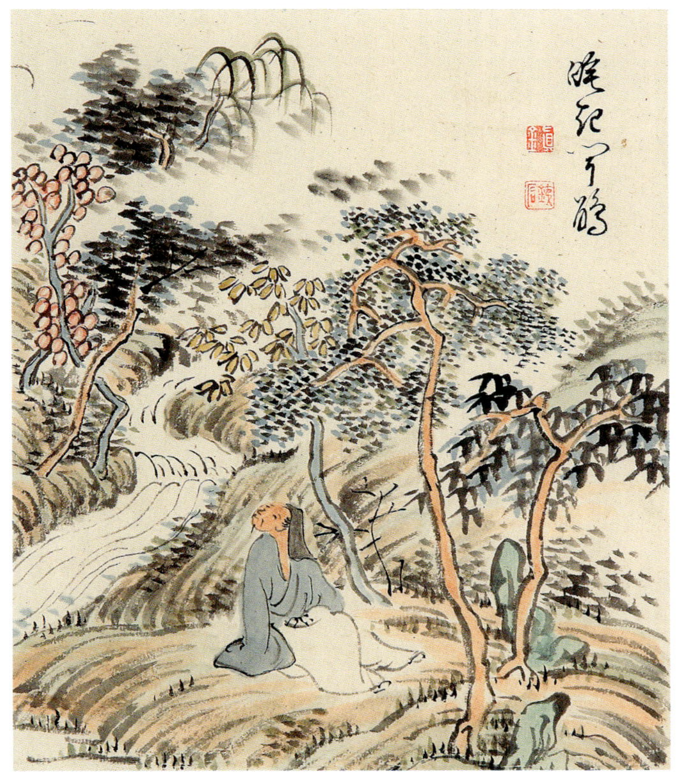

9 睡起聞鵑 Awoken from sleep by hearing a *hotogisu*

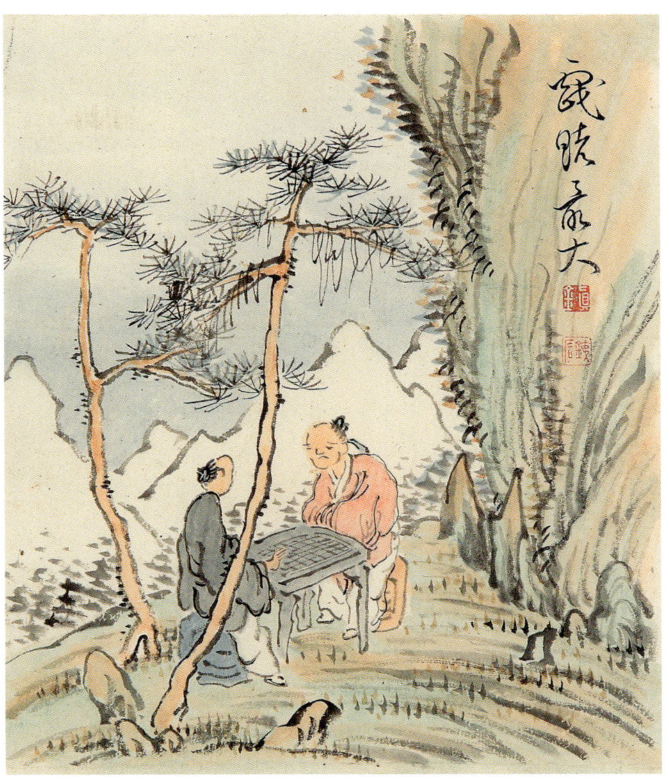

10 戲跣最大 Playing barefoot is the greatest

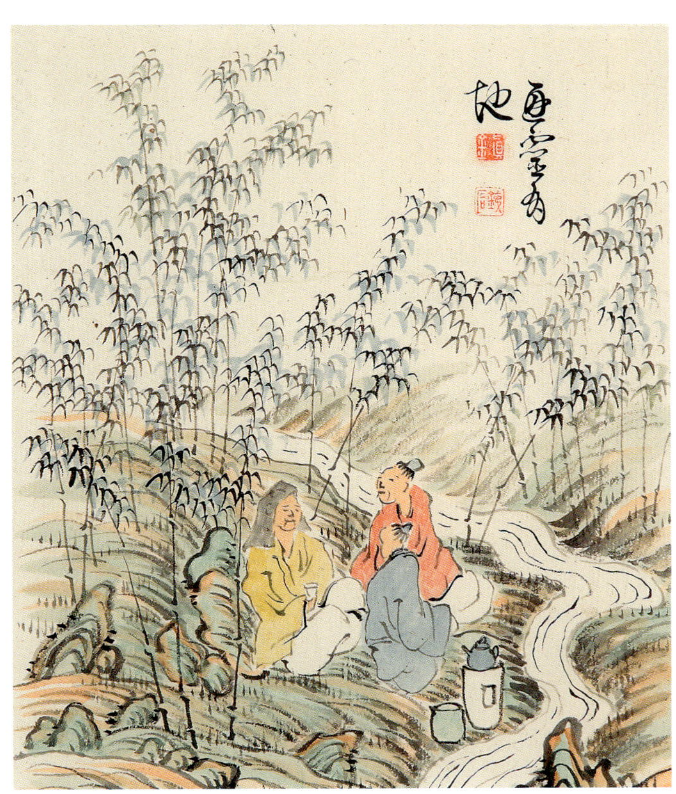

11 通靈有地 A magical place

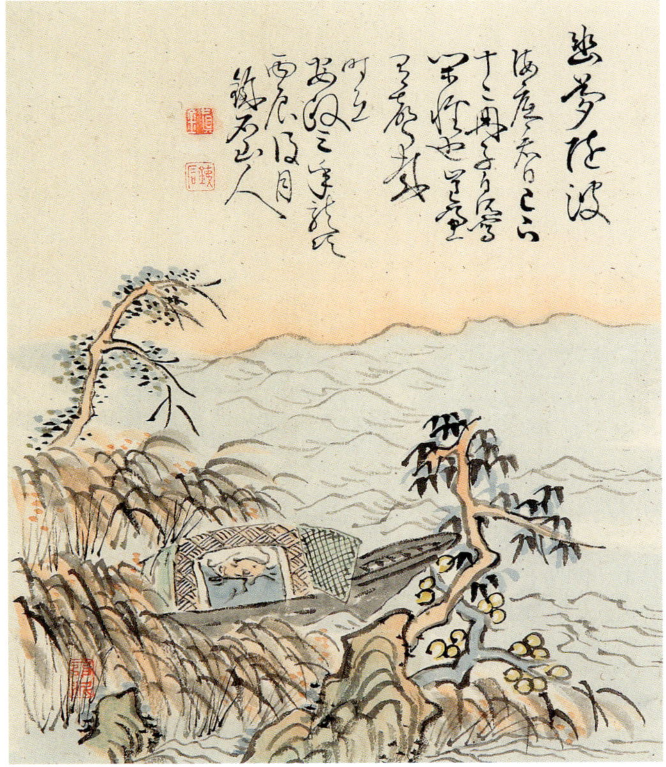

12 幽夢随波。Lonely dreams following the waves

海底看日己下十二冊子自所寫閑惟也□□有聲哉。
時在安政三年新次丙辰後月。鐵石山人。
From "Viewing the sun in the depths of the sea," the following twelve album leaves were drawn by me, third year of Ansei [1856], a month after the heishin New Year's. Tesseki Sanjin.

Hazama Seigai 磵西涯 (羽様西崕)

1811–1878

The theme of this painting is derived from one of the most famous narratives in East Asian history, *Romance of the Three Kingdoms* (Sanguo yanyi 三国演義).[1] Attributed to Luo Guanzhong 羅貫中 of the fourteenth century, this long historical epic was compiled from earlier records and legends dealing with the politics and warfare of the Three Kingdoms period in the early third century, at the close of the Han dynasty. This narrative, filled with friendship and betrayal, ambition and failure, conquest and collapse, has spawned endless variations up to the present, with *manga,* animation, and computer games still based on the story.

The three heroes of the title, the noted generals Guan Yu 関羽 (160–219), Zhang Fei 張飛 (d. 221), and Liu Bei 劉備 (also known as Xuande 玄徳, 161–223), pledge eternal brotherhood in the first chapter of the *Romance.* Because of the depth of their vow, which included the wish that they all die on the same day, paintings of the meeting have come to symbolize fidelity in East Asia. In the text, the meeting occurs in a garden filled with peach blossoms with the burning of incense and animal sacrifice, but later paintings of the theme employed a wide variety of compositions.

Seigai's striking interpretation is dominated by exaggeratedly large peach trees, drawn with arching branches that resemble the growth pattern of plum trees, the slight pink color of the emerging peach blossoms reminding the viewer of their identity. Horizontal black rocks contrast with the dramatic frenzy of the branches, stabilizing the composition while providing an effective backdrop to the figures. The key figure, Guan Yu, sitting on a horse while breaking off a branch of flowers, is identified by his large beard and renowned curved-blade weapon, the Green Dragon Crescent Moon Blade (Qinglong yanyue dao 青龍偃月刀, similar to the European glaive), held by one of the attendants. Although all three generals attained great fame, Guan Yu eventually became a popular folk deity throughout East Asia.

Seigai was a student of Oda Kaisen 小田海僊 (1785–1862),[2] and this work shows the influence of Nagasaki paintings that were themselves based on imported Chinese works like those studied by Kaisen. The figures' minutely detailed clothing and strongly colored skin tones are typical of many paintings done in Nagasaki in the late eighteenth century. Guan Yu's horse, with its slightly awkward position, tilted head, and roughly attempted suggestion of volume, shows the impact, some generations removed, of Western modeling, which was popularized in China through the works of the Italian Jesuit painter Giuseppe Castiglione (1688–1766). Horses created under his influence by Shen Nanping 沈南蘋 (1682–c. 1760) were adopted in the work of many Japanese artists,[3] such as Yosa Buson 与謝蕪村 (1716–1783).[4]

One of the delights of this work is the minute rendering of the figures. In another sign of their mutual dependence, one general bears a bow in a decorated sling, while his compatriot carries a quiver loaded with arrows. The distinctive facial features and clothing of the two attendants, one holding a banner decorated with a dragon motif, indicates their origin in distant areas outside China. These aspects contribute a striking exoticism to this portrayal of an ancient symbol of brotherhood. PB

77. *Three Heroes of the Peach Blossom Garden*
桃園三傑
(Tōen sanketsu)[5]
Hanging scroll: ink and heavy colors on silk
110.4 × 51 cm

SIGNATURE: *Seigai sei Hazama kyo* 西涯生硼恭

SEALS: *Hazama Kyo azana Daimi* 硼恭字大未 (sig. upper)
Seigai gain 西涯畫印 (sig. middle, impressed upside down)
□陽如雪 (sig. lower)

Purchase, 2005
13184.1

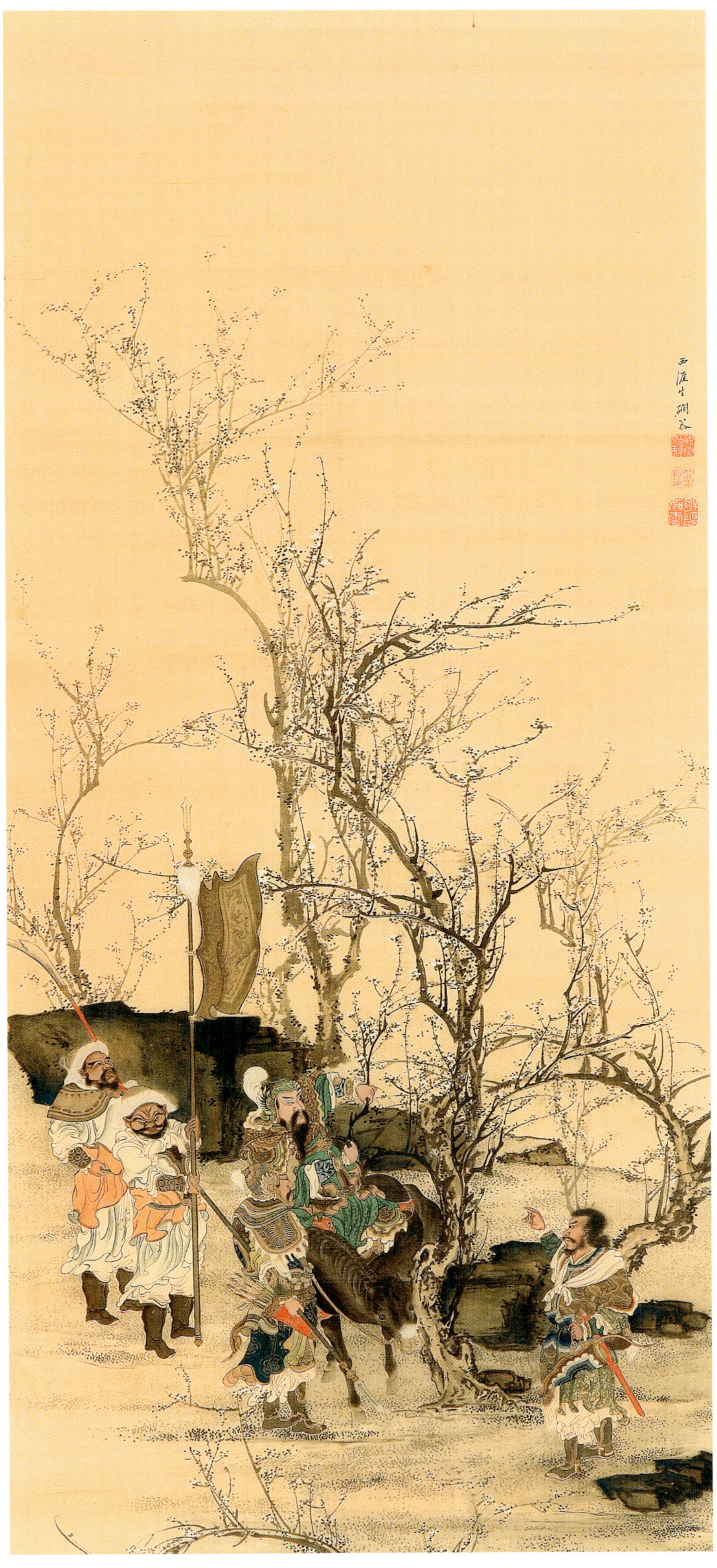

NOTES

1. A complete translation is available in Moss Roberts, *Romance of the Three Kingdoms* (Beijing: Foreign Language Press, 2005).

2. See the Internet site on famous people from Hagi, which lists information about the artist: http://www.hagibukkyo.com/2-jinbutugaido/jinbutu-kensaku.htm (accessed March 2008).

3. Shen visited Japan from 1731 to 1733, and thereafter his Chinese and Japanese disciples continued to popularize his style in Japan.

4. See the similar horses after Shen's style in Buson paintings in Sasaki Johei, *Yosa Buson*, Nihon no bijutsu 109 (Tokyo: Shibundō, 1975), illustrations 21 and 43.

5. The twentieth-century title on the box mistakenly labels the work "Three Generals of the Plum Grove" (*Bairin sanshō* 梅林三将), revealing how the specifics of the theme have gradually faded from common memory.

Doi Gōga 土井聱牙

1817–1880

78. *Screens of Human Figures and Bamboo* (rearranged)
人物/竹図 (Jinbutsu take zu)

1865
Ink on paper
133.9 × 48.7 cm each panel
Gift of Terry Welch, in honor of Paul Berry, 2005
13145.1 & 2

The eccentric Confucian scholar Doi Gōga was most renowned for his prolific output of bamboo paintings. He also painted many sparse landscapes, including a small number in which he embedded stones and hillocks with the bulging eyes of demonic faces. He was also well regarded for his calligraphy, usually in cursive script but occasionally in well-controlled clerical style. Most unusual, however, were his many depictions of emaciated, skeletal figures. Most Japanese viewers take them to be hungry ghosts (*gaki*), animated corpses, demons, or some other supernatural being, but Gōga's inscriptions show them to be satires on the nature of human life.

Screens like this pair are very rare among Gōga's works. In this case, he made two different sets of six paintings, one featuring bamboo and the other with figures. The bamboo set was painted on a darker paper quite distinct from that of the figure paintings, and the seal usage is fairly consistent within each group, factors that point to their separate origins. These sets may have been made within a short time of each other, but it was the decision of some later owner to mount them as they are today with the sets mixed together. For the purposes of clarity and to aid comparison, the images are illustrated here in their original, separate groupings of figures and bamboo. Their intended sequence, if one was planned, cannot be known.

The grotesque facial expressions and comically animated, spindly limbs of Gōga's remarkable figures often produce amazement in first-time viewers. The bizarre brushwork of the paintings seems a rejection of every earlier figural style. The standard etiquette for display in a Japanese home would never encompass their presence, and it would seem that no nineteenth-century artist could have painted many such works. That Gōga actually made a considerable number of these strikingly odd figure paintings suggests that he did indeed find an audience for them. Wherein did the appeal of these dancing, running, shouting, stone-embracing, head-scratching figures lie? The answer can be found in their varied inscriptions, which are best described as didactic declarations, not verse.

The message on the first panel of the figure paintings, "Seeking the mind is not possible; giving you a calm mind is possible," is denied on the third: "A calm mind is not possible; ending up as dried bones is possible." This seeming cynicism is reinforced by the text of the sixth panel: "It doesn't matter that you are blessed with a beautiful form; just look at the actions of your skull." From these inscriptions and others like them, it is clear that Gōga is not thinking about death, ghosts, or demons but commenting on the human condition. Such statements have a long history in Japanese culture, often in a Buddhist context. Buddhist perceptions of the meaning of life derive in part from ancient traditions of philosophic reflection on aging and the dissolution of the body after death[1] as well as a focus on the internal elements, not the outward form, of the living body. Indeed, the closest parallel to the way these figures have been painted lies in *zenga* works by various Edo-period priests. Gōga must have seen such *zenga* in various temple settings, yet his own works focus exclusively on his unique perspective on Confucian teachings.

Among these figure paintings, the most emphatic message is repeated on the second and fifth panels: "The ultimate truth of humanity resembles smoke, resembles a fart, appearing, yet quickly dispersed." This brash, even offensive, declaration of the human tendency to avoid the true nature of things was reinforced in Gōga's own writings on the nature of sages.[2] His main aim, however, was not to condemn human society but to shock people into looking more deeply into the nature of life. This is made quite clear in an inscription[3] on a Gōga painting of three figures that suggest parents and a child:

和志伽於満辺可	わしかおまへか	Is this me? Is that you?
於満辺伽和志可	おまへかわしか	Is that you? Is this me?
皮我尾葉井多羅	ひかおはいだら	If you take off the skin
和可利也勢奴	わかりやせぬ	It is impossible to know.

The common essence of all people stressed by this verse may have been Gōga's guiding principle in creating these macabre yet comic works.

Turning to Gōga's bamboo painting is to enter a different, more peaceful realm. Perhaps 80 percent of his production consists of varied compositions of this popular topic. He set out his ideas for painting bamboo in a lengthy treatise sprinkled with quotations from classic Chinese texts on the theme.[4] His various seals carved with the expression "*samadhi* of painting bamboo" indicate his feelings of mastery. It has long been said that Gōga adopted the motif upon seeing a bamboo painting by the Ōbaku priest Taihō 大鵬 (1691–1774),[5] a Chinese monk who twice became head priest of Manpukuji. Taihō's expressive bamboo paintings were well liked despite the variety of "faults" they display if assessed by traditional standards. Indeed, Gōga's use of basket-weave brushwork in a too-regular pattern where leaves overlap may be a direct influence from Taihō, who often emphasized this "fault" in his own paintings. Gōga's contrarian spirit was likely attracted to this transformation of flaws into virtues.

Traditionally bamboo paintings were a means by which the artist could prove his accomplishments with the brush. In the inscription on the first bamboo panel, Gōga didactically reminds the viewer of the high-quality materials and spiritual qualities requisite for fine brushwork: "Wanting to know the marvels of the brush tip, it is good to look at each of the four treasures and three fundamentals."[6] In another, shorter treatise on painting bamboo, *Discourse on Nourishing Bamboo* (Yōchikusetsu 養竹説), Gōga clearly identifies painting with calligraphy: "The heart of calligraphy is painting; the heart of painting is calligraphy."[7] Yet he was also interested in observing growing bamboo. All around his house he planted specimens that people had given him in return for his bamboo paintings.[8]

Gōga composed the statements on the figure paintings, but three of the verses found on the bamboo panels are couplets from Tang-dynasty poems. The verses on the second and fourth panels are the last two lines of quatrains from two poems (from a set of eleven) on the theme of bamboo by the poet Chen Tao 陳陶 (c. 812–c. 885). The verse on the fifth panel is a couplet from "Nighttime Flute" 夜笛 by Shi Jianwu 施肩吾 (act. c. 815).[9] It was common to quote poems without citation in the Edo period, and the other poems may likewise be Chinese compositions. That these are not especially famous examples demonstrates Gōga's erudition.

Gōga's compositions for this array of six bamboo paintings are impressively varied. Culms thick and thin shoot upward and hang down, the arrangements of foliage filling each panel with dramatic forms and brushwork. The leaves, being far too slender and long for actual bamboo, are not shaped in the standard manner, yet the energy of their sweeping curves and overlapping patterns compensates for this loss in realism. These portrayals are equal to the finest of Gōga's many bamboo scroll paintings. The poetic sensibility of his bamboo is well expressed by the inscription on the fifth panel: "Moonlight still slants through the unsullied western chamber; a flute's lonely sound enters the eastern house."

PB

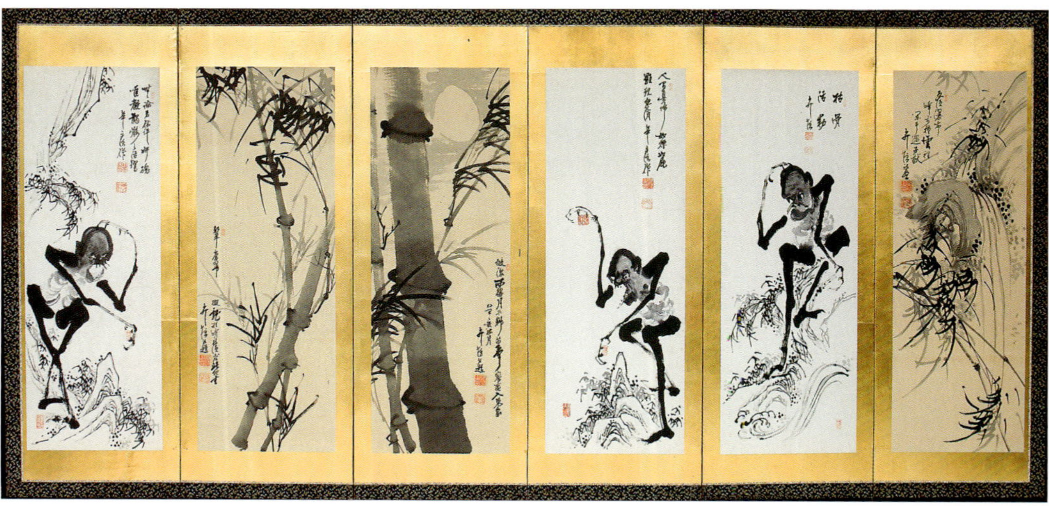

ABOVE AND AT RIGHT: Present arrangement of *Screens of Human Figures and Bamboo*

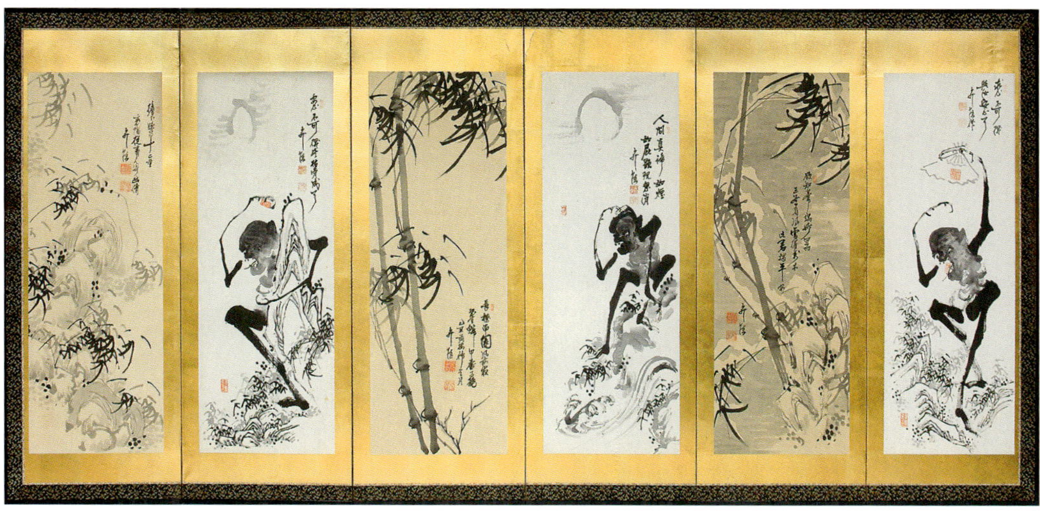

NOTES

1. See Kanda Fusae's article surveying this theme, "Behind the Sensationalism: Images of a Decaying Corpse in Japanese Buddhist Art," *Art Bulletin* 87, no. 1 (2005): 24–49.

2. See the discussion in the biography of Gōga in this volume.

3. Thanks to Maezawa Seiichi for cracking the puzzle of this inscription, which was written in *ateji*, or homophonic characters. The painting is in the Hakutakuan collection, Kyoto.

4. See Doi Gōga, *Chikuseki kogen* (Tokyo: Buneidō, 1916).

5. Stephen Addiss, "Nanga koki no sannin no kojin shugi gakatachi" in *Bakumatsu Meiji no gakatachi—Bunmei kaika no hazama ni*, edited by Tsuji Nobuo (Tokyo: Perikansha, 1992), 225–26.

6. The "four treasures" are the four necessities for calligraphy and painting: brush, paper, ink, and inkstone. The "three fundamentals" are the spiritual requisites for good brushwork: spirit, breath energy, and inspiration.

7. Aspects of this treatise are summarized in Hashimoto Eiji, *Saitō Setsudō Doi Gōga*, Sōsho Nihon no shisoka, 39 (Tokyo: Meitoku Shuppansha, 1993), 164–70. This quotation appears on page 168. The text of *Yōchikusetsu* is found in the seventh *kan* of Gōga's *Gōga iko*, 16 *kan*. Doi Buji, 1895.

8. Gōga relates this anecdote in the same treatise; ibid., 165–66.

9. See the *Complete Tang Poems* (Chuan Tang shi 全唐詩) for Shi's verse, 494–128.

10. The expression on this seal, frequently used by Gōga, comes from a passage in chapter 15 of the *Analects* (Lunyu 論語), attributed to Confucius. The full passage goes, "To be so absorbed in thought as to go all day without eating and all night without sleeping does not resemble learning." The idea is that real study is active, not passive. For those unaware of the source, the phrase on the seal seems a humble expression of one's efforts, yet in the original context it is an exhortation for genuine learning.

11. "Gentleman" may be a metaphoric reference to bamboo, as in the expression "Four Gentlemen," which refers to bamboo, orchids, plum, and chrysanthemum.

12. See note 6 above.

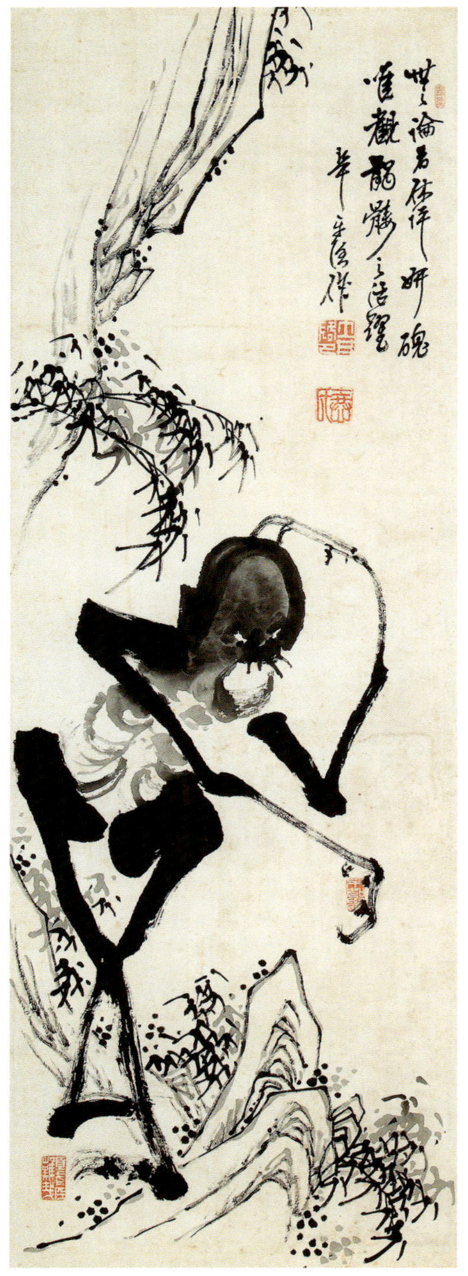

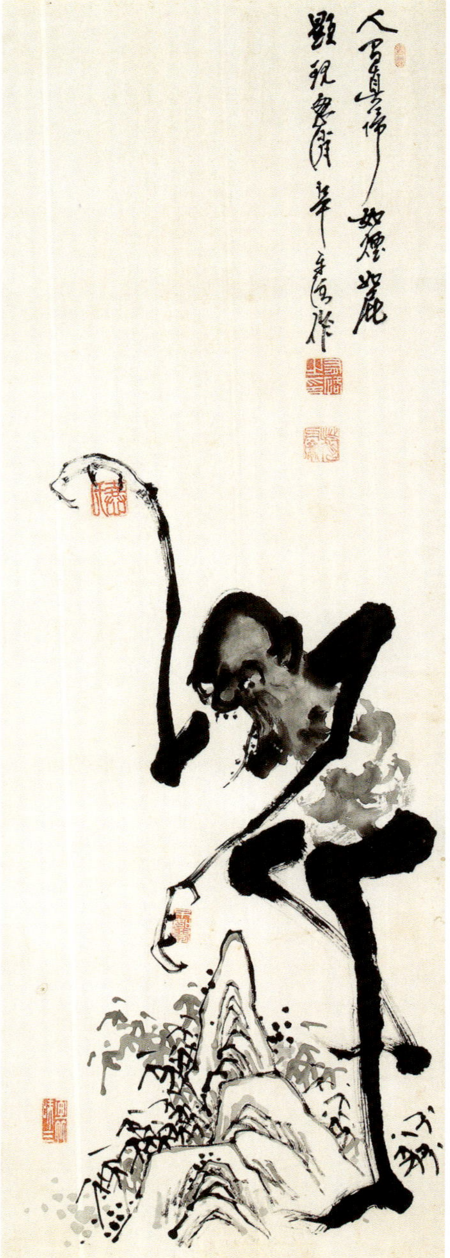

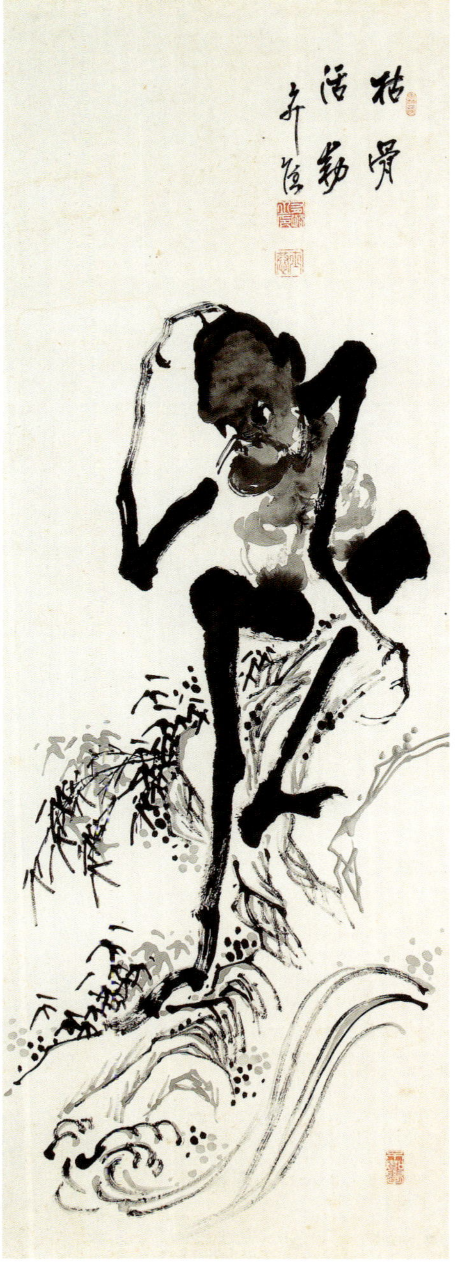

Panel 6:
Figure under a Cliff Scratching His Head

SIGNATURE: *Gōga Kaku saku* 聱牙恪作

SEALS: *gachiku sanmai* 画竹三昧 *samadhi* of painting bamboo (upper right)
Doi Kaku sen 土井恪卩 (sig. upper)
Kyō shi 恭氏 (sig. lower)
funyo gaku 不如學 doesn't resemble learning (lower hand)
頁□□難哉 (bottom left)

INSCRIPTION: 無論君休妍魄。唯觀髑髏之活躍
It doesn't matter that you are blessed with a beautiful form; just look at the actions of your skull.

Panel 5:
Shouting Figure Holding Seals

SIGNATURE: *Gōga Kaku saku* 聱牙恪作

SEALS: *gachiku sanmai* 画竹三昧 *samadhi* of painting bamboo (upper right)
Yūkaku no in 有恪之印 (sig. upper)
Gōgasai 聱牙斎 (sig. lower)
Kyō shi 恭氏 (upper hand)
funyo gaku 不如學 doesn't resemble learning (lower hand)
gachiku sanmai 画竹三昧 *samadhi* of painting bamboo (bottom left)

INSCRIPTION: 人間真諦如煙如屁顕現忽消
The ultimate truth of humanity resembles smoke, resembles a fart, appearing, yet quickly dispersed

Panel 4:
Figure Scratching His Head by a Stream

SIGNATURE: *Doi Kaku* 土井恪

SEALS: *gachiku sanmai* 画竹三昧 *samadhi* of painting bamboo (upper right)
Yūkaku no in 有恪之印 (sig. upper)
Shikyō 士恭 (sig. lower)
funyo gaku 不如學 doesn't resemble learning (bottom right)

INSCRIPTION: 枯骨活動
Activities of dried bones

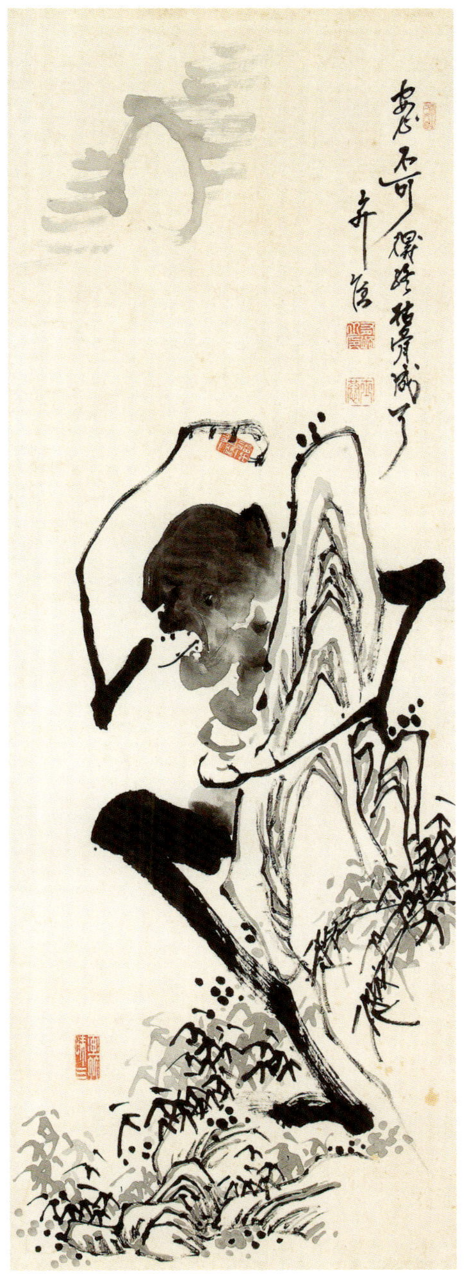

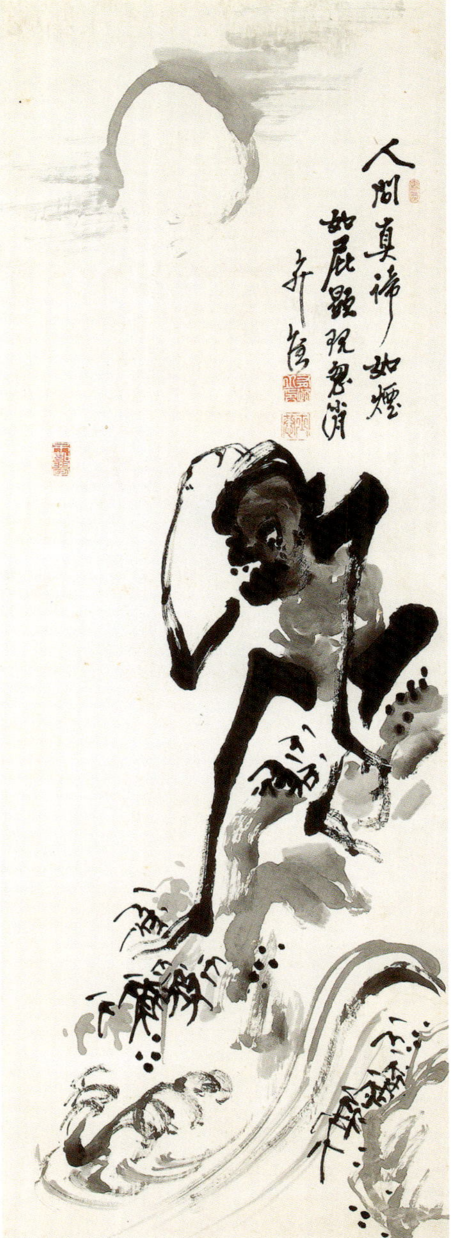

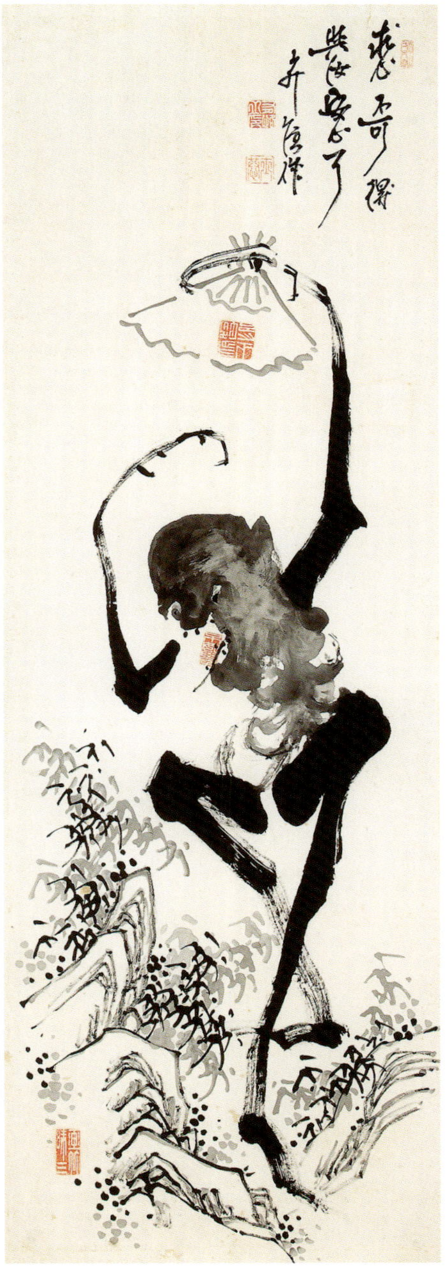

Panel 3:
Figure Embracing a Stone in Moonlight

SIGNATURE: *Doi Kaku* 土井恪

SEALS: *Tensei ippen shin* 天生一片心 naturalness is part of the mind (upper right)
Yūkaku no in 有恪之印 (sig. upper)
Shikyō 士恭 (sig. lower)
kono e kono toki ittan isshō this painting, this time, one chat, one laugh (in hand)
gachiku sanmai 画竹三昧 *samadhi* of painting bamboo (bottom left)

INSCRIPTION: 安心不可得。終枯骨成可。
A calm mind is not possible; ending up as dried bones is possible.

Panel 2:
Figure Scratching His Head by a Moonlit Stream

SIGNATURE: *Doi Kaku* 土井恪

SEALS: *gachiku sanmai* 画竹三昧 *samadhi* of painting bamboo (upper right)
Yūkaku no in 有恪之印 (sig. upper)
Shikyō 士恭 (sig. lower)
funyo gaku 不如學 doesn't resemble learning (left)

INSCRIPTION: 人間真諦如煙如屁顕現忽消
The ultimate truth of humanity resembles smoke, resembles a fart, appearing, yet quickly dispersed.

Panel 1:
Figure Waving a Fan

SIGNATURE: *Doi Kaku saku* 土井恪作

SEALS: *Tensei ippen shin* 天生一片心 naturalness is part of the mind (upper right)
Yūkaku no in 有恪之印 (sig. upper)
Shikyō 士恭 (sig. lower)
Yūkaku no in 有恪之印 (on fan)
funyo gaku 不如學 doesn't resemble learning (in mouth)[10]
gachiku sanmai 画竹三昧 *samadhi* of painting bamboo (bottom left)

INSCRIPTION: 求心不可得。與汝安心可。
Seeking the mind is not possible; giving you a calm mind is possible.

Bamboo

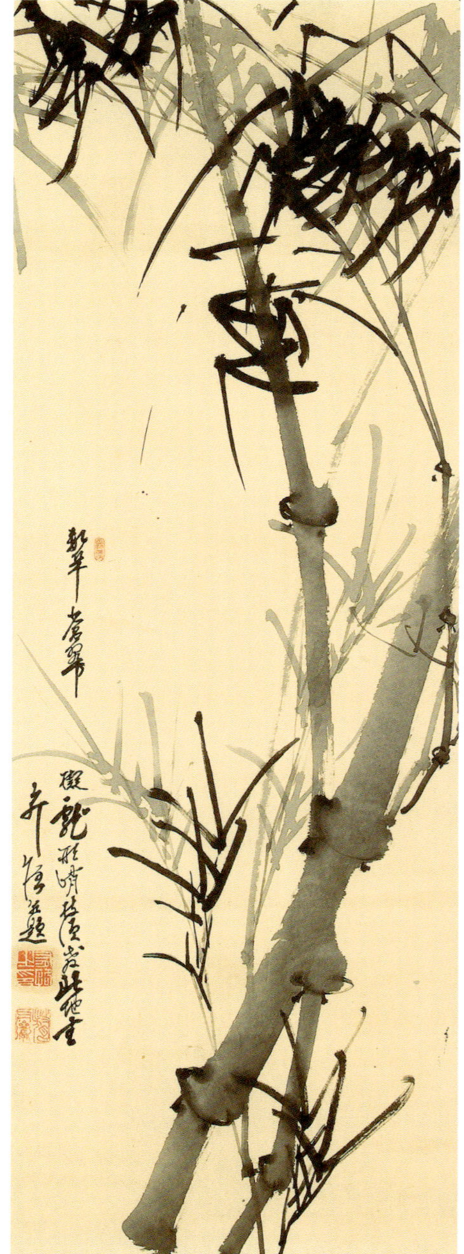

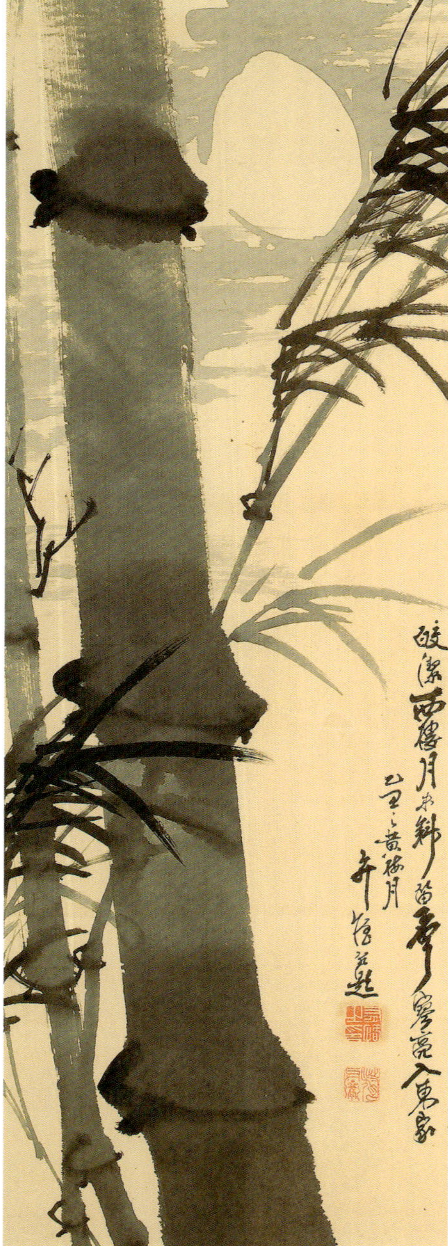

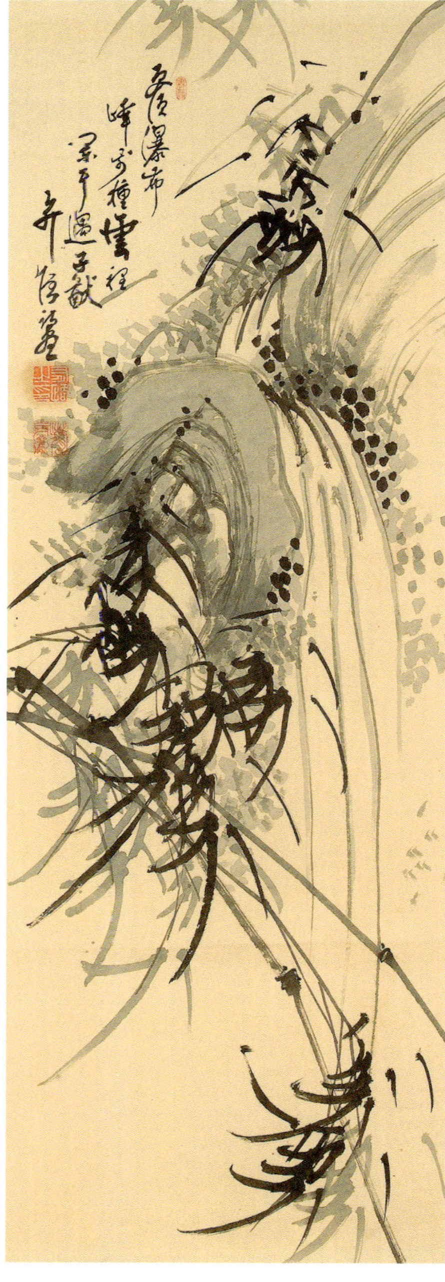

Panel 6:
Slender Bamboo

SIGNATURE: *Doi Kaku heidai* 土井恪并題

SEALS: *gachiku sanmai* 画竹三昧 *samadhi* of painting bamboo (upper right)
Yūkaku no in 有恪之印 (sig. upper)
Gōgasai 聱牙斎 (sig. lower)

INSCRIPTION: 數竿翠蒼擬龍形。峭枝須教此地生。
Several bright green bamboo shoots resemble a dragon's shape; vigorous stems are made to sprout from this earth.

Panel 5:
Moonlit Bamboo

SIGNATURE: *kinoto ushi* [1865] *kobai tsuki Doi Kaku heidai* 黄梅月土井恪并題

SEALS: *gachiku sanmai* 画竹三昧 *samadhi* of painting bamboo (upper right)
Yūkaku no in 有恪之印 (sig. upper)
Gōgasai 聱牙斎 (sig. lower)

INSCRIPTION: 皎潔西樓月未斜。笛聲寥亮入東家。
Moonlight still slants through the unsullied western chamber; a flute's lonely sound enters the eastern house.

Panel 4:
Bamboo by a Waterfall

SIGNATURE: *Doi Kaku shiga* 土井恪詩画

SEALS: *gachiku sanmai* 画竹三昧 *samadhi* of painting bamboo (upper right)
Yūkaku no in 有恪之印 (sig. upper)
Gōgasai 聱牙斎 (sig. lower)

INSCRIPTION: 更須瀑布峰前種。雲裡欄杆遇子猷。
Of course, this is the kind found by a mountain waterfall; within the clouds a railing to serve the gentleman's plan.[11]

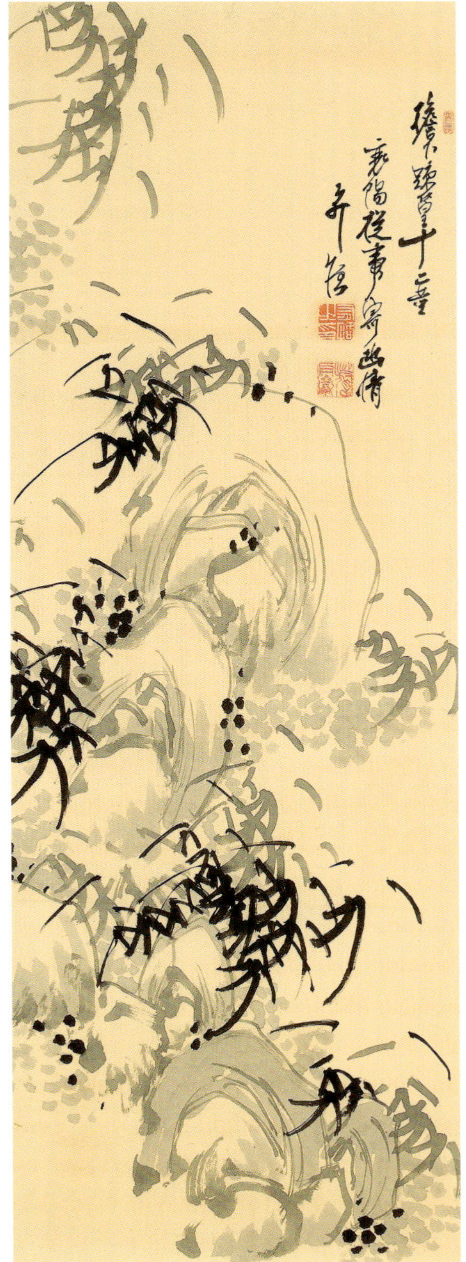

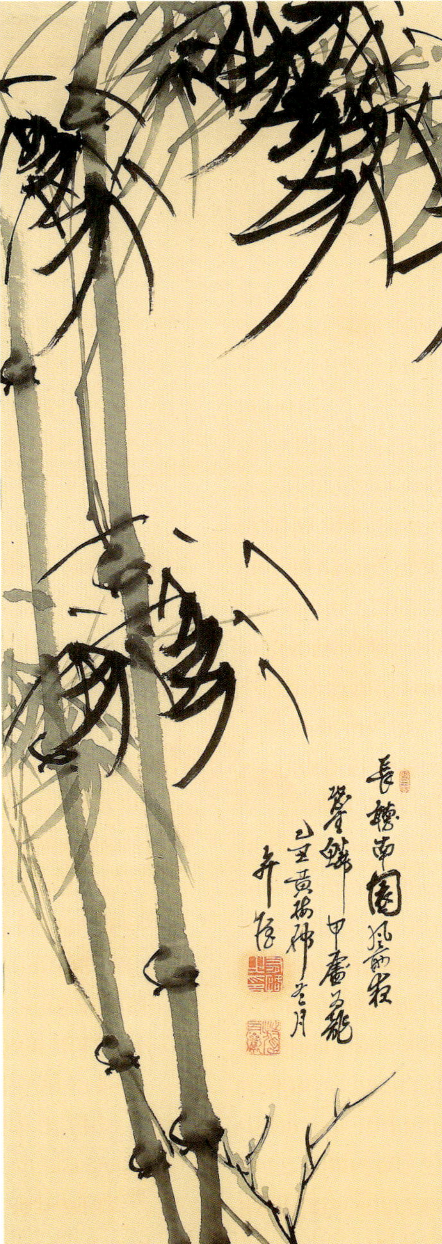

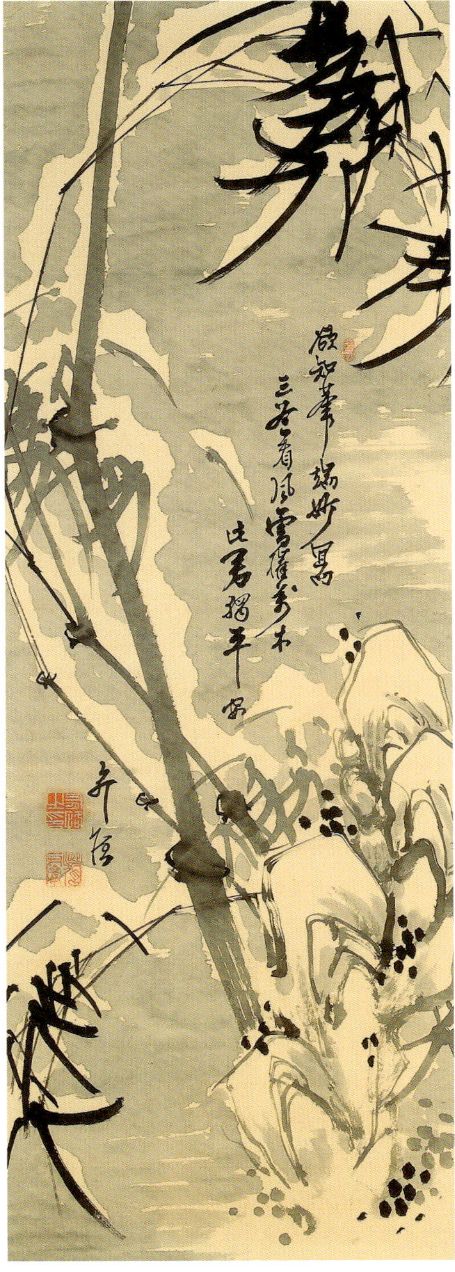

Panel 3:
Scattered Bamboo

SIGNATURE: *Doi Kaku* 土井恪

SEALS: *gachiku sanmai* 画竹三昧 *samadhi* of painting bamboo (upper right)
Yūkaku no in 有恪之印 (sig. upper)
Gōgasai 聱牙斎 (sig. lower)

INSCRIPTION: 檐下疎篁十二茎。衰陽従事寄幽情。
Under the eaves, twelve shafts of scattered bamboo; the fading sun bestows elegance.

Panel 2:
Windswept Bamboo

SIGNATURE: *kinoto ushi* [1865] *kōbai shin tōgetsu Doi Kaku* 黄梅神冬月土井恪

SEALS: *gachiku sanmai* 画竹三昧 *samadhi* of painting bamboo (upper right)
Yūkaku no in 有恪之印 (sig. upper)
Gōgasai 聱牙斎 (sig. lower)

INSCRIPTION: 長聴南園風雨夜。恐生鱗甲盡為龍。
Listening long in the southern garden to the nighttime wind and rain; fearful of the scaly birth of the dragon.

Panel 1:
Bamboo in Snow

SIGNATURE: *Doi Kaku* 土井恪

SEALS: *gachiku sanmai* 画竹三昧 *samadhi* of painting bamboo (upper right)
Yūkaku no in 有恪之印 (sig. upper)
Gōgasai 聱牙斎 (sig. lower)

INSCRIPTION: 欲知筆端妙。宜四三各看。風雪積萬木。此君獨平安。
Wanting to know the marvels of the brush tip, it's good to look at each of the four treasures and three fundamentals.[12] Windswept snow covers the myriad trees; your solitude is peaceful and calm.

Tanomura Chokunyū 田能村直入

1814–1907

Literati painters were best known for their knowledge of Confucian texts and Chinese poetry, but they usually maintained a simultaneous interest in various forms of Buddhism. Not only were many Buddhist priests active patrons or even participants in literati gatherings; the temples themselves were often the location for *sencha* gatherings and exhibitions of paintings and calligraphy. These associations occasionally resulted in the creation of iconic Buddhist paintings, yet among the many possible themes, two stand out, the White-robed Kannon and the original disciples of the Buddha called Rakan 羅漢. Although the reasons for this preference are many, the main motive derived from the popularity of these themes in the Zen tradition. The Zen temples of Kyoto are noted for their collections of Song- and Yuan-dynasty paintings of these figures. The main influence, however, may have been Manpukuji 萬福寺, the headquarters of the Ōbaku Zen 黄檗 sect in Uji, which played a key role in the origins of the literati movement in Japan. The immigrant Chinese monks there not only made many paintings of the Kannon and the Rakan but also brought with them old examples from China that were studied by visiting artists. Ike Taiga 池大雅 (1723–1776) famously fingerpainted eight *fusuma* panels depicting five hundred Rakan in 1764 after studying the figures in the handscroll version of that theme attributed to Wang Zhenpeng 王振鵬 (c. 1270–c. 1330) in the temple collection.

Although originally a very serious theme, by the late Ming period, paintings of Rakan were often treated more humorously, a tendency that increased even more in the hands of Japanese literati painters. The misshapen heads and peculiar poses traditional for Rakan neatly dovetailed with Confucian iconography, wherein an oddly shaped head was often a sign of wisdom in legendary figures such as the deity of agriculture, Shennong 神農. In the nineteenth century, in particular, large numbers of semicomic paintings of Rakan were created by Fujimoto Tesseki 藤本鐵石 (1817–1863), Hine Taizan 日根對山 (1813–1869), and Tomioka Tessai 富岡鐵斎 (1836–1924).

Tanomura Chokunyū, too, was captivated by this theme; he painted more images of Rakan than of any other topic except landscapes. His Rakan paintings can be divided into two categories, those created in large sets to be donated to temples or to raise money and those, like the present work, created as a solitary image. His earliest recorded set of Rakan paintings is a group of sixteen scrolls given to Saikōji temple in Taketa in 1835, soon after the death of his teacher and foster father, Tanomura Chikuden (1777–1835).[1] In 1847 Chokunyū created a "complete" set of all five hundred Rakan in order to raise funds for the repair of a building at Osaka's noted Shitennōji temple.[2] These paintings, although fairly simple, bore the correct name of each Rakan and included a verse in Chinese.[3] Sometime later he created a set of one thousand Rakan paintings for a similar fund-raising activity. His biggest group was the five thousand Rakan he created in 1889 for the fifty-fifth memorial ceremony of Chikuden's death, painted and inscribed in a simple, repetitive manner with an unusual grass brush. Chokunyū was said to have painted ten of these works every morning.[4]

Chokunyū's individual paintings of Rakan were usually more complex than those created in huge sets. They ranged from the extremely detailed, heavily colored example from 1853 at the Hakutsuru Museum, Kobe, to the more lighthearted example seen here.[5] Chokunyū signed this painting by stating the generations of spiritual transmission from the Buddha.[6] As this is usually done only by Buddhist priests, especially by Ōbaku Zen monks, it is likely that he made this painting between 1899 to 1902, when he was head priest of Shishirin'in 獅子林院. Chokunyū remained a very vigorous painter and calligrapher even in his last years. The drama of the bold brushwork in the rocks and bare tree, the humor of the Rakan as they chat together and gaze at the moon, and the power of Chokunyū's sweeping calligraphy reveal all his talents at top form. PB

79. *Sixteen Rakan* 十六羅漢図 (Jūroku rakan zu)

c. 1900
Hanging scroll: ink and color on satin
140.3 × 50 cm

SIGNATURE: *Shakuson nanajunana sei hoei Chokunyū Koji Chi* 釋尊七十七世法裔直入居士癡 Seventy-seventh-generation dharma descendant from Sakyamuni, layperson Chokunyū Chi

SEALS: 竹翠□鑄書 (upper right)
Chokunyū Koji 直入居士 (sig. upper)
chayū 茶友 friend of tea (sig. lower)
enran shinsho ze go kyo 煙嵐深處是吾居 I reside in a deep space of mist and storms (bottom right)

INSCRIPTION:
十有六尊者,悉皆存異胥,一霄乘清風,偶然出幽窟,步上巉巌頭,相會賞圓月,身心清且閒,禅機自然發,各到着一言,戎喝又戎咄,意味深更深,惟能得窮竭,妙用否神通,水雲何日歇,遊戲弄天與,逸性廟法闕,岫畔無心雲,往成環出没,觀空不頂帰,呼茶勢丈笏,天上与人間,婆婆又恍惚,低頭現脚根,渓澗雲勃々

Sixteen sacred disciples, all of them extraordinary,
As soon as the pure breeze arises, unwittingly emerge from the dark grotto.
Walking atop the precipitous slopes, assembling to appreciate the round moon,
Body and mind pure and dignified, Zen actions spontaneously arise.
Each arrives with one word, a great shout or a great cry;
The meaning is deep and deeper still, obtainable only after complete exhaustion.
Marvels that deny supernatural powers, waters and clouds rest for how many days?
Playing with heaven's gifts, indolence as the temple rules are lost.
Mountain peaks level with mindless clouds, perfectly encircled coming and going,
Watching the sky not returning from the summit, crying out at the tablet of age.
Heavens above give humanity, old women and senility;
Lowering one's head deeply to the feet, mountains, streams, and clouds suddenly change.

Purchase, 2005
13203.1

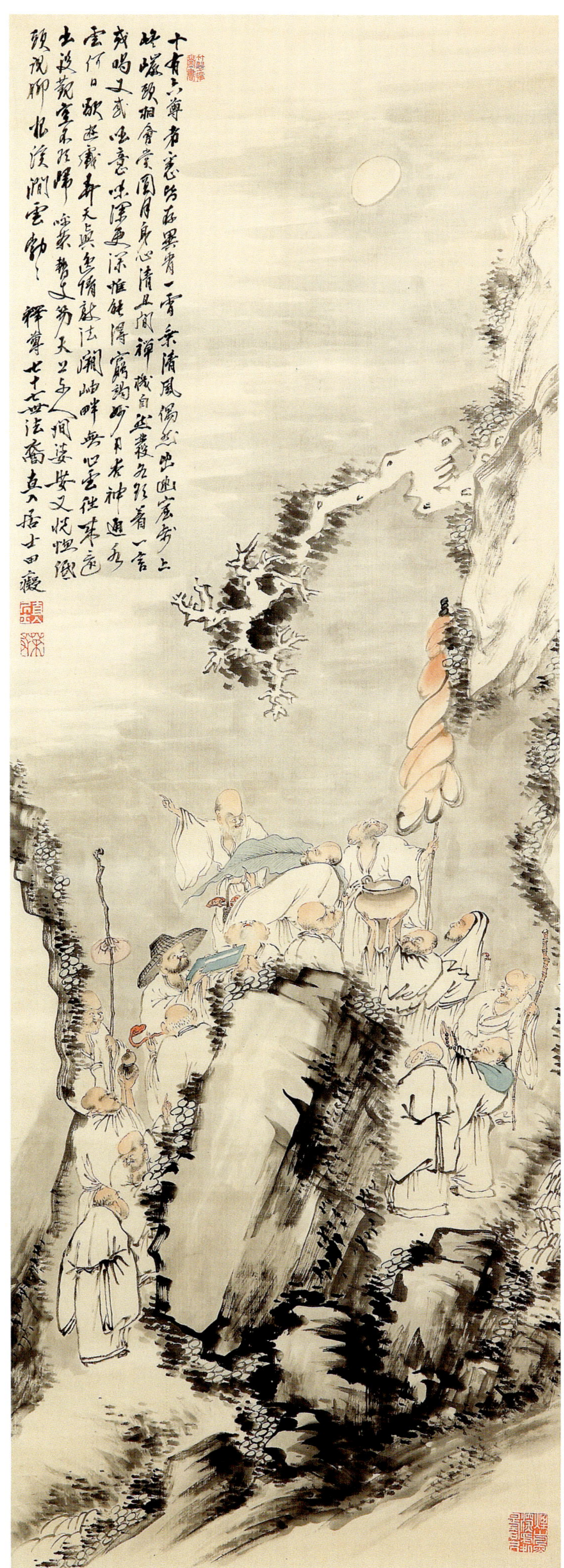

NOTES

1. Watanabe Masura, *Chokunyū Koji ihō* (Kyoto: Gashindō, 1925), 22.

2. Ibid., 44. There are five hundred named Rakan recorded in Buddhist tradition, although paintings more often show them as a group of sixteen or eighteen figures.

3. See one example from this set in Paul Berry and Yokoya Kenichirō, *Unexplored Avenues of Japanese Painting* (Ōtsu: Ōtsu Shiritsu Rekishi Hakubutsukan; Seattle: University of Washington Press, 2001), plate 31.

4. Ibid., 87.

5. See Kyōto Furitsu Sōgō Shiryōkan, *Tanomura Chokunyū to Tomioka Tessai* (Kyoto, 1985), plate 4.

6. Chokunyū had two different sets of seals that claimed he was a fortieth- or forty-first-generation descendant from Rinzai, suggesting that there was some controversy concerning from whom he had received dharma transmission. He used the fortieth-generation seal in the early Meiji period and the forty-first-generation seal while resident at Shishirin'in. Both types appear in the undated Chokunyū seal book in the Hakutakuan collection, Kyoto.

Tomita Keisen 冨田溪仙

1879–1936

Su Dongpo was the pseudonym of Su Shi 蘇軾 (1037–1101), a superb calligrapher and painter as well as a celebrated poet and scholar-official with a tumultuous political career in Song China. Su and his elite circle of friends formulated the literati ideal of painting as a means of personal expression that valued the character of the artist over technical dexterity. In the subsequent development of the Chinese and Japanese literati tradition, Su came to be revered not only for his poetry and calligraphy but for many events from his life which sparked the imaginations of scholar-amateur artists throughout the centuries.

In modern Japan, Tomioka Tessai (see cat. nos. 11, 46), who shared the same birthday as Su, greatly admired the poet and produced numerous paintings inspired by his life. A favorite subject was *Su Dongpo in a Borrowed Hat* (Sokō tairyū zu 蘇公戴笠図), which derived from an incident during Su's exile to Hainan Island 海南島 late in his life. For those depictions, Tessai typically portrayed the eminent scholar caught in a sudden rain wearing a borrowed peasant hat and clogs.[1] The story goes that his humorous appearance caused women and children to laugh, but Su remained composed and unaffected.

As indicated by the inscription, Keisen's painting also represents a rain-related episode, but from Su's early life. After passing the imperial examination in 1061, Su received an appointment as assistant magistrate of Fengxiang 鳳翔 district in Shannxi 陝西 province, where he built a pavilion. During his sojourn, the area experienced a severe drought. When rain finally came, local residents and officials rejoiced hand in hand, the sight of which compelled Su to name his building Joy-Rain Pavilion.[2]

In this small painting, the renowned scholar is dressed in a billowy robe and looms large under an umbrella held by his servant. Although roughly portrayed by light washes and seemingly clumsy lines, the expansive figure exudes a quiet dignity. Rows of vivid green on the ground indicate a cultivated field rejuvenated by fresh rain. In the background, three herons are cursorily outlined with a wavy line. Emulating the spontaneity and expressiveness of Tessai's style and unhampered by technical concerns, Keisen achieved a similar naïveté here. His brush style, however, is distinctively his own, displaying less structure and greater playfulness than that of the older artist.

By the time Keisen painted *Su Dongpo,* his unconventional painting style had attracted a great deal of attention from *yōga* artists. One of them, Saitō Yori 齋藤與里 (1885–1959), pointed out as early as 1917 that what made Keisen's art unique were his brush lines of "non-beauty" (*fukirei* 不綺麗) and "disorderliness" (*ranzatsu* 乱雑).[3] Yori's words capture the heart of Keisen's art, as exemplified by this work.

MM

80. *Su Dongpo* 蘇東坡 (Sotōba) T

1920
Hanging scroll: ink and color on silk
47.1 × 42.2 cm

SIGNATURE: *Keisen* 溪仙

SEAL: 鎮□

INSCRIPTION:
Sotōba Kiutei 蘇東坡喜雨亭
Su Dongpo['s] Joy-Rain Pavilion

Purchase, 2005
13215.1

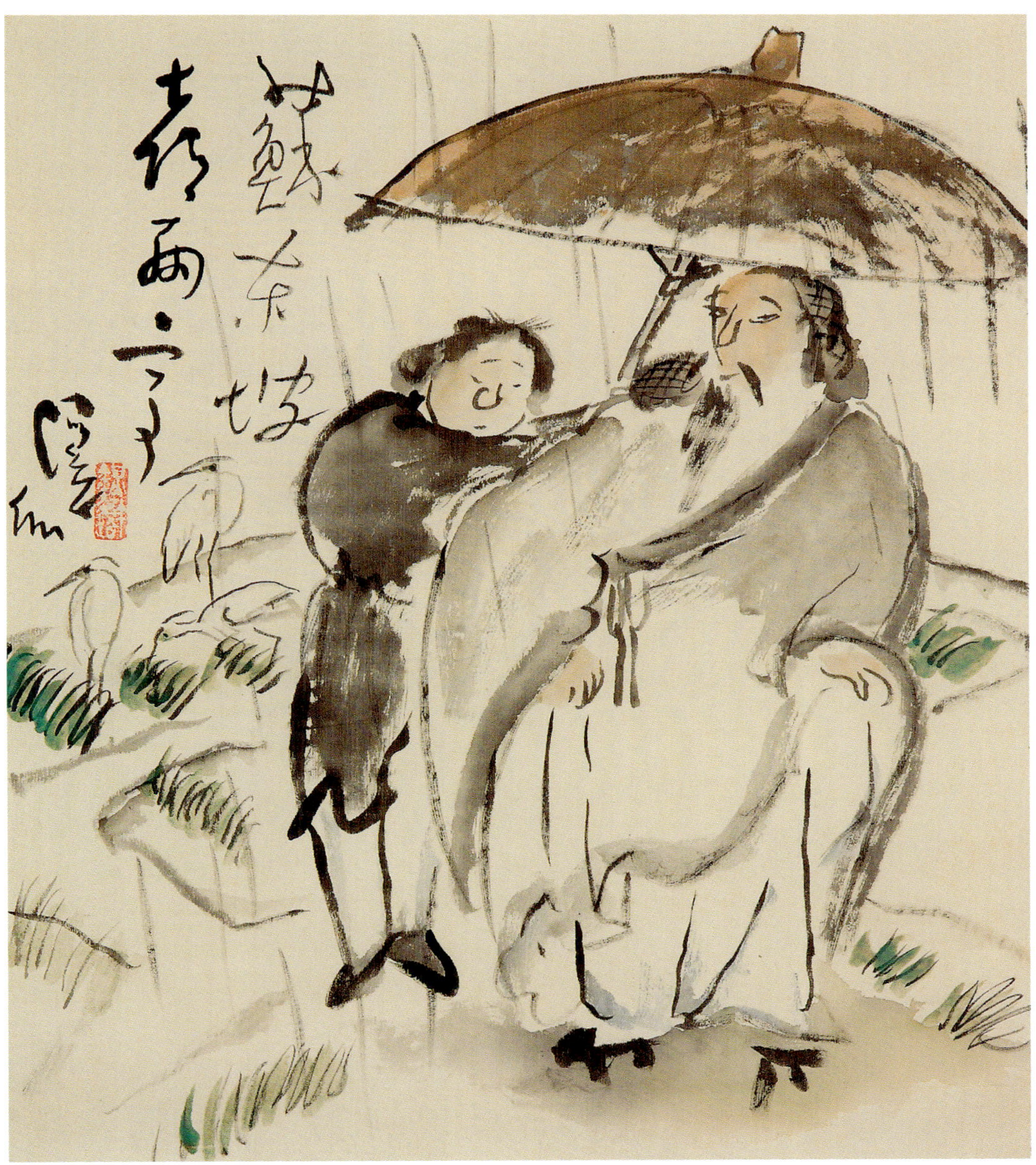

NOTES

1. See Kyōtoshi Bijutsukan, *Seitan hyakugojūnen kinen Tomioka Tessai ten*, exh. cat. (Kyoto: Kyōto Shinbunsha, 1985), plates 106, 137, and 209.

2. Morohashi Tetsuji, *Dai kanwa jiten*, 5th ed. (Tokyo: Daishūkan Shoten, 1976), 2: 1090.

3. Saitō Yori, "Tomita Keisen ron," *Chūō bijutsu* 3, no. 8 (August 1917): 30.

Nakajima Kahō 中島華鳳

1866–1939

The first question asked in viewing this painting might be, "What is that demon (*oni* 鬼) so fiercely biting?" The answer reveals the pun upon which the painting is based. The large object is an *oni senbei,* a kind of roasted rice cracker. The *senbei* cracker in Japan is variously said to have appeared in the seventh to ninth centuries, when the technique for making it was imported from China. According to an early reference to *oni senbei* in *Kefukikusa* 毛吹草, the 1638 haiku manual by Matsue Shigeyori 松江重頼 (1602–1680), the cracker was being produced in the Rokujō 六条 area of Kyoto and in Izumi Sakai 和泉堺, south of Osaka. The puffy, roasted surface of the *senbei* was said to resemble the face of an *oni.* Although methods of manufacture varied over time, *oni senbei* was known for being especially hard and so big that it was broken up for eating. The string that runs through the giant *senbei* was likely used for hanging it in the shop before sale. The joke, of course, is that it takes a real *oni* with fangs to eat the hard, oversize *oni senbei.*

This dramatic rendition of a clever idea was first created by Maruyama Ōkyo's 円山應擧 (1777–1795) most individualistic disciple, Nagasawa Rosetsu 長沢蘆雪 (1754–1799). Known for his flamboyant, yet elegant brushwork, Rosetsu is now considered one of the great eccentric painters of the late eighteenth century. The intense expression of the *oni* as its fangs bite down on the huge *senbei* firmly grasped in its claws conveys a comic impression of desire and imminent satisfaction. Rosetsu's most distinctive seal is the large, roughly circular one seen here. At some point this seal suffered a large chip in the upper right corner, but on this scroll its form is complete, revealing that the painting was done in the earlier part of his career. Rosetsu's original painting appeared in a prewar sale catalogue, and comparison with it shows how fully Kahō captured not only the form but the spirit of the painting and the calligraphy (fig. 1).[1]

Making copies or inspired revisions of older works is an ancient practice in Japan; the endless versions of certain paintings by Sesshū 雪舟 (1420–1506) are among the best-known examples. Although an accomplished and prolific painter in his own right, Kahō frequently made new versions of older paintings, especially those by Itō Jakuchū 伊藤若冲 (1716–1800),[2] Rosetsu, and his older friend Tomioka Tessai. The copying of such works simultaneously demonstrated an appreciation of the original composition and the talent to re-create it. In this case, Kahō indicated his authorship by placing a square seal with his name over the edge of the Rosetsu seal.[3]

The striking dotted design of the paper mounting is typical of those Kahō sometimes employed in the Taishō period. Although the spirit of experimentation that swept through so many painting circles during that time was usually confined to the painting itself, Kahō's unique mountings declare the modernity of his work. The mounting of this painting, itself based on an eighteenth-century composition, establishes just this sense of delightful freshness.

PB

NOTES

1. Kyōto Bijutsu Kurabu, *Tōshi Ueno Kyokushōan shozōhin nyūsatsu mokuroku* (November 16, 1925): plate 64.

2. For a Kahō version of a Jakuchū composition, see Paul Berry and Yokoya Kenichiro, *Unexplored Avenues of Japanese Painting* (Ōtsu: Ōtsu Shiritsu Rekishi Hakubutsukan, 2001), plate 89.

3. Most copies of the seals from the original work are painted in with red ink, yet this copy of Rosetsu's seal appears to have been recarved and impressed, a much more difficult and time-consuming process.

81. *Oni Senbei* 鬼煎餅

After Nagasawa Rosetsu
Hanging scroll: ink and color on paper
131.2 × 46.3 cm

SIGNATURE (after Rosetsu): *suichūgo sha Rosetsu* 醉中後寫 蘆雪 Drawn after becoming drunk. Rosetsu

SEALS: *Gyo* 魚 (after Rosetsu)
Kahō 華鳳

Purchase, 2005
13207.1

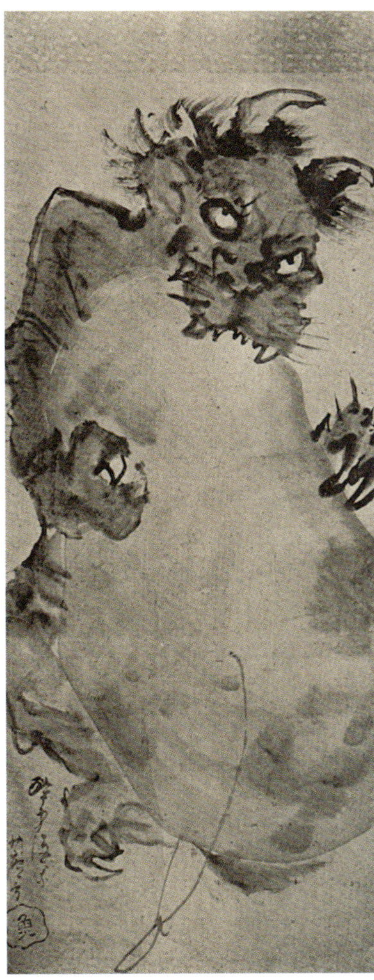

Figure 1. Nagasawa Rosetsu, *Oni Senbei*. Hanging scroll: ink and light color on paper. Ex–Ueno Kyokushōan collection.

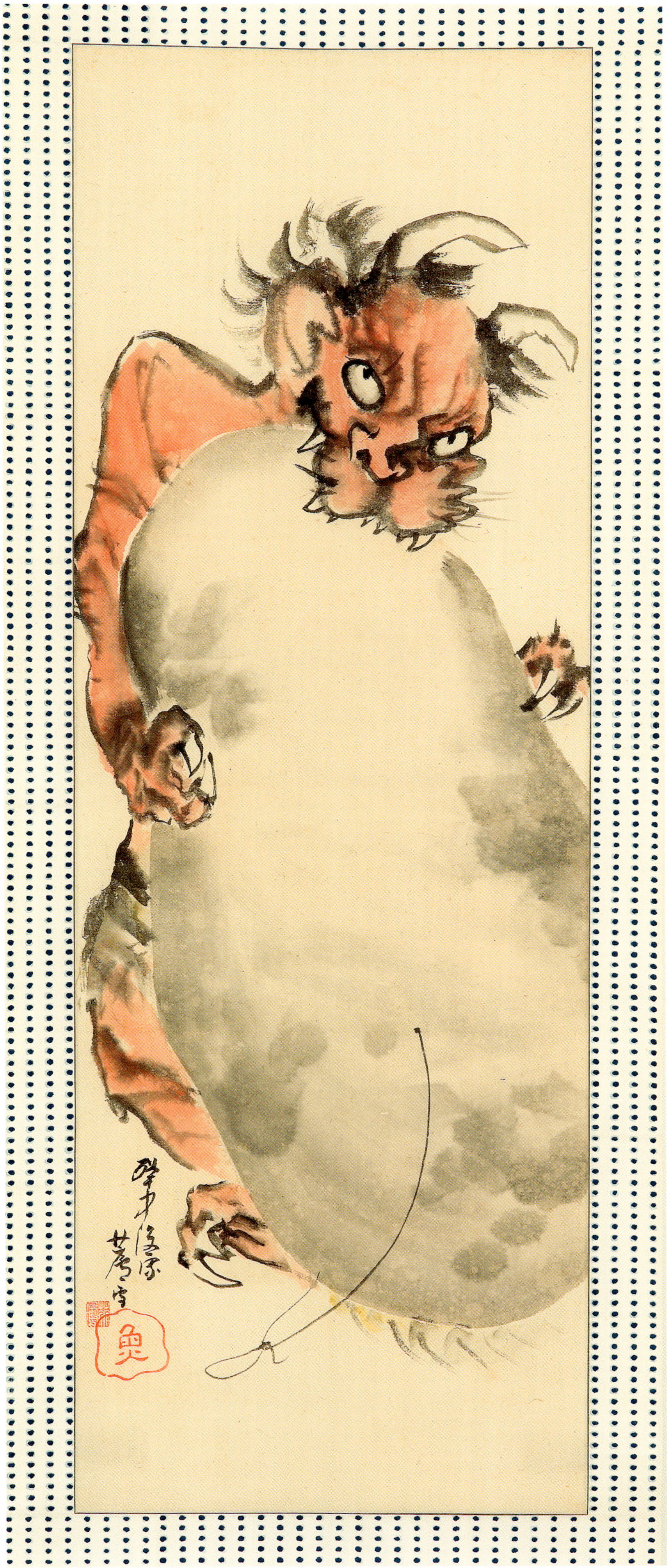

Takakura Kangai　高倉観崖

B. 1884

82. *Album of Chinese Landscapes and Figures* 中国山水人物画帖 (Chūgoku sansui jinbutsu gajō)

1920
Album of ten leaves: ink and color on silk
33 × 24 cm each

SIGNATURES: *Kangai sanshō sha* 観崖山樵写 Painted by Kangai the recluse (leaves 1–6, 8, 10)
Kangai sha 観崖写 (leaves 7, 9)

SEALS: *Kanshun* 涵蓁 (leaves 1, 4, 8)
Kōjo 鏗如 (leaves 2, 3, 5–7, 9, 10)

Purchase, 2005
13159.1

A decisive turning point in Kangai's artistic career was his two-month trip to China with Hashimoto Kansetsu 橋本関雪 (see cat. no. 13) in the spring of 1918.[1] Traveling to Jiangnan 江南, in the Yangtze River delta, they visited famous sites in Suzhou 蘇州 and Hangzhou 杭州 before proceeding to Shanghai. Although they had intended to visit Nanjing and Beijing, an outbreak of plague in Nanjing forced them to return to Japan from Shanghai. By 1918 Kansetsu had firmly established himself as one of the most illustrious Kyoto painters of his generation through spectacular achievements at the Bunten, the government exhibition. The son of a Confucian scholar, he had a profound interest in China and had already visited the continent twice. Thus, despite the fact that Kansetsu was only a year older, Kangai referred to him reverentially as "*sensei* [teacher], who is erudite about Chinese history."[2]

In the 1910s Kangai himself had achieved considerable success at the government exhibition with his sumptuous screen paintings of popular female subjects. Upon returning from China in 1918, however, he took a radically different direction. For the Bunten that year, Kangai submitted a triptych of Chinese landscapes titled *Scenes from Zhejiang* 浙江所見, based on his visits, to famous Chinese sites.

This album, dated "spring of the *kōshin* year 庚申春日" (1920) on the fifth, eighth, and tenth leaves, exemplifies Kangai's post-1918 style and represents his new enthusiasm for Chinese subjects, both real and imaginary. The scene shown opposite is the fourth leaf, *Farmer Working on a Long Spring Day* 耕人遅日之図. The most striking aspect of the composition is Kangai's animated brushwork combined with the bright palette of Taishō *nihonga*. In the sea of dots that blend to form the trees and flowers in an exuberant pointillist pattern, the only stable area is the patch of flat land where the man is busy at work. In the background, a tall green-blue mountain juts up suddenly, breaking the flow of Kangai's inscription. Although Kansetsu's influence can be detected in the long-legged figure, the painting is distinctly Kangai's in its inventive composition, strong color, and playful brushwork.

In some examples Kangai's compositions are unconventional to the point of quirkiness. In the third leaf, he placed a mountain in the foreground, soaring through the center of the composition, and highlighted it with vibrant blue strokes and green dots. The acute bird's-eye view of the background distorts the perspective, making the distant land appear to be a green cloud above the mountain with the boat floating in the sky. Kangai imaginatively transformed a generic mountain-and-water landscape into an arresting image.

In other scenes Kangai employed explosive colors to personalize orthodox subjects. The ninth leaf portrays the famous scholar-poet Rin Nasei 林和靖 (Ch., Lin Hejing, 967–1028), who lived as a recluse by the West Lake, Hangzhou. This is the only historical figure prominently featured in the album, no doubt inspired by a visit to his grave during the 1918 trip.[3] Kangai depicted the scholar walking alongside blossoming white plums, accompanied by a magnificent crane. By dressing the poet in a bright red robe and showing him with his beloved plum and crane, Kangai created a joyous, intimate portrait of the revered Northern Song poet.

The eighth leaf stands out for Kangai's mischievous use of ink. In *Evening Bell at Misty Temple* 烟寺晩鐘之図, Kangai let dark ink spread with no defining brushwork. With the addition of blue and green, the wet forms suggest a mountain, while the unpainted area in the middle is to be read as a band of mist. But Kangai's mountain appears as if an organic growth about to engulf the tiny structure in the upper right. Perhaps the most unusual scene is the sixth, *Harvesting Water Chestnuts at the West Lake* 西湖所見採菱之図,

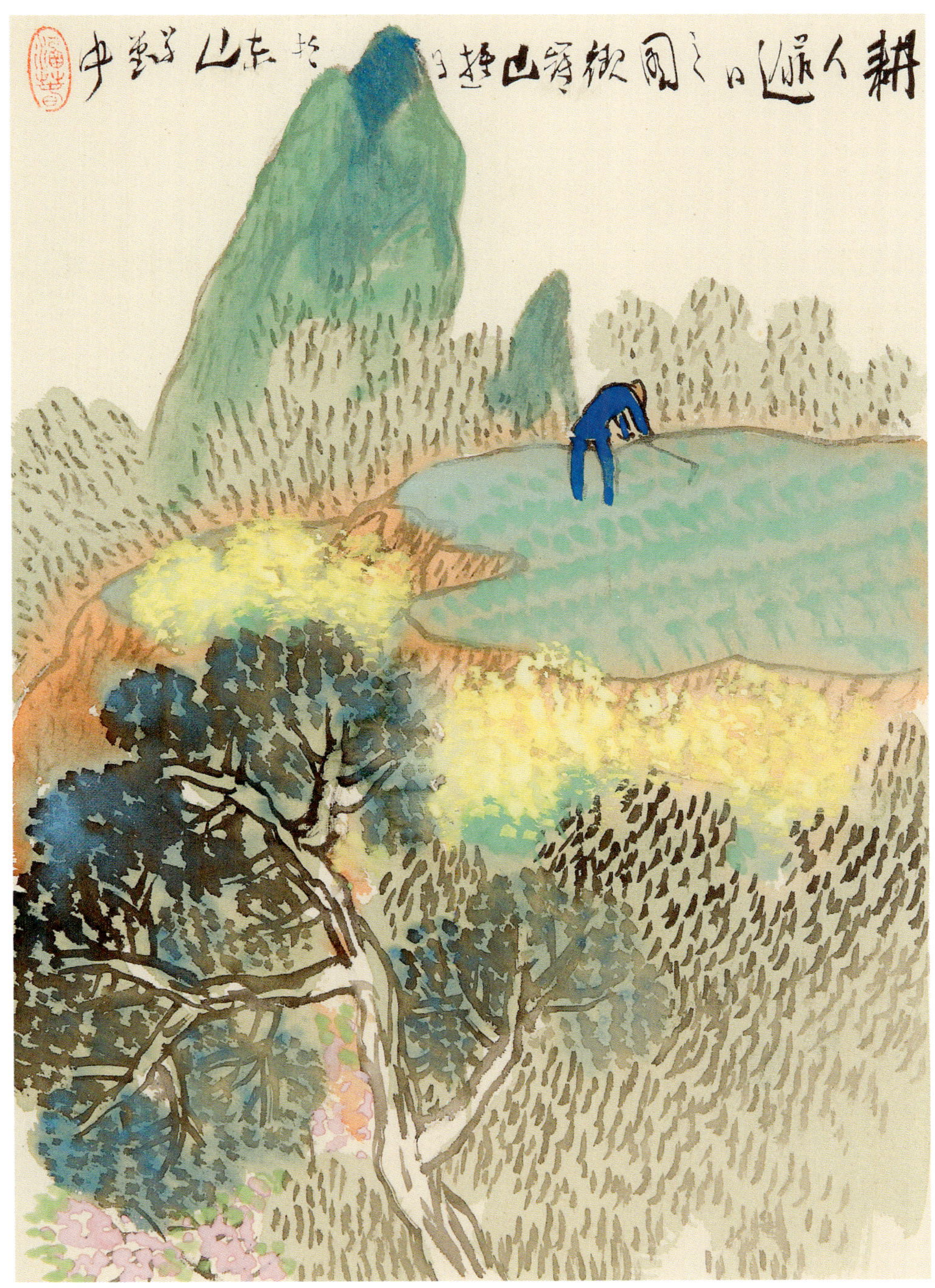

in which two figures lie side by side in their boat to scoop up their harvest. Their unusual work posture is both humorous and endearing, and the restrained color imbues the scene with a quiet lyricism.

After 1919 Kangai seems to have withdrawn from national competitions to pursue painting independently. Except for paintings that appeared in the art periodical *Daimai bijutsu* after the late 1920s, the facts of his later life and artistic career remain unknown. This delightful album gives us a welcome glimpse into the talent of this intriguing artist. MM

NOTES

1. For more details of their trip, see Takakura Kangai, "Shina ni asobite," *Kyōto bijutsu*, no. 45 (June 1918): 15–19, and two essays by Hashimoto Kansetsu, "Shina man'yū miyage banashi," *Kaiga seidan* 6, no. 6 (June 1918): 41, and "Kōnan ni mitaru shizen to jin'i no chōwa," *Kyōto bijutsu*, no. 45 (June 1918): 9–11.

2. Takakura, "Shina ni asobite," 15.

3. Ibid., 17.

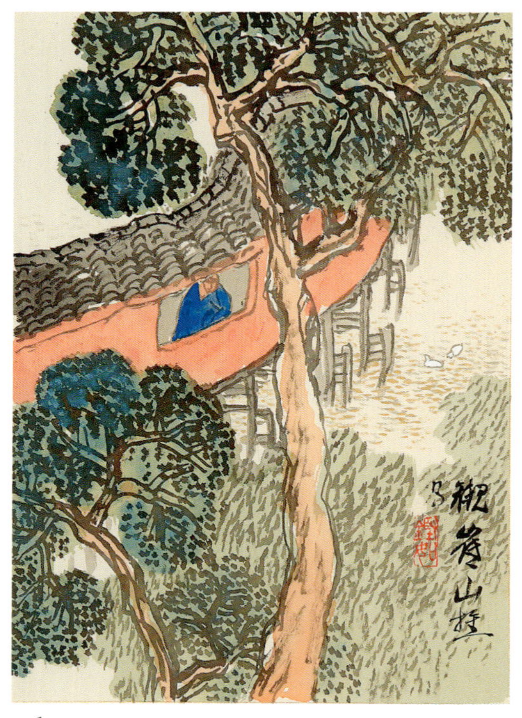

1

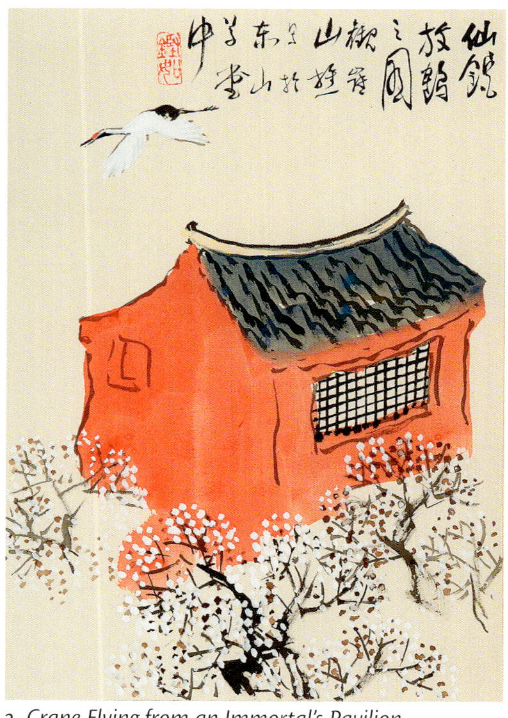

2 *Crane Flying from an Immortal's Pavilion*
仙館放鶴之図

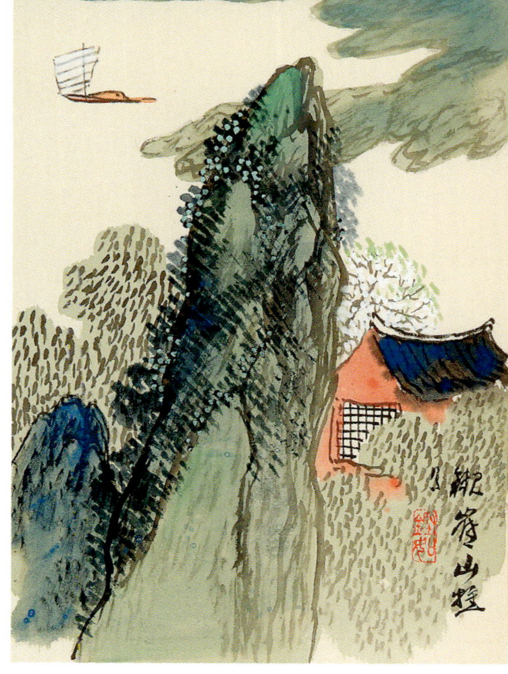

3

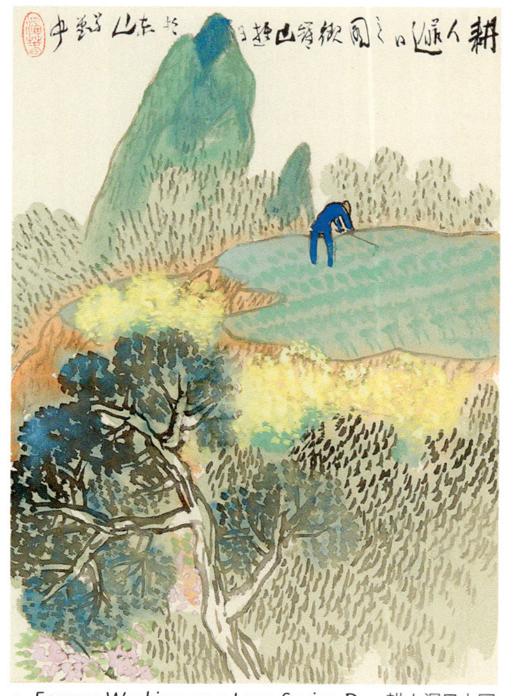

4 *Farmer Working on a Long Spring Day* 耕人遲日之図

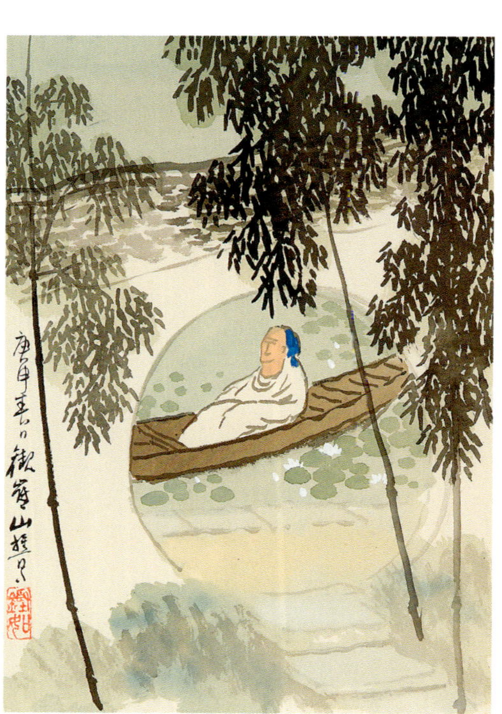

5

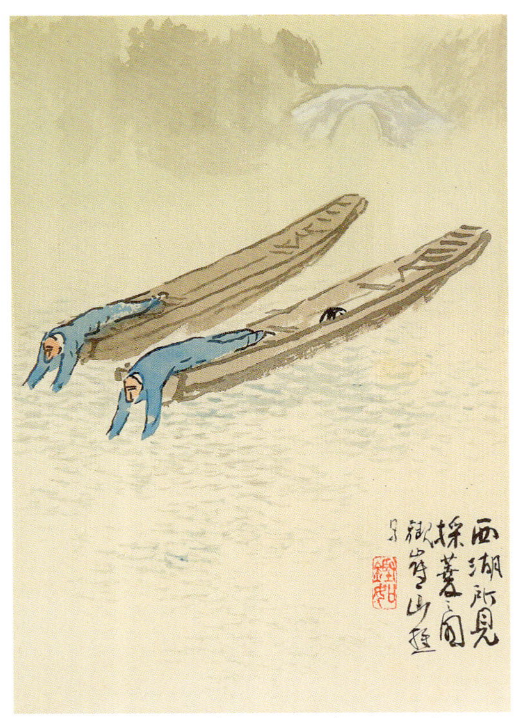

6 *Harvesting Water Chestnuts at the West Lake*
西湖所見採菱之図

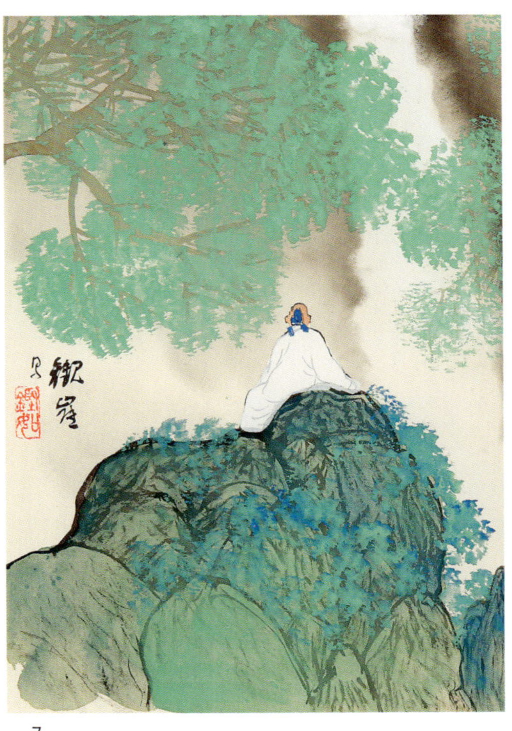

7

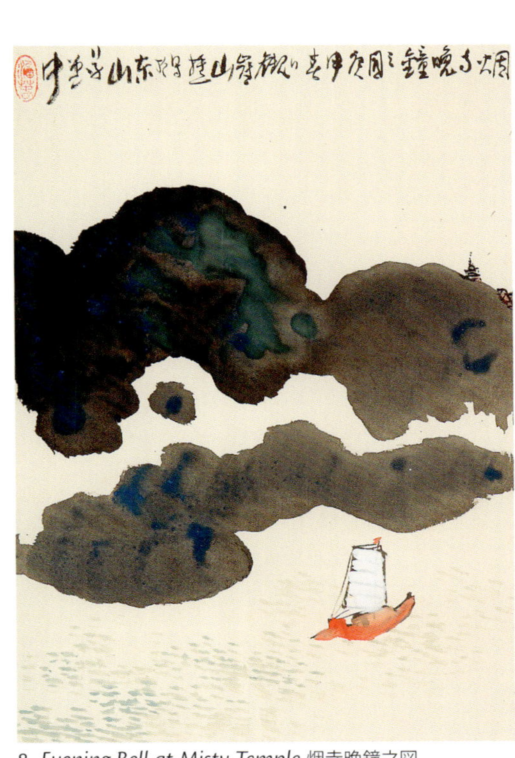

8 *Evening Bell at Misty Temple* 烟寺晩鐘之図

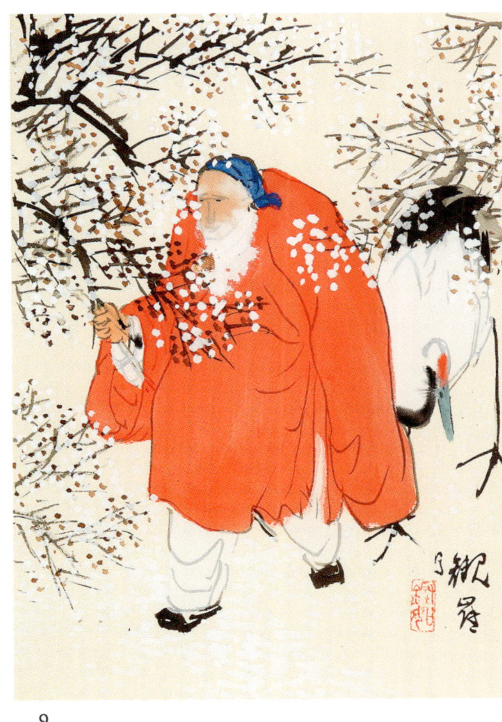

9

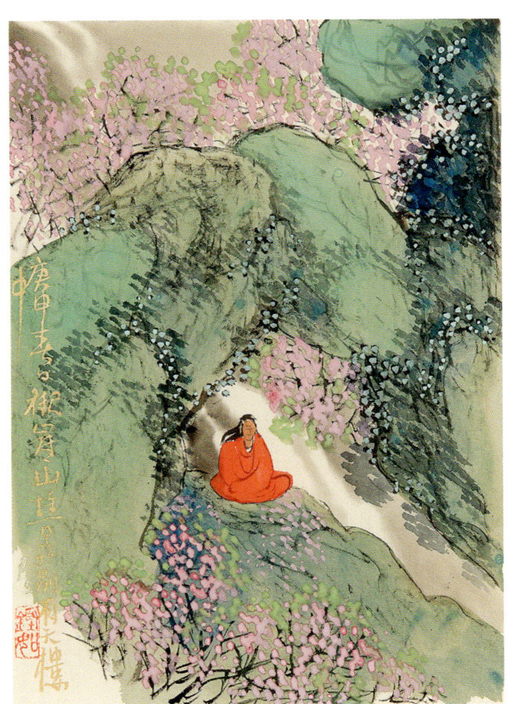

10

Ogawa Sen'yō 小川千甕

1882–1971

Gyoran Kannon represents a female form of Kannon (Ch., Guanyin), one of the thirty-three manifestations of the bodhisattva of compassion. With its origin in Tang China, the legend of Gyoran Kannon is inseparable from that of Merōfu Kannon (馬郎婦, Ch., Malangfu). In the story, a beautiful young woman promises to marry the man who can quickly learn a series of Buddhist sutras. Of many eager suitors, only one meets the final challenge of memorizing the entire Lotus Sutra (Hokkekyō 法華経) within three days. (In the Merōfu version, the man is identified as Master Ma.) On the wedding day, however, the woman suddenly dies. Several days later, a monk comes by and opens the casket of the dead woman to find the bones of her skeleton linked by a golden chain. He proclaims the woman to be a manifestation of a great being who helps believers to follow Buddhist teachings and attain enlightenment. In later versions of the story, the woman's identity is revealed as Kannon.

Merōfu Kannon and Gyoran Kannon became the most important feminine manifestations of Kannon in China, while Gyoran Kannon gained wide popularity in seventeenth-century Japan.[1] In art, both deities are portrayed as attractive women—but with one major iconographic difference: a basket of fish identifies Gyoran Kannon as a fish seller while Merōfu Kannon holds a scroll in her hands. In this painting, Ogawa Sen'yō created his own version of Gyoran Kannon holding a woven bamboo basket filled with fish in one hand and a book of sutras in the other.

During the initial fifteen years of his artistic pursuit, Sen'yō maintained a parallel interest in Japanese and Western styles of painting. Around 1904 and 1905, while working as a painter of Buddhist images and studying ink brushwork under Tanaka Ikka 田中一華 (1864–1924), Sen'yō also received instruction in oil painting from Asai Chū 浅井忠 (1856–1907). With other young *nihonga* artists under Asai's tutelage, Sen'yō founded Heigokai 丙午会, which provided a venue for exhibiting their Western-influenced works.[2] In turn, during the 1910s, when he made a serious foray into oil painting, Sen'yō joined the *yōga*-trained painters of the Coral Group (Sangokai 珊瑚会), where he explored new *nihonga* possibilities. Finally, during the 1920s, to which *Fish-basket Kannon* can be dated, Sen'yō reestablished himself as a *nihonga* artist with a growing focus on modern interpretations of literati painting.

Gyoran Kannon, a deity manifested as a beautiful young woman, challenges an artist to capture both her sensuality and her spirituality. In this, Sen'yō succeeded. Represented with great sensitivity and freedom, his Gyoran Kannon is an alluring woman of ethereal beauty. The reddish outline of the figure, a widespread convention during the Taishō period, conveys her tangible human presence and sensuousness. Her delicately depicted face, encircled by a halo, is serene in expression. The unusual but elegant colors of her gently swaying, soft garment grant her an unworldly charm. The spiritual ambience of the image is further enhanced by the subtle, pervasive sheen of the satin ground. Although Sen'yō employed none of the brushwork associated with established literati modes, the roughly outlined foliage and freely textured tree trunk indicate the influence of Tomioka Tessai's expressive style. Sen'yō's adoption of *yōga* technique can be seen in the loose depiction of the deity's garment, its form defined by long strokes of directly applied color. The surprisingly detailed representation of the fish and basket introduces an unexpected degree of visual interest. Despite success at the Japan Art Institute (Nihon Bijutsuin 日本美術院) during the 1920s, Sen'yō was at times troubled by what he called the "bad *yōga* elements" in his work.[3] Nonetheless, it is his accomplished synthesis of various styles and techniques that resulted in the stunningly fresh expression of this painting.

MM

83. *Fish-basket Kannon*
魚籃観音 (Gyoran kannon) T
1920s
Hanging scroll: ink and color on satin
134.2 × 40.8 cm

SIGNATURE: *Sen'yō sō* 千甕叟
Sen'yō an old man

SEAL: *Sen'yō* 千甕

Terry Welch Collection

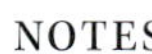

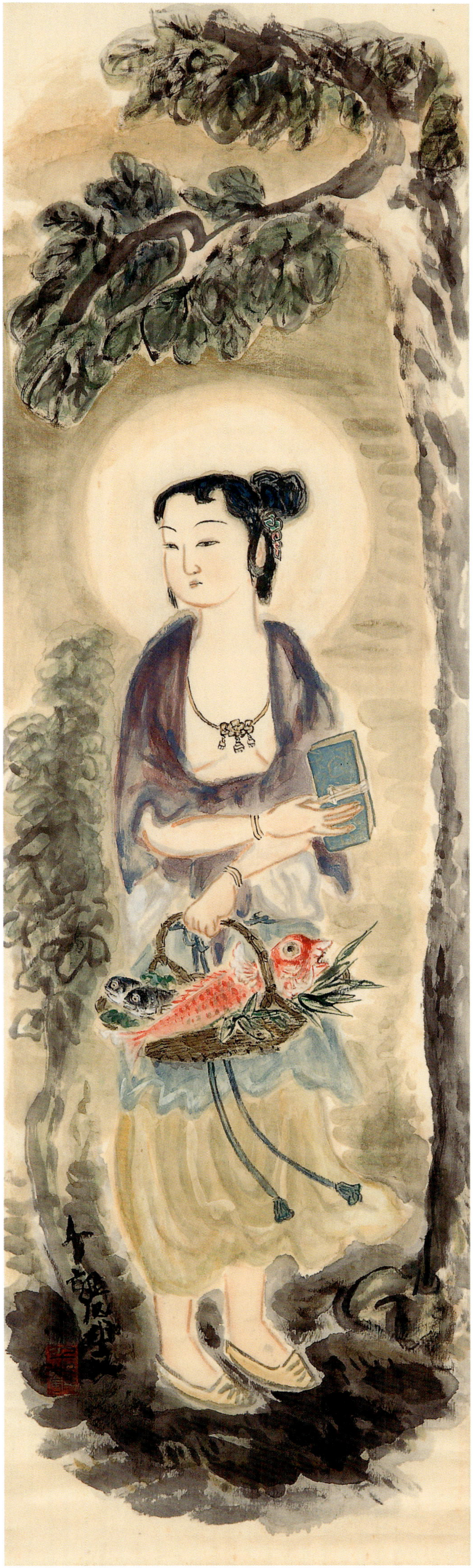

NOTES

1. For a detailed discussion of the origin and historical development of Merōfu Kannon and Gyoran Kannon, see Patricia Fister, "Merōfu Kannon and Her Veneration in Zen and Imperial Circles in Seventeenth-Century Japan," *Japanese Journal of Religious Studies* 34, no. 2 (2007): 419–24 (http://www.nanzan-u.ac.jp/SHUBUNKEN/publications/jjrs/jjrsMain.htm).

2. See Sen'yō's reminiscences of Heigokai and its members in "Kaikyū manki," *Bi no kuni* 1, no. 8 (December 1925): 20–23.

3. Ogawa Sen'yō, *Gashū: Ogawa Sen'yō* (Kyoto: Benridō, 1967), 16.

Appendices

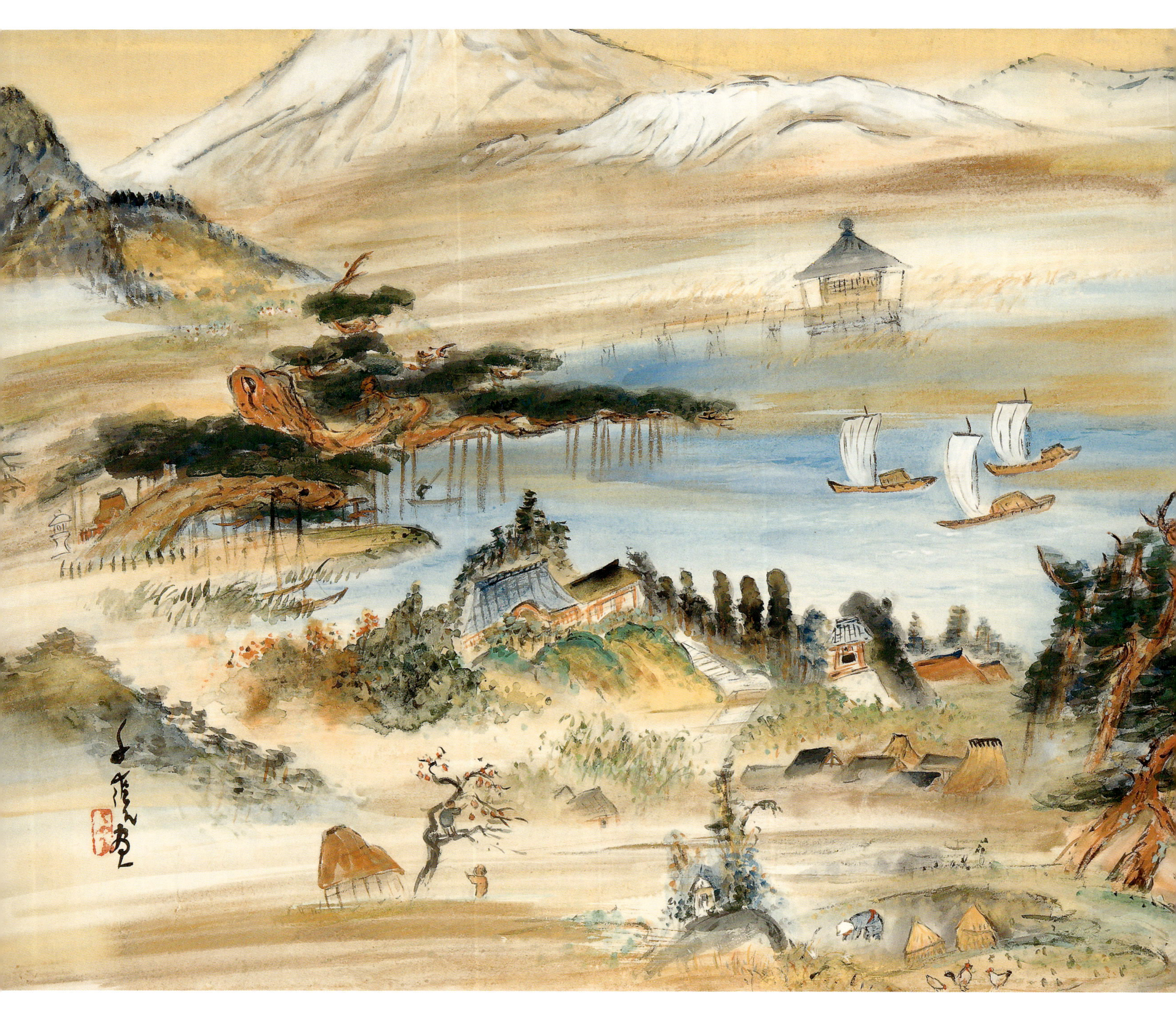

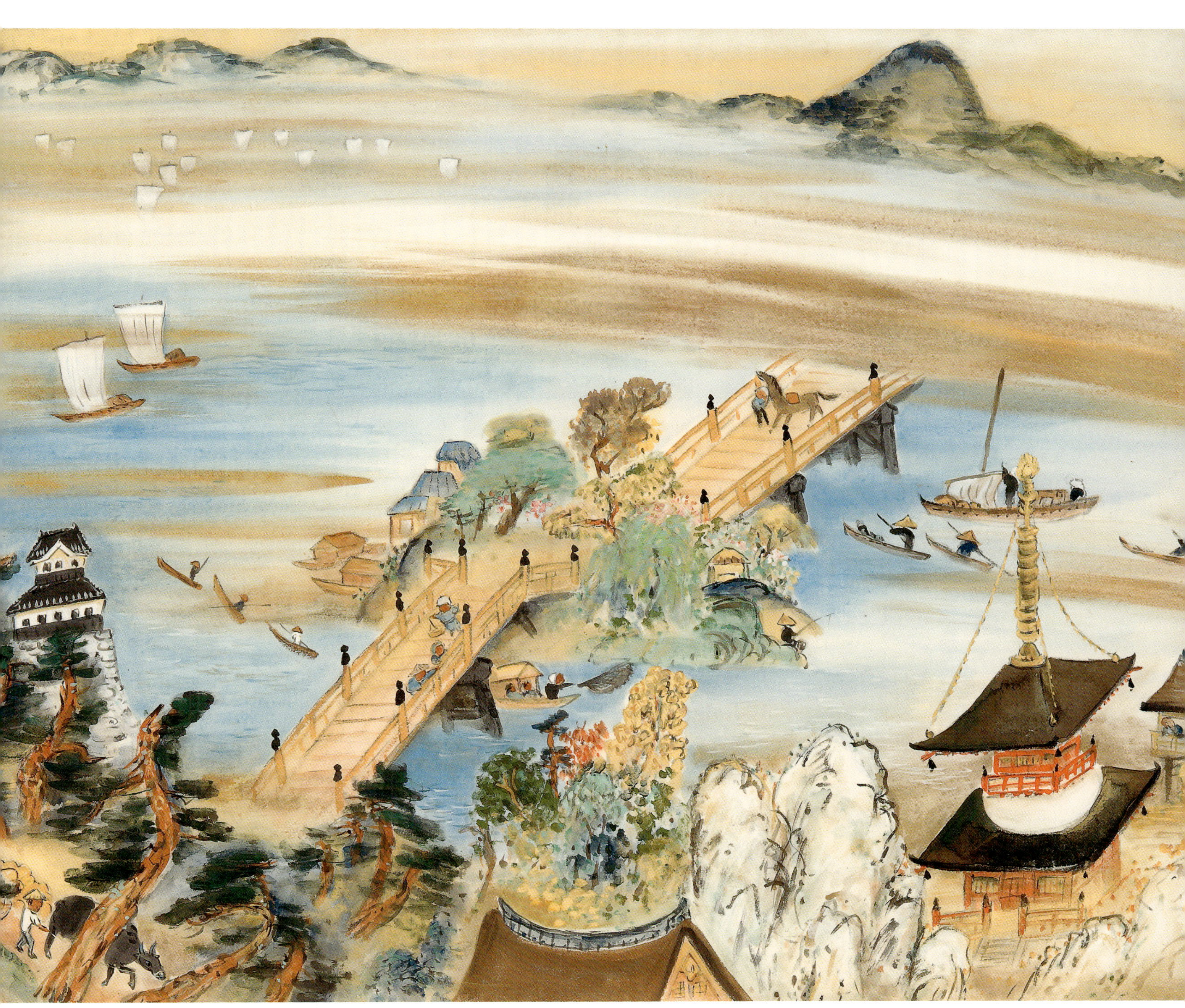

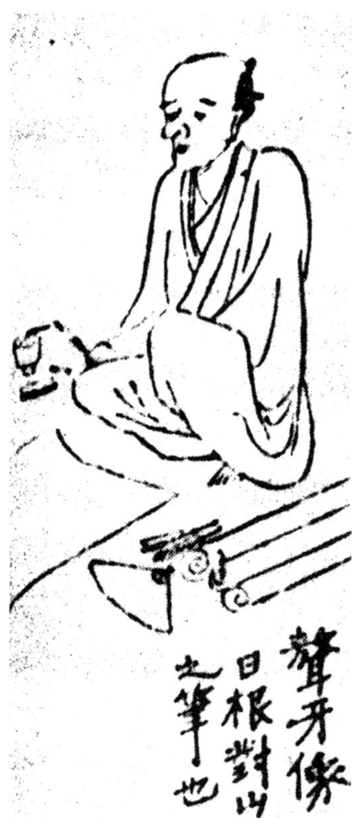

Doi Gōga 土井聱牙 1817–1880

The usual image of a Confucian scholar is of a teacher whose sedate life of erudition and conservative values upheld the established ranks of Edo-period society. Although there is some truth to this, some Confucian scholars differed markedly from the norm, especially in the latter part of the Edo period, as a few took issue with the state of society. Ōshio Heihachirō 大塩平八郎 (1793–1837) ended his life as the leader of an abortive rebellion in Osaka, and Rai San'yō 頼山陽 (1780–1832), the noted literati calligrapher and painter, devoted much time to his *Unofficial History of Japan* (Nihon gaishi 日本外史, 1807–), a social critique cloaked as history.

Among these iconoclasts was the scholar-painter Doi Gōga. His name itself was chosen for its dual meaning of "something difficult to understand" and "reluctance to listen to others," two qualities well reflected in his life. Although he lectured widely and had many students, his writings were not published until after his death.[1] It may well have been that his critiques of the history and meaning of Confucianism were considered so extreme that it would have been dangerous to publish them during the political upheaval of the late Edo period. The directness of Gōga's commonsense criticism of received teachings was expressed in its most extreme form in the inscriptions he added to his many skeletal figure paintings (see cat. no. 78).

Gōga was the second son in a family who originally had practiced acupuncture in the Ise Ueno area; his father later became a physician for the local Tōdō *han*. When the *han* opened a school, his father became its Confucian teacher. A prodigy in reading and writing, Gōga succeeded to the family's hereditary stipend at the age of twelve after the deaths of his father and elder brother. At the age of eighteen, he became blind in one eye and later in life was called the "One-eyed Dragon" of Confucianism. It is said that his fear of totally losing his sight drove Gōga to excel at memorization, and he gained fame for his ability to recall the exact location of quotes from the classics.[2] He had studied with the noted Confucian scholar Saitō Setsudō 斎藤拙堂 (1797–1865) since he was a child and had progressed so rapidly that he was invited to write the postscript to the *Essays of Setsudō* (Setsudō bunwa 拙堂文話). Setsudō was very well connected in literati painting circles, being well acquainted with Rai San'yō, Okada Hankō 岡田半江 (1782–1846), Shinozaki Shōchiku 篠崎小竹 (1781–1851), and many others. Setsudō helped introduce the precocious young Gōga into the more cosmopolitan world of scholar-artists, and he became the most famous of Setsudō's many students.

After serving for six years as a private lecturer to the *han* lord, Gōga opened his own school when he was thirty-eight and maintained it until the end of the Edo period. Some have interpreted this period without employment by the *han* government as a sign that Gōga had offended officials with his blunt criticism of the status quo. Setsudō himself may have felt the irony of his most talented student not having a significant position.[3]

Gōga's startling presentation of Confucianism pointed out the contradictions between tradition and everyday attitudes. In his *Discourse on Sages* (Seijinron 聖人論) Gōga said that learning from the Confucian classics was like trying to eat a whale when only the skin and bones were left.[4] He pointed out that Confucius traveled about giving advice to the rulers of his day, but none put his teachings into practice —yet it was still commonly said that society would be well ordered if one had the virtue of Confucius.[5] Most shockingly, Gōga maintained that identifying Confucius as a sage because he was the founder of Confucianism would be the same as calling the famous Chinese bandit of antiquity, Daozhi 盗跖, a sage because he had founded a gang.[6] With these and other blunt comments, Gōga meant not to destroy Confucianism but to strip it of hypocrisy and cant, making it a believable and practical philosophy for daily life rather than a set of antiquated rituals and standards.

The artwork that Gōga produced reflects several aspects of his personality. His bamboo studies and landscapes disclose a poetic sensibility centered on nature, while his bizarre figure paintings reveal his iconoclasm with the acerbic wit and shock value of their inscriptions. The boldness of his works limited their reception outside his home prefecture, yet his unique vision continues to draw attention today. PB

BIBLIOGRAPHY

Addiss, Stephen. "Nanga koki no sannin no kojin shūgi gakatachi" 南画後期の三人個人主義画家たち. In Tsuji Nobuo 辻惟雄, ed., *Bakumatsu・Meiji no gakatachi—Bunmei kaika no hazama ni* 幕末・明治の画家たち一文明開花のはざまに. Tokyo: Perikansha ペリカン社, 1992.

Doi Gōga 土井聱牙. *Gōga sensei zuihitsu* 聱牙先生随筆. Tokyo: Buneidō 文永堂, 1916.

Hashimoto Eiji 橋本英治. *Saitō Setsudō. Doi Gōga* 斎藤拙堂・土井聱牙. Sōsho・Nihon no shisoka 叢書・日本の思想家 39. Tokyo: Meitoku Shuppansha 明徳出版社, 1993.

Saitō Masakazu 斎藤正和. *Saitō Setsudō den* 斎藤拙堂伝. Tsu: Mie-ken Ryōsho Shuppankai 三重県良書出版会, 1993.

NOTES

1. The first collection of his writings, *Gōga iko*, was published in 1885.
2. Hashimoto, *Saitō Setsudō. Doi Gōga*, 127.
3. See the presentation of Gōga's career in Saitō, *Saitō Setsudō den*, 287–90.
4. Ibid., 142.
5. Ibid., 153.
6. Ibid., 152.

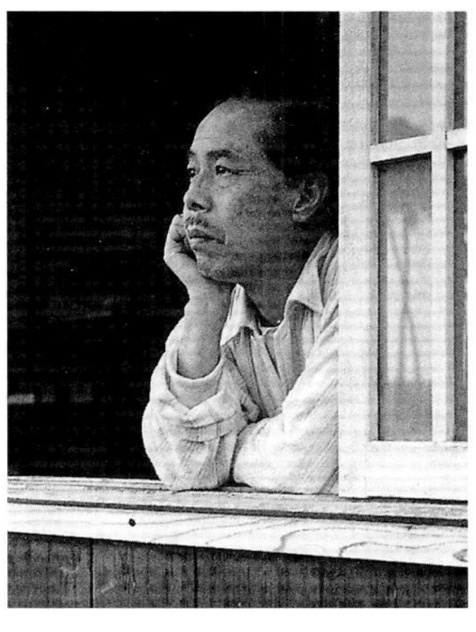

Dōmoto Inshō
堂本印象 1891–1975

Few modern Japanese painters have demonstrated such dramatic diversity and breadth in their work as Dōmoto Inshō. Born the son of a sake brewery merchant in Kyoto, Inshō had a long, thriving career, which the Japanese government recognized with the Order of Cultural Merit (Bunka Kunshō) in 1961. His older brother was the celebrated lacquer artist Shikken 漆軒 (1889–1964). A creatively restless painter, Inshō constantly made stylistic changes, culminating most dramatically with pure abstraction in his postwar work. Moreover, his artistic pursuit took him far beyond the confines of painting. In 1966 he established the Dōmoto Inshō Art Museum in Kyoto. For this ambitious multimedia art project, Inshō designed the entire building, from the white exterior with its ornamented façade to the details of the interior decoration and furnishings, including stained glass, wall tapestry, doorknobs, lighting fixtures, tables, and chairs.

Upon graduating in 1910 from the Design Division of the Kyoto Municipal School of Arts and Crafts (Kyōto Shiritsu Bijutsu Kōgei Gakkō 京都市立美術工芸学校), Inshō began working in a textile company to support his family, who had suffered bankruptcy. For the next eight years, while he drew designs for Nishijin textile patterns, he faced financial struggle and artistic disappointment as the Bunten national exhibition continued to reject his submissions. Determined to become a professional painter, he entered the Kyoto Municipal Special School of Painting (Kyōto Shiritsu Kaiga Senmon Gakkō 京都市立絵画専門学校) in 1918 and also joined the private studio of Nishiyama Suishō 西山翠嶂 (1879–1958), a successful Kyoto painter and a son-in-law of Takeuchi Seihō 竹内栖鳳 (1864–1942). Among Inshō's classmates at the Special School of Painting was another older and talented student, Fusen Tetsu (see cat. no. 60). In 1919 both artists, still in the initial phases of their training, made auspicious debuts at the Bunten, although their career paths would diverge afterward.

The 1920s marked Inshō's emergence as one of the most watched *nihonga* painters. His eclectic approach became the topic of critical discussion, but he continued to shine at the national exhibitions, winning the highest award in 1921 and a special Imperial Art Institute Award at the 1925 Teiten. Among the themes of Inshō's major paintings from this period were Kyoto scenery, Chinese landscapes, portraits and other figural subjects, birds-and-flowers, and religious subjects, executed in styles drawn from sources as varied as Maruyama-Shijō, *yamatoe,* the literati movement, and Western oil painting. Some critics viewed Inshō's mastery of multiple styles as an "arrogant display of talent," but others interpreted it as the artist's earnest efforts to achieve self-discovery and fulfillment.[1] Indeed, for Inshō, staying with the same style and expression signified stagnancy: "Once a painter perfects one style, he should immediately break away from it. . . . He must abandon what he achieved and move on to the next phase. When the next phase is completed, a painter must again abandon it, repeating this process of creative development over and over. . . . By doing so, his art becomes elevated."[2]

During the late Taishō period, Inshō's success as a painter brought him temple commissions for large-scale works, beginning in 1925 with the thirty-two paintings on the wall and sliding doors at Ryūshōji 龍翔寺 within the

Daitokuji complex. Numerous other commissions followed at major establishments in Kyoto such as Ninnaji, Tōfukuji, and Daigoji and also in Nara, Wakayama, and Osaka. Inshō's engagement with temple commissions would continue through the early 1970s, sometimes taking him as far as Tokyo and Shikoku Island.

Like many artists, Inshō painted historical subjects and military themes to express his patriotism during World War II. The changes that occurred in his art after the war stunned viewers. In the late 1940s, Cubist-inspired compositions of contemporary women began to appear in Inshō's works. After a 1952 trip to Europe, Inshō moved beyond a tentative rejection of naturalism to explore pure abstraction. His Mondrian-inspired abstract painting *Consciousness* (Ishiki 意識) caused great controversy at the 1956 government exhibition.[3] Thereafter, Inshō continued to experiment and transform his art, sometimes reintroducing strong ink brush lines, representational motifs, and even religious symbolism into his new style. Executed in Japanese traditional pigments, gold, and silver, his abstract paintings achieved great popularity in Europe and were championed by Michel Tapié (1909–1987), a French writer and advocate of Art Informel.[4] Until his death, Inshō continued to occupy a prominent position in the Kyoto art world, participating in both national and local exhibitions.

MM

BIBLIOGRAPHY

"Dōmoto Insho shi shinsakuga ten" 堂本印象氏新作画展. *Bijutsu no Nihon* 美術之日本 15, no. 2 (February 1923): 19–20.

Kanzaki Ken'ichi 神崎憲一. "Dōmoto Inshō shi koten" 堂本印象氏個展. *Tōei* 搭影 9, no. 7 (August 1933): 50–51.

Katayama Naotake 片山尚武. "Mikiki no mama" 見聞の儘. *Daimai bijutsu* 大毎美術 5, no. 4 (April 1926): 10–11.

Kyōto Furitsu Dōmoto Inshō Bijutsukan 京都府立堂本印象美術館. *Dōmoto Inshō*. Kyoto: Kyōto Bunka Zaidan 京都文化財団, 1992.

———. *Botsugo nijūnen Dōmoto Inshō ten* 没後20年堂本印象展. Exh. cat. Kyoto, 1995.

———. *Dōmoto Inshō no keifu: Seihō・Suishō・Inshō* 堂本印象の系譜：栖鳳・翠嶂. Kyoto, 1997.

Morioka, Michiyo, and Paul Berry. *Modern Masters of Kyoto: The Transformation of Japanese Painting Traditions, Nihonga from the Griffith and Patricia Way Collection.* Seattle: Seattle Art Museum, 1999.

Nishiyama Suishō 西山翠嶂, Fukuda Heihachirō 福田平八郎, Nakamura Daizaburō 中村大三郎, Tsukushi Harusaburō 筑紫春三郎, and Kanzaki Ken'ichi. "Dōmoto Inshō ron." *Atorie* 7, no. 5 (May 1930): 141–48.

NOTES

1. Kanzaki Ken'ichi, "Dōmoto Inshō ron: Daikansei no katei ka tazaijukugi no koji ka," *Atorie* 7, no. 5 (May 1930): 146.

2. Quoted by Yoshida Yōichi, "Dōmoto Inshō · gagyō no hensen," in Kyōto Furitsu Dōmoto Inshō Bijutsukan, *Dōmoto Inshō no keifu*, 18.

3. Kyōto Furitsu Dōmoto Inshō Bijutsukan, *Botsugo nijūnen Dōmoto Inshō ten*, 116.

4. In 1952 Tapié authored the book *Un art autre* (Art of Another Kind) and coined the term Art Informel to define a new style of painting that broke from traditional, structured compositions. Emphasizing spontaneity, it often resulted in highly gestural and calligraphic expressions. Abstract Expressionism is considered its American counterpart. For a discussion of Tapié's influence on *nihonga* painters during the 1950s and 1960s, see Ellen P. Conant, Steven D. Owyoung, and J. Thomas River, *Nihonga: Transcending the Past, Japanese-Style Painting, 1868–1968* (Saint Louis: Saint Louis Art Museum, 1995), 66–68.

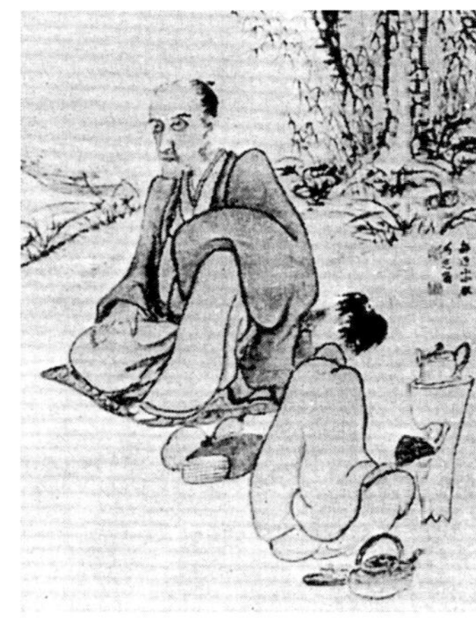

Fujimoto Tesseki
藤本鐵石 1817–1863

A great many of the literati artists of western Japan during the late Edo period were associated with the rising opposition to the policies of the shogunate and the aspiration to restore imperial rule. Yet Tesseki was among the few who gave their lives for this cause and was regarded as a martyr, inspiring others to take up arms. After the old regime was overthrown, Tesseki was so esteemed for his loyalty to the imperial cause that his painting and calligraphy were valued more for having been created by this self-sacrificing idealist than for their own merit. Even his like-minded friend Yamanaka Shinten'ō 山中信天翁 (1822–1885), also noted for literati painting and calligraphy (see cat. nos. 8, 39, 40, 67), discussed only the political career of Tesseki in his Meiji-period essay devoted to his memory.[1]

Tesseki was the second son of Katayama Sakichi 片山佐吉 (1763–1830) from the small town of Higashikawahara 東川原 on the outskirts of Okayama city. At the time of his father's death in 1830, he was adopted by Fujimoto Shige 藤本重賢 (d. 1832), and upon the death of his elderly adoptive father, Tesseki became the head of the Fujimoto family as a retainer of the local *han*.

In 1833 Tesseki began to study literati painting with the local artist Itō Kachiku 伊藤花竹 (1805–1881).[2] Following the pattern of such aspiring literati painters as Uragami Gyokudō 浦上玉堂 (1745–1820), Rai San'yō 頼山陽 (1780–1832), and Tanomura Chikuden 田能村竹田 (1777–1835), Tesseki resigned his position with the *han* in 1840 and left home to travel about the country. For more than a decade he criss-crossed Japan, visiting Ise, Edo, Nikkō, Niigata, Nagano, Onomichi, Hagi, Nagasaki, the dramatic landscape of the Yabakei 耶馬渓 valley, Izumo, Nagoya, and Shikoku. These travels not only developed his skills and reputation as an artist but also brought him into contact with many people who hoped to change Japan's political future.

Tesseki improved his swordsmanship in 1856, becoming proficient in the Ittō Shinryū 一刀新流 school. During this time he broadened his connections with scholars committed to restoring imperial power such as the poet-painter Yanagawa Seigan 梁川星巌 (1789–1858) and Umeda Unpin 梅田雲浜 (1815–1859). In 1857 Tesseki stayed for more than a month in the Itami area outside Osaka, where he visited the many wealthy sake brewers in the region, repaying his hosts with paintings, as was the custom.[3] Back in Kyoto in 1858, Tesseki met Murayama Hanboku 村山半牧 (1825–1868), a young literati painter from Echigo. Although Haboku was never a formal student of Tesseki's, his painting and calligraphy reveal a striking resemblance to his admired senior's works.[4]

Later in 1858 the shogunate cracked down on the supporters of the imperial cause in a sweeping series of arrests called the *Ansei no taigoku* 安政大獄. Many of Tesseki's close friends, including San'yō's son, Rai Mikisaburō 頼三樹三郎 (1825–1859), and Umeda Unpin, were among those jailed. In the next year, Mikisaburō and others were executed, and Unpin died in prison. Political unrest and violence mounted after the 1860 assassination in Edo of Ii Naosuke 井伊直弼 (1815–1860), the shogunal advisor who had recommended the crackdown. The loss of his friends seems to have further increased Tesseki's commitment to the cause to "revere the emperor, expel the barbarians" (*sonnō jōi* 尊王攘夷), and he plunged into even closer involvement with like-minded *rōnin* 浪人 (samurai who had left their *han* appointments) from western Japan.

Tesseki's political activity culminated when he joined with thirty-some activists, many of them *rōnin* from the Tosa *han* in Shikoku and the Kurume *han* in Kyushu, to form the Tenchūgumi 天誅組 (Heaven's Punishment Association). Members included Buddhist and Shinto priests, scholars, and farmers; most were in their late teens and twenties. Tesseki was chosen as one of three leaders, along with Yoshimura Toratarō 吉村寅太郎 (1836–1863) and the noted scholar Matsumoto Keidō 松本奎堂 (1831–1863), and charged with raising funds for arms. The group's naïve idealism was typified by the choice of the charismatic Nakayama Tadamitsu 中山忠光 (1845–1864) as its military leader, despite his being only eighteen years old.

Their moment of action arrived in the eighth month of 1863, prompted by the scheduled visit of Emperor Kōmei 孝明天皇 (1831–1866) to pray for the expulsion of foreigners at the tumulus of the first emperor, Jinmu Tennō 神武天皇 (trad. b. 711 BCE). On the seventeenth the Tenchūgumi attacked the chief magistrate's office at Gojō 五条 in Nara, beheaded the magistrate, burned the office to the ground, and declared a new government. When the news reached Kyoto, however, the emperor canceled his journey, and the *han* groups that might have supported the group were effectively discouraged from taking action. The Tenchūgumi withdrew to the Tōtsukawa 十津川 district of southern Nara prefecture, where its members gathered almost a thousand supporters—mostly farmers—from among the local people. Unprepared and desperate, they unsuccessfully tried to fashion cannons from the hollowed-out trunks of pine trees. On the twenty-sixth day they attempted to take Taketori Castle, which was defended by only two hundred soldiers. Yet the Taketori forces, well trained and armed with real cannons, soon threw the much larger attacking group into disarray. Having suffered great losses, the Tenchūgumi withdrew to Tōtsukawa. Yoshimura was badly wounded, and Nakayama fled to Shikoku and Kyushu in a futile attempt to raise support for the rebellion.

By early in the ninth month the shogunate had assembled an army of 14,000, and, despite the exhortations of the recently returned Nakayama, morale collapsed as many members and supporters deserted the group. Even though Nakayama ordered the dissolution of the Tenchūgumi on the nineteenth, the remaining members were hunted down. Tesseki died in battle on the twenty-fourth, the injured Keidō committed suicide, and Nakayama was killed in 1864.

Tesseki and the other members of the Tenchūgumi were quickly regarded as martyrs for the imperial cause and may have inspired Hanboku to commit suicide in order to avoid capture on the eve of the Meiji Restoration in 1868. The perceived nobility of their quixotic efforts was reinforced during the war years of the 1930s and 1940s, resulting in the publication of a 1943 novel about Tesseki.[5] The first in-depth study of Tesseki's life was written by Ashida Motohiro 芦田林弘 (1916–1945), one of the Great East Study Group (Daitō-juku 大東塾), whose members committed group *seppuku* in Tokyo on August 25, 1945, in apology to the emperor for losing the war.[6]

Although the drama of Tesseki's death has long overshadowed his career as an artist, his greatest aesthetic legacy may be found in the stylistic similarities between his work and many of the early paintings of Tomioka Tessai 富岡鐵齋 (1836–1924), who so admired Tesseki that he eventually portrayed him in paintings as an ideal *bunjin.* The casual, yet sensitive brushwork and humor of Tesseki's paintings have attracted many Western collectors. PB

BIBLIOGRAPHY

Ashida Motohiro 芦田林弘. *Fujimoto Tesseki* 藤本鐵石. Okayama, Tsuyamashi, 1979.

Takeno Tōsuke 武野藤介. *Ishin hiwa Fujimoto Tesseki* 維新秘話 藤本鐵石. Tokyo: Kagaku Nihonsha 科学日本社, 1943.

Watanabe Chisui 渡辺知水. *Fujimoto Tesseki* 藤本鐵石. Okayama City: Fujimoto Tesseki Sensei Kenshōkai 藤本鐵石先生顕彰会, 1962.

Yamanaka Shinten'ō 山中信天翁. "Fujimoto Tesseki" 藤本鐵石. *Tōzai* 東西、, no. 4 (1906).

NOTES

1. The essay was published posthumously in the journal *Tōzai,* in 1906; see Yamanaka, "Fujimoto Tesseki."

2. Watanabe, *Fujimoto Tesseki,* 208. The majority of biographical information presented here comes from this work, the most detailed study of Tesseki's life.

3. A survey of collections of sake-brewing families in the Itami area in the 1980s located about seventy works by Tesseki that are presumably from this period.

4. Hanboku wrote an honorific text about Tesseki in 1863; see Watanabe, *Fujimoto Tesseki,* 36–37.

5. Takeno, *Ishin hiwa Fujimoto Tesseki.*

6. Ashida's study of Tesseki was discovered among his belongings after his death and not published until 1979. In its preface, Ashida calls the work his last will and testament.

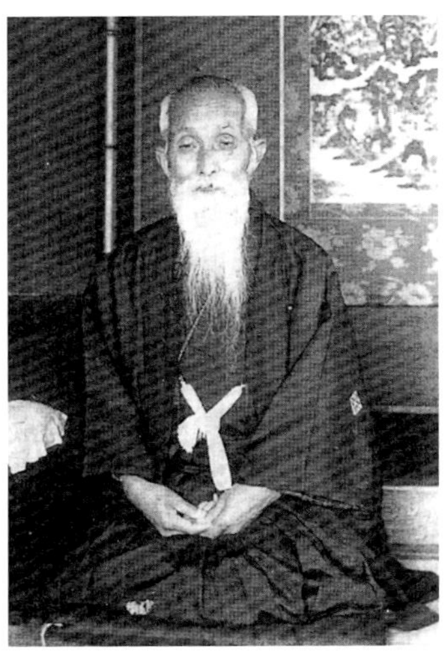

Fukuda Kodōjin
福田古道人
1865–1944

Kodōjin was born in the small town of Shingō in rural Wakayama prefecture. Even though he was skilled enough in Chinese poetry to publish a collection of verse while in his twenties, he switched to modern-style haiku after becoming a follower of Masaoka Shiki 正岡子規 (1867–1902) in 1889. Writing under his *haijin* name, Haritsu 把栗, Kodōjin frequently published haiku in poetry magazines in the late Meiji period and became widely known as Shiki's disciple. In the last years of his life, he again wrote Chinese verse and began to make distinctive literati landscapes signed with his painting name, Kodōjin. He also made simple paintings of plants and flowers that emphasized his dramatic brushwork and inscriptions of Chinese poetry. Kodōjin contributed the title calligraphy to Tomita Keisen's 富田溪仙 (1879–1936) illustrated account of his travels in Taiwan and China, the *Manga Travelogue of Taiwan and China* (Tai Shin manga kikō 台清漫画紀行, 1910). He must have appreciated Keisen's taste for unusual compositions and unconventional brushwork.

Most literati painters affiliated themselves with formal associations such as the Japanese Nanga Association (Nihon Nanga Kyōkai 日本南画協会), the Japan Nanga Institute (Nihon Nangain 日本南画院) and, in the Tokyo region, the Japan Nanga Group (Nihon Nangakai 日本南画会) and the Japan Southern School Group (Nihon Nanshūga Kai 日本南宗画会). But some painters, often self-taught, operated on the fringes of these groups, including artists such as Irie Shikai 入江之介 (1862–1940), who developed a style based on his study of Tanomura Chikuden 田能村竹田 (1777–1835), and Maeda Mokuhō 前田黙鳳 (1853–1918), a well-known calligrapher who created many unusual, strongly colored landscapes.

Kodōjin was one of these outsiders. In 1879 he began his study of painting with Suzuki Hyakunen 鈴木百年 (1825–1891) in Kyoto.[1] Kodōjin appears to have been more influenced by Hyakunen's literati painting than by his teacher's earlier background in the Shijō school. It seems likely that he studied only the fundamentals of painting technique, as even his earliest work reveals no clear influence of Hyakunen's style. Kodōjin showed no interest in the competitive exhibition environment, where paintings were hung, row upon row, in massive galleries in the Western-style exhibition halls of the national shows. In order to make an impact, paintings required large formats, but the individualists were creating intimate works best viewed in isolation in small rooms or tokonoma. Although the major *nihonga* painters also made smaller works for similar circumstances, they established and maintained their reputations through their successes in national shows. Literati painters like Kodōjin relied instead on private patronage developed through individual contacts and a few special exhibitions.[2] Operating outside formal art organizations and exhibitions, Kodōjin and other similar literati painters were rarely noted by critics. Yet they were successful on their own terms in satisfying a small group of supporters who appreciated their independent stance.

Although Kodōjin lived on a modest income for most of his life, patronage of his work reached extraordinary levels in the early Shōwa period, and the Kodōjin club was formed to promote the exhibition of his work. Among its members were an array of powerful figures: Kuhara Fusanosuke 久原房之助 (1869–1965), whose extraordinary wealth, built on interests in oil, shipping, steel, life insurance, and copper mining, allowed him to promote right-wing causes in the 1930s; Nakagawa Kojūrō 中川小十郎 (1866–1944), a founder and later president of Ritsumeikan University; Minami Hiroshi 南弘 (1869–1946), once governor of Toyama prefecture and secretary for the first two Saionji cabinets; Ogura Masatsune 小倉正恒 (1875–1961), the foremost director of Sumitomo concerns in the 1930s; and Naitō Konan 内藤湖南 (1866–1934), a prominent China scholar and art historian at Kyoto University.[3] Kodōjin made two paintings for presentation to the powerful elder statesman and imperial advisor Saionji Kinmochi 西園寺公望 (1849–1940) on his eightieth birthday. One was a small depiction of the isle of immortals drawn in gold on red paper and the other an orchid painting brushed with silver leaves and gold flowers. These wealthy backers were responsible for the high prices at Kodōjin's 1929 show at the Tokyo Mitsukoshi department store. For the eighty-six exhibited works, prices ranged from 100 to 2,500 yen for hanging scrolls and up to 5,000 yen for pairs of screens. These are extraordinary figures for an independent artist in the early Shōwa period. It is one of the ironies of Kodōjin's career that his celebrations of reclusive retreats, free of the mundane world, were so avidly sought by those who were most embroiled in politics and finance. It may have been just such men who most desired a kind of fantastic escape from the day-to-day pressures of their busy lives.

Kodōjin frequently painted landscapes and occasionally approached other literati themes. Some landscapes recall the eccentricities of Hosokawa Rinkoku 細川林谷 (1779–1843), yet the outlines Kodōjin often made with wet, horizontal dots were a new feature that parallels the rejection of line in some contemporary *nihonga* paintings. His paintings of plants and rocks reflect his veneration of the enduring spirit of the aged so admired in East Asian tradition. The majority of his works are in ink or ink with slight color, but he sometimes used bright mineral pigments and even gold.

The eccentricity of Kodōjin's paintings has parallels with the work of many self-taught literati painters in Japan. Even though Chinese literati ideals celebrated the idea of amateurism, Chinese practitioners usually established near professional levels of brush technique. In Japan, however, many artists, Kodōjin among them, respected this amateur ideal by training themselves, achieving satisfaction with their naive but vigorous brushwork. PB

BIBLIOGRAPHY

Addiss, Stephen, and Jonathan Chaves. *Old Taoist: The Life, Art, and Poetry of Kodōjin.* New York: Columbia University Press, 2000.

Kokufu Shūtoku 国府重徳. *Kodōjin-kai shushi* 古道人会趣旨. Privately published broadside, 1928.

Matsumoto Akira 松本皎, "Kumano Shingū no Kodōjin." *Kumanoshi* 熊野誌, no. 50 (2004): 81–98.

———. "Seisho Fukuda Isajirō" 静処福田伊佐次郎. *Kumanoshi,* no. 51 (2005): 97–119.

———. "Tokushū: Haritsu haiku shūgō" 特集：はりつ俳句聚合. *Saryūtei, Guan, Kodōjin kenkyū,* no. 2 (January 2007): 1–83.

———. "Tokushū: Haritsu no aforizumu" 特集：把栗のアフォリズム. *Saryūtei, Guan, Kodōjin kenkyū* 簑笠亭・愚庵・古道人研究, no. 2 (January 2008): 1–190.

NOTES

1. See the Kodōjin chronology by Matsumoto, "Seisho Fukuda Isajirō," 116–19. Matsumoto's ongoing research on Kodōjin has uncovered a wealth of historical materials that has been presented in a variety of recent publications.

2. In 1927 Kodōjin held an exhibition supported by the famous Shunpōdō 春芳堂 mounting studio at the Kyōto Bijutsu Kurabu and at the Mitsukoshi department store in Tokyo in 1929; ibid., 119.

3. The full list of fifty-nine members of the Kodōjin group is given in ibid., 112. It includes former prime ministers, heads of many corporations, members of parliament, and so on. The aims of the group were set out by its leader Kokufu Shūtoku in a 1928 broadside.

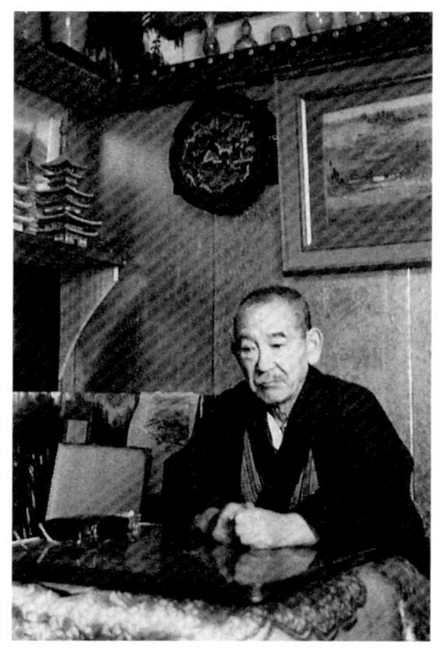

Fusen Tetsu 不染鉄 1891–1976

Fusen Tetsu refused to conform to popular trends and achieved an intensely personal painting style. At the Teiten government exhibitions, large paintings vied for attention, but Tetsu's works eschewed the immediate appeal of eye-catching color or daring composition. One insightful critic commented on *Painting of Mountain and Sea* (Sankai zue 山海圖繪), Tetsu's 1925 Teiten entry:

> With Mount Fuji as its focus, the artist depicts everything in the painting—the fields, mountains, ocean, boats, villages, harbor, people, and fish—without missing anything. By thoroughly portraying all elements with great care in precise detail, he expresses his unique philosophy on nature and human life. His obstinate lines and gloomy colors are not readily attractive, but as you keep looking at this work, you become deeply drawn to his character. There is no one at this exhibition who is more faithful to the expression of his individuality than this artist.[1]

For his subjects Tetsu chose ordinary scenes drawn from his own memories and experiences. He frequently incorporated prose or poems, making his biographical paintings at times confessional. Later in his life, living alone in a humble studio at Nara, Tetsu formed friendships with several young women students at a nearby college. He corresponded with them by postcard—more than three hundred—freely written and beautifully illustrated in a delicately expressive style. These poetic postcard-diaries,[2] direct and self-probing, encapsulate Tetsu's practice of art as a fundamental means of self-expression.

Born in Koishikawa 小石川, Tokyo, the son of a Buddhist priest, Tetsu was sent to a small fishing village in Chiba at the age of eleven for preliminary Buddhist training. Instead of the priesthood, however, he turned to art, joining the Japan Art Institute (Nihon Bijutsuin 日本美術院) as a student member in 1914. He may have also studied with Yamada Keichū 山田敬中 (1868–1934),[3] a Tokyo artist who achieved a distinguished career at the government exhibitions. After a brief association with the Japan Art Institute, Tetsu went to Izu Ōshima 伊豆大島, a remote island southwest of Tokyo, where he worked as a fisherman for three years. The themes of island, seaside village, and ocean were to appear later in many of his paintings. In 1918 he began the five-year course at the Kyoto Municipal Special School of Painting (Kyōto Shiritsu Kaiga Senmon Gakkō 京都市立絵画専門学校). Surrounded by students a decade younger, Tetsu took up a happy, free-spirited lifestyle of "traveling, drinking, and womanizing,"[4] but he also confirmed his artistic gift during this period. His paintings were accepted twice at the Teiten, and he graduated from the school with first-place honors in 1923. Thereafter he participated in the Teiten almost annually through 1934 while moving every few years between the Kyoto/Nara and Kanagawa/Tokyo areas.[5]

Tetsu finally settled in Nara during the early 1940s and began a reclusive life except for a brief spell as a high school principal. Although he received an appointment to the government exhibition committee in 1947, he never again participated in large national competitions. Instead he showed his work at locally organized solo shows and in group exhibitions of Nara artists. Besides painting and teaching a small number of pupils, he found pleasure in exploring other media such as ceramic decoration and painting on kimono. After his death, Tetsu was largely forgotten in the Japanese art world. But passionate connoisseurs admired him as an "illusive literati painter" (*maboroshi no bunjin gaka* 幻の文人画家),[5] and there has been a resurgence of interest in Tetsu's life and art in recent years.

MM

BIBLIOGRAPHY

Fusen Tetsuji 不染鐵二. "Ōkochi kun no koto" 大河内君の事. *Bi no kuni* 美之国 4, no. 9 (September 1928): 60–63.

Hoshino Keizō and Hoshino Mamiko 星野桂三・万美子. *Maboroshi no bunjin-gaka: Fusen Tetsu isaku ten* 幻の文人画家：不染鉄遺作展. Exh. cat. Kyoto: Hoshino Garō 星野画廊, 1996.

———. *Botsugo sanjūnen・Fusen Tetsu isaku ten* 没後 30 年・不染鉄遺作展. Exh. cat. Kyoto: Hoshino Garō 星野画廊, 2007.

Kyōto Kokuritsu Kindai Bijutsukan 京都国立近代美術館. *Kyōto no nihonga, 1910–1930* 京都の日本画, 1910–1930. Exh. cat. Kyoto, 1986.

Nara Kenritsu Bijutsukan 奈良県立美術館. *Botsugo nijūnen kinen tokubetsu ten: Junjō no gaka, Fusen Tetsu ten* 没後 20 年記念特別展：純情の画家、不染鉄展. Exh. cat. Nara, 1996.

———. *Gaka Fusen Tetsu no ehagakishū* 画家不染鉄の絵はがき集. Nara, 2000.

NOTES

1. Nittenshi Hensan Iinkai, *Nittenshi 7, Teitentenhen 2* (Tokyo: Nitten, 1982), 532. The painting is reproduced in color in Nara Kenritsu Bijutsukan, *Botsugo nijūnen kinen tokubetsu ten*, 21, and Kyōto Kokuritsu Kindai Bijutsukan, *Kyōto no nihonga, 1910–1930*, 83.

2. Two hundred postcards by Tetsu were published in Nara Kenritsu Bijutsukan, *Gaka Fusen Tetsu no ehagakishū.*

3. Hoshino and Hoshino, *Maboroshi no bunjingaka*, 27.

4. The artist inscribed these sentiments on a painting; see Nara Kenritsu Bijutsukan, *Botsugo nijūnen kinen tokubetsu ten*, plate 94-6 on p. 63.

5. Hoshino and Hoshino, *Maboroshi no bunjin gaka*, 29.

6. Ibid.

Gotō Shūgai 後藤秋涯 1886–1979

Biographical information on Shūgai is scarce. Born in Gifu prefecture, he lived in Kyoto and studied painting under Tajika Chikuson 田近竹邨 (1864–1922) while pursuing Chinese studies with Fujisawa Nangaku 藤沢南岳(1842–1920), a Confucian scholar in Osaka.[1] Chikuson had been a pupil of Tanomura Chokunyū 田能村直入 (1814–1907), who in turn had trained under the Edo-period literati master Tanomura Chikuden 田能村竹田 (1777–1835). Thus Shūgai followed in the illustrious lineage of orthodox literati painting. His many surviving works attest to a prolific career. In the late 1920s the periodical *Daimai bijutsu* published illustrations of Shūgai's blue-and-green landscapes, which were available for sale, and indicated that his paintings were in demand among collectors and connoisseurs.[2] Indeed, the 1938 *Paintings by Shūgai* (Shūgai gafu 秋涯画譜) includes more than fifty works of superb quality, many of which were owned by wealthy patrons.[3] Shūgai may have been one of the many accomplished artists who chose to pursue their careers quietly by fulfilling private commissions and giving painting instruction. MM

BIBLIOGRAPHY

Araki Nori 荒木矩, ed. *Dai Nihon shoga meika taikan, denki gehen* 大日本書畫名家大鑑：傳記下編. 1934. Reprint. Tokyo: Daiichi Shobō 第一書房, 1975.

Nihon Chūō Nanshūgakai 日本中央南宗畫會. *Shitai ōsei* 姿態横生. Nagoya, 1911.

Tuchihashi Kahei 土橋嘉兵衛, ed. *Shūgai gafu* 秋涯画譜. Kyoto: Unsōdō 芸艸堂, 1938.

NOTES

1. Araki, *Dai Nihon shoga meika taikan*, 1319, and Nihon Chūō Nanshūgakai, *Shitai ōsei.*

2. *Daimai bijutsu* 6, no. 10 (October 1927), plate 163, and *Daimai bijutsu* 6, no. 11 (November 1927), plate 22.

3. Among the patrons were Naiki Seibei, a noted connoisseur and collector of modern-period paintings in Kyoto; Iida Shinshichi, founder of the retail shop (later Takashimaya department store); and Ōhara Magosaburō, who established the Ōhara Museum of Art; see Tuchihashi, *Shūgai gafu.*

Hagura Katei 羽倉可亭 1799–1887

The usual image of Confucian scholars and Shinto priests is of dignified, conservative men much concerned about propriety. Katei's unusual life, including a long period of dissolute wandering about Japan, reveals how mistaken these common assumptions can be. As a seal carver and painter, Katei was well known in the literati circles of mid-nineteenth-century Kyoto; his many friends included the much younger Tomioka Tessai (1836–1924).

Katei was born into the Hagura family of the Kada 荷田 clan that had served the Fushimi Inari shrine since the middle of the Muromachi period. His father died when he was five months old, but he was adopted by another branch of the same family. Raised to be a shrine priest, he had already attained several of the lower ranks by the age of eighteen. But despite his swift rise in the shrine hierarchy, when he was twenty-four, Katei abruptly left his post, assumed everyday garb, and went to Edo. His adoptive father submitted a letter of resignation on behalf of his son, whom he described as having an illness caused by depression.[1]

After spending some time in Edo, Katei roamed Japan for many years, traveling the length of the country from Kagoshima in Kyushu to Matsumae in southern Hokkaido. Remarkably, an account in his own hand, "The Villainous Strange Events of a Half-crazy Man Outside of Heaven" (Tengai hankyōjin burai kiji), has recently come to light and provides many anecdotes of these wanderings, illustrated with small sketches.[2] Although written in 1861, the account covers miscellaneous events from the late 1820s through the 1830s. Katei describes his meetings with various scholars and artists around Japan, including the female painter Ema Saikō 江馬細香 (1787–1861), the calligrapher Ōkubo Shibutsu 大窪詩仏 (1766–1837), and the famous Zen priest-painter Sengai 仙厓 (1750–1837). On numerous occasions his hosts asked him to create paintings or carve seals, indicating that his talents were already well regarded. While in Nagasaki for a year, he attended an exhibition of calligraphy and painting at the famous Kagetsurō 花月楼 establishment in the Maruyama pleasure quarters. The honorific biography inscribed on his grave states that Katei was not attracted by either sex or sake, yet he describes so many events in the pleasure districts of the areas he visited that it is hard to believe he was truly abstemious. Although literati commonly traveled widely during the later Edo period, this little-known record is one of the few surviving first-person accounts.

Although the chronology of his studies is incomplete, Katei is known to have been a pupil when he was young of the noted Kyoto Confucian scholar Murase Kōtei 村瀬栲亭 (1746–1818). He first learned painting and seal carving from the monk Sō Geppō (see cat. no. 22), and later, presumably in Edo, he deepened his study with the master seal carver Hosokawa Rinkoku 細川林谷 (1779–1843). Rinkoku was known for creating large sets of seals that taken together formed famous Chinese texts. His influence is exemplified in a famous incident related to Katei's seal-carving prowess. After Katei introduced himself at an inn as a seal carver, the innkeeper asked to see examples of his work; otherwise he would conclude Katei was an imposter. Not having any completed seals with him, Katei stayed up the whole night carving the different faces of twenty-eight seal stones with the complete text of Li Bo's 李白 (701–762) poem "Preface to Enjoying a Spring Evening in a Peach Blossom Garden." Impressions of the set of seals still exist today.[3]

Katei further polished his painting technique by studying with the Shijo-school painter Okamoto Toyohiko 岡本豊彦 (1773–1845). His painting evolved in a pattern similar to that of many literati artists whose fairly detailed and precise styles gradually loosened up in the last years of the shogunate and became much bolder and more abbreviated in the first decades of the Meiji period. In 1884 he was twice invited to teach at the newly formed Kyoto Prefecture Painting School (Kyōto-fu Gagakkō), but he declined due to his great age. Today, Katei is most often noted as one of the senior friends of Tessai who helped shape his interest in literati painting and its lifestyle. PB

BIBLIOGRAPHY

Fushimi Inari Taisha 伏見稲荷大社. *Bakumatsu ishinki no bungajin・Hagura Katei botsugo hyakunijūnen kinen shazō sakuhin ten* 幕末維新期の文雅人・羽倉可亭 没後百二十年記念 社蔵作品展. Kyoto, 1999.

Hagura Keishō 羽倉敬尚. "Bungajin Hagura Katei Yoshinobu o megutte" 文雅人 羽倉可亭良信をめぐって. In *Kinsei gakugei ronko: Hagura Keisho ronbunshu.* Tokyo: Meiji Shobō, 1992.

Kanda Kiichiro 神田喜一郎, ed. *Shōdō zenshū, bekkan ni* 書道全集、別巻二. Tokyo: Heibonsha 平凡社, 1968.

Shiomura Ko 塩村耕. "Bakumatsu ichi bunjin no seishun horoki—Hagura Katei no 'Tengai hankyojin burai kiji.'" 幕末一文人の青春放浪記一羽倉可亭の「天外半狂人無頼奇事」. In *Sugiyama Jogakuen Daigaku Tankidaigakubu nijū shūnen kinen ronshū* 椙山女学園大学短期大学部二十周年記念論集. Nagoya: Sugiyama Jogakuen Daigaku Tankidaigakubu, 1989.

NOTES

1. The most detailed information on Katei's family background and upbringing is in Hagura, "Bungajin Hagura Katei Yoshinobu o megutte."

2. The text and some of the illustrations are provided in Shiomura, "Bakumatsu ichi bunjin no seishun horoki."

3. This account is given in Hagura, "Bungajin Hagura Katei Yoshinobu o megutte," 275. An *inpu* of the complete set was displayed at the 1999 Katei exhibition at Fushimi Inari. Impressions of the first four seals of the set are shown in Kanda, *Shōdō zenshū, bekkan ni*, plate 84.

Haruki Nanmei 春木南溟 1795–1878

Many talented Japanese painters whose lives bridged the transition from the late Edo to early Meiji periods have been largely neglected in the subsequent study of Japanese art history. Haruki Nanmei is no exception, as indicated by the paucity of biographical information available today. During the final years of the shogunate regime, Nanmei established himself as a respected literati painter in the city of Edo and continued his successful career into the first decade of the Meiji era, enjoying the strong appreciation and patronage of the new government officials. He witnessed the emergence of modern Japan under the restored imperial power, participated in the first Domestic Industrial Exposition (*Naikoku kangyō hakurankai* 内国勧業博覧会) in 1877,[1] and died before the popularity of literati painting began to wane in the following decade.

Nanmei's father, Nanko 南湖 (1759–1839), was a noted literati painter in Edo. Nanko led a comfortable life in the service of Masuyama Sessai 増山雪斎 (1755–1820), the daimyo of the Nagashima fief and a serious literati artist, who financed Nanko's trips to the Kyoto-Osaka area and Nagasaki to study painting. As a participant in the Small Society for the Preservation of Poetry Chanting (Shō Fukyū Ginsha 小不朽吟社),[2] an elegant literati gathering in Edo, Nanko was well acquainted with major *bunjin* painters and poets vying with Tani Bunchō 谷文晁 (1763–1840) for renown as the preeminent artist of the day.

Brought up in a privileged artist's home, Nanmei received training from his father and Bunchō, and studied the later copies of Yuan and Song Chinese paintings. His paintings ultimately surpassed his father's in technical finesse and decorative flair. Extremely eclectic, Nanmei painted in a variety of styles, usually employing fine, detailed brushwork, as demonstrated by his *Immortal's Pavilion in Spring Daybreak* (cat. no. 35). His impressive painting skill and warm personality attracted many high-ranking samurai *bunjin,* among whom were Matsudaira Kakudō 松平確堂 (1814–1891), Yamauchi Yōdō 山内容堂 (1827–1872), and Akizuki Kokō 秋月古香 (1833–1904); Yōdō even built a house for Nanmei next to his own villa.[3] Many of these prominent samurai would hold important administrative positions in the Meiji government. Thus, Nanmei followed in his father's footsteps as a distinguished literati painter whose career was sustained by elite patrons. Nanmei's younger brother Seiko 西湖 (dates unknown), son Nanka 南華 (1819–1866), and grandson Nankei 南溪 (b. 1846), who also became literati painters, maintained the artistic lineage of the Haruki family.[4]

MM

BIBLIOGRAPHY

Araki Nori 荒木矩, ed. *Dai Nihon shoga meika taikan, denki gehen* 大日本書畫名家大鑑：傳記下編. 1934. Reprint. Tokyo: Daiichi Shobō 第一書房, 1975.

Atsumi Kuniyasu 渥美国泰. *Kameda Bōsai to Edo Kaseiki no bunjin tachi* 亀田鵬斎と江戸化政期の文人達. Tokyo: Geijutsu Shinbunsha 芸術新聞社, 1995.

Kawakita Michiaki 河北倫明, comp. *Kinadi Nihon bijutsu jiten* 近代日本美術事典. Tokyo: Kōdansha 講談社, 1989.

Umezawa Seiichi 梅澤精一. *Nihon nangashi* 日本南畫史. Tokyo: Nan'yōdō 南陽堂, 1919.

NOTES

1. Kawakita, *Kindai Nihon bijutsu jiten,* 290.

2. Umezawa, *Nihon nangashi,* 505.

3. Araki, *Dai Nihon shoga meika taikan, denki gehen,* 1348. Matsudaira Kakudō, the lord of Tsuyama (Okayama), was known for his promotion of academic learning. Akizuki Kokō, an accomplished painter and calligrapher, was the son of the lord of the Takanabe fief (Miyazaki). He held a series of government positions in the early Meiji period, as did Yamauchi Yōdō, a daimyo of Tosa (Kōchi) who was known for his support of artists including Nanmei and Okuhara Seiko.

4. Kawakita, *Kindai Nihon bijutsu jiten,* 290.

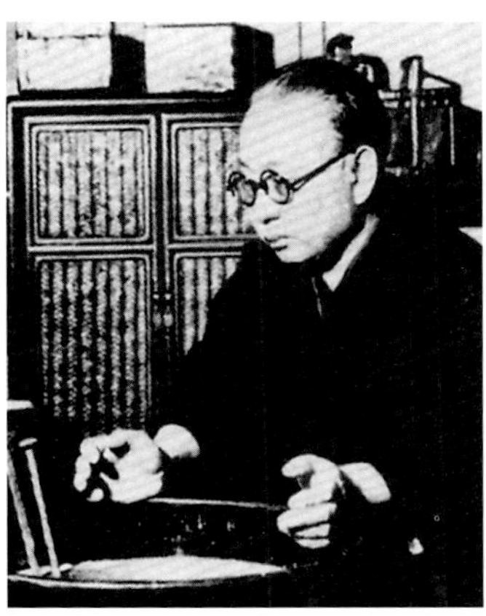

Hashimoto Kansetsu 橋本関雪 1883–1945

Among the *nihonga* artists of his generation, Hashimoto Kansetsu stood out for his impressive literati (*bunjin*) pedigree. He attained national acclaim as a Kyoto artist through his Shijō-based painting, but his love of Chinese art and culture, instilled by the cosmopolitan environment of his youth in Kobe, underlined his life and art. Kansetsu made more than thirty trips to China and in his paintings regularly represented Chinese themes derived from history and literature or from his personal observations on the continent. Unyielding and opinionated, Kansetsu was prone to stirring up controversy in Kyoto, which valued the etiquette of refinement and restraint. His contentious relationship with his teacher, Takeuchi Seihō 竹内栖鳳 (1864–1942), a powerful representative of the Kyoto painting circle, is widely known.[1] Kansetsu disparaged the conservatism of the Kyoto art community and complained about the politically entrenched judging system of the government exhibitions.[2] Kansetsu was an artist of compelling talent and a man of strong self-conviction, not easily deflated by outside disapproval or criticism. Before his premature death, he achieved a spectacular artistic career and enormous wealth, leaving behind a complex artistic legacy, which included propagandist activities during World War II.

Kansetsu's father, Kaikan 海関 (1855–1935), came from a family of Confucian scholars and once served the Matsudaira clan of the Akashi fief 明石藩 (Hyōgo prefecture). In 1868, Kaikan moved his family to Kobe and made a living as a teacher of Chinese studies. When Kansetsu was five years old, his mother left the family. He was brought up by his grandmother, who recited Chinese poems to him as if they were lullabies.[3] Kansetsu later credited her for his lifelong love of Chinese literature. At about age twelve, while receiving instruction in Chinese literature from his father, Kansetsu began studying painting with a Shijō-school artist named Kataoka Kōkō 片岡公曠.

Kansetsu's adolescence was full of challenges and difficulties. He went to Tokyo at the age of fifteen to pursue painting, but the family's financial difficulties forced him to return to Kobe the next year. For the next several years, Kansetsu shifted among relatives and acquaintances, earning a livelihood by painting. Resolved to make a name for himself, he moved to Kyoto in 1903 and became a pupil of Seihō, whose paintings of exotic Western landscapes and realistic lions had distinguished him as an exciting new leader of the Kyoto painting circle. Kansetsu is said to have been a vocal critic of other pupils' works shown at Chikujōkai, Seihō's private studio.[4] Two years later, Kansai left Kyoto to serve as a military artist during the Russo-Japanese War.

Kansetsu's financial fortunes began to change when one of his paintings was accepted into the 1908 Bunten, the government-sponsored exhibition. Throughout the next decade, he continued to participate in the Bunten, showcasing his talent by often submitting two works of contrasting nature. For example, in 1912, when the *nihonga* section was split to form conservative and more progressive divisions, Kansetsu entered works to both and won an award in each. In 1914 he submitted *Southern Country* (Nangoku 南国), a dynamic representation of Chinese boats bustling with working-class people in expressive postimpressionist color, and *Palace Garden* (Kōen 後苑), a delicate portrayal of a refined Chinese lady in a secluded setting. In the next year, Kansetsu's paintings of two distinct genres demonstrated even more impressive technical mastery and versatility: *Hunt* (Ryō 猟) displayed his dazzling command of figural and animal depictions in a Chinese hunting scene, while *Xiajiang in June* (Kyōkō no rokugatsu 峡江の六月) represented a panoramic landscape of a Chinese river in a combination of literati brushwork and *yōga* technique. Kansetsu's works received the highest award in 1916, 1917, and 1918, resulting in his appointment to a judging panel in 1919. To win the top award consecutively for three years was an extraordinary and rare feat. A commentator proclaimed in 1919 that "only one or two artists in one hundred years" would be born with talent that might equal Kansetsu's.[5] At the height of his national success, however, Kansetsu was described as a "bad boy" (*nikumarekko* 憎まれっ子) of the art world, and when he built a luxurious house near Ginkakuji, he faced criticism for an ostentatious display of wealth.[6] His soaring popularity might have triggered envy, but more likely it was the self-importance with which he boasted of his talent and flaunted his elite literati background that provoked the antagonism of other Kyoto painters.[7] Aware of his isolation in Kyoto, Kansetsu once wrote that he felt a closer affinity with Tokyo artists.[8]

During the 1920s, having established himself as a master artist and living comfortably, Kansetsu continued to visit China and twice made long trips to Europe with his family.[9] He officially left Seihō's Chikujōkai, published a book titled *Path to Literati Painting* (Nanga e no dōtei 南画への道程), and disbanded his private school in order to recover his "true self."[10] Although his involvement with the government show continued, Kansetsu focused more on solo exhibitions, which largely featured literati-style hanging scrolls accompanied by his calligraphies.

Kansetsu's reputation as a painter of animals grew after 1930 with skillful depictions such as *Dark Gibbons* (Gen'en 玄猿, 1933) and *Foreign Dogs* (Tōken zu 唐犬図, 1935), which recalled the Shijō naturalism and technical finesse of his old teacher Seihō. As war fervor heightened in the late 1930s, Kansetsu became an ardent supporter of Japan's expansionist effort and thereafter took part in numerous war-related exhibitions. His unexpected death at the age of sixty-one makes one ponder what directions his art might have taken had he lived to experience the radical alterations that took place in postwar Japan.[11] MM

BIBLIOGRAPHY

Asahi Shinbunsha 朝日新聞社. *Seitan hyakunen: Hashimoto Kansetsu ten* 生誕百年：橋本関雪展. Exh. cat. Osaka, 1984.

———. *Botsugo gojūnen kinen: Hashimoto Kansetsu ten* 没後五十年記念：橋本関雪展. Exh. cat. Nagoya, 1994.

Hakusasonjin 白沙村人. "Nigacha hiyameshi" 苦茶冷飯. *Daimai bijutsu* 5, no. 10 (October 5, 1926): 30–31.

Hashimoto Kansetsu 橋本關雪. "Kōnan ni mitaru shizen to jin'i no chōwa" 江南に観たる自然と人為の調和. *Kyōto bijujtsu* 京都美術, no. 45 (June 1918): 9–11.

———. *Nanga e no dōtei* 南畫への道程. Tokyo: Chōū Bijutsusha 中央美術社, 1924.

———. "Teiten shinsain o ji shite" 帝展審査員を辭して. *Daimai bijutsu* 大毎美術 4, no. 9 (September 1925): 1–4.

———. "Shinpen zakki" 身邊雜記. *Bi no kuni* 美之国 2, no. 10 (October 1926): 12–15.

———. "Amari jōzu sugiru" 餘り上手過る. *Daimai bijutsu* 7, no. 8 (August 1928): 32–33.

———. "Dattan zakki" 脱胆雜記. *Daimai bijutsu* 7, no. 9 (September 1928): 32–35.

Higashino Gajin 東野畫人. "Yowatari to e no gūgen—Hashimoto Kansetsu shi ni tsuite" 世渡りと繪の寓言—橋本關雪氏について. *Daimai bijutsu* 5, no. 12 (December 1926): 46–49.

Kanzaki Bansokei 神崎蠻楚桂. "Kikuchi Keigetsu to Hashimoto Kansetsu" 菊池契月と橋本關雪. *Bi no kuni* 3, no. 2 (February 1927): 136–41.

Kikuchi Keigetsu 菊池契月. "Yoi imi no tasshasa" よい意味の達者さ. *Daimai bijutsu* 4, no. 10 (October 1925): 12–13.

Kotenrōshujin 壺天樓主人. "Shijin gaka Kansetsu" 詩人畫家關雪. *Daimai bijutsu* 4, no. 10 (October 1925): 17–19.

Matsubayashi Keigetsu 松林桂月. "Hashimoto Kansetsu ron: Ki o ou no hito" 橋本關雪論：気を負ふの人. *Chūō bijutsu* 中央美術 5, no. 11 (November 1919): 104–7.

Miyazaki Ichisada 宮崎市定. "Hashimoto Kansetsu to kangaku" 橋本関雪と漢学. In *Miyazaki Ichisada Zenshū* 宮崎市定全集 22. Tokyo: Iwanami Shoten 岩波書店, 1992.

Morioka, Michiyo, and Paul Berry. *Modern Masters of Kyoto: The Transformation of Japanese Painting Traditions, Nihonga from the Griffith and Patricia Way Collection.* Seattle: Seattle Art Museum, 1999.

Nishimura Goun 西村五雲. "Netsu no aru seisaku" 熱のある製作. *Daimai bijutsu* 4, no. 10 (October 1925) 14–16.

Tsukada Kan 塚田幹. "Hashimoto Kansetsu ron: Kanjō no hito Kansetsu" 橋本關雪論：感情の人關雪. *Chūō bijutsu* 5, no. 11 (November 1919): 107–11.

NOTES

1. See Paul Berry's essay on Kansetsu in Morioka and Berry, *Modern Masters of Kyoto*, 224–25.

2. See Hashimoto, *Nanga e no dōtei*, 125–27, and Hashimoto, "Teiten shinsain o ji shite," 2–3.

3. Takaori Taeko, "Chichi Kansetsu no koto," in *Seitan hyakunen: Hashimoto Kansetsu ten*, exh. cat. (Osaka: Asahi Shinbunsha, 1984), 8–9.

4. Kimura Shigeyoshi, "Hashimoto Kansetsu: Sono hito to geijutsu," in *Botsugo gojūnen kinen: Hashimoto Kansetsu ten*, exh. cat. (Nagoya: Asahi Shinbunsha, 1994), 18.

5. See the comment in Nittenshi Hensan Iinkai, *Nittenshi 6, Teitenhen 1* (Tokyo: Nitten, 1982), 529.

6. See Matsubayashi, "Hashimoto Kansetsu ron," 106, and Tsukada, "Hashimoto Kansetsu ron," 110–11.

7. See the discussion by Miyazaki, "Hashimoto Kansetsu to kangaku," 371–75.

8. Kansetsu named Kaburaki Kiyokata and Hirafuku Hyakusui as his Tokyo friends; see Hashimoto, "Shinpen zakki," 15.

9. In 1921 Kansetsu went to Europe for six months, visiting France, Germany, Holland, and Italy. He traveled to Europe with his family again in 1927 and began collecting Western art, including Greek vases, around this time; see Asahi Shinbunsha, *Botsugo gojūnen kinen*, 133–35.

10. Hashimoto, "Shinpen zakki," 12. His private school, Shinkōkai, resumed operation in 1936.

11. In 1926 Kanzaki Ken'ichi wrote that he would be interested in seeing Kansetsu's art when he reached Tessai's ripe old age; see Kanzaki, "Kikuchi Keigetsu to Hashimoto Kansetsu," 140. After Kansetsu's death, Inoue Yasushi expressed a similar sentiment, saying that Kansetsu's art needed "old-age maturity"; quoted by Hashimoto Kiichi, "Hashimoto Kansetsu no sekai," in *Seitan hyakunen: Hashimoto Kansetsu ten*, exh. cat. (Osaka: Asahi Shinbunsha, 1984), 107.

Hazama Seigai 磵西涯 (羽様西崕) 1811–1878

Seigai's identity has long been obscured due to his having used different sets of characters with the same pronunciation to write his name.[1] Based on the signatures on his paintings, it seems that he employed the three-character version 磵西涯 in his earlier years and then adopted the four-character name 羽様西崕 late in his life. Best known in his home city of Hagi 萩,[2] Seigai studied with the noted painter Oda Kaisen 小田海僊 (1785–1862), who was raised in the neighboring city of Shimonoseki. Kaisen had studied with Matsumura Goshun 松村呉春 (1751–1811) in Kyoto and later traveled widely, working for the Hagi *han* residence in Edo, where he and Seigai may have met, as well as studying paintings in Nagasaki. Ultimately it was Kaisen's close study of newly imported Chinese works that had the most influence on the literati paintings he produced.

Seigai became especially well known for his birds-and-flowers compositions. They reveal the influence of Qing-dynasty painters mixed with a strong, almost aggressive, quality of line that may be attributed to his viewing the work of Tani Bunchō's 谷文晁 (1763–1840) followers. That Seigai had traveled in Japan is demonstrated by a reference to an earlier trip to Fukui in a long inscription he wrote on an 1870 work inspired by the sight of a Wang Mian 王冕 (1278–1359) plum painting.[3] Although the details of his career remain unclear, his paintings show his talent for creating vivid, dramatic compositions. Despite his gifts, Seigai has remained obscure, much like the large number of skilled artists who were known only in their home districts, far from the major cities, during the Edo and Meiji periods.

PB

BIBLIOGRAPHY

Araki Nori 荒木矩, ed. *Dai Nihon shoga meika taikan* 大日本書画名家大鑑. 1934. Reprint. Tokyo: Daiichi Shobō 第一書房, 1975.

NOTES

1. Although the information recorded separately under these differing names generally matches, separate accounts listing the same personal name, Sōshirō 宗四郎, and the name Shiko 師古 are decisive. See the entry under Hazama Seigai at the Internet site listing the famous people of Hagi: hagibukkyo.com/2-jinbutsugaido/jinbutu-kensaku, and in Araki, *Dai Nihon shoga meika taikan*, vol. 1, 710.

2. Seigai's grave is on the grounds of the Kōunji 広雲寺 temple in the center of Hagi city.

3. In a private collection in Japan.

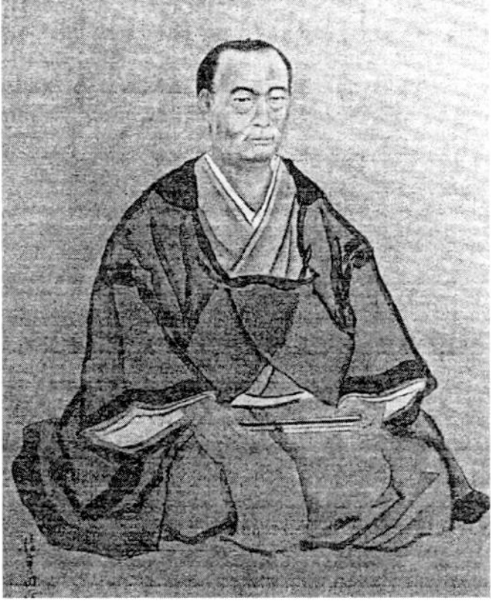

Hine Taizan 日根対山 1813–1869

Hine Taizan was one of the most successful and prolific Kyoto literati painters at the end of the Edo period. Various accounts and anecdotes portray him as a professional artist of enormous talent and personal complexity. When Hidaka Tetsuō 日高鉄翁 (1791–1871), a monk-painter from Nagasaki respected for his firsthand knowledge of Chinese artists, traveled to Kyoto around 1846, Taizan and others flocked to hear his instruction on painting. Tetsuō commended Taizan for attaining "sophisticated elegance" in painting and praised him as "the only person who grasped ten after learning one" among the Kyoto artists he taught. At the same time, the monk-painter chided Taizan for letting inattentiveness creep into his work as he rushed to complete paintings for sale.[1] According to another story, Taizan kept a heap of paper and silk provided by patrons in his studio so he could dash off paintings one after another in drunken abandon.[2] Unflattering profiles and criticisms of his professionalism aside, it is beyond question that Taizan grounded his art in the serious study of Chinese masters. Many of his works attest to his deep understanding of literati aesthetics and display commanding brushwork and attention to delicate details.

Taizan was the third son of a farmer in Izumi 和泉 (southern Osaka prefecture), and the details of his early training are unclear. While studying painting under Momoda Eiun 桃田栄雲 (d. 1855), a *yamatoe*-school painter of the nearby Kishiwada 岸和田 domain, Taizan enjoyed the patronage of Satoi Fukyū 里井浮丘 (1799–1866), a wealthy shipping merchant in his hometown. Fukyū commissioned Taizan to paint a portrait of his deceased brother around 1834, indicating that the artist was already accomplished at a young age.[3] Well versed in arts and literature, Fukyū encouraged Taizan to copy paintings in his collection. In 1842 Fukyū introduced young Taizan to Okada Hankō 岡田半江 (1782–1846), a respected Osaka literati painter and, shortly thereafter, to Nukina Kaioku 貫名海屋 (1778–1863), an esteemed Confucian scholar and painter-calligrapher in Kyoto.[4] Although the nature of their teacher-pupil relationship remains ambiguous, it is believed that Kaioku's encouragement was crucial in Taizan's decision to focus on literati painting. For example, on Kaioku's advice, Taizan made numerous trips to the Kumano 熊野 area (Wakayama prefecture) to study its scenic mountains.[5]

In 1846 Taizan settled in Kyoto and quickly established himself as a painter. The *List of Kyoto Painters and Calligraphers* (Kōto shogajin meiroku 皇都書畫人名録), published the following year, describes him as a "Southern-school painter and calligrapher."[6] As his reputation spread, Taizan enjoyed the support of many samurai lords and aristocrats and became acquainted with illustrious members of the Kyoto *bunjin* circle such as Yanagawa Seigan 梁川星巌 (1789–1858), Nakabayashi Chikkei 中林竹渓 (1816–1867), Fujimoto Tesseki 藤本鉄石 (1817–1863), Rai Shihō 頼支峰 (1823–1889), and Rai Mikisaburō 頼三樹三郎 (1825–1859). He traveled to Tsu (Mie prefecture) in 1850, where he also met and drew a portrait of Doi Gōga 土井贅牙 (1817–1880), a brilliant young scholar in the service of the Tōdō fief 藤堂藩.[7]

There are numerous anecdotes about Taizan's volatile behavior. One relates an incident at a banquet hosted by Lord Shimazu. Taizan accepted a request to paint on the spot, and inspired by the magnificence of Taizan's work, a well-known *waka* poet composed a poem and added an unsolicited inscription. Infuriated, Taizan vehemently denounced the poet's action as defiling his painting.[8] Taizan is also said to have criticized his teacher Kaioku for lacking brush power, proposed a duel with Chikkei after a particularly explosive argument, and temporarily broken off his relationship with Fukyū, who had consistently contributed to the advancement of his career.

The last ten years of Taizan's life coincided with the dramatic closure of the feudalistic era and the emergence of modern government in Japan. Unlike some of his *bunjin* friends, Taizan kept his distance from political activities during this turbulent period. Later scholars' interpretations are ambivalent: Taizan's self-esteem as a great artist may have led him to remain aloof, or his sharp instinct for self-preservation may have caused him to avoid dangerous political entanglements.[9] But his career undeniably flourished during this time as a new generation of literati painters entered his studio. Among them, two women, Noguchi Shōhin 野口小蘋 (1847–1917) and Atomi Kakei 跡見花蹊 (1840–1926), in particular, would achieve noteworthy success in Meiji Japan.

MM

BIBLIOGRAPHY

Harada Heisaku 原田平作. *Bakumatsu Meiji Kyōraku no gajin tachi* 幕末明治京洛の画人たち. Kyoto: Kyōto Shinbunsha 京都新聞社, 1985.

Izumisanoshishi Hensan Iinkai 泉佐野市史編纂委員会. *Izumisanoshishi shiryō dai nishū: Hine Taizan Sakuhinshū* 泉佐野市史資料第二集・日根対山作品集. Izumisano, Osaka, 2001.

Izumisanoshi Kyōiku Iinkai 泉佐野市教育委員会. *Hine Taizan*. Exh. cat. Izumisano, Osaka, 1970.

Kanmuri Toyoichi 冠豊一. *Meiji no nangaka: Kōin sagen* 明治の南画家・篁蔭瑣言 4. Osaka: Kinki Shuppan Insatsu 近畿出版印刷, 1990.

Kyōtoshi Bijutsukan. *Kyōto gadan: Edomatsu・Meiji no gajintachi* 京都画壇江戸末・明治の画人たち. Kyoto: Ātosha アート社, 1975.

Rekishikan Izumisano 歴史館泉佐野. *Kyōdo ga unda gajin, sono 2: Hine Taizan* 郷土が生んだ画人その２・日根対山. Exh. cat. Izumisano, Osaka, 2001.

NOTES

1. Tetsuō's comment is quoted by Umezawa Seiichi, *Nihon nangashi* (Tokyo: Nan'yōdō, 1919), 952–53, and by Kanmuri Toyoichi, "Hine Taizan no gafū to sakuhin," in Izumisanoshi Kyōiku Iinkai, *Hine Taizan*, 48.

2. Kanmuri, "Hine Taizan no gafū to sakuhin," 50.

3. Kanmuri Toyoichi, "Hine Taizan no seinenki hoi," *Hōshun*, no. 222 (June 1973): 2.

4. It has been suggested that Taizan did not get along with Hankō because of differences in artistic opinion. See the discussion by Kanmuri Toyoichi, "Hine Taizan to Okada Hankō," in Izumisanoshi Kyōiku Iinkai, *Hine Taizan*, 73–78.

5. Kanmuri Toyoichi, "Taizan no nan'yū o meguru hitobito," *Hōshun*, no. 217 (January 1973): 1.

6. Nagata Yasuhiro, "Hine Taizan—Zenhanki no geijutsu," in Rekishikan Izumisano, *Kyōdo ga unda gajin, sono 2*, 5.

7. Kanmuri Toyoichi, "Ryōgaemachi no Taizan to sono shūhen," *Hōshun*, no. 220 (April 1973): 23.

8. Mizohashi Tsunejirō, "Hine Taizan shōden," in Izumisanoshi Kyōiku Iinkai, *Hine Taizan*, 36. See also Harada, *Bakumatsu Meiji Kyōraku no gajin tachi*, 28–29.

9. The former is the opinion of Harada, *Bakumatsu Meiji Kyōraku no gajin tachi*, 27–28, and the latter, of Kanmuri Toyoichi, "Hine Taizan to Nakabayashi Chikkei (shōzen)," *Hōshun*, no. 242 (April 1975): 22–23.

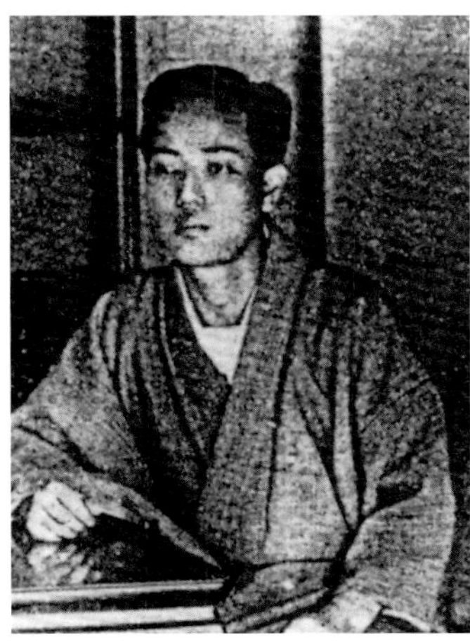

Hirai Baisen 平井楳仙 1889–1969

Hirai Baisen's artistic career was marked by a meteoric rise and fall. Born in Kyoto, Baisen attended the Painting Division of the Kyoto Municipal School of Arts and Crafts (Kyōto Shiritsu Bijutsu Kōgei Gakkō 京都市立美術工芸学校) and graduated in 1906. The eighteen-year-old painter became an instant star in the Kyoto art world the next year after having a painting accepted at the first Bunten 文展 and receiving an award at the Exhibition of New and Old Art (*Shinko bijutsuhin tenrankai* 新古美術品展), Kyoto. Throughout the Taishō period, Baisen continued to garner recognition at the annual government exhibition, and he received a prestigious appointment to its jury in 1924. Shunning the common practice of entering an established painter's studio to advance one's career, Baisen remained independent after graduation,[1] making his accomplishment even more noteworthy. Consistent success in the national arena brought much prestige and wealth to young Baisen. In 1925 he was ranked as the painter with the sixth-highest income in the Osaka and Kyoto areas, surpassing many older, renowned artists.[2] The Plum Promotion Society (Baisuikai 楳推会), founded in 1922 by his patrons, included several hundred members and supported Baisen by organizing annual exhibitions and sales of his works.[3] In the early Shōwa period, however, the enthusiastic acceptance of his paintings began to dissipate. In his seminal book on *nihonga* painting in Kyoto (*Kyotō ni okeru nihongashi* 京都に於ける日本画史), published in 1929, Kanzaki Ken'ichi 神埼憲一 described Baisen as an artist whose premature peak had passed as if "a flash of lightning."[4]

Baisen's late-Meiji entries at the Bunten were still grounded in tradition and included several examples of history paintings, a popular genre at the time. Eager to create new *nihonga*, he and other graduates of the Kyoto Municipal School of Arts and Crafts founded a study group, the Peach Blossom Society (Tōkakai 桃花会), in 1910 and held group exhibitions for the next several years. During the Taishō period, Baisen tackled a new range of subjects and styles. He visited China in 1913 and submitted two paintings of Chinese scenes to the 1914 Bunten: *Palace Garden* (Kyūen 宮苑) and *Summer at Liaohe River* (Ryōga no natsu 遼河の夏). Both earned praise for their fresh decorative flair, achieved through imaginative compositions and strong color contrasts.[5] For the 1915 Bunten, Baisen produced *Summer* (Natsu 夏), a set of three panel paintings that juxtaposed urban and rural scenes of dramatically different moods. His layering of color to build a thick surface as if working in *yōga* led one prominent reviewer to commend the paintings as daring and innovative, "free from the established rules of traditional *nihonga*."[6] A year later Baisen submitted *Thirty Scenes of the Capital* (Miyako sanjūkei 都三十景), a set of three albums with brilliant color depictions of thirty separate Kyoto scenes. In each painting Baisen varied the viewpoint and adopted different styles referencing the Tosa school, *yōga*, and *nanga*. Reviewers' responses were mixed: some applauded Baisen's skill and ambitious approach, but others criticized the work as shallow and unrefined.[7] For the 1919 government exhibition, Baisen changed direction again and created *High Noon* (Hizakari 日盛り), a pair of screens featuring the Western-inspired realism then in vogue among young artists in a striking portrayal of two goats resting under a grapevine trellis.[8] Baisen sought a new direction year after year, producing works of stunning diversity.

In light of his accomplishments during the 1910s, the subsequent critical dismissal and decline of Baisen's art are disheartening. Baisen's experimental attitude, in which he constantly changed his artistic vision, was not valued by all. In 1926 Kitano Tsunetomi 北野恒富 (1880–1947), a talented Osaka artist, criticized Baisen for following popular crowd-pleasing trends rather than developing his true individual style.[9] Others saw Baisen's diverse *nihonga* expressions as products of a superficial ingenuity devoid of true artistic depth.[10] Baisen himself contributed to these negative perceptions by displaying a cavalier attitude toward painting. As the recipient of a second-place award at the 1915 Bunten, the highest given that year, Baisen went to Tokyo to attend the exhibition and stayed for three weeks. Interviewed by an art journal, the twenty-six-year-old artist proclaimed that he enjoyed playing tennis more than painting and had stayed so long in Tokyo to practice tennis with his brother, a music student.[11] Although Baisen was a much more serious artist than his comment conveyed, such remarks neither endeared him to fellow artists nor dispelled his image as an artist lacking gravitas. He continued to work without affiliating himself with a senior master or an art group and had become alienated from other painters by the late 1920s.[12] Ultimately, the increasingly rigid, academic nature of the *nihonga* world may have suffocated Baisen's creative spirit.[13] Financial need caused a further decline in his work. It is believed that Baisen was the guarantor of his son-in-law's business, and when it went bankrupt, the artist incurred the debt, which he paid off by churning out paintings.[14]

Although Baisen continued to show at the government exhibition almost annually until the mid-1930s, and again in 1941 and 1943, he did not participate in public exhibitions after the war. Instead he spent the last two decades of his life fulfilling private commissions and painting small-scale works for the Plum Promotion Society.[15] Six paintings included in this catalogue (see cat. nos. 54–57, 73, 74) provide a glimpse into the stylistic breadth and originality that this gifted artist achieved during his most innovative period.

MM

BIBLIOGRAPHY

"Gaka shūnyū shirabe" 畫家收入調べ. *Daimai bijutsu* 大毎美術 5, no. 7 (July 1926): 42–44.

Hoshino Keizō 星野桂三. *Ishi o migaku: Bijutsushi ni kakureta shugyoku* 石を磨く:美術史に隠れた珠玉. Tokyo: Sankei Shinbunsha 産経新聞社, 2004.

Kitano Tsunetomi 北野恒富. "Seison Baisen no taihi" 青邨楳仙の對比. *Daimai bijutsu* 大毎美術 5, no. 12 (December 1926): 30–34.

Kyō-waranbe 京わらんべ. "Baisen san wa Bukkōji san" 楳仙さんは佛光寺さん. *Daimai bijutsu* 大毎美術 5, no. 12 (December 1926): 38.

Morioka, Michiyo, and Paul Berry. *Modern Masters of Kyoto: The Transformation of Japanese Painting Traditions. Nihonga from the Griffith and Patricia Way Collection.* Seattle: Seattle Art Museum, 1999.

Murakami Ayame 村上文芽. "Hirai Baisen shi" 平井楳仙氏. *Daimai bijutsu* 大毎美術 5, no. 12 (December 1926): 41–42.

Shindō Tōnosuke 新道陶之助. "Kinbenka no Baisen kun" 勤勉家の楳仙君. *Daimai bijutsu* 大毎美術 5, no. 12 (December 1926): 35–36.

Yui Kazuto 油井一人. *Nijusseiki bukko nihongaka jiten* 20 世紀物故日本画家事典. Tokyo: Bijutsunenkansha 美術年鑑社, 1998.

NOTES

1. Murakami, "Hirai Baisen shi," 41.
2. "Gaka shūnyū shirabe," 43.
3. Kyō-waranbe, "Baisen san wa Bukkōji san," 38, and Murakami, "Hirai Baisen shi," 42.
4. Kanzaki Ken'ichi, *Kyōto ni okeru nihongashi* (Kyoto: Kyōto Seihan Insatsusha, 1929), 191.
5. See the comments on this work in Nittenshi Hensan Iinkai, *Nittenshi* 3, *Buntenhen* 3 (Tokyo: Nitten, 1980), 376. The painting is illustrated in the same issue, pp. 342–43.
6. See the long commentary by Matsumoto Matatarō, "Bunten no nihonga o hyōsu," *Shinbi* 4, no. 11 (November 1915): 59–60.
7. "Dai jikkai Bunten nihonga gōhyō," *Bijutsu no Nihon* 8, no. 11 (November 1916): 22–23, and Sawamura Koi, "Bunten nihonga hyō," *Shinbi* 5, no. 11 (November 1916): 56.
8. For a color reproduction of this work, see Kyōto Kokuritsu Kindai Bijutsukan, *Kyōto Kokuritsu Kindai Bijutsukan shozō meihinshū: Nihonga* (Kyoto: Mitsumura Suiko Shoin, 2002), 84–85.
9. Kitano, "Seison Baisen no taihi," 32.
10. Shindō, "Kinbenka no Baisen kun," 36.
11. "Kinosaki to Kamogawa to ima hitotsu wa risōteki ni kaita," *Kaiga seidan* 3, no. 10 (November 1915): 68.
12. Kitano, "Seison Baisen no taihi," 31.
13. See Paul Berry's biography of Hirai Baisen in Morioka and Berry, *Modern Masters of Kyoto,* 271.
14. Hoshino Keizō, "Michizane no tsuisō, 'kyonen no kon'ya': Hirai Baisen," in Hoshino, *Ishi o migaku,* 44–45.
15. Yui, *Nijusseiki bukko nihongaka jiten 20,* 325.

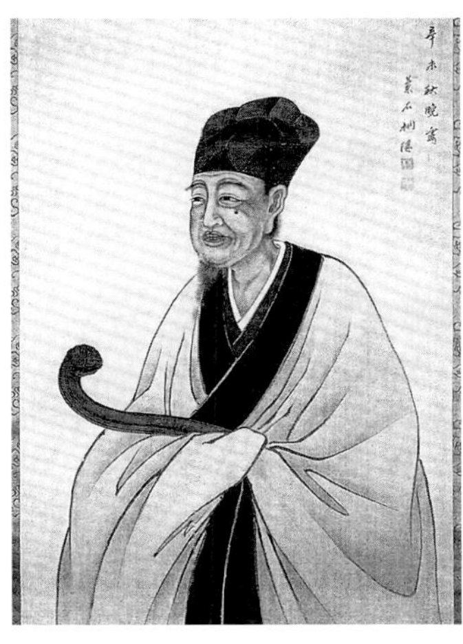

Hirose Taizan 廣瀬臺山 1751–1813

During his lifetime, Hirose Taizan was better known as an administrator of economic affairs than as an artist. He spent most of his adult life dutifully fulfilling his obligations as the head of a samurai family, and only for a decade, after his retirement, did he enjoy the leisurely lifestyle of gentleman-scholar. Yet Taizan was an accomplished poet and painter, and an active member of the Edo *bunjin* circle. Tanomura Chikuden 田能村竹田 (1777–1835) and Kanai Ujū 金井烏州 (1796–1857) treated him with high regard in their painting treatises.[1] Taizan excelled at landscape painting. The majority of his extant oeuvre dates from the last twenty years of his life and reveals an orthodox approach based on the broad study of various Chinese masters. Many works, however, display exceptionally imaginative, complex compositions with a strong feeling for spatial expression. Furthermore, the examples Taizan left of true-view painting of Mount Fuji and the Atami coast, based on actual observation, display the breadth of his interests and styles. His relative obscurity today is attributed largely to the fact that he neither took formal pupils, who could carry on his lineage and spread his reputation, nor wrote an extensive painting treatise for posterity.[2]

Taizan was born into a samurai family who served the Tsuyama 津山 fief (Okayama prefecture). His *gō*, Taizan, comes from Mount Tai 臺山, a peak that rises in a village north of Tsuyama, where his father's warlord ancestor had established a small castle during the sixteenth century.[3] Taizan spent most of his early years in Osaka, where he was born and where his father was responsible for the Tsuyama fief's economic affairs. In 1767, at the age of sixteen, Taizan began formal training as a samurai and soon afterward received his appointment to serve the fief. Until the family's return to Tsuyama in 1775, Taizan busied himself as a young samurai in Osaka. During this period he also acquired a solid *bunjin* foundation, receiving painting instruction from Fukuhara Gogaku 福原五岳 (1730–1799), an Osaka painter and a pupil of Ike Taiga 池大雅 (1723–1776), and studying poetry and the *qin* (*shichigen-goto* 七弦琴) with the Confucian scholar Hosoai Hansai 細合半斎 (1727–1803).

With his father's retirement in 1779, Taizan at age twenty-eight became the head of the Hirose family, and shortly thereafter, he received an important appointment that took him to Edo, where he was in charge of his lord's residence. Despite the demands of his work, Taizan pursued artistic activities as much as time allowed, becoming acquainted with major *bunjin* painters and poets, among them Tani Bunchō 谷文晁 (1763–1840), Uragami Gyokudō 浦上玉堂 (1745–1820), and Masuyama Sessai 増山雪斎 (1755–1820).[4] Sometime in the late 1790s, Taizan assumed leadership of the Small Society for the Preservation of Poetry Chanting (Shō Fukyū Ginsha 小不朽吟社). One literati artist described this elegant Edo cultural group, popular in the eighteenth and nineteenth centuries, as producing "poetry and painting in abundance."[5]

Besides painting, Taizan enjoyed carving seals and playing the seven-string *qin*. A *qin* cloth cover, believed to have belonged to Taizan, verifies his close ties with the Edo *bunjin* community and demonstrates the expression of friendship so crucial to literati ideals and activities. Twenty-six *bunjin*, including Bunchō, Gyokudō and his son Shunkin, and the noted priest-painter-poet Unshitsu 雲室 (1753–1827), decorated Taizan's *qin* cover with calligraphic inscriptions and paintings of figures and bird-and-flower subjects.[6]

Taizan enjoyed a happy marriage with a wife who shared his devotion to the arts. But they lost four children to illness,[7] and the recurring tragedy may have driven Taizan and his wife to pursue literati activities with an even greater passion in search of solace. During the late 1790s Taizan tried to withdraw from service on several occasions because of illness, and he finally retired from his official duties in 1803. He returned to Tsuyama in 1811 and died there two years later.

MM

BIBLIOGRAPHY

Hirose Tetsushi 廣瀬哲士. "Hirose Taizan o kataru" 廣瀬臺山を語る 1. *Shoga kottō zasshi* 書畫骨董雑誌, no. 333 (March 1936): 1–3.

———. "Hirose Taizan o kataru 2." *Shoga kottō zasshi,* no. 334 (April 1936): 4–6.

———. "Hirose Taizan o kataru 3." *Shoga kottō zasshi,* no. 336 (June 1936): 4–6.

———. "Hirose Taizan o kataru 4." *Shoga kottō zasshi,* no. 340 (October 1936): 4–6.

Kurihara Tadashi 栗原直. *Hirose Taizan.* Tokyo: Miki Shobō 三樹書房, 1991.

Nishimura Nangaku 西村南岳. "Hirose Taizan ni tsuite: Hyakunijūgoshūki kinen iboku ten ni sai shi" 廣瀬臺山について－百廿五周忌記念遺墨展に際し－. *Nanga kanshō* 南畫鑑賞 6, no. 10 (October 1937): 6–13.

Tsuyama Kyōdo Hakubutsukan 津山郷土博物館. *Hirose Taizan—Nenki no aru sakuhin kara* 広瀬臺山－年記のある作品から. Exh. cat. Tsuyama, 1992.

Umezawa Seiichi 梅澤精一. *Nihon nangashi* 日本南畫史. Tokyo: Nanyōdō 南陽堂, 1919.

NOTES

1. See Hugh Wylie, "Nanga Painting Treatises of Nineteenth-Century Japan: Translations, Commentary, and Analysis" (PhD diss., University of Kansas, 1991), 107–8, 167–68.
2. Umezawa, *Nihon nangashi*, 496–97.
3. Kurihara, *Hirose Taizan*, 24.
4. For Taizan's wide circle of *bunjin* friends, see ibid., 313–64.
5. The literati painter Kanai Ujū (1796–1857) made this comment in his *Musei shiwa* (Talks on "Silent Poetry"); see Wylie, "Nanga Painting Treatises," 168–69.
6. The paintings and calligraphies were added over a span of several years, starting in 1800; see Kurihara, *Hirose Taizan*, 295–96.
7. Hirose, "Hirose Taizan o kataru 3," 5.

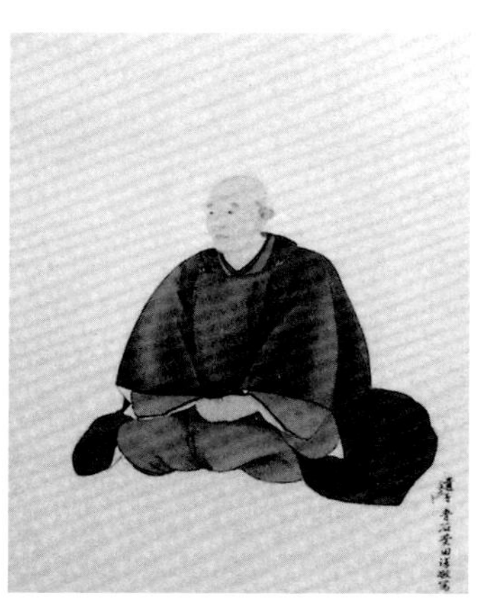

Hoashi Kyōu 帆足杏雨 1810–1884

Kyōu, Takahashi Sōhei 高橋草坪 (1802–1835), and Tanomura Chokunyū 田能村直入 (1814–1907) were the top three disciples of Tanomura Chikuden 田能村竹田 (1777–1835). Initially their work closely resembled that of their teacher, yet Kyōu and Chokunyū (Sōhei died the same year as Chikuden) would gradually develop their own distinctive approaches.

Kyōu, the fourth son of a prominent family in Hetsugi 戸次, near present-day Ōita city, had begun studying with Chikuden in 1824 and frequently traveled with his teacher during the last five years of Chikuden's life. In this way Kyōu met many top artists in Osaka and Kyoto, including Rai San'yō 頼山陽 (1780–1833), Shinozaki Shōchiku 篠崎小竹 (1781–1851), and Uragami Shunkin 浦上春琴 (1779–1846).[1] One of the most impressive of Kyōu's early works is the album *Paintings and Poems of Enjoying the Capital* (Kyōyū shigajō 京遊詩画帖), made during a trip with Chikuden in 1832 and 1833. These delicate paintings are almost indistinguishable from his teacher's finest work, and each leaf bears an inscription by Chikuden.

The year after Chikuden's death, Kyōu assembled many inscriptions from his mentor's major works and added them to the collection Chikuden had begun to form the multivolume *Inscriptions on My Paintings* (Jigadaigo 自畫題語), published in 1839.[2] As Chikuden's inscriptions often included long prose passages as well as original poetry, this text has been a primary source for information about Chikuden's attitudes and major life experiences. Chikuden had urged his students to carefully study Chinese paintings and poetry, and Kyōu energetically followed his lead. During the subsequent decades of the Edo period, Kyōu found his mature style, mixing some aspects of Chikuden's works with various approaches he had seen in Qing-period paintings. Although these works occasionally refer to Chikuden's compositions, they are mostly meticulously painted, complex landscapes that reveal a close study of Chinese works.[3]

Like many of his literati compatriots, Kyōu transformed his painting style during the social upheaval that occurred in the late 1860s and 1870s with the formation of the new Meiji government. Kyōu developed a distinctive type of wavering line that typified his works during the last decades of his life. He made large numbers of complex landscapes using pale ink and light colors and inscribed with long, sometimes original poems. His works in this style became extremely popular around Japan, although he remained largely in Kyushu during the Meiji period. In 1872 his painting of the fantastic peaks of the nearby Yabakei 耶馬渓 valley was among those selected for exhibition at the 1873 International Exposition in Vienna. As Chokunyū had left Kyushu for Osaka and Kyoto, Kyōu came to be considered Chikuden's main successor in his home province of Ōita.

PB

BIBLIOGRAPHY

Hoashi Susumu 帆足進, ed. *Kyōu yōteki* 杏雨餘滴. 2 vols. Tokyo: Katō Suzunosuke 加藤鎮之助, 1912.

Ōita Kenritsu Geijutsu Kaikan 大分県立芸術会館. *Hoashi Kyōu ten zuroku* 帆足杏雨展図録. Ōita City, 1984.

Oguri Ken'ichi 小栗憲一. *Hōkai shishi* 豊繪詩史. 3 vols. Kyoto, 1884.

Taketani Chōjirō 竹谷長二郎. *Bunjin gaka Tanomura Chikuden* 文人画家田能村竹田. Tokyo: Meiji Shoin 明治書院, 1981.

NOTES

1. The biographical information included here is drawn largely from the essay and chronology by Munakata Ken'ichi 宗像健一 in *Hoashi Kyōu ten zuroku*, which accompanied the exhibition at the Ōita Kenritsu Geijutsu Kaikan.

2. See the complete annotated translation into modern Japanese in Taketani, *Bunjin gaka Tanomura Chikuden.*

3. A large number of Kyōu's study sketches (*funpon* 粉本) of Chinese paintings remain in the collection of the Ōita Kenritsu Geijutsu Kaikan. The bulk of the Hoashi family collection of paintings, including many famous works by Chikuden, was given to the Ōita-shi Bijutsukan.

Honkō Fūgai 本高風外 1779–1847

Many more Rinzai Zen 臨済禅 than Sōtō Zen 曹洞禅 priests attained prominence as practitioners of Zen painting and calligraphy in Japan. This striking difference is due to the Sōtō sect's emphasis on seated meditation, or *zazen* 座禅. In order to facilitate this practice, Sōtō temples were located in quiet rural areas away from the disturbances of city life. Rinzai temples, in contrast, were often located in cities, and monks sought out interaction with wealthy patrons and the ruling class. Rinzai priests were encouraged to develop their talents at poetry, painting, and calligraphy, but in the Sōtō context such activities were often viewed as distractions. Despite these differing attitudes, a number of Sōtō priests in the Edo period developed reputations for their painting and calligraphy; among them, Fūgai Ekun 風外慧薫 (1568–1650) and the later Honkō Fūgai were especially prominent.[1]

Born Azuma Taiji 東泰二 in a farming family in Mie prefecture, Fūgai was taken into a local temple and raised by the priest Tokugan Donzui 徳岩曇瑞 from the age of four.[2] He is believed to have begun painting when he was about ten years old, first copying paintings in the temple collection and then advancing to the works of the painter Gessen 月僊 (1741–1809).[3] In 1800 he adopted the name Fūgai 風外, and the alternate name Kōyū 好幽 is frequently found on his seals. In 1802 he began studying the works of the noted literati painter Tanomura Chikuden 田能村竹田 (1777–1835). Fūgai became head priest, in 1818, of the small temple Entsūin 円通院 in the Tenma district of Osaka, where he completed a painting of five hundred *rakan* on eight sliding *fusuma* panels in 1821. Residing in Osaka allowed him contact with the painters and patrons in that prosperous merchant city. Fūgai began to deeply explore the works of Ike Taiga 池大雅 (1723–1776) in local collections in 1826 and announced in a letter his intention to follow Taiga's approach to painting.[4] For the rest of Fūgai's career, Taiga's influence is evident in most of his works. Fūgai often traveled to the Matsue area in Shimane prefecture, visiting temples such as Tenrinji 天輪寺, where, in 1832, he made some of his most accomplished works in a burst of creativity that continued for several years.

From 1834 to 1840 Fūgai was the twenty-fifth head priest of the Kōjakuji 高積寺 temple in Toyota city outside Nagoya. He was quite prolific during his tenure, and every November the temple holds an exhibition of Fūgai's works from its collection. Fūgai retired in 1841 to the Ujakurō 烏鵲楼 in Osaka where he stayed active, giving lectures on Zen and painting vigorously. Along with the noted literati painters of the area, Fūgai participated in the 1842 exhibition of calligraphy and paintings on the occasion of the seventh anniversary of Chikuden's death. Fūgai had one major disciple, Yokoyama Unnan 横山雲南 (1813–1880), the second son of a doctor from Matsue. Although Unnan's style was eventually most influenced by the Chinese literati paintings he studied, his surviving letters reveal that he admired Fūgai above the other prominent painters of the period.[5] PB

BIBLIOGRAPHY

Endō Tomohiko 遠藤友彦, ed. *Ujakurō kōkan roku* 烏鵲楼高閑録. Tokyo: Kokusho Kankokai 国書刊行会, 2004.

Fujimoto Mokusen 藤本黙仙. *Fūgai* 風外. Nagoya: Fūgai Hakkan Iinkai 風外発刊委員会, 1987.

Hisamatsu Shin'ichi. *Zen and the Fine Arts.* Tokyo and Palo Alto: Kodansha International, 1971.

NOTES

1. Other than being Sōtō priests and sharing the name Fūgai, these two figures are unrelated in their careers and styles.

2. The biographical information on Fūgai presented here is based primarily on the biography by Fujimoto Mokusen, *Fūgai.*

3. Although Gessen's birth date is often given as 1721, a record at his home temple Jakushōji 寂照寺 that gives 1741 for his birth is introduced in *Shoga kottō zasshi* 書画骨董雑誌, no. 217 (July 1926): 7.

4. Ibid., 70–71.

5. Ibid., 76–85.

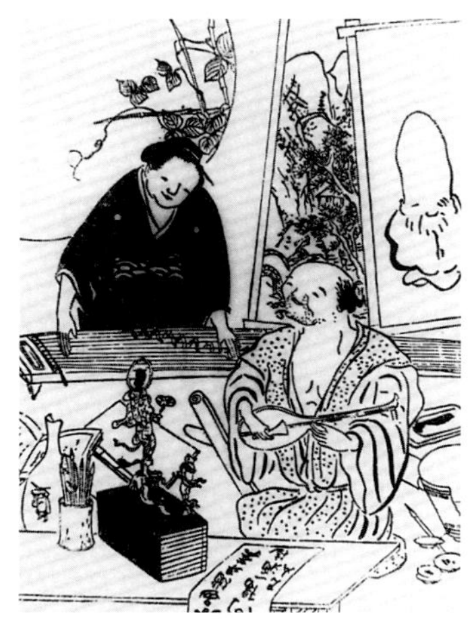

Ike Gyokuran
池玉瀾 1727/8–1784

Ike Gyokuran and her husband, Ike Taiga 池大雅 (1723–1776), were likely the most celebrated artistic couple of the Edo period. The memory of their bohemian lifestyle has been shaped and immortalized in various anecdotes and images of the Japanese *bunjin* world. The famous portrayal of the couple by Mikuma Katen 三熊花顛 (1730–1795), published in *Biographies of Extraordinary Persons of Recent Times* (Kinsei kijin den 近世畸人伝), shows Taiga playing the samisen and Gyokuran the koto in a room cluttered with paintings, books, calligraphies, brushes, and rolled-up papers.[1] Gyokuran's posthumous fame would derive from her identity as Taiga's wife, but during her lifetime and for a short while after her death, she enjoyed a reputation in her own right as an accomplished poet and painter. Both Gyokuran's and Taiga's names appear in the list of noted painters in the 1768 edition of *Record of Famous People of Kyoto* (Heian jinbutsu shi 平安人物誌). Several decades after Gyokuran's death, Tanomura Chikuden 田能村竹田 (1777–1835) praised her as the best among Japan's female painters in his well-known painting treatise *The Prattling of a Mountain Hermit* (Sanchūjin jōzetsu 山中人饒舌).[2]

Gyokuran's given name was Machi 町. She represented a lineage of famous female poets that began with her grandmother Kaji 梶 (act. early eighteenth century), who operated a teahouse called Matsuya 松屋 in Kyoto while gaining fame for her *waka* compositions. Kaji's adopted daughter, Yuri 百合 (1694–1764), continued the tradition, establishing a reputation for her literary talent. Machi was born to Yuri and a samurai named Tokuyama 徳山, a retainer of the Tokugawa shogun. When Tokuyama was called back to Edo, Yuri and her daughter stayed in Kyoto. Although Gyokuran carried on the family legacy of *waka* composition, she also became well versed in painting, receiving instruction from the distinguished literati painter Yanagisawa Kien 柳沢淇園 (1706–1758) from an early age. It is believed that Kien was a customer at Yuri's teahouse and gave his pupil the name Gyokuran (Jade Orchid), taking a character from Gyokkei 玉桂, one of his artist names.

Kien also taught Taiga painting during his youth, and Taiga and Gyokuran may have come to know each other through Kien.[3] Their marriage, arranged by her mother, occurred sometime between 1746 and 1752.[4] At the time, Taiga was making a living as an artist and calligrapher. Even after her marriage, Gyokuran may have continued to use her surname Tokuyama, and some suggest that she and Taiga may not have legalized their union.[5] Living in a three-room atelier/house in Makuzugahara 真葛ヶ原 near the Gion shrine, Gyokuran pursued painting under her husband's tutelage, studying his model works and directly copying his paintings. She eventually developed a brush mode influenced by Taiga's distinct style. The compilation of Gyokuran's overall oeuvre and understanding of her development and activities as a painter remain at an early stage today. Gyokuran's known paintings, however, convey an unmistakable individuality. In comparison to Taiga's works, her manner is more whimsical and her brushwork unconventional, with exaggerated outlines, unusual texture strokes, and eccentric geometric forms. Although Gyokuran painted large screens, her intimate works are more widely known. Her numerous fan paintings are admired for their imaginative, playful compositions.

By all accounts, Gyokuran and Taiga were well matched in their art-focused interests and temperaments. While Gyokuran learned painting from her husband, she in turn introduced him to *waka* poetry, and both studied classical poetry with the courtier Reizei Tamemura 冷泉為村 (1712–1774). *Biographies of Extraordinary Persons* relates a famous episode in which Taiga forgot a box of brushes he meant to take to a gathering sponsored by Kimura Kenkadō 木村兼葭堂 (1736–1802) in Osaka, and Gyokuran rushed to deliver it to him. Taiga absentmindedly thanked the messenger without noticing it was his wife, and Gyokuran simply bowed without a word and returned home.[6] Upon her mother's death in 1764, Gyokuran became the owner of the Matsuya teahouse, and the couple continued to sell paintings and calligraphies. After Taiga died, Gyokuran maintained her artistic activities and enjoyed friendships with the artists in Taiga's circle such as Kenkadō, Kō Fuyō 高芙蓉 (1722–1784), Fukuhara Gogaku 福原五岳 (1730–1799), and Aoki Shukuya 青木夙夜 (c. 1737–1806).[7]

MM

BIBLIOGRAPHY
Fischer, Felice, et al. *Ike Taiga and Tokuyama Gyokuran: Japanese Masters of the Brush*. Exh. cat. Philadelphia: Philadelphia Museum of Art, 2007.

Fister, Patricia. *Japanese Women Artists, 1600–1900*. Exh. cat. Lawrence: Spencer Museum of Art, 1988.

Hitomi Shōka 人見少華. "Gyokuran." *Nanga kenkyū* 南画研究 2, no. 9 (September 1958): 4, 10–11.

Mori Senzō 森銑三. "Taiga ibun 大雅遺聞 17: Taiga to Gyokuran 大雅と玉瀾." *Nanga kenkyū* 2, no. 10 (October 1958): 12.

Suzuki Susumu 鈴木進. "Taiga to Gyokuran." *Ko bijutsu* 古美術, no. 44 (April 1974): 37–50.

Takeuchi, Melinda. *Taiga's True Views: The Language of Landscape Painting in Eighteenth-Century Japan*. Stanford: Stanford University Press, 1992.

NOTES

1. For this illustration, see Kyoko Kinoshita, "The Life and Art of Tokuyama Gyokuran," in Fischer et al., *Ike Taiga and Tokuyama Gyokuran*, 34; Fister, *Japanese Women Artists*, 74; and Takeuchi, *Taiga's True Views*, 76.
2. See the translation by Hugh Wylie, "Nanga Painting Treatises of Nineteenth Century Japan: Translations, Commentary, and Analysis" (PhD diss., University of Kansas, 1991), 116.
3. Kinoshita, "The Life and Art of Tokuyama Gyokuran," 38.
4. Scholarly opinion differs about the year of their marriage; see Suzuki Susumu, "Taiga to Gyokuran," 40, and Kinoshita, "The Life and Art of Tokuyama Gyokuran," 33–40.
5. Kinoshita, "The Life and Art of Tokuyama Gyokuran," 33 and 40.
6. As conveyed by Mori, "Taiga ibun 17: Taiga to Gyokuran," 12.
7. Kinoshita, "The Life and Art of Tokuyama Gyokuran," 40.

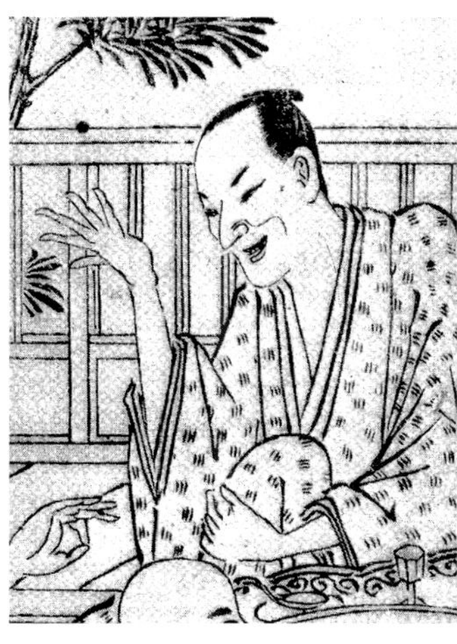

Kameda Bōsai
亀田鵬斎 1752–1826

Bōsai was the son of a manager of a tortoiseshell products store in Nihonbashi in Edo. His skill as a calligrapher had been encouraged from childhood, when he trained under two prominent calligraphers, Mitsui Shinna 三井親和 (1700–1782) and Inoue Kinga 井上金峨 (1732–1784). Bōsai supported himself by lecturing on Confucianism and opened his own school. He was truly prolific, and a great many of his calligraphies survive to this day.[1] His son Kameda Ryōrai 亀田綾瀬 (1778–1853) learned the several styles of his father's calligraphy and frequently created high-quality works. Bōsai's eccentric paintings appeal through their simple compositions with dramatic brushwork that typically displays the spreading of ink beyond the brushstroke (*nijimi* 滲み) and the uneven inking of the brush tip which produces a range of tones within a stroke (*katabokashi* 片暈かし).

Compared to the refined literati circles of Kyoto and Osaka, Edo literati were flamboyant. The new forms of popular culture that proliferated in the confluence of political and economic power in Edo may have been less constrained by the older traditions prevalent in western Japan. Even so, Bōsai stood out from his contemporaries for his celebration of intoxication. Although poets in East Asia have always praised the benefits of drink, few have written as many poems on the theme as Bōsai. He went so far as to print a parody of a Buddhist text in praise of sake in 1827, *Sutra of the Buddhist Teachings on Sake as a Marvelous Medicine* (Bussetsu maka shu myōyaku kyō 仏説摩訶酒妙薬経), and a popularized version, *Sutra on the Virtues of Sake* (Shutoku kyō 酒徳経).[2] His reputation for drinking has influenced the perception that Bōsai's freely brushed paintings and seemingly wild cursive script were an outgrowth of his love of wine. Yet his skill in a formal regular script was so prominent that he was often asked to create texts for stele engraving, and the resulting stone monuments that display his firm, rectilinear script still survive in many locations around northern Japan.[3]

Bōsai's circle of friends was nearly identical to those surrounding the noted painter Tani Bunchō 谷文晁 (1763–1840), including the calligraphers Ichikawa Beian 市河米庵 (1779–1858) and Ōkubo Shibutsu 大窪詩佛 (1766–1837), as well as the painters Sakai Hōitsu 酒井抱一 (1761–1828), Haruki Nanko 春木南湖 (1759–1839), and others. Among the many records of their association are a large number of joint works, often composed impromptu on the occasion of a gathering (for an example, see cat. no. 3).[4] Bōsai's travels to northern Japan from 1809 to 1811 gave him an opportunity to meet other literati, most notably Kushiro Unsen 釧雲泉 (1759–1811) and Ryōkan 良寛 (1758–1851), the poet-priest renowned for calligraphy.[5] The appeal of Bōsai's relaxed and entertaining personality seems well matched by the engaging eccentricity of his artwork. PB

BIBLIOGRAPHY
Addiss, Stephen. *The World of Kameda Bosai*. New Orleans: New Orleans Museum of Art; Lawrence: University Press of Kansas, 1984.

Atsumi Kuniyasu 渥美国泰. *Kameda Bōsai to Edo kaseiki no bunjintachi* 亀田鵬斎と江戸化政期の文人達. Tokyo: Geijutsu Shinbunsha 芸術 新聞社, 1995.

Kameda Bōsai. *Mountains of the Heart*. New York: George Braziller, 2007.

Kameda Bōsai Sōshū 亀田鵬斎総集. Ojiyashi: Ojiyashi Kameda Bōsai-ten Jikkō Iinkai 小千谷市亀田鵬斎展実行委員会, 2007.

Morita Shiryū 森田子龍, ed. "Kameda Bōsai" 亀田鵬斎. *Bokubi* 墨美, no. 148 (June 1965).

Setagaya Kuritsu Kyōdo Shiryōkan 世田谷区立郷土資料館. *Edo no bunjin kōyūroku: Kameda Bōsai to sono nakamatachi* 江戸の文人交友録: 亀田鵬斎とその仲間たち. Tokyo, 1998.

Sugimura Eiji 杉本英治. *Kameda Bōsai* 亀田鵬斎. Tokyo: Kinsei Fūzoku Kenkyūkai 近世風俗研究会, 1978.

———. *Kameda Bōsai no sekai.* 亀田鵬斎の世界. Tokyo: Miki Shobō 三樹書房, 1985.

———, ed. *Kameda Bōsai shibun shoga shū* 鵬斎詩文書画集. Tokyo: Miki Shobō 三樹書房, 1982.

NOTES

1. The 2007 *Kameda Bōsai sōshū* illustrates more than four hundred works (mostly calligraphy) gathered from locations in Niigata prefecture. Bōsai's popularity as a calligrapher is further attested by the many forgeries generated in the decades following his death.

2. See illustrations of the text and a brief discussion in Atsumi, *Kameda Bōsai to Edo kaseiki no bunjintachi*, 280–81. A facsimile edition of *Bussetsu maka shu myōyaku kyō* is included in Sugimura, *Kameda Bōsai*, 251–69.

3. See the many examples illustrated in Atsumi, *Kameda Bōsai to Edo Kaseiki no bunjintachi*, 33–86, and Sugimura, *Kameda Bōsai no sekai*, 37–91.

4. There are two main types of joint works, those composed at the same time and often including the date and the reason for the gathering, and those compiled over time by a patron who desired small examples of his favorite artists' work. One of the seals on the work in cat. no. 3 uses the term *sekijō* 席上, or "written on the spot," suggesting that these works were made at a gathering.

5. See cat. no. 2 in this volume for a discussion of the relationship of Bōsai's calligraphy to that of Ryōkan.

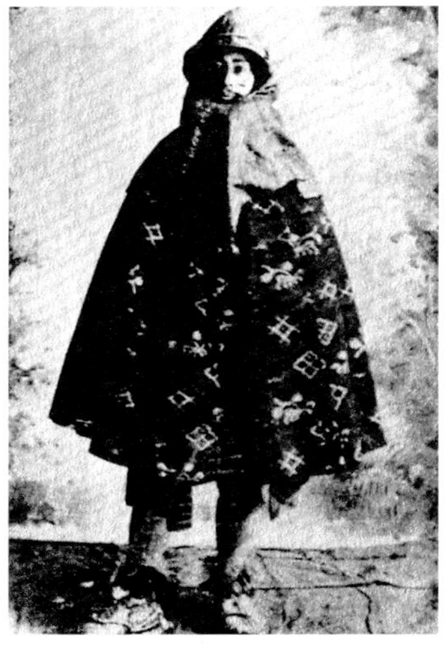

Kawahigashi Hekigotō 河東碧梧桐 1873–1937

Twentieth-century Japan saw many innovations in calligraphy, yet few could match the daring eclecticism of Hekigotō's fusion of ancient Chinese calligraphy with Japan's tradition of haiku, the poetry of the enduring moment. Not only did he reconcile styles that were viewed as antithetical; his irregular arrangements of characters produced startling compositions that had no precedent. Beyond influencing the styles of some friends and associates, Hekigotō's calligraphy had no following after the early 1930s, yet his work stands as the major prewar precedent for the explosion of abstract calligraphy in the 1950s whose practitioners would include great talents such as Morita Shiryū 森田子龍 (1912–1999), Inoue Yūichi 井上有一 (1916–1985), Teshigahara Sōfū 勅使河原蒼風 (1900–1990), and Suda Kokuta 須田剋太 (1906–1990).

Hekigotō was born and raised in the castle town of Matsuyama on Shikoku Island, an unlikely and remote location for fostering the transformation of the haiku movement. It was here that Matsuoka Shiki 松岡子規 (1867–1902) would initiate a new approach to haiku that succeeded in revitalizing the poetic form. His Matsuyama disciple Takahama Kyoshi 高浜虚子 (1874–1959) extended Shiki's popularity while maintaining the traditional structure of haiku as having a 5-7-5 division of syllables and a seasonal reference. Kyoshi's conservative modernism contrasts with Hekigotō's abandonment of the syllabic structure and even the set length of haiku in his search to strengthen the immediacy that is key to the poetic life of this most brief verse form.[1]

Hekigotō was the fifth son of Seikei, a Confucian scholar who founded a short-lived school in Matsuyama. After receiving a traditional education in the Confucian classics, Hekigotō went to a local school where he befriended the young Kyoshi. Oddly it was Hekigotō's desire to learn about American baseball that first prompted him to seek out Shiki, who was a great fan of the game and had just returned to Matsuyama in 1889 from a sojourn in Tokyo. Kyoshi and Hekigotō both became close to the slightly older Shiki, and they encouraged each other's literary efforts, especially in haiku. Hekigotō matured so quickly in haiku composition that Shiki placed him in charge of his important newspaper column on haiku at *Nihon shinbun* when he left to cover the Sino-Japanese War in 1895. Hekigotō's devotion to Shiki is best seen in his book *Speaking of Shiki* (Shiki o kataru), which covers their relationship until the mid-1890s and also discusses Hekigotō's early development as a poet. While Hekigotō was in the hospital recovering from smallpox in 1897, Kyoshi became involved with his girlfriend. The consequent strain on their friendship was amplified as their poetic inclinations diverged. Kyoshi eventually edited the influential, yet comparatively traditional haiku magazine *Hototogisu,* and Hekigotō came to advocate a new direction (*shinkeikō* 新傾向) for haiku that put vital immediacy over adherence to traditional structure.

Hekigotō was equally interested in finding a new visual expressiveness for calligraphy that would be as direct and unornamented as his verse. Hekigotō admired the early poems of the Man'yoshu anthology for these same qualities, and the idea of reaching deep into the past for inspiration seemed a possibility. The turning point came during his eighteen-month journey around the countryside of Japan. After setting out in August 1906, he settled in for a forty-day stay at the Asamushi hot spring in northern Aomori prefecture in January and February 1907. During this time he received several ink rubbings of Chinese Six Dynasties calligraphy from the *yōga* painter Nakamura Fusetsu 中村不折 (1866–1943). Fusetsu had long been a friend of Shiki's, and his ideas on life drawing (*shasei* 写生) had strongly influenced the early development of Shiki's approach to haiku.[2] Yet, one of Fusetsu's greatest contributions lay in his passionate exploration of ancient Chinese calligraphy and his accumulation of tens of thousands of calligraphies, rubbings, bronzes, steles, and inscribed ceramics.[3]

Hekigotō poured over the rubbings he had received, admiring the seeming awkwardness of their straight, blunt lines and unusual sense of balance and composition. He immediately altered his own calligraphy to express his interpretation of these qualities.[4] The enthusiasm for creating new styles of calligraphy based on the study of ancient Chinese examples spread among a number of calligraphers and painters in the late Meiji period. The Ryūminkai 龍眠会 association, formed in 1913, promoted this trend in calligraphy, and claimed such prominent members as Fusetsu, Hekigotō, the calligrapher-painter Maeda Mokuhō 前田黙鳳 (1853–1918), and the innovative artist Tomita Keisen 富田渓仙 (1879–1936).[5]

Hekigotō was unique in this group for applying the new Chinese-based style to the writing of the most Japanese form of poetry, the haiku. Most other members of the group restricted their use of these new styles to Chinese characters. Since the origins of haiku in the seventeenth century, a great many styles of cursive calligraphy had been used for its mixture of *hiragana* syllables and characters, yet all had been dominated by fluid, graceful lines and compositions. Hekigotō's heavily inked, bold lines, often angular and arranged in startling compositions, were a seeming affront to the entire tradition of haiku calligraphy.

Hekigotō refined his approach to calligraphy throughout his life, finally reaching a well-balanced blend of fluid and angular strokes in an ongoing variety of new compositions. Although he had his biggest impact in verse in midcareer, many of his finest calligraphies date from the last decade of his life, in the Shōwa period.[6] Under his influence, a few other haiku poets adopted similar calligraphy styles for their poems, notably Shiodani Uhei 塩谷鵜平 (1877–1940). Among Hekigotō's other achievements was his authorship of the earliest book (1926) on Yosa Buson 与謝蕪村 (1716–1783) as a painter; most of Hekigotō's contemporaries had ignored Buson's artwork while excitedly reevaluating his importance as a creator of haiku.[7] Hekigotō's considerable research led him to the Tango area, to develop a better understanding of Buson's origins, and his book was the first to highlight this formative period of Buson's life. His biggest contribution, however, may have been his arresting, idiosyncratic style, which established the expressive potential of calligraphy and a way of being inspired but not restricted by the past.

PB

BIBLIOGRAPHY

Hayashi Makoto 林誠, ed. *Nakamura Fusetsu no subete ten* 中村不拙のすべて展. Ina: Nagano-ken Ina-shi Bunkakan 長野県伊那市文化館, 2006.

Izawa Motoyoshi 井沢元美. *Hekigotō, Seisensui, Santōka* 碧梧桐,井泉水山頭火. Haijin no shoga bijutsu 俳人の書画美術, vol. 9. Tokyo: Shūeisha 集英社, 1979.

Kakimori Bunko 柿衛文庫. *Hanshinkan to Kawahigashi Hekigotō* 阪神間と河東碧梧桐. Itami: Kakimori Bunkō 柿衛文庫, 2002.

Kawahigashi Hekigotō 河東碧梧桐. *Gajin Buson* 画人蕪村. Tokyo: Chūō Bijutsusha 中央美術社, 1926.

———. *Shiki o kataru* 子規を語る. Tokyo: Hanbunsha 汎文社, 1934.

Keene, Donald. *Dawn to the West: Japanese Literature in the Modern Era: Poetry, Drama, Criticism.* New York: Henry Holt, 1984.

Morita Shiryū 森田子龍, ed. "Kawahigashi Hekigotō" 河東碧梧桐. *Bokubi* 墨美, no. 164 (December 1966).

———, ed. "Tokushū Ryūminkai" 特集龍眠会. *Bokubi* 墨美, no. 159 (June 1966).

Onodera Keiji 小野寺敬治. "Hekigotō to Ryūminkai" 碧梧桐と龍眠会. *Sumi* 墨, no. 36 (May 1982): 52–53.

Sawada Taigyō 沢田大暁. "Kyo Heki no sho, sono hensen o miru" 虚碧の書、その変遷を見る. *Sumi* 墨, no. 36 (May 1982).

Takahama Kyoshi 高浜虚子 and Kawahigashi Hekigotō 東碧梧桐. *Kawahigashi Hekigotō. Takahama Kyoshi, Kawahigashi Hekigotō shū* 高浜虚子,河東碧梧桐集. Meiji bungaku zenshū 明治文学全集, 56. Tokyo: Chikuma Shobō 筑摩書房, 1977.

Takii Kosaku 瀧井孝作. *Hekigotō zenkushu* 碧梧桐全句集. Tokyo: Kagyūsha 蝸牛社, 1982.

NOTES

1. A brief overview of the relations between Shiki, Kyoshi, and Hekigotō is found in Keene, *Dawn to the West*, 99–118.

2. Ibid., 98. Shiki maintained such a close lifelong association with Fusetsu that he spent his last years in a house very close to Fusetsu's Tokyo residence.

3. Fusetsu's collection is now housed in the new building of the Shodō Hakubutsukan on the site of his home in Ugisudani. Although proceeding steadily, a full inventory of the huge collection is still far from completion.

For a survey of his life and collecting activities, see Hayashi, *Nakamura Fusetsu no subete ten.*

4. The notes, letters, and postcards Hekigotō wrote during his stay at the hot springs all show this sudden transformation in style; see Sawada, "Kyo Heki no sho, sono hensen o miru," 60.

5. A brief history of the group is given in Onodera, "Hekigotō to Ryūminkai," 52–53. A more detailed treatment with many examples of calligraphies by group members is found in Morita, "Tokushū Ryūminkai." Five Keisen paintings with inscriptions by Hekigotō appear in Kakimori Bunko, *Hanshinkan to Kawahigashi Hekigotō,* 17–19.

6. The best visual survey of his calligraphy is provided in Morita, "Kawahigashi Hekigotō."

7. Kawahigashi, *Gajin Buson.*

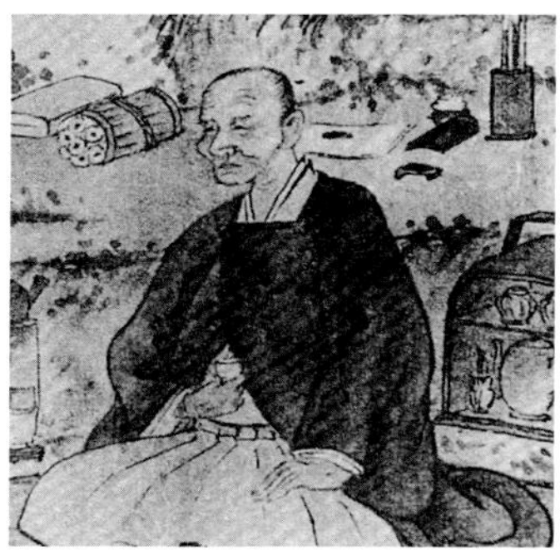

Kinoshita Itsuun 木下逸雲 1799–1866

The Kinoshita family had been doctors in Nagasaki for some generations, and Itsuun, the third son, also studied medicine, investigating newly imported Western techniques as well as traditional Japanese and Chinese procedures. In addition, he assumed the hereditary role of *otona* 乙名, or district (*chō* 町) leader, that had been abdicated by his eldest brother and passed to him through the early death of another brother.[1] Even with these responsibilities, Itsuun developed an interest in painting early in his life and first studied with Ishizaki Yūshi 石崎融思 (1768–1846), who painted Chinese-style landscapes and practiced an early form of oil painting. He joined the Zen priest Tetsuō 鐵翁 (1791–1871) in studying with the visiting Chinese merchant-painter Jiang Jiapu 江稼圃 (b. c. 1745, act. in Japan from 1804). One of the most influential of the Chinese painters to come to Japan, Jiang had a huge impact on Itsuun and many other painters in Nagasaki.

Tetsuō, Miura Gomon 三浦梧門 (1809–1860), and Itsuun became the three prominent literati painters of their generation in Nagasaki. Itsuun and Tetsuō were especially close, and most of the Japanese artists who came to learn literati painting in Nagasaki studied with both of them. Tanomura Chikuden 田能村竹田 (1777–1835) held them in high regard, visiting them in Nagasaki and carrying on a long correspondence with both men. Itsuun was deeply involved in promoting the local blue-and-white porcelain called Kameyama-yaki 亀山焼. He often painted designs for the wares used in *sencha,* and he encouraged Chikuden and others to try their hand. The kiln was located on the grounds of the Wakamiya Jinja 若宮神社, close to the Kinoshita family temple, Zenrinji 禅林寺. Itsuun's romantic sense of the literati life inspired him to import lotus from West Lake in Hangzhou and raise them in the pond at Zenrinji for the enjoyment of his friends.[2]

Itsuun became quite close to visiting Chinese artists such as Xu Yuting 徐雨亭 (b. 1824) and Wang Kesan 王克三 (act. c. 1862).[4] They joined Tetsuō in urging painters, including Yasuda Rōzan 安田老山 (1830–1882) and Nagai Unpei 長井雲坪 (1833–1899), to visit China to deepen their understanding of Chinese painting. When Tomioka Tessai visited Nagasaki in 1861, he found Itsuun more congenial than Tetsuō and spent much time studying in Itsuun's library.[5]

Itsuun painted many subjects, but landscapes form the bulk of his work. He excelled at large, complex compositions with dense, layered brushwork.[6] His skills as a painter, his wide variety of interests, and the ease with which he held lasting friendships made him a well-known figure in literati circles around Japan. His life was cut short unexpectedly in 1866, when he died at sea while returning from a visit to his brother in Edo.[3]

PB

BIBLIOGRAPHY

Hayashi Genkichi 林源吉. "Kameyama-yaki to Kinoshita Itsuun" 亀山焼と木下逸雲. *Nagasaki dansō* 長崎談叢, no. 20 (October 1937): 34–37.

Katō Ruiko 加藤類子, ed. *Tessai to sono shiyūtachi: Bunjinga on kindai* 鉄斎とその師友たち: 文人画の近代. Kyoto: Kyōto Kokuritsu Kindai Bijutsukan 京都国立近代美術館, 1997.

Shimizu Hiroshi 清水博. *Gajin Nagai Unpei* 画人長井雲坪. Naganoshi: Shinano Kyōiku Shuppansha 信濃教育出版社, 1976.

Tsuruta Takeyoshi 鶴田武良. "Ō Kokusan to Jo Utei" 王克三と徐雨亭, *Kokka* 国華, no. 1070 (1989).

NOTES

1. Shimizu, *Gajin Nagai Unpei,* 29–30.

2. Hayashi, "Kameyama-yaki to Kinoshita Itsuun," 34–35.

3. Shimizu, *Gajin Nagai Unpei,* 64–65.

4. While visiting Shanghai in 1872, Sano Zuigan took a painting by Kinoshita Itsuun to Wang Kesan for an inscription; see Tsuruta, "Ō Kokusan to Jo Utei," 22.

5. Shimizu, *Gajin Nagai Unpei,* 47–49.

6. Refer to the seven color plates of his work in Katō, *Tessai to sono shiyūtachi,* plates 174–180.

Kobayashi Shunshō 小林春樵 1888–1929?

The striking image of Kobayashi Shunshō's *Plum Trees in Tsukigase* included in this volume (cat. no. 47) indicates a painter of great artistic gifts. But much remains unknown about him, except for his given name, Umejirō 梅次郎, and that he studied under Yamamoto Shunkyo 山元春挙 (1871–1933) and participated in the government exhibitions.[1]

It is likely that Shunshō began his training with Shunkyo sometime at the end of the Meiji period. By then, Shunkyo had emerged as one of the new leaders of *nihonga*, epitomizing modernity with his elegant Western clothes and use of photography for his majestic landscape compositions. His private school (*juku*), founded in 1900 and named Rice Seedling Society (Sanaekai 早苗会) in 1909, was one of the most prosperous in Kyoto. Shunkyo not only scheduled art lectures and sketching trips to the mountains but also organized annual exhibitions of his pupils' paintings, a tradition that lasted until his death in 1933. Under Shunkyo's tutelage, Shunshō must have participated in many of those activities, steadily developing his skill as a *nihonga* painter. As late as 1929 he was still recorded as a member of the Rice Seedling Society.[2]

Shunshō's inclusion at the government exhibition was sporadic: 1915, 1922, and 1929. His 1915 submission, titled *Morning* (Asa 朝), received an honorable mention. A representation of a tree-dotted hilltop with an open distant vista, this panoramic landscape displayed the influence of Shunshō's teacher.[3] His 1922 entry, *Mountain Villa* (Sansō 山荘), demonstrated a more personal approach, featuring an intimate landscape with a rustic residence rather than the grandeur of nature. Five years later, at the 1929 competition, Shunshō again depicted traditional architecture in *Enseian Hermitage* (Enseian 圓成庵). The painting's style is markedly more refined, with crisp details that indicate the artist's awareness of the conservative trend that had become pervasive in early Shōwa *nihonga*.

Shunshō's life story subsequent to the 1929 exhibition is unclear. He may have maintained low-key artistic activities, free from the pressure of competitions and exhibitions, or some circumstances might have ended his career. It is also highly possible that he died soon thereafter.[4] MM

BIBLIOGRAPHY

Araki Nori 荒木矩, ed. *Dai Nihon shoga meika taikan, denki gehen*, 大日本書畫名家大鑑:傳記下編. 1934. Reprint. Tokyo: Daiichi Shobō 第一書房, 1975.

Kanzaki Ken'ichi 神崎憲一. *Kyōto ni okeru nihongashi* 京都に於ける日本画史. Kyoto: Kyōto Seihan Insatsusha 京都精版印刷社, 1929.

NOTES

1. Araki, *Dai Nihon shoga meika taikan, denki gehen*, 1310.

2. Kanzaki, *Kyōto ni okeru nihongashi*, 286.

3. Shunshō's government exhibition entries of 1915, 1922, and 1929 are illustrated respectively in Nittenshi Hensan Iinkai, *Nittenshi 4, Buntenhen 4* (Tokyo, 1981), 91; *Nittenshi 6, Teitenhen 1* (1982), 421; and *Nittenshi 9, Teitenhen 4* (1983), 114.

4. A year after Shunkyo's death, *Gasei Yamamoto Shunkyo to Kyōto gadan* (Kyoto: Toshi to Geijutsusha, 1934) was published as a tribute to the artist. It included a long list of Shunkyo's pupils who were still active when he died. Shunshō's name does not appear in the list.

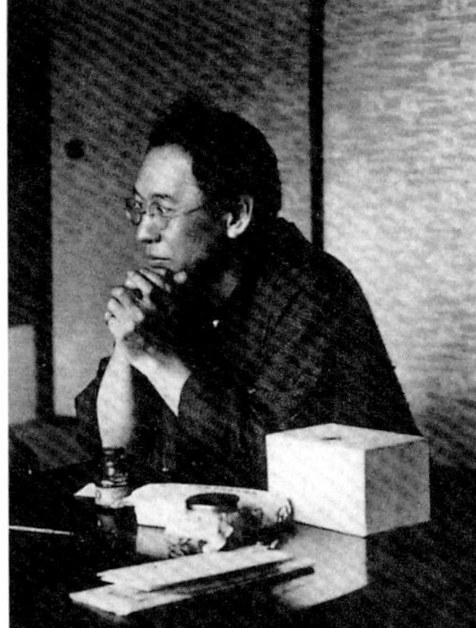

Kondō Kōichiro 近藤浩一路 1884–1962

Kondō Kōichiro's artistic career defies easy categorization. Originally trained in Western-style oil painting, he worked as a successful cartoonist-illustrator, explored *nihonga* techniques, and eventually achieved fame as an innovative ink painter. Today, he is best known for pushing the medium of ink further than anyone else in order to portray air and light effects in his objective yet lyrical paintings.

Kōichiro was born in a small town in southern Yamanashi. He lost his father when he was four and was brought up by his grandfather, a local statesman involved with the economic and cultural development of the region.[1] Complying with his family's wish, Kōichiro moved to Tokyo in 1902 to pursue medical studies but found himself drawn to arts and literature. In 1904 he gathered the courage to show his watercolors to Wada Eisaku 和田英作 (1874–1959), a respected *yōga* painter. Astonished by the quality of Kōichiro's work, Wada accepted him on the spot as his live-in pupil.[2] In 1905 Kōichiro enrolled in the Western-style oil painting division at the Tokyo School of Fine Arts (Tōkyō Bijitsu Gakkō) and graduated five years later. Among the students he encountered there were Fujita Tsuguji 藤田嗣治 (1886–1968) and Okamoto Ippei 岡本一平 (1886–1948), with whom he formed lifelong friendships. At the Tokyo School of Fine Arts Kōichiro also began studying haiku under Watanabe Suiha 渡辺水巴 and later published his poems under the name Shichō 柿腸.

Kōichiro enjoyed an auspicious start as a young artist: while still a student, he showed his works at the 1907 exhibition of the White Horse Society (Hakubakai 白馬会), a premier *yōga* institution, and in 1910, the year of his graduation, his entry was accepted at the Bunten 文展, a prestigious government exhibition. Subsequently, he held a series of jobs, among them, painting a ceiling and a wall at the Imperial Theater in Tokyo with Wada, and teaching at a women's art school in Kyoto, where he met his future wife. Kōichiro participated in the Bunten for the last time as a *yōga* artist in 1913.

Kōichiro took a job as a cartoonist for a newspaper company in 1915. With his friend Ippei, who was also a cartoonist, Kōichiro organized exhibitions for the Tokyo Cartoonist Group (Tokyo Mangakai 東京漫画会) between 1916 and 1921. During this period, Kōichiro switched to *nihonga* and also participated in the activities of two groups (Sekiyōkai 赤甕会 and Sangokai 珊瑚会), whose artists, like Kōichiro, worked in *nihonga* despite their *yōga* training.

In 1919 Kōichiro's three entries were accepted at the Reestablished Japan Art Institute (Saikō Nihon Bijutsuin 再興日本美術院) exhibition, and he became a member of the institute two years later. Throughout this time, he worked in both bright *nihonga* colors and ink. His ink handscroll, *Six Views of Cormorant Fishing* (Ukai rokudai 鵜飼六題), shown at the 1923 Japan Art Institute exhibition, established him as a premier modern ink painter. A set of six handscrolls, each nearly three meters in length, this ambitious work synthesized bold ink brushwork, a quirky figural style, and a Western sense of light to evoke the exotic ambience of a night scene.

When the Kantō earthquake of 1923 destroyed Kōichiro's house in Tokyo, he moved his family to Kyoto, his wife's hometown, and opened the private Ink Heart School (Bokushinsha 墨心舎) but continued to participate in the Japan Art Institute exhibitions. From the mid-1920s into the early 1930s, he explored the ink medium and formats in works varying from those strongly influenced by the exuberant brush style of Tomioka Tessai 富岡鉄斎 (1836–1924) to others more grounded in Western pictorial space and perspective.[3] Although Kōichiro would increasingly focus on Western-influenced ink painting, the *nanga* approach, with its loose brushwork and traditional East Asian pictorial space, would not completely disappear from his oeuvre.

Tired of the politics within the Japan Art Institute, Kōichiro withdrew from the organization in 1936. Although he returned to Tokyo, he concentrated on intimate one-person exhibitions, showing as few as six (1939 Nihonbashi Takashimaya exhibition) and never more than twenty-five works.[4] By this time he had achieved a unique style that employed ink brushwork as a realist tool to portray light, air, and the changing weather and seasons. He returned to the government exhibition in 1954 and continued to participate until 1961, one year before his death. MM

BIBLIOGRAPHY

Kikuya Yoshio 菊屋吉生. "Sangokai ronkō" 珊瑚会論考. *Bijutsu kenkyū* 美術研究, no. 377 (February 2003): 30–58.

Kōichiro sakuhinshū 浩一路作品集. Kyoto: Yamada Naosaburō 山田直三郎 (Unsōdō), 1925.

Komatsu Kiyoshi 小松清. "Kondō Kōichiro." *Geijutsu shinchō* 芸術新潮 4, no. 11 (November 1953): 207–14.

Kumamoto Kenjirō 隅元謙次郎. "Kondō Kōichiro no sakuhin," *Hōshun* 萌春, no. 42 (March 1957): 13–20.

Morioka, Michiyo, and Paul Berry. *Modern Masters of Kyoto: The Transformation of Japanese Painting Traditions, Nihonga from the Griffith and Patricia Way Collection.* Exh. cat. Seattle: Seattle Art Museum, 1999.

Noji Kōichiro 野地耕一郎 and Hirabayashi Akira 平林彰, eds. *Hikari no suibokuga: Kondō Kōichiro no zenbō* 光の水墨画：近藤浩一路の全貌. Exh. cat. Tokyo: Yomiuri Shinbun Tokyo Honsha and Bijutsukan Renraku Kyōgikai 読売新聞東京本社・美術館連絡協議会, 2006.

Sano Bijutsukan 佐野美術館. *Bokusai no shijin: Kondō Kōichiro* 墨彩の詩人：近藤浩一路. Exh. cat. Mishima, 2002.

Tokubi Daiyōdo 徳美大容堂. "Kōichiro kun no koto" 浩一路君のこと. *Daimai bijutsu* 大毎美術 5, no. 11 (November 1926): 42–43.

Yamanashi Kenritsu Bijutsukan and Kanagawa Kenritsu Kindai Bijutsukan 山梨県立美術館・神奈川県立近代美術館. *Kondō Kōichiro ten.* Exh. cat. Kōfu: Yamanashi Kenritsu Bijutsukan, 1979.

Yamatane Bijutsukan 山種美術館. *Kindai no nanga—Yūshin no sekai: Hyakusui・Hōan・Tsunetomo・Kōichiro* 近代の南画—遊心の世界：百穂・放菴・恒友・浩一路. Exh. cat. Tokyo, 1993.

NOTES

1. Kawauchi Eriko, "Kondō Kōichiro—Sumi tono taiwa," in Sano Bijutsukan, *Bokusai no shijin,* 88.

2. Hirabayashi Akira, "Kondō Kōichiro no gagyō—Inten jidai o chūshin ni," in Noji and Hirabayashi, *Hikari no suibokuga,* 12.

3. In 1920 Kōichiro listed Tessai as his favorite artist; see Kondō Kōichiro, "Watashi no seikatsu," *Chūō bijutsu* 6, no. 9 (September 1920): 107. *Kōichiro sakuhin-shū,* published in Kyoto in 1925, includes many hanging scrolls in a pure literati mode, displaying expressive brushwork and the artist's poetic inscriptions in Chinese characters. See also his Tessai-inspired works published in "Keisen, Kōichiro gahaku shinsakuhin," *Daimai bijutsu* 5, no. 9 (September 1926): 7–8.

4. For an insightful critique of the 1939 exhibition, see Kanzaki Ken'ichi, "Kondō Kōichiro shi dai gokai koten," *Tōei* 15, no. 12 (December 1939): 36–37.

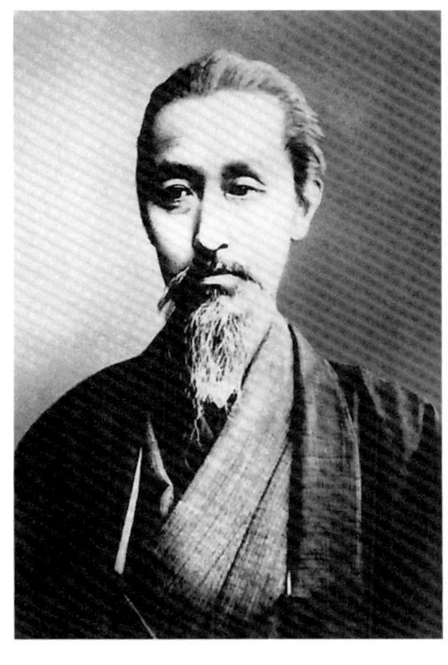

Kōno Bairei
幸野楳嶺 1844–1895

A young, impoverished artist at the time of the Meiji Restoration, Kōno Bairei emerged as a leading Kyoto painter and teacher during the 1880s. His contribution to the advancement of the Kyoto art world is immeasurable. Convinced that art could help perfect culture and aid national prosperity, Bairei tirelessly promoted a modern system of art education that would nurture not only painters but also artisans working in the traditional craft industries of Kyoto. The Kyoto Prefecture Painting School (Kyōto-fu Gagakkō 京都府画学校), which he helped establish in 1880, developed into the most important art institution in Kyoto and continues in operation today as the Kyoto City University of Arts (Kyōto Shiritsu Geijutsu Daigaku 京都市立芸術大学).[1]

Bairei, the son of a Kyoto moneylender, became a pupil of Nakajima Raishō 中島来章 (1796–1871), a Maruyama-school artist, at age eight. Although established as a professional painter in 1867, he was financially destitute during the early years of his career. With Raishō's permission, Bairei began studying in 1871 with Shiokawa Bunrin 塩川文麟 (1801–1877), a renowned Shijō artist.[2] Soon after, in 1873, both Bairei and Bunrin were among fifty traditional-style painters selected to showcase their talent in a painting demonstration at the second Kyoto Exposition (*Kyōto hakurankai* 京都博覧会). Like many Kyoto artists at that time, Bairei wanted to expand his artistic learning beyond the foundation provided by the *shasei*-based Maruyama and Shijō schools. Thus, while learning Chinese literature from Kamiyama Hōyō 神山鳳陽 (dates unknown), Bairei sought advice and instruction from such noted literati painters as Maeda Chōdō 前田暢堂 (1817–1878), Nakanishi Kōseki 中西耕石 (1804–1884), Yamanaka Shinten'ō 山中信天翁 (1822–1885), and Ema Tenkō 江馬天江 (1825–1901).[3]

During the late 1870s, Bairei's career took an upward turn. He began winning awards at numerous exhibitions, including the Kyoto Exposition and the Domestic Industrial Exposition (*Naikoku kangyō hakurankai* 内国勧業博覧会). Furthermore, Bunrin's introduction brought the patronage of the Higashi Honganji temple, whose head priest, Ōtani Kōshō 大谷光勝 (1817–1894), had once studied painting under Matsumura Keibun 松村景文 (1779–1843).[4] Besides commissioning paintings, Kōshō took Bairei to Kyushu in 1877 and to the Tokyo area in 1885, and Bairei sketched the various locales they visited.[5] Upon Bunrin's death, Bairei assumed leadership of the Shijō school, and many promising pupils flocked to his studio. Bairei had more than sixty students in 1883,[6] by which time his four greatest pupils, Kikuchi Hōbun 菊池芳文 (1862–1918), Takeuchi Seihō 竹内栖鳳 (1864–1942), Taniguchi Kōkyō 谷口香嶠 (1864–1915), and Tsuji Kakō 都路華香 (1870–1931), who would lead Kyoto *nihonga* into the twentieth century, had all entered the studio. Although a compassionate teacher, Bairei was stern and short-tempered, and even his four gifted pupils were temporarily expelled on his orders from time to time.[7]

In 1878, Bairei and Mochizuki Gyokusen 望月玉泉 (1834–1913) submitted a proposal for the establishment of a painting school, cosigned by Kubota Beisen 久保田米僊 (1852–1906) and Kose Shōseki 巨勢小石 (1843–1919), to the governor of Kyoto prefecture. The Kyoto Prefecture Painting School was founded two years later, with Tanomura Chokunyū 田能村直入 (1814–1907) as its first director (Chokunyū had been the first to petition for the school). Bairei was appointed with Suzuki Hyakunen (1825–1891) to head the Northern division of the school, but an existing rivalry between the men caused Hyakunen to withdraw afer only a month. The continuing conflict with the Suzuki school compelled Barei to leave the school a year later, and Hyakunen's son Shōnen (1848–1918) took over the position. In 1888 Bairei returned to the school, but a drastic restructuring he proposed caused such controversy that he left again two years later. Despite factional discord and frequent restructuring in its early history, the Kyoto Prefecture Painting School became the most significant educational institution for the city's artists.

In 1886 Bairei collaborated with his friend Kubota Beisen and personally financed the establishment of the Kyoto Young Painters Study Group (Kyōto Seinen Kaiga Kenkyūkai 京都青年絵画研究会). By providing opportunities for open competition, this interschool group marked the first serious attempt to promote young Kyoto artists based on ability rather than the prestige of their lineage. The group's first exhibition was successful, but Bairei's zealotry so offended others involved that the group immediately dissolved. In the unpleasant aftermath, Bairei temporarily relocated to Nagoya.[8] During the 1880s he served as a judge at various painting venues such as the Domestic Competitive Painting Exhibition (*Naikoku kaiga kyōshinkai* 内国絵画共進会) and other shows held in Osaka, Nagoya, and Ishikawa.

In 1890 Bairei and Beisen formed the Kyoto Art Association (Kyōto Bijutsu Kyōkai 京都美術協会), which published *Kyōto bijutsu kyokai zasshi*, one of the earliest art journals in the city, and they launched the Exhibition of New and Old Art (*Shinko bijutsuhin tenrankai* 新古美術品展覧会) in 1895, the first important competitive painting exhibition in Kyoto. It offered a gateway to success for Kyoto artists well into the 1910s. That same year Bairei traveled to Tokyo to participate as a member of the jury panel for the third Domestic Industrial Exhibition. Finding himself trapped in a power struggle between traditional and modernizing factions, however, he abruptly returned to Kyoto. When younger artists demanded an explanation for his action, Bairei became so disillusioned that he announced his retirement from teaching the following year.

But Bairei continued to paint, producing his famous *Farmhouse in Autumn* (Shūjitsu denka zu 秋日田家図), subtitled *Life of Young Ninomiya Sontoku* (Ninomiya Sontoku yōji zu 二宮尊徳幼時図), commissioned by the Japanese government for the 1893 World's Columbian Exposition in Chicago. Sontoku (1787–1856), Bairei's subject, was a respected economist, with expertise in agrarian reform and development, who had overcome his humble origins through hard work and perseverance. In the late Meiji period, the government promoted him as the embodiment of an ideal Japanese citizen, erecting statues of him and lauding his accomplishments in school textbooks, and Tomioka Tessai (1836–1924) is believed to have recommended Sontoku as a subject to Bairei.[9] The monumental painting, featuring young Sontoku returning home with a load of firewood on his back while reading a book, demonstrates an ambitious synthesis of panoramic landscape with detailed narrative elements. This didactic approach is only one aspect of Bairei's oeuvre. He worked in diverse styles, some witty and lighthearted, relating to his haiku practice; others are wistful expressions in lyrical brushwork.[10]

A man of integrity and high idealism, Bairei did not hesitate to openly criticize those who did not agree with him, causing many controversies. Nonetheless, he and his colleagues pushed the Kyoto painting circle to modernize, and he achieved spectacular success as a teacher, nurturing many prominent artists who would carry on his legacy. Bairei's contribution was fully recognized when he was designated an Imperial Household Artist (*teishitsu gigeiin* 帝室技芸員) in 1893. Although his health was in decline, he dutifully completed painting commissions for the Higashi Honganji temple during the fall and winter of 1894, shortly before his death. MM

BIBLIOGRAPHY

"Geien Sōwa: Teishitsu gigeiin Kōno Bairei kun rireki" 藝苑叢話: 帝室技藝員幸野梅嶺君履歴. *Kyōto bijutsu kyōkai zasshi* 京都美術協会雑誌, no. 19 (December 1893): 18–22.

Kanzaki Bansokei 神崎蠻楚桂. "Kōno Bairei no shōgai: Kare no seikatsu—kare to Kyōto gadan, ichi ~ jū" 幸野楳嶺の生涯：彼の生活—彼と京都画壇、一～十. *Daimai bijutsu* 大毎美術 7, no. 10 (October 1928); 7, no. 12 (December 1928); 8, no. 1 (January 1929); 8, no. 4 (April 1929); 8, no. 6 (June 1929); 8, no. 8 (August 1929).

Kanzaki Ken'ichi 神崎憲一. *Kyōto ni okeru nihongashi* 京都に於ける日本画史. Kyoto: Kyōto Seihan Insatsusha 京都精版印刷社, 1929.

Kōno Toyokazu 幸野豊一, ed. *Kōno Bairei: Botsugo hyakunen kinen shuppan* 幸野楳嶺：没後百年記念出版. 2 vols. Kyoto: Unsōdō 芸艸堂, 1995.

Kyōtoshi Bijutsukan 京都市美術館. *Kyōto gadan: Edo matsu Meiji no gajin tachi* 京都 画壇江戸末・明治の画人たち. Kyoto: Ātosha アート社, 1977.

———. *Sansui kara fūkei e, Kyōto nihonga no nagare: Bunrin, Bairei, Seihō* 山水から風景へ、京都日本画の流れ：文麟、楳嶺、栖鳳. Exh. cat. Kyoto, 1995.

Misumi Masahiro 三澄正博. "Kōno Bairei no gyōseki ni tsuite" 幸野楳嶺の業蹟について. *Bijutsu kenkyū* 美術研究, no. 62 (February 1937): 16–25.

Morioka, Michiyo, and Paul Berry. *Modern Masters of Kyoto: The Transformation of Japanese Painting Traditions. Nihonga from the Griffith and Patricia Way Collection.* Exh. cat. Seattle: Seattle Art Museum, 1999.

Shiga Kenritsu Kindai Bijutsukan 滋賀県立近代美術館 and Kyōto Shinbunsha 京都新聞社. *Kyōto gadan kyoshō no keifu・Kōno Bairei to sono ryūha* 京都画壇巨匠の系譜・幸野楳嶺とその流派. Exh. cat. Ōtsu: Shiga Kenritsu Kindai Bijutsukan and Kyōto Shinbunsha, 1990.

NOTES

1. The most complete document on the history of the school is Kyōto Shiritsu Geijutsu Daigaku Hyakunenshi Henshū Iinkai, *Hyakunenshi: Kyōto Shiritsu Geijutsu Daigaku* (Kyoto, 1981).

2. Bairei's decision to study with Bunrin may not have been based entirely on artistic reasons. Bairei married Raishō's daughter around 1870 but divorced her shortly thereafter. This situation may have compelled him to leave Raishō's tutelage; see Kanzaki Bansokei, "Kōno Bairei no shōgai," 12–13.

3. "Geien Sōwa," 19.

4. "Kōno Bairei-ō den," *Kaiga sōshi*, no. 100 (May 1895): 7.

5. "Geien Sōwa," 19.

6. Kanzaki Ken'ichi, *Kyōto ni okeru nihongashi*, 66.

7. One such incident occurred in 1890, when Bairei entrusted Hōbun, Seihō, Kōkyō, and Kakō with evaluating his pupils' submissions to his private school (*juku*) exhibition. When the four reported their decision, Bairei disagreed

and demanded they rescind it. They stood their ground, and Bairei expelled them. Several months later, the priest of Kitano Shrine intervened and won their reinstatement; see Kanzaki Bansokei, "Kōno Bairei no shōgai," 50–52.

8. Misumi, "Kōno Bairei no gyōseki ni tsuite," 20. For a slightly different view, see Kanzaki Bansokei, "Kōno Bairei no shōgai," 22–23.

9. Asano Nagatake, Kobayashi Yukio, and Hosokawa Goryū, comps., *Genshoku Meiji hyakunen bijutsukan* (Tokyo: Asahi Shinbunsha, 1967), 18.

10. See Harada Heisaku's discussion of Bairei's art in Kyōtoshi Bijutsukan, *Kyōto Gadan*, 240–43.

Kushiro Unsen 釧雲泉 1759–1811

Unsen was born in the town of Shimabara 島原 at the base of Mount Unsen 雲仙 in Nagasaki prefecture. Taking *un* 雲 from the mountain's name and *sen* 泉 from the *onsen* 温泉, or hot springs, of his hometown, he created an artist's name that sounds the same as the name of the volcanic peak. It is thought that Unsen's family once had samurai status, yet for some reason Unsen's father took his son to Nagasaki, where he was able to study Chinese language and painting with immigrant merchants.[1] Unsen left Nagasaki to travel throughout much of Japan on a journey that would last for the rest of his life. Although his early itinerary remains unclear, inscriptions on paintings indicate that he was in the Okayama region from 1791 to 1793. The paintings from this period are those of a fully matured painter and some of his finest, with a certain casual sophistication of brushwork. The assurance of these works demonstrates that Unsen must have been painting for many years already, although dated works from earlier times have yet to be published. His Okayama paintings are scarce compared to those made later in Kyoto, Edo, and Niigata.

Documentation of his career is slim, composed of Kameda Bōsai's 亀田鵬齋 (1752–1826) 1814 eulogy, selected letters, and scattered references to him in the writings of other literati he encountered during his travels.[2] Although it is not known when he moved to the Osaka/Kyoto area, the noted Confucian scholar and amateur painter Minagawa Kien 皆川淇園 (1734–1807) dedicated a calligraphy to him in 1798, which suggests that Unsen had arrived in Kyoto by that time.[3] Unsen is believed to have associated with the most prominent artists of the time, including Kimura Kenkadō 木村蒹葭堂 (1736–1802), Okada Beisanjin 岡田米山人 (1742–1820), Totoki Baigai 十時梅厓 (1749?–1804), among many others. Although this was a time of ferment in literati circles, only a few dated works by Unsen are known from his stay in the Kansai area.[4]

Unsen is believed to have moved by 1802 to the Edo area, where he associated with the artists and calligraphers around Tani Bunchō 谷文晁 (1763–1840). He stayed in Edo until 1806, and it is notable that his paintings from this period do not reveal Bunchō's influence, despite this artist's dominant impact on most literati painters in the area. An unusual record of Unsen is found in the writings of the noted economist and amateur painter Kaiho Seiryō 海保青陵 (1755–1817), who mentioned meeting Unsen in his residence, near the back door of Yushima Tenjin 湯島天神, the Michizane shrine in Edo. Seiryō noted Unsen's skill in creating Chinese-style landscape paintings and his interesting personality, labeling him a true *rōnin* 浪人, a wandering samurai unattached to a domain.[5]

Unsen left Edo in 1806 with the noted calligrapher and painter of bamboo Ōkubo Shibutsu 大窪詩佛 (1766–1837) for a trip to northern Japan. Eventually Shibutsu returned to Edo, but Unsen stayed on, settling in the village of Izumozaki, the same area where the famous calligrapher Ryōkan 良寛 (1757–1831) lived. Bōsai later traveled from Edo to visit them both. Unsen died at a time when he seems to have been contemplating a return to Edo.

Unsen's travels distributed his paintings widely across Japan; he seems to have sold paintings to local patrons wherever he went. His landscapes show an unusually clear grasp of Chinese literati painting. The comparative freedom of his early Okayama works gradually gave way to a more orthodox focus on reserved brushwork and stable compositions, yet his remarkable personality and grasp of literati painting impressed people everywhere he went. PB

BIBLIOGRAPHY

Adams, Celeste, and Paul Berry. *Heart Mountains and Human Ways.* Houston: Museum of Fine Arts, 1983.

Mori Senzō 森銑三. "Kushiro Unsen zakki" 釧雲泉雑記. 1938. Reprint. Vol. 4, *Mori Senzō chosakushū* 森銑三著作集. Tokyo: Chūō Kōronsha 中央公論社, 1971.

Ōmura Seigai 大村西崖, ed., *Unsen ibokushū* 雲泉遺墨集. Osaka: Hōko Shoin 仿古書院, 1923.

NOTES

1. Ōmura, *Unsen ibokushū*, unpaginated. Unsen's father may have died while they were in Nagasaki.

2. Using these sources Mori Senzō pieced together some aspects of Unsen's career in his article "Kushiro Unsen zakki," first published in 1938. Although Unsen's paintings have appeared in a variety of exhibitions, there has yet to be a serious attempt to study his career despite the general recognition of his importance.

3. Illustrated as one of the frontispieces in Ōmura, *Unsen ibokushū*.

4. The best source is Ōmura's *Unsen ibokushū*, which includes many dated works among the fifty-some paintings illustrated there.

5. Seiryō's comments are quoted in Mori, "Kushiro Unsen zakki," 250–51.

Kuwayama Gyokushū 桑山玉洲 1746–1799

The Kuwayama family operated cargo boats and a money exchange in the town of Wakaura in Wakayama, where Gyokushū was born. The origin of his interest in painting is unknown, but he wrote about some aspects of his artistic development in a 1790 manuscript (*Gyokushū gashu* 玉洲畫趣).[1] In this account he describes his acquaintance with major literati painters such as Ike Taiga 池大雅 (1723–1776), Kō Fuyō 高芙蓉 (1722–1784), and Kimura Kenkadō 木村蒹葭堂 (1736–1802). In addition to meeting the key literati of western Japan, Gyokushū repeatedly traveled to Edo in the late 1760s and early 1770s and met many painters there.[2] The usual pattern would be for a young artist to become the disciple of a noted senior figure, yet Gyokushū decided to train himself by studying different styles.

It is likely that Gyokushū became aware of Nagasaki-style paintings during his visits to Edo, as themes and approaches from that southern port were very popular in the capital in the late eighteenth century. Some of his first datable paintings from the early 1770s are strongly colored depictions of horses, flowers, and fish. He even painted an advancing tiger whose dramatic curvilinear pose had been popularized by Yūhi 熊斐 (1712–1772) and his disciples, and eventually became an iconic composition in Nagasaki painting.[3] Sprinkled among these works were paintings based on Chinese landscapes and illustrations from woodblock books.

The majority of Gyokushū's works are undated, and it is difficult to ascertain when in the late 1770s he turned toward landscape painting in a more purely literati vein. Ink landscapes with light colors in vertical compositions replaced the brightly colored, Nagasaki-influenced themes. Although he continued to paint such reserved landscapes until the end of his life, in the 1790s he began to employ a remarkable style typified by strong, smooth outlines for trees and hills whose interiors he developed through layers of ink and color washes rather than the typical literati reliance on stringy texture strokes (*shun* 皴). The atmosphere created by these skillfully applied transparent color washes makes the landscapes of Gyokushū's last years dramatically different from the paintings of his contemporaries.

In addition to this new landscape style, Gyokushū developed an interest in so-called true-view paintings (*shinkeizu* 真景圖).[4] A Japanese version of a Chinese practice, true-view paintings were intended to display the real character of actual places, with the understanding that "real" meant an aestheticized, intuitive perception rather than a literal Western-style depiction. Gyokushū made handscrolls, albums, scrolls, and even a screen with this approach.[5]

Gyokushū also made a significant contribution as a writer on painting. The most influential of his works was *Comments on Painting* (Kaiji higen 絵事鄙言). Published by Kenkadō shortly after Gyokushū's death, it is regarded as Japan's first scholarly treatise on literati painting. This and several other unpublished treatises add to the impressive accomplishments of this independent artist during his comparatively brief career. PB

BIBLIOGRAPHY

Kondō Takashi 近藤壮, ed., *Tokubetsu ten–Kuwayama Gyokushū* 特別展–桑山玉洲. Wakayama: Wakayama Shiritsu Hakubutsukan 和歌山市立博物館, 2006.

Matsushita Hidemaro 松下英麿. *Ike Taiga* 池大雅. Tokyo: Shunjūsha 春秋社, 1967.

———. *Kuwayama Gyokushū* 桑山玉洲. Tokyo: Chūō Kōronsha, 1959.

Tatsumi Mitsuru 辰巳充, ed. *Kuwayama Gyokushū ten* 桑山玉洲展. Wakayama Prefecture: Tanabe Shiritsu Bijutsukan 田辺市立美術館, 2001.

Wylie, Hugh. "Nanga Painting Treatises of Nineteenth-Century Japan: Translations, Commentary, and Analysis." PhD diss., University of Kansas, 1991.

NOTES

1. The full text is provided in an appendix to Kondō, *Tokubetsu ten–Kuwayama Gyokushū*, 100–103. This catalogue also introduces a painting treatise by Gyokushū newly discovered on the inner surface of the folded pages in one of his bound manuscripts. A portion of the contents is reproduced on p. 104. The full text is being prepared for publication.

2. The chronology in Tatsumi, *Kuwayama Gyokushū ten*, mentions Gyokushū's second visit to Edo as occurring in the spring of 1771 (p. 95).

3. See illustration in ibid., pl. 15.

4. See Melinda Takeuchi, *Taiga's True Views: The Language of Landscape Painting in Eighteenth-Century Japan* (Stanford: Stanford University Press, 1994).

5. See the examples illustrated in Kondō, *Tokubetsu ten–Kuwayama Gyokushū*, 37–52.

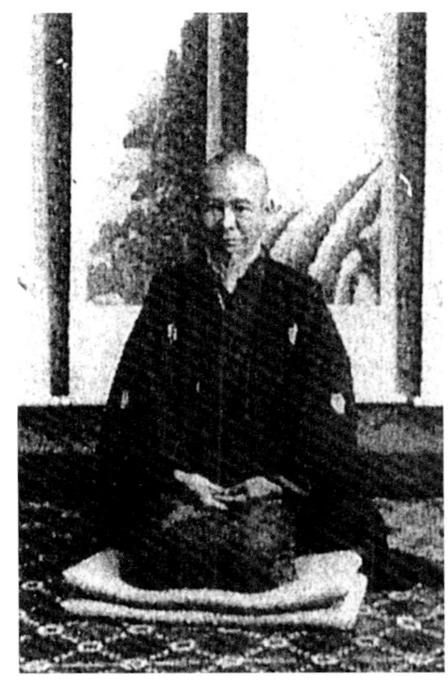

Maeda Mokuhō
前田黙鳳 1853–1918

Mokuhō was the son of Maeda Chūsaku 前田忠作, a retainer of the Tatsuno 龍野 domain in Hyōgo prefecture. In 1873 he took a job in Tokyo as a clerk at the Hakubunkan 博文館 bookstore. By 1882 Mokuhō was able to open his own bookstore, which published classic reference books on Chinese literature and culture such as the 1720 *Peiwen yunfu* 佩文韻府, an index to Chinese expressions found in literary texts.[1] His enthusiasm for publishing these works led him to make repeated brief trips to China, but insufficient sales forced him to close the store in 1888. Freed from the responsibilities of publishing, in 1901 Mokuhō began traveling in China as he researched calligraphy.[2] When he returned to Japan in 1908, he formed Kenpitsukai 健筆会, which supported the study of early Chinese calligraphy and the exhibition of contemporary works inspired by stone stele inscriptions from the Six Dynasties period (220–589). The members of the group included such prominent calligraphers as Nakamura Fusetsu 中村不折 (1866–1943), Kawahigashi Hekigotō 河東碧梧桐 (1873–1937), and Nomura Soken 野村素軒 (1842–1927). Fusetsu formed a related group, Ryūminkai 龍眠会, with largely the same membership and intentions in 1913.[3]

Mokuhō created a number of calligraphy style dictionaries in the last several decades of his life, and these remained in print in Japan and China until the 1970s. His most interesting publication was the 1910 *Calligraphy and Painting Research Method* (Shoga kenkyūhō), which laid out his ideas on the relationship between calligraphy and painting. Mokuhō asserted that painting was fundamentally rooted in the brushstrokes used in calligraphy. In his book he divided his text into sections based on the different modes of calligraphy and compared illustrations of the brushwork in characters and in simple elements of painting. Although this was an ancient idea, the appreciation of calligraphy as artwork was coming under criticism from painters trained in Western modes of realism, and this work seems to have been Mokuhō's defense of the traditional connection between the two.

Mokuhō created many calligraphies in cursive, clerical, and archaic styles. In addition, he made many paintings on themes including flowers, ancient bronzes, and landscapes. Among his landscapes, a number show bizarre compositions of cliffs.[4] The bold, thick outlines he used in his paintings are clearly related to the brushwork in his calligraphy. Other members of Kenpitsukai and Ryūminkai shared his enthusiasm for studying calligraphy, and collectively they represented a movement that aimed to create new art inspired by ancient forms. PB

BIBLIOGRAPHY

Campbell, Robert ロバート・キャンベル. "Tōkyō Hōbunkan no saigetsu" 東京鳳文館の歳月. Parts 1 and 2. *Edo bungaku* 江戸文学., nos. 15 and 16 (May and October 1996).

Dai Nihon Jinmei Jisho Kankō Kai大日本人名辭書刊行会. *Dai Nihon jinmei jisho* 大日本人名辭書, vol. 4. 1937. Reprint. Tokyo: Kōdansha 講談社, 1980.

Ishikawa Kyūyō 石川九楊. "Rittaiha fū no sho no tanjō Maeda Mokuhō 'shigon ku'" 立体派風の書の誕生前田黙鳳「四言句」. *Sumi* 墨 (November/December 2000): 61–64.

Itō Takao 伊藤隆夫. "Maeda Mokuhō no ichidanmen shodō zasshi *Shokan* no meiun" 前田黙鳳の一断面—書道雑誌『書鑑』の命運」. *Sumi* 墨 no. 77 (1988).

Maeda En 前田圓. *Shoga kenkyūhō* 書畫研究法. 2 vols. Tokyo: Kōkadō 光華堂, 1910.

———. *Shoketsu* 書訣. Tokyo: Saitō Shobō 西東書房, 1912.

———. *Mokuhō bokugi* 黙鳳墨戲. Tokyo: Tōa Geijutsusha 東亜芸術社, 1915.

"Maeda Mokuhō sensei o kokusu" 前田黙鳳先生を哭す. *Shosei* 書勢 (December 1918).

Morita Shiryū 森田子龍, ed. "Tokushū Ryūminkai" 特集龍眠会. *Bokubi* 墨美, no. 159 (June 1966).

Shimonaka Kunihiko 下中邦彦, ed. *Shodō zenshū* 書道全集, vol. 25. Tokyo: Heibonsha 平凡社, 1965–68.

NOTES

1. The main source of biographical information on Mokuhō remains the remembrance published in 1918 shortly after his death, "Maeda Mokuhō sensei o kokusu." Mokuhō's significant career as a publisher is discussed in Robert Campbell's detailed article, "Tōkyō Hōbunkan no saigetsu."

2. Dai Nihon Jinmei Jisho Kankō Kai, *Dai Nihon jinmei jisho*, vol. 4, 2526.

3. See the biographical entry on Kawahigashi Hekigotō in this catalogue for more information on this group.

4. See the landscapes in Paul Berry and Yokoya Kenichirō, *Unexplored Avenues of Japanese Painting* (Ōtsu: Ōtsu Shiritsu Rekishi Hakubutsukan; Seattle: University of Washington Press, 2002), plate 58 and p. 137.

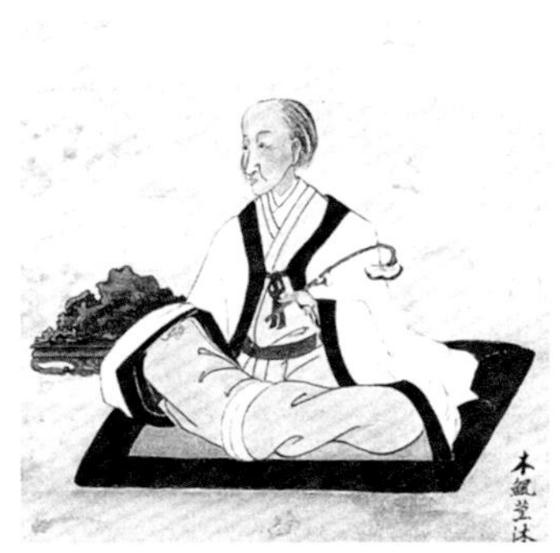

Masuyama Sessai 増山雪斎 1754–1820

Sessai was the eldest son of Masuyama Masayasu 増山正贇 (1726–1776), the fourth-generation daimyo of the Nagashima domain. Located on the delta formed where three rivers enter the ocean at the border between present-day Mie and Aichi prefectures, this small domain of moderate wealth was often threatened by flooding. But it prospered due to an arrangement with Osaka whereby the daimyo was often appointed director of a supplementary police force. The yearly stipend paid to the domain was doubled if a year passed without any significant trouble in the district.[1] This position not only stabilized the *han* finances; it gave the Nagashima daimyo a prominent social position in Osaka. When Masakata 正賢 (Sessai's proper name) became the fifth Masuyama daimyo, this important connection allowed him to develop lasting relationships with the prominent literati Kimura Kenkadō 木村蒹葭堂 (1736[1749]–1802), Totoki Baigai 十時梅厓 (1732–1804), and calligrapher Chō Tōsai 趙陶齋 (1713–1786).

When Kenkadō fell afoul of a revision in the sake production code, Sessai invited him to stay at Nagashima for two years and then helped him restore his fortune in Osaka through the sale of writing implements. This new venture led to Kenkadō's greatest prominence as the patron of a literati salon in Osaka. Sessai shared an interest in literati pursuits with Baigai and appointed him a Confucian scholar at the school newly established for the Nagashima domain in 1784. Tōsai, the son of a Nanjing merchant and a courtesan from the Maruyama district in Nagasaki, became an Ōbaku monk in 1727 while a teenager and eventually lived at the sect headquarters, Manpukuji, near Kyoto. In 1750 he left the order and began a career as a calligrapher and seal carver. Sessai and Baigai were among the many followers of his style of calligraphy.

Sessai's interest in painting developed in several directions. In bird-and-flower painting, he was strongly influenced by trends initiated by immigrant Chinese painters and their Japanese followers. Although these colorful paintings with dramatic compositions of peacocks and other appealing birds were popular across Japan, he may have been exposed to such works during his frequent visits to Edo, where Nagasaki trends were especially in vogue. Sessai's many bird-and-flower paintings, while not following any specific Chinese artist, have compositions similar to those popular in Nagasaki.

Landscapes by Sessai are reserved compared to the flamboyance of his bird-and-flower works. The restrained brushwork and stable compositions in ink and light colors seem to express his appreciation for the quiet atmosphere found in some forms of the Chinese literati tradition.

Sessai retired from his position as daimyo in 1801 and spent much of his final years in the large Nagashima-*han* residence in the Sugamo area of Edo. He amused himself with the study of insects he found in the estate's extensive gardens, producing four large albums of detailed paintings of insects sorted according to the seasons. Known as the *Chūchijō* 虫豸帖, these precise studies made from life reveal his extraordinary ability.[2] Sessai's son, Masayasu 正寧 (1785–1842), practiced his father's style of detailed colorful painting under the artist name Setsuen 雪園.[3] Sessai and Setsuen exemplify the larger pattern of scattered daimyo who became involved in literati circles in the late Edo period.

PB

BIBLIOGRAPHY

Kuwanashi Hakubutsukan 桑名市博物館. *Masuyama Sessai: Daimyō no biishiki* 増山雪斎: 大名の美意識. Kuwana, 2007.

Mie Kenritsu Bijutsukan 三重県立美術館. *Masuyama Sessai ten: Edo no fūryū saishi* 増山雪斎展: 江戸の風流才子. Tsū, 1993.

Tamamushi Satoko 玉蟲敏子, ed. *Satake Shozan Masuyama Sessai: Hakubutsu gafu* 佐竹曙山・増山雪斎: 博物画譜. Edo meisaku gajō zenshū 江戸名作画帖全集, vol. 8. Tokyo: Shinshindō Shuppan 駸々堂出版, 1995.

NOTES

1. This special situation is discussed in Kuwanashi Hakubutsukan, *Masuyama Sessai*, 34–36.

2. These four albums are in the collection of the Tokyo National Museum and are reproduced in Tamamushi, *Satake Shozan Masuyama Sessai.*

3. See the title calligraphy by Setsuen on the right scroll of a pair of paintings by Edo artists from 1831 to 1832 in Paul Berry and Yokoya Ken'ichi, *Unexplored Avenues of Japanese Painting* (Ōtsu: Ōtsu Shiritsu Rekishi Hakubutsukan; Seattle: University of Washington Press, 2001), plate 91. These paintings reveal Setsuen's association with the top literati of the Edo area at that time.

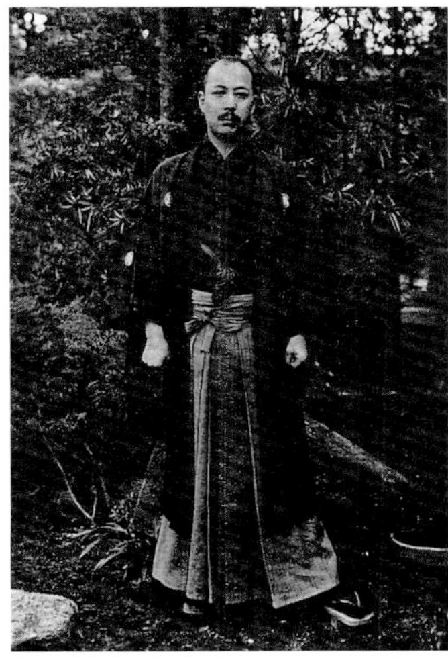

Mizuta Chikuho 水田竹圃 1883–1958

Born and raised in Osaka, Mizuta Chikuho and his colleague Yano Kyōson 矢野橋村 (1890–1965) became the foremost leaders of the twentieth-century literati movement in the Kyoto-Osaka area. Chikuho's three younger brothers—Mizuta Kōgyū 黄牛 (1897–1968), Mizuta Kenzan 硯山 (1902–1988), and Kaname Juhei 要樹平 (1906–1994)—also had successful artistic careers. Both at the government salon and at the Japan Nanga Institute (Nihon Nangain 日本南画院), Chikuho strove to achieve what he called "creative *nanga*" (*sōsakuteki nanga,* 創作的南画)[1] by actively integrating personal observations of nature with Chinese-derived literati ideals and brush formulas. The balance Chikuho sought between nature and art, the external world and one's imagination, encapsulated one of the major challenges faced by literati painters in modern Japan.

At the age of fourteen, Chikuho began his art training under Himejima Chikugai 姫島竹外 (1840–1928), a leading Osaka literati painter with a prosperous private studio. Chikuho had early public success in 1903 when his entry at the Fifth Domestic Industrial Exposition received an award. Within a decade his career had blossomed. His painting at the 1912 Bunten won an honorable mention, and more awards followed, including the highest prize, which was awarded to his landscape in 1916. Although he was a tradition-minded artist who valued the established literati aesthetic, Chikuho was part of the modernizing trend toward artistic freedom and individualism in the Taishō art world. In 1918 nine Osaka artists, including Chikuho, organized the Osaka Discussion Group (Ōsaka Sawakai 大阪茶話會) to proclaim the creative independence of painters;[2] in the same year, young Kyoto artists launched the Association for the Creation of National Painting (Kokuga Sōsaku Kyōkai 国画創作協会) in protest against the conservatism of the government exhibition. Two years later Chikuho participated in the founding of the Japan Independent Painting Group (Nihon Jiyū Gadan 日本自由画壇), which opened yet another venue for artists. Although generally considered more moderate than the Association for the Creation of National Painting, the artists of Chikuho's group experimented widely with painting styles.

Chikuho sought inspiration for his work by traveling to China frequently, often with his friend Kyōson. Dressed in Chinese clothes to better blend in, they visited sites celebrated by Chinese scholars such as West Lake 西湖 in Hangzhou 杭州, made numerous sketches of people and exotic scenery, and collected unusual seal stones.[3] Their 1915 trip included a visit to Mount Hua 華山 in Shaanxi 陝西 province, one of the five sacred mountains of China, where several important Daoist monasteries were located. *Real View of Mount Hua* (Taikazan jikkei 太華山實景), Chikuho's submission to the Bunten that year, represents the picturesque rise of a mountain ridge with small buildings perched precariously on its side. The fresh subject, based on actual observation, offered a perfect theme for Chikuho, who sought to create novel ink expressions while honoring the time-honored rules of brush method and scholarly ideals.

During the 1920s, the Japan Nanga Institute was central to Chikuho's activities. Established in 1921 in Kyoto, the institute provided a major venue for contemporary literati painters from all over Japan, including Kyōson, Ogawa Sen'yō 小川千甕 (1882–1971) and Shirakura Jihō 白倉二峰 (1906–1974). As a founding member, Chikuho participated in its annual exhibition until its closure in 1936, all the while maintaining an approach to painting often described as "calm," "refined," and "classic."[4] He resumed participation in the government exhibition in 1926 and continued his activity there until 1957, one year before his death in Kyoto. MM

BIBLIOGRAPHY

"Mizuta Chikuho gahaku shōden" 水田竹圃畫伯小傳. *Kaiga seidan* 繪畫清談 5, no. 8 (August 1917): no pagination.

"Mizuta Chikuho shi sakuga tenrankai" 水田竹圃氏作畫展覽會. *Kaiga seidan* 5, no. 8 (August 1917): 48–49.

Yui Kazuto 油井一人. *Nijū seiiki bukko nihongaka jiten* 20世紀物故日本画家事典. Tokyo: Bijutsu Nenkansha 美術年鑑社, 1998.

NOTES

1. Mizuta Chikuho, "Dai jūyonkai Nanten ni attate—Seisaku kansō," *Nanga kanshō* 4, no. 6 (June 1935): 17.

2. The group included Kyōson, Kitano Tsunetomi (1880–1947), and Shima Seien (1892–1970) and was described as a gathering of the "most earnest young Osaka artists" in "Bijutsukai kahō," *Bijutsu no Nihon* 10, no. 2 (February 1918): 34. See also "Ōaka Sawakai no kanshōka keihatsu no risō,"

originally published in *Waseda bungaku* (September 1918) and cited in Nittenshi Hensan Iinkai, *Nittenshi 5, Buntenhen 5* (Tokyo: Nitten, 1981), 494–95.

3. See Yano Kyōson, "Shina man'yū nisshi," *Kaiga seidan* 5, no. 8 (August 1917): 35–37, and "Bijutsukai kahō," *Bijutsu no Nihon* 9, no. 1 (January 1917): 35.

4. See Hagisato Sanshi, "Nihon Nangain tenrankai o miru," *Kaiga seidan* 11, no. 1 (January 1923): 22; Soeda Tatsurei, "Nangain dai gokai ten o miru," *Bi no kuni* 3, no. 2 (February 1927): 88; and Komuro Suiun, "Nangain tenrankai zensakuhin hyō—Seinen shosakka ni ataete," *Tōei* 9, no. 5 (June 1933): 5.

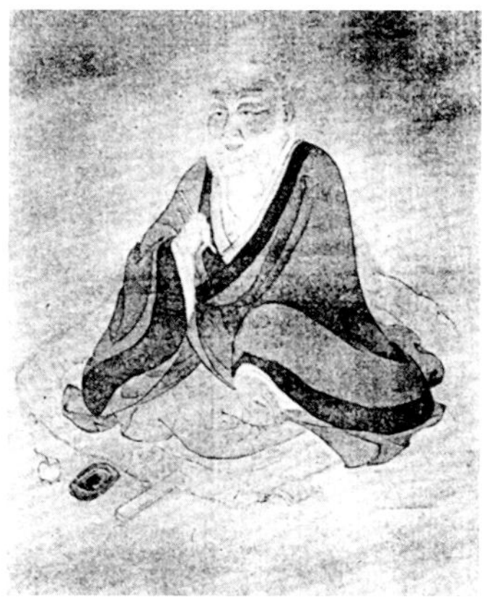

Nakabayashi Chikutō 中林竹洞 1776–1853

Nakabayashi Chikutō and Yamamoto Baiitsu 山本梅逸 (1783–1856) are considered to be among the leading exponents of Owari *nanga* 尾張南画, or literati painting in Nagoya, despite the fact that both men spent many years as artists in Kyoto.[1] They each had illustrious careers, but of the two, Chikutō remained more loyal to the Chinese-introduced scholar-painter ideal.

Born the only child of a gynecological doctor, Chikutō began studying painting with Yamada Kyūjō 山田宮常 (1747–1793) at age thirteen.[2] The following year Kyūjō introduced his young student to a wealthy Nagoya merchant, Kamiya Ten'yū 神谷天遊 (1721–1801). This collector of Chinese and Japanese paintings and calligraphies invited Chikutō to live at his house to study the works he owned. Baiitsu later joined Ten'yū's household and became Chikutō's lifelong friend. It is believed that Ten'yū created artist names for Chikutō and Baiitsu after viewing Chinese paintings with them at a temple. He picked the name Chikutō (Bamboo Grotto) because the young painter admired a work purported to be by Li Kan (1245–1320), a famous Chinese bamboo painter, and Baiitsu (Plum Elegance) because the other artist marveled at a work attributed to Wang Mian (1287–1359), best known for his ink plum paintings.[3] In 1795 Chikutō left Ten'yū's house and began earning a living as an independent painter.

Attracted by a thriving *bunjin* community and the Chinese paintings and calligraphies held in the collections of the city's temples and wealthy merchants, Chikutō first went to Kyoto with Baiitsu in 1802 and eventually settled there in 1815. He joined the literati circle around Rai Sanyō 頼山陽, the noted historian and *bunjin*, and met other literati masters of the time, including Uragami Shunkin 浦上春琴 (1779–1846), Aoki Mokubei 青木木米 (1767–1835), Nukina Kaioku 貫名海屋 (1778–1863), and Tanomura Chikuden 田能村竹田 (1777–1835). Remaining loyal to literati ideals, Chikutō studied Chinese classics and advocated a return to the brushwork traditions of Chinese masters. Furthermore, he believed in the validity of copying from nature in a personal, intuitive manner rather than taking the scientific approach introduced from the West. In a youthful painting treatise completed in 1802, Chikutō criticized the realist school founded and popularized by Maruyama Ōkyo 円山応挙 (1733–1795) and his followers, asserting that they were moving in the wrong direction.[4] He denounced their paintings as merely "crowd pleasing" and their brushwork as "lacking in bone."[5]

Chikutō's reputation emerged as early as 1813, when his name appeared in the literati painting section of *Record of Famous People of Kyoto* (Heian jinbutsu shi 平安人物誌).[6] Even after establishing a flourishing painting career, he adhered to the values of the scholar-amateur and sometimes turned down prestigious commissions. When Chikutō received an imperial order to create a painting for a new palace building in 1842, he was instructed to submit a preliminary sketch. He declined on the grounds that he could transmit his mind's inspiration only after picking up a brush to execute the actual work,[7] thus affirming the literati concept of painting as a spontaneous act of self-expression. By all accounts, Chikutō was a man of few words but was respected for his scholarly demeanor and mild temperament.[8]

In 1838 Chikutō withdrew to his studio in the outskirts of Kyoto and thereafter led an increasingly reclusive life. A prolific writer, he composed numerous treatises and instruction books on painting in his lifetime. Chikutō's son Chikkei 竹渓 (1816–1867) and daughter Seishuku 清淑 (1831–1912) also became accomplished literati painters.

MM

BIBLIOGRAPHY

Adams, Celeste, and Paul Berry. *Heart Mountains and Human Ways: Japanese Landscape and Figure Painting.* Exh. cat. Houston: Museum of Fine Arts, 1983.

Cahill, James. *Scholar Painters of Japan: The Nanga School.* Exh. cat. New York: The Asia Society, 1972.

Kanematsu Romon 兼松蘆門. *Chikutō to Baiitsu* 竹洞と梅逸. Tokyo: Gahōsha 畫報社, 1910.

Kurokawa Shūichi 黒川修一 and Kamiya Hiroshi 神谷浩. *Nihon kaigaron taisei* 日本絵画論大成, vol. 6. Tokyo: Perikansha ぺりかん社, 2000.

Nagoyashi Hakubutsukan 名古屋市博物館. *Owari no kaigashi: Nanga* 尾張の絵画史・南画. Exh. cat. Nagoya, 1981.

Rosenfield, John M., and Fumiko E. Cranston. *Extraordinary Persons: Works by Eccentric, Nonconformist Japanese Artists of the Early Modern Era (1580–1868) in the Collection of Kimiko and John Powers*, vols. 2, 3. Cambridge, MA: Harvard University Art Museum, 1999.

Takeuchi Umematsu 竹内梅松. "Chūkyō nanga no nimeika: Chikutō to Baiitsu ni tsuite" 中京南画の二名家・竹洞と梅逸に就いて. *Nanga kanshō* 南畫鑑賞 3, no. 10 (October 1934): 28–33.

NOTES

1. Owari *nanga* is considered to have specific characteristics by Kobayashi Motoaki, "Owari nanga no tokushitsu," in Nagoyashi Hakubutsukan, *Owari no kaigashi*, 86–87.

2. Kanematsu, *Chikutō to Baiitsu*, Chikutō chronology, 2.

3. Ibid., 4–5, and Rosenfield and Cranston, *Extraordinary Persons*, vol. 3, 67. The Li Kan and Wang Mian paintings Chikutō and Baiitsu saw are today in the Imperial Household Collection, Tokyo. See *Gyobutsu, Chūgoku bijutsu*, Kōshitsu no shihō, vol. 13 (Tokyo: Mainichi Shinbunsha, 1993), plates 27 and 28.

4. Addis, *Nanga Painting*, 58, and Rosenfield, *Extraordinary Persons*, vol. 2, 240.

5. For Chikutō's 1802 treatise (*Chikutō garon*), see Kanematsu, *Chikutō to Baiitsu*, 124.

6. Kobayashi, "Owari nanga no tokushitsu," 85.

7. This incident and others are mentioned by Kanematsu, *Chikutō to Baiitsu*, 28–30.

8. See comments by Sanyō, Baiitsu, and others, quoted in ibid., 23–24.

Nakajima Kahō 中島華鳳 1866–1939

Nakajima Kayō 中島華陽 (1813–1877), the Shijo-school painter believed to be Kahō's father, was a disciple of the Kyoto painter Yokoyama Kazan 横山華山, who had studied with Ganku 岸駒 (1749[1756]–1838) and Matsumura Goshun 松村呉春 (1752–1811). Kayō's elder daughter, Tatsu 多津 (d. 1869), married the noted painter Tomioka Tessai 富岡鐵齋 (1834–1924) in 1867. This family connection is believed to have been the initial basis for Kahō's lifelong friendship with the much older artist. Throughout his career Kahō employed a Tessai-like style for some works, and his most famous painting is a 1907 portrait of Tessai, complete with an inscription by his subject.[1] Kahō also painted many works in the style of Buson's *haiga*, including Buson's manner of fluid, cursive calligraphy.

Like many of his contemporaries, Kahō occasionally decorated lacquer and ceramic utensils. In addition he took great interest in the mountings of his paintings. Mountings for a number of his Taishō-period creations have bold designs and startling combinations of fabrics and papers that give these works great graphic appeal.

Kahō often did renditions of the works of other artists, such as Nagasawa Rosetsu 長沢蘆雪 (1754–1799) and Itō Jakuchū 伊藤若冲 (1716–1800). He was so deeply interested in Jakuchū that he helped restore the Sekihōji 石峰寺 temple, which had been the focus of the older artist's attentions, most importantly the large number of stone *rakan* 羅漢 statues in the rear garden. Kahō sold paintings he had created in Jakuchū's style to raise money for the repair of some of the temple buildings.[2]

Kahō continued to have deep connections to the Sekihōji temple, which is not far from the famous Fushimi Inari shrine. Even today, a number of his works survive in the temple collection, including a massive painting of geese and reeds that roughly approximates Muruyama Ōkyo's 応挙 (1733–1795) style. Kahō and his children are buried in the Sekihōji graveyard. One of his children predeceased him, and Kahō's name was later engraved on that child's headstone. Because the stone gives only the date of the child's death, Kahō's death date has long been obscure. Yet the Sekihōji graveyard record book clearly marks his death as occurring in 1939.[3] Kahō's low-profile career is typical of many artists who successfully maintained themselves through the private sale of their works without ever attempting to gain prominence by way of the major public exhibitions.

PB

BIBLIOGRAPHY

Berry, Paul, and Yokoya Kenichiro. *Unexplored Avenues of Japanese Painting*. Ōtsu: Ōtsu Shiritsu Rekishi Hakubutsukan, 2001.

Katō Ruiko 加藤類子 et al. *Bunjinga no kaindai Tessai to sono shiyūtachi* 文人画の近代鐵齋とその師友たち. Kyōto Kokuritsu Kindai Bijutsukan 京都国立近代美術館, 1997.

NOTES

1. See color plate 196 (p. 17) in Katō, *Bunjinga no kindai Tessai to sono shiyūtachi*.

2. See an example of a Kahō painting after Jakuchu's colorful treatment of Fushimi dolls in Berry and Yokoya, *Unexplored Avenues of Japanese Painting*, plate 89 and pp. 175–76.

3. These observations are based on a personal investigation of records and works at the temple.

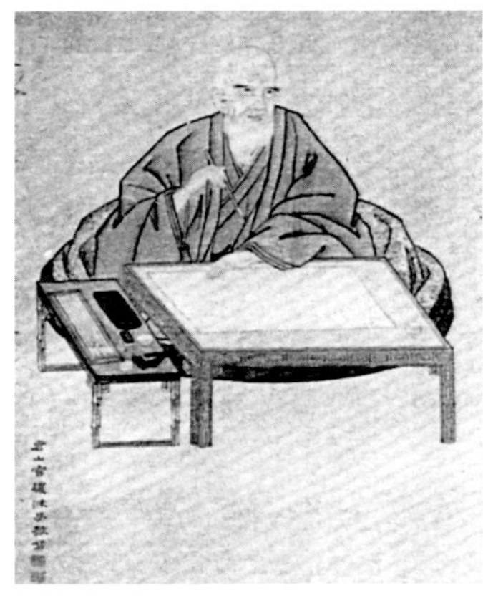

Noro Kaiseki
野呂介石 1747–1828

Noro Kaiseki was one of the principal literati painters in Kii 紀伊 province (Wakayama prefecture). As one of the so-called Four Celestial Kings of painting—the other three being Nagamachi Chikuseki 長町竹石 (1747–1806), Kushiro Unsen 釧雲泉 (1759–1811), and Hamada Kyōdō 濱田杏堂 (1766–1806)—he had many followers during his lifetime. Unlike his colleagues, who had itinerant *bunjin* lifestyles and supported themselves by painting, Kaiseki established a respectable career as a samurai and enjoyed a comfortable life. Deeply concerned with using correct models, Kaiseki relied on the pictorial vocabulary and compositional formulas of Chinese predecessors for his orthodox painting style. He particularly admired the Yuan master Huang Gongwang 黄公望 (1269–1354) and Yi Fujiu 伊孚九, a Chinese merchant who transmitted the styles of old literati masters during his visits to Nagasaki in the early eighteenth century. Kaiseki was best known for his landscape paintings, especially his depictions of the Nachi waterfall in his native province.

Kaiseki was the fifth child of a well-established sake merchant in Kii. His samurai ancestors had served the Toyotomi clan until the beginning of the seventeenth century. After clan's fall, the family settled in Kii as townsmen. Socially prominent and wealthy, the family provided its children with excellent educations and training in the military arts. Among Kaiseki's nine siblings, two brothers became physicians, two others earned samurai status as did Kaiseki, and one established himself as a Confucian scholar.[1] Around the age of ten, Kaiseki began studying under Itō Rangū 伊藤蘭嵎 (1693–1778), an eminent scholar of Neo-Confucianism. Rangū's teachings on the importance of following the Confucian ideal profoundly influenced Kaiseki. Moreover, Kaiseki's interest in painting may have been triggered by Rangū, who amused himself by painting orchids in ink.[2]

According to one source, Kaiseki went to Kyoto in 1760 to study ink painting under the Ōbaku Zen monk Kakutei 鶴亭 (d. 1785).[3] In 1767, at the age of twenty, Kaiseki returned to Kyoto and became a pupil of Ike no Taiga 池大雅 (1723–1776), from whom he received instruction on and off for three or four years. He eventually settled in Kii but frequently traveled to Kyoto and Osaka. During this formative period Kaiseki also learned painting from Kuwayama Gyokushū 桑山玉州 (1746–1799), his contemporary in Kii province, and began to form what would be a lifelong friendship with Kimura Kenkadō 木村兼葭堂 (1736–1802), a wealthy Osaka merchant and respected connoisseur and patron of the arts. Guided by great teachers and friends, Kaiseki happily devoted himself to the study of painting for several decades. According to his own account, he made an effort to paint ten scenes a day for ten years.[4]

In 1793, when he was forty-six years old, Kaiseki was appointed an official for the Kii fief. This position required extensive travel in his native province as he was responsible for overseeing copper mining, sugarcane production, and forestry. Thereafter Kaiseki resolutely adopted the lifestyle and ethics of a samurai in active service. When Murase Shūsui 村瀬秋水 (1795–1876), an aspiring literati painter from Mino province (Gifu prefecture), visited Kaiseki's residence, he was surprised to see several men practicing with swords and spears as if it were a fencing studio.[5] *Shihekisai's Talks on Painting* (Shihekisai gawa 四碧斎画話), a record of Kaiseki's reminiscences, includes incidents that point to his serious-minded approach to life and art. In one episode Kaiseki refused his pupils' offer to celebrate his eightieth birthday, proclaiming that the event held for his seventieth had been sufficient for one lifetime.[6]

Esteemed highly by his lord for his artistic ability, Kaiseki regarded it as his responsibility to paint on orders from the fief officials. While serving his domain, however, he never abandoned his literati pursuits. He became well acquainted with distinguished members of the Kyoto-Osaka literati circle such as Rai Sanyō 頼山陽 (1780–1832), Shinozaki Shōchiku 篠崎小竹 (1781–1851), and Tanomura Chikuden 田能村竹田 (1777–1835), all of whom visited him. Kenkadō also came to see Kaiseki on several occasions before his death in 1802. Kaiseki's artistic reputation eventually spread beyond Kyoto and Osaka, and requests for his work arrived even from distant Edo. One such request came from Ōkubo Shibutsu 大窪詩佛 (1766–1837), a well-known scholar-poet in Edo who sent a poem to the artist in 1809.[7] Kaiseki continued to busy himself with painting until his death at the age of eighty-one.

MM

BIBLIOGRAPHY

Adams, Celeste, and Paul Berry. *Heart Mountains and Human Ways: Japanese Landscape and Figure Painting.* Exh. cat. Houston: Museum of Fine Arts, 1983.

Furukawa Hokka 古川北華. "Takaku Aigai to Noro Kaiseki, jō" 高久靄厓と野呂介石, 上. *Nanga kanshō* 南畫鑑賞 7, no. 11 (November 1938): 23–31.

———. "Takaku Aigai to Noro Kaiseki, ge." *Nanga kanshō* 7, no. 12 (December 1938): 34–39.

Matsushita Hidemaro 松下秀麿. *Ike Taiga* 池大雅. Tokyo: Shunjūsha 春秋社, 1967.

Minamoto Toyomune 源豊宗, comp., and Sasaki Jōhei 佐々木丞平, ed. *Kyōto gadan no jūkyūseiki 2: Bunka・Bunseiki* 京都画壇の十九世紀 2:文化・文政期. Kyoto: Shibunkaku Shuppan 思文閣出版, 1994.

Mochizuki Nobunari 望月信成. "Noro Kaiseki." *Nanga kenkyū* 南画研究 3, no. 6 (September 1959): 1–3.

Mori Senzō 森銑三. *Mori Senzō chosakushū, dai sankan* 森銑三著作集第三巻. Tokyo: Chūō Kōronsha 中央公論社, 1988.

Rosenfield, John M., and Fumiko E. Cranston. *Extraordinary Persons: Works by Eccentric, Nonconformist Japanese Artists of the Early Modern Era (1580–1868) in the Collection of Kimiko and John Powers.* Vol. 2. Cambridge, MA: Harvard University Art Museum, 1999.

Seikadō Bunko Bijutsukan 静嘉堂文庫美術館. *Nihon no bunjinga ten I* 日本の文人画展 I. Exh. cat. Tokyo, 1995.

Wakayama Kenritsu Hakubutsukan 和歌山県立博物館. *Noro Kaiseki tokubetsuten* 野呂介石特別展. Exh. cat. Wakayama, 1978.

Wylie, Hugh. "Nanga Painting Treatises of Nineteenth-Century Japan: Translations, Commentary, and Analysis." PhD diss., University of Kansas, 1991.

NOTES

1. See the Noro family chart by Sakai Tetsurō, "Noro Kaiseki no shōgai to geijutsu—Zentaizō tsuikyū no tame no joron," in Wakayama Kenritsu Hakubutsukan, *Noro Kaiseki tokubetsuten,* no pagination.

2. Mori, "Noro Kaiseki," in *Mori Senzō chosakushū, dai sankan,* 315.

3. Mori identifies the source as *Sanmeika ryaku nenpu* by Tamaoki Hyakurei; ibid., 310 and 315.

4. From *Shihekisai gawa,* Kaiseki's reminiscences recorded by his students; see Wylie, "Nanga Painting Treatises of Nineteenth-Century Japan," 40.

5. Furukawa, "Takaku Aigai to Noro Kaiseki, jō," 29. Shūsui's visit occurred in 1822 according to the chronology in Wakayama Kenritsu Hakubutsukan, *Noro Kaiseki tokubetsuten,* no pagination.

6. Discussed by Wylie, "Nanga Painting Treatises of Nineteenth-Century Japan," 317–18.

7. Sakai, "Noro Kaiseki no shōgai to geijutsu," no pagination.

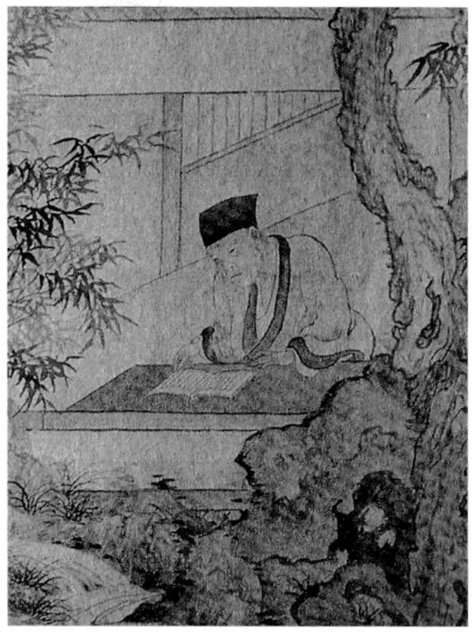

Nukina Kaioku
貫名海屋 1778–1863

Kaioku was the second son of the Yoshii 吉井 family, who served the daimyo of the Awa 阿波 *han* domain in Tokushima prefecture, on the island of Shikoku. In 1806 Kaioku reverted to using the name Nukina, an earlier name of the Yoshii family. Kaioku first studied painting with his mother's father, the local Kanō-school artist Yano Michimasa 矢野典雅, who was in service to the Awa domain and had studied under Kanō Michinobu 狩野典信 (1730–1790). Kaioku's desire to become a painter is said to have been ignited when he viewed a set of fifteen landscape paintings attributed to the Ming literati painter Qian Gu 錢穀 (1508–1578) at the Tokushima Zen temple Kanchōin 観潮院. His first calligraphy teacher was Nishi Noriyuki 西宣行 (1764–1826), who lived nearby, and it was the calligraphy of the famous priest Kōbō Daishi 弘法大師 (774–835) that drew Kaioku to the Shingon temples on Kōyasan in 1794. In 1799, he entered the noted Kaitokudō 懐徳 Confucian school run by Nakai Chikuzan 中井竹山 (1730–1804) in Osaka.[1] Kaioku lived in Kyoto from 1811, yet from 1822 through 1852 the various editions of the *Record of Famous People of Kyoto* (Heian jinbutsu shi 平安人物誌) list Kaioku only in the categories of Confucian scholar and poet, suggesting that his public image was not based on his accomplishments in calligraphy and painting. In this sense, he fulfilled the literati ideal of amateurism by avoiding the perception of being a professional painter.

It is believed that Kaioku visited Nagasaki three times, yet only the second visit in 1836 can be clearly dated. During this visit Kaioku studied painting with the Zen priest Tetsuō 鐵翁 (1791–1871). Even though Kaioku already had much experience as a painter, his time with Tetsuō seems to have had a lasting effect on his work. Certain aspects of his brushwork and his fondness for using satin may have been influenced by his admiration for the senior artist, who had extensively studied recently imported Chinese paintings and knew immigrant Chinese artists.

After moving to Kyoto, Kaioku continued to pursue calligraphy, which would become his principal art form. He mastered a great variety of styles with the help of woodblock-printed model books (*hōjō* 法帖) made after the works of famous Chinese calligraphers. Although most calligraphers could work in various script forms, their main talent was often limited to one or two types. Kaioku's accomplishments in standard, clerical, and cursive scripts established his renown.[2] His principal occupation was as a Confucian scholar, yet his knowledge of Chinese calligraphy grew to be so encyclopedic that he became one of the key figures in the Kyoto literati world from the 1820s onward. An 1827 handscroll (cat. no. 24) by Uragami Shunkin 浦上春琴 (1779–1846) appears to have been designed to give Kaioku's inscription pride of place at the end of the landscape while emphasizing his connections with the calligrapher Shinozaki Shōchiku 篠崎小竹 (1781–1851) and Tanaka Kakuō 田中鶴翁 (1782–1848), the key figure in the Osaka *sencha* tea world.

Kaioku taught painting to many students, his most noted disciple being the talented Hine Taizan 日根對山 (1813–1869), with whom he created a number of joint works. Kaioku was a prolific artist, and his paintings were often quickly sketched affairs, yet a large number of complex, fully realized landscapes also remain.[3] His landscape compositions are diverse, suggesting that he examined many Chinese paintings during his travels around Japan.[4] An artist whose quality improved with age, Kaioku produced calligraphies in his last years whose profundity exceeds that of his polished earlier works. In the prewar collecting world, Kaioku's paintings and calligraphy were very highly valued, ranking alongside those of his close friend Rai San'yō 頼山陽 (1780–1833). PB

BIBLIOGRAPHY

Hashimoto Yoshifumi 橋本吉文. "Sūō nenpu" 菘翁年譜. *Shoron* 書論, no. 17 (Fall 1980): 103–34.

Katō Ruiko 加藤類子, ed. *Tessai to sono shiyūtachi: Bunjinga on kindai* 鉄斎とその師友たち: 文人画の近代. Kyoto: Kyōto Kokuritsu Kindai Bijutsukan 京都国立近代美術館, 1997.

Nakata Yūjirō 中田勇次郎. "Ichikawa Beian to Nukina Kaioku" 市川米庵と貫名海屋. In Shimonaka Kunihiko 下中邦彦, ed., *Shodō zenshū* 書道全集, vol. 23, 17–19. Tokyo: Heibonsha 平凡社, 1958.

Tanaka Sōkaku 田中双鶴. "Awa no Sūō" 阿波の菘翁. *Shoron* 書論, no. 17 (Fall 1980): 97–102.

———. *Nukina Sūō seisetsu* 貫名菘翁精説. Tokyo: Ueno Shoten 上野書店, 1983.

———. *Nukina Sūō shoga shū* 貫名菘翁書画集. Tokyo: Ueno Shoten, 1983.

Ueda Sōkaku 上田双鶴 and Nakata Yūjirō 中田勇次郎. *Nukina Sūō* 貫名菘翁. Tokyo: Nigensha 二玄社, 1962.

NOTES

1. There are conflicting accounts about when Kaioku first arrived in Osaka; see Hashimoto, "Sūō nenpu," 106–7.

2. See the variety of works illustrated in Shimonaka, *Shodō zenshū*, plates 78–89.

3. See the paintings illustrated in Katō, *Tessai to sono shiyūtachi*, plates 17–19. There are hundreds of paintings by Kaioku reproduced from prewar auction catalogues in Sasaki Jōhei 佐々木丞平 and Sasaki Masako 佐々木正子, eds., *Koga sōran* 古画総覧, *Bunjinkei* 文人系, vol. 1 (Tokyo: Kokusho Kankōkai 国書刊行会, 2006).

4. See the pair of twelve-panel screens by Kaioku that includes his versions of various paintings by Chinese painters in Harada Heisaku and John Teramoto, eds., *Japanese Masterworks: Paintings from the Indianapolis Museum of Art* (Seattle: University of Washington Press, 2005). Kaioku created many works like this based on Chinese paintings he had studied.

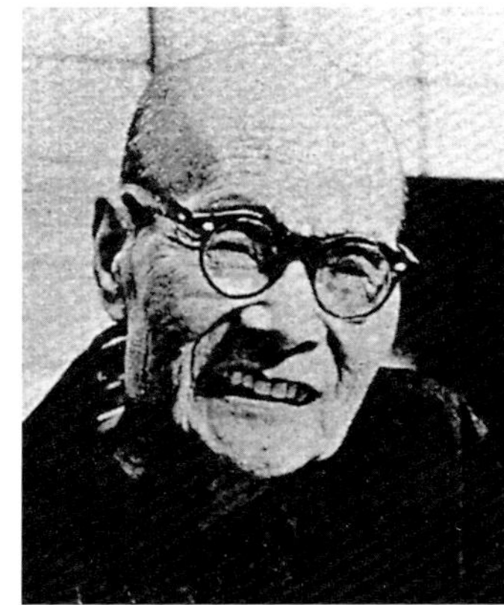

Ogawa Sen'yō 小川千甕 1882–1971

Sen'yō's career demonstrates the vitality of the literati tradition in Japan well into the postwar world. Like Tomioka Tessai 富岡鐵齋 (1836–1924), Sen'yō reached the peak of his popularity in the last years of his life with roughly brushed paintings filled with bright colors. Some critics have seen more than a passing resemblance to Tessai's work, yet Sen'yō was quick to say his early influences were the childlike works of Sengai 仙厓 (1750–1837) and the bold creations of the Zen master Hakuin 白隠 (1685–1768).[1] Having established himself as an oil painter, he followed his own path in his gradual evolution into a *nanga* painter without basing his work on that of earlier artists.

Sen'yō's family operated a bookstore that for several centuries published Buddhist texts in Kyoto. Sen'yō first apprenticed in 1897 as a painter of iconic imagery with Kitamura Keijū 北村敬重. Although he was still painting Buddhist images by day in 1904, at night he was studying Western-style oil painting at the private school of Asai Chū 浅井忠 (1856–1907). He became friends with the young Umehara Ryūsaburō 梅原龍三郎 (1888–1986) and Yasui Sōtarō 安井曾太郎 (1888–1955), who were to become leading oil painters in Japan, and joined them at the Kansai Bijutsuin painting school when it opened in 1906. In 1908 Sen'yō began painting decorations on pottery at the Kyoto Municipal Ceramic Testing Studio (Kyōto Shiritsu Tōjiki Shikenjō

京都市立陶磁器試験場). Watching the tremendous output of ceramics from the studio's new electric kiln inspired him to adopt the name Sen'yō, which means "A Thousand Pots." Although he preferred the "Chinese" pronunciation of Sen'yō, an early publication gave an alternate pronunciation, Chikame, and to his frustration, he was often called by that name until the end of his life.[2]

In 1913 Sen'yō traveled to Europe by boat via India to study Western painting and returned to Kyoto in 1914 after touring France and Italy. He joined with Kawabata Ryūshi 川端龍子 (1885–1966), Hirafuku Hyakusui 平福百穂 (1877–1933), Ogawa Usen 小川芋銭 (1868–1938), Morita Tsunetomo 森田恒友 (1881–1933), and Kondō Koichiro 近藤浩一路 (1884–1962) to form the Coral Group (Sangokai 珊瑚会), where they could explore new forms of painting. Although these artists eventually went their own ways, they shared an interest in the free brushwork and strong elements of fantasy found in *manga* and *haiga* paintings.[3] Even though Sen'yō had exhibited an oil painting at the fifth show of the re-inaugurated Inten in 1918, the exhibition works that followed, appearing almost yearly from 1921, were Western-influenced *nihonga* paintings that gradually shifted toward new interpretations of literati styles. When the Great Kantō Earthquake struck the Tokyo area in 1923, Sen'yō was living behind the Shinshōji 真性寺 temple in Sugamo 巣鴨. He joined fellow artists interested in *haiga* and *manga* to produce many handscrolls showing the massive fires that destroyed the city and the painful aftermath for people forced to live among the burned-out streets.

In 1930 Sen'yō exhibited a brightly colored literati painting of the Kurama fire festival at the Inten show, but he left the Inten in 1933 for the newly formed Japan Nanga Institute (Nihon Nangain), which exhibited contemporary literati painting. Sen'yō had a deep interest in *haiga,* which he viewed as one aspect of literati painting. Although *haiga* ordinarily combine a haiku verse with a related, simply brushed painting, Sen'yō interpreted the format loosely; the illustrations he made for his 1933 book on how to paint *haiga* rarely include poems. After a 1931 trip to Hangzhou, Suzhou, and Shanghai, he embarked on repeated visits to China, Taiwan, Korea, and Manchuria over the next decade. The series of illustrated volumes of his work published in the mid-1930s reveal the successful reception his individualistic works enjoyed. These stylistically diverse paintings were chosen from private collections all over Japan, and the book, whose title refers to his patronage group, Saiyōkai 采甕会, was likely produced by his supporters.[4]

Sen'yō restarted his career after the war, increasing his production of literati paintings gradually and exhibiting his works. He almost succumbed to illness in 1958 but recovered his health and continued to hold solo exhibitions, which garnered considerable acclaim, until the end of his long life. His last paintings employ especially rich colors and seem to radiate good humor, forming a kind of climax to his decades-long exploration of wide-ranging styles. Today he is often viewed as a solitary, eccentric literati painter, yet this perception is due largely to his having outlived most of his contemporaries. Sen'yō's career came to fruition in association with many of the other major artists of the twentieth century who mixed Japanese and Western painting traditions in their search for new forms of expression. **PB**

BIBLIOGRAPHY

Kikuya Yoshio 菊屋吉生. "Sangokai ronkō" 珊瑚会論考. *Bijutsu kenkyū* 美術研究, no. 377 (February 2003): 30–58.

Kikuya Yoshio and Shiotani Jun 塩谷純, eds. "Kenkyū shiryō Sangokai shiryō shū" 研究資料珊瑚会史料集. *Bijtusu kenkyū* 美術研究, no. 376 (March 2002): 39–68.

Morita Shiryū 森田子龍, ed. "Ogawa Sen'yō" 小川千甕. *Bokubi* 墨美, no. 142 (November 1964).

———, ed. "Saibannen no Sen'yō" 最晩年の千甕. *Bokubi* 墨美, no. 217 (January 1971).

Nihon Bijutsuin Hyakunenshi Henshūshitsu 日本美術院百年史編集室. *Nihon Bijutsuin hyakunen shi* 日本美術院百年史. Vols. 4–6. Tokyo: Nihon Bijutsuin 日本美術院, 1994–97.

Ogawa Sen'yō 小川千甕. *Gashū Ogawa Sen'yō* 画集小川千甕. Kyoto: Benridō 便利堂, 1967.

———. *Saiyōkai gazon dai san satsu* 采甕会画存第三冊. Nagoya: Nagoya Insatsu Kabushiki Gaisha 名古屋印刷株式会社, 1935.

———. *Shinsan haiga hō* 新纂俳画法. Tokyo: Kōransha 交蘭社, 1933.

NOTES

1. See the interview in *Bokubi*, no. 142 (November 1964): 8.

2. Sen'yō describes his frustration in an interview in ibid., 7.

3. For the Coral Group and its exhibitions, refer to Kikuya Yoshio's articles listed above.

4. See Ogawa, *Saiyōkai gazon dai san satsu.*

Okada Hankō 岡田半江 1782–1846

The Okada family was comparatively wealthy due to their operation of rice storehouses (*kurayashiki* 蔵屋敷) that exchanged rice from the *han* domains around Japan for money. This business often extended to making loans to local rulers, giving the operators of rice storehouses a critical role in the economy and a social position akin to bankers. Hankō's father, Okada Beisanjin 岡田米山人 (1744–1820), was a prominent literatus in the Osaka area. He had an unusual style of painting, and he and his friend Uragami Gyokudō 浦上玉堂 (1745–1820) are often linked as eccentric literati painters of the period. A close friend of Kimura Kenkadō 木村蒹葭堂 (1736–1802), Beisanjin was a patron of fellow artists and had a large collection of paintings and art objects that was studied by the painters of the area.[1]

Hankō grew up in the rich aesthetic environment of a lively literati salon. He was already making paintings by his early teens, often with a bold, simplified brushwork that resembled that of this father. He rapidly developed his skills as a painter and by his twenties had begun working in the style he would build on for the rest of his career. Much like Gyokudō's son Shunkin 春琴 (1779–1846), Hankō moved away from the extremes of his father's style and, through his careful study of Qing-period painting, developed a sophisticated brushwork with which he created complex, layered compositions that were most admired in the first half of the nineteenth century.

Hankō's most famous works are typified by the subtle use of horizontal Mi-dots (*beiten* 米点) combined with washes that produce a remarkable sense of the misty atmosphere of mountain valleys.[2] His close friend, the Osaka painter Kaneko Sessō 金子雪操 (1794–1857), wrote an inscription in 1855 on Hankō's *Scholar Viewing a Waterfall from a Bridge* that well describes his technique:

> Master Dong Xuanjai 董玄宰 [Dong Qichang 董其昌 1555–1636] said: "In painting mountains and clouds, it is not necessary to wash in or to outline. They are better painted in such a way that they appear like steam floating up and down in the air. Then one may say that they have life rhythm." However, do not press your brush too heavily or the ink will be clumsy and airless. Also, it is better to use both a wet and a dry brush alternately; only then can it be said to have no defects.[3]

Hankō's life was interrupted by a traumatic event in the second month of 1837. Like many other literati, he was very close to Ōshio Heihachirō 大塩平八郎 (1793–1837), who operated a school in Osaka based on the teachings of Wang Yangming 王陽明 (1472–1558), whose radical Neo-Confucianism had been continually critiqued by the Edo government. Responding to conditions of rising poverty, Ōshio organized a rebellion in Osaka, and while the police were suppressing the rebels, a fire broke out and burned a large part of the city, including the Okada family residence with its famous collection of paintings and books. This disaster forced Hankō to move south of the city to Sumiyoshi, where he lived quietly for five years. When he returned to the center of Osaka, he resumed painting at a great pace, and many of his finest works date from these years. Hankō was a much more celebrated painter during his lifetime than his father, yet in the twentieth century the quiet beauty of his works has been less appreciated than the quirky boldness of his father's landscape and figure painting. PB

BIBLIOGRAPHY

Ishihama Tsuneo 石濱恒夫, et al. *Okada Beisanjin* 岡田米山人. Bunjinga suihen 文人画粋編, vol. 15. Tokyo: Chūō Kōronsha 中央公論社, 1978.

Kōyama Noboru 神山登. "Okada Beisanjin・Hankō no shōgai" 岡田米山人・半江の生涯. *Kobijutsu* 古美術, no. 53 (July 1977): 52–71.

Monroe, Betty. "Okada Beisanjin." PhD diss., University of Michigan, 1974.

Ōsaka Shiritsu Bijutsukan 大阪市立美術館大阪市立美術館. *Beisanjin narabini Hankō ten zuroku* 米山人並半江展圖録. Kyoto: Benridō 便利堂, 1941.

Yabumoto Kōzō 薮本公三. "Okada Beisanjin nenpu kō" 岡田米山人年譜稿. *Kobijutsu* 古美術, no. 53 (July 1977): 72–88.

NOTES

1. The best biographical information on Beisanjin and Hankō is in Kōyama, "Okada Beisanjin・Hankō no shōgai"; Yabumoto, "Okada Beisanjin nenpu kō"; and Monroe, *Okada Beisanjin.*

2. The most noted example of this technique is *Crows Rising in Spring Mist* at the Toyama Kinenkan 遠山記念館.

3. This painting is one of a pair of Hankō landscapes dated to 1838 at the University of Michigan Museum of Art; see Celeste Adams and Paul Berry, *Heart Mountains and Human Ways: Japanese Landscapes and Figure Painting* (Houston: Museum of Fine Arts, 1983), 78–79.

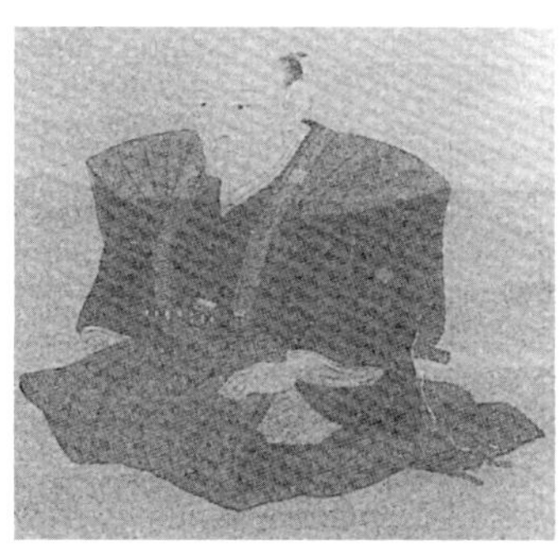

Okamoto Toyohiko 岡本豊彦 1773–1845

The Okamoto family ran a sake business in Kurashiki in Okayama prefecture.[1] From an early age Toyohiko showed an interest in drawing, and the local literati painter Kuroda Ryōzan 黒田綾山 (1755–1814) became his first teacher. Originally from Takamatsu in Shikoku, Ryōzan had been a student of Fukuhara Gogaku 福原五岳 (1730–1799), who in turn had studied with Ike Taiga (1723–1776). Ryōzan had also been close to another of Gogaku's disciples, Hayashi Rōen 林閬苑 (d. 1810).[2] Toyohiko is thought to have entered Gogaku's school in Osaka in 1791.[3]

Toyohiko moved in 1798 to Kyoto, where he studied and lived with Matsumura Goshun 松村呉春 (1752–1811). In more than a decade of work with Goshun, Toyohiko became regarded, along with Goshun's younger brother Keibun 松村景文 (1779–1847), as one of his top disciples. Toyohiko adopted Goshun's softer version of Maruyama Ōkyo's 円山応挙 (1733–1795) approach as well as the literati style of Goshun's first teacher, Yosa Buson 与謝蕪村 (1716–1883). Most famous for his many landscapes, Toyohiko was also skilled in painting figures and birds-and-flowers. Although his career as an artist was successful, his personal life was tragic, with his six children and two wives dying of various causes over a period of years.[4] Left without an heir, Toyohiko adopted one of his disciples, Okamoto Tsukehiko (1823–1883), as his successor.

Toyohiko may have made his greatest impact through the accomplishments of his primary students, such as the lacquer painter Shibata Zeshin 柴田是真 (1807–1891), Tanaka Nikka 田中日華 (d. 1845), and most especially Shiokawa Bunrin 塩川文麟 (1808–1877). In turn, Bunrin's student Kōno Bairei 幸野楳嶺 (1844–1895) taught some of the key *nihonga* painters of the first part of the twentieth century, including Takeuchi Seihō 竹内栖鳳 (1864–1942). To some degree Toyohiko's legacy was the Shijō-school style that fostered the development of *nihonga* painting in the Kyoto area.

PB

BIBLIOGRAPHY

Kojō Shin'ichi 古城真一, Yasuhara Shūkai 安原秀魁, and Hara Mitsumasa 原三正. *Kurashiki sandai gajinden: Kuroda Ryōzan • Okamoto Toyohiko • Furuichi Kinga* 倉敷三代画人伝：黒田綾山・岡本豊彦・古市金峨. Kurashiki 倉敷: Kurashiki Shidankai 倉敷史談会, 1983.

Sakakibara Yoshirō 榊原吉郎. *Maruyama–Shijōha no nagare* 円山・四条派の流れ. *Kindai no bijutsu* 近代の美術, no. 25. Tokyo: Shibundō 至文堂, 1974.

NOTES

1. The complexities of his mother's situation and background are given in Kojō et al., *Kurashiki sandai gajinden*, 102–7. The account of Ryōzan and Toyohiko given here is based on materials presented in this work, the most detailed account of their careers.

2. Ibid., 43–49.

3. Ibid., 131.

4. Ibid., 116.

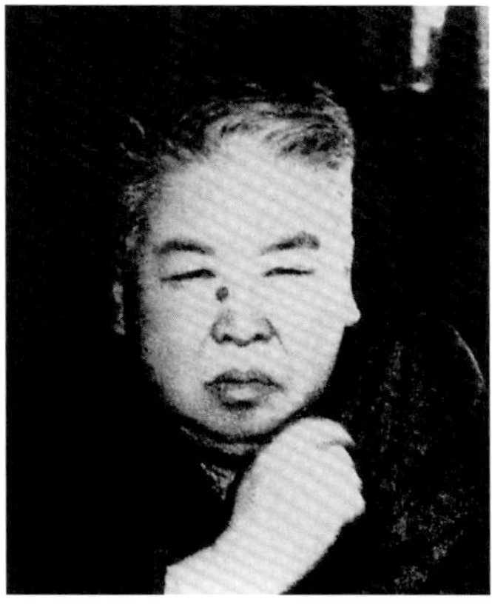

Okuhara Seiko 奥原晴湖 1837–1912

Okuhara Seiko transcended the gender barrier to become one of the most celebrated Meiji-period literati painters in Tokyo, patronized by the new political leaders of the Meiji government. A nonconformist who wore men's clothes and cropped her hair, she left many amusing anecdotes.[1] Her impressive artistic achievement, however, was based on her indisputable talent and unyielding self-determination.

Seiko was born the fourth daughter of a high-ranking samurai family in the service of the Koga domain 古河藩 (Ibaraki prefecture). A tomboy, she trained in martial arts such as judo and *naginata* (a form using a pole weapon). She also demonstrated a remarkable gift for painting and scholarship. At the age of seventeen, Seiko became a pupil of Hirata Suiseki 枚田水石, who had studied painting under Tani Bunchō 谷文晁 (1763–1840), a leading Edo literati painter. For the next decade Seiko made copies of Chinese paintings as well as Japanese literati works in local collections. Fortunately for Seiko, there were many accomplished scholars active in the Koga domain. Along with her pursuit of painting, she studied Chinese poetry with Ōnuma Chinzan 大沼沈山 and received instruction from Chine Ichiō 茅根一鷗, who excelled in Chinese studies and *waka* poetry.

Her practice of calligraphy with Koyama Kagai 小山霞外, celebrated for his grass-style writing, and his son Gooka 呉岡, known for seal script, gave her a solid foundation for the later development of her individual style.[2] Seiko's family was related through marriage to Takami Senseki 鷹見泉石 (1785–1858), a chief retainer of the Koga domain and a respected scholar of Western learning. Seiko enjoyed the privilege of visiting him until his death.[3]

In 1865 Seiko moved to Edo to pursue an artistic career and settled in Shitaya, where many scholars and artists lived. She quickly began accepting pupils, a remarkable feat for a woman barely thirty years old. Around the time of the Meiji Restoration in 1868, Seiko moved temporarily to Kumagaya 熊谷 (Saitama prefecture), to escape the political turmoil and violence in the capital, but soon returned to Tokyo (formerly Edo) and gained patrons among the new government's leading politicians, among them Yamauchi Yōdō 山内容堂 (1827–1872) and Kido Takayoshi 木戸孝允 (1833–1877). In 1872, at Kido's recommendation, Seiko received an audience with the empress, the first time a female painter had been granted such an honor.

During the 1870s and 1880s Seiko's career flourished. Her paintings, which increasingly showed a bold brushwork influenced by the style of the Chinese painter Zheng Xie 鄭燮 (or Zheng Banqiao 鄭板橋, 1693–1765), were sought after not only by individual collectors but by dining establishments, which purchased them for display. As many as three hundred pupils were enrolled at one time at the private painting school Seiko established in 1871.[4] Her stature was such that other respected literati artists such as Yasuda Rōzan 安田老山 (1830–1882) and Sugawara Hakuryū 菅原白龍 (1833–1898) visited her to exchange artistic ideas. In 1878 Seiko traveled beyond Tokyo to Kansai and met leading *bunjin* of the area, including Yamanaka Shinten'ō 山中信天翁 (1822–1885), Tomioka Tessai 富岡鉄斎 (1836–1924), Doi Gōga 土井贅牙(1816–1880), and Itakura Kaidō 板倉塊堂 (d. 1879).

During the late 1880s the popularity of Chinese-derived literati painting began to wane with the government push for modernization, the influence of Western culture, and the rise of nationalistic sentiments. When established in 1888, the Tokyo School of Fine Arts (Tōkyō Bijutsu Gakkō 東京美術学校) offered classes only in sculpture, metal and lacquer works, and *nihonga* (or Japanese-style modern painting). Recognizing the tenor of the times, Seiko withdrew from the Tokyo art scene and retired to a small village in Kumagaya in 1891.

Many consider Seiko's paintings from her Kumagaya period to be the most representative of her entire oeuvre, even though her earlier works in the daring, free brush style inspired by Zheng Xie had established her reputation.[5] In Kumagaya Seiko's style became more carefully detailed in execution, sometimes using rich color. Like a true *bunjin*, she immersed herself in reading and painting, and traveled to Tōhoku, Kansai, and Hokuetsu to mingle with connoisseurs and collectors, all the while seeking new stimulation for her art. After the turn of the century, people from distant places requested her paintings and many came to Kumagaya to visit her. Due to failing health, Seiko stopped accepting commissions in 1912 but continued to paint until her death the following year.

MM

BIBLIOGRAPHY

Aimi Kōu 相見香雨. "Okuhara Seiko, jō." *Saitama shi dan* 埼玉史談 1, no. 3 (1930): 154–60.

———. "Okuhara Seiko, chū." *Saitama shi dan* 1, no. 4 (1930): 249–55.

Fister, Patricia. *Japanese Women Artists, 1600–1900*. Exh. cat. Lawrence, Kansas: Spencer Museum of Art, 1988.

Fujikake Shizuya 藤懸静也, ed. *Okuhara Seiko gashū* 奥原晴湖画集. Tokyo: Kōgeisha 巧藝社, 1933.

Irabaki Kenritsu Rekishikan 茨城県立歴史館. *Okuhara Seiko ten*. 2 vols. Mito, 2001.

Kawashima Junji 川島恂二. *Gasan kara miru Okuhara Seiko* 画賛から見る奥原晴湖. Tokyo: Rin Shobō りん書房, 1991.

Koga Rekishi Hakubutsukan 古河歴史博物館. *Okuhara Seiko funpon shiryō mokuroku* 奥原晴湖粉本資料目録. Koga, 2002.

McClintock, Martha. "Okuhara Seiko (1837–1913): The Life and Arts of a Meiji Period Literati Artist." PhD diss., University of Michigan, 1991.

Saitama Kenritsu Hakubutsukan 埼玉県立博物館. *Okuhara Seiko ten*. Exh. cat. Ōmiya, 1978.

NOTES

1. See a discussion of Seiko's life in Fujikake, *Okakura Seiko gashū*, 1–37.

2. Ibid., 6.

3. See Kawashima, *Gasan kara miru Okuhara Seiko*, 863–86.

4. Fujikake, *Okakura Seiko gashū*, 15.

5. Paul Berry observes that this is a matter of personal preference. He argues that later art historians seem to approve of Seiko's relatively low profile as a female artist in the countryside over the assertive, high-status painter who outshone most of her male colleagues. Personal correspondence with the author, October 1, 2007.

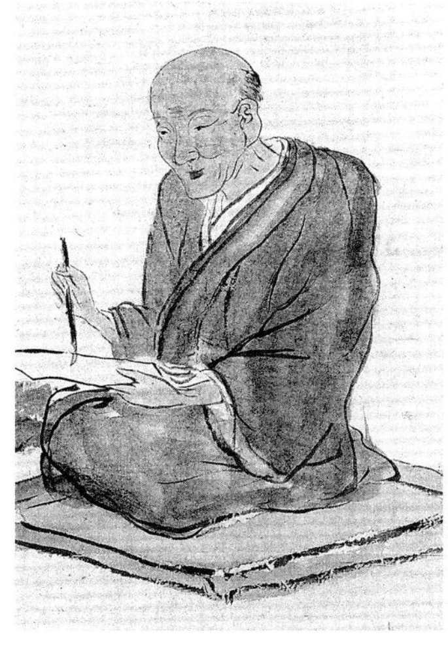

Ōtagaki Rengetsu
大田垣蓮月 1791–1875

Ōtagaki Rengetsu was not a sinophile. Unlike most literati artists, she did not devote herself to the study of Chinese poems or paintings. Her literary and artistic accomplishments and humble lifestyle, however, easily validate her as a model of *bunjin* ideals and values. A Buddhist nun, Rengetsu is best known for her *waka* 和歌 poetry. She was also a talented calligrapher, painter, and potter who decorated her simple wares with her own poems. Her artistic legacy, coupled with her unusual life story, place her as one of the most endearing female artists of Meiji Japan.

Rengetsu was adopted soon after birth by the Ōtagaki family, samurai serving at Chion'in 知恩院 temple in Kyoto. Her biological parents are believed to have been a high-ranking samurai and the daughter of a merchant family or nobleman.[1] Around the age of seven, Rengetsu was sent to Kameoka Castle 亀岡城 in Tanba, west of Kyoto, to serve as a lady-in-waiting. During the following decade, surrounded by cultured women tutored in art and literature, she received the best education then available to a young woman. While Rengetsu was away, her stepbrother, the family's heir, died. She dutifully returned home and at age seventeen entered into an arranged marriage to carry on the Ōtagaki family name. In the next fifteen years, she would face the tragic deaths of two husbands and five children. After her second husband died in 1823, she became a nun and received the name Rengetsu (Lotus Moon). Her stepfather also renounced the world, and the two retired to a cottage within the Chion'in complex. There, Rengetsu dedicated herself to the arts and in the next decade lived quietly with her stepfather, a well-educated man knowledgeable of literature and poetry and a master of the board game *go*.

The death in 1832 of her stepfather, the last member of her family, devastated Rengetsu. Paradoxically, it opened the door to her pursuit of an independent life as a respected *bunjin* artist. Rengetsu moved to the Okazaki 岡崎 area and began earning a living by making pottery. She hand-modeled and decorated her pieces with her own poems, which she incised or inscribed into or on the clay surface. Her unpretentious tea utensils appealed to scholars and connoisseurs of discriminating taste who practiced Chinese-derived *sencha* 煎茶. The increasing popularity of both her pottery and her calligraphy, which extended beyond the *bunjin* circle, is believed to have caused Rengetsu to move more than thirty times in the next three decades in order to escape the excessive attention.[2]

Rengetsu gave invaluable help to the literati master Tomioka Tessai 富岡鉄斎 (1836–1924) during the start of his career. When she was about sixty years old, young Tessai became her live-in assistant and a close friend. A few years later, in 1862, Tessai opened his first private school at Rengetsu's house in Shōgoin 聖護院 village, near Kumano shrine. To help launch Tessai as a scholar and a painter, Rengetsu inscribed her poems on his works, transforming them into marketable commodities.

Around 1866 Rengetsu finally settled in a tea hut at the Jinkōin 神光院 temple. Despite the political and social upheaval of the time, she lived quietly in her humble abode, receiving many guests and pursuing her creative endeavors. Until her death she remained unconcerned with material luxury and was compassionate toward the unfortunate and the poor. Rengetsu's tombstone, a small unadorned rock in a natural shape, is engraved with an inscription by Tessai.

MM

BIBLIOGRAPHY

Bokubi 墨美, no. 103 (January 1961), and no. 109 (July 1961).

Eastburn, Melanie; Lucie Folan; and Robyn Maxwell. *Black Robe White Mist: Art of the Japanese Buddhist Nun Rengetsu.* Exh. cat. Canberra: National Gallery of Australia, 2007.

Fister, Patricia. *Japanese Women Artists, 1600–1900.* Exh. cat. Lawrence: Spencer Museum of Art, 1988.

Fudokukaku Shujin 不讀閣主人. "Rengetsuni, jō." *Shoga kottō zasshi* 書畫骨董雑誌, no. 168 (June 1922): 12–15.

———. "Rengetsuni, ge." *Shoga kottō zasshi*, no. 169 (July 1922): 17–19.

Kimura Sekiryū 木村夕立, "Rengetsu o omou" 蓮月を憶ふ. *Daimai bijutsu* 大毎美術 4, no. 6 (June 1925): 30–34.

Kono Miki 菰野美紀. "Rengetsuni no uta" 蓮月尼の歌. *Daimai bijutsu* 5, no. 10 (October 1926): 10–15.

Maeda Toshiko 前田訣子. *Bunjin shofu 11: Rengetsu.* Kyoto: Tankōsha, 1979.

Morooka Emiko 師岡笑子. "Otagaki Rengetsu." *Bakumatsu shihi no tegami* 幕末志士の手紙. Edited by Naramoto Tatsuya 奈良本辰也. Tokyo: Gakugei Shorin, 1969.

Murakami Sodō 村上素道, ed. *Rengetsuni zenshū.* 3 vols. Kyoto: Rengetsuni Zenshū Hanpukai 蓮月尼全集頒布会, 1926–27.

Sayama Sei 佐山濟. "Ōtagaki Rengetsu no uta." *Joryū bungaku hyōronshū: Chūsei kinseihen* 女流文学評論集中世近世編. Edited by Imai Kuniko 今井邦子. Nagano: Meikō Shobō, 1948.

Sumi 墨, no. 44 (September 1983).

Tokuda, Kōen 徳田光圓. *Rengetsuni no shin kenkyū.* Kyoto: Sanmitsudō Shoten, 1958.

———. *Ōtagaki Rengetsu.* Tokyo: Kōdansha 講談社, 1982.

NOTES

1. Rengetsu's mother may have been a courtesan, but this possibility was considered least likely; see Fister, *Japanese Women Artists*, 144 and 158, and Tokuda, *Rengetsuni no shin kenkyū*, 10–12.

2. One scholar suggests, however, that Rengetsu's restlessness was partly due to the emotional trauma caused by the tragic loss of her family members; see Maeda, *Bunjin shofu 11*, 65–66.

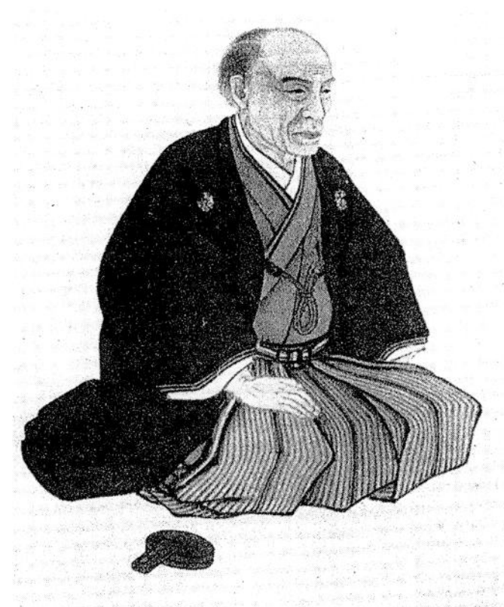

Shiokawa Bunrin 塩川文麟 1808–1877

Due to the attention given to the new ideas and styles in Kyoto *nihonga* painting circles of the early twentieth century, precursors of these developments, like Bunrin, often have been overlooked. In 1868 Bunrin helped sponsor an early association, the Cloudlike Society (Jōunsha 如雲社), which counted among its members many of the top Kyoto painters, including Mori Kansai 森寛斎 (1814–1894), Nakajima Raishō 中島来章 (1796–1871), and Maruyama Ōritsu 円山応立 (1817–1875). Their periodic exhibitions helped foster public display as a key feature in shaping new attitudes toward painting.[1] Traditionally, most paintings were viewed only by the patrons who commissioned them and their friends. Public exhibitions not only allowed many more people, including other artists, to view new works but also encouraged the growth of art criticism in the newspapers and magazines of the Meiji period. Bunrin exhibited his work publicly throughout his life, even showing a painting at the Centennial International Exhibition of 1876 in Philadelphia.

The Shiokawa family had long served as retainers to the Takatsukasa 鷹司 family, who became attached to the Yasui no Miya Rengekōin Monzeki 安井宮蓮華光門跡, a temple in Okazaki[2] connected to the imperial family, where Bunrin's father would serve. Bunrin's parents both died in 1820, and the following year the young Bunrin went to study painting in Fushimi. His talent soon recognized, he was employed as a painter at the Rengekōin Monzeki and shortly thereafter entered the atelier of the Shijō-school painter Okamoto Toyohiko 岡本豊彦 (1773–1845).[3] Bunrin, one of Toyohiko's most successful students, had a great many disciples. The most important of these was Kōno Bairei 幸野楳嶺 (1844–1895), who went on to teach some important *nihonga* painters in Kyoto, including Takeuchi Seihō 竹内栖鳳 (1864–1942).

Bunrin's Shijō-school training is evident in figure paintings that sometimes show the influence of Maruyama Ōkyo 円山応挙 (1733–1795); his later landscapes are often indebted to Yosa Buson 与謝蕪村 (1716–1783). He became especially well known for night scenes with fireflies and sparklers (*hanabi senkō* 花火線香). Although many of Bunrin's large-scale works are tranquil in nature, he also made many lively, humorous paintings on the spur of the moment. The works of this prolific painter are found in many public and private collections, yet a comprehensive study of his career has yet to be undertaken. PB

BIBLIOGRAPHY

Conant, Ellen, Steven Owyoung, and J. Thomas Rimer. *Nihonga, Transcending the Past: Japanese Style Painting, 1868–1968.* Saint Louis: Saint Louis Art Museum, 1995.

Kyōtoshi Bijutsukan 京都市美術館. *Kyōto Nihonga no nagare: sansui kara fūkei e: Bunrin, Bairei, Seihō* 京都日本画の流れ：山水から風景へ: 文麟, 楳嶺, 栖鳳. Kyoto: Kyōto Shinbunsha 京都新聞社, 1995.

Morioka, Michiyo, and Paul Berry. *Modern Masters of Kyoto: The Transformation of Japanese Painting Traditions, Nihonga from the Griffith and Patricia Way Collection.* Seattle: Seattle Art Museum, 1999.

Nomura Bunkyo 野村文擧, ed. *Bunrin-ō sanjū kaiki kinen iboku tenrankai gashū* 文麟翁卅三回忌記念遺墨展覽會畫集 Tokyo: Gahōsha 畫報社, 1910.

NOTES

1. Refer to Harada Heisaku's brief history of the Cloudlike Society in Conant et al., *Nihonga*, 76–77.

2. Founded in the Kamakura period, this temple had become quite small by this time and has since disappeared.

3. Most of the biographical information given here is drawn from Kyōtoshi Bijutsukan, *Kyōto Nihonga no nagare*, 8–9. See also Morioka and Berry, *Modern Masters of Kyoto*, 58–59.

Shirakura Jihō 白倉二峰 1896–1974

During the 1920s Shirakura Jihō made his name as one of the leaders of the new literati painting (*shin nanga* 新南画) movement at both the Japan Nanga Institute (Nihon Nangain 日本南画院) and the Teiten exhibition. His *Forest in Evening* (Shinrin boshoku 深林暮色), which received the highest award at the 1930 Teiten, stood out for its "rough and forceful" quality among the more sedate entries typical of the government exhibition.[1] Although depicting the conventional literati subject of a scholar in his retreat, *Forest in Evening* displayed an unorthodox composition and a distinctive brush style with an "eccentric flavor" reminiscent of postimpressionism.[2] For his experimental approach, the critics called Jihō a rare and unusual talent (*kisai* 奇才).[3]

It was not uncommon for artists of this era to switch from *yōga* to *nihonga* at some juncture in their careers (see, for example, the biographical entries on Kondō Kōichiro and Ogawa Sen'yō). In Jihō's case, the process was more circuitous than usual. Born in Niigata 新潟, Jihō first apprenticed under Hattori Gorō 服部五老 (1871–1930), a literati painter trained under Tanomura Chokunyū 田能村直入 (1814–1907) in Kyoto. During his teens, Jihō moved to Tokyo and began studying watercolor and drawing under Ishii Hakutei 石井柏亭 (1882–1958). Jihō must have been something of a prodigy, as the *yōga* paintings he submitted in 1914 and 1915 under the name of Shirakura Kinrō 欣郎 were accepted at the Bunten. He was not yet twenty. Jihō's *yōga* pieces were distinguished by strong calligraphic lines, confirming the aesthetic sensibility that would draw him back to literati painting soon thereafter.

In 1917 Jihō moved to Kyoto and began studying with Tajika Chikuson 田近竹邨 (1864–1922), a prominent literati master and a top pupil of Chokunyū. Only two years later his landscape, entered under the name Jihō, was accepted in the *nihonga* section of the Teiten. Titled *Secluded Dwelling, Healing Worldliness* (Shindō izoku 深堂醫俗), it was a pure literati work in both subject and execution, with its vigorous brush mode.[4] Determined to pioneer a new path, Jihō joined the Japan Nanga Institute soon after it was established in 1921 to promote the modernization of the literati tradition, and after Chikuson's death he became a pupil of Komuro Suiun 小室翠雲 (1874–1945), the leader of the institute. Jihō enjoyed continued recognition at the government exhibition and was appointed to its jury in 1941. During this time, Suiun called him "the Sanraku of *nanga*" 南画の山楽 for his daring compositional approach,[5] but others criticized some of his works as being too busy or confusing because of his excessive use of texture strokes.[6]

The assertive brushwork began to disappear from Jihō's work around 1940, when he changed his *gō* to Kanyū 嘉入. A more delicate style began to prevail in his oeuvre.[7] As exemplified by *Misty Rain over Stream* (Saiu ryūsui 細雨流水), 1941, and *Morning Twilight* (Reimi 黎明), 1942,[8] his deliberate, labored style, with refined color and carefully rendered details, blurred the distinction between *nanga* and *nihonga*. Kanyū continued to participate in the government exhibition through 1962. MM

BIBLIOGRAPHY

Komuro Suiun 小室翠雲. "Nangain tenrankai zensakuhin hyō" 南畫院展覧會全作品評. *Tōei* 搭影 9, no. 5 (June 1933): 2–6.

Kyōto Kokuritsu Kindai Bijutsukan 京都国立近代美術館. *Kankoku Kokuritsu Chūō Hakubutsukan shozō: Nihon kindai bijutsuten* 韓国中央博物館所蔵：日本近代美術展. Tokyo: NHK and Asahi Shinbunsha 朝日新聞社, 2003.

Soeda Tatsurei 添田達嶺. "Nangain daigokaiten o miru" 南畫院第五回展を観る. *Bi no kuni* 美之国 3, no. 2 (February 1927): 84–89.

———. "Nangainten hyō" 南畫院展評. *Tōei* 搭影 11, no. 6 (June 1935): 24–27.

Tomita Keishi 冨田啓子. "Shirakura Jihō-shi koten" 白倉二峰氏個展. *Tōei* 16, no. 6 (June 1940): 29.

Yui Kazuto 油井一人. *Nijū seiiki bukko nihongaka jiten* 20世紀物故日本画家事典. Tokyo: Bijutsu Nenkansha 美術年鑑社, 1998.

NOTES

1. See the comments published in Nittenshi Hensan Iinkai, *Nittenshi 9, Teitenhen 4* (Tokyo: Nitten, 1983), 542.

2. Ibid.

3. Soeda, "Nangainten hyō," 26.

4. For an illustration of this work, see Nittenshi Hensan Iinkai, *Nittenshi 6, Teitenhen 1* (Tokyo: Nitten, 1982), 96.

5. Sanraku (1559–1635) was a Kanō-school painter in Kyoto known for dramatic, stylized compositions; see Komuro, "Nangain tenrankai zensakuhin hyō," 3.

6. Soeda, "Nangain daigokaiten o miru," 87, and Nittenshi Hensan Iinkai, *Nittenshi 9, Teitenhen 4*, 526.

7. See Tomita, "Shirakura Jihō-shi koten," 29.

8. For color illustrations of these works, see Kyōto Kokuritsu Kindai Bijutsukan, *Kankoku Kokuritsu Chūō Hakubutsukan shozō*, 55, and Nittenshi Hensan Iinkai, *Nittenshi 15, Shinbuntenhen 3* (Tokyo: Nitten, 1985), 13.

Sō Geppō 僧月峰 1760–1839

Eventually to become the thirty-fourth generational head of the Sōrinji 双林寺 temple in Kyoto, the young Geppō studied with the noted literati painter Ike Taiga 池大雅 (1723–1776), who lived close to the temple. Originally a Tendai facility, Sōrinji was reestablished as a Pure Land temple of the Jishū sect in the fourteenth century, returning to the Tendai sect only in the Meiji period. It became famous during the Edo period as a place to view cherry blossoms, and most of the temple grounds were incorporated into the newly established Maruyama Park in the early Meiji period.

Taiga's lifelong friend Ken'a Shōnin 謙阿上人 (1724–1784), the thirty-first head of Sōrinji, adopted Geppō when he was eight years old. After Taiga's death, his wife, the talented painter Gyokuran 玉瀾 (1728–1784), continued to live in their home. When Gyokuran died, Taiga's disciple Aoki Shukuya 青木夙夜 (d. 1802) maintained the residence, which was rebuilt inside the Sōrinji grounds. Eventually Geppō (priestly name, Shinryō 辰亮) assumed responsibility for the upkeep of the home, becoming the third-generation Taigadō. Well known for landscape paintings that are mostly in styles unrelated to Taiga, Geppō supported himself in part by authenticating the master's paintings.[1] He was succeeded in his caretaker role by his sons Giryō 義亮 (1798–1865) and Seiryō 清亮 (1807–1869). The fifth-generation Taigadō, Teiryō 定亮 (1839–1910), saw the building dismantled in 1903 by the Kyoto city government, which a few years later erected a large stele in its memory.

Besides authenticating paintings by Taiga and maintaining his career as a painter and seal carver, Geppō had a reputation as a haiku poet and as an illustrator of woodblock books.[2] For his landscape paintings Geppō usually employed heavy outlines and often used strong colors. He was unusual among Taiga's many disciples in showing little influence from his teacher's multiple styles, but he did help to propagate Taiga's work by creating the *Taigadō gafu* 大雅堂画譜. This 1804 work contains Geppō's copies of figures Taiga drew from the Chinese *Mustard Seed Garden Painting Manual* (Kaishien gaden 芥子園画伝), a preface by the Kyoto poet Murase Kōtei 村瀬栲亭 (1746–1818), and a postscript by the equally famous Confucian scholar Minagawa Kien 皆川淇園 (1734–1807). Due to his reputation in painting and seal carving, Geppō was repeatedly listed among the major artists in editions of the *Record of Famous People of Kyoto* (Heian jinbutsu shi 平安人物志) from 1813 to 1838.[3] Other than his descendants, his primary disciple was Hagura Katei 羽倉可亭 (1799–1887).

In the latter half of his life, Geppō associated with the principal literati active in the Kyoto area, including Aoki Mokubei 青木木米 (1767–1833), Rai San'yō 頼山陽 (1780–1832), and Tanomura Chikuden 田能村竹田 (1777–1835). Undoubtedly painters sought out his Taigadō residence out of respect for the earlier artist, but Geppō's sponsorship of yearly exhibitions of new paintings and calligraphy also must have been a factor. Minagawa Kien hosted the semiannual Exhibition of New Calligraphies and Paintings (*Shin shoga tenkan* 新書画展観) at Sōrinji from 1794, and Geppō seems to have continued the spring and autumn shows at least until 1820.[4] These exhibitions attracted the major artists of the region, making Sōrinji a focal point for literati gatherings. PB

BIBLIOGRAPHY

Kyōto Bunka Hakubutsukan 京都文化博物館. *Miyako no eshi wa hyakka ryōran: "Heian jinbutsushi" ni miru Edo jidai no Kyōto gadan.* Kyoto, 1999.

Matsushita Hidemaro 松下英麿. *Ike Taiga* 池大雅. Tokyo: Shunjūsha 春秋社, 1967.

Mitchell, C. H. *The Illustrated Books of the Nanga, Maruyama, Shijo, and Other Related Schools of Japan: A Bibliography.* Los Angeles: Dawson's Book Shop, 1972.

Roberts, Laurance. *Dictionary of Japanese Artists.* New York: Weatherhill, 1976.

Tanabe Nahoko 田邉菜穂子. "Sōrinji no gasō Geppō no koto" 双林寺の画僧月峰のこと. *Gobun kenkyū* 語文研究 (Kyūshū Daigaku Kokugo Bungakkai 九州大学国語文学会), no. 103 (2007): 19–35.

NOTES

1. The standard account of Geppō's life is in Matsushita, *Ike Taiga*, 318–20. I follow Matsushita in calling Geppō the third-generation Taigado (see the chart in Matsushita, p. 283), although some sources call him second generation (depending upon whether Ike Taiga is considered the first generation). The Western tradition of Geppō's family name being Yamaoka and coming from Wakayama, details given in Roberts, *Dictionary of Japanese Artists*, and Mitchell, *The Illustrated Books of the Nanga, Maruyama, Shijo, and Other Related Schools of Japan*, cannot be confirmed with Japanese sources.

2. Geppō's haiku were published in several anthologies; refer to Tanabe, "Sōrinji no gasō Geppō no koto," 34n.3. See the titles of works that include his illustrations in Mitchell, *The Illustrated Books*, 50–51, and Tanabe, 34n.2.

3. Tanabe, "Sōrinji no gasō Geppō no koto," 20–21.

4. Ibid., 30–33.

Suzuki Fuyō 鈴木芙蓉 1749–1816

Born in Kitagatamura 北方村, now a part of Iida city in Nagano prefecture, Fuyō was the second son of the farmer Kinoshita Kanbei 木下甚平.[1] It appears that he studied with several local artists while young, but records of his activities become clearer only after his arrival in Edo in 1778. He apparently began using the Suzuki family name after being adopted as the successor to his first wife's family.[2]

Although he associated with many painters, it is likely that Fuyō's primary teacher was Watanabe Gentai 渡辺玄對 (1749–1822), who had studied with the literati pioneer Nakayama Kōyō 中山高陽 (1717–1780).[3] Gentai's eclectic approach to painting encompassed many so-called Northern-school styles from China as well as an array of literati themes and brushwork. Fuyō's style mirrored the variety of influences embraced by his teacher, including Ming-dynasty Zhe 浙 school compositions and brush modes. Fuyō's landscape brushwork often resembled that found in the mountains and rocks of Tang Yin's 唐寅 (1470–1524) paintings.[4]

Although Tani Bunchō 谷文晁 (1763–1840) is frequently listed as both a student and then later a teacher of Fuyō's, it seems that only the former is true. Very early in his career, from 1782, Bunchō studied with Fuyō, who would have been among those who encouraged Bunchō's eclecticism and interest in Zhe-school compositions. Despite Bunchō's growing fame, Fuyō maintained his own distinctive brushwork throughout his career and rarely reveals anything resembling Bunchō's trademark flourishes.

Fuyō created several books illustrated with Chinese themes. One of the most interesting is *Hi Kangen's Landscape Painting Style* (Hi Kangen sansui gashiki 費漢源山水画式) of 1789,[5] purportedly Fuyō's copy of a Hi Kangen manuscript in his possession. Hi Kangen 費漢源 (Fei Hanyuan, act. 1734–1763) was one of the important Chinese artists to visit Japan, yet only a few works can be reliably attributed to him today. Fuyō's book is evidence of the high regard accorded Hi Kangen in the Edo period.

Fuyō regularly traveled in Japan, visiting the noted literatus Kimura Kenkadō 木村蒹葭堂 (1736–1802) in Osaka in 1790, 1793, and 1796, and possibly going as far as Nagasaki in 1807.[6] These excursions gave Fuyō a considerable national reputation that nonetheless was eclipsed after his death by Bunchō's widespread popularity. Fuyō's many landscape and figure paintings are now being reevaluated for their important role in the development of literati painting in the Edo area.

PB

BIBLIOGRAPHY

Murasawa Takeo 村沢武夫. *Suzuki Fuyō den* 鈴木芙蓉伝. Matsumoto: Kyōdo Shuppansha 郷土出版社, 1983.

Naganoken Shinano Bijutsukan 長野県信濃美術館. *Suzuki Fuyō* 鈴木芙蓉. Nagano: Nagano-ken Shinano Bijutsukan 長野県信濃美術館, 1991.

Suzuki Fuyō to sono shuhen: Wasarerareta bujin gaka 鈴木芙蓉とその周辺：忘れられた文人画家. Tokushima: Tokushima Shiritsu Tokushimajō Hakubutsukan 徳島市立徳島城博物館, 2004.

Tani Bunchō to Suzuki Fuyō 谷文晁と鈴木芙蓉. Iida: Iidashi Bijutsu Hakubutsukan 飯田市美術博物館, 1999.

NOTES

1. Older accounts give the name of Fuyō's father as Kannai 甚内, but the 2004 *Suzuki Fuyō to sono shuhen* presents a genealogy of his family written in 1805 that lists the name as Kanbei; see p. 68.

2. Naganoken Shinano Bijutsukan, *Suzuki Fuyō*, 40–41.

3. Ibid., 41–44. Much of the little that is known of Fuyō's relations with other artists comes from Sō Unshitsu's 僧雲室 (1753–1827) *Unshitsu zuihitisu* 雲室随筆; see Mori Senzō 森銑三 and Kitakawa Hirokuni 北川博邦, eds., *Zoku Nihon zuihitsu taisei* 続日本随筆大成, vol. 1 (Tokyo: Yoshikawa Kōbunkan 吉川弘文館, 1979).

4. See the examples illustrated in Anne De Coursey Clapp, *The Painting of T'ang Yin* (Chicago: University of Chicago Press, 1991). Even though authentic works by this noted Ming painter were rare in Japan at this time, copies, forgeries, and works in his style by minor painters were widely available.

5. *Hi Kangen sansui gashiki* 費漢源山水画式, 3 vols. (Edo: Suwaraya Mohei 須原屋茂兵衛, 1789). Bunki 文熙 and Suzuki Shinbei 鈴木新兵衛, the names given as editor and illustrator of this work, are both alternate names of Suzuki Fuyō.

6. See the chronology in Naganoken Shinano Bijutsukan, *Suzuki Fuyō*, 49–51. Fuyō's visits to Osaka are noted in Kenkadō's diary.

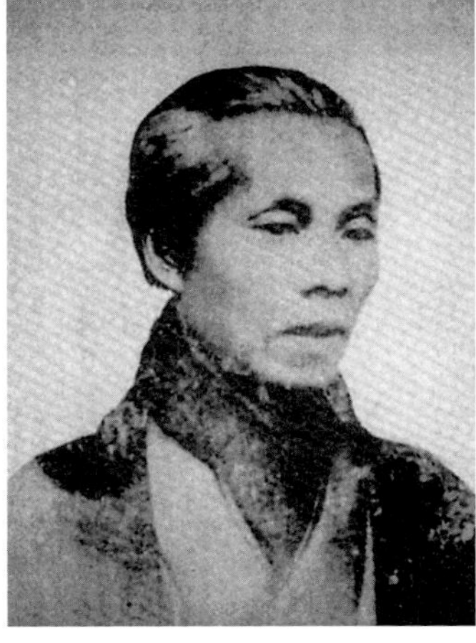

Suzuki Hyakunen 鈴木百年 1825–1891

During the 1860s, when Japanese society was in transition from feudal rule to the modern era, Suzuki Hyakunen established a new "school" of painting characterized more by its eclecticism than by stylistic or thematic unity. His school quickly found a niche in the early-Meiji Kyoto art world, attracting many patrons and pupils. When the city's traditional-style painters gathered to showcase their talent in a painting demonstration at the second Kyoto Exposition (Kyōto Hakurankai 京都博覧会) in

1873, Hyakunen's school outnumbered all others. Of the fifty Kyoto painters selected, nearly one-quarter represented Hyakunen's lineage, including his son Shōnen 松年 (1848–1918) and pupils Imao Keinen 今尾景年 (1845–1924) and Kubota Beisen 久保田米遷 (1852–1906).[1] Through the 1880s, Western visitors with an interest in Japanese painting who came to Kyoto usually called at Hyakunen's studio.[2] Mild-tempered and knowledgeable of Chinese literature and poetry, Hyakunen enjoyed friendships with Kyoto *bunjin* such as Ema Tenkō 江馬天江 (1825–1901), Yamanaka Shinten'ō 山中信天翁 (1822–1885), and Tomioka Tessai 富岡鉄斎 (1836–1924).[3] His wife Shunkō 春香 was said to be an accomplished painter and calligrapher as well as a poet and potter.[4]

Hyakunen's lifelong literati interests derived from his upbringing. His father was a scholar of astronomy and Daoist divination in Kyoto who once had been a samurai in service to the Akō fief 赤穂藩 in Harima 播磨 (Hyōgo prefecture). Hakunen, the eldest son, learned to draw astronomical diagrams and charts at an early age, and during his mid-teens he was sent to Akō for two years, to broaden his education by studying with a scholar-physician.[5] After he returned to Kyoto, Gantai 岸岱 (1782–1865) and Kishi Renzan 岸連山 (1804–1859), frequent guests of his father, recognized the young man's talent and encouraged him to pursue painting. The details of Hyakunen's formal artistic training are obscure. It is generally accepted that he was largely self-taught, although he did receive some instruction from Ōnishi Chinnen 大西椿年 (1792–1851), who had studied literati painting under Tani Bunchō and briefly trained in the Maruyama tradition. The last syllable of the name Hyakunen relates to one character from Chinnen's name, and his teacher's broader approach to painting might have influenced him to explore numerous styles.[6] Hyakunen's endeavors encompassed not only the literati lineage but also the Maruyama-Shijō, Tosa, Kanō, and Kishi schools.[7] By his early twenties Hyakunen was active as a professional painter, and he secured his first major imperial commission in 1846.[8]

During the early Meiji years Hyakunen's career flourished. He gained an appointment as one of the principal instructors at the newly founded Kyoto Prefecture Painting School (Kyōto-fu Gagakkō 京都府画学校) in 1880 and won awards at the Domestic Competitive Painting Exhibition (*Naikoku kaiga kyōshinkai* 内国絵画共進会) in 1882 and 1884. Eventually Hyakunen entrusted his school to Shōnen, the eldest and most gifted of his three sons. In the last decade of his life Hyakunen recognized the talent of the young Fukuda Kodōjin 福田古道人 (1865–1944), the wildly individualistic literati painter who became his pupil for several years.[9] Always fond of travel, Hyakunen visited the regions surrounding Kyoto and central and northern Honshu, especially in his later years. He died of illness in Tokyo on his way home from a trip to Akita. MM

BIBLIOGRAPHY

Akō Shiritsu Bijutsu Kōgeikan Tabuchi Kinenkan 赤穂市立美術工芸館田淵記念館. *Akō yukari no gaka: Suzuki Hyakunen・Shōnen* 赤穂ゆかりの画家：鈴木百年・松年. Exh. cat. Akō, 2006.

Harada Heisaku 原田平作. *Bakumatsu Kyōraku no gajin tachi* 幕末京洛の画人たち. Kyoto: Kyōto Shinbunsha 京都新聞社, 1985.

Kanzaki Ken'ichi 神崎憲一. *Kyōto ni okeru nihongashi* 京都に於ける日本画史. Kyoto: Kyōto Seihan Insatsusha 京都精版印刷社, 1929.

Kyōtoshi Bijutsukan 京都市美術館. *Kyōto gadan: Edo matsu Meiji no gajin tachi* 京都画壇江戸末・明治の画人たち. Kyoto: Ātosha アート社, 1977.

Morioka Michiyo, and Paul Berry. *Modern Masters of Kyoto: The Transformation of Japanese Painting Traditions, Nihonga from the Griffith and Patricia Way Collection.* Seattle: Seattle Art Museum, 1999.

"Suzuki Hyakunen den, fu tsuma Shunkō" 鈴木百年傳, 附妻春香. *Kyōto bijutsu kyōkai zasshi* 京都美術協会雑誌, no. 89 (November 1899): 11–13.

NOTES

1. See Kanzaki, *Kyōto ni okeru nihongashi*, 14–15.

2. Ibid., 38.

3. Akō Shiritsu Bijutsu Kōgeikan Tabuchi Kinenkan, *Akō yukari no gaka*, 9. This catalogue is the best source for illustrations of works by Hyakunen and Shōnen.

4. "Suzuki Hyakunen den, fu tsuma Shunkō," 13.

5. Akō Shiritsu Bijutsu Kōgeikan Tabuchi Kinenkan, *Akō yukari no gaka*, 9.

6. Harada Heisaku, "Sakka to Sakuhin," in Kyōtoshi Bijutsukan, *Kyōto gadan*, 249.

7. Harada, *Bakumatsu Kyōraku no gajin tachi*, 85.

8. "Suzuki Hyakunen den," 12.

9. Stephen Addiss, *Old Taoist: The Life, Art, and Poetry of Kodōjin (1865–1944)* (New York: Columbia University Press, 2000), 2.

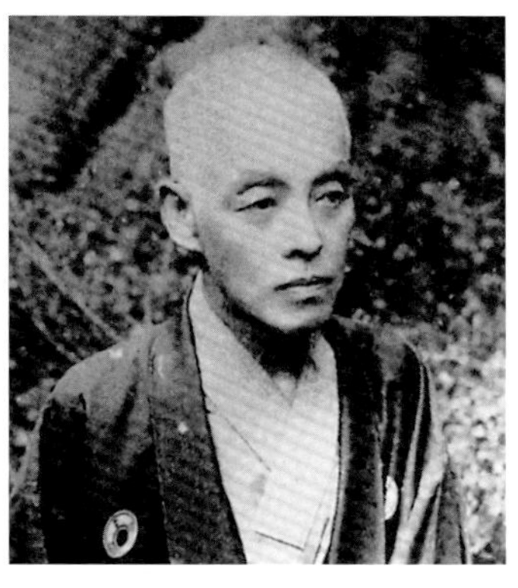

Suzuki Shōnen
鈴木松年 1848–1918

Suzuki Shōnen's bold paintings and flamboyant lifestyle reflect the dynamic tenor of Meiji society. Shōnen, who succeeded the Suzuki school founded by his father, Hyakunen 百年 (1825–1891), achieved prominence as a major Kyoto artist at the turn of the century. Hyakunen's three sons became artists, but Shōnen was the most talented. Nicknamed "Present-day Shōhaku" (Ima Shōhaku) after the proud, eccentric Edo-period artist Soga Shōhaku 曽我蕭白 (1730–1781), Shōnen built a reputation for his bravura brushwork that was matched by his supreme self-confidence and outspokenness. Both in painting and in personality, Shōnen contrasted with his father. The mild-mannered Hyakunen enjoyed quiet literati pursuits, while Shōnen flaunted his talent and wealth. He built a magnificent house resembling a temple[1] and kept several mistresses, fathering more than ten children with them and his wife.[2] His well-known affair with the celebrated artist Uemura Shōen 上村松園 (1870–1949) produced a son who also became a successful painter, Uemura Shōkō 松篁 (1902–2001).

Shōnen trained under his father and made an early public appearance as one of the fifty Kyoto artists selected to demonstrate painting at the second Kyoto Exposition (Kyōto Hakurankai 京都博覧会) in 1873. He actively participated in the newly organized public shows of the 1880s and 1890s such as the Domestic Competitive Painting Exhibition (*Naikoku kaiga kyōshinkai* 内国絵画共進会), the Domestic Industrial Exposition (*Naikoku kangyō hakurankai* 内国勧業博覧会), and the Exhibition of New and Old Art (*Shinko bijutsuhin tenrankai* 新古美術品展覧会). Shōnen received awards at the 1893 World's Columbian Exposition in Chicago and the Paris International Exposition of 1900. Although he was best known for his landscapes, he was a consummate professional who could paint any subject including figures and birds-and-flowers. In a set of *rakan* 羅漢 paintings from his mature period, figures portrayed in color are defined by a strong, modulating outline and set against an expressive ink landscape in which layers of wash are combined with forceful brushwork showing traces of a split brush.[3]

Fiercely competitive and headstrong, Shōnen did not hesitate to criticize others. In the Kyoto art world, artists often had to supplement their incomes by painting textile designs, but Shōnen shunned such work, proclaiming it unworthy of a true artist,[4] and he disparaged Imao Keinen 今尾景年 (1845–1924), a colleague who also trained under Hyakunen, as a "*yūzen* artisan." In particular, the mutual animosity between Shōnen and Kōno Bairei 幸野楳嶺 (1844–1895) was legendary. Their antagonism purportedly began when a wealthy merchant gathered a group of Kyoto artists to create a "mandala of vegetables" (*aomono zukushi no mandara* 青物づくしの曼荼羅) to be presented to a nobleman.[5] Besides Shōnen and Bairei, the invited aritsts included Yokoyama Seiki 横山清暉 (1793–1865), Nakajima Raishō 中島来章 (1796–1871), Shiokawa Bunrin 塩川文麟 (1801–1877), and Suzuki Hyakunen, accompanied by their pupils. The merchant urged the assembled artists to start with a daikon, a kind of radish, to represent Buddha, but the painters were hesitant. Suddenly, Shōnen, barely sixteen years old, walked up to the front and shocked everyone by painting a large daikon with a sweeping motion of his brush. Shōnen's brazen behavior, an insult to the older masters, infuriated Bairei, and the two young painters brawled. Their hostility later grew into a full-blown rivalry as they emerged as the leaders of the Suzuki and Shijō schools respectively.

When the Meiji government established a national art exhibition in 1907, an official urged Shōnen to become a member of its jury, but he obstinately declined, reasoning that too many art-ignorant bureaucrats would meddle with the experts' decisions.[6] Although Shōnen had many students, only a few achieved successful careers, and this may have cast a shadow on his reputation after his death. But as true prowess with the brush has largely disappeared from contemporary Japanese painting, scholars have gained renewed admiration for Shōnen's work.[7] MM

BIBLIOGRAPHY

Donguri 鈍愚理. "Suzuki Shōnen ni atauru no sho" 鈴木松年に與ふるの書. *Chūō bijutsu* 中央美術 2, no. 7 (July 1916): 88–89.

"Gendai meigaka den 5: Suzuki Shōnen" 現代名畫家傳(五). *Kaiga seidan* 繪畫清談 5 (May 1914): 52–54.

Harada Heisaku 原田平作. *Bakumatsu Kyōraku no gajin tachi* 幕末京洛の画人たち. Kyoto: Kyōto Shinbunsha 京都新聞社, 1985.

Hata Senrei 畑仙齢. "Yukeru Suzuki Shōnen" 逝ける鈴木松年. *Kaiga seidan* 6, no. 3 (March 1918): 34–36.

Kanzaki Ken'ichi 神崎憲一. *Kyōto ni okeru nihongashi* 京都に於ける日本画史. Kyoto: Kyōto Seihan Insatsusha 京都精版印刷社, 1929.

Konishi Fukunen 小西福年. "Shōnen'ō tsuioku" 松年翁追憶. *Daimai bijutsu* 大毎美術 8, no. 3 (March 1929): 10–15.

Kyōtoshi Bijutsukan 京都市美術館. *Kyōto gadan: Edo matsu Meiji no gajin tachi* 京都画壇江戸末・明治の画人たち. Kyoto: Ātosha アート社, 1977.

Morioka, Michiyo, and Paul Berry. *Modern Masters of Kyoto: The Transformation of Japanese Painting Traditions, Nihonga from the Griffith and Patricia Way Collection.* Seattle: Seattle Art Museum, 1999.

Okada Han'yō 岡田播陽. "Suzuki Shōnen'ō no shōgai" 鈴木松年の生涯. *Chūō bijutsu* 4, no. 3 (March 1918): 88–94.

"Shōnen gahaku to kataru" 松年畫伯と語る. *Shoga kottō zasshi* 書畫骨董雜誌 43 (December 1911): 21–24.

NOTES

1. See "Shōnen gahaku to kataru," 21.
2. Okada, "Suzuki Shōnen'ō no shōgai," 92.
3. For a color illustration of this work, see Kyōtoshi Bijutsukan, *Kyōto gadan,* 84–85.
4. Hata, "Yukeru Suzuki Shōnen," 35. Senrei points out that Shōnen did not have to paint textile designs due to his comfortable inheritance from Hyakunen.
5. The anecdote is described in great detail by Okada, "Suzuki Shōnen'ō no shōgai," 89–91.
6. Hata, "Yukeru Suzuki Shōnen," 36. See also Konishi, "Shōnen'ō tsuioku," 12–13.
7. See Harada Heisaku, "Edomatsu Meiji no Kyōto no gajintachi," in Kyōtoshi Bijutsukan, *Kyōto gadan,* 248.

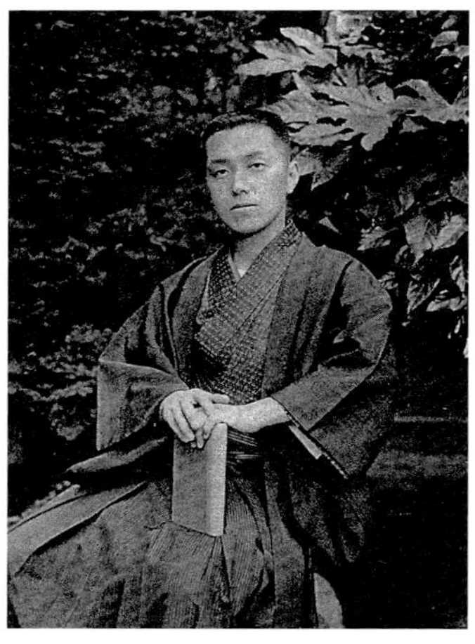

Takakura Kangai 高倉観崖 1884–1957?

Occasionally, a particular event in an artist's life has such an impact that it transforms his or her art completely. This was certainly the case with Takakura Kangai, whose artistic direction made a 180-degree turn after he traveled to China in 1918.

Biographical data about Kangai are scarce. Born in Beppu 別府 in Ōita, Kyushu, he graduated in 1905 from the Painting Division of the Kyoto Municipal School of Arts and Crafts (Kyōto Shiritsu Bijutsu Kōgei Gakkō 京都市立美術工芸学校).[1] Hirai Baisen 平井楳仙 (1889–1969) was in the class a year behind him. Sometime after graduation, Kangai entered the studio of Takeuchi Seihō 竹内栖鳳 (1864–1942).[2]

Kangai was first accepted at the Bunten in 1914 with a *bijinga* (painting of female subjects). This pair of screens titled *Spring at Kamo River* (Kamogawa no haru 鴨川の春) depicted a young woman drying *yūzen* textiles by a river. Kangai deftly represented numerous colorful floral textiles to contrast with the unadorned beauty of the woman. The next year, he repeated the theme of a woman at work in *Mandarin Oranges* (Mikan 蜜柑). In this representation of a woman harvesting fruits in an orchard, Kangai displayed his skill not only in his depiction of the figure but also in the detailed landscape background. Both paintings reflected the popularity of contemporary subjects in a naturalistic style among Kyoto painters during the early 1910s. For the 1916 Bunten, Kangai turned to a complex multiple-figure composition. In *Spring Outing* (Haru no asobi 春の遊び), Edo-period women enjoy a picnic in a scene filled with luxurious garments and ornately decorated objects such as parasols, tea utensils, and portable furniture.[3] Among many *bijinga* accepted at the Bunten that year, Kangai's work stood out for its intricate decorative patterns and attention to minute details.

By 1917 Kangai had established a reputation for large-scale *bijinga* generously embellished with expensive pigments. *Spring at Kamo River* was priced at 1,000 yen, one of the highest amounts that year, when the cost of most paintings ranged from 50 to 500 yen.[4] Thus, upon previewing Kangai's painting of flowers for the 1917 Bunten, one reporter wrote, "As usual, hardworking Kangai has produced an attention-grabbing, eye-blinding painting of dazzling color. He has invested about 600 yen–worth of pigments—gold, azurite blue, malachite green, powdered coral, powdered crystal, and everything else he can find—to cover the surface of a pair of six-fold screens that already have *urahaku* 裏箔 [gold leaf applied to the back of silk]."[5] Despite Kangai's effort, the painting was rejected.

It is likely that Kangai became acquainted with Hashimoto Kansetsu 橋本関雪 (1883–1945) through Seihō's private school, of which both were members. In the spring of 1918 they embarked on a trip to China. Traveling to Jiangnan 江南, the area immediately south of the lower reaches of the Yangtze River 揚子江, they visited Suzhou 蘇州, Hangzhou 杭州, and Shanghai 上海.[6] That fall Kangai submitted the triptych *Scenes from Zhejiang* (Sekkō shoken 浙江所見) to the Bunten.[7] Drawn from his firsthand experiences in

China, three elaborate landscapes represent exotic Chinese architecture, including the famous seven-story pagoda of Tiger Hill in Suzhou. In the following year Kangai was reported to be painting a Chinese subject again,[8] but there is no record of his participation in the government exhibition in 1919 or thereafter.

The details of Kangai's career after this time are unknown. Apparently deciding to pursue painting independently, away from the politics of the national competitions, Kangai organized private exhibitions at the public hall in Kyoto's Okazaki Park in 1920 and 1921.[9] In the late 1920s his Chinese landscapes in literati style began to appear in the advertising section of an art magazine, *Daimai bijutsu* 大毎美術. One such work, dated 1929, included the artist's inscription stating that he had painted it during a visit to Ube in Yamaguchi prefecture.[10] Supported by collectors in his hometown, Kangai may have also traveled to make a living, as many free-spirited literati painters had done in earlier times. MM

BIBLIOGRAPHY

Takakura Kangai 高倉観崖. "Shina ni asobite" 支那に遊びて. *Kyōto bijutsu* 京都美術, no. 45 (June 1918): 15–19.

———, ed. *Sosetsu shoken* 蘓浙所見. Beppu, Ōita: Takakura Kangai Kōenkai 高倉観崖後援会, 1928.

Yui Kazuto 油井一人. *Nijū seiiki bukko nihongaka jiten* 20世紀物故日本画家事典. Tokyo: Bijutsu Nenkansha 美術年鑑社, 1998.

NOTES

1. Araki Nori, ed., *Dai Nihon shoga meika taikan, denki gehen* (1934; reprint, Tokyo: Daiichi Shobō, 1975), 2785, and *Gagakkō-Geidai 100 shūnen kinen dōsōsei meibo, 1880–1980* (Kyoto: Kyōto Shiritsu Geijutsu Daigaku Bijutsu Gakubu Dōsōkai, 1980), 30.

2. Kangai is referred to as a member of Chikujōkai, Seihō's private school, in "Nyūsen rakusen uchimaku banashi," *Kaiga seidan* 5, no. 11 (November 1917): 54.

3. *Spring at Kamo River* is illustrated in Nittenshi Hensan Iinkai, *Nittenshi 3, Buntenhen 3* (Tokyo: Nitten, 1980), 318–19. For *Mandarin Oranges* and *Spring Outing*, see Nittenshi Hensan Iinkai, *Nittenshi 4, Buntenhen 4* (Tokyo: Nitten, 1981), 110–11, 404–5.

4. "Dai hakkai Bunten no chinretsuhin mokuroku," *Kaiga seidan* 2, no. 10 (November 1914): 2–5.

5. "Nyūsen rakusen uchimaku banashi," 54.

6. See Takakura, "Shina ni asobite," 15–19, and two essays by Hashimoto Kansetsu, "Shina man'yū miyage banashi," *Kaiga seidan* 6, no. 6 (June 1918): 41, and "Kōnan ni mitaru shizen to jin'i no chōwa," *Kyōto bijutsu*, no. 45 (June 1918): 9–11.

7. The painting is illustrated in Nittenshi Hensan Iinkai, *Nittenshi 5, Buntenhen 5* (Tokyo: Nitten, 1981), 327.

8. "Teiten to shosakka," *Bijutsu no Nihon* 11, no. 9 (September 1919): 19.

9. Azuma Seijirō, "Sosetsu jūran shōhin ni daisu," in Takakura, *Sosetsu shoken*, n.p.

10. See *Daimai bijutsu* 9, no. 5 (May 1930): 26.

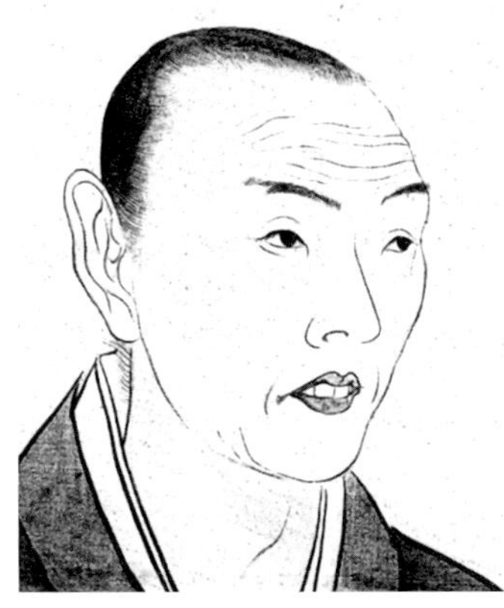

Tani Bunchō 谷文晁 1763–1840

Bunchō was born to a samurai family who lived in Edo while serving the Tayasu 田安 family from Omi (Shiga prefecture). His father, Tani Rokkoku 谷麓谷 (1729–1809), was a well-known poet who encouraged Bunchō to study painting from an early age. When he was about ten years old, Bunchō became a pupil of the Kanō-school artist Katō Bunrei 加藤文麗 (1706–1782). This early exposure sparked an interest in the Kanō-school style that would surface in Bunchō's career on many occasions.

When he was eighteen, Bunchō began to study with the painter Watanabe Gentai 渡辺玄對 (1749–1822), who had recently arrived in Edo from Nagasaki, where he had studied the latest Chinese influences. Gentai had been exposed to a range of Chinese painting—Southern and Northern schools, professional and amateur. He owned many Chinese paintings, including twelve by Lan Ying 藍瑛 (1585–c. 1664), of which a number are still extant. This group of Lan Ying paintings influenced Bunchō and was copied by many painters around Japan, including Yamamoto Baiitsu 山本梅逸 (1783–1856). Lan Ying was a popular professional artist who often mixed Northern and Southern styles in his painting, just as Bunchō did in many of his later works. Bunchō was also influenced by Zhe 浙 school paintings of the Ming period and landscapes by Xie Shichen 謝時臣 (1487–1567), which were available in Japan by the eighteenth century.

Bunchō's early exposure to so many foreign ideas in painting encouraged him, as it did many literati artists, to be wide-ranging in his interests. He worked in most of the major styles, including *yamatoe* 大和絵, Buddhist iconic paintings, Rinpa 琳派, blue-and-green landscapes, hastily painted ink landscapes, compositions drawn from Song paintings, formal portrait paintings, "true view" (*shinkeizu* 真景圖) landscapes, and recently imported Chinese and even Western styles. Amid this astonishing array, Bunchō achieved a level of excellence in each form. His versatility had a formative effect on the development of literati painting in the Edo area. Literati painting in Japan is distinguished from its Chinese counterparts by its eclecticism; Japanese artists continually incorporated influences of all kinds, while many Chinese literati sought to more clearly define and delimit their sources. Though eclecticism is a general feature of Japanese literati painting, it was most striking among Bunchō, his friends, and their followers.

Bunchō's earliest paintings are fairly simple compositions of roughly brushed landscapes; these were followed by precisely painted ink landscapes of the Kansei 寛政 period (1789–1800), which show a soft delicacy that is often associated with literati brushwork. In the last decades of Bunchō's life, complex blue-and-green landscapes on silk with moderately stiff brushwork alternated with ink landscapes on paper that featured loose, wet brushwork and washes. He was one of the most popular painters in Edo, and he matched the great demand for his work with his tremendous output. Even during his lifetime some critics felt that his professionalism at times overwhelmed his sensitivity, imparting a mechanical quality to some works.[1]

Bunchō had hundreds of students, including many of the most talented Edo-area artists of the following generation, such as Watanabe Kazan 渡辺華山 (1793–1841), Tachihara Kyōsho 立原杏所 (1786–1840), and Takaku Aigai 高久靄崖 (1796–1843). PB

BIBLIOGRAPHY

Atsumi Kuniyasu 渥美國泰. *Shazanrō Tani Bunchō no subete* 写山楼谷文晁のすべて. Tokyo: Ribun Shuppan 里文出版, 2002.

Chance, Frank. "Fealty and Patronage: Notes on the Sponsorship by Matsudaira Sadanobu of Tani Bunchō and His Painting." *Early Modern Japan* 12, no. 2 (Fall–Winter 2004): 68–76.

———. "Tani Bunchō and the Edo School of Japanese Painting." PhD diss., University of Washington, 1986.

Fukushima Kenritsu Hakubutsukan 福島県立博物館. *Sadanobu to Bunchō: Matsudaira Sadanobu to shūhen no gajintachi* 定信と文晁：松平定信と周辺の画人たち. Aizu Wakamatsu 会津若松, 1992.

Hosono Masanobu 細野正信. *Kindai kaiga no reimei: Bunchō–Kazan to yōfūga* 近代絵画の黎明：文晁・華山と洋風画. Nihon bijutsu zenshū 日本美術全集, vol. 25. Tokyo: Gakushū Kenkyūsha 学習研究社, 1994.

Kōgeisha 巧藝社. *Bunchō ibokushū* 文晁遺墨集. Tokyo, 1930.

Kōno Motoaki. 河野元昭. "Tani Bunchō" 谷文晁. *Nihon no bijutsu*, no. 257 (1987).

Onshi Kyōto Hakubutsukan 恩賜京都博物館. *Bunchōihō* 文晁遺芳. Kyoto: Benridō 便利堂, 1938.

Sasaki Eiriko 佐々木英理子. *Tani Bunchō to sono ichimon* 谷文晁とその一門. Tokyo: Itabashi Kuritsu Bijutsukan 板橋区立美術館, 2007.

Tochigi Kenritsu Bijutsukan 栃木県立美術館. *Shazanrō Tani Bunchō* 写山楼谷文晁. Utsunomiya 宇都宮, 1979.

Yamato Bunkakan 大和文華館. "Bunchō–Tairō tokushū" 文晁・大浪特輯. *Yamato Bunka* 大和文華, no. 105 (2001).

Yorozu Tetsugorō 萬鉄五郎. *Bunchō* 文晁. Tokyo: ARS アルス, 1926.

NOTE

1. Tanomura Chikuden 田能村竹田 (1777–1835) occasionally expressed such criticisms of Bunchō's work, as in his inscription to a 1828 handscroll of Mount Unzen: "At Hashimoto Chikka's house there is a long landscape handscroll made by Tani Bunchō. It is thought to have been made during his best period. The brush and ink method and color technique are scrupulous, completely exhausting the good and the beautiful without going to excess. However, looking critically, not a few mechanical aspects can be seen; therefore this handscroll does not achieve the first rank." See Paul Berry, "Tanomura Chikuden 1777–1835: Man Amidst the Mountains" (PhD diss., University of Michigan, 1985), 111.

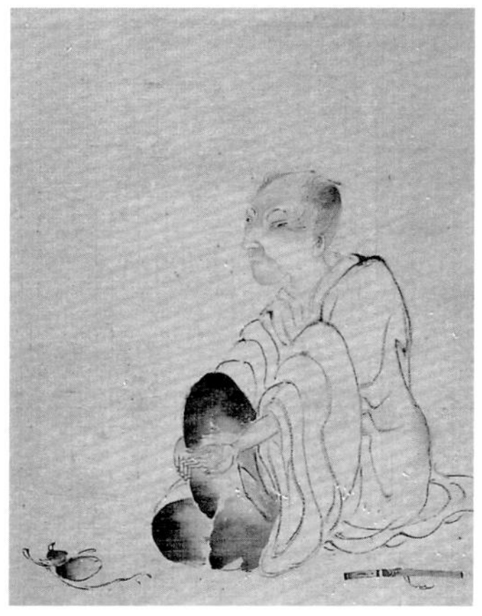

Tanomura Chikuden 田能村竹田 1777–1835

Chikuden is commonly acknowledged as one of the most skilled painters and sophisticated scholars of Chinese painting and verse of his generation. This high reputation continued well into the middle of the twentieth century, and because his most famous works have passed from one important collection to another, they are in excellent condition even today.

The Tanomura family were the hereditary physicians for the daimyo of the Oka *han*, the Nakagawa. As the second son, Chikuden was allowed to study Chinese poetry and painting with two local artists, Fuchino Shinsai 淵野真斎 (1760–1823) and Watanabe Hōtō 渡辺蓬島 (1752–1833). In 1798 he received permission to abandon the family occupation of physician for that of scholar. His first duty was to participate in the the compilation of the *Bungo kokushi* 豊後国誌, the gazetteer of the local province. Chikuden's three years of work on the gazetteer had two major influences on his life. When a draft of the gazetteer was completed, Chikuden traveled to Edo to consult with domain officials over revisions to the text. Arriving in the summer of 1801, he briefly enrolled in the Confucian school of the noted scholar Hayashi Jussai 林述斎 (1768–1841), and he met repeatedly with the painter Tani Bunchō 谷文晁 (1763–1840). This was Chikuden's only experience of the Edo literati world. Yet his impressions of the literati groups in Osaka and Kyoto, where he stayed on his travels to and from Edo, would have a lasting impact on his attitudes toward painting.[1] In addition, his survey of the conditions in local towns and farming communities, part of his preparation for writing the gazetteer, exposed him to the severe conditions of peasant life, laying the foundation for his later petitions for reform of the *han* government.

Early in 1805 Chikuden took a leisurely, circuitous tour through Nagasaki, Shimonoseki, and Osaka on his way to Kyoto, meeting the major scholars, poets, and painters of western Japan. He became friends with many of the top literati of Kyoto and Osaka, staying, for example, for forty days with Uragami Gyokudō 浦上玉堂 (1745–1820) at the small temple Jimyōin 持明院 in Osaka. The relationships formed at this time so bonded Chikuden to Osaka and Kyoto that he would travel back and forth between these cities and his hometown of Taketa for the rest of his life.

Near the end of 1811 Chikuden wrote a petition of protest in response to the rioting of peasants in the Oka *han* domain. He wrote several more the following year and finally resigned his position as Confucian scholar to the domain when his missives were ignored. From then on, Chikuden focused on developing his skills in painting, traveling around western Japan, and meeting fellow literati. His talent as a painter matured, and his reputation rose over the years. In autumn 1826 he began a fateful yearlong stay in Nagasaki. He immersed himself in the study of recently imported Chinese paintings and found a new impetus for his own work. In both painting and poetry he achieved a level of understanding of Chinese cultural traditions that was remarkable for his time. He was one of the few literati painters who could express himself freely in long Chinese inscriptions on his works. The last eight years of his life saw the production of his most renowned albums and hanging scrolls. This fruitful period was cut short by his illness and sudden death. He continued to influence later generations through the works of his disciples, especially his adopted son Tanomura Chokunyū (1814–1907) and Hoashi Kyoū (1810–1884). PB

BIBLIOGRAPHY

Berry, Paul. "Tanomura Chikuden 1777–1835: Man Amidst the Mountains." PhD diss., University of Michigan, 1985.

Idemitsu Bijutsukan 出光美術館. *Tanomura Chikuden* 田能村竹田. Tokyo, 1997.

———. *Tanomura Chikuden* 田能村竹田. Tokyo: Heibonsha 平凡社, 1992.

Iijima Isamu 飯島勇. "Tanomura Chikuden" 田能村竹田. *Nihon no bijutsu* 日本の美術, no. 165 (1980).

Kizaki Aikichi 木崎愛吉. *Daifūryū Tanomura Chikuden* 大風流田能村竹田. 8 vols. Tokyo: Minyūsha 民友社, 1929.

Kōno Motoaki 河野元昭. *Gyokudō • Chikuden • Beisanjin* 玉堂・竹田・米山人. Edo meisaku gajō zenshū 江戸名作画帖全集, vol. 2. Tokyo: Shinshindō Shuppan 駸々堂出版, 1993.

Munakata Ken'ichi 宗像健一. *Tanomura Chikuden* 田能村竹田. Ōita: Ōita-ken Kyōiku Iinkai 大分県教育委員会, 1993.

Ōita-ken Kyōiku 大分県教育庁管理部文化課編. *Tanomura Chikuden shiryōshū* 田能村竹田資料集. 4 vols. Ōita: Ōita-ken Kyōiku Iinkai, 1992.

Ōita Kenritsu Geijutsu Kaikan 大分県立芸術会館. *"Chikuden to sono kōyūtachi" ten*「竹田とその交友たち」展. Ōita, 1994.

Sasaki Gōzō 佐々木剛三. *Mokubei / Chikuden* 木米/竹田. Nihon bijutsu kaiga zenshū 日本美術絵画全集, vol. 21. Tokyo: Shūeisha 集英社, 1980.

Takahashi Hiromi 高橋博巳, ed. *Sanchūjin; Jigadaigo; Chikuden shiyū garoku* 山中人饒舌；自画題語；竹田荘師友 画録. Tokyo: Perikansha ぺりかん社, 1996.

Taketani Chōjirō 竹谷長二郎. *Bunjin gaka Tanomura Chikuden* 文人画家田能村竹田. Tokyo: Meiji Shoin 明治書院, 1981.

Tanomura Chikuden 田能村竹田. Bunjinga suihen 文人画粋編, vol. 17. Tokyo: Chūō Kōronsha 中央公論社, 1975.

Togari Soshinan 外狩素心庵. *Chikuden meiseki daizushi* 竹田名蹟大図誌. 2 vols. Tokyo: Benridō 便利堂, 1935.

Woodson, Yoko. "Traveling Bunjin Painters and Their Patrons: Economic Lifestyle and Art of Rai San'yō and Tanomura Chikuden." PhD diss., University of California at Berkeley, 1983.

NOTE

1. The most comprehensive treatment in English of Chikuden's career is Berry, "Tanomura Chikuden 1777–1835." The most detailed treatment of Chikuden's career, letters, and day-to-day activities is the classic eight-volume text by Kizaki Aikichi, *Daifūryū Tanomura Chikuden*, of 1929. The best recent treatment of Chikuden's life in Japanese is Munakata Ken'ichi's 1993 *Tanomura Chikuden*. The information presented in this brief biography is found in all three of these sources.

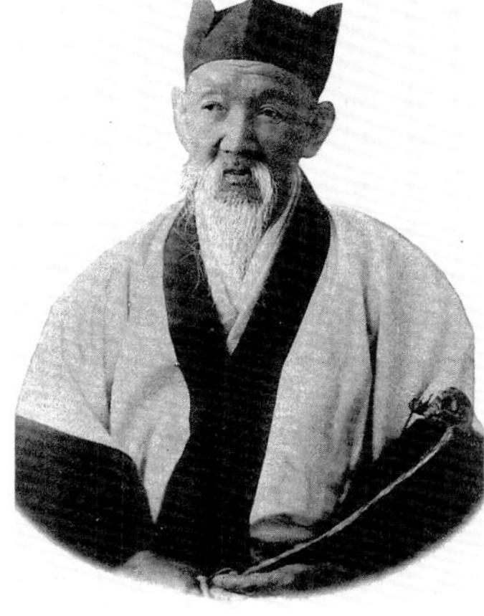

Tanomura Chokunyū 田能村直入 1814–1907

Tanomura Chokunyū was the third son of Sannomiya Den'emon 三宮伝右衛門, an official with a hereditary position in the Oka *han* silver office and a village headman for the town of Taketa in central Ōita prefecture. Raised among Taketa's many artists, Chokunyū first studied Kanō painting with Okamoto Baisetsu 岡本梅雪 in 1820. Two years later he became a student of Tanomura Chikuden 田能村竹田 (1777–1835), who realized the young boy's talent and adopted him into his family. Chokunyū often accompanied Chikuden on his many journeys. On a trip to Osaka in the ninth month of 1834, Chikuden enrolled

Chokunyū in the Senshindō 洗心堂 school organized by Ōshio Chūsai 大塩中斎 (1792–1837), the revolutionary proponent of the thought of Wang Yangming 王陽明 (1472–1528) and a friend of many Osaka-area literati.

After Chikuden's death in 1835, Chokunyū spent four years in Ōita prefecture working on commissions for Buddhist temples. Tired of the isolation of his home province, he returned to the Kansai area in 1839 and eventually established his residence in the port city of Sakai, where he maintained a home until moving to Osaka in 1846. Chokunyū is recorded as having several hundred students in Sakai, yet he continued to expand his stylistic repertoire by avidly copying Chinese paintings.

In the eighth month of 1878, a decade after moving to Kyoto, Chokunyū petitioned the Kyoto prefectural government for the creation of Japan's first publicly supported painting school, the Kyoto Prefecture Painting School (Kyōto-fu Gagakkō 京都府画学校). He pledged to use the proceeds of his painting activities to help support the school, and in the months that followed he canvassed the countryside, raising substantial funds. Further support for the establishment of the school came the next year, when four artists of the Maruyama and Shijō schools submitted a similar proposal to the prefectural government. In 1882 Chokunyū opened a private school for teaching *nanga* in his home. It merged in 1896 with the newly established Japan Nanga Association (Nihon Nanga Kyōkai 日本南画協会), which attained a national membership of more than 1,500.

Chokunyū's study of Zen began in his youth in Taketa. In 1862 he signed a portrait of Baisaō 賣茶翁 (1672–1763) in the manner of an Ōbaku Zen priest, identifying his lineage in the fortieth generation from the Tang Zen master Linqi 臨濟 (J., Rinzai, d. 867).[1] Around this time, Chokunyū visited the Shōindō 松陰堂 at Manpukuji 萬福寺 at the invitation of the Ōbaku priest Daishin 大心 (n.d.). Here he encountered the teenaged monk Daiyū Kōhō 大雄弘法 (1849–1929), who would become the forty-sixth head of the Ōbaku Zen headquarters of Manpukuji from 1919 to 1925. Chokunyū, as the old friend of Daiyū's teacher Daishin, received much consideration from the high-ranking younger priest. After consultations with priests at Manpukuji, Chokunyū became head priest at the Shishirin-in 獅子林院 subtemple (1898–1902). He later moved to a retreat in eastern Kyoto.[2]

Chokunyū became known for creating many large series of paintings such as his one hundred portraits of Baisaō (1672–1763), which commemorated the hundredth anniversary of the death of the founder of *sencha* tea practice in Japan. Chokunyū was one of the major *sencha* enthusiasts in the Kansai area, arranging large gatherings and concomitant displays of artworks. He also made many Buddhist paintings, including a complete set of five hundred paintings of Rakan, the legendary group of the Buddha's original disciples and a very popular subject in Ōbaku Zen. Chokunyū usually created such sets to raise funds for restoring temples, supporting painting academies, and similar large projects.

Chokunyū's descendants start with his son, Shōsai 小斎 (1845–1909), adopted in 1850, and Shōsai's son, Shōkō 小篁 (1879–1910); the three generations sometimes created joint works during Chokunyū's last years. The most prominent of Chokunyū's many disciples were Tajika Chikuson 田近竹邨 (1864–1922), Kodama Katei 児玉果亭 (1841–1913), Yamada Kaidō 山田介堂 (1869–1924), Tanaka Hakuin 田中伯陰 (1871–1930), Hattori Gorō 服部五老 (1871–1930), and Hirao Chikka 平尾竹霞 (1856–1939). Chokunyū's influence on twentieth-century literati painting became pervasive through the careers of these popular artists and their students. In the late Meiji period, Chokunyū and Tomioka Tessai 富岡鐵斎 (1836–1924) were known as the two senior figures in literati painting. Although they associated in a variety of ways, they had quite different temperaments. Chokunyū's lasting influence was through his disciples, while Tessai's legacy was his artistic vision and the style of painting he developed near the end of his life.

PB

BIBLIOGRAPHY

Kyōto Furitsu Sōgō Shiryōkan 京都府立総合資料館. *Tanomura Chokunyū to Tomioka Tessai* 田能村直入と富岡鉄斎. Kyoto, 1985.

Morioka, Michiyo, and Paul Berry. *Modern Masters of Kyoto: The Transformation of Japanese Painting Traditions, Nihonga from the Griffith and Patricia Way Collection.* Seattle: Seattle Art Museum, 1999.

Onshi Kyōto Hakubutsukan 恩賜京都博物館. *Chokunyū bokuhō* 直入墨芳. Kyoto: Benridō 便利堂, 1937.

Shimada Yasuhiro 島田康寛. *Kyōto no nihonga* 京都の日本画. Kyoto: Kyōto Shinbunsha 京都新聞社, 1991.

Tanomura Shōkō 田能村小篁, ed. *Chokuyū Koji myōsekishū* 入居士妙蹟集. 10 vols. Kyoto: Yamada Unsōdō 山田芸艸堂, 1909–.

Watanabe Masaru 渡辺勝. *Chokunyū Koji ihō* 直入居士遺芳. 2 vols. Kyoto: Gashindō 画神堂, 1925.

Yamamoto Hidemaro 山本英麿. "Tanomura Chokunyū to Kodama Katei: Meiji no bunjinga seisui ni tsuite" 田能村直入と児玉果亭: 明治の文人画盛衰について. *Ueda Joshi Tanki Daigaku kiyō* 上田女子短期大学紀要, no. 18 (1995): 11–22.

NOTES

1. Because Chokunyū also referred to himself as the forty-first generation in this lineage, there must have been some controversy over who approved his entry into the lineage.

2. The details of Chokunyū's career as an Ōbaku monk and most of the other biographical information in this entry are drawn from Watanabe, *Chokunyū Koji ihō*, the most detailed biography of Chokunyū. His time at Manpukuji is discussed on pp. 105–10.

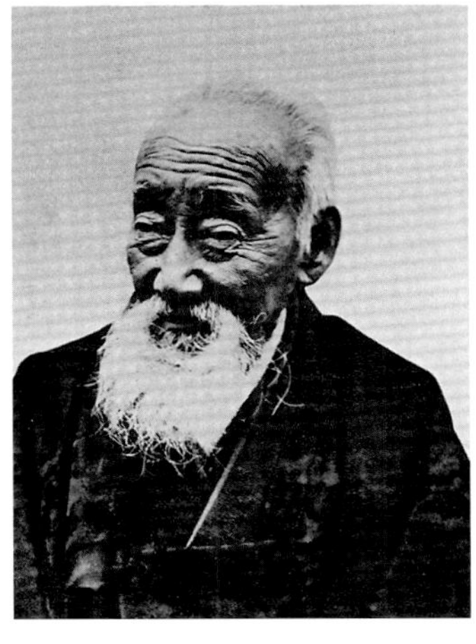

Tomioka Tessai 富岡鉄斎 1836–1924

Tomioka Tessai reached the pinnacle of his career in old age, when his physical appearance—flowing, white beard, dark robe and scholar's hat, and cane in hand—resembled that of a Daoist immortal. Mirroring his creative powers during the last decade of his life, his keen intellectual curiosity kept him engaged in the contemporary art scene. Ogawa Sen'yō 小川千甕 (1882–1971) remembered encountering the nearly eighty-year-old Tessai, dressed in his trademark robe and carrying his cane, studying newly introduced French art at an exhibition sponsored by the White Birch (Shirakaba 白樺) group.[1]

Tessai's mature painting style, characterized by exuberant ink brushwork and bright colors, emerged after a lifelong study of not only Chinese and Japanese literati traditions but also the practices of the Kanō school, *yamatoe*, Rinpa, and *ukiyoe*. He even experimented with Western-style painting. Yet Tessai regarded himself as a scholar and not a painter, urging viewers to read his inscriptions in order to understand the meaning of his paintings. Extolling the literati virtue of "reading ten thousand books and traveling ten thousand miles," Tessai journeyed throughout Japan from north to south and amassed a huge collection of books which included classical Chinese publications no longer available on the continent. Naitō Konan 内藤湖南 (1866–1934), a prominent sinologist at Kyoto Imperial University, is said to have prized Tessai's personal library as an invaluable resource in his field.[2] When financial rewards came to him late in life, Tessai spent generously to acquire art objects he fancied. Much to the chagrin of antique dealers, Tessai casually left valuable items, including a hibachi by Aoki Mokubei 青木木米 (1767–1833), an earthenware piece decorated by Ogata Kezan 尾形乾山 (1663–1743), and a painting by Tanomura Chikuden 田能村竹田 (1777–1835), in his cluttered studio, insisting that ownership is meaningless if the objects are locked up in storage.[3]

The second son of a Buddhist robe merchant in Kyoto, Tessai suffered hearing problems from childhood, and for this reason his parents encouraged him to establish a livelihood other than the family business. With the intention of becoming a scholar, Tessai pursued Japanese and Chinese studies and began painting by the mid-1850s. Kubota Setsuyō 窪田雪鷹 (act. mid-19th c.) and Ōsumi Nankō 大角南耕 (act. mid-19th c.) are believed to have given young Tessai painting lessons. During his early career, the most significant influence came from the poet-nun Ōtagaki Rengetsu 大田垣蓮月 (1791–1875), an accomplished calligrapher, potter, and painter. She hired the teenage Tessai as a live-in assistant for her pottery-making endeavor and later promoted him to painting her calligraphy compositions on the wares. In 1861 Tessai traveled to Nagasaki to seek guidance from Hidaka Tetsuō 日高鉄翁 (1791–1871) and Kinoshita Itsuun 木下逸雲 (1799–1866), and in 1868, through Rengetsu, Tessai met Tanomura Chokunyū 田能村直入 (1814–1907), a leading exponent of literati painting in Kyoto. Yamanaka Shinten'ō 山中信天翁 (1823–1885), a celebrated calligrapher-painter and connoisseur of Chinese painting, also influenced Tessai's development as a painter. It is likely, however, that Tessai was basically self-taught, using the works of other artists as models and investigating an array of past painting styles.

After a brief career as a Shinto priest at Ōtori Shrine in Osaka during the late 1870s, Tessai returned to Kyoto to take care of his mother. In subsequent decades he played an active role in the Kyoto art world. He was appointed to the judging panel of the first modern competitive painting exhibition in Kyoto, the 1886 Kyoto Young Painters Study Group (Kyōto Seinen Kaiga Kenkyūkai 京都青年絵画研究会) organized by Kōno Bairei 幸野楳嶺 (1844–1895) and Kubota Beisen 久保田米僊 (1852–1906). In 1892 Tessai and Bairei were fellow jurors at the Kyoto City Exhibition of Arts and Crafts (*Kyōtoshi bijutsu kōgeihin ten* 京都市美術工芸品展). Tessai continued to serve on prestigious juries and participate in exhibitions through the late 1890s. In 1896 he joined Chokunyū and twenty-three other Kyoto literati painters to launch the Japan Nanga Association (Nihon Nanga Kyōkai 日本南画協会), with the aim of advancing literati painting in the modern era. Furthermore, from 1894 to 1904, Tessai taught ethics at the Kyoto Municipal School of Arts and Crafts (Kyōto Shiritsu Bijutsu Kōgei Gakkō 京都市立美術工芸学校). Through his activities, Tessai formed friendships beyond the literati circle with many *nihonga* painters, including Mori Kansai 森寛斎 (1814–1894), Kishi Chikudō 岸竹堂 (1826–1897), Kōno Bairei, and Imao Keinen 今尾景年 (1845–1924). As Tessai was not a professional painter, he did not take pupils, but Hashimoto Dokuzan 橋本獨山 (1869–1928), who would become head priest of Shōkokuji 相国寺, a Rinzai-sect Zen temple in Kyoto, is believed to have studied under Tessai during the mid-1880s.[4]

In the last decade of the Meiji era Tessai's artistic fame spread beyond Kyoto and Osaka, and during the Taishō period, his painting reached the height of creative freedom, featuring a lavish use of ink, exhilarating brushwork, and accents of vivid *yamatoe* color. In some of his late works, Tessai achieved an ink expression of unusual richness and complexity by drawing with an old ink stick directly onto the wet surface of layered brushwork.[5] Appreciation of Tessai's painting transcended the *nihonga-yōga* division, and he inspired younger artists such as Tomita Keisen 冨田溪仙 (1879–1936), Kondō Koichiro 近藤浩一路 (1884–1962), Morita Tsunetomo 森田恒友 (1881–1933), and Masamune Tokusaburō 正宗得三郎 (1883–1962). Tokusaburō, an oil painter from Tokyo, visited Tessai on numerous occasions and published many essays on the elder master. For these painters, Tessai's nonconformist lifestyle and art not only represented the embodiment of the Japanese literati tradition but also resonated with the modern ideals of individualism and expressionism introduced from the West. MM

BIBLIOGRAPHY

Atorie アトリエ 15, no. 4 [Tessai gō 鐵齋号] (March 1938).

Katō Ruiko 加藤類子, Shimada Yasuhiro 島田康寛, et al., eds. *Bujnjinga no kindai: Tessai to sono shiyūtachi* 文人画の近代：鉄斎とその師友たち. Exh. cat. Kyoto: Kyōto Kokuritsu Kindai Bijutsukan 京都国立近代美術館, 1997.

Kyōtoshi Bijutsukan 京都市美術館. *Seitan 150-nen kinen Tomioka Tessai ten* 生誕 150 年記念富岡鉄斎展. Exh. cat. Kyoto, 1985.

Misawa Kyūkō 三澤九皐. "Fukkatsu shita Tessaiō no seikatsu" 復活した鉄斎翁の生活. *Kaiga seidan* 繪畫清談 3, no. 8 (August 1915): 34–37.

Morioka, Michiyo, and Paul Berry. *Modern Masters of Kyoto: The Transformation of Japanese Painting Traditions, Nihonga from the Griffith and Patricia Way Collection.* Seattle: Seattle Art Museum, 1999.

Nanga kanshō 南畫鑑賞 5, no. 10 [Tomioka Tessai tokushū 富岡鐵齋特輯] (October 1936).

Nanga kanshō 6, no. 11 [Tomioka Tessai tokushū] (November 1937).

Ogawa Sen'yō 小川千甕. "Tessai sensei ni kakawaru zakkan" 鐵齋先生に關はる雜感. *Atorie* 2, no. 2 (February 1925): 18–21.

Uchiyama Takeo 内山武夫. "Tessai to Kyōto gadan" 鉄斎と京都画壇. In Shiga Kenritsu Kindai Bijtsukan 滋賀県立近代美術館, *Tomioka Tessai ten—Fuse Bijutsukan shozōhin o chūshin ni* 富岡鉄斎展—布施美術館所蔵品を中心に. Exh. cat. Ōtsu, 1993.

NOTES

1. Ogawa Sen'yō, "Tessai sensei ni kakawaru zakkan," 20–21.
2. Misawa, "Fukkatsu shita Tessaiō no seikatsu," 35.
3. Masamune Tokusaburō, "Waga konomu gajin: Tomioka Tessai sensei," *Atorie* 11, no. 4 (April 1934): 26.
4. Misawa, "Fukkatsu shita Tessaiō no seikatsu," 36.
5. Masamune, "Waga konomu gajin," 26.

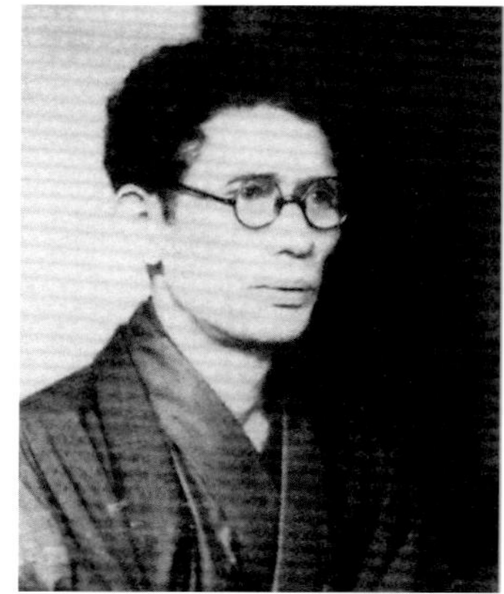

Tomita Keisen
冨田溪仙 1879–1936

Tomita Keisen was tall and muscular with a tanned face, generous nose, and penetrating eyes. But his most prominent feature was his exceptionally large head with naturally curly hair, which one writer compared to Buddha's.[1] For some observers, his striking appearance symbolized not only the fortitude of his character but also his artistic greatness.[2] Although initially trained in the Shijō-school technique, Keisen was inspired more by the individualism and freedom of the literati tradition. Moreover, he was one of the few Kyoto artists to center his activities at the Tokyo-based Japan Art Institute (Nihon Bijutsuin 日本美術院). Known for his artistic independence and frank, unyielding personality, Keisen achieved a reputation—and notoriety—as an eccentric (*kijin* 奇人) and unconventional (*hakaku* 破格) painter by the end of the 1920s.[3]

Born in Fukuoka to a well-known noodle manufacturer, Keisen acquired a solid foundation in painting while still a youngster under a Kanō-school artist. In 1896 he moved to Kyoto and the following year became a live-in pupil of Tsuji Kakō 都路華香 (1870–1931). In the subsequent decade he mastered the Shijō style under Kakō and participated in various competitions such as the Exhibition of New and Old Art (*Shinko bijutsuhin tenrankai* 新古美術品展覧会) and the Domestic Industrial Exposition (*Naikoku kangyō* hakurankai 内国勧業博覧会). At the same time, he began a process of self-searching that led him to Zen meditation practice, the study of Christianity and ancient Chinese philosophy, and an examination of Nara- and Heian-period Buddhist paintings. His interest in the art of Sengai 仙厓 (1750–1837), a Zen monk, and literati masters such as Ike Taiga 池大雅 (1723–1776) and Yosa Buson 与謝蕪村 (1716–1783) continued to grow, and he visited Tomioka Tessai 富岡鉄斎 (1836–1924) to seek guidance. In 1909 Keisen traveled to Taiwan and China for six months and the next year went on an extensive sketching trip to northern Japan. By the end of the Meiji period, Keisen's distinctive painting style had begun to emerge.

During the early Taishō period, Keisen achieved recognition at the Bunten exhibition. His *Cormorant Fishing Boats* (Ubune 鵜船), derived from his China trip, received an award at the 1912 competition. This informally composed ink depiction of multiple boats crowded with birds and people shows loose brushwork and a spontaneous flair, even though Keisen used an entire trunkful of paper before settling on the final version.[4] Urged by Yokoyama Taikan 横山大観 (1868–1958), who as a Bunten juror had recognized unusual talent in his entries, Keisen participated in the first exhibition sponsored by the reestablished Japan Art Institute in 1914 and remained an active member thereafter. His exuberant brush style and intense color found appreciative viewers among Tokyo's artists, but these features set his work apart from Kyoto *nihonga*, generally characterized by descriptiveness and technical mastery. Yamamoto Shunkyo 山元春挙 (1871–1933), a leading Kyoto painter, once remarked that Keisen's art was more like "amateur play" and did not represent the main current of painting.[5]

Although Keisen remained aloof from the Kyoto art community, he was not a recluse. Kawahigashi Hekigotō 河東碧梧桐 (1873–1937), who sought to modernize haiku and calligraphy by advocating direct, immediate expression, recognized a kindred spirit in Keisen's art and maintained a close friendship with him through the 1910s. Hekigotō often stayed at Keisen's house and once worked with him on a screen at a restaurant at the owner's request.[6] Keisen's exchange with Paul Claudel (1868–1955), French ambassador to Japan from 1921 to 1927, is also well known. A poet, playwright, and admirer of Japanese art, Claudel visited Keisen's thatched-roof house in Saga, Kyoto, in the spring of 1923.[7] Later the two men collaborated on an album, *Twelve Scenes of the Inner Moat at Edo Castle* (Edojō uchibori jūnikei 江戸城内濠十二景), and several other projects.

Convinced that art should be a solitary endeavor, Keisen rejected the common practice of opening a private studio to train students. He was, however, deeply aware of his indebtedness to his teacher Kakō, who had shown great kindness to him early in his career. Upon Kakō's death, Keisen helped to organize his retrospective exhibition at the Imperial Museum of Kyoto and financed the publication of a large book, *Kakō's Ink Trace* (Kakō bokushō 華香墨蹤), which commemorated his accomplishments. Some believed that these were acts of atonement on Keisen's part for having pursued his career with the Tokyo group rather than under Kakō.[8] Regardless, Keisen's effort revealed the tender side of an artist known for his sarcasm and nonconformity. Regrettably, only five years after Kakō's demise, Keisen died of a cerebral hemorrhage.

MM

BIBLIOGRAPHY

Haga Tōru 芳賀徹 and Hayashi Yōko 林洋子, eds. *Pōru Kurōderu to Kyōto gadan* ポール・クローデルと京都画段. Tokyo: Kurōderu Botsugo Gojūnen Kinen Kikaku Iinkai クローデル没後50年記念企画委員会, 2005.

Kawahigashi Hekigotō 河東碧梧桐, Yasuda Yukihiko 安田靫彦, Kobayashi Kokei 小林古径, and Saitō Yori 齋藤與里. "Ko Tomita Keisen tsuitō" 故冨田溪仙追悼. *Bijutsu shinron* 美術新論 11, no. 8 (August 1936): 88–94.

Kotenrō-shujin 壺天樓主人. "Keisen to Hyakusui" 溪仙と百穂. *Daimai bijutsu* 大毎美術 4, no. 11 (November 1925): 17–19.

Kyōtoshi Bijutsukan 京都市美術館. *Botsugo rokūjunen kinen: Tomita Keisen ten* 没後六十年記念冨田溪仙展. Exh. cat. Kyoto, 1996.

Morioka, Michiyo, and Paul Berry. *Modern Masters of Kyoto: The Transformation of Japanese Painting Traditions, Nihonga from the Griffith and Patricia Way Collection.* Seattle: Seattle Art Museum, 1999.

Saitō Yori. "Tomita Keisen ron" 冨田溪仙論. *Chūō bijutsu* 中央美術 3, no. 8 (August 1917): 26–31.

Sakakibara Shihō 榊原紫峰, Sotokari Soshin'an 外狩素心庵, Kanzaki Ken'ichi 神埼憲一, and Shimomise Seiichi 下店静市. "Tomita Keisen shi o kataru" 冨田溪仙氏を語る. *Atorie* アトリエ 6, no. 4 (April 1929): 95–103.

Shimomise Seiichi. "Tomita Keisen ron." *Nihon bijutsu* 日本美術 2, no. 6 (June 1943): 15–18.

———, ed. *Keisen hachijūichiwa* 溪仙八十一話. Tokyo: Kaizōsha 改造社, 1925.

Tanaka Hisao 田中日佐夫. "Tomita Keisen ten o mite" 冨田渓仙展を見て. *Sansai* 三彩 no. 339 (November 1975): 42–43.

Tokubi Yō 徳美容. "Keisen kun no hanmen" 溪仙君の半面. *Daimai bijutsu* 4, no. 11 (November 1925): 19–21.

Tsuruta Heihachirō 弦田平八郎 and Masuda Hiromi 増田洋. *Gendai Nihon no bijutsu 2: Hirafuku Hyakusui / Tomita Keisen* 現代日本の美術 2：平福百穂 / 冨田渓仙. Tokyo: Shūeisha 集英社, 1977.

Yamakawa Sōkichi 山川草吉. "Tomita Keisen isaku ten o mite" 冨田溪仙遺作展を観て. *Nanga kanshō* 南畫鑑賞 6, no. 6 (June 1937): 39–40.

Yoshimura Teiji 吉村貞司. "Tomita Keisen no sekai" 冨田渓仙の世界. *Sansai*, no. 339 (November 1975): 44–50.

NOTES

1. Shimomise Seiichi, "Tomita Keisen sensei o kataru," *Atorie* 6, no. 4 (April 1929): 101–2.

2. Ibid., 102.

3. See Sotokari Soshin'an, "Tomita Keisen kei o kataru," *Atorie* 6, no. 4 (April 1929): 97–98; Kanzaki Ken'ichi, "Iwayuru henkijinteki ichirei to jinseikanteki geijutsukanteki riron," *Atorie* 6, no. 4 (April 1929): 101; and Kobayashi Kokei, "Ko Tomita Keisen tsuitō: Rikai no chikara," *Bijutsu shinron* 11, 8 (August 1936): 92.

4. Tsuruta and Masuda, *Gendai Nihon no bijutsu* 2, 97.

5. Ibid.

6. Kawahigashi Hekigotō, "Ko Tomita Keisen tsuitō: Keisen o omou," *Bijutsu shinron* 11, no. 8 (August 1936): 89.

7. See Claudel's poetic depiction of his visit to Keisen's house in Haga and Hayashi, *Pōru Kurōderu to Kyōto gadan*, 5.

8. Kanzaki Ken'ichi, "Keisen kan hisō hen," *Bi no kuni* 8, no. 8 (August 1932): 64.

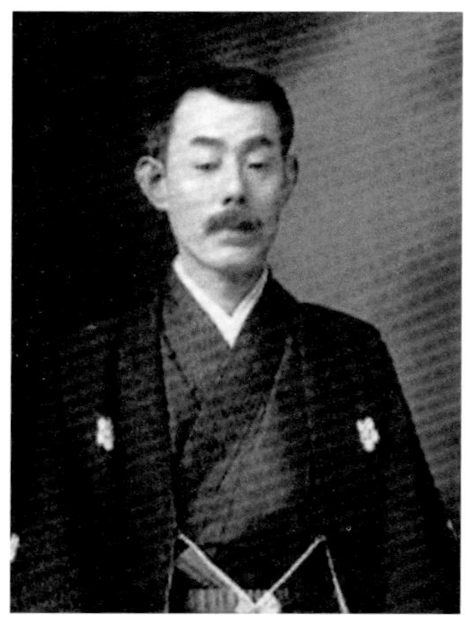

Tsuji Kakō 都路華香 1870–1931

The modern concepts of artistic freedom and individualism had barely begun to emerge in Japan at the end of the Meiji era, but among the Kyoto *nihonga* painters of his generation, Tsuji Kakō stood out for his strong advocacy of individual expression. His oeuvre from the 1910s and 1920s demonstrates his imaginative approach and displays a stunning range of styles, often described as "original" or "eccentric" by his contemporaries. Although he fell into near obscurity after his death, recent exhibitions in the United States and Japan have rekindled an appreciation of Kakō's unique artistic legacy.[1] His study of the wave represents one of the most fascinating and memorable experiments in the twentieth-century *nihonga* world.

Born to a *yūzen* artisan's family and encouraged by his father, Kakō began his apprenticeship at the age of ten under Kōno Bairei 幸野楳嶺 (1844–1895). During the 1890s he began participating in competitive exhibitions such as the Domestic Industrial Exposition (*Naikoku kangyō hakurankai* 内国勧業博覧会) and the Exhibition of New and Old Art (*Shinko bijutsuhin tenrankai* 新古美術品展) in Kyoto, spreading his name first as a figure painter. The subsequent diversity of his painting modes emerged from his examination of various traditions of the past, which he synthesized in his more individual, modern style. Throughout the 1890s, following a widespread practice among Kyoto artists, Kakō painted textile designs for the dry-goods store Takashimaya to supplement his income. His close relationship with Takashimaya continued through several decades: Kakō's *Green Waves* (Ryokuha 緑波), c. 1910, one of his most breathtaking works, once belonged to the Iida family, the founders of the shop that later became the Takashimaya department store.

In his well-chronicled experimentation with the wave theme during the last decade of the Meiji era, Kakō sought to capture the constant movement of water. At the peak of this investigation, he prepared five pairs of screens to test different styles of portraying waves. Through this decade-long process, Kakō transcended established techniques and formulas, and he gradually began to shift the emphasis in his art from objectivity toward subjectivity. The wave, the major catalyst for this transformation, subsequently remained an important motif in his painting.

Kakō's mature style featured bright color and an inventive brush style, as exemplified by his Taishō works such as *Diamond Gate* (Kongōmon 金剛門), 1921, and *Entering Mount Kōya* (Kōya mōde 高野詣), 1926.[2] Kakō was also a superb ink painter whose images at times verged on pure abstraction in their adroit tonal gradation and dynamic brushwork.[3]

Although he was one of Kyoto's most promising artists, Kakō had only tenuous success in the national arena. After the government exhibition was established in 1907, he submitted ambitious compositions almost annually, but although his work was consistently accepted, he did not win a high award until 1916. His unconventional approach and unwillingness to conform to the taste of the time did not impress the judging panel, which in general favored moderate, conservative styles. By the time Kakō received a prestigious appointment to the jury in 1924, almost two decades later than his Kyoto colleagues Takeuchi Seihō 竹内栖鳳 (1864–1942) and Yamamoto Shunkyo 山元春挙 (1871–1933), he had ceased to participate in the government exhibition.

Outspoken and at times honest to a fault, Kakō was admired by the members of the Kyoto art community for his integrity and dignity. In 1926 he became the principal of two schools where he had taught, the Kyoto Municipal

School of Arts and Crafts (Kyōto Shiritsu Bijutsu Kōgei Gakkō 京都市立美術工芸学校) and the Kyoto Municipal Special School of Painting (Kyōto Shiritsu Kaiga Senmon Gakkō 京都市立絵画専門学校). Despite his responsibilities at the schools, Kakō continued to paint. Shortly before his death, Kakō completed his last work, a formal portrait of Mokurai 黙雷 (1854–1930), the Zen master at Kenninji 建仁寺 under whom Kakō had begun his spiritual training thirty years earlier. MM

BIBLIOGRAPHY

Kyōto Kokuritsu Kindai Bijutsukan 京都国立近代美術館 and Kasaoka Shiritsu Chikkyō Bijutsukan 笠岡市立竹喬美術館. *Tsuji Kakō.* Exh. cat. Kyoto and Kasaoka, 2006.

Morioka, Michiyo, and Paul Berry. *Modern Masters of Kyoto: The Transformation of Japanese Painting Traditions, Nihonga from the Griffith and Patricia Way Collection.* Exh. cat. Seattle: Seattle Art Museum, 1999.

Uchiyama Takeo 内山武夫, comp. *Shiatoru Bijutsukan kara no satogaeri: Griffith & Patricia Way Collection, Kindai no Kyōto gadan* シアトル美術館からの里帰り:グリフィス&パトリシア・ウェイコレクション、近代の京都画壇. Exh. cat. Kobe: Kōbe Shinbunsha 神戸新聞社, 2001.

NOTES

1. Morioka and Berry, *Modern Masters of Kyoto;* Uchiyama, *Shiatoru Bijutsukan kara no satogaeri;* and Kyōto Kokuritsu Kindai Bijutsukan and Kasaoka Shiritsu Chikkyō Bijutsukan, *Tsuji Kakō.*

2. Both paintings are illustrated in Morioka and Berry, *Modern Masters of Kyoto,* 52 and 170, and Kyōto Kokuritsu Kindai Bijutsukan, *Tsuji Kakō,* 130 and 141.

3. See *Kamo Riverbank in the Misty Rain,* in Morioka and Berry, *Modern Masters of Kyoto,* 175.

Uragami Shunkin 浦上春琴 1779–1846

Shunkin was the eldest son of the noted eccentric literati painter Uragami Gyokudō 浦上玉堂 (1745–1820). A retainer of the Okayama Shinden *han* 岡山新田藩 (known as the Kamogata *han* 鴨方藩 since the Meiji period), Gyokudō devoted himself to playing and popularizing the seven-stringed horizontal lute or *qin* (J., *kin*), the most esteemed instrument in Chinese literati culture.[1] His enthusiasm led him to name his eldest son Shunkin (Spring *Qin*) and his second son Shōkin 秋琴 (Autumn *Qin*, 1785–1871). Even though Gyokudō rose to the high position of *ōmetsuke* (a kind of police supervisor), he and his two children eventually left the *han* in 1794.[2] After traveling for several years, including to Osaka, Edo, and the Aizu *han*, Gyokudō and Shunkin finally settled in Kyoto around 1799. Gyokudō spent the last decades of his life developing his skill with the *qin* while making increasingly impressive landscape paintings with his distinctive brushwork.

Shunkin had studied painting with his father from childhood, and his skills grew rapidly when he returned to Kyoto in 1811 after studying Chinese paintings in Nagasaki.[3] Shunkin's main theme was landscape, yet he also painted figures and birds-and-flowers. Shunkin benefited from his close association with Kimura Kenkadō 木村蒹葭堂 (1736–1802), Rai San'yō 頼山陽 (1780–1832), Tanomura Chikuden 田能村竹田 (1777–1835), and other painters steeped in knowledge of Chinese paintings. Like the paintings of other literati artists of his time, such as Yamamoto Baiitsu 山本梅逸 (1783–1856) and Nakabayashi Chikutō 中林竹洞 (1776–1853), Shunkin's works did not resemble those of the earlier generation. These painters deeply studied the Chinese paintings at hand and formed their own styles.[4] As did Okada Hankō 岡田半江 (1782–1846), Shunkin forsook the eccentricity of his father's style for a much more polished, technically adept approach that emphasized sophistication over a forceful expression of individuality. The painters of Shunkin's generation in western Japan each possessed their own style yet collectively can be seen to follow the orthodox trend in Qing literati painting. Their devotion to carefully constructed landscapes was superseded by more freely composed and expressively painted works by Fujimoto Tesseki 藤本鉄石 (1816–1863), Yamanaka Shinten'ō 山中信天翁 (1822–1885), Tomioka Tessai 富岡鉄斎 (1836–1924), and other artists active in supporting the rise of imperial power at the end of the Edo period. PB

BIBLIOGRAPHY

Fukushima Kenritsu Hakubutsukan 福島県立博物館. *Gyokudō to Shunkin–Shūkin: Uragami Gyokudō fushi no geijutsu* 玉堂と春琴・秋琴：浦上玉堂父子の芸術. Aizu Wakamatsu 会津若松：Fukushima Kenritsu Hakubutsukan 福島県立博物館, 1994.

Nakamura Shin'ichirō 中村真一郎, Matsushita Hidemaro 松下英麿, et al. *Rai San'yō* 頼山陽. Bunjinga suihen 文人画粋編, vol. 18. Tokyo: Chūō Kōronsha 中央公論社, 1976.

Ryūkawa Kiyoshi 竜川清. *Uragami Gyokudō: Hito to geijutsu* 浦上玉堂：人と芸術. Tokyo: Kokusho Kankōkai 国書刊行会, 1976.

Taketani Chōjirō 竹谷長二郎. *Bunjinga ron: Uragami Shunkin "Rongashi" hyōshaku* 文人画論：浦上春琴「論画詩」評釈. Tokyo: Meiji Shoin 明治書院, 1988.

Uragami Shunkin 浦上春琴. *Suian seihi roku* 睡菴清秘録. Facsimile edition, 1915. Manuscript, 1830.

NOTES

1. Gyokudō's passion for the *qin* and its music is discussed in depth in Stephen Addiss, *Tall Mountains and Flowing Waters: The Arts of Uragami Gyokudō* (Honolulu: University of Hawaii Press, 1987). The high regard for the *qin* in Chinese culture is surveyed in Robert Hans van Gulik, *The Lore of the Chinese Lute,* 2d ed. (Rutland, VT: Tuttle, 1968).

2. Gyokudō held this rank from 1781 to 1887. The chief events of his life and the lives of his sons are noted in the chronology in Fukushima Kenritsu Hakubutsukan, *Gyokudō to Shunkin–Shūkin*, 143–44.

3. Ibid., 99.

4. In his 1830 manuscript *Suian seihi roku*, Shunkin discussed the depth of inspiration he received from some Chinese paintings.

Yamamoto Baiitsu 山本梅逸 1783–1856

Baiitsu's father, Yamamoto Tomouemon 山本友右衛門 (d. 1794), was a sculptor in service to the Nagoya-area Owari *han*. Baiitsu is thought to have asserted his desire to become a painter shortly after his father's death, yet his earliest teachers are unknown.[1] The biggest influence on the young artist was his first patron, Kamiya Ten'yū 神谷天遊 (1710–1801), a major collector of Chinese painting who encouraged Baiitsu's study of literati works.

Early in their lives Baiitsu and his older friend Nakabayashi Chikutō 中林竹洞 (1776–1853) visited the Nagoya Sōtō Zen temple Banshōji 萬松寺. They spent the day making careful copies of two Yuan-period paintings, *Bamboo and Rocks* by Li Kan 李衎 (1245–1320) and *Ink Plum Blossoms* by Wang Mian 王冕 (1287–1359). Chikutō later adopted his name, meaning "bamboo grotto," after Li's work, and Baiitsu eventually took his name, meaning "plum elegance," from Wang's work. Some forty years later, Baiitsu was delighted to see the paintings again at the home of his Nagoya pupil Hirano Deikō 平野泥江 (1813–1878).[2]

In 1802, after their patron Ten'yū's death, Baiitsu and Chikutō went to Kyoto to further their painting careers. But a year later Baiitsu left Kyoto to travel around Japan, using Nagoya as his base. During this time he painted *fusuma* panels for Kanazawa Castle and spent considerable time in Edo, where he associated with Tani Bunchō 谷文晁 (1763–1840), Ōkubo Shibutsu 大窪詩佛 (1767–1837), and other prominent literati.[3] Baiitsu's periods in Kyoto gradually lengthened, and from the 1830s he spent most of his time there.[4] In 1854, growing weaker in old age, he returned to Nagoya for his last few years.

Baiitsu was primarily recognized for his skillful landscape paintings and his complex compositions of birds-and-flowers. Using a distinctive, comparatively dry brushwork that sometimes resembles that of his friend Chikutō, Baiitsu established a high level of quality built upon his careful study of Chinese paintings. His deep knowledge of literati painting and meticulous technique fit well with similar attitudes held by other major painters of his generation, including Uragami Shunkin 浦上春琴 (1779–1846), Okada Hankō 岡田半江 (1782–1846), and Tanomura Chikuden 田能村竹田 (1777–1835).

Beyond his painting activities, Baiitsu became a major figure in the *sencha* tea-drinking circles that were central to the literati lifestyle. At these gatherings, friends studied painting and calligraphy as well as *sencha* utensils, many of Chinese origin. Antique and contemporary paintings were displayed at some larger meetings, a precursor of the public displays of artwork that emerged in the Meiji period.[5]

PB

BIBLIOGRAPHY

Graham, Patricia. *Tea of the Sages: The Art of* Sencha. Honolulu: University of Hawaii Press, 1998.

———. "Yamamoto Baiitsu: His Life, Literati Pursuits, and Related Paintings." PhD diss., University of Kansas, 1983.

Kanematsu Romon 兼松蘆門. *Chikutō to Baiitsu* 竹洞と梅逸. Tokyo: Gahō sha 画報社, 1910.

Mori Senzō 森銑三. "Baiitsu to Shibutsu" 梅逸と詩佛. 1939. Reprinted in *Mori Senzō chosakushū* 森銑三著作集, vol. 4. Tokyo: Chūō Kōronsha 中央公論社, 1970–72.

Nagoyashi Hakubutsukan 名古屋市博物館. *Nangaka Yamamoto Baiitsu: Karei naru kachō—Sansui no fūga: Tokubetsuten* 南画家山本梅逸：華麗なる花鳥・山水の風雅：特別展. Nagoya, 1998.

Tokugawa Yoshihiro 徳川義寛 and Inoue Yasushi 井上靖, eds. *Kōshitsu no shihō* 皇室の至宝, vol. 13, *Bekkan* 別巻. Tokyo: Mainichi Shinbunsha 毎日新聞社, 1991–93.

Yoshida Toshihide 吉田俊英. "Yamamoto Baiitsu kenkyū jōsetsu" 山本梅逸研究序説. *Nagoyashi Hakubutsukan kenkyū kiyō* 名古屋市博物館研究紀要, no. 2 (1979).

NOTES

1. The basic account of Baiitsu's life given here relies upon that presented in Nagoyashi Hakubutsukan, *Nangaka Yamamoto Baiitsu*, 1998.

2. Deikō's account of Baiitsu's relation to this painting is given in his lengthy manuscript, kept with the Li Kan and Wang Mian paintings, which have been in the Imperial Household Collection since their donation by Banshōji in 1880. See the discussion of these works in Tokugawa and Inoue, *Kōshitsu no shihō*, plates 27–28 and pp. 155–56.

3. Baiitsu's repeated meetings with the calligrapher and painter Shibutsu are examined in detail in Mori, "Baiitsu to Shibutsu."

4. In the six times the *Record of Famous People of Kyoto* (Heian jinbutsu shi 平安人物志) was issued during his career, Baiitsu is listed only in the 1838 and 1852 editions.

5. See the account of his involvement with *sencha* in Graham, *Tea of the Sages*, 107–13.

Yamamoto Chikuun 山本竹雲 1820–1888

Chikuun was known for his painting and seal carving and was a close associate of Yamamoto Shinten'ō 山本信天翁 (1822–1885), Tani Tesshin 谷鐵臣 (1822–1905), and Kumagai Suikō 熊谷醉香 (Kyūkyodō Naotaka 鳩居堂直孝, 1817–1875), owner of the famous painting supply store Kyūkyodō 鳩居堂. He was a connoisseur of *sencha* 煎茶 utensils, and his evaluations of tea utensil boxes (*hakogaki* 箱書) were so esteemed that they greatly increased the value of the contents. Chikuun's father was from the Abe 阿部 family, retainers to the Okayama *han*. His mother, Shika (1791–1833), was the third daughter of Yamamoto Kinho 山本琴浦 (1757–1835), a painter from the Kurashiki Kojima 倉敷児島 area of Okayama.[1] Chikuun's original name was Abe Yujirō 阿部, but when his parents divorced, he and his mother returned to her family's home and Chikuun adopted the Yamamoto name. His mother died after suffering some form of mental illness, and the teenage Chikuun crossed the nearby strait to Shikoku to live with his aunt in Takamatsu 高松. Some have theorized that Chikuun's nervous temperament, reflected in his peculiarly compacted cursive calligraphy, may have had its origin in these childhood difficulties.

Chikuun left Takamatsu around 1840 and spent the next several decades traveling across the country, with extended stays in Fukui and Osaka, before settling in Kyoto at the beginning of the Meiji period. Although he studied seal carving with Hosokawa Rinkoku 細川林谷 (1779–1843) and Confucian classics with Shinozaki Shōchiku 篠崎小竹 (1781–1851), Chikuun was largely self-taught as a painter. His works cover a range of styles from twelve-fold landscape screens in strong colors to simply sketched, whimsical scenes. This latter style may have been inspired by Rinkoku's often comically eccentric landscape paintings. An example of this striking type is a pair of scrolls Chikuun made depicting Yabakei Rakanji 耶馬渓羅漢寺, a temple popular for its views of the unusual rock formations of the Yabakei valley in Ōita prefecture. Yabakei was famous among nineteenth-century literati artists for its dramatic cliffs, which were thought to resemble the distinctive terrain of China. Chikuun's inscription records that he had painted it on the spot, yet the peaks that twist upward like tree branches reveal the full expression of his imagination. Chikuun was also a popular seal carver in the Meiji period, making seals for many of the top painters and calligraphers.[2] His most lasting impact, however, remains his highly regarded *sencha* utensil-box inscriptions.[3]

Chikuun, who combined the roles of painter, seal carver, and connoisseur, was a model literatus in the early Meiji period. But his unstable personality led him, after an argument with his wife, to drown himself in the Chigogaike 稚児ケ池 pond in the mountains behind Kiyomizudera 清水寺 in eastern Kyoto.[4] PB

BIBLIOGRAPHY

Hasegawa Shōshōkyo 長谷川瀟々居. *Sencha shi* 煎茶志. 1965. Reprint. Tokyo: Heibonsha 平凡社, 1983.

Kibi Gaishi 吉備外史. "Kodoku no gajin Yamamoto Chikuun" 孤独の画人山本竹雲. *Shoga kottō zasshi* 書画骨董雑誌, no. 336 (June 1936): 10–11.

Shimonaka Naohiko 下中邦彦, ed. *Shodō zenshū* 書道全集. Vols. 25 and *Bekkan* 2. Tokyo: Heibonsha 平凡社, 1968.

NOTES

1. A basic biography is found in Shimonaka, *Shodō zenshū*, vol. 25, 169.
2. Mention of his seal carving and examples of his work are included in Shimonaka, *Shodō zenshū, bekkan* 2, plate 87, pp. 17 and 110. See also the essay on seals in this volume.
3. The status of Chikuun's inscriptions on *sencha* utensils is discussed in Hasegawa, *Sencha shi*, 145–46.
4. Another report says that he drowned in Midorogaike in the northern outskirts of Kyoto city; see ibid., 144–45.

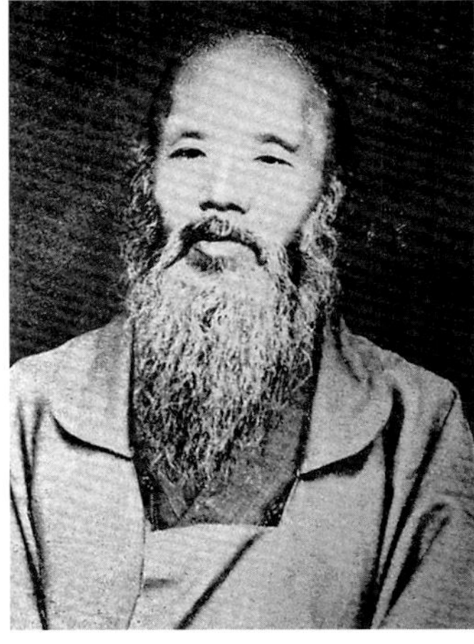

Yamanaka Shinten'ō 山中信天翁 1822–1885

One of the key figures in the Kyoto literati world during the early Meiji period was Yamanaka Shinten'ō. Due to his connections with the leaders of the new government in Tokyo, associations with the imperial court, and considerable personal wealth, Shinten'ō became a chief patron of and participant in Kyoto's literati affairs. He was born near Nagoya in the village of Higashiura 東浦 (now Hekinan-shi), the second son of a wealthy farming family that traditionally had been the official purveyor of goods for the daimyo of the Numazu *han* near Mount Fuji. He began his studies in Osaka with the noted Confucian scholar and calligrapher Shinozaki Shōchiku 篠崎小竹 (1781–1851). In the 1850s Shinten'ō moved to Kyoto, where he associated with members of the anti-

bakufu movement, including Yanagawa Seigan 梁川星巌 (1789–1858) and Rai San'yō's third son Mikisaburō 三樹三郎 (1825–1859).[1]

As he recorded in the preface to *Shin meika ronga shū* 新名家論画集, a woodblock-printed collection of Chinese texts on literati painting published in 1861, Shinten'ō met a Chinese merchant in Nagasaki in 1857 who had recently arrived with several hundred scrolls of Chinese calligraphy and painting. During the same trip, Shinten'ō obtained a number of Chinese books on painting from the Nagasaki literati painter Miura Gomon 三浦梧門 (1809–1860). This concentrated contact with Chinese culture in Nagasaki made a strong impression on him, as it had on so many earlier artists.

After the shogunate arrested and executed opposition figures during the 1858 Ansei repression (*Ansei no taigoku* 安政の大獄), Shinten'ō went to Ise to study with Saitō Setsudō 斉藤拙堂 (1791–1865) for three years before returning to Kyoto. As the government's suppression of rebellious samurai intensified in 1863, Shinten'ō became an active patron of the imperial loyalists still under suspicion in the Kyoto area. Finally, he provided food and money to troops fighting in the Fushimi area during the first month of 1868 as the new regime was establishing itself. In recognition of his services on behalf of the imperial forces, Shinten'ō was appointed to a wide variety of posts during the next six years, including the governorship of areas that are now part of Miyagi prefecture. From the account given in Shinten'ō's diary (which he kept from 1869 until his death), this period of official service kept him extremely busy with travel. He went repeatedly to Tokyo to meet with his friends in the government, including Kido Kōin 木戸孝允 (1833–1877), Iwakura Tomomi 岩倉具視 (1825–1883), and the premier, Sanjō Sanetomi 三条実美 (1837–1891). He also visited Sendai, the capital city of the province he briefly governed.

After Shinten'ō retired from government service in 1873, the frequency of his meetings with literati friends greatly increased. He built a house called Villa of the Two Waters (Nisuisō 二水荘) after the Kamo and Takano rivers that flanked the site, in the Shimogamo area of Kyoto. He adopted the alternate name of Nisui 二水, perhaps a reference to the same name used by Zhang Ruitu 張瑞圖 (1570–1641), whose works he admired. Landscape paintings by this noted late-Ming painter, whose simple, powerful brushwork may have influenced him, are among the few Chinese paintings mentioned in Shinten'ō's diary.

Shinten'ō spent most of his final decade at his large villa in Arashiyama called Tairansanbō 對嵐山房. It was an ideal location for literati gatherings, with an excellent view of the famous Arashiyama spring cherry blossoms and autumn maple leaves. It was so well regarded that the Meiji emperor stayed there during his 1877 visit to Kyoto. Shinten'ō was called to Tokyo in 1885 for consultations with officials of the imperial household, when he abruptly took ill and died.

Although Shinten'ō sometimes inscribed his paintings with references to Tanomura Chikuden 田能村竹田 (1777–1835), and reportedly had briefly studied with one of Chikuden's disciples in Kyoto, he seems to have been largely self-taught. His tendency to compose paintings with bold brushwork and only a few tones of ink was already established in his few known Edo-period works, which are more reserved than later examples. His mature landscape style of the Meiji period is characterized by spatial distortion, bold brushwork, and ink washes (often on satin) that recall the equally individualistic paintings of early seventeenth-century artists including Zhang Ruitu and Li Liufang 李流芳 (1575–1629), whose works were well known in Japan.

Shinten'ō shared his contemporaries' interest in large scroll paintings of unusual stones, vigorous pine trees representing long life, and miscellaneous topics rendered in albums.[2] On rare occasions he employed color, but he preferred unadorned ink and brushwork. Beyond painting and calligraphy, he also decorated ceramics used for *sencha*. A seal carver himself, he possessed a large collection of seals and liberally applied them to his paintings. As a connoisseur, he inscribed the boxes of many Chinese paintings with the biographies of the painters. This mixture of activities formed one model for a literati lifestyle that so impressed his younger compatriot Tomioka Tessai 富岡鐵斎 (1836–1924). A number of Tessai's early Meiji paintings are close in style to Shinten'ō's landscapes, and the explosive irregularity of Tessai's Taishō-period works can be seen as an outgrowth of Shinten'ō's influence.

The characters for the name Shinten'ō may also be pronounced *ahodori*, or "stupid bird," equivalent to the English-language term "gooney," for the albatross. The albatross's stumbling, hopping gait on land gives rise to these pejorative terms for a bird that is astonishingly elegant when gliding at altitude, forming an interesting metaphor for the awkward but inspiring creations of a self-taught painter. Such reflections may have given an additional level of meaning to a name that could also be interpreted as "the old man with faith in the emperor." This last reading is reinforced by his apparent adoption of the name Shinten'ō near the beginning of the Meiji period.

Shinten'ō's calligraphy was very popular, and he met many requests for book titles, studio names, and poems. He was devoted to the study of Chinese calligraphy; in a postscript to an 1879 exhibition catalogue of his collection of Chinese and Japanese books of calligraphy ink rubbing (*hōjō* 法帖), he claimed to own more than a thousand such volumes. According to Tessai, Shinten'ō began to develop his own style while studying the semicursive script of Yan Zhenqing 顔真卿 (709–785) as seen in the 764 draft of a letter known as *Zhengzuowei tie* 争座位帖, which was available as an ink rubbing. Rubbings of *Zhengzuowei tie* had been very popular during the *bakumatsu* 幕末 period. Dissatisfied with his own worm-eaten copy, Rai San'yō 頼山陽 (1780–1832) had appropriated Shinozaki Shōchiku's more perfect rubbing. After San'yō's death, his copy passed into the hands of the Confucian scholar Sakuma Shōzan 佐久間象山 (1811–1864), who became famous for his advocacy of Western learning. Shōzan based his later script style on his studies of this text and published a new printing of it some years before his political assassination in Kyoto. Shinten'ō combined various Chinese and Japanese influences to form the twisting brushwork that emphasizes the bold, curving movements typical of his style. The rough vigor of the abrupt transitions and ample use of "flying-white" make Shinten'ō's cursive script one of the most distinctive of the early Meiji period. PB

BIBLIOGRAPHY

Addiss, Stephen. "Yamanaka Shinten'ō." *Monumenta Nipponica* 48, no. 3 (Autumn 1993): 315–36.

Katō Ruiko 加藤類子, Shimada Yasuhiro 島田康宏, et al., eds. *Tessai to sono shiyūtachi: Bunjinga no kindai* 鐵斎とその師友たち文人画の近代. Kyoto: Kyōto Kokuritsu Kindai Bijutsukan 京都国立近代美術館, 1997.

Okajima Ryōhei 岡島良平. *Shinten'ō ibokushū* 信天翁遺墨集. Hekinan: Hekinan-shi Kyōiku Iinkai 碧南市教育委員会, 1981.

———. *Yamanaka Shintenō botsugo hyakunen kinen mokuroku* 山中信天翁没後百年記念目録. Hekinan: Hekinan-shi Kyōiku Iinkai, 1985.

Shintenkai 信天会. *Shinten'ō* 信天翁. Hekinan: Hekinan-shi Shintenkai 碧南市信天会, 1915.

NOTES

1. The majority of the biographical information presented here is from the extensive materials found in Shintenkai, *Shinten'ō*.

2. Illustrations of Shinten'ō's works can be found in the works listed above and in Paul Berry and Yokoya Ken'ichirō, *Unexplored Avenues of Japanese Painting*, exh. cat. (Ōtsu: Ōtsu Shiristu Rekishi Hakubutsukan; Seattle: University of Washington Press, 2001), plates 10, 11, 59, 63.

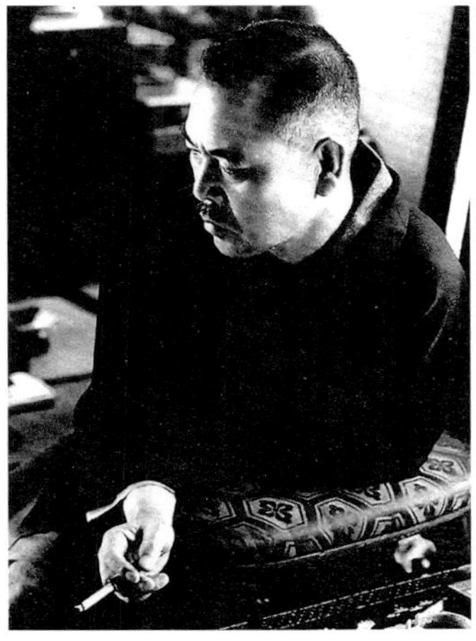

Yano Kyōson
矢野橋村 1890–1965

Yano Kyōson once wrote, "In general, there is no such thing as a genius. . . . Rather, more formidable is the one who keeps working with steadfastness and perseverance."[1] True to his word, Kyōson overcame a series of setbacks in his life through sheer determination and tenacity. Foremost, he was a painter who carried the banner of the modern literati movement. He was also a passionate educator, gifted illustrator and calligrapher, and excellent essayist. Furthermore, endowed with political astuteness and a generous spirit, Kyōson tirelessly organized and financed art groups and schools in order to elevate the cultural position of Osaka. Described as a man of "many hobbies and many talents" (*tashu tagei* 多趣多芸),[2] Kyōson represented a type of *bunjin* who pursued literati ideals not in a reclusive lifestyle but by fully engaging with the worldly affairs of modern society.

Born in a seaside village in Ehime prefecture, Kyōson was the last of six children. He lost his father in 1906, and the next year, the seventeen-year-old Kyōson moved to Osaka to study painting. To support himself, he apprenticed at an arms factory near Osaka Castle, but after only a week his left hand was crushed in an accident. This misfortune, instead of dispiriting him, strengthened his resolve to become a painter. Garnering his family's promise to support him for three years, Kyōson started his artistic training full-time. He wished to enter the studio of Himejima Chikugai 姫島竹外 (1840–1928), but this leading Osaka literati painter already had more than two hundred students.[3] Thus, in 1909, Kyōson became a pupil of Nagamatsu Shunyō 永松春洋 (1849–1931), who had studied under the

Kyoto literati master Tanomura Chokunyū 田能村直入 (1814–1907).

In 1913 Kyōson received an honorable mention at the government-sponsored Bunten for the pair of screens he submitted, *Fresh Morning at Mountain and Lake* (Kozan seigyō 湖山清暁). A depiction of Lake Biwa in ink on a gold background, the painting is Kyōson's reinterpretation of literati style with the addition of Western perspective. Tokyo and Kyoto groups dominated the Bunten that year, and Kyōson was one of only four Osaka painters whose names appeared. Soon after the exhibit, a magazine article introduced Kyōson as a "one-armed painter" and described how the artist had enlisted a loyal friend to help move the large screens over nearly one hundred days as he worked to complete them.[4] Kyōson continued to receive awards at the annual Bunten through 1915. His success at the prestigious exhibition spread his reputation as a promising *nanga* painter and gave him the financial security to take a month-long trip to China in 1917.[5]

Kyōson's career during the latter half of the Taishō period reflected changes occurring in Japan's art world. Dissatisfied with the conservatism of the government exhibition, Kyōson turned to the Japan Art Institute (Nihon Bijutsuin 日本美術院), a newly reorganized Tokyo group known for progressive ideas. His literati-based entry was included in the institute's exhibition in 1917, but his work was rejected the following year. Frustration with the established venues led Kyōson to organize a private exhibition, which came to be associated with the Shuchōsha Society 主潮社. Established in 1920 by Kyōson and his close friend Uemura Sōichi 植村宋一 (1891–1934),[6] the group sought to invigorate the cultural ambience of modern Osaka, which was considered inferior to those of Tokyo and Kyoto. The group launched annual art exhibitions, shown in both Osaka and Tokyo, and promoted monthly public lectures on art and literature. Kyōson not only participated in the Shuchōsha exhibitions but supported the group financially until the Kantō earthquake of 1923 caused it to disband.

During the late 1920s and 1930s, Kyōson's activities expanded in multiple directions. In 1921 he joined the Japan Nanga Institute (Nihon Nangain 日本南画院), founded to promote contemporary literati painting. For the next fifteen years, the group offered an important national venue for modern literati artists, including Komuro Suiun 小室翠雲 (1874–1945), Ogawa Sen'yō 小川千甕 (1882–1971), Mizuta Chikuho 水田竹圃 (1883–1958), and Shirakura Jihō 白倉二峰 (1906–1974). Kyōson was one of the younger members and remained the principal representative of Osaka literati artists at the Japan Nanga Institute, showing ambitious monumental works at its annual exhibitions. Meanwhile, in 1924, Kyōson established and became the principal of the Osaka Art School (Ōsaka Bijutsu Gakkō 大阪美術学校), where he nurtured many successful local artists. He returned to the government exhibition in 1927. Kyōson also busied himself as an illustrator. Among his many works for newspaper serials, his daily contribution to "Miyamoto Musashi" 宮本武蔵 by Yoshikawa Eiji 吉川英二, published in *Asahi Shinbun* in 1935, achieved unprecedented popularity.[7] Wanting to provide a new venue for literati painters, unconstrained by the politics that hampered other organizations, Kyōson established the Heaven and Earth Society (Kenkonsha 乾坤社) in 1939 and organized the society's annual exhibition through 1943.

During World War II, the Osaka Art School was requisitioned by the military, but in 1946 Kyōson helped the Osaka Municipal Art Museum (Ōsaka Shiritsu Bijutsukan 大阪市立美術館) to open a new institution in the war-devastated neighborhood by donating all the supplies that had been preserved from his old school.[8] In that same year, he resumed showing at the government exhibition. Kyōson received numerous awards for his artistic contributions in Osaka before his death from a stroke in 1965. MM

BIBLIOGRAPHY

Hirakatashi Kyōiku Iinkai 枚方市教育委員会. *Yano Kyōson ten: Kindai suiboku no seisui* 矢野橋村展—近代水墨の精粋. Exh. cat. Hirakata, 2002.

Kanai Shiun 金井紫雲. "Kenkonsha to Yano Chidōjin" 乾坤社と矢野知道人. *Nihon bijutsu* 日本美術 2, no. 2 (February 1943): 59–60.

Mochizuki Nobunari 望月信成. *Yano Kyōson meisaku senshū* 矢野橋村名作選集. Osaka: Seibundō Shuppan Kabushiki Gaisha 清分堂出版株式会社, 1975.

Yano Kyōson. "Daiichinin gabō zatsuwa" 第一人畫房雑話. *Daimai bijutsu* 大每美術 5, no. 2 (February 1926): 22–26.

———. "Hirakata Gotenyama ni utsuru Ōsaka Bijutsu Gakkō ni tsuite" 枚方御殿山に移る大阪美術学校に就て. *Daimai bijutsu* 8, no. 5 (May 1929): 22–24.

———. "Hajimete no Teiten shinsain o shite" はじめての帝展審査員をして. *Daimai bijutsu* 9, no. 5 (May 1930): 8–13.

———. "Dai ni mohō jidai" 第二模倣時代. *Tōei* 塔影 8, no. 3 (March 1932): 10–12.

———. "Nihon Nangain kaisan go ni" 日本南画院解散後に. *Tōei* 12, no. 10 (October 1936): 55–56.

———. "Shinpen zakkan" 身邊雑感. *Tōei* 16, no. 11 (November 1940): 53–56.

NOTES

1. Yano, "Hajimete no Teiten shinsain to shite," 12.

2. Mochizuki, *Yano Kyōson meisaku senshū*, 19.

3. Kitagawa Hisashi, "Shuchōsha to wa?—Yano Kyōson to Uemura Sōichi," in Hirakatashi Kyōiku Iinkai, *Yano Kyōson ten*, 59, and Mochizuki, *Yano Kyōson meisaku senshū*, 2.

4. "Kataude gaka no kōmyō," *Shinbi* 2, no. 12 (December 1913): 22–23.

5. See Yano Kyōson, "Shina manyū nisshi," *Kaiga seidan* 5, no. 8 (August 1917): 35–37.

6. For a detailed account of Shuchōsha activities, see Kitagawa, "Shuchōsha to wa?" 57–61. Uemura, a writer, journalist, and literary/art critic, later became a prominent novelist under the pen name Naoki Sanjūgo. In 1935 Naoki's name was given to an award for popular fiction, the Naoki Prize, one of the most prestigious literary awards in Japan today.

7. Kitagawa, "Shuchōsha to wa?" 65.

8. For a detailed account, see Mochizuki, *Yano Kyōson meisaku senshū*, 6–7.

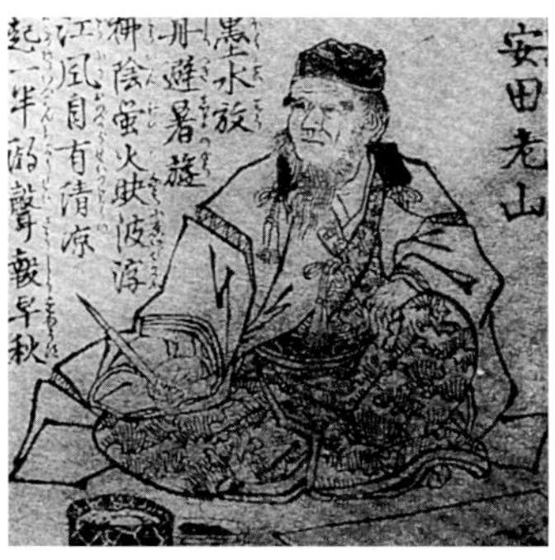

Yasuda Rōzan
安田老山 1830–1882

Rōzan was the first Japanese literati artist to actually study for a long period with a major Chinese literati artist on the mainland, and this training made his paintings seem quite fresh in Japan. He was raised near the small town of Kaizu 海津 in Gifu prefecture, where his father held the hereditary position of doctor for the Takasu *han* 高須藩. Rōzan adopted the personal name Yō 養, from the neighboring mountain of Yōrōzan 養老山, and his artist name Rōzan (Old Mountain) was derived from the same source.

Said to have loved painting as a youth, Rōzan eventually moved to Nagasaki to study Chinese literati painting. Although it is unclear when he arrived in Nagasaki, he is known to have studied with Hidaka Tetsuō 日高鐵翁 (1791–1871) and the immigrant artist Xu Yuting 徐雨亭 (b. 1824). In Nagasaki he could be assured of seeing the most recently imported Chinese paintings as well as meeting immigrant Chinese artists, who, if not famous in their own country, at least offered an unmediated connection to Chinese culture and art.

Rōzan's desire to understand Chinese painting and culture in depth was matched by a group of young artists in Nagasaki who were studying with Tetsuō and Kinoshita Itsuun 木下逸雲 (1799–1866). They included Nagai Unpei 長井雲坪 (1833–1899) of Niigata, Ishikawa Kansen 石川澗泉 (Gozan 呉山, 1844–1917) from Toyama prefecture, and Ihara Kōfu (1847–1872). The sole woman in the group, Kōfu (also known as Teisha) was married to Rōzan and had already studied painting with Chō Kōran 張紅蘭 (1804–1879), presumably in the Gifu area, before the couple had set out for Nagasaki. Through the services of the Dutch-born Guido Verbeck (1830–1898) of the Dutch Reformed Church of America, these artists smuggled themselves into Shanghai in 1867. After Kōfu's arrival in 1870, Rōzan and his wife became students of one of Shanghai's leading artists, Hu Yuan 胡遠 (Gongshou 公壽, 1823–1886). Kōfu died in Wusong 呉淞 in 1872.

Hu Gongshou's most notable influence of on Rōzan is seen in Rōzan's repeated use of the side of the brush tip to create swollen flourishes in many of his outlines, but the Japanese artist's tendency toward relatively dry brushwork and dramatically unstable compositions reveals his independence from his Chinese mentor. His career lasted barely a decade after his return to Japan in 1873, and the large number of high-quality works that remain is evidence of the popularity his work enjoyed in the Meiji period. Rōzan received such acclaim for his art that he quickly became wealthy and acquired a large residence in Tokyo. In the twentieth century, Asakura Fumio 朝倉文夫 (1883–1964), the noted Western-style sculptor, was an avid collector of Rōzan's works, and several dozen of Rōzan's paintings are preserved in the Asakura Chōsokan 朝倉彫塑館 museum in Tokyo.

The strong brushwork and eccentric compositions commonly found in Rōzan's many landscapes are also present in his paintings of bamboo, pines, potted plants, and stones. These topics were vehicles for Rōzan's bravura brushwork, the highly prized expression of his sophisticated training and personal character. Rōzan rarely applied color to his works, relying instead on ink tonalities to effectively suggest a range of surfaces and forms. His paintings bear inscriptions in the emaciated, irregular calligraphy that was one of his trademarks. Rōzan was the most famous of the many artists who studied painting in China during the Meiji period. PB

BIBLIOGRAPHY

Araki Nori 荒木矩, ed. *Dainihon shoga meika taikan* 大日本書画名家大鑑, vol. 1. 1934. Reprint. Tokyo: Daiichi Shobō 第一書房, 1975.

Fogel, Joshua. "Lust for Still Life: Chinese Painters in Japan and Japanese Painters in China in the 1860s and 1870s." In *Acquisitions: Art and Ownership in Edo-Period Japan*, ed. Elizabeth Lillehoj. Warren, CT: Floating World Editions, 2007.

Lai Yu-chih. "Surreptitious Appropriation: Ren Bonian (1840–1850) and Japanese Cutlture in Shanghai, 1842–1895." PhD diss., Yale University, 2005.

Shimizu Hiroshi 清水博. *Gajin Nagai Unpei* 画人長井雲坪. Naganoshi 長野市: Shinano Kyōiku Shuppansha 信濃教育出版社, 1976.

Wong, Aida Yuen. *Parting the Mists: Discovering Japan and the Rise of National-style Painting in Modern China.* Honolulu: University of Hawaii Press, 2006.

Yanagi Ryō 柳亮. *Kindai kaiga to bunjinga no chisei: Nagai Unpei no geijutsu* 近代絵画と文人画の知性：長井雲坪の芸術. Yokohama: Kotobuki Garō Tōkyō Bijutsu Shuppan Dezain Sentaa コトブキ画廊 東京 美術出版デザインセンター, 1974.

Yonezawa Hideo 米沢秀雄. *Shanhai shiwa* 上海史話. Tokyo: Bōbō Shobō 畝傍書房, 1942.

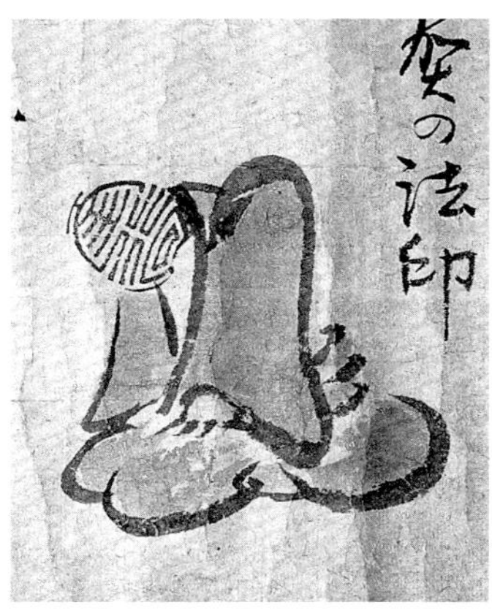

Yokoi Kinkoku
横井金谷 1761–1832

The concept of the eccentric, or *kijin* 奇人, was so popular during the Edo period that the stories of unusual personalities of the day were collected in *Anecdotes of Extraordinary People of Recent Times* (Kinsei kijin den 近世奇人伝).[1] *Kijin* came from all walks of life, and some were so unusual that they became legends in their lifetimes. Kinkoku is remarkable for having recorded his own eccentricities in *The Life of Kinkoku Shōnin* (Kinkoku Shōnin ichidaiki 金谷上人一代記), which, resembling a prototype of autobiographical fiction (*shishōsetsu* 私小説), comically exposed bizarre and potentially embarrassing incidents.[2] Kinkoku's promotion of his unusual qualities helped to advance his career and reached such heights that at one point he claimed his works had the protective powers of an amulet.[3]

Born in Kusatsu in Shiga prefecture, Kinkoku became a priest of the Jodo sect at the age of eight. In 1781, he became head of a small Kyoto temple, the Kinkoku-zan Gokurakuji. He adopted his artist name, Kinkoku, at this time. When the temple was destroyed by fire, he left Kyoto to travel around the country before settling in Nagoya, where he became acquainted with a variety of literati painters. Kinkoku's most significant religious involvement was with Shūgendō 修験道, whose mountain-climbing priests (*yamabushi* 山伏) combine Shinto with esoteric Buddhism. Some of his most dramatic landscapes portray *yamabushi* processions and initiations in the mountains. While mountain landscapes were his central theme, he also painted Buddhist icons, courtesans, and *haiga.*

Kinkoku's classic landscape image is of prominent mountains vibrating with the bold brushwork he made famous. These dynamic works constitute a large percentage of his output, and it might seem natural enough that the rustic, self-taught artist would develop this manner of painting. But a number of paintings from the turn of the nineteenth century show that Kinkoku was making extremely careful studies of Yosa Buson's 与謝蕪村 (1716–1783) works. His best examples are difficult to distinguish from the originals, aside from their signatures and seals. That Kinkoku could so thoroughly penetrate not only the form but the sense of Buson's brushwork and color reveals his real talent as a painter. The high quality of these early studies demonstrates that the much rougher style he maintained in his later career was a matter of choice, not lack of talent or training in the subtler aspects of the art. Kinkoku's style of landscape painting in the last several decades of his life became increasingly wild and energetic, at times dissolving the forms he was describing. His clientele was predominantly made up of the wealthy farmers and merchants from the area around Lake Biwa; he also created many screen paintings for shrines and temples.

Although the seventeenth- and eighteenth-century eccentrics that fill the pages of the *Anecdotes of Extraordinary People* were mostly from Kyoto, Kinkoku never found favor in that city, whose residents consistently preferred the polished work of Matsumura Goshun 松村呉春 (1752–1811) and his Shijō-school followers. Kinkoku's later *yamabushi* paintings must have seemed like the creations of a country ruffian. Although this perception may be attributed to some extent to a certain snobbishness on the part of Kyotoites, it may have been equally true that eccentric behavior was more widely appreciated in the eighteenth century. PB

BIBLIOGRAPHY

Fister, Patricia. *Yokoi Kinkoku: The Life and Painting of a Mountain Ascetic.* Ann Arbor, MI: University Microfilms, 1983.

———. "The Impact of Shugendo on the Painting of Yokoi Kinkoku." *Ars Orientalis* 18 (1990): 163–95.

———. "The Legacy of Yosa Buson." In *An Enduring Vision*, ed. Lisa Rotondo-McCord. New Orleans: New Orleans Museum of Art, 2002.

Rittō Rekishi Minzoku Hakubutsukan 栗東歴史民族博物館. *Ōmi Kotō-Konan no gajintachi* 近江湖東・湖南の画人. Ritto, 1999.

Rosenfield, John, and Fumiko Cranston. *Extraordinary Persons: Works by Eccentric, Non-conformist Japanese Artists of the Early Modern Era (1580–1868) in the Collection of Kimiko and John Powers.* 3 vols. Cambridge, MA: Harvard University Art Museums, 1999.

Yokoi Kinkoku 横井金谷. *Kinkoku Shōnin kōjōki* 金谷上人行状記. Vol. 37, *Tōyō bunko* 東洋文庫, ed. Fujimori Seikichi 藤森成吉. Tokyo: Heibonsha 平凡社, 1965.

Yokoya Ken'ichirō 横谷健一郎. *Baitei・Kinkoku* 楳亭・金谷. Ōtsu: Ōtsushi Rekishi Hakubutsukan 大津市歴史博物館, 2008.

NOTES

1. Ban Kōkei's 伴蒿蹊 (1733–1806) *Kinsei kijinden* was first published in 1790 and was followed by a sequel in 1798. John Rosenfield uses this concept to frame his discussion of many Edo-period painters in Rosenfield and Cranston, *Extraordinary Persons.*

2. Refer to the annotated text of the *Ichidaiki* 一代記 edited by Fujimori Seikichi, *Kinkoku Shōnin kōjōki.*

3. Found in a letter from Kinkoku to his relative Yokoi Yasozaemon; see Fister, "The Legacy of Yosa Buson," 66 n.44.

Seals | Art of the Microcosm

Paul Berry

The prominent appearance of reddish seal impressions is one of the defining aspects of East Asian painting and calligraphy, with most works having one, often several, or sometimes a great many. The artist places these seals, whose characters frequently provide his or her name, on the work to signify its completion. Because seal characters are inscribed in various ancient styles, most viewers rarely attempt to read them but simply accept them as part of the customary appearance of a painting. Yet what are these seals? What is their origin? Why are there so many, and what rules govern their placement on an artwork? Do seals give only the name of the artist, or are there other meanings? Most seals were carved with great care, but what are their aesthetics? To pursue these and related questions is to step into a miniature world that unites the earliest forms of Chinese characters with the aesthetic sensibilities of the seal carvers and the various periods and social circles in which they lived. This arcane world combines the directness of effective graphic design with stylistic and literary references that reverberate over the centuries, leaping across the barriers of time and geography as the use of seals spread throughout East Asia.

To fully explore even a microcosm such as this would require an encyclopedic work. This essay provides a brief introduction to some aspects of seal history, usage, and aesthetics, with a focus on seals employed in Japan on works of the nineteenth and early twentieth centuries.

Chinese Seals

The practice of carving seal characters relates to the earliest surviving form of Chinese characters. Although the invention of the Chinese writing brush is often placed some centuries before the Christian era, the Neolithic painted potteries of Yangshao 仰韶 (4500–2500 BCE) show some hint of brushwork, which varies in width from thick stroke to thin line, one of the defining characteristics of a writing brush. Additionally, some Neolithic materials have markings that may be the precursors of characters. Even if there had been an ancient practice of writing characters with a brush, what has survived as the earliest form of writing in

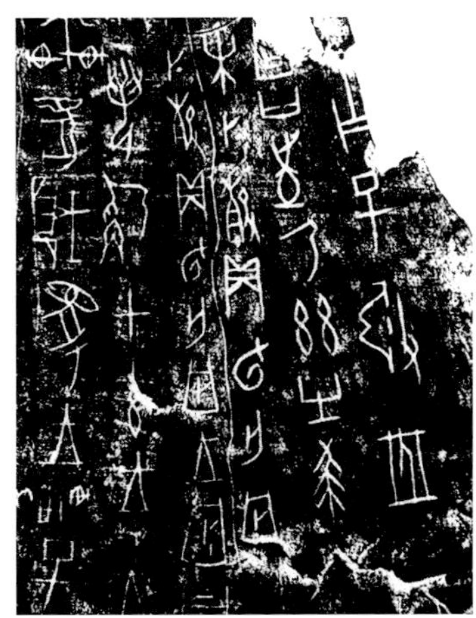

1. Shang-period (1523–1046 BCE) *jiagu* 甲骨 script, part of a longer inscription on a scapula.

China are the script characters known as *jiagu* 甲骨 (shell and bone, often called oracle bones; no. 1), which were inscribed on ox scapulae and tortoiseshell as part of a divinatory practice of the Shang dynasty. The rough, irregular appearance of these characters appealed to the modern sensibilities of some seal carvers when the script style was rediscovered around 1900. These earliest characters scratched with straight lines gave way to single characters representing family groups and to increasingly long inscriptions about ritual and political events which were cast into the surfaces of bronze vessels. It was long thought that the bronze inscriptions were cut in relief on the molds used to cast the vessels, but a new theory suggests they were applied to the mold surface as lines of soft clay.[1]

The characters in late Shang and Western Zhou bronze inscriptions, known as *dazhuan* 大篆, or large seal script, are irregular in size and form when compared with the later *xiaozhuan* 小篆, or small seal script, which was regularized in the Qin dynasty. The section of a longer *dazhuan* bronze inscription shown here (no. 2) reveals the irregularity of line and overall form as well as the pictographic quality of some characters. The composition of the Qin seal illustrated here (no. 3) achieves an interesting balance of forms, being divided into four squares, each containing one character created with thin, rectilinear lines.

There were many later styles of brush-written calligraphy, such as clerical, cursive, semicursive, and regular, yet the characters found in the large seal and, most especially,

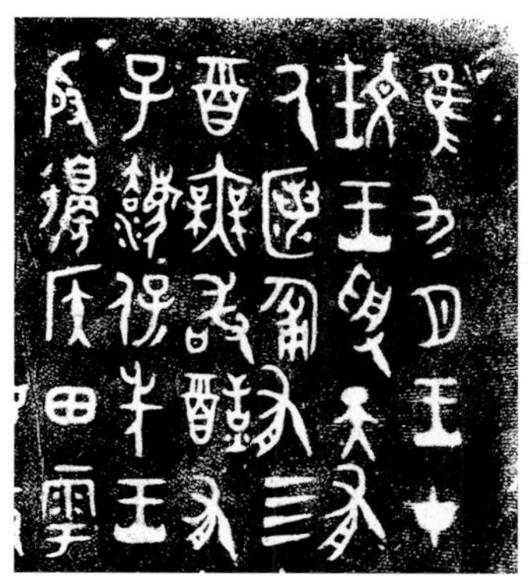

2. Western Zhou–period (1046–771 BCE) *dazhuan* 大篆, or large seal script, part of a longer inscription on a bronze vessel.

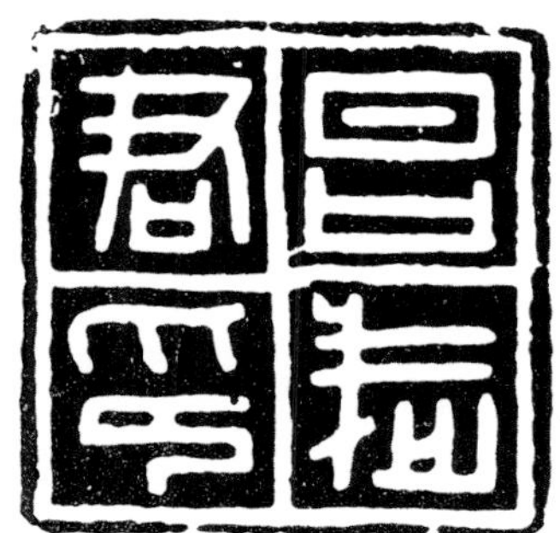

3. Qin-period (221–207 BCE) seal inscribed with *xiaozhuan* 小篆, or small seal script: 昌武君印

4. Han-period (206 BCE–220 CE) official seal, or *kuanyin* 官印: 朐長之印

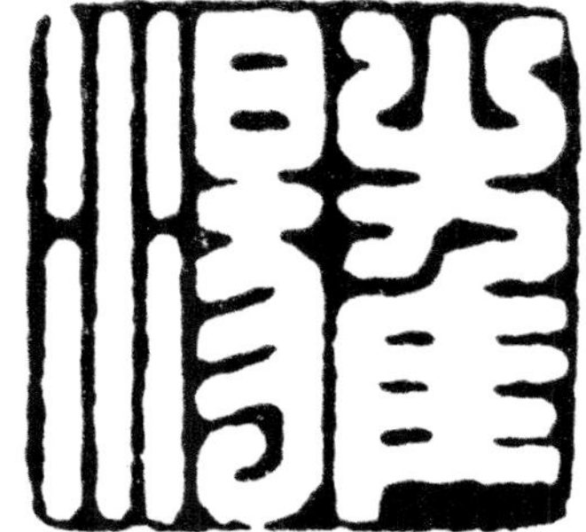

5. Han-period private seal, or *heyin* 私印: 崔湯

the small seal scripts would form the visual foundation for most seal inscriptions throughout East Asia down to modern times. Small seal script became, and remains, standard for most characters carved on seals. Large seal script gradually gained an audience in the later part of the Qing period and continues in occasional use today.

The historical study of the orthography of Chinese script styles has changed greatly over the centuries, and the forms and meanings traditionally ascribed to many large seal-script characters increasingly have been found to be incorrect as greater numbers of authentic bronze inscriptions are collated. This has complicated the reading of Qing-period seals, whose carvers often referred to highly inaccurate dictionaries of large-seal characters. Thus modern dictionaries based on archaeological materials are preferred for reading ancient bronze inscriptions, while the older dictionaries are best for reading later seal inscriptions.

Although there are examples of seals in earlier periods, they first became widespread during the Qin and Han dynasties. These early seals made of cast bronze mostly fell into the categories of official seals (*kuanyin* 官印), such as one used by a district official (no. 4), or private seals (*heyin* 私印, no. 5). Usually square or rectangular, with either single characters or two- to four-character inscriptions of titles or names, these seals were used to mark documents or to indicate private possessions. Characters were created in the small seal-script style, and at times the abstract forms of animals were employed. The majority of these seals had intaglio, or so-called white-character (*hokubun* 白文), inscriptions. Rulers had seals made from jade, pure gold, and other precious materials. Han-period seals have been appreciated from the Song period onward as the forms of the characters and their arrangements became viewed as the classic prototypes for seal creation. As emblems of identification and authority, seals and their carving maintained a close connection to antique precedents: the Han period for the seals themselves, and the much greater antiquity of the Shang period for the origin of early forms of seal script.

In the Six Dynasties period the increasing size of the *kuanyin* was accompanied by a simultaneous lowering of quality in both character design and line, which often became irregular and weak. Even so, some high-quality seals were still made early on, such as a famous gold seal from the Wei period (no. 6). The design of this seal, with its swollen white lines expanding slightly as they end, leaving only narrow red areas in the interior of each character, represents an approach still greatly favored among seal carvers today. These trends persisted during the Tang period as seals became even larger, primarily for use on official documents. The majority of these large seals had *rilievo*, or red-character (*shubun* 朱文), inscriptions. The use of seals to record collections or as evidence of having viewed a work arose in association with the appreciation of calligraphy scrolls during the late Tang period.

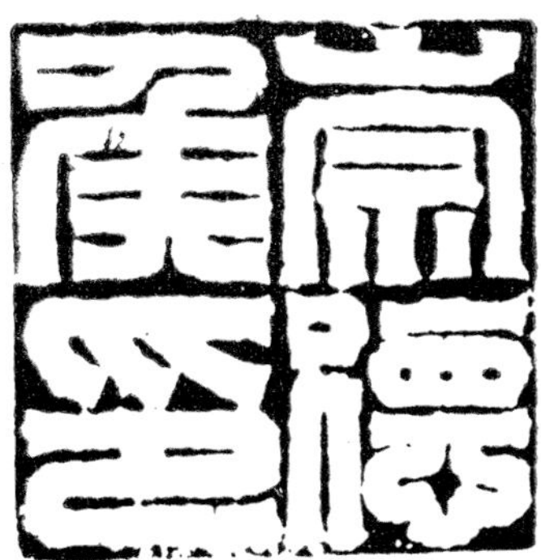

6. Wei-period (220–264) gold seal: 崇德侯印

Antiquarianism reached unparalleled heights during the reign of the Song emperor Huizong 徽宗 (1082–1135), who commissioned the first known publication on antique seals, the *Xuanhe yinpu* 宣和印譜.[2] In the Song period the practice of impressing seals on works gradually became more widespread among calligraphers, and then painters, although it was far from universal. The scholar-artist Mi Fu 米芾 (1051–1107) marked his evaluation of paintings with seals, giving this practice a boost outside the imperial circles, where seals were already used for this purpose.

It was the rise of the literati class, with its focus on new forms of painting and calligraphy, in the Yuan period that stimulated the proliferation of seal usage and brought a new level of quality to seal design. Literati promoted the appreciation of seals as a part of their artistic lifestyle. Zhao Mengfu 趙孟頫 (1254–1322) wrote a history of seals using examples from the Han and Wei periods.[3] This work, along with several other publications on seals, discloses the Yuan literati's growing emphasis on the aesthetics of seals among their antiquarian pursuits. During this period seals were cast in metal and made from ivory or wood. Craftspeople rather than the artists themselves are presumed to have been the carvers. Seal ink was a mixture of cinnabar and water.

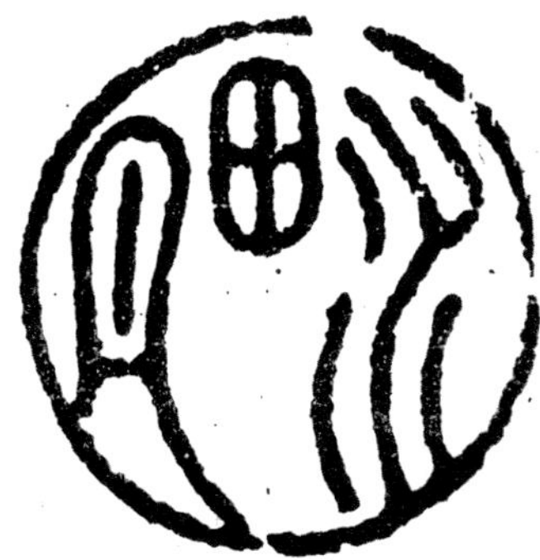

7. Hsu Wei (1521–1593) seal: 渭

The Ming period witnessed a widening interest in seals, especially in literati circles. The literati soon went beyond placing name seals next to their signatures and began developing seals for other locations on their works. Their fascination with seal design encouraged the production of many seals with the same inscriptions but arranged differently in varying script styles or cut with similar designs either in red or white characters. Seals continued to be made from multiple materials, and soft, easily carved, and colorful steatite (soapstone) became increasingly popular. Even professional artists began to assert their identity with signatures accompanied by single seals.

Generally speaking, the number of seals an artist applied to a single work gradually increased from one or two to more by the end of the Ming period. The number of seals placed on a work by the artist was affected by many factors, not the least being the artist's own enthusiasm for them. The dramatic painter-calligrapher Hsu Wei 徐渭 (1521–1593) was known to pepper his works with seals, putting many impressions on his handscrolls of plants and fish (no. 7).

The vogue for seals led to the publication of woodblock-printed books of the designs of ancient seals, the oldest extant example being the *Collection of Selected Antique Seals* (Ji guyin pu 集古印譜) of 1575.[4] Such compilations soon multiplied, and copies eventually found their way to Japan. Various schools of seal carving developed during the Ming period, and artists increasingly carved some of their own seals. A few, like Wen Zhengming's 文徵明 (1470–1559) eldest son Wen Peng 文彭 (1498–1573), became especially renowned for their talent. Wen designed one of his father's most famous seals (no. 8), and he was among the first to carve seals with poetic expressions unrelated to an artist's names or studio titles. Wen Peng's younger contemporary from Anwei, He Zhen 何震 (1530–c. 1604), extolled the simplicity of ancient Han seals, a quality seen in his seal dated 1604 (no. 9). Seals had long been considered art objects in themselves, and noted carvers like Wen and He often added lengthy cursive inscriptions on the sides of their seals that suggested their meaning and included their signatures and the date of carving (no. 9a).[5] By the seventeenth century these two seal carvers were regarded as the founders of the Wen school of Jiangsu and the Anhui school, often called Huipai 徽派.

In the seventeenth century many artists created boldly designed seals for their paintings and calligraphy, especially favoring white-character inscriptions, which could be executed more simply and directly than those with red characters. These seals, although not as sophisticated as those of the famous carvers, are appealing for their rough vitality and awkward amateurism, which were often hallmarks of literati painting. A seal by the famous calligrapher Wang Duo 王鐸 (1592–1652) is an excellent example, with its robust design in irregular, roughly chipped lines (no. 10).

By the eighteenth century the widespread popularity of *jinshi* 金石 (metal and stone) studies, the examination of inscriptions on bronzes and stone steles, began to influence styles in calligraphy and seal carving. Although reverence for the ancient Han styles continued, professional seal carving had drifted away from that high standard in the late Ming and early Qing periods. *Jinshi* studies, with an emphasis on examining old monuments, and the ink rubbings made from them, brought a renewed interest in strength of line and composition that reinvigorated seal designs. Major schools of seal carving proliferated, and the exploration of old forms and the creation of modern variants increased through the nineteenth century. The discovery of early script on Shang oracle bones in 1899 brought this most ancient style into use in seals of the early twentieth century. Modern interpretations of ancient script styles became a dominant trend in artistic calligraphy and was pushed further by carvers such as Wu Changshuo 吳昌碩 (1844–1927) in seals that play with the graphic qualities of large seal script (no. 11). The assertiveness of the amateur seals carved by

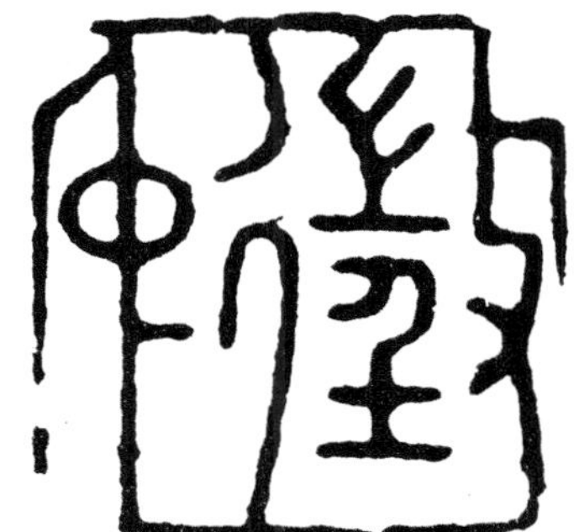

8. Seal carved by Wen Peng (1498–1573) for his father, Wen Zhengming (1470–1559): 徵仲

9. Sealed carved by He Zhen (1530–c. 1604) and dated 1604: 雲中白鶴

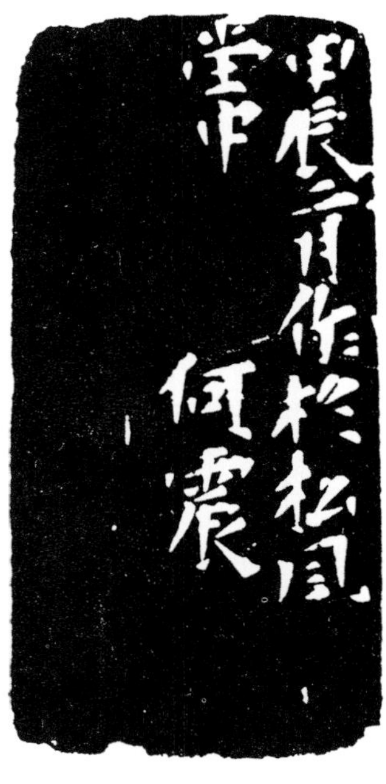

9a. Inscription on the side of seal 9: 甲辰二月作松風堂中何震

10. Seal used by Wang Duo 王鐸 (1592–1652): 煙潭漁叟

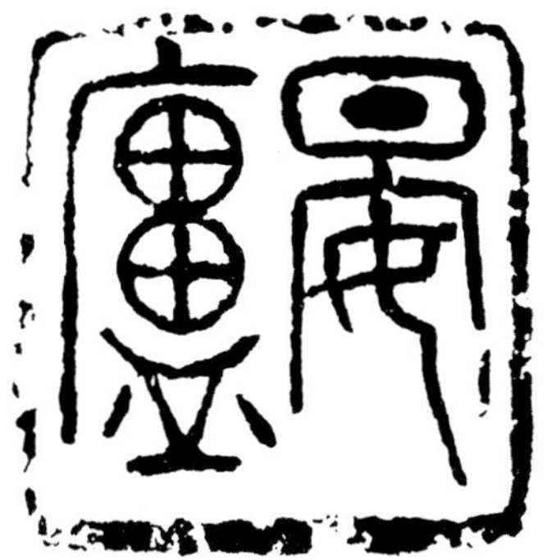

11. Seal carved in 1914 by Wu Changshuo (1844–1927): 晏盧

12. Seal carved by Qi Baishi (1863–1957): 中国長沙湘潭人也

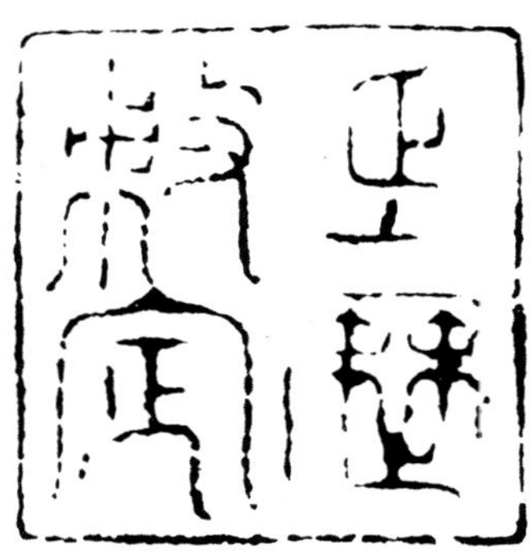

13. Nara-period (Enreki, 782–8CE) ambassador seal impression: 延歴勅定

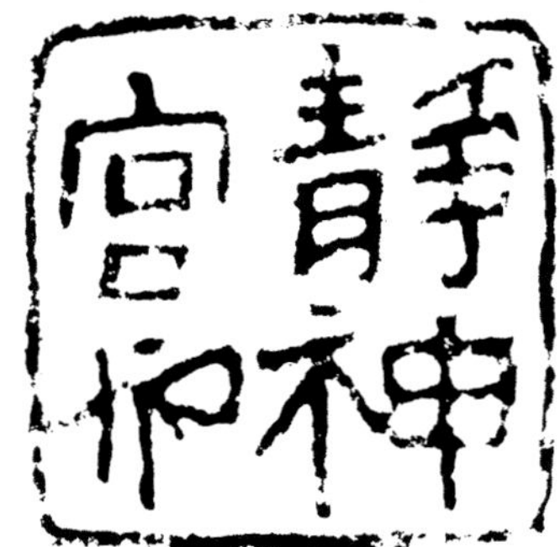

14. Heian-period (794–1185) bronze shrine seal: 静神宮印

late Ming and early Qing calligraphers was extended in the even more dramatic seals (no. 12) by prominent artists such as Qi Baishi 斎白石 (1863–1957), whose roughly engraved style is similar to some aspects of the early *jiagu* script (see no. 1).

The Development of Japanese Seal Traditions

Although the actual beginnings of seal usage in Japan have yet to be determined, it appears that Chinese seals played a symbolic role in international relations before being adopted for practical use. A gold seal discovered under a giant stone in 1784 near Hakata in Kyushu appears likely to be the Later Han seal sent as a gift with an embassy to Japan in 57 CE.[6] Since then several other Han-period gold seals discovered in Japan have established that the symbolic political significance of seals likely preceded their use in Japan.

The early chronicle of Japan, the *Nihon shoki* 日本書紀, contains a brief reference to a wooden seal in 692, indicating that seals likely were gradually coming into use around this time. Official seals and temple seals appear on multiple documents and calligraphies kept at the Hōryūji 法隆寺 and the Shōsōin 正倉院 in Tōdaiji 東大寺 (no. 13).[7] Most appear to have been impressed from cast bronze, red-character seals whose large size and weak design and line reflect the changes that had occurred in China during the Sui and early Tang periods. These features are seen in a Heian-period shrine seal (no. 14) whose simple, naïve line has a charm of its own.

Kao 花押, or flower signatures, had developed in Japan by the mid-ninth century as decorative, cursive anagrams with which to identify a writer. These fixed cursive forms were sometimes cut into wood and applied as seals, in accord with a Chinese practice popular in the Song and Yuan periods.[8] Handwritten or stamped *kao* became so appealing during the Kamakura period that the use of seals slackened. The *kao* shown here (no. 15) is that of an imperial relative, Kajiimiya Saiinhosshinnō 梶井宮最胤法親王 (1563–1639). Sometimes a *kao* suggests an image, and this one resembles a handcart.

As Zen sects developed in Japan in the mid-Kamakura period, Japanese priests began traveling in China, and large numbers of Chinese calligraphies entered Japan, transmitting the growing trend toward personal seals in the Song period. Such seals were fashionable in Zen circles, which may have been the impetus behind the custom of personal seal use in Japan and explains why the earliest stylistic models were found in the seals impressed on calligraphies and paintings by Song-period Zen monks. Although the practice of carving personal seals in stone is thought to have begun in the Yuan period, it did not become prevalent in China until the sixteenth century. In Japan some seals were still cast in bronze, but following Chinese practice, ivory and especially wood became most common. Under this Chinese influence a variety of new seal shapes appeared, including round seals and those shaped like *ding* 鼎, the archaic, bronze tripod cauldron (see no. 18). These seal

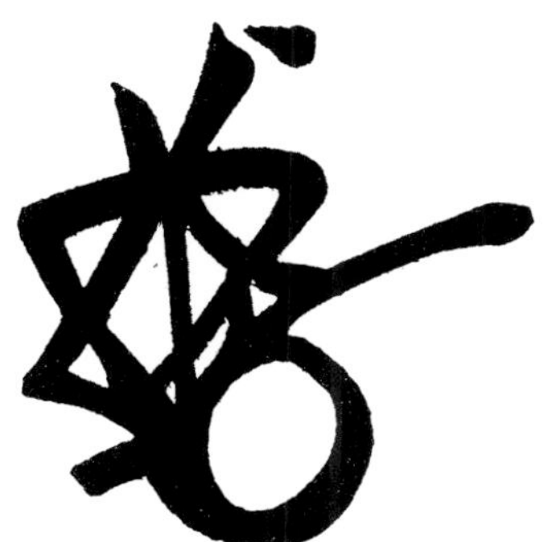

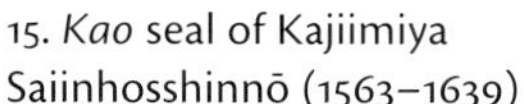

15. *Kao* seal of Kajiimiya Saiinhosshinnō (1563–1639)

16. Seal used by Sesshū (1420–1506): 雪舟

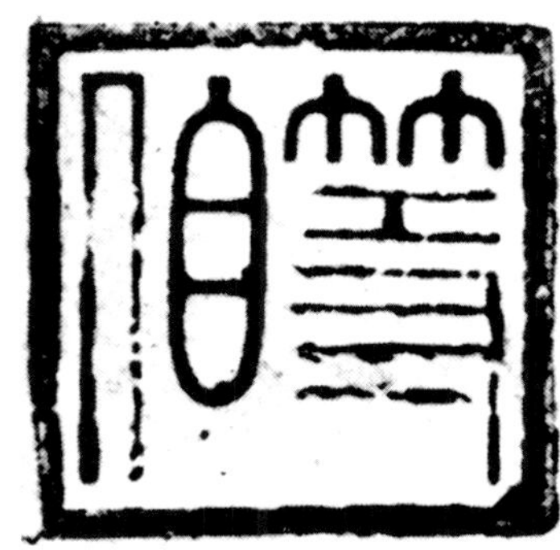

17. Seal used by Hasegawa Tōhaku (1539–1610): 等伯

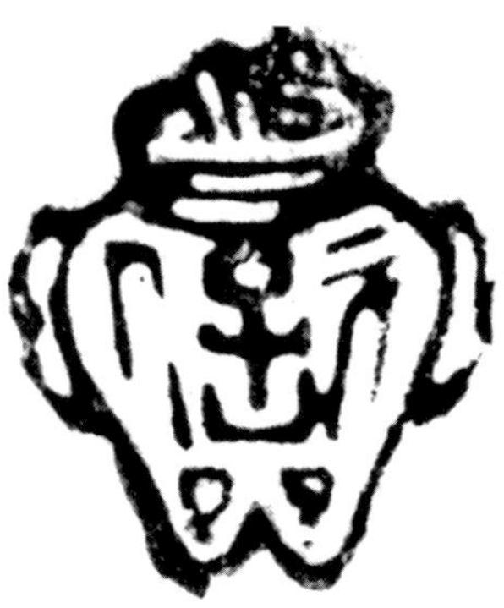

18. Seal in shape of tripod cauldron used by Kanō Motonobu (1476–1559): 元信

materials, shapes, and character styles were to remain popular throughout the Muromachi and Momoyama periods and well into the middle of the Edo period. Although most Kamakura-period seals have some form of the small seal script popular in China, certain Buddhist temples also began to employ regular script (*kaisho* 楷書), a tradition that would also continue into the Edo period.

In the Muromachi period, the continued importation of Chinese calligraphies and paintings had some effect, making seals smaller and more sophisticated; however, the antiquarian styles favored by the Yuan-period literati and their Ming successors were little known in Japan. The patterns of the late Kamakura-period seals were generally maintained into the late seventeenth century, when Chinese monks connected with the Ōbaku school of Zen gradually introduced the influence of the sixteenth-century Wen and He schools. At the beginning of the Muromachi period, seals tended to appear more on calligraphy than on painting. The bulk of early ink paintings in Japan had neither signatures nor seals; many of the artist seals now found on them were apparently added centuries later. The simple style of the large, square seals associated with Sesshū 雪舟 (1420–1506, no. 16) were followed for centuries by artists in the Unkoku 雲谷 and Hasegawa 長谷川 schools (no. 17). The Kanō tradition maintained a special fondness for the bronze tripod cauldron shape, which other schools also widely used (no. 18).

Well into the eighteenth century, wood was the preferred material for seals in Japan, even for the wealthiest and most prominent artists, such as Kanō Tan'yū 狩野探幽 (1602–1674).[9] The use of wood affected not only possible designs but also the quality of line when compared to seals from bronze or stone. Early Edo-period seals sometimes have very thin red lines or fanciful shapes, such as Tan'yū's Mount Fuji (no. 19), effects that are easier to achieve in wood than in stone. The characters carved in wooden seals tend to have smoother lines and a certain fluidity, unlike the more rugged and forceful lines that result from standard stone-carving techniques. Some of the large seals associated with Honami Kōetsu 本阿弥光悦 (1558–1637, no. 20), Tawaraya Sōtatsu 俵屋宗達 (act. 1620s–40s), and Ogata Kōrin 尾形光琳 (1658–1716, no. 21) used this fluidity to great effect in uniquely Japanese designs that sometimes include characters in regular, semicursive, or cursive forms rather than in seal script. Their seals established a certain aesthetic among those artists later grouped under the term Rinpa 琳派.

With increasing use came a greater appreciation of seals themselves. Two woodblock-printed compilations of rough copies of seals attributed to the earlier artists of China appeared in 1647.[10] From these primitive beginnings, employing awkward renditions of seals that were themselves frequently spurious, books of seal images, called *inpu* 印譜, gained an audience in the eighteenth century, reaching a peak in the late Meiji period. Subsequent woodblock-printed

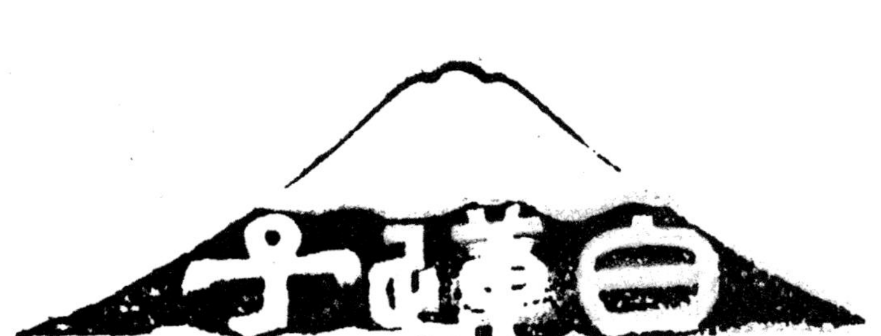

19. Fuji-shaped seal used by Kanō Tan'yū (1602–1674): 白蓮子

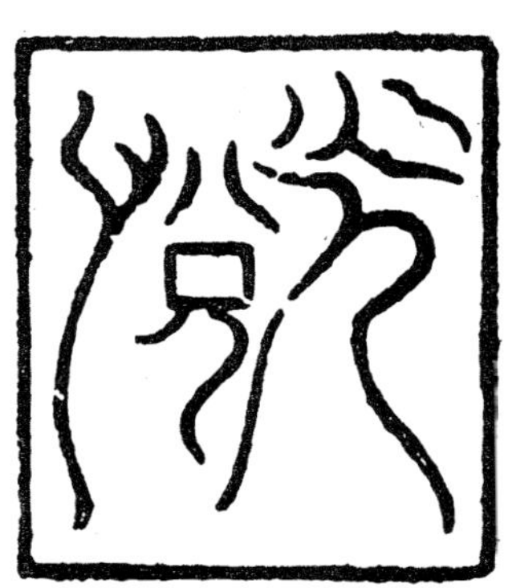

20. Seal used by Honami Kōetsu (1558–1637): 光悦

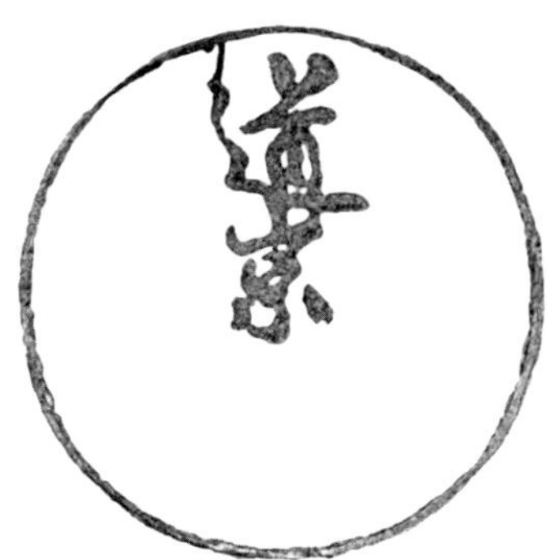

21. Seal used by Ogata Kōrin (1658–1716): 道崇

inpu recorded the shapes of original seal impressions more precisely, and some even used cinnabar seal ink (*shuniku* 朱肉) for the woodblock reproductions.

The gradual introduction of Ōbaku Zen to Japan during the last decades of the seventeenth century brought many aspects of late Ming culture to Japan, including new forms of seal carving. Overall Ōbaku seals, often cut in stone, tend to be large and rather simply carved. But the seals made by the Ōbaku monk Dokuryū 獨立 (1596–1672) were more varied and sophisticated (no. 22). His seals, and those of the even more skilled Chinese Sōtō monk Shin'etsu 心越 (1639–1695), introduced some of the trends in sixteenth-century Chinese literati seal usage to Japan. A white-character seal by Shin'etsu (no. 23) has much of the full, rounded quality of line found in Han seals, coupled with prominent curves in the character composition. His red-character seal (no. 24) has a sharp, bristling line, with the character for "crane" (*tsuru* 鶴) derived from the pictographic aspect of large seal script. Shin'etsu helped popularize seals with long poetic inscriptions (no. 25). These new ideas had begun to spread widely in Japanese literati painting and calligraphy circles by the mid-eighteenth century. Just as the popularity of literati painting, with its poetic and historical allusions, spurred the use of seals with many kinds of inscriptions during the Ming, the development of Japanese literati painting also often relied on famous poems or references to them. Artists, who once might have had only a few seals, enjoyed following the Chinese practice of affixing a great variety of seals for many reasons beyond naming the artist. The popular *bunjin* 文人 painter Ike Taiga 池大雅 (1723–1776) used more than one hundred seals in his comparatively brief career.[11] The burgeoning enthusiasm for seals encouraged artists to develop careers as seal carvers, and their efforts likewise stimulated the further appreciation and growing diversity of styles and types.

Taiga's close friend Kō Fuyō 高芙蓉 (1722–1784) was central to the increasing sophistication of seals in the eighteenth century. Active in the Kyoto area, Fuyō was talented in painting and calligraphy but was best known for the seals he carved for many top artists of his day and for his publication of influential *inpu*. Fuyō's students extended his impact.[12] His seals reveal a range of styles, including a more accurate understanding of the classic Han style as reinterpreted in the Ming period (no. 26), and they helped raise the standard for sophisticated, elegant carving (no. 27) well beyond the Kyoto area.[13] Although most seals were carved by individuals who devoted their lives to the work, a growing number of artists from the time of Taiga onward occasionally made seals themselves. This kind of talented amateurism in seal carving, which became more prevalent with time, was common among Meiji-period calligraphers and literati painters.

The last decades of the nineteenth-century Edo period saw the flowering of many styles of seal carving and a multitude of noted practitioners. The eccentric painter Hosokawa Rinkoku 細川林谷 (1782–1842) was a prolific carver. Active in

22. Seal carved and used by Dokuryū (1596–1672): 遺世獨立

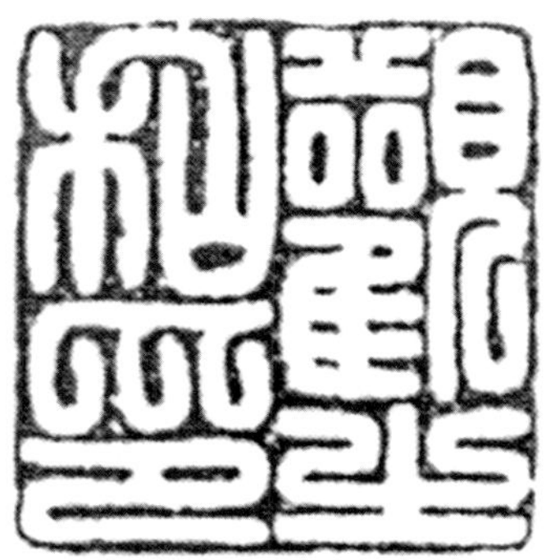

23. Seal carved by Shin'etsu (1639–1695): 觀之私印

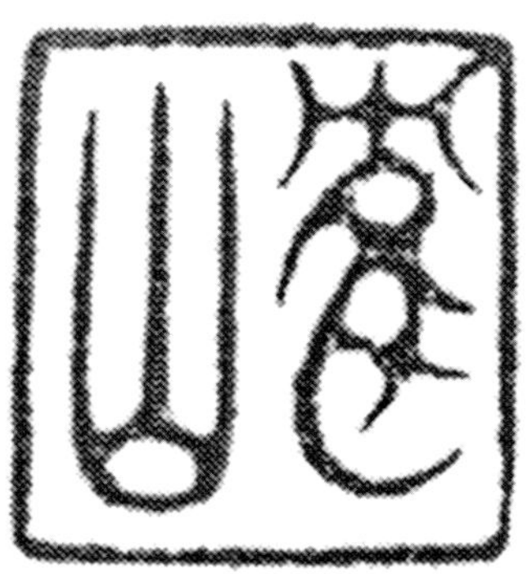

24. Seal carved by Shin'etsu: 鶴山

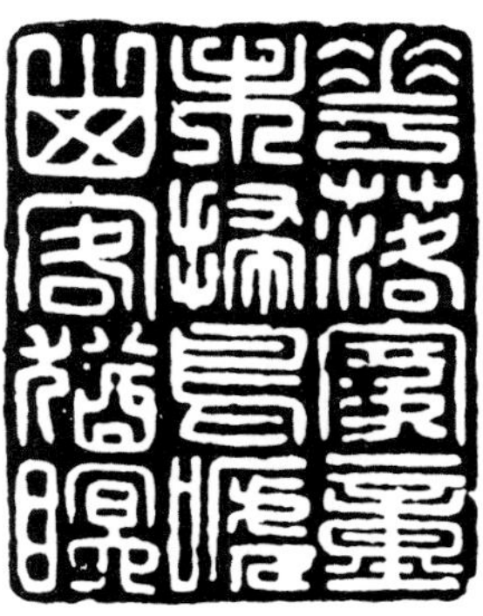

25. Seal carved by Shin'etsu: 華落家童未採鳥啼山客猶眠

Edo, he traveled widely, visiting Nagasaki, the ideal haunt for anyone desiring the latest Chinese imports, and spending time in Kyoto and Osaka. His seals show great exuberance in their variety of styles and designs.[14] Rinkoku's white-character "Enjoying activities of an honorable family" 樂事世家 (no. 28) has a stable, simple composition that suggests the monumentality of antiquity. His influence was predominant in the Edo area and extended beyond the Tokugawa period to seal carvers such as Yamamoto Chikuun 山本竹雲 (1820–1888) in Kyoto. Chikuun's white-character "Distant mountains have no brushstrokes, distant water has no waves" 遠山無皴遠水无波 (no. 29) was intended to combine a sense of modernism with antiquity through the rough, vigorous carving of angular lines. This seal, which offers ancient advice for painting landscapes, would have been placed in the corner of a painting.

By the mid-nineteenth century, the enthusiasm for seals was so great that some artists owned hundreds of them. Many bore the various names of the artist, often carved in different styles and sizes. Other seals contained lines of poetry or philosophical expressions. Artists would commission seals, receive them as gifts from friends, or carve their own seals. Antique seals or seals made by noted carvers were collected. Among a large group of seals owned by a single artist, a great many would have seen infrequent or perhaps no use, while a few would become favorites, appearing on many works. Long-lived artists often used different seals during different periods of their lives, reflecting

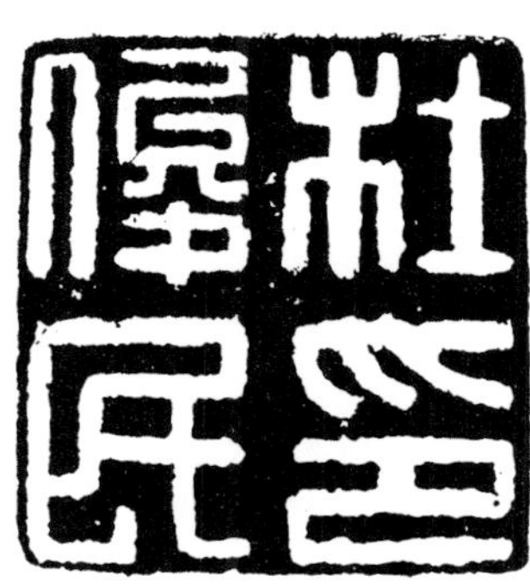

26. Seal carved by Kō Fuyō (1722–1784): 杜俊民印

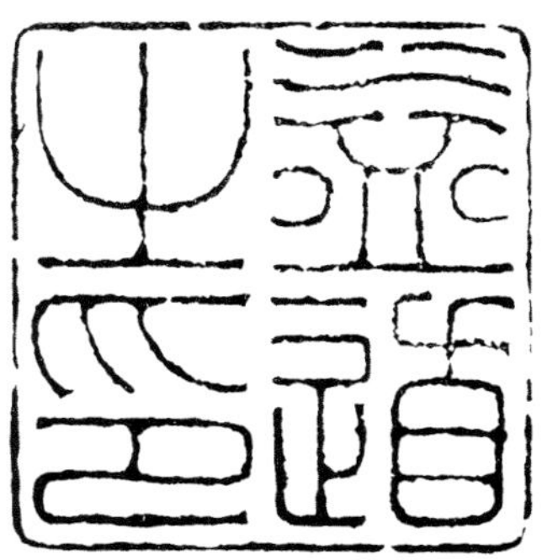

27. Seal carved by Kō Fuyō: 益道之印

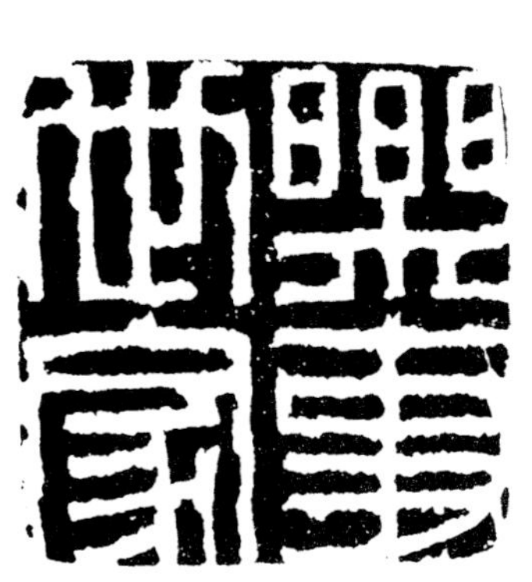

28. Seal carved by Hosokawa Rinkoku (1782–1842): 樂事世家

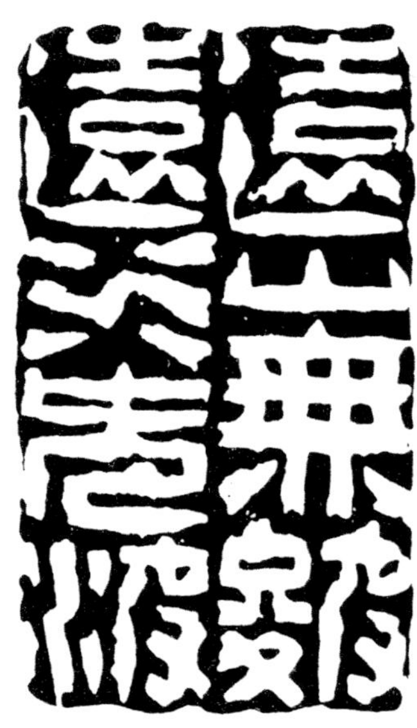

29. Seal carved by Yamamoto Chikuun (1820–1888): 遠山無皴遠水无波

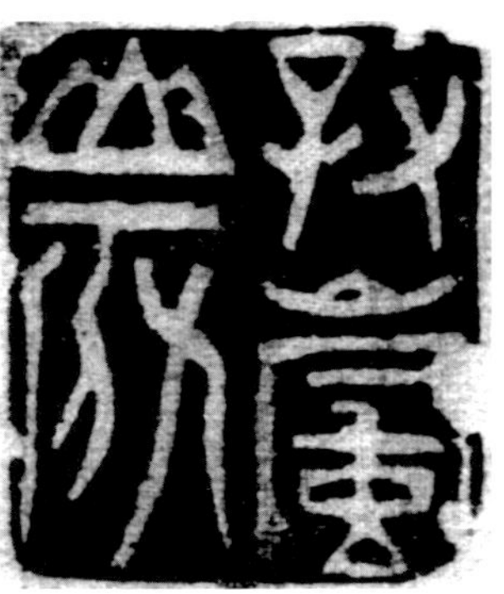

30. Seal used by Yamanaka Shinten'ō (1822–1885): 對嵐山房

changing fashions in seal styles, the adoption of new names, and new directions in their painting practice. Broken or lost seals naturally disappeared from use.

Among the artists in this catalogue, three were especially known for employing large numbers of seals. Yamanaka Shinten'ō 山中信天翁 (1822–1885) used as many as twelve seals on a single painting and twenty in an album.[15] Although he sometimes impressed two seals with his names near his signature, and another at the head of the inscription in the standard fashion, he often added seals with a variety of meanings (see the seal appendix in this volume). At the center of the Kyoto area literati world, Shinten'ō received seals as gifts and commissioned others from the carvers he knew, but the stylistic similarity among his seals suggests that he carved many himself. He also carved seals for his friends, including Tessai (see no. 39a). Although there is no comprehensive publication of his seals, an informal survey of about fifty works showed sufficient variety to suggest that he possessed hundreds of them.

Shinten'ō's white-character "Tai Ranzan bō" 對嵐山房 (no. 30) is typical of his boldly carved seals that employ a modernized rendition of the irregular forms of large seal script. Shinten'ō frequently impressed his large, oval red-character "butterfly hermitage" 蜨廬, with its curves and bending lines, as an additional seal on his works (no. 31). Gaps in the encircling line of a seal are ordinarily accidental chips caused by wear, yet such breaks were sometimes intentional, meant to give an impression of age. The regular spacing of the gaps in Shinten'ō's seal suggests they may be an intentional component of his design. Shinten'ō had a number of seals reading "Seiitsu" 静逸, a name he frequently used early in his career. This white-character "Seiitsu" seal (no. 32) has the full lines and swelling ends typical of a high-quality Han-period seal and those made in that style, such as the gold seal from the Wei period (see no. 6). Shinten'ō also had many seals reading "getsukyō" 月橋 (moon bridge), after the famous Togetsukyō 渡月橋 bridge in Arashiyama near his Kyoto villa. This red-character "getsukyō" seal (no. 33) uses a version of large seal script as it was interpreted in much later times. The slight variation of line width and irregularity in the curves impart suggestions of awkwardness and age to the design. The large number of fine seals Shinten'ō used indicates his passion for the art form and his interest in communicating to the viewer the variety of meanings in their inscriptions.

Due to his great longevity, Tanomura Chokunyū 田能村直入 (1814–1907) accumulated a selection of seals that reflect trends from the Edo period to the early twentieth century, including antique seals, Chinese seals, and seals by many different carvers. A collection of Chokunyū's seal impressions made shortly after he died included 292 examples but omitted most of the ones he used in the Edo period. He may well have used as many as four hundred different seals during the course of his life.

Chokunyū's white-character seal "Sauntering beyond the human" 人外之游 (no. 34), carved in 1852,[16] has wide,

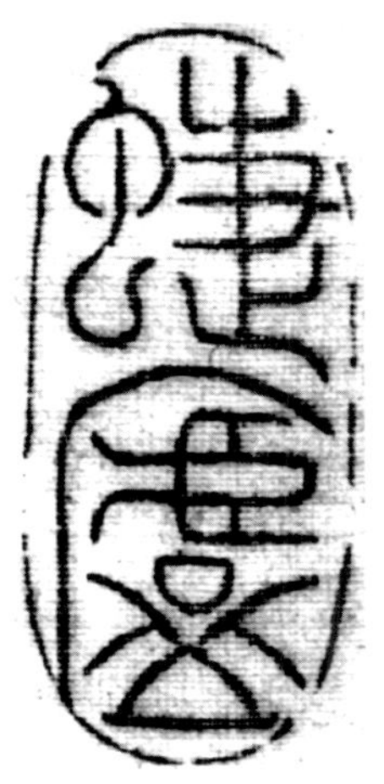

31. Seal used by Yamanaka Shinten'ō: 蜨廬

32. Seal used by Yamanaka Shinten'ō: 静逸

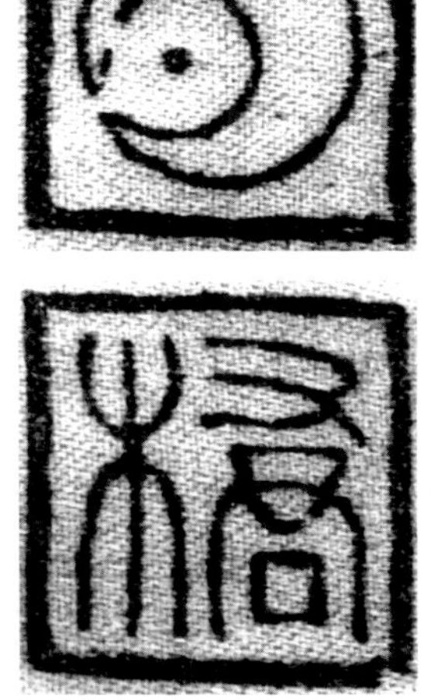

33. Seal used by Yamanaka Shinten'ō: 月橋

34. Seal used by Tanomura Chokunyū (1814–1907): 人外之游

soft lines in an old style. It is the mirror image of a seal well known for being used by the famous immigrant Chinese painter Yi Fujiu 伊孚九 (1698–1746).[17] The seal is hard to read, as both the characters and their positions are reversed, yet as important as catching its meaning is recognizing its reference to a painter who is considered one of the founding figures of literati painting in Japan. Although creating a mirror image of a noted seal is unusual, repeating the expression or design of a famous older one is common.

Another Chokunyū seal bears the old Chinese expression "A person grinds ink, ink grinds a person" 人磨墨墨磨人 (no. 35). The saying, which refers to the practice of grinding an ink stick to create ink, implies that while people make ink, it is the ink that creates the artist. The white characters, written in a standard form of small seal script with full, intentionally rugged lines, gain some of their visual appeal from their repetition in reverse order on the left side. Another pleasing seal design celebrates Chokunyū's birth in 1814 in red characters written in a later interpretation of large seal script, "Bunka 11, mid-spring began my first year" 文化甲戌仲春望□生弌年 (no. 36). This style is especially hard to read today, yet the pictographic quality of large seal script has remained attractive to modern seal carvers. Another example of a Chokunyū seal, one of several that commemorates his role as head of a subtemple at Manpukuji temple, reads "Rinzai true-sect, forty-first generation, Ōbaku Shishirin head priest, Chokunyū Dōjin" 臨濟正宗四十弌世黄檗獅子林住職直入道人掌 (no. 37).[18] The white-character text is written in small seal script, as is standard for seals with long inscriptions.

Even though Shinten'ō and Chokunyū were devoted to the seal art form, Tomioka Tessai 富岡鐵斎 (1836–1924) exceeded other painters of his day in his commitment to collecting and using a wide variety of seals, including many by famous carvers of the Edo period, those made by his prominent friends, and a variety of Chinese seals. An extensive, five-volume collection of impressions from his seals has 309 examples yet is far from complete.[19] Tessai owned a wooden seal carved by the noted scholar and calligrapher Rai San'yō 頼山陽 (1780–1832), "Mountains are blue, waters are bright" 山碧水明 (no. 38). Its design is deceptively simple, with an unusual form for the character "bright" 明 in the lower left corner. He also had several seals made by his older friend Shinten'ō. One of them, the wooden white-character "Now there is no mist, guest" 今無霞客 (no. 39), has bold, rough, and irregular lines that give the seal a sense of both antiquity and modernity. Shinten'ō carved his name into its side 信天翁記 (no. 39a). Tessai commissioned a number of excellent seals from the talented carver Zhao Shuru 趙叔孺 (1874–1945), including a white-character seal made in 1921 in the style of Han-period seals, "Peaceful—small retreat" 安蔬小隱 (no. 40). Zhao's close study of Han-period precursors is apparent in the formality of the composition and the subtle placement of lines. Zhao also made Tessai's red-character "Kuixing Pavilion" 魁星閣 (no. 41). Kuixing, a deity of the Pole Star and the patron of literature, was a

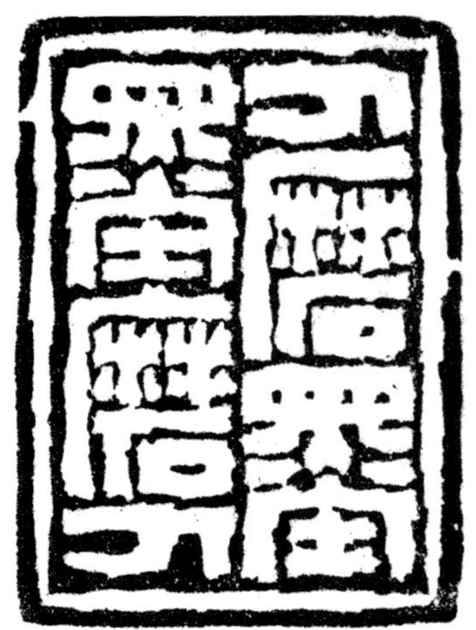

35. Seal used by Tanomura Chokunyū: 人磨墨墨磨人

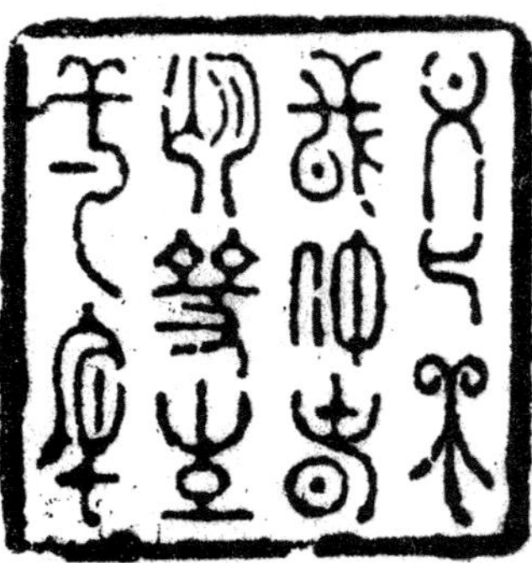

36. Archaic-style seal used by Tanomura Chokunyū: 文化甲戌仲春望□生弍年

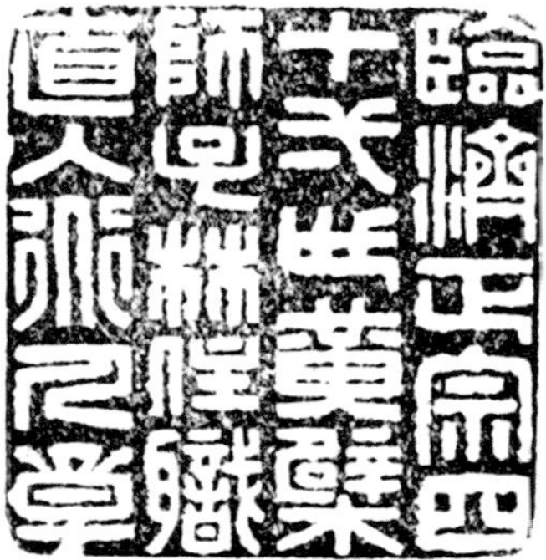

37. Seal used by Tanomura Chokunyū: 臨濟正宗四十弍世黄檗獅子林住職直入道人掌

38. Seal carved by Rai San'yō (1780–1832), used by Tomioka Tessai (1836–1924): 山碧水明

favorite of Tessai's, and several of the artist's seals relate to him. The elegant composition and crisp, thin lines make this a fine example of the modern reworking of large seal script. Tessai's interest in contemporary Chinese seal carving was but one part of a larger interchange that led to the establishment in 1913 at West Lake in Hangzhou of the Xiling Seal Society 西泠印社, which came about through the combined efforts of Chinese and Japanese scholars and artists.

Enthusiasm for carving, collecting, and using seals peaked in the Meiji and Taishō periods, a time that was also the height of artistic interaction between seal carvers in Japan and China. The use and appreciation of seals were integral to literati painting and calligraphy, and paralleled interest in the literati lifestyle, including *sencha* gatherings where seals and seal impressions in *inpu* were often displayed. The dramatic decline in the study of Chinese language and culture in the postwar years has seen a corresponding contraction in literati painting, as few people can now even read Chinese inscriptions written in cursive or seal scripts much less understand the historical and stylistic referents. Seal carving has retained much of its popularity in China, where the graphic appeal of archaic scripts has attracted artists working in various media. Currently, the study of Chinese is growing steadily in Japan, and this renewed interest in the language may eventually lead to a new appreciation of those aspects of Japanese art that are historically connected to China.

Categories of Seals

Seals are divided into categories depending on the nature of their inscriptions. For instance, many seals contain the artist's names, including family name, personal name, aliases (*azana* 字), style names (*gō* 号), studio names, and many others. Some artists had dozens of names, which often evolved over the course of their careers.

Small seals placed at the upper right corner of inscriptions or calligraphy are known as *kanbōin* 冠帽印, as they "crown" the beginning of the text. They contain a variety of expressions, and style-name seals are sometimes employed along with the *kanbōin*. Seals with poetic expressions placed in the corners or along the edges of works are known as *yūin* 遊印, or "playful" seals, and bear lines of poetry, favorite expressions, philosophical concepts, and so on. *Shūzōin* 収蔵印, which indicate ownership, are sometimes applied by collectors and usually give the name of the collection. Although often seen on Chinese paintings, they are much rarer in Japan and are more often found impressed inside the wooden storage box than on the surface of a work. Seals of appreciation, or *kanshōin* 鑑賞印, which indicate the approval of a connoisseur, are also customarily placed inside boxes. Although there are many additional categories and subcategories of seals, the above divisions are the principal ones.

Patterns of Seal Use

So-called white-character, or *hakubun* 白文, seals and red-character, or *shubun* 朱文, seals are often used in alternation.

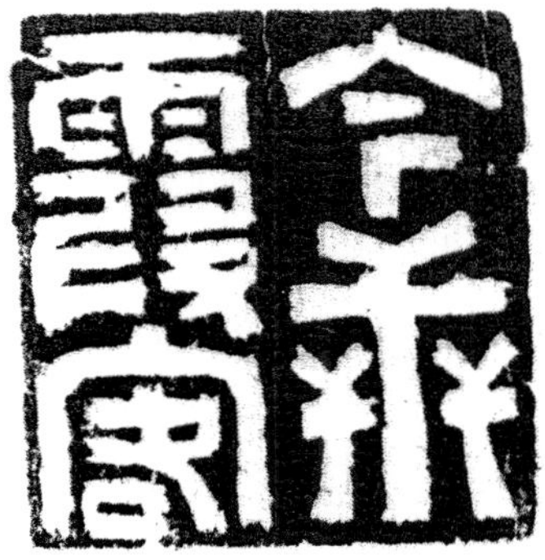

39. Seal carved by Yamanaka Shinten'ō for Tomioka Tessai: 今無霞客

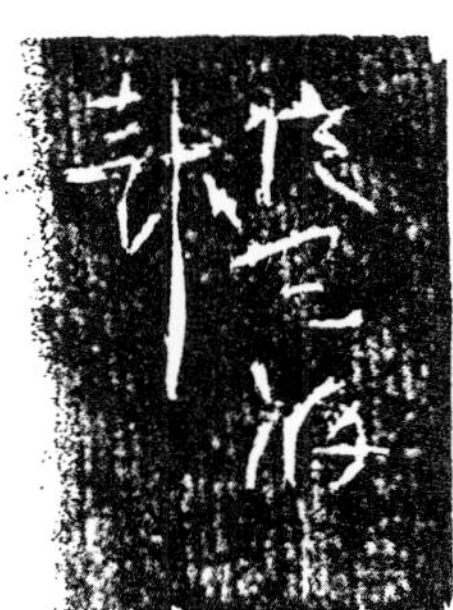

39a. Side inscription by Shinten'ō on seal 39: 信天翁記

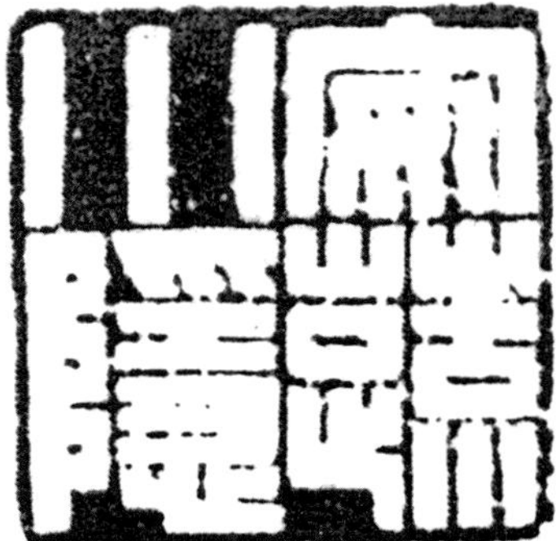

40. Seal carved by Zhao Shuru (1874–1945) for Tomioka Tessai: 安蔬小隱

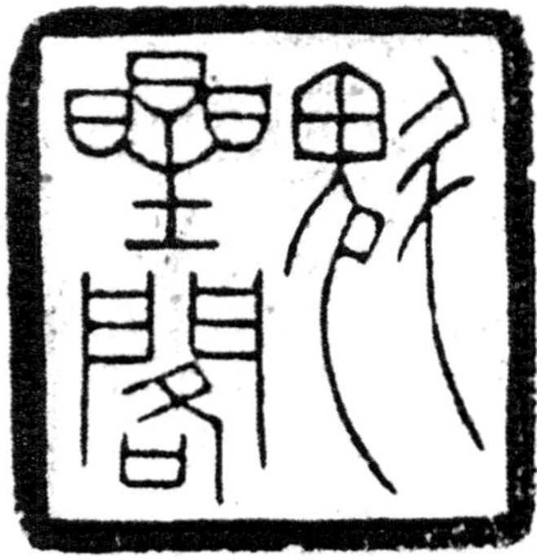

41. Seal carved by Zhao Shuru for Tomioka Tessai: 魁星閣

Especially when two seals appear next to the artist's signature, one typically employs white characters and the other red. A pleasing mixture of different shapes, styles, and red or white characters is considered ideal when an artist applies many seals to a work.

Impressing a single seal on a completed work is usually considered a necessary minimum, while the most common pattern is two name seals by the signature plus a *kanbōin* seal, if there is an inscription. Yet there is no specific limit to the number of *yūin* 遊印 on a work. Artists establish their own patterns for the kind and number of seals on their paintings.

As enthusiasm for seals mounted in the nineteenth century, new ways of using and thinking about seals developed. Hosokawa Rinkoku, Hagura Katei 羽倉可亭 (1799–1887), and other seal carvers inscribed classic Chinese texts with a linked series of seals in various script styles and designs and impressed them on handscrolls and albums. Collections of seal impressions, or *inpu,* were usually placed in albums, and applying the seals of a specific artist to a sheet of paper in tandem with a painting and mounting the work as a hanging scroll became a popular practice in the Meiji period. This led some artists to integrate their seals into the paintings themselves. A dramatic example is the 1901 *Sumo Wrestlers* by Suzuki Shōnen 鈴木松年 (1848–1918), which incorporates five seals into the decorative designs on the wrestlers' *keshōmawashi* skirts (no. 42). Parts of the seal on the far left of the painting were carefully masked off to fit the shape of the skirt. Shōnen repeatedly used his bold seals in paintings. Doi Gōga 土井贅牙 (1817–1880) often made paintings of demonic-looking figures that are shown squeezing, throwing, or chewing the seal impressions they appear to hold in their hands. The 1865 Gōga screen in this catalogue (cat. no. 78) provides many examples of this startling application of seal imagery. Seals were even used to represent the self, as in the dramatic self-portrait by Yokoi Kinkoku 横井金谷 (1761–1832) in which his most common seal, reading "Kinkoku," represents the artist's head (no. 43). The Edo-period haiku poet Furuta Ryūko 古田龍湖 had a seal with the artist name meaning "dragon lake," and the image of a twisting dragon is superimposed over the character for "lake" (no. 44). Unusual seals such as these are unforgettable, a desirable quality for an artist who wanted to be noticed.

In the first few decades of the twentieth century, it became fashionable for prominent painters to have the designs of their seals woven into fabrics to be used exclusively in mountings for their hanging scrolls, thus fully integrating the seals into their artworks. Yet the enthusiasm for seals had begun to wane by the 1930s, as many artists reverted to smaller seals, often placing only one next to their signature.

Seals as Expression of Identity

From the beginning, painters used seals for the purpose of confirming their identity with a unique mark. But this practice gradually merged into an expression of the artist's inner

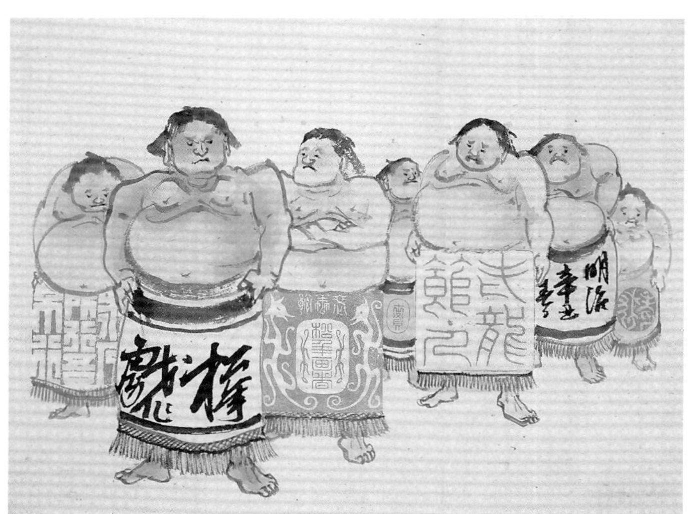

42. Suzuki Shōnen (1848–1918), *Sumo Wrestlers*, dated 1901. Hanging scroll: ink and color on paper, 44.7 × 59.2 cm. Hakutakuan collection, Kyoto.

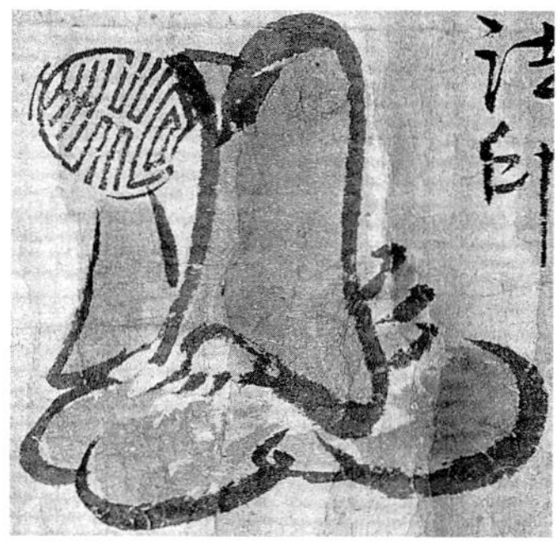

43. Self-portrait by Yokoi Kinkoku (1761–1832) with seal representing his head: 金谷

44. Seal used by Furuta Ryūko: 龍湖

identity. This major transformation occurred in tandem with a shift in the status of painters, from craftspeople creating decorations to artists expressing high aesthetic and poetic values. The rise of literati painting in Japan, with its Chinese precedents, emphasis on Chinese poetry, and paintings meant to reveal the character of the artist, was the greatest factor in changing perceptions of the possibilities of painting as an expressive art form.

At first painters' seals bore the name of the artist, and over time the number of names an artist used multiplied, in part to represent different aspects of identity that the artist wished to associate with the painting. A single painting could be impressed with the many different names of the same artist, thus focusing attention on the complexity of the painter's identity. With the development of *kanbōin* and especially *yūin*, seals could be inscribed with poetry and other sentiments that the artist wished to convey in association with the painting. Artists could place any inscription they liked on a work, yet it is significant that the inscriptions on seals rarely relate directly to a painting's theme. Instead, the seals reveal the attitudes of the artists themselves. Each time one views a work by an artist, previously unseen seal inscriptions add to the perception of the artist's character.

A brief consideration of a few seals used by Tanomura Chikuden 田能村竹田 (1777–1835) demonstrates how they express his self-perceptions. Chikuden began his career as a poet and only later became accomplished as a painter. Early on he sometimes applied a seal with two lines based on a Wang Wei 王維 (699–761) poem: "In this age mistakenly a poet, in an earlier life I must have been a painter" 当代誤詞客前身應畫師.[20] These lines not only express his situation; they rather boldly associate him with the figure traditionally considered the founder of literati painting in China. In a lighter vein, another seal used by Chikuden reads, "In a previous life I was a butterfly" 前身胡蝶, recalling Zhuangzi's 荘子 (c. fourth century BCE) story about dreaming he was a butterfly.[21] Another seal of Chikuden's quotes four characters from Li Bo's 李白 (701–762) famous poem "Question and Answer amid the Mountains" 山中問答: "Laughing but not answering" 笑而不答.[22] A seal given to Chikuden by his close friend Rai San'yō 頼山陽 bears the name "Ko Hakusekiō" 小白石翁, meaning Little White Stone Old Man 白石翁, a reference to one of the alternate names of the famous literati Shen Zhou 沈周 (1427–1509), suggesting that Chikuden was a "little Shen Zhou."[23] In a similar fashion, a great many artists expressed their ideas and revealed aspects of their personalities and interests through their seals. Seals became, in effect, a highly referential visual language that transmits the artists' visions of themselves and their art.

NOTES

The illustrations of seals in this essay are not actual size. For ease of viewing, most have been enlarged; a few large seals have been reduced. Ultimately the size of a seal is part of its aesthetic character, but it was not possible to consider this complex issue in this short essay.

1. See the new theory of some types of bronze casting in Lukas Nickel, "Imperfect Symmetry: Re-thinking Bronze Casting Technology in Ancient China," *Artibus Asiae*, vol. 66, no. 1 (2006): 5–39.

2. Shimonaka Yasaburō et al., *Shodō zenshū* 書道全集 [hereafter SZ] (Tokyo: Heibonsha, 1954–68), B1, 7.

3. Although only the preface survives; see ibid.

4. SZ, B1, 8.

5. SZ, B1, plates 38–40.

6. The seal is mentioned in the fifth-century *History of the Later Han* (Hou Han shu 後漢書); see SZ, B2, 1.

7. SZ, B2, 1–2.

8. SZ, B2, 3–4.

9. See the photograph of the surviving Tan'yū seals in Sakakibara Satoru 榊原悟 et al., *Kanō Tan'yū ten: Seitan yonhyaku nen kinen* 狩野探幽展: 生誕四〇〇年記念 (Tokyo: Nihon Keizai Shinbunsha 日本経済新聞社, 2002), plate 8.

10. Nakata Yūjirō 中田勇次郎, *Nihon no tenkoku* 日本の篆刻 (Tokyo: Nigensha 二玄社, 1966), 113.

11. The most extensive collection of Taiga's seals is inserted in the first folio of Kosugi Hōan 小杉放庵 and Suzuki Susumu 鈴木進, eds., *Ike Taiga gafu* 池大雅画譜, 5 folios (Tokyo: Chūō Kōron Bijutsu Shuppan 中央公論美術出版, 1957–59).

12. Nakata, *Nihon no tenkoku*, 132–39, 147–68.

13. SZ, B2, 63–65.

14. Stephen Addiss, "Hosokawa Rinkoku: Seal-carver, Poet, and Literati Painter," *Kaikodo Journal*, no. 3 (Spring 1997); Addiss, SZ, B2, 100; Nakata, *Nihon no tenkoku*, 140–41.

15. See his 1878 painting of unusual rocks impressed with twelve of his seals in Paul Berry and Yokoya Ken'ichirō, *Unexplored Avenues of Japanese Paintings* (Ōtsu: Ōtsu Shiritsu Rekishi Hakubutsukan; Seattle: University of Washington Press, 2001), plate 63 and seal appendix p. 149. For the 1876 album employing twenty different seals, see plate 10 and pp. 136–37.

16. The date of this seal is carved on its side. This inscription is visible in the large Chokunyū *inpu* in the Hakutakuan collection. This phrase appears in old Chinese texts connected to tea practice.

17. See the discussion of him in cat. no. 24 in this volume on Uragami Shunkin's *Laughter on Spring Wind*.

18. See the discussion of Chokunyū's role as head of Shishirin-in in his biography in this catalogue.

19. Tomioka Masutarō, ed. 富岡益太郎, *Muryōjubutsudō inpu* 無量壽佛堂印譜, 5 vols. (Kyoto: Sunkōdō 寸紅堂, 1926). This remarkable work was limited to three hundred copies with impressions from the original seals.

20. See Paul Berry, "Tanomura Chikuden 1777–1835: Man Amidst the Mountains" (PhD diss., University of Michigan, 1985), 352, seal 6.

21. Ibid., 356, seal 16.

22. Ibid., 354, seal 11.

23. Ibid., 367, seal 44.

Signatures and Seals

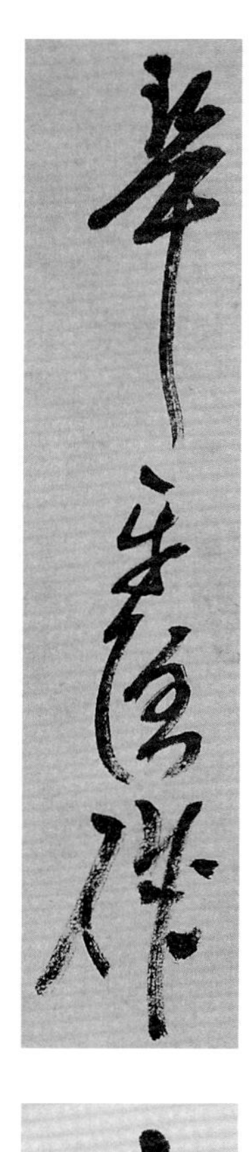

Doi Gōga
土井贅牙

Screens of Human Figures and Bamboo, 1865
人物/竹図

CAT. NO. 78

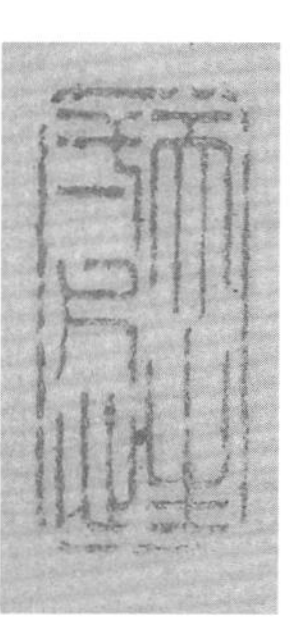
天生一片心

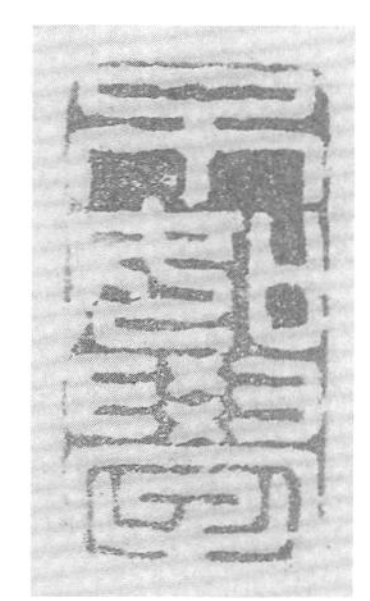
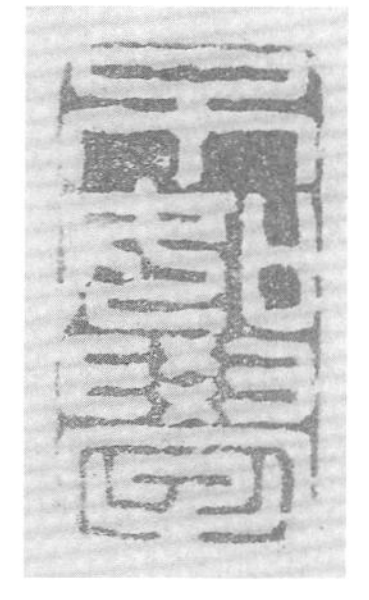
不如學

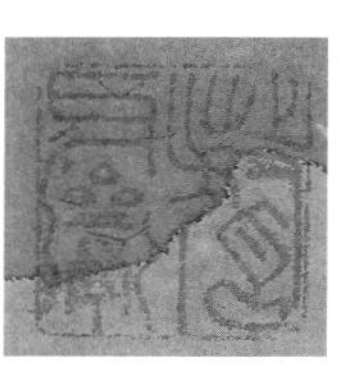
贅牙斎

有恪之印

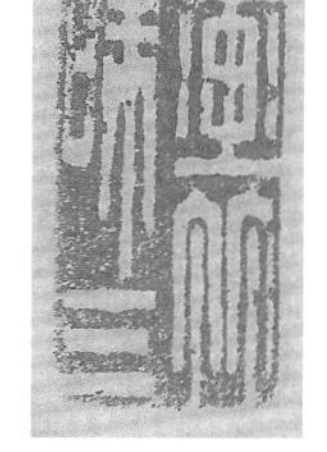
画竹三昧

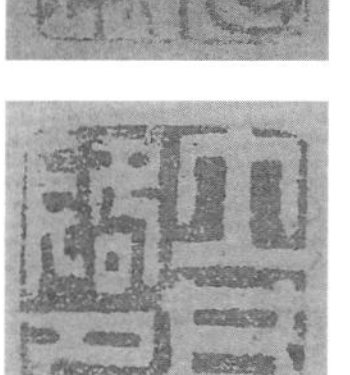
土井恪卩

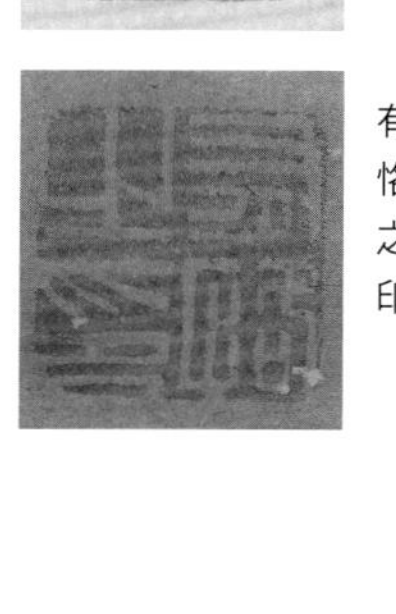
士恭

有恪之印

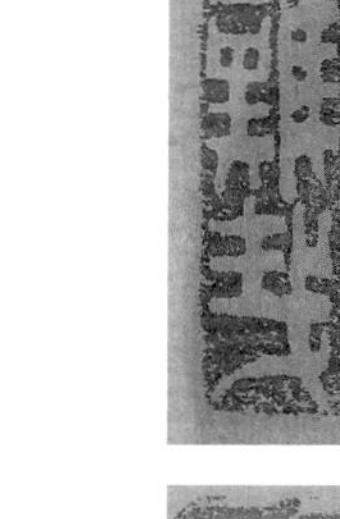
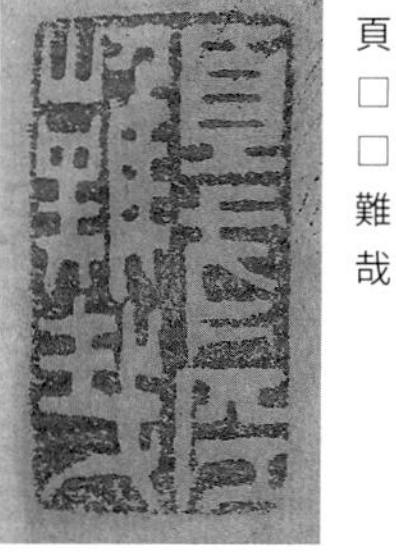
頁□□難哉

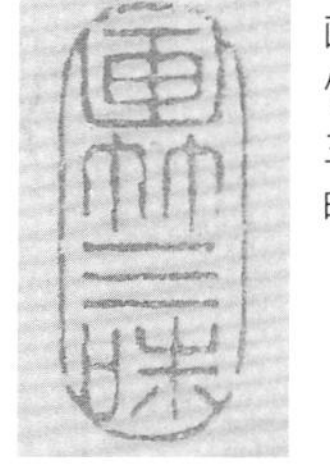
画竹三昧

恭氏

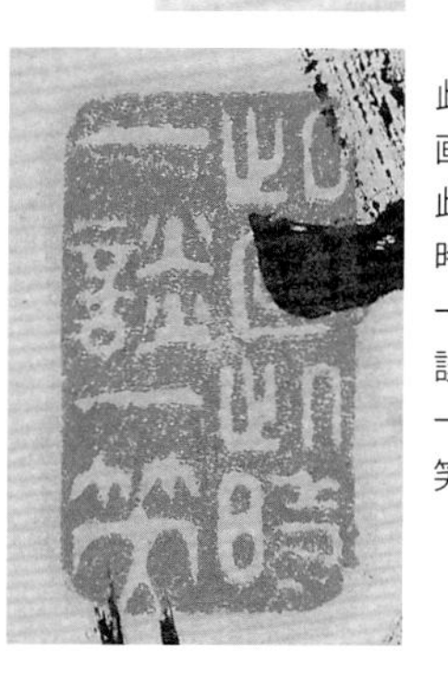
此画此時一談一笑

Dōmoto Inshō
堂本印象

Chinese Garden, 1923
中国庭園図

CAT. NO. 75

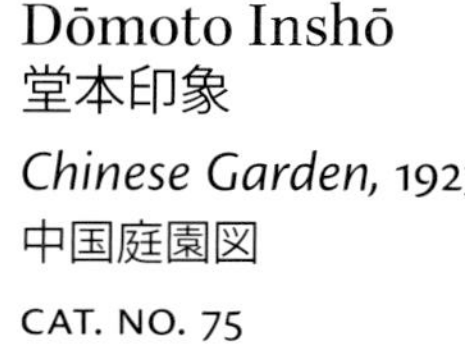

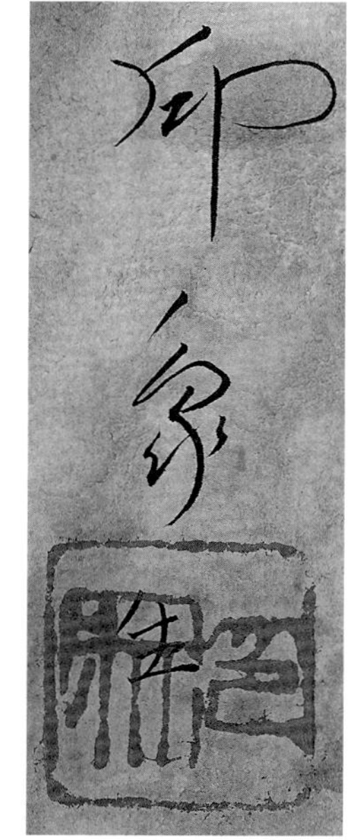
印象

The signatures and seals reproduced here are not shown at actual size. The seals found on individual paintings, however, are proportionate to each other.

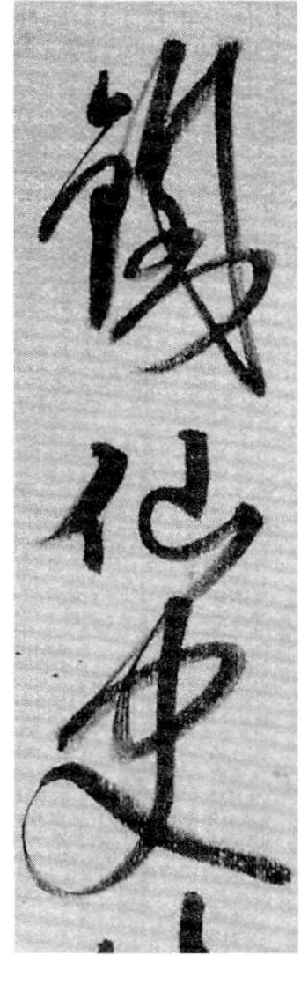

Fujimoto Tesseki
藤本鉄石

Pleasures of the Literati Life, 1856
人生一楽帖
CAT. NO. 76

真金

銕石

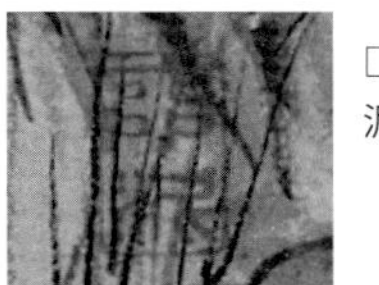

□泥

Old Pine, 1859
老松図
CAT. NO. 65

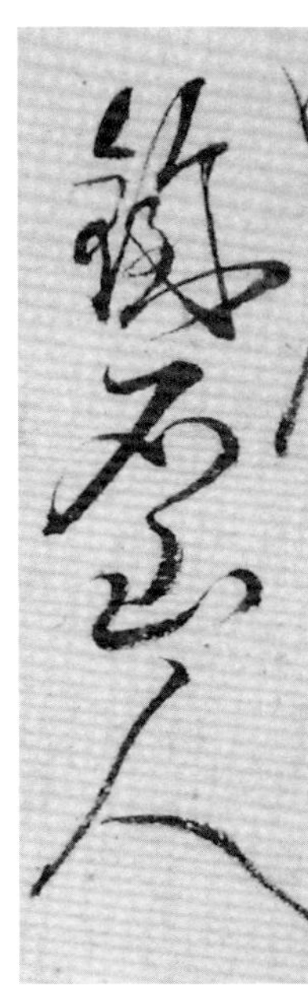

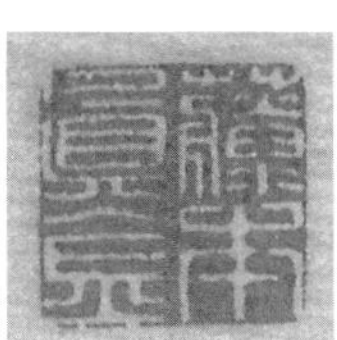
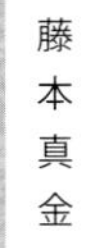

藤本真金

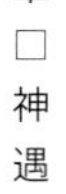

筆□神遇

藤本真金
壽樂
都門賣菜
吉備男子

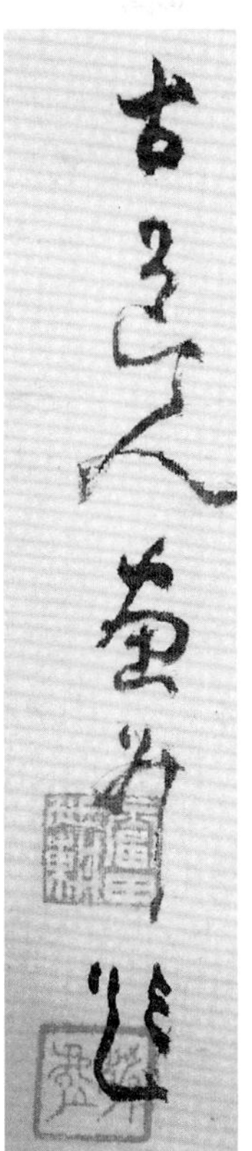

Fukuda Kodōjin
福田古道人

Mountain Valley in Quiet Mood, 1912
溪山幽趣図
CAT. NO. 49

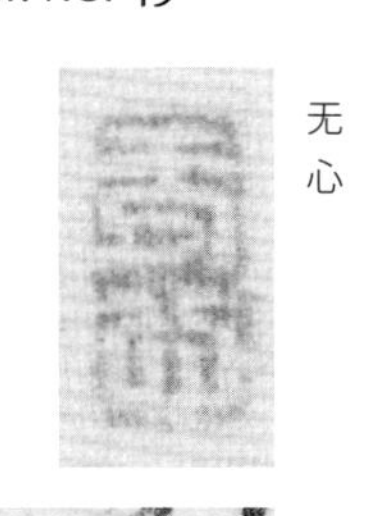

无心

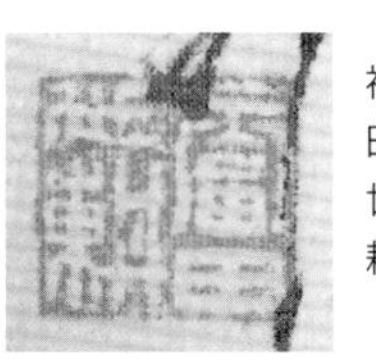

福田世耕

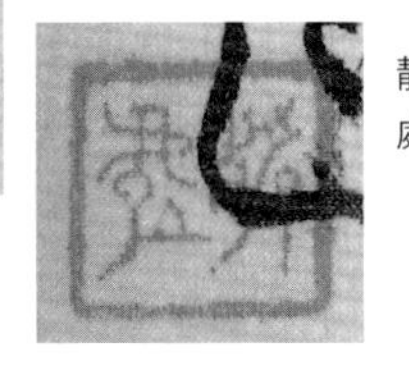

静處

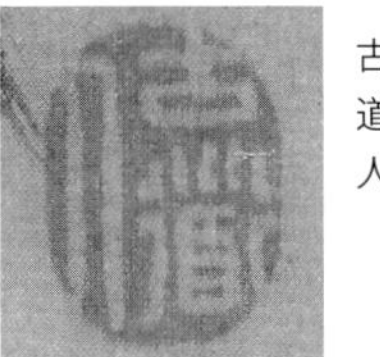

古道人

Autumn Spirit—One Pavilion, 1933
秋心一宇図
CAT. NO. 50

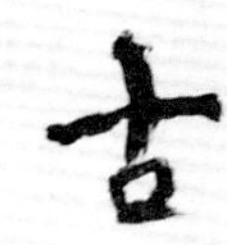
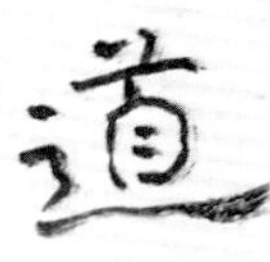
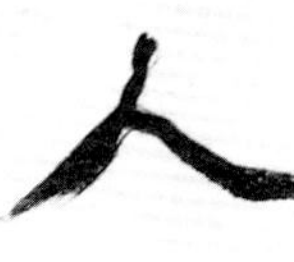

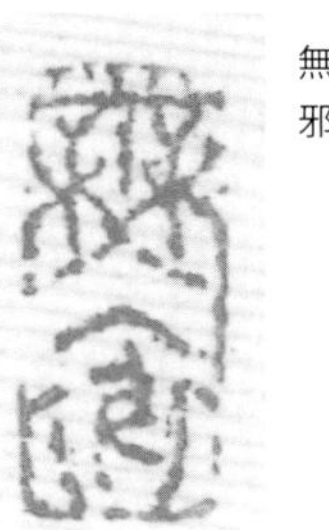

無邪

福田世耕

静處

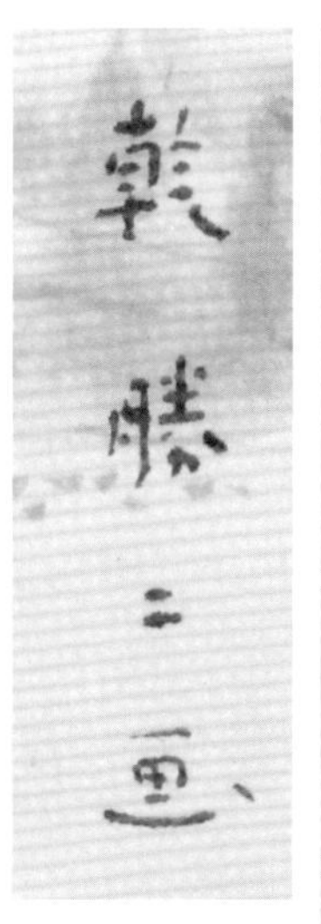

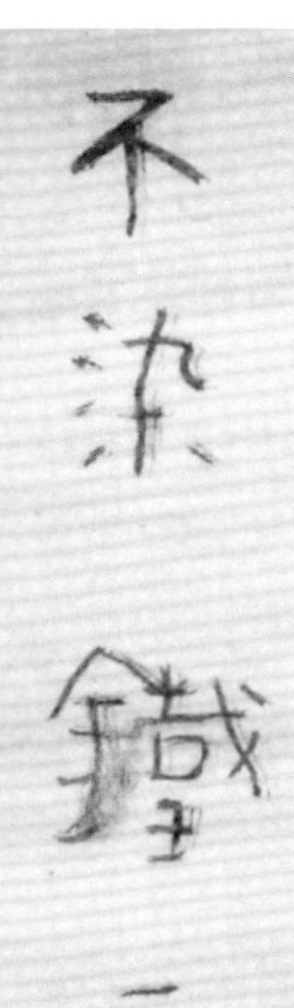

Fusen Tetsu
不染鉄
with Inui Katsuji
乾勝二

Scenes of the South Sea Islands, 1944
南洋の風景

CAT. NO. 60

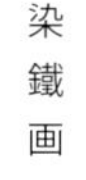

不染鐵画

鐵

鐵

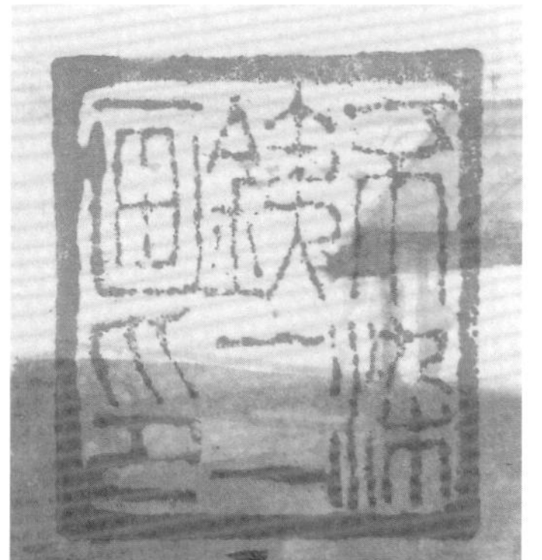

不染銕二画印

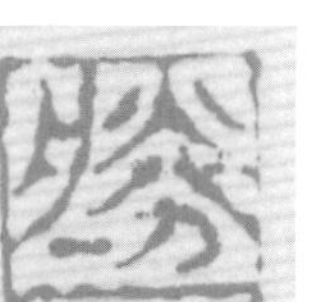

勝二

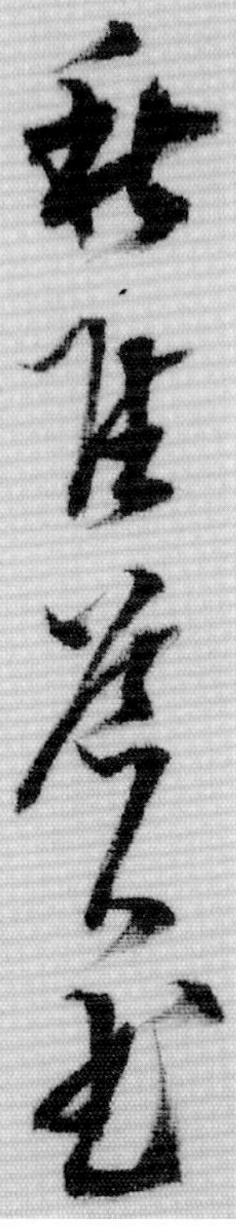

Gotō Shūgai
後藤秋涯

Idle Pleasures, 1920s
閒怡

CAT. NO. 53

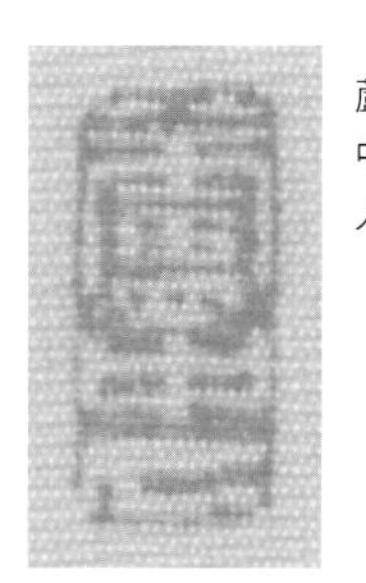

蘆中人

半雲山荘

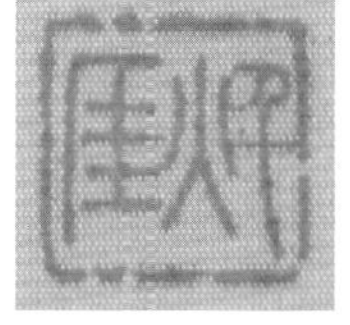

秋涯

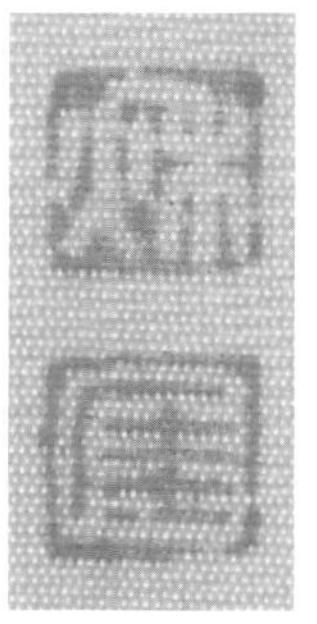

秋厓

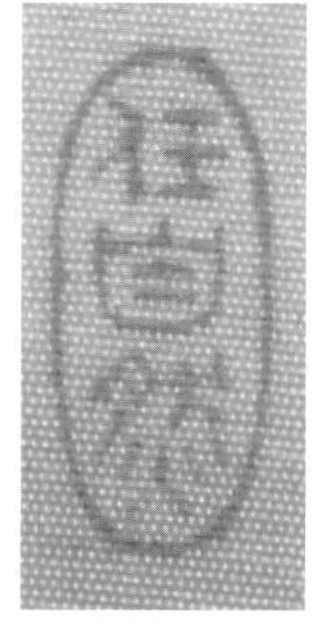

任自然

無息

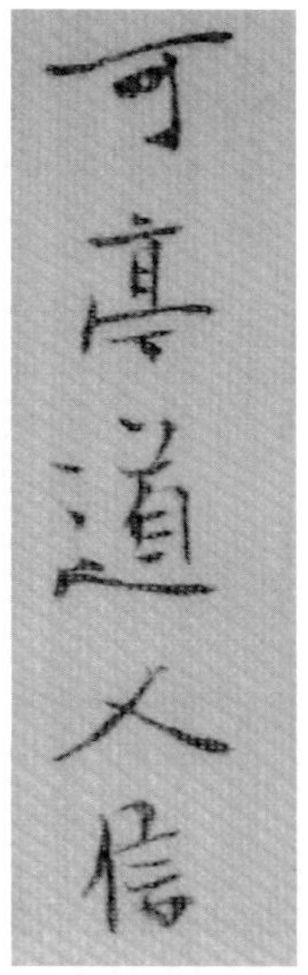

Hagura Katei
羽倉可亭

Elegant Gathering in the Western Garden, 1882
西園雅集図

CAT. NO. 9

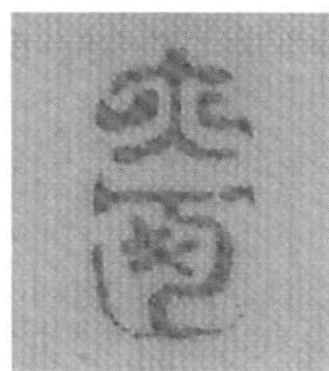
亦可

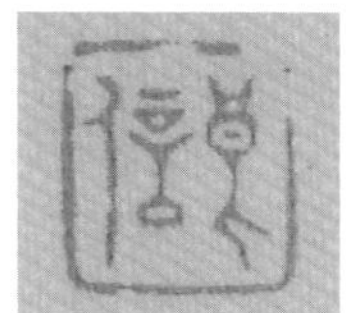
良信

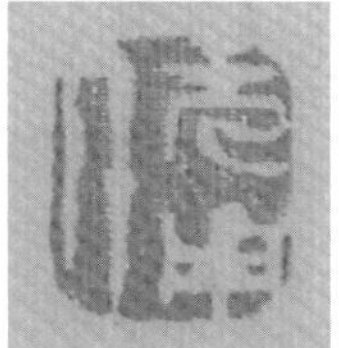
無用人

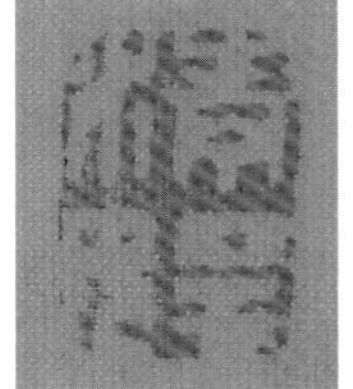
清娯

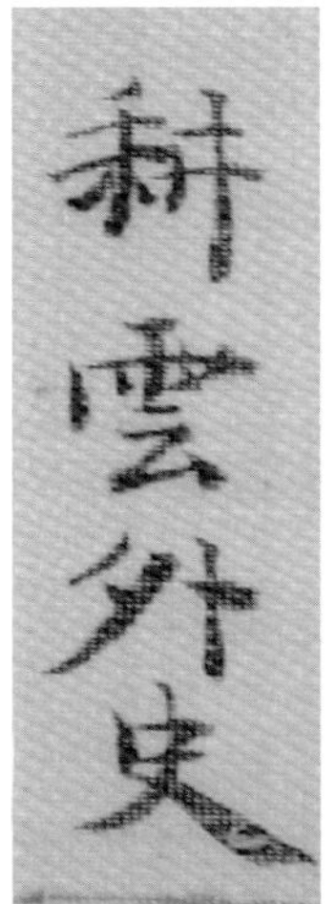

Haruki Nanmei
春木南溟

Immortal's Pavilion in Spring Daybreak, 1853
僊閣春曙図

CAT. NO. 35

南溟

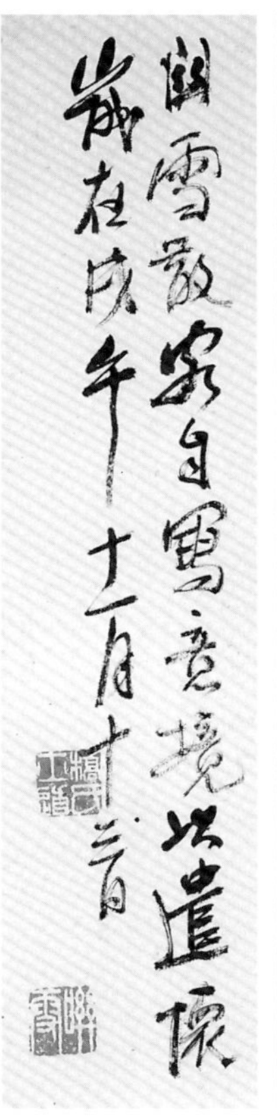

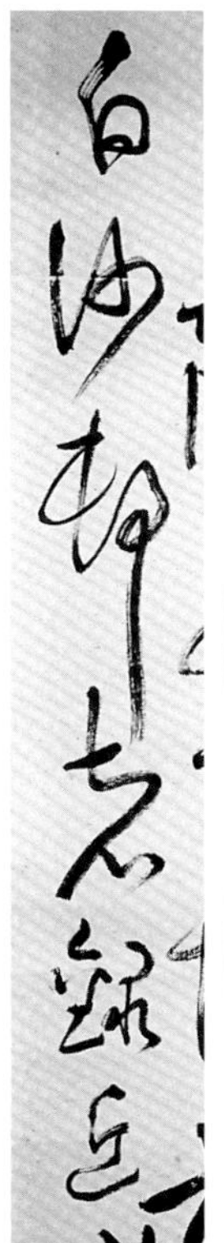

Hashimoto Kansetsu
橋本関雪

Sound of the Wind in the Pines / Seven-Character Line Calligraphy, 1918
松濤満地図並七古書

CAT. NO. 13

滄海遺珠

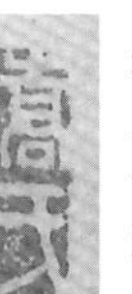
橋氏士道

関雪

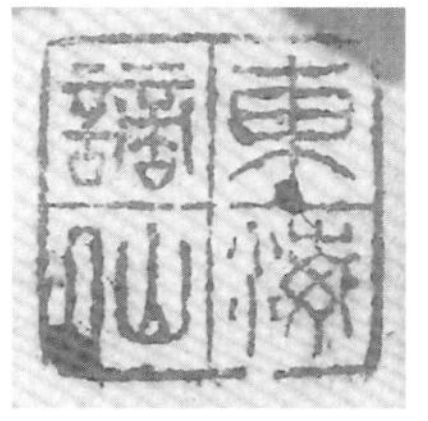
東海謫仙

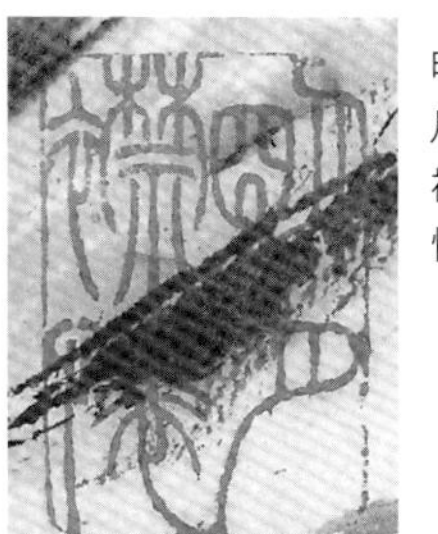
明月襟懐

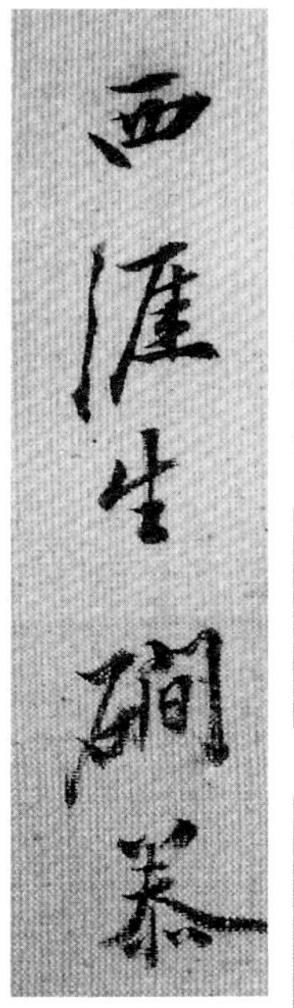

Hazama Seigai
西涯

Three Heroes of the Peach Blossom Garden
桃園三傑

CAT. NO. 77

磵恭字大未

西涯畫印

□陽如雪

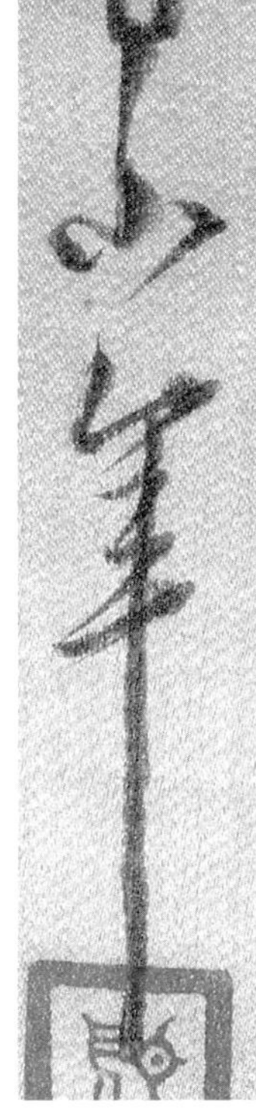

Hine Taizan
日根対山

Rain Passing over the Spring Forest, 1857
春林過雨図

CAT. NO. 33

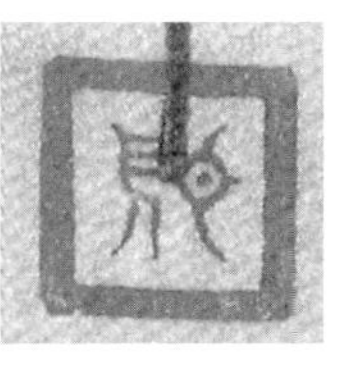

日長

小年父

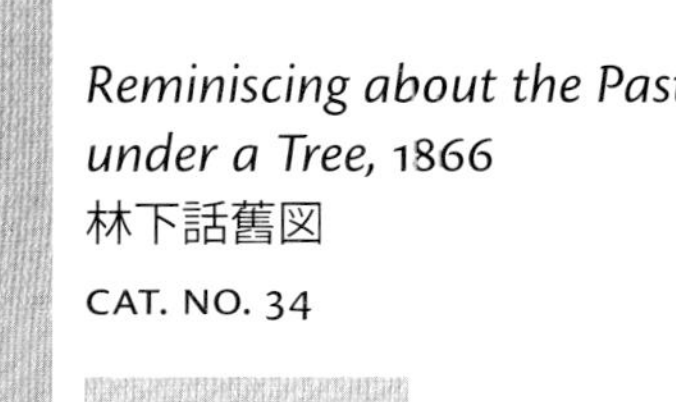

Reminiscing about the Past under a Tree, 1866
林下話舊図

CAT. NO. 34

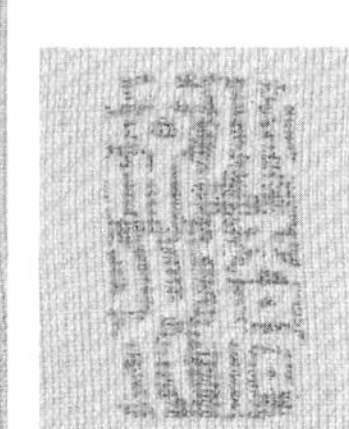

小橋流水

山静似太古

日長如小年

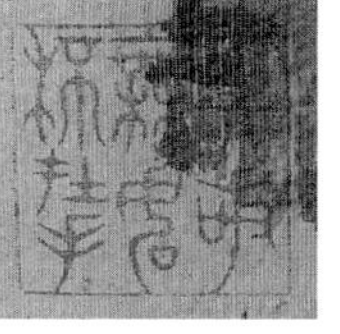

萬事無如在杯手

Hirai Baisen
平井楳仙

White Lotus, 1915
白蓮
CAT. NO. 73

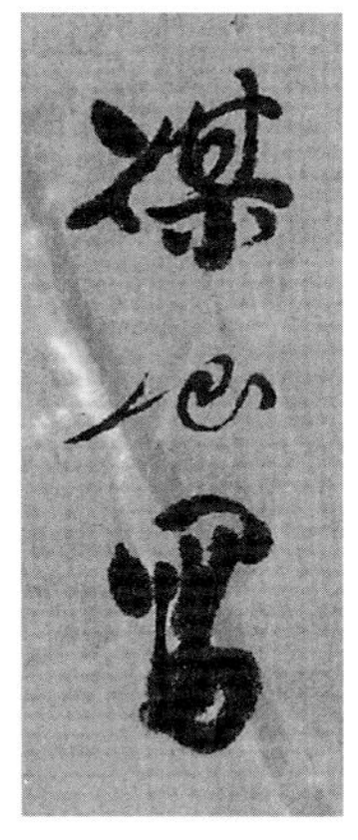

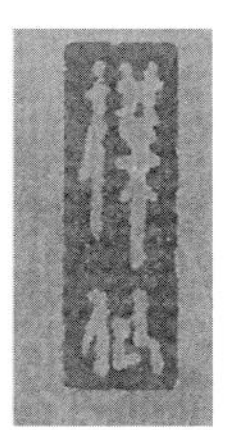

楳
仙

Cloud over Mount Hiei,
late 1910s 比叡雲峰
CAT. NO. 55

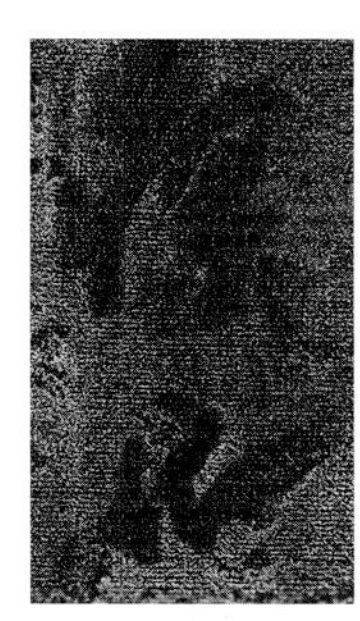

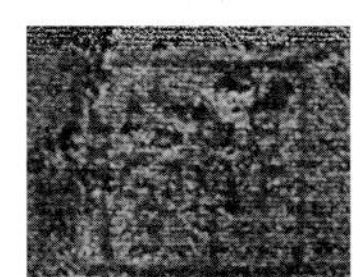

楳
僊

Mountains in China,
late 1920s 中国山岳図
CAT. NO. 56

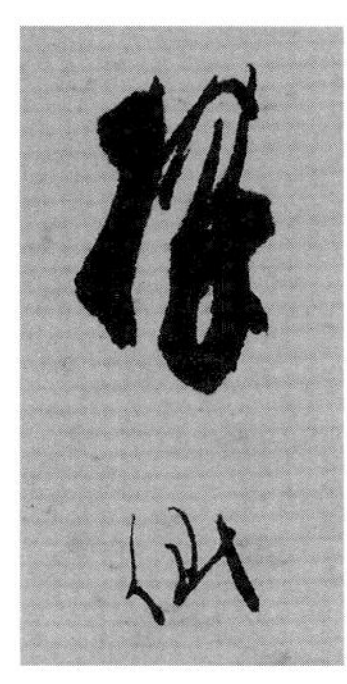

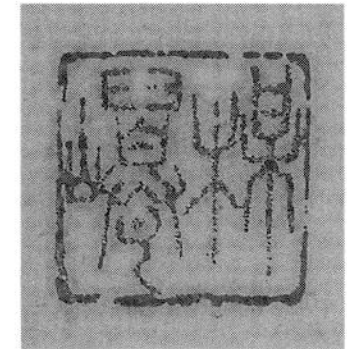

楳
僊

Shower over a Mountain Village,
1916 山市驟雨
CAT. NO. 54

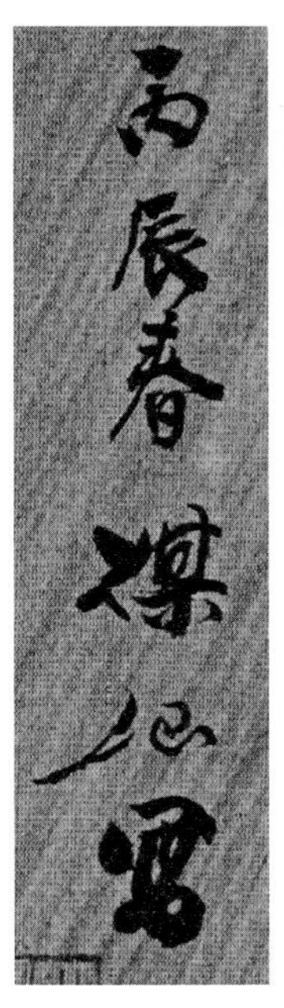

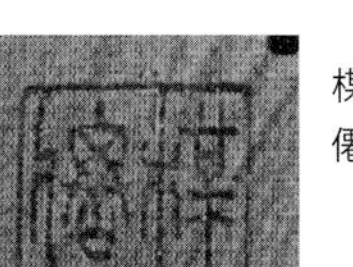

楳
僊

Plum in Snow / Rising Sun,
late 1910s 梅と日の出図
CAT. NO. 74

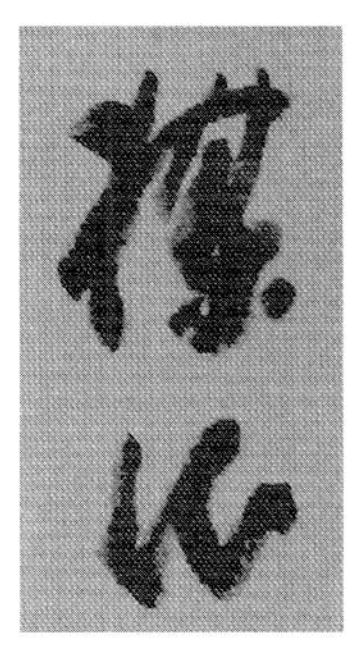

楳
僊

Mount Hōrai,
c. 1930 蓬莱山
CAT. NO. 57

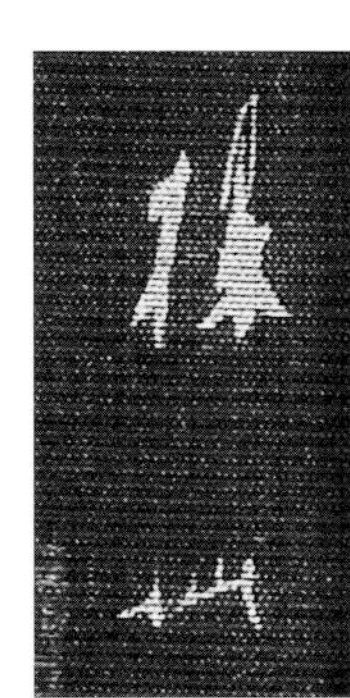

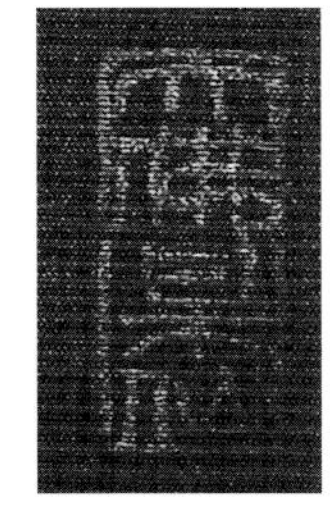

大
佛
某
仙

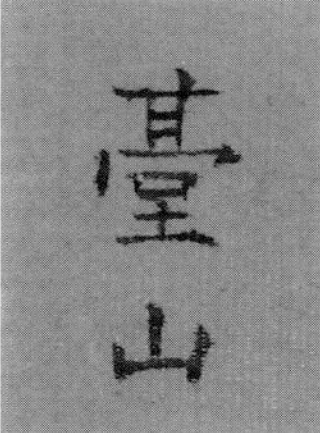

Hirose Taizan
広瀬臺山

Plum Blossom Studio, c. 1800
梅華書屋図

CAT. NO. 17

清
風

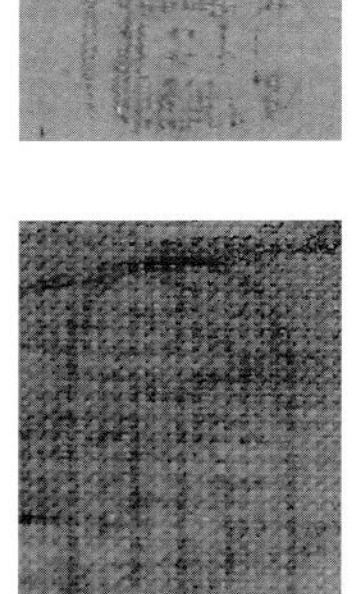

雲 (?)

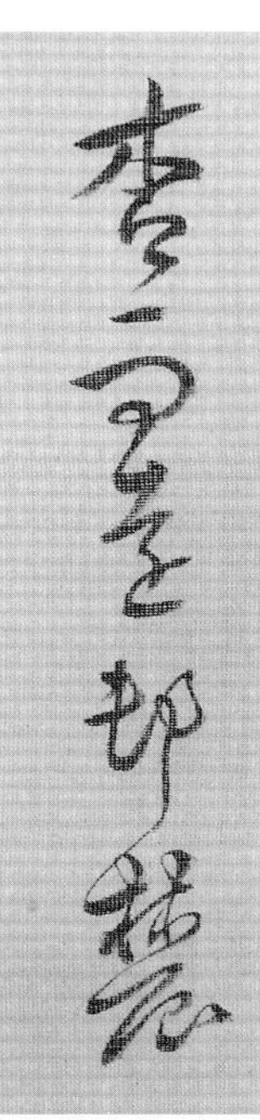

Hoashi Kyōu
(traditional attribution)
帆足杏雨

Landscape in Snow
雪山水景図

CAT. NO. 38

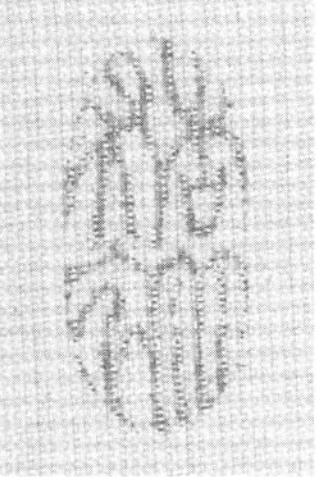

杏
雨
布
衣

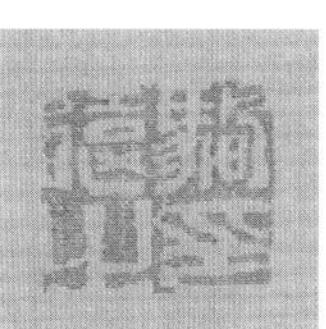

驅
遠
之
印

comparison seal

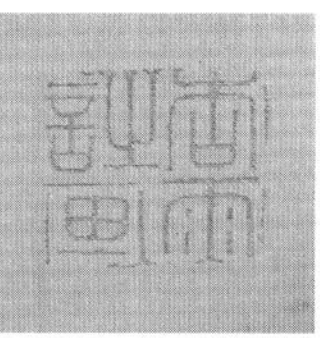

杏
雨
詩
画

comparison seal

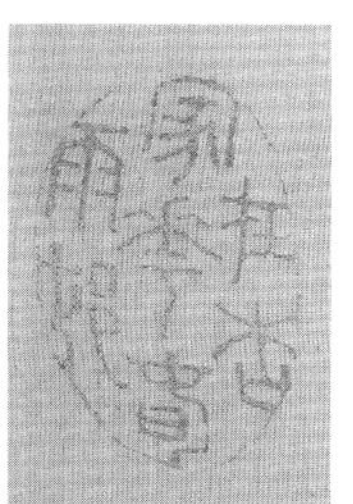

家
在
杏
華
春
雨
邨

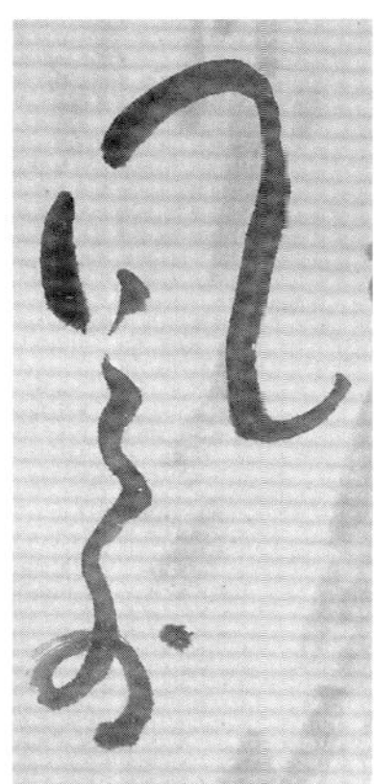

Honkō Fūgai
(traditional attribution)
本高風外

Visiting a Mountain Valley
山渓入客圖

CAT. NO. 27

好
幽

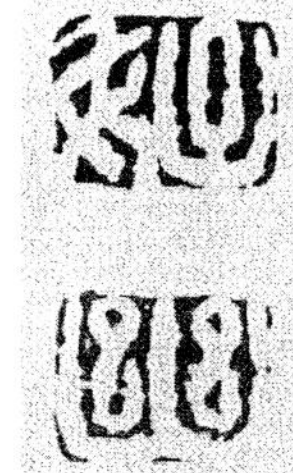

comparison seal

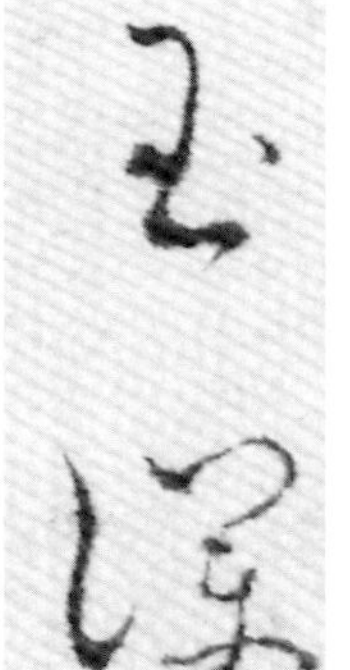

Ike Gyokuran
(traditional attribution)
池玉瀾
Willows on the Riverbank
柳蔭山水図
CAT. NO. 14

玉
瀾

comparison seal

松
風

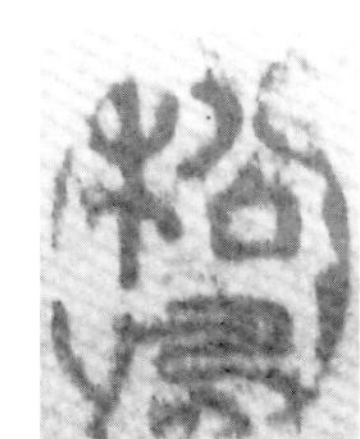

comparison seal

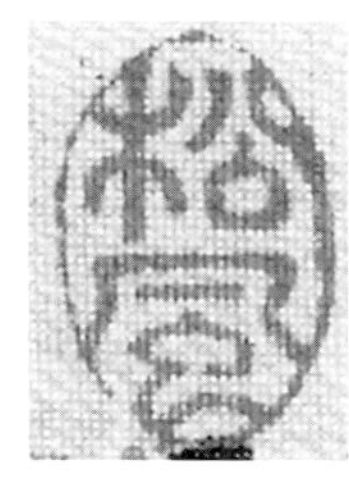

comparison seal

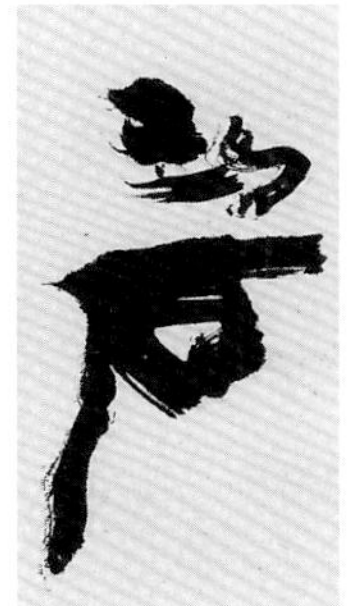

Kawahigashi Hekigotō
河東碧梧桐
Potted Plum Haiku, 1930s
盆梅俳句
CAT. NO. 12

碧
梧
桐

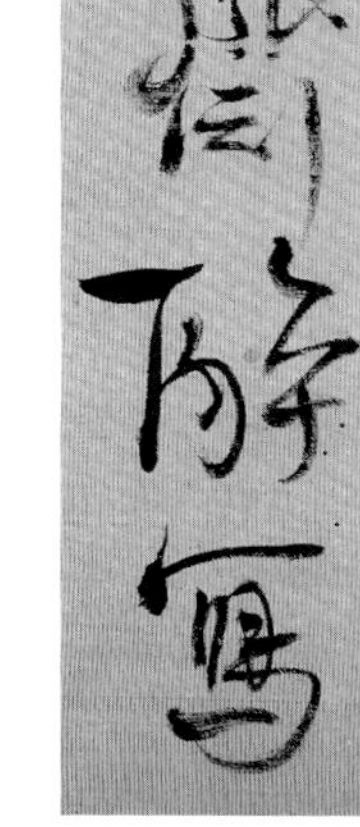

Kameda Bōsai
亀田鵬斎
Clearing after Rain, Clustered Peaks, 1807
雨霽群峯図
CAT. NO. 19

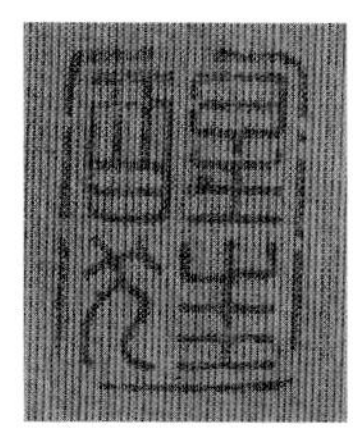
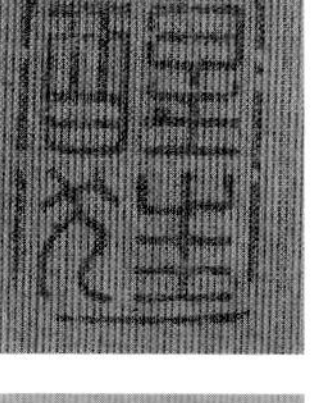

醒
狂

鵬
斎
閒
人

長
興
私
印

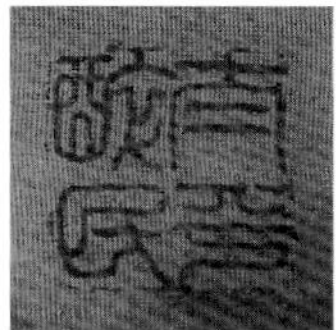

太
平
酔
民

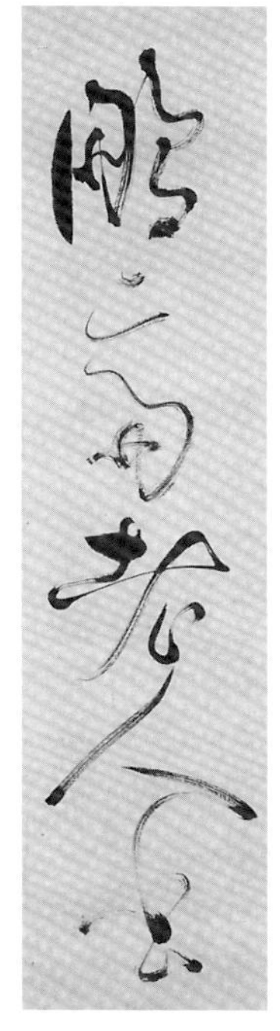

A Life of Drinking Sake, c. 1820
一生飲酒
CAT. NO. 2

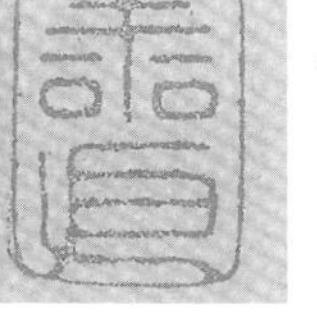

善
身

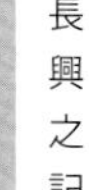

長
興
之
記

鵬
斎

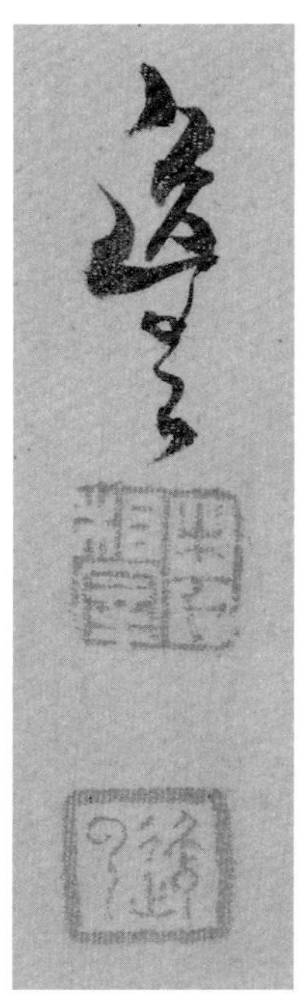

Kinoshita Itsuun
木下逸雲
Boat Returning in Autumn Mountains, 1844
秋山帰船図
CAT. NO. 32

木下相宰

逸雲

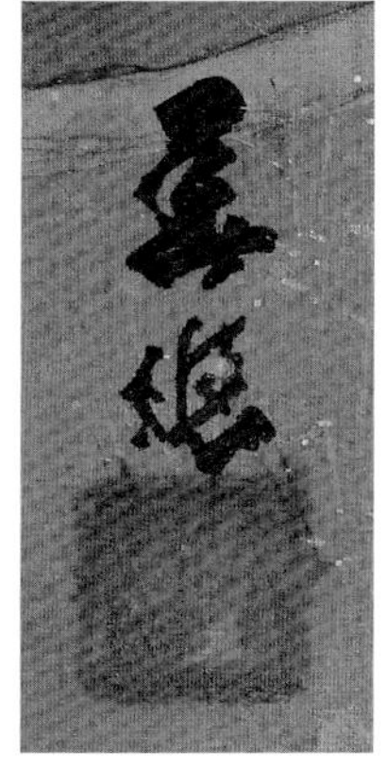

Kobayashi Shunshō
小林春樵
Plum Trees in Tsukigase, 1910s 月ヶ瀬梅林之図
CAT. NO. 47

□春樵

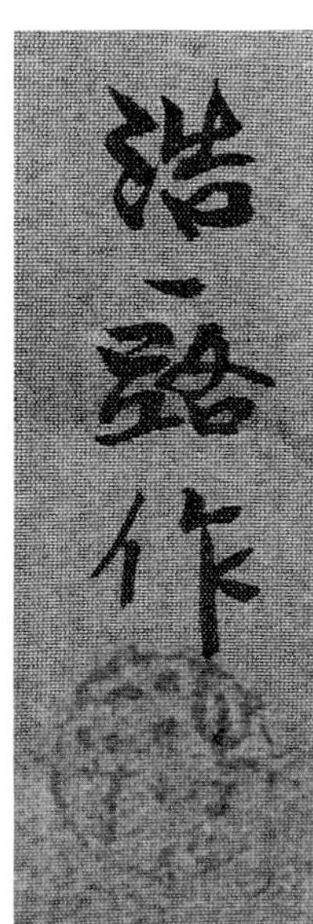

Kondō Kōichiro
近藤浩一路
Winter Mountain, c. 1920
冬乃山
CAT. NO. 51

浩浩乎(?)

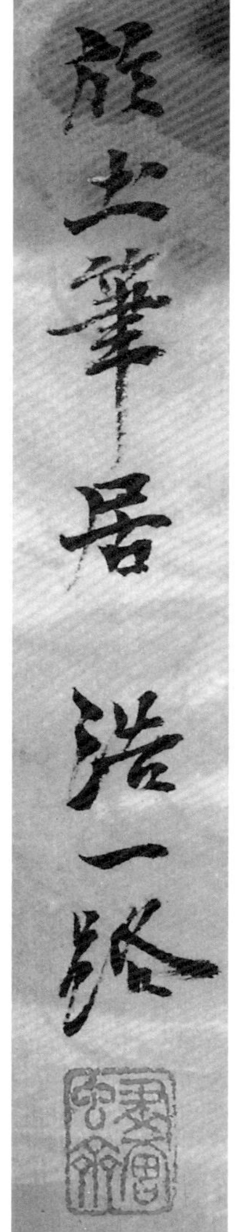

Rocky Seashore, late 1930s
荒磯
CAT. NO. 52

画虫斎

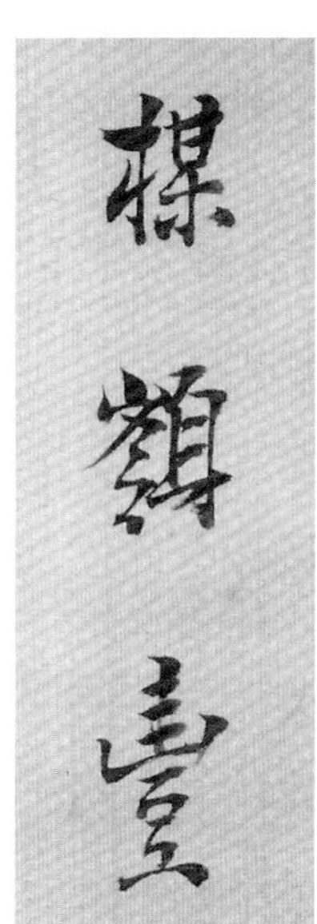

Kōno Bairei
幸野楳嶺
White Fox Jumping over a Torii Gate, 1875
華表白狐図
CAT. NO. 68

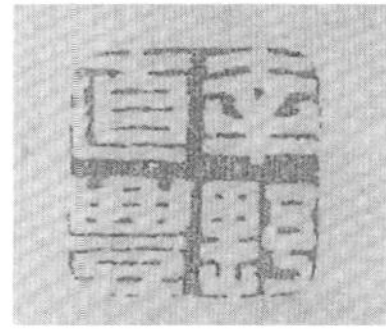

幸野直豊

楳嶺

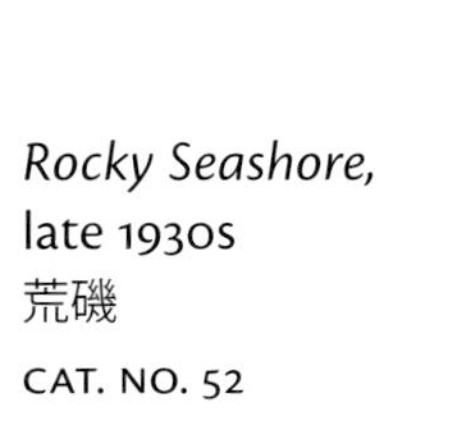

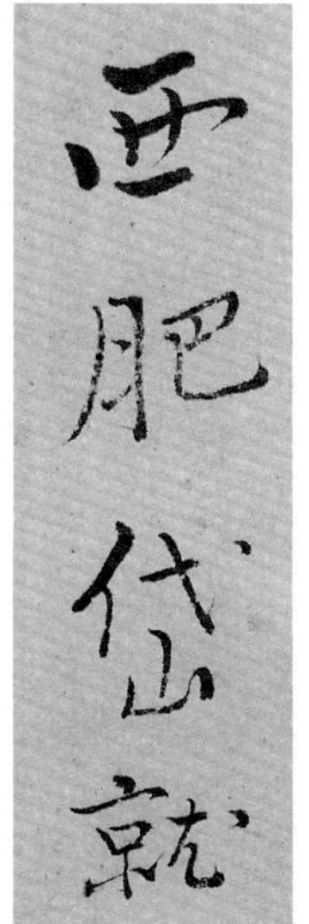

Kushiro Unsen
釧雲泉
Visiting a Friend—Discussing Antiquity, 1793
訪友論古図
CAT. NO. 16

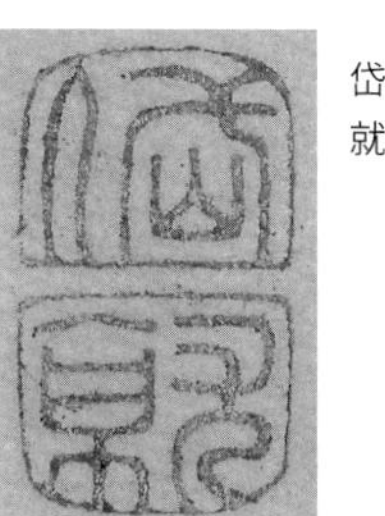

岱
就

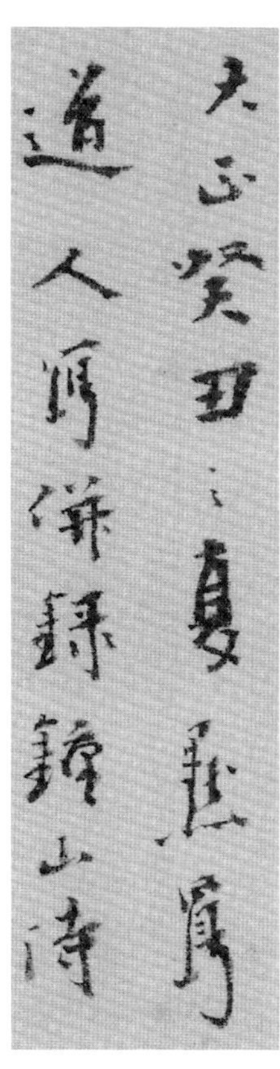

Maeda Mokuhō
前田黙鳳
Landscape Inspired by a Poem on Zhongshan, 1913
鍾山詩意山水図
CAT. NO. 45

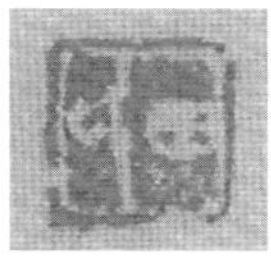

田
氏

黙
鳳

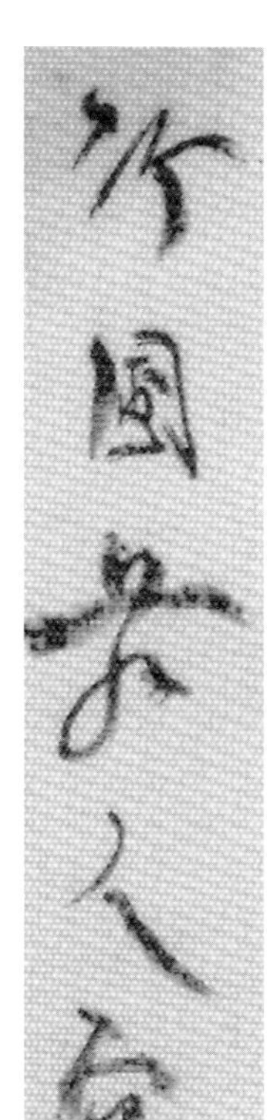

Mizuta Chikuho
水田竹圃
Gibbons Grasping at the Moon, 1930s
猿猴捉月図
CAT. NO. 71

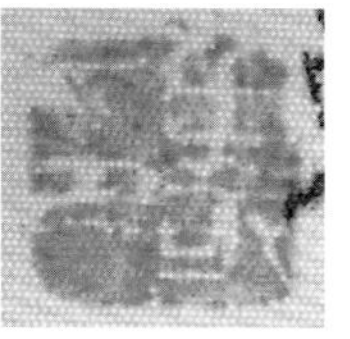

田
敬
印

竹
圃

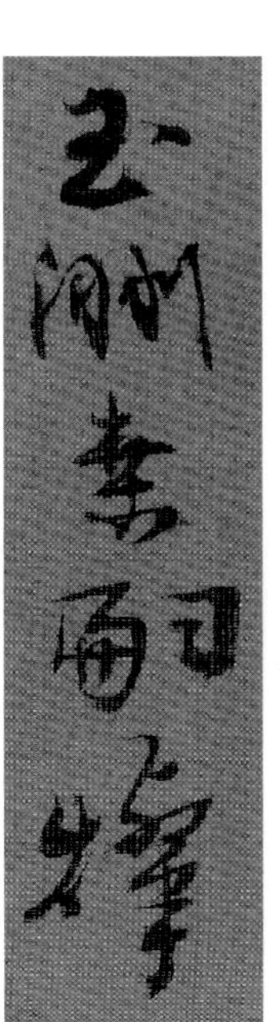

Kuwayama Gyokushō
桑山玉州
Spring Landscape, c. 1797
春景山水図
CAT. NO. 15

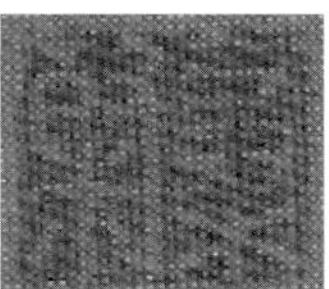

桑
燦

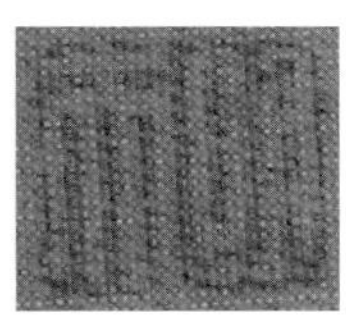
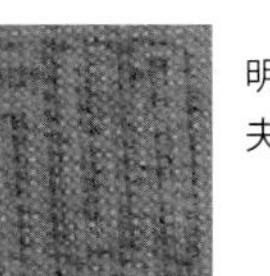

明
夫

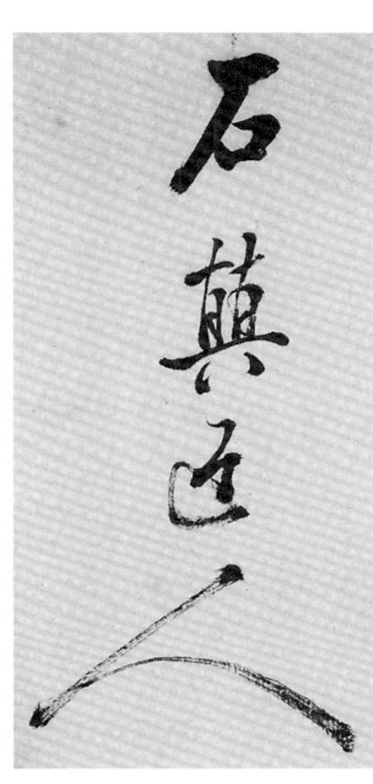

Masuyama Sessai
増山雪斎
Pure Conversation among Green Mountains, c. 1816
青山中清談図
CAT. NO. 18

雪
斎

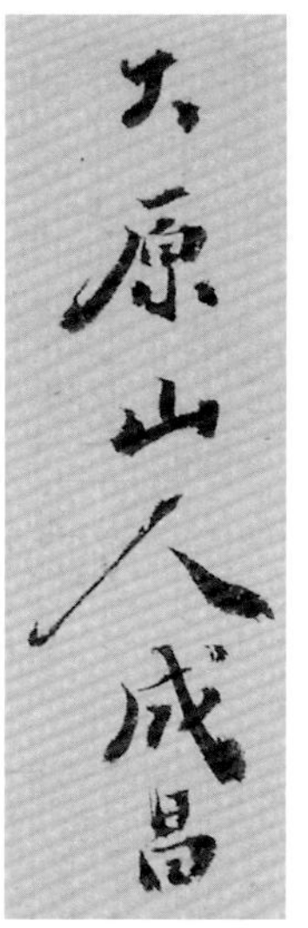

Nakabayashi Chikutō
中林竹洞
Elegant Orchid, 1827
幽蘭図
CAT. NO. 62

心
□
元
微

成
昌
之
印

字
伯
明

竹
洞

冰
清
雪
白

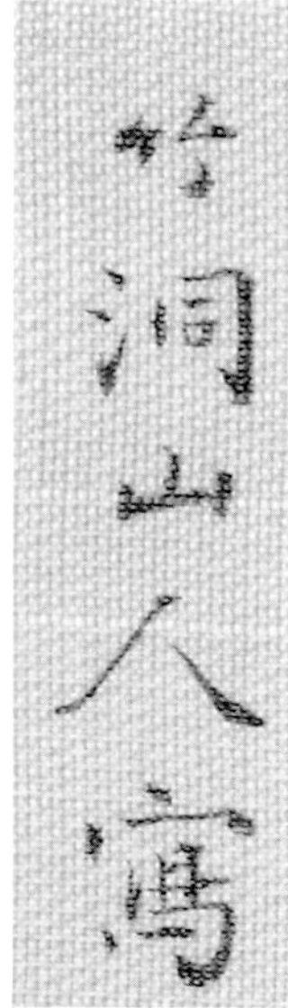

Cranes and Pine Trees, 1830s
群鶴松泉図
CAT. NO. 28

成
昌
之
印

字
伯
明

Nakajima Kahō
中島華鳳
Oni Senbei
鬼煎餅
CAT. NO. 81

華
鳳

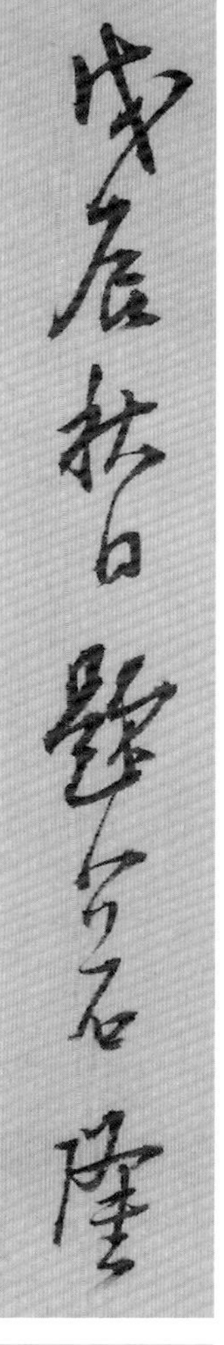

Noro Kaiseki
野呂介石
Nachi Waterfall, 1808
那智滝図
CAT. NO. 20

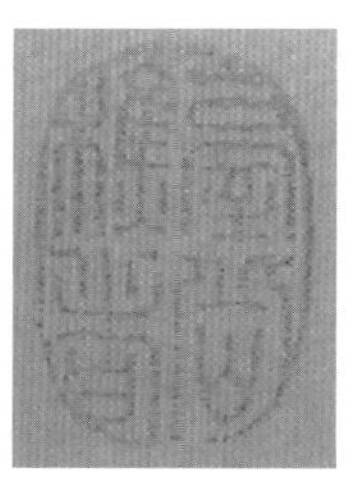

臺
岳
樵
者

第
五
隆
印

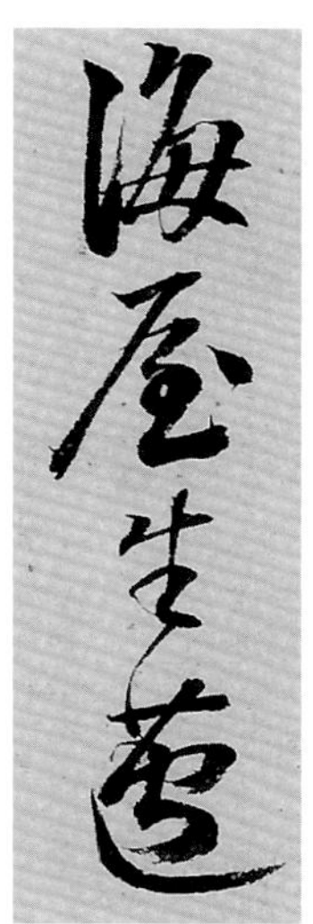

Nukina Kaioku
貫名海屋

Unzen Waterfall in Autumn, 1837
雲泉秋景圖

CAT. NO. 29

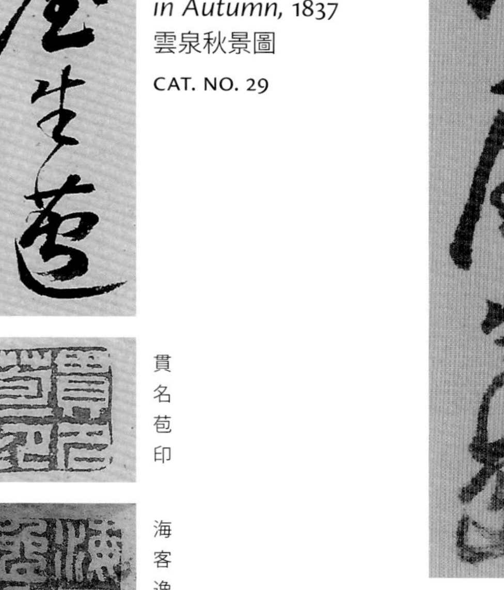

貫名苞印

海客逸興

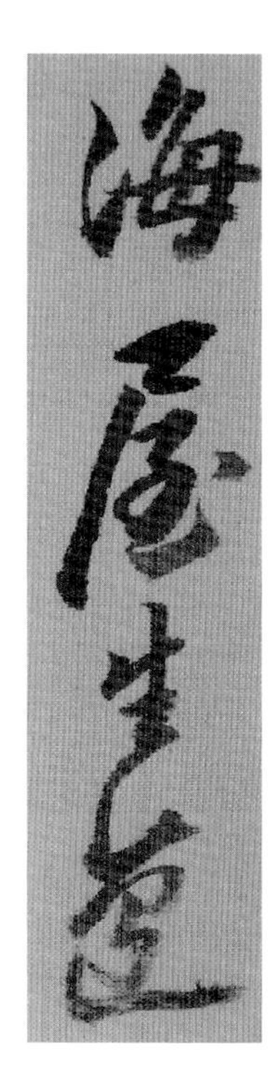

Landscape with Bamboo Grove in Light Red Wash, 1847
竹林山水図

CAT. NO. 31

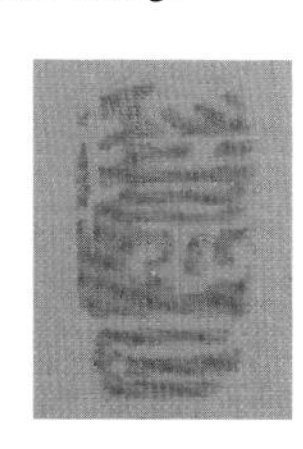

隱己

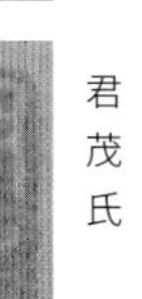

君茂氏

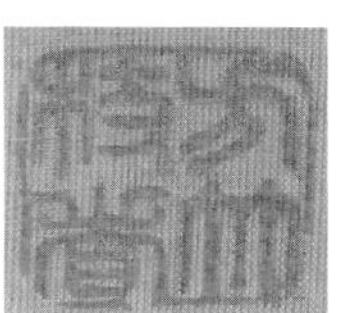

方竹杖者

Quatrain on Mountain Springs, 1860
山泉七言絶句

CAT. NO. 5

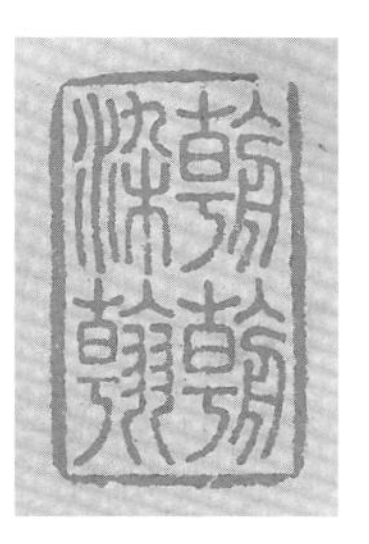

朝朝染翰

君茂

世味老来薄似紗

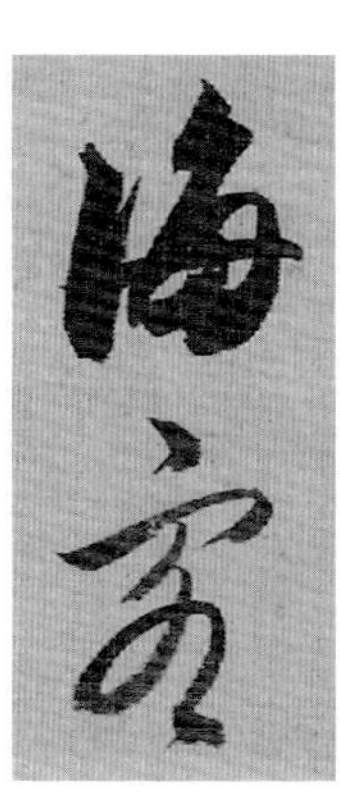

Viewing Plum Flowers in Snow, 1841
雪中見楳図

CAT. NO. 30

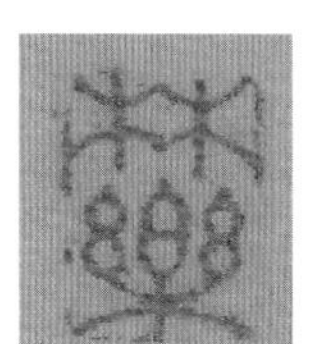

林樂

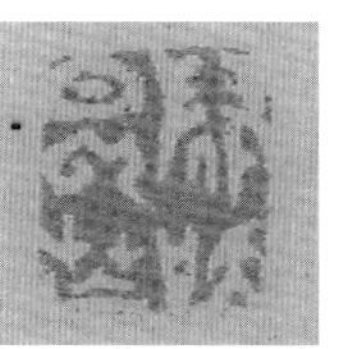

閒和白雲芒

我愛其静

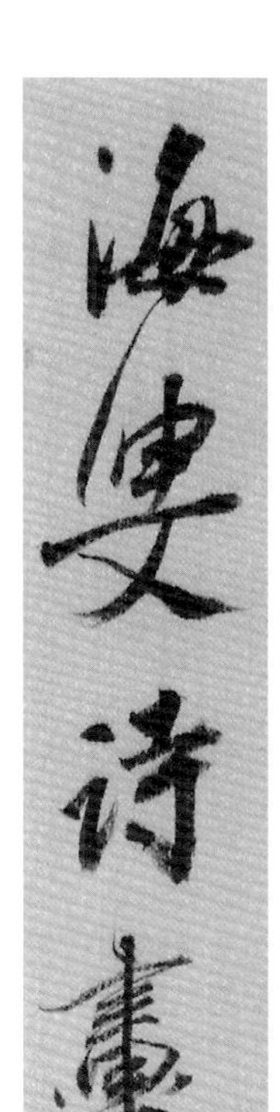

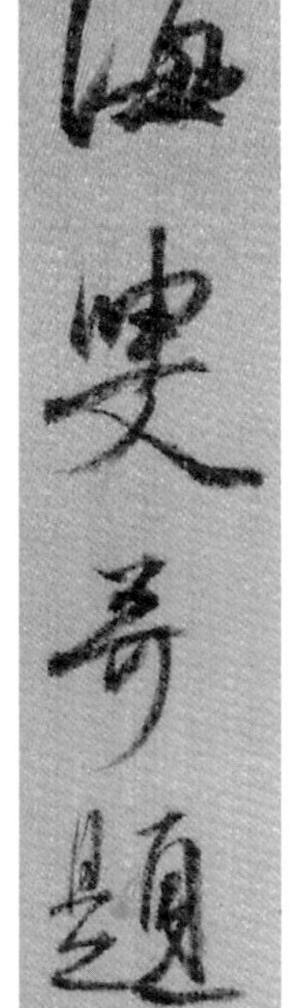

Plants of Four Seasons, 1840s
四時花卉図

CAT. NO. 64

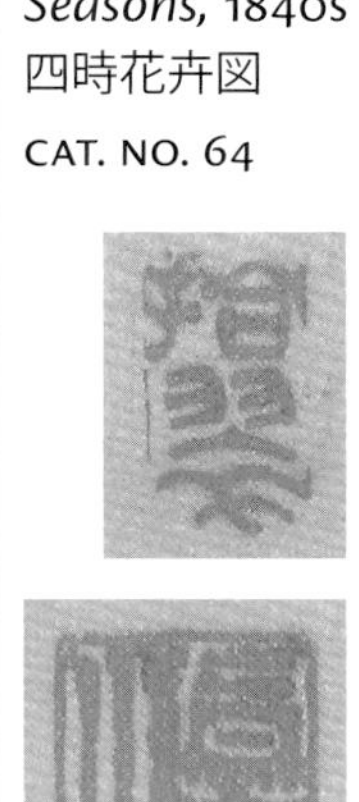

拾翠

君茂氏

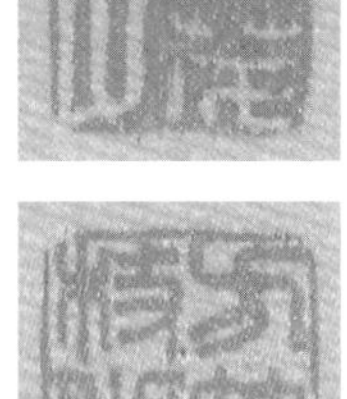

方竹杖者

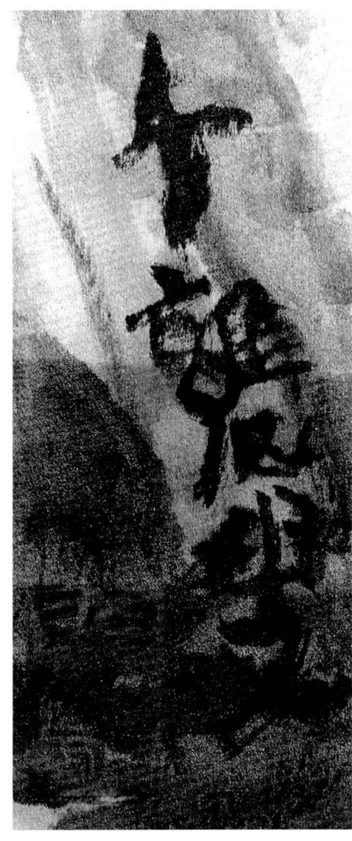

Ogawa Sen'yō
小川千甕
Fish-basket Kannon, 1920s
魚籃観音
CAT. NO. 83

千
甕

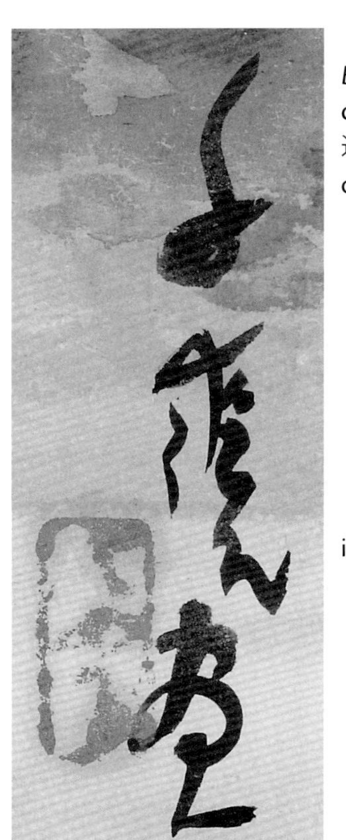

Eight Views of Ōmi,
c. 1933
近江八景図
CAT. NO. 58

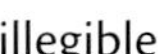
illegible

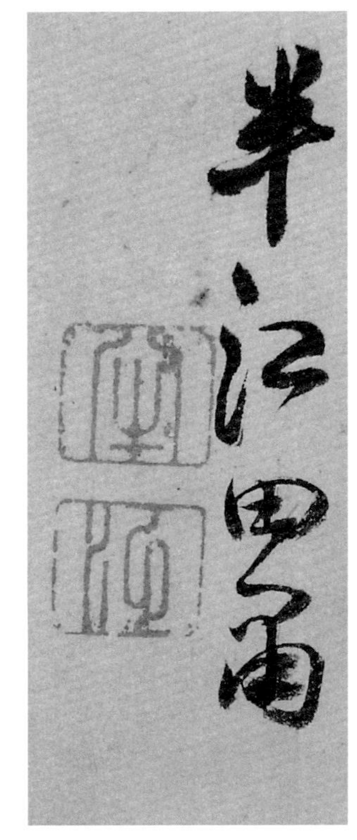

Okada Hankō
岡田半江
Pulling a Boat Upstream,
1836
船引之図
CAT. NO. 25

半
江

風
外
人
雲

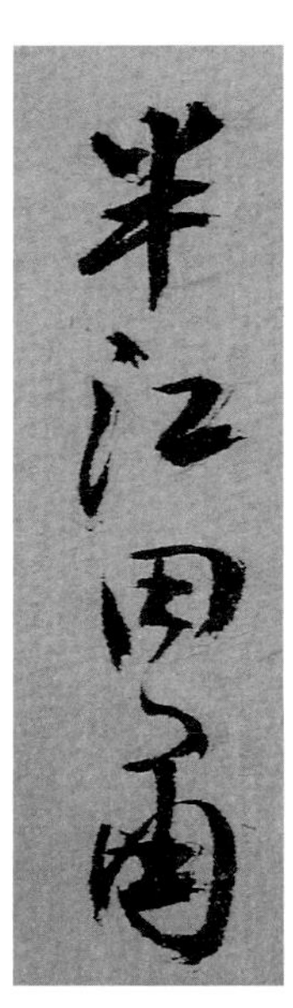

Lofty Pine Expressing Longevity, 1838
喬松供寿図
CAT. NO. 26

田
粛

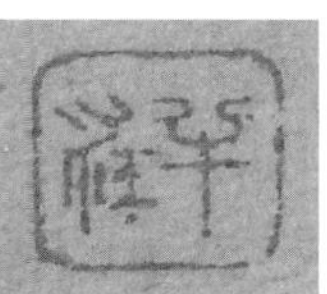

半
江

生
涯
画
筆
隷
詩
筆

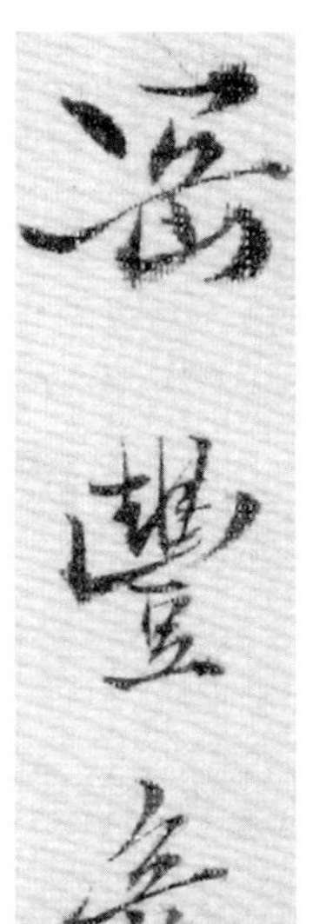

Okamoto Toyohiko
岡本豊彦

Summer Mist, 1820s
夏霞

CAT. NO. 23

豊彦

子彦

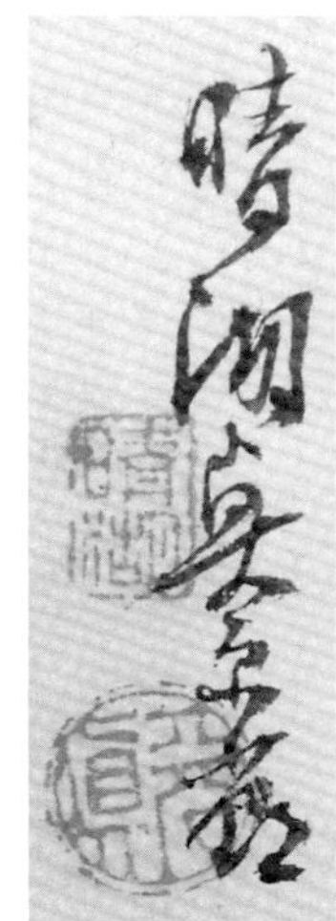

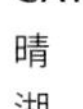

Okuhara Seiko
奥原晴湖

Elegant Mood of Mountain Residence, late 1860s
山荘幽韻図

CAT. NO. 44

晴湖

天真

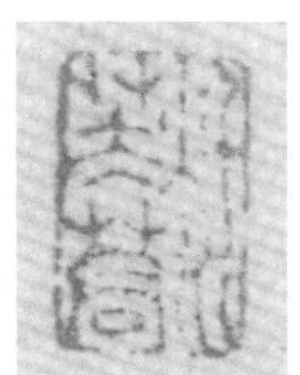

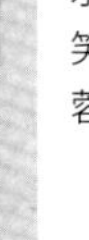

秋水笑蓉

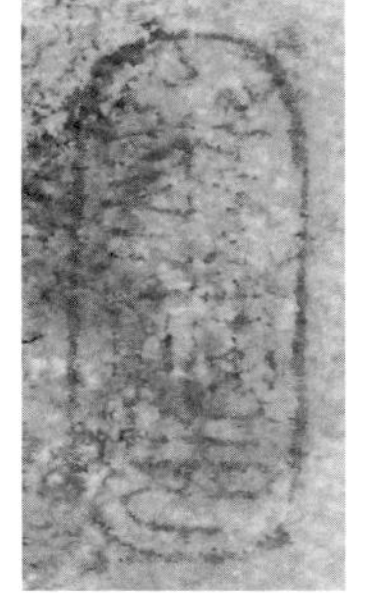

墨吐烟雲

Ōtagaki Rengetsu
大田垣蓮月

Sake cup, 1860s
杯

CAT. NO. 6

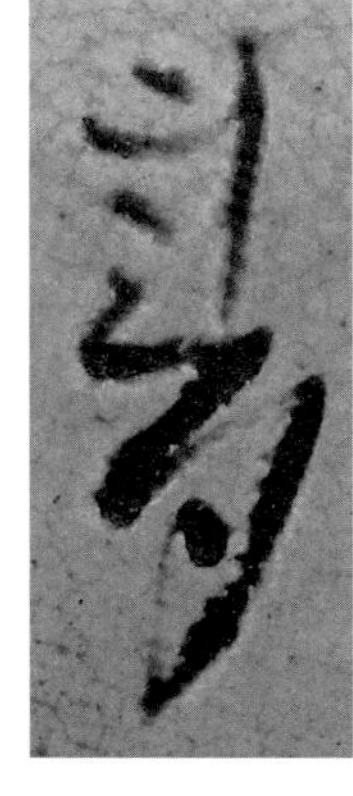

Tea caddy, 1860s
茶入れ

CAT. NO. 7

Sakai Hōitsu, Tani Bunchō, and others

Collaborative Work by Edo Literati Artists, mid-1810s

江戸文人合作

CAT. NO. 3

Sakai Hōitsu

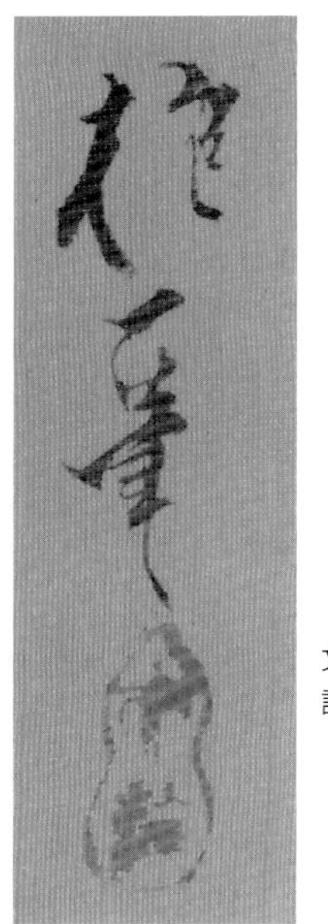

文詮

Kuwagata Keisai

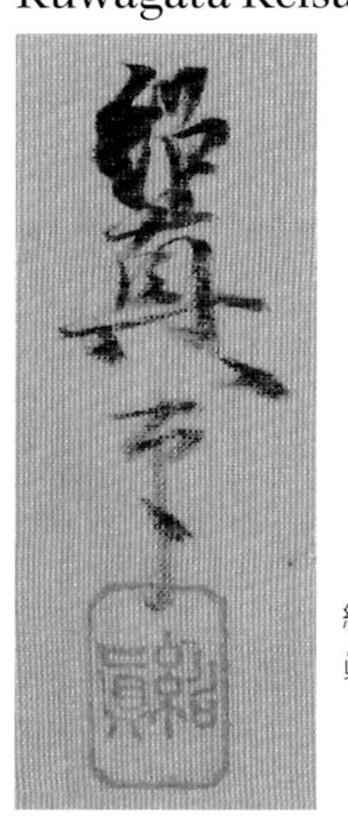

紹眞

Kubo Shunman

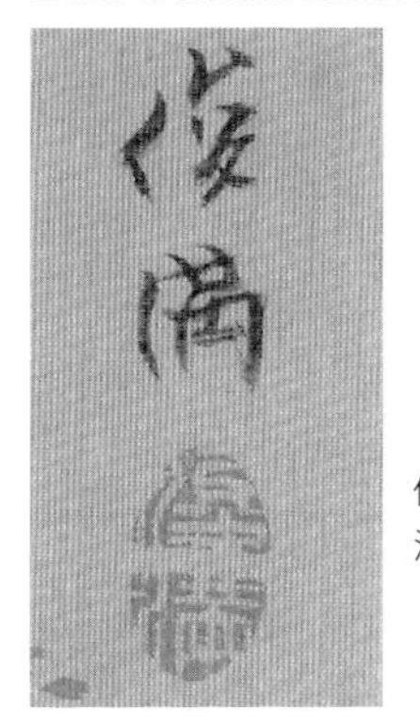

俊満

Tani Bunchō

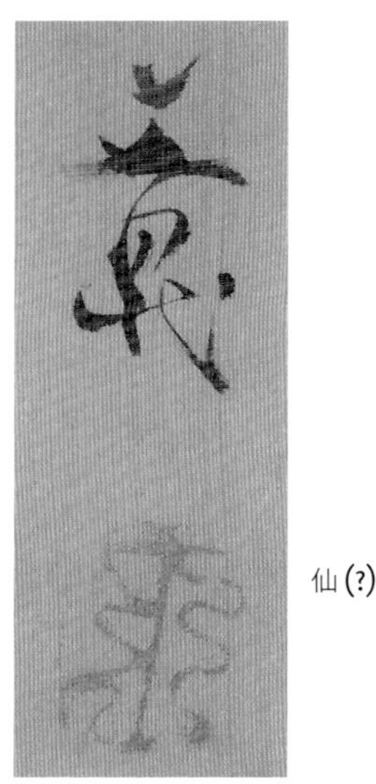

仙 (?)

Tani Bun'ichi

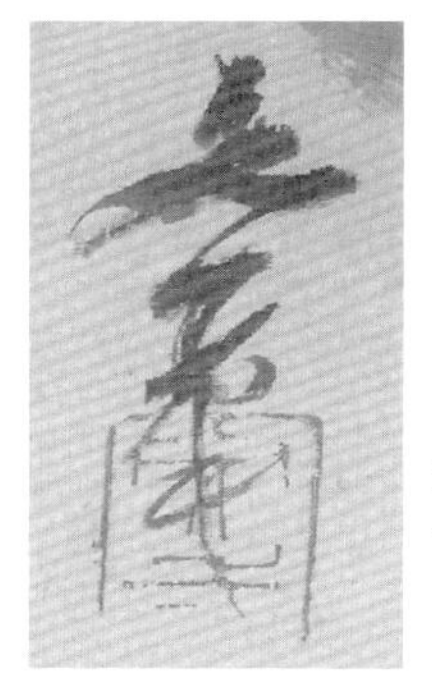

文一

Ichikawa Beian

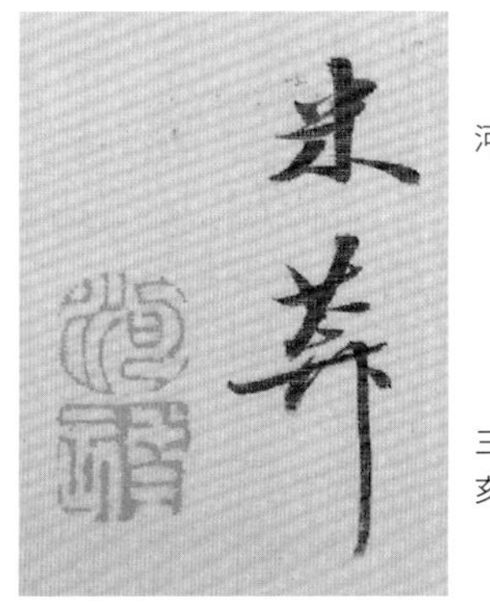

河

三亥

Ōkubo Shibutsu

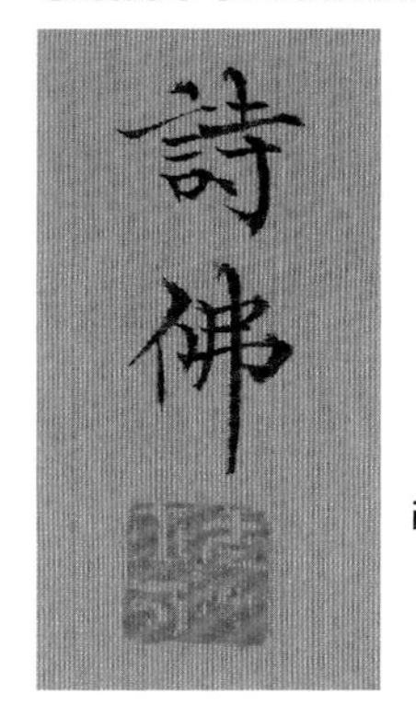

illegible

Kameda Bōsai

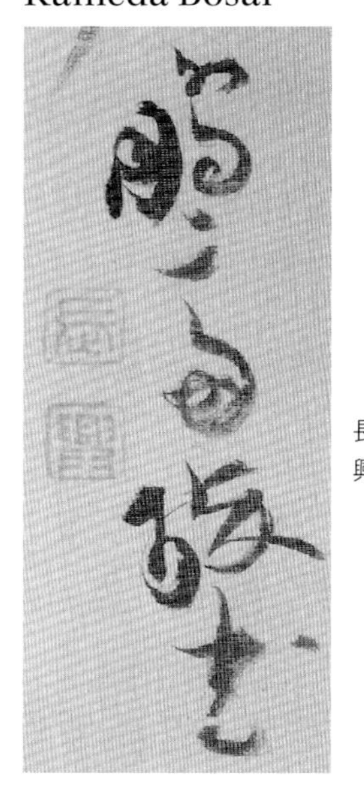

長興

Kikuchi Gozan

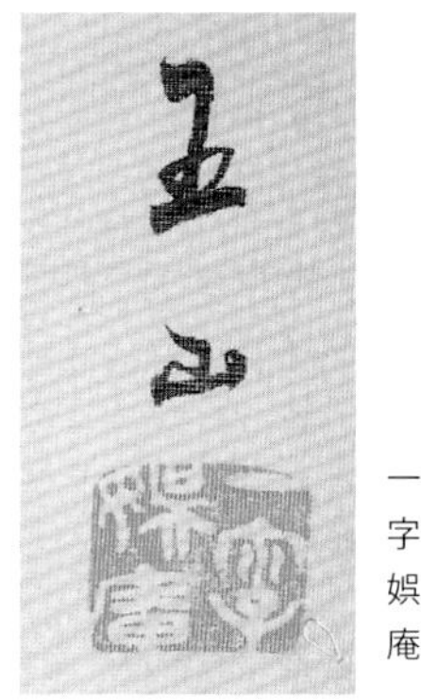

一字娯庵

Nakai Keigi

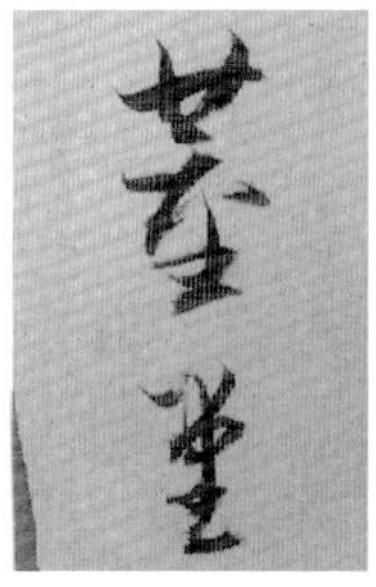

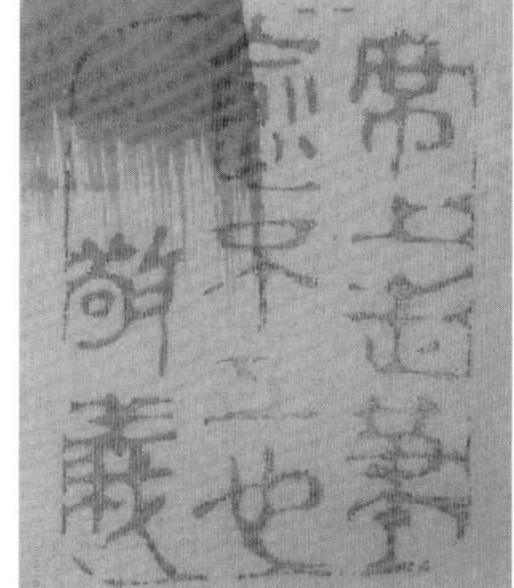

席上走筆愈不工也敬義

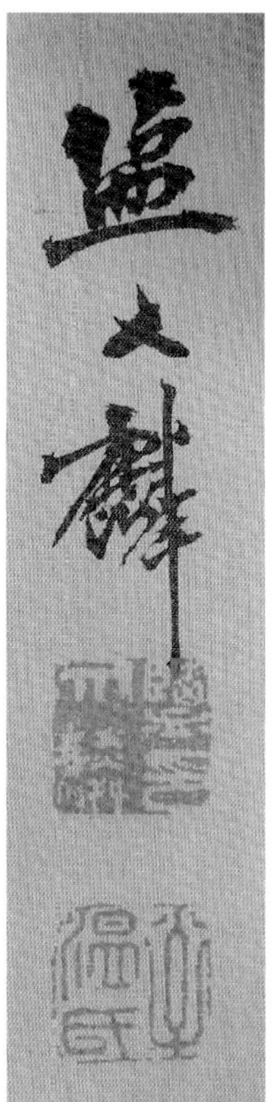

Shiokawa Bunrin
塩川文麟
White Fox on a Moonlit Night
月夜白狐図
CAT. NO. 66

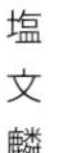

塩文麟印

子温氏

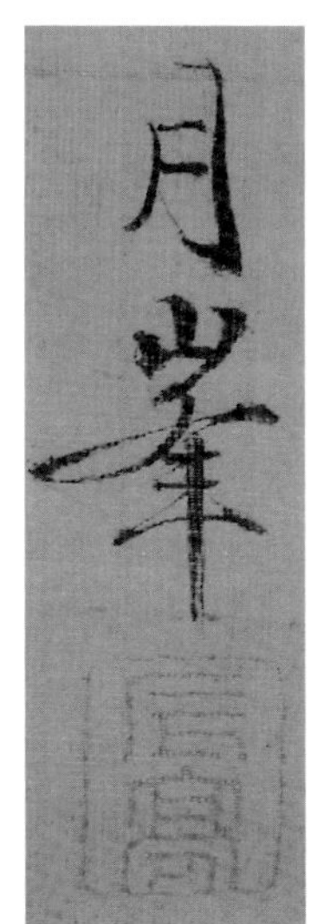

Sō Geppō
僧月峯
Moonlit Fishing Village
月下漁邨図
CAT. NO. 22

辰亮

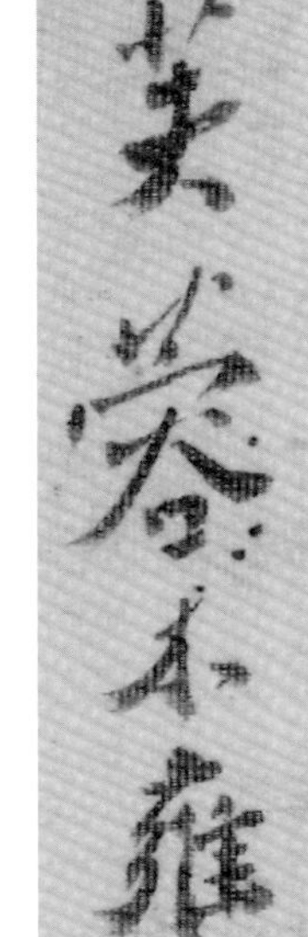

Suzuki Fuyō
鈴木芙蓉
Meandering Stream at Lanting, 1806
蘭亭曲水之図
CAT. NO. 1

木雍之印

文熙氏

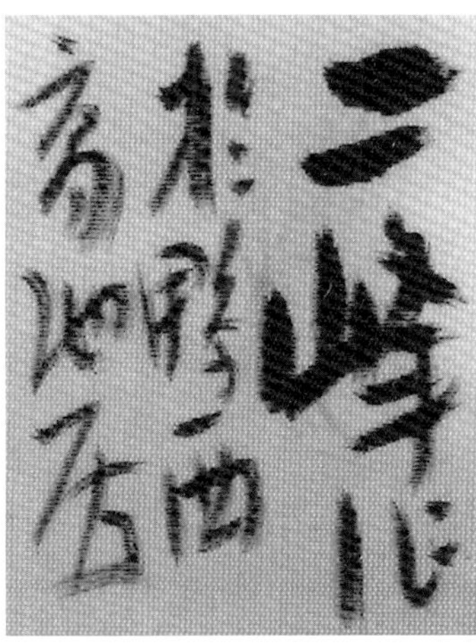

Shirakura Jihō
白倉二峰
Viewing Plum Blossoms, 1922
梅花書窓
CAT. NO. 59

□□山人

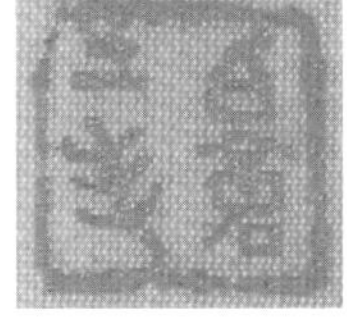

白倉二峰

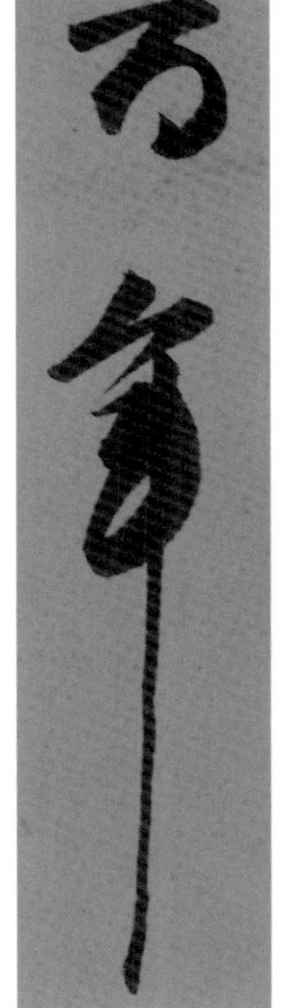

Suzuki Hyakunen
鈴木百年
Spring and Autumn Landscapes, 1866
春秋山水図
CAT. NO. 41

画仙堂主

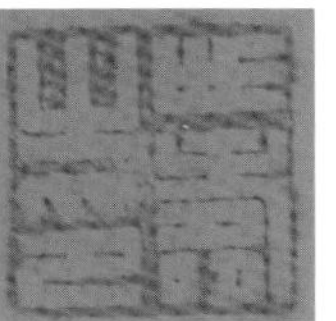

世壽之印

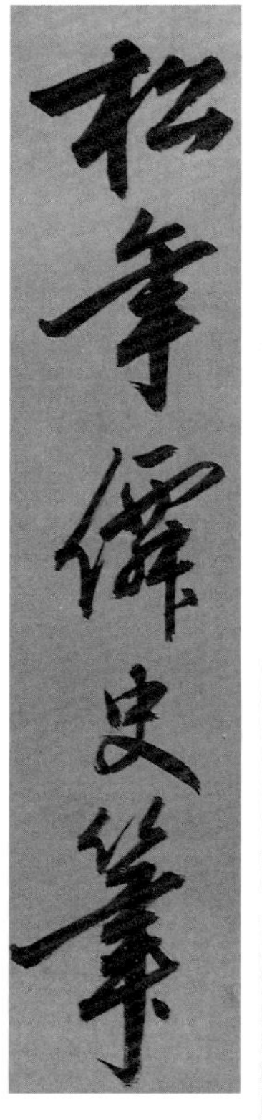

Suzuki Shōnen
鈴木松年
Old Pine, 1900
老松図
CAT. NO. 69

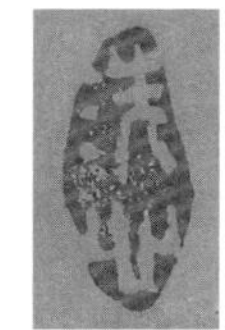

洗心

鈴木世賢

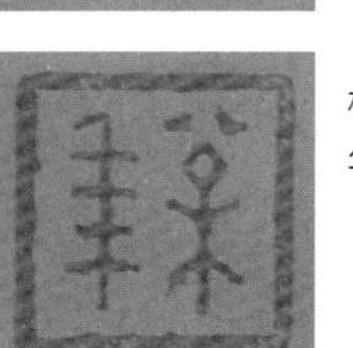

松年

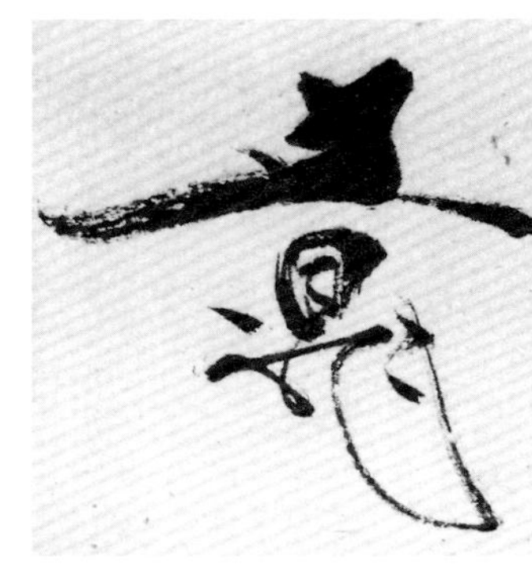

Tani Bunchō
谷文晁
Landscape and Bamboo, 1804
山水竹図
CAT. NO. 61

谷文晁寫

文晁

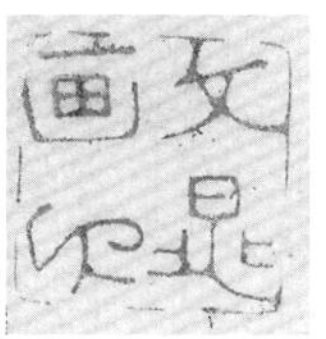

文晁画印

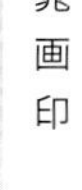

illegible

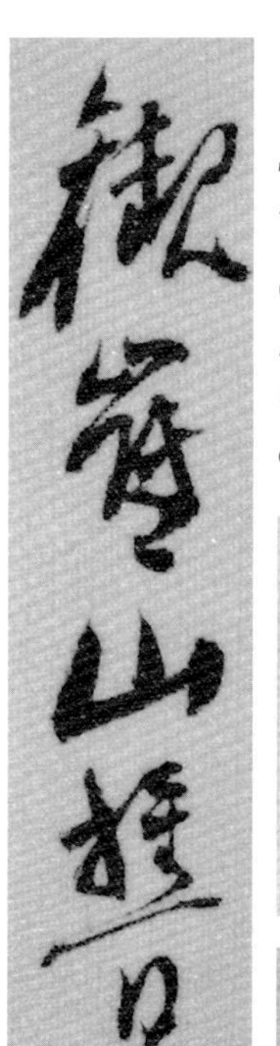

Takakura Kangai
高倉観崖
Chinese Landscapes and Figures, 1920
中国山水人物画帖
CAT. NO. 82

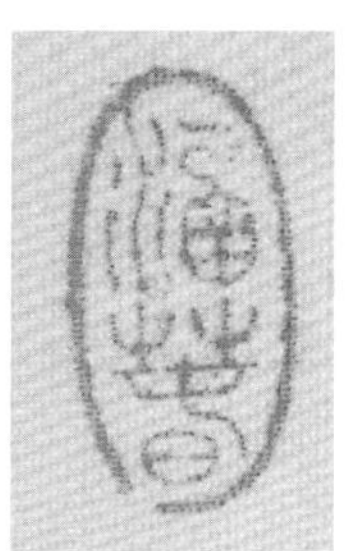

涵碁

鏗如

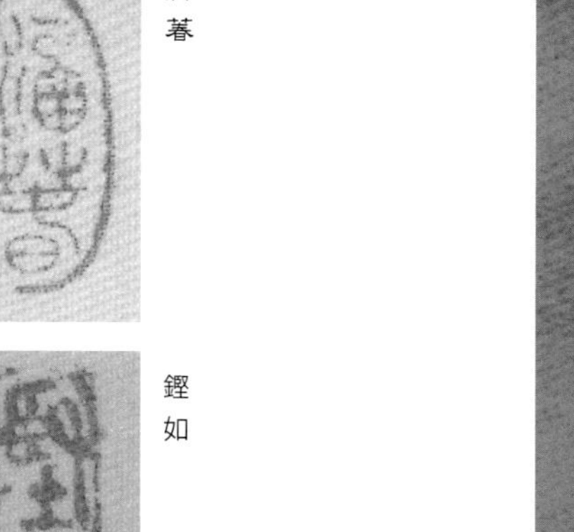

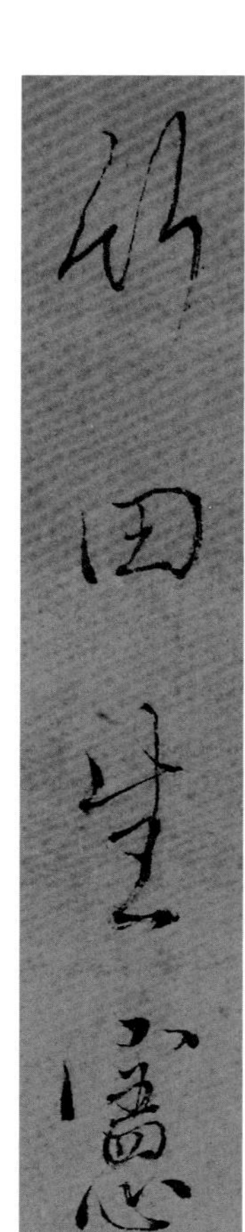

Tanomura Chikuden
田能村竹田
Crossing a River in Wind and Rain, 1829
風雨渡江図
CAT. NO. 21

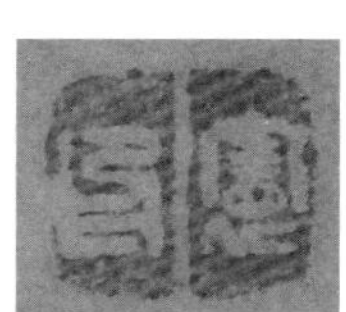

憲印

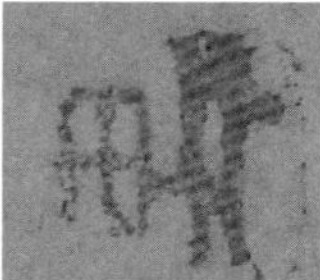

竹田

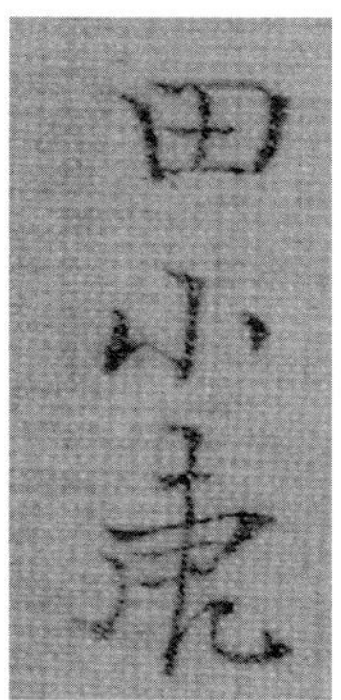

Tanomura Chokunyū
田能村直入
Landscape in the Style of Wang Meng, 1850
摹黄鶴山樵之圖意
CAT. NO. 42

小
虎

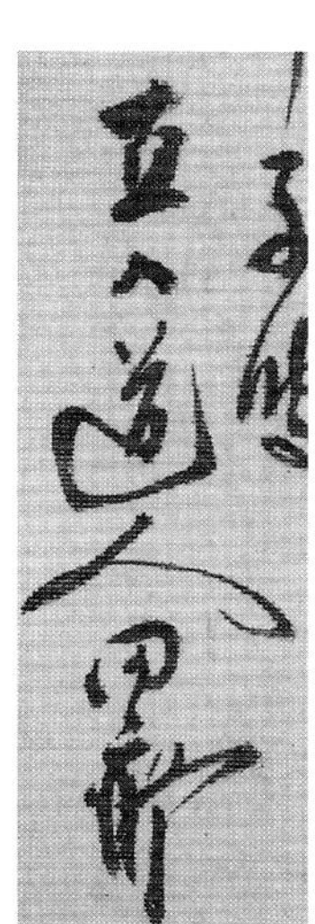

Great View of Rivers and Mountains, 1896
江山大観図
CAT. NO. 43

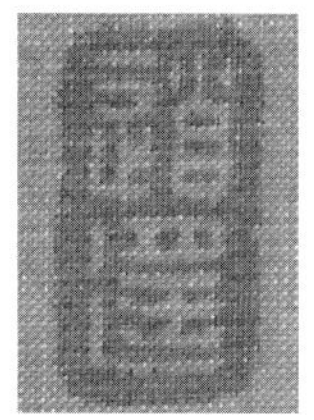

逍
遥

癡

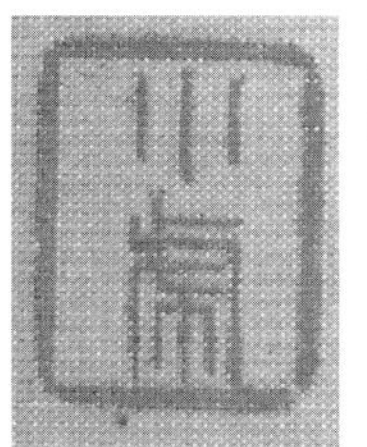

小
虎

自
然
天
然

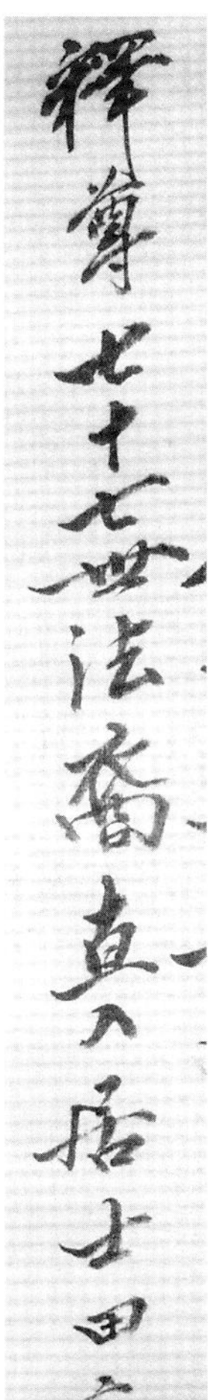

Sixteen Rakan, c. 1900
十六羅漢図
CAT. NO. 79

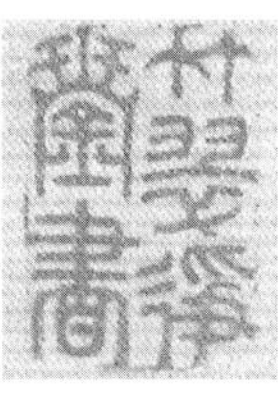

竹
翠
□
鑄
書

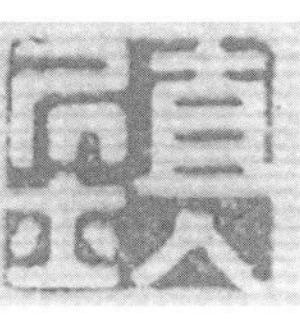

直
入
居
士

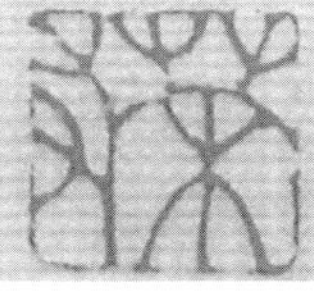

茶
友

煙
嵐
深
處
是
吾
居

Tomioka Tessai
富岡鉄斎

Sweeping Away the World's Dust, 1916
掃蕩俗塵

CAT. NO. 46

鐵
齋

富
岡
百
錬

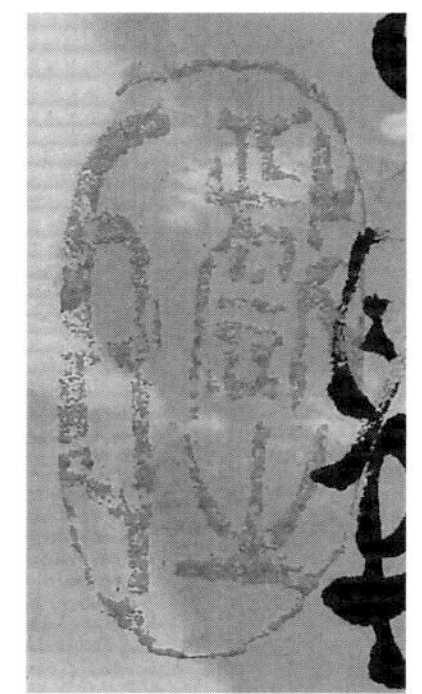

戲
之
耳

Tsuji Kakō
都路華香

Cranes, c. 1908
鶴図

CAT. NO. 70

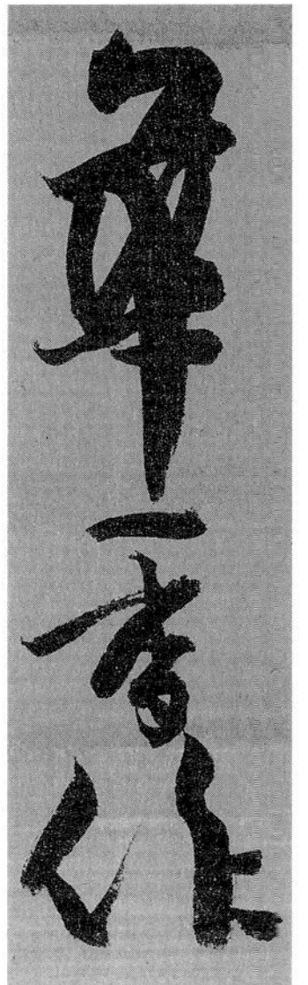

都
良
景
印

華
香

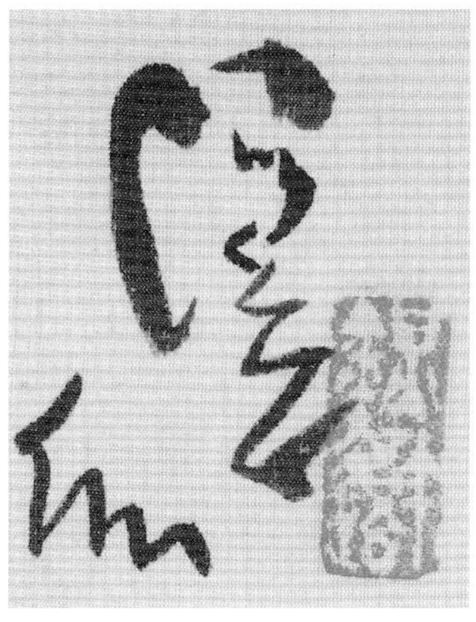

Tomita Keisen
冨田溪仙

Su Dongpo, 1920
蘇東坡

CAT. NO. 80

鎮
□

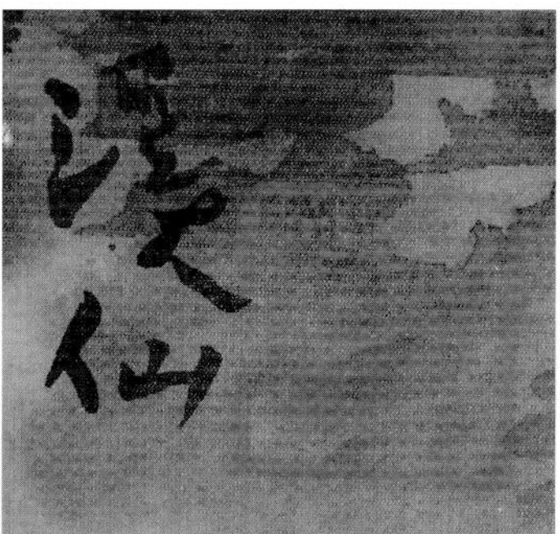

A Boat Crossing a Large River, 1926
泛 舟横大江図

CAT. NO. 48

燕
巣
楼
人

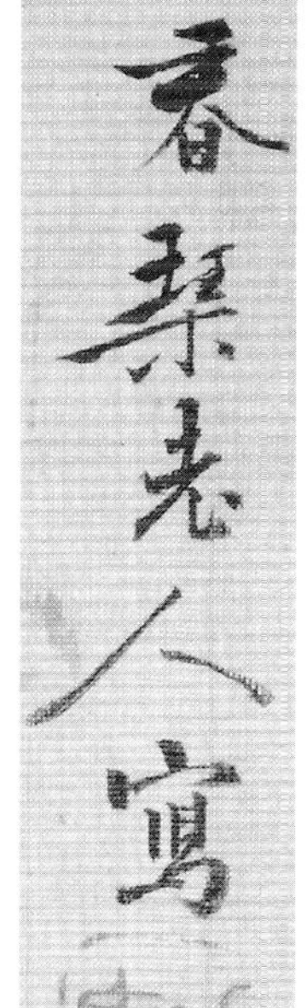

Uragami Shunkin
浦上春琴

Laughter on Spring Wind, 1827
笑春風図

CAT. NO. 24

睡
庵

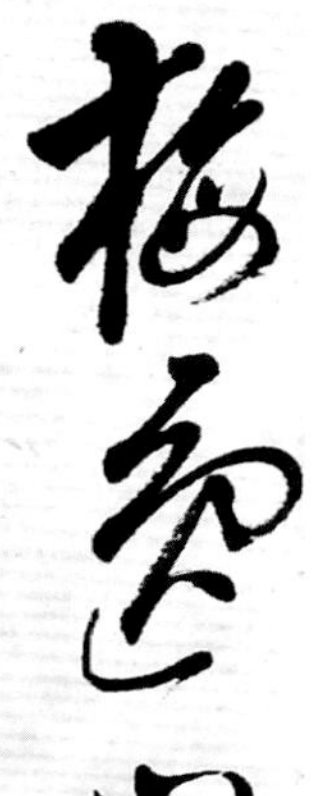

Yamamoto Baiitsu
山本梅逸
Plum Blossoms and Bamboo, 1835
梅竹図
CAT. NO. 63

山本亮印

玉禅居士

Yamamoto Chikuun
山本竹雲
Floating Mists over Green Forest, 1882
浮嵐曖翠図
CAT. NO. 10

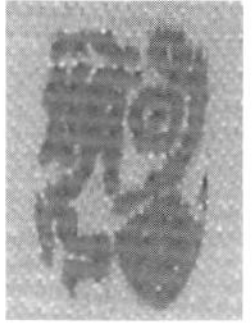

明西□人

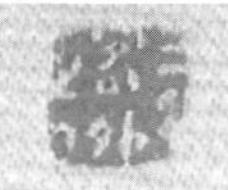

□□外□□

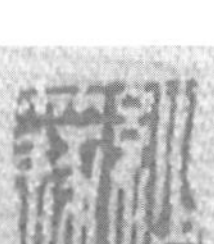

紗箋

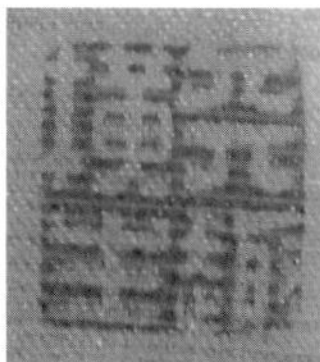

天趣横生

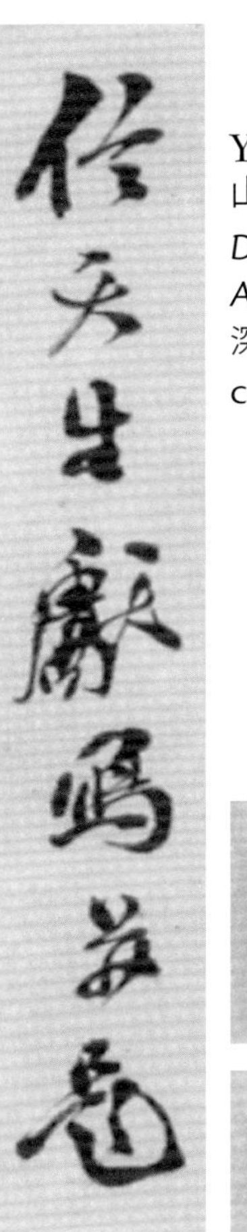

Yamanaka Shinten'ō
山中信天翁

Deep in the Woods, A Thatched Hut, 1875
深林草廬之図

CAT. NO. 39

會經我眼即戊有

山中献印

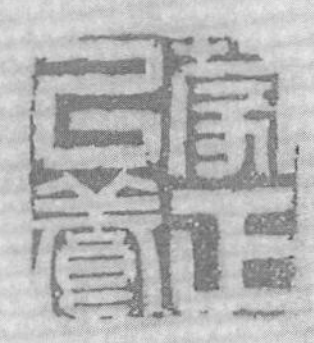

蒙以養正

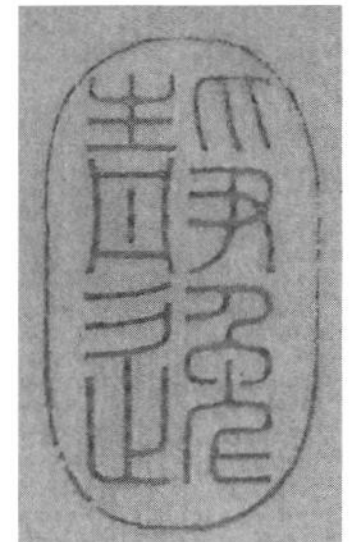

静逸

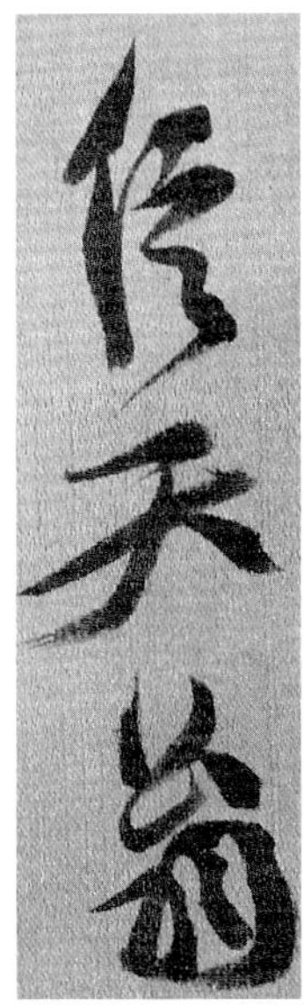

Visiting a Friend through Weeping Willows, 1870s
垂柳訪友図

CAT. NO. 40

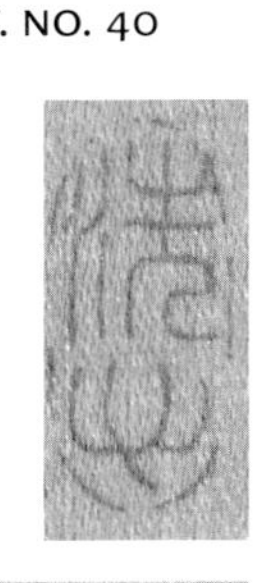

洗心

蒙以養正

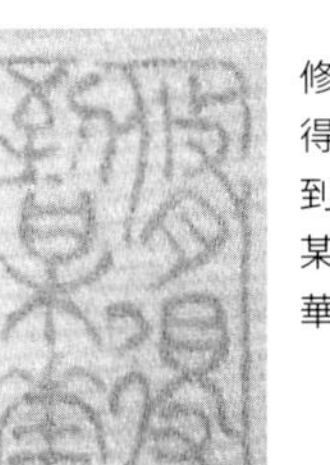

修得到某華

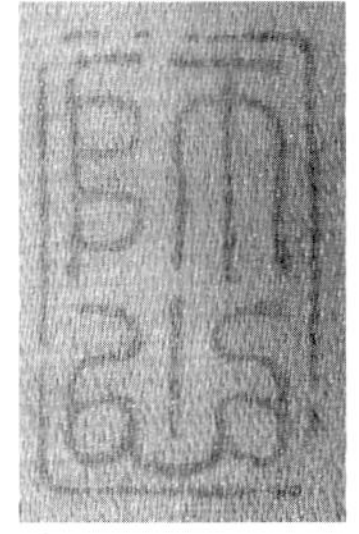

師心

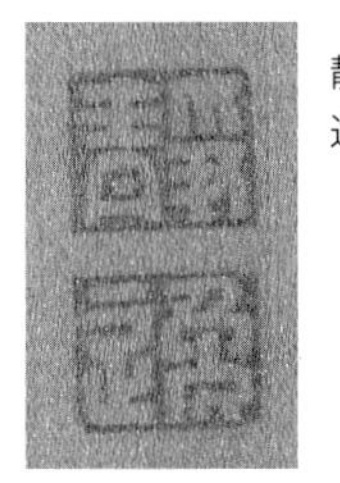

静逸

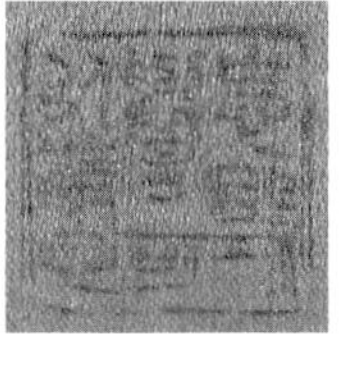

忘毀誉可以清心

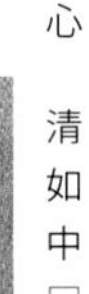

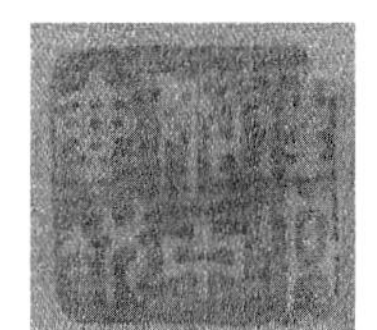

清如中□□

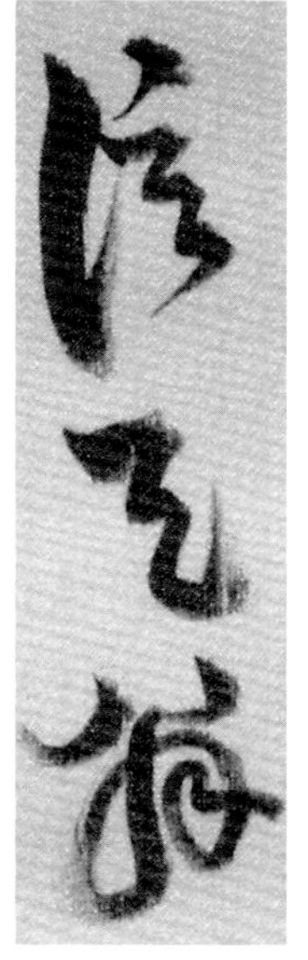

One Hundred Things as You Wish, 1878
百事如意図
CAT. NO. 67

蕩浮漚

静逸

忘毀譽可以清心

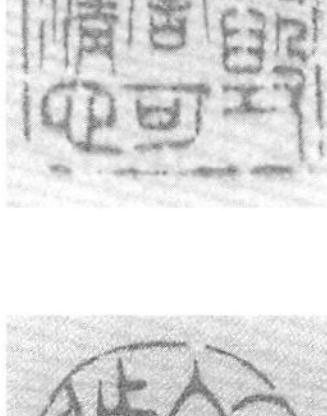

餘時作詩人

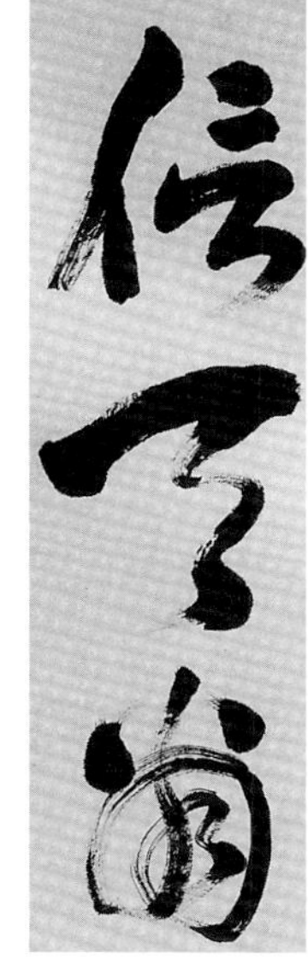

Quatrain in Cursive Calligraphy / Bamboo in Snow, 1884
七言絶句草書 / 雪中竹図
CAT. NO. 8

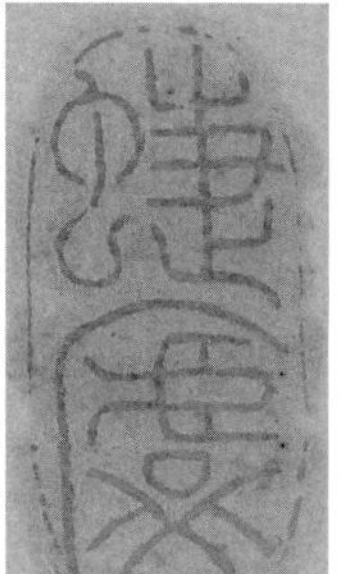

蝶鹿

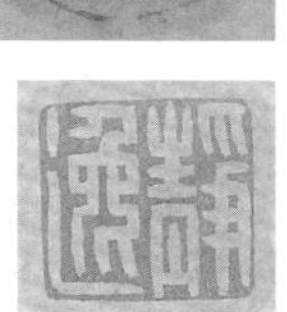

静逸

侶鳳道人

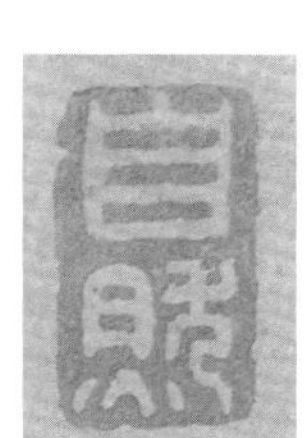

自然

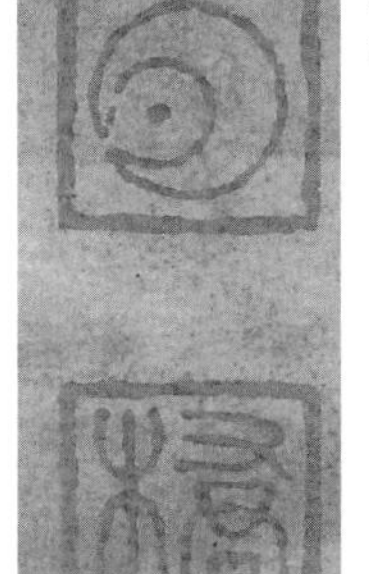

月橋

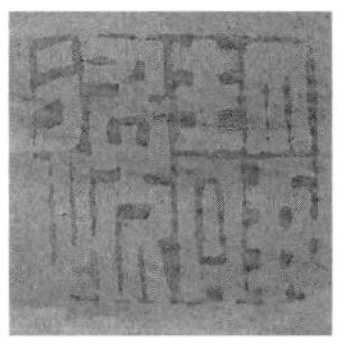

静逸

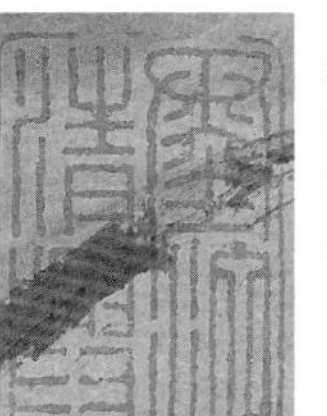

墨池清興

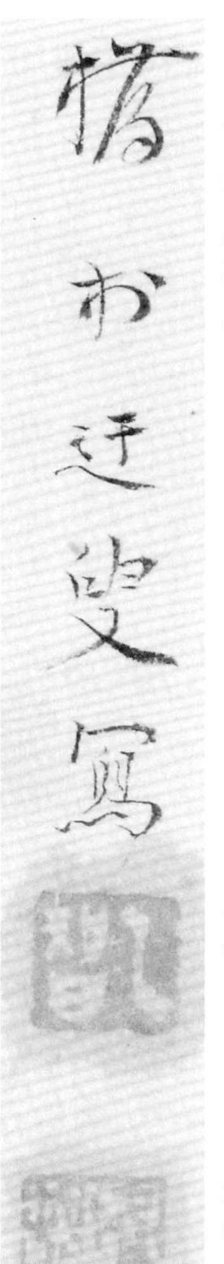

Yano Kyōson
矢野橋村
Mother's Breast, 1939
乳
CAT. NO. 72

一
智

橋
村

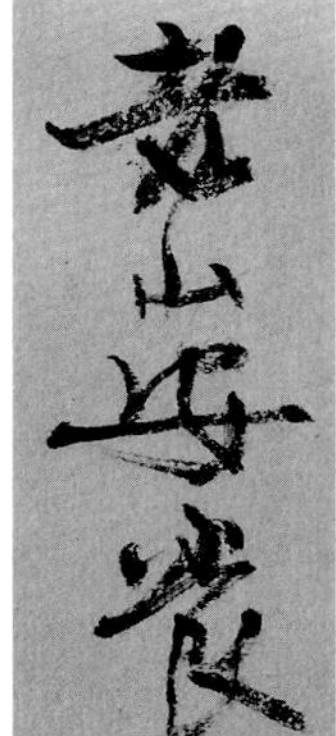

Yasuda Rōzan
安田老山
Autumn Landscape, 1878
秋景山水図
CAT. NO. 36

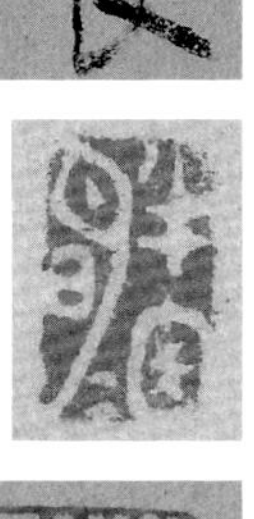

半
窓
明
月

臾
聞
子
印

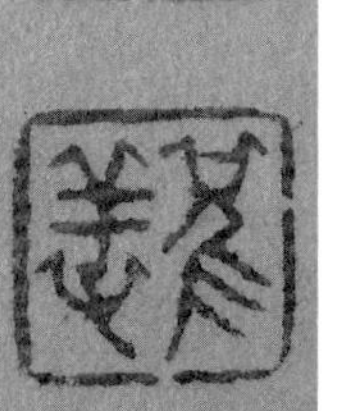

老
養

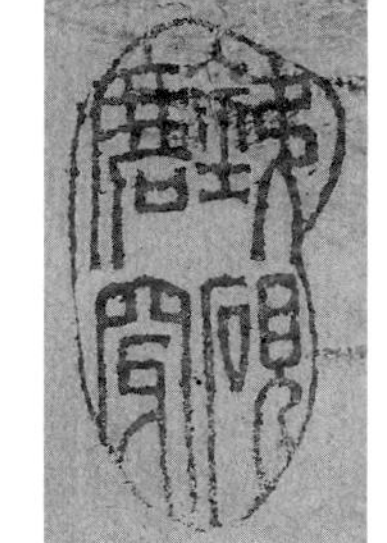

銕
硯
磨
穿

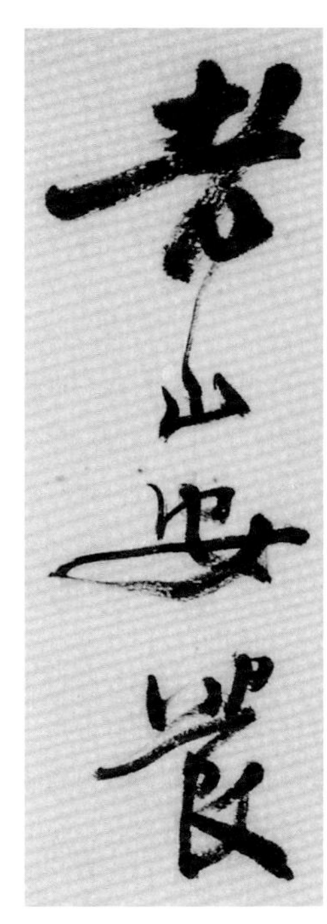

Spring Landscape, 1881
春景山水図
CAT. NO. 37

友
石
山
房

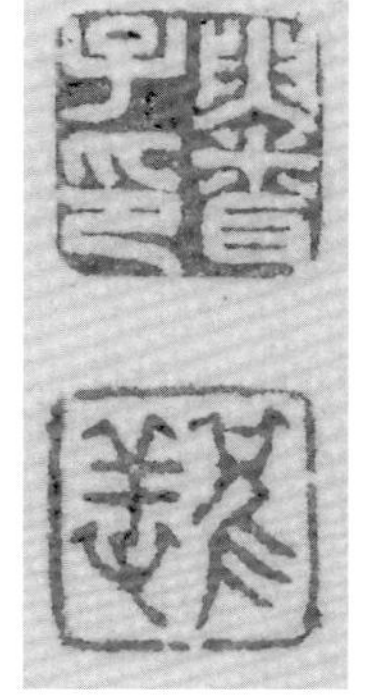

臾
聞
子
印

老
養

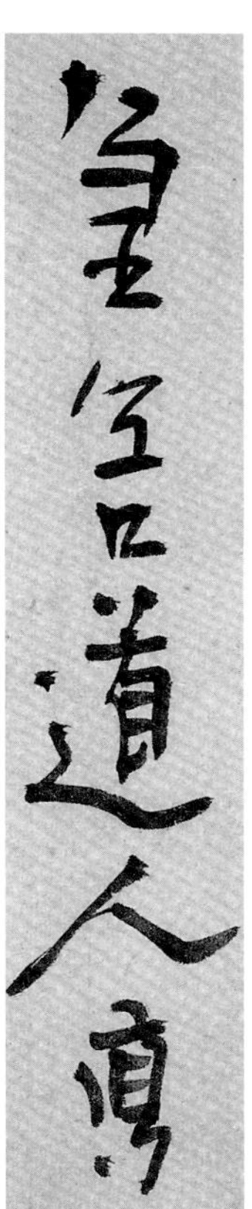

Yokoi Kinkoku
横井金谷

Drawing Pure Spring Water to Compare Tea, early 1800s
汲清泉闘茗

CAT. NO. 4

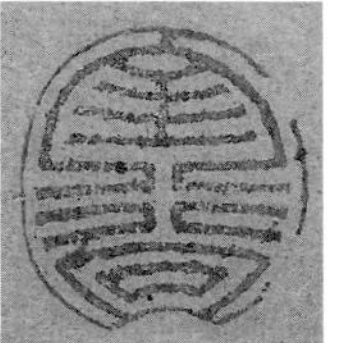

金
谷

Authors' Acknowledgments

We offer our foremost thanks to collector Terry Welch, whose profound love of nature and Japanese art propelled him to build his impressive collection. Our gratitude also goes to William Jay Rathbun, former Curator of Japanese Art at the Seattle Art Museum, who had the prescience to encourage Terry to pursue the area of literati painting; Griffith Way, whose own collecting activities were a continual source of inspiration; and Cheney Cowles, for sharing his deep appreciation of Japanese painting.

In bringing this project to fruition, we were assisted by many individuals to whom we owe our heartfelt gratitude. Uchiyama Takeo, former Director of the National Museum of Modern Art, Kyoto, kindly examined the collection in the early stages of the exhibition's preparation. The enthusiasm for the project expressed by Stephen Little, Director of the Honolulu Academy of Arts; Julia White, former Curator of Asian Art at the Academy; and Shawn Eichman, present curator, was indispensable. We also extend our thanks to Academy staff members Sati Benes, Megan Callan, and Sawako Chang for their assistance throughout the various phases of this project.

In the formidable task of transcribing and translating inscriptions, we were helped initially by Tamaki Maeda and John Szostak. Transcribing the cursive inscriptions and archaic seal script was a challenge. The Chinese texts are filled with literary and historical references that we could only partially uncover, and the ambiguity contained in poetry triggered varying interpretations. To create fluid verse in English would have caused even greater distortions of the original meanings of the poems, and so we opted for more literal translations that, despite their prosaism, convey much of the content of the works. We hope to have taken the study of the literary side of these works a step forward, regardless of remaining insufficiencies. For any mistakes or misinterpretations, we take full responsibility.

We are based across the ocean from one another, but distance did not impede our collaboration. Michiyo made multiple trips to Japan to collect extensive research materials. With impeccable professionalism, the staff at the National Diet Library, National Research Institute for Cultural Properties, Tokyo, and Osaka Prefectural Library, assisted in amassing voluminous information. In Seattle, the librarians at the East Asian Library, University of Washington, provided tireless help in searching out books and journals. Furthermore, the scholarship of Jan Hwang (Wang Jue) was crucial to the completion of the translations of painting inscriptions.

Meanwhile, Paul, based in Kyoto, received assistance from the staff of the Kansai Gaidai University Library and the libraries of several dozen universities, prefectures, cities, museums, and other institutions. Many libraries showed great generosity by copying or loaning extremely rare materials, often going beyond their usual practices out of regard for the research being conducted. A great many individuals assisted Paul's research and writing, and a partial list of those to whom he is indebted includes Thomas Ebrey, Patricia Fister, Patricia Graham, Hoshino Keigo, Kaneko Shin'ya, Kawasaki Hiroshi, Kawasaki Masatsugu, Kawasaki Masaharu, Elizabeth Kenney, Kimura Mineyo, Maezawa Eiichi, Matsumoto Akira, Matsumoto Kenjirō, Mizutani Michikazu, Tanaka Dai, Yamamoto Kō, Yamazoe Haruki, Yanagi Takashi, and Yokoya Ken'ichirō.

The catalogue's superb photography is owed to Tim Siegert, with additional contributions by Jeff Engelstad and Paul Macapia, and its beautiful design, to John Hubbard. Throughout the preparation and production of the catalogue, the staff at Marquand Books, including Marie Weiler, Tina Kim, and Sara Billups, provided seamless support despite the difficult tasks we asked of them.

Lastly, this catalogue would not have materialized without the meticulous reading, perceptive questions, and good humor of our editor, Suzanne Kotz.

Paul Berry and Michiyo Morioka

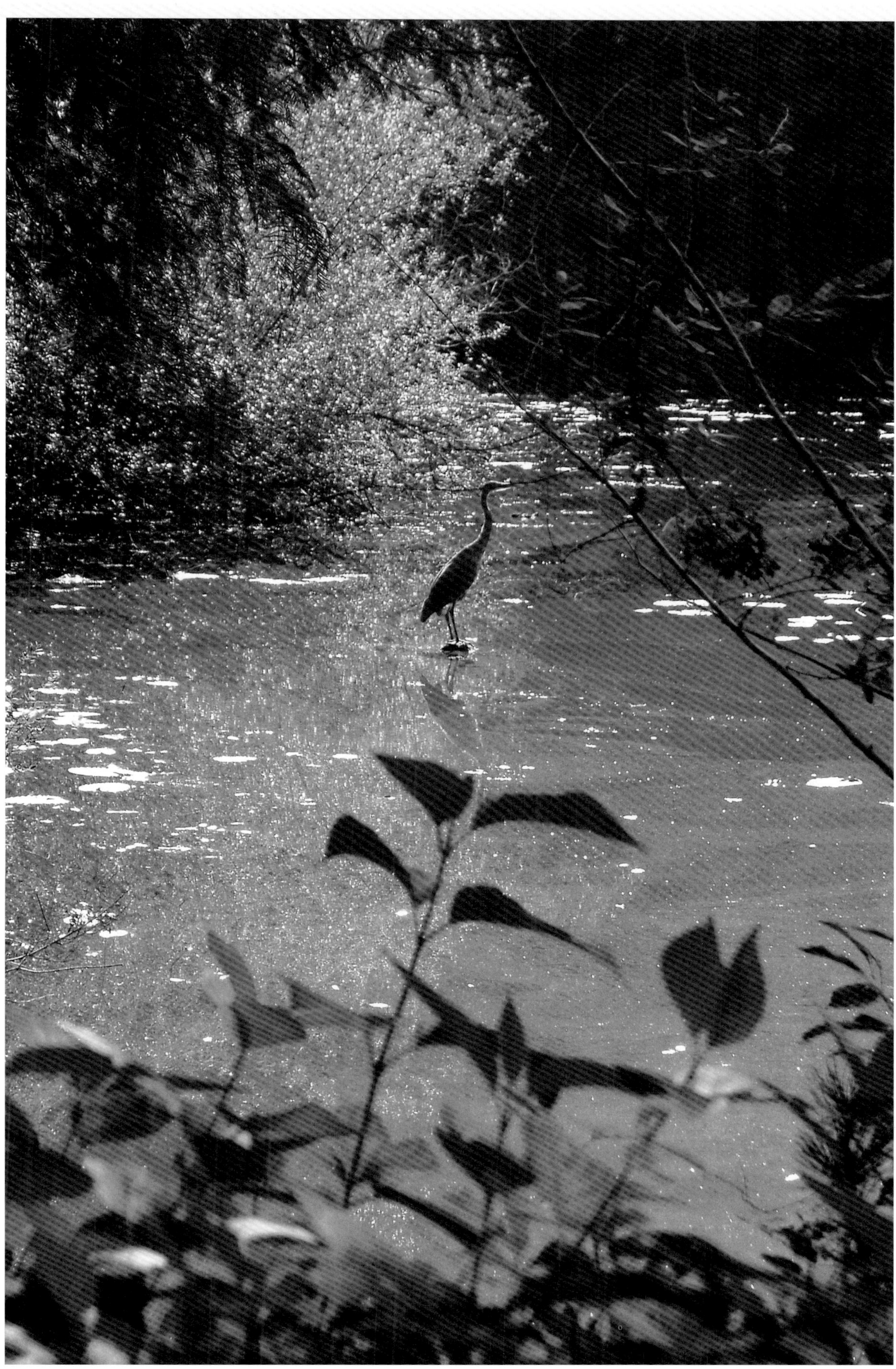

Terry Welch garden, near Seattle, Washington

Selected Bibliography

Addiss, Stephen. *77 Dances: Japanese Calligraphy by Poets, Monks, and Scholars 1568–1868*. New York: Weatherhill, 2006.

Araki Nori 荒木矩, ed. *Dai Nihon shoga meika taikan* 大日本書畫名家大鑑. 4 vols. 1934. Reprint. Tokyo: Daiichi Shobō 第一書房, 1975.

Berry, Paul, and Yokoya Ken'ichirō. *Shirarezaru Nihon kaiga: Shiatoru Hakutakuan korekushon* 知られざる日本絵画：シアトル白澤庵コレクション. Ōtsu: Ōtsu Shiritsu Rekishi Hakubutskan 大津市立歴史博物館, 2001.

Cahill, James. *Scholar Painters of Japan: The Nanga School*. New York: The Asia Society, 1972.

Chūō bijutsu 中央美術 3, no. 7 [*Nanga kenkyū* 南畫研究] (July 1917).

Ehime Kenritsu Bijutsukan 愛媛県美術館. *Kindai Nihon no bijutsu: Yōgaka・nihongaka tachi no mosaku to tenkai* 近代日本の美術：洋画家・日本画家たちの模索と展開. Exh. cat. Matsuyama, 1998.

Fister, Patricia. *Japanese Women Artists, 1600–1900*. Lawrence: Spencer Museum of Art, University of Kansas, 1988.

Fujiwara Kakurai 藤原鶴来, ed. *Shin shodō jiten* 新書道字典. Tokyo: Nigensha 二玄社, 1985.

Fushima Chūkei 伏見冲敬. *Shodō daijiten* 書道大字典. Tokyo: Kadokawa Shoten 角川書店, 1974.

Gunma Kenritsu Kindai Bijutsukan. *Shizen ni asobi shizen ni utau—Kindai nanga ten* 自然に遊び、自然に謳う—近代南画展. Exh. cat. Takasaki 高崎, 1999.

Hirabayashi Akira 平林彰, ed. *Noguchi Shōhin to kindai nanga : Meiji no kyūtei gaka* 野口小蘋：明治の宮廷画家. Kōfu: Yamanashi Kenritsu Bijutsukan 山梨県立美術館, 2005.

Hyōgo Kenritsu Bijutsukan 兵庫県立美術館. *Nangatte nanda?! Kindai no nanga—Nihon no kokoro to bi* 南画って何だ?! 近代の南画—日本のこころと美. Exh. cat. Kobe, 2008.

Ibaraki Kenritsu Kindai Bijutsukan 茨城県立近代美術館, Tochigi Kenritsu Bijutsukan 栃木県立近代美術館, and Gunma Kenritsu Kindai Bijutsukan 群馬県立近代美術館. *Kita Kantō no bunjinga* 北関東の文人画. Exh. cat. Mito: Utsunomiya 宇都宮, Takasaki 高崎, 1995.

Iijima Shunkei 飯島春敬. *Shodō jiten* 書道辞典. Tokyo: Tōkyōdō Shuppan 東京堂出版, 1995.

———, ed. *Sōgō shodō daijiten* 綜合書道大辞典. 14 volumes. Tokyo: Tōkyōdō Shuppan 東京堂出版, 1982.

Kaiga seidan 繪畫清談 4, no. 2 [*Nanga gō* 南畫號] (February 1916).

Kanai Shiun 金井紫雲, ed. *Tōyō gadai sōran* 東洋畫題綜覧. 1938. Tokyo: Kokusho Kankōkai 国書刊行会, 1997.

Kanō Kōkichi 狩野亨吉 and Iwakami Hōgai 岩上方外. *Shoga rakkan inpu taizen* 書画落款印譜大全. 2 vols. 1932. Tokyo: Kashiwa Shobō 柏書房, 1996.

Katō Ruiko 加藤類子 and Shimada Yasuhiro 島田康寛 et al., eds. *Bujnjinga no kindai: Tessai to sono shiyūtachi* 文人画の近代：鉄斎とその師友たち. Exh. cat. Kyoto: Kyōto Kokuritsu Kindai Bijutsukan 京都国立近代美術館, 1997.

Kawakita, Michiaki 河北倫明, comp. *Kinadi Nihon bijutsu jiten* 近代日本美術事典. Tokyo: Kōdansha 講談社, 1989.

Kawakita Michiaki 河北倫明 and Takashina Shūji 高階秀爾, *Kindai Nihon kaigashi* 近代日本絵画史. Tokyo: Chūō Kōronsha中央公論社, 1978.

Kawakita Michiaki 河北倫明 and Horie Tomohiko 堀江知彦. *Genshoku Gendai Nihon no bijutsu 12: Bunjinga to sho* 原色現代日本の美術12：文人画と書. Tokyo: Shōgakukan 小学館, 1979.

Kikuya Yoshio 菊屋吉生. "Sangokai ronkō" 珊瑚会論考. *Bijutsu kenkyū* 美術研究 no. 377 (February 2003): 30–58.

Kitakawa Hirokuni 北川博邦. *In to injin* 印と印人. Tokyo: Nigensha 二玄社, 1982.

Kobayashi Tadashi 小林忠, ed. *Bijutsu kankei zasshi mokuji sōran* 美術関係雑誌目次綜覧. 4 vols. Tokyo: Kokusho Kankōkai 国書刊行会, 2000.

Kodama Kōta 児玉幸多. *Kuzushiji kaidoku jiten* くずし字解読辞典. 1975. Reprint. Tokyo: Tōkyōdō Shuppan 東京堂出版, 1999.

Kokusho sōmokuroku 國書總目錄. 9 vols. Tokyo: Iwanami Shoten 岩波書店, 1989–91.

Kuo, Jason (Chi-sheng). *Word as Image: The Art of Chinese Seal Engraving*. Seattle: University of Washington Press, 1992.

Kyōto Kokuritsu Kindai Bijutsukan 京都国立近代美術館. *Ishoku no suibokugaka: Nozawa Joyō, Hijiya Bunkei, Ogawa Sen'yō* 異色の水墨画家：野沢如洋・泥谷文景・小川千甕. Exh. cat. Kyoto, 1975.

———. *Ishoku no suiboku gaka: Mizukoshi Shōnan, Yamaguchi Hachikushi, Kusunoki Keishū* 異色の水墨画家: 水越松南・山口八九子・楠瓊州. Exh. cat. Kyoto, 1976.

———. *Ishoku no suiboku gaka: Nishi Seiun, Kondō Kōichiro, Yamashita Maki* 異色の水墨画家：西晴雲・近藤浩一路・山下摩起. Exh. cat. Kyoto, 1979.

Kyōtoshi Bijutsukan 京都市美術館. *Kyōto gadan: Edo matsu Meiji no gajin tachi* 京都画壇江戸末・明治の画人たち. Kyoto: Ātosha アート社, 1977.

Lai Yu-chih. "Surreptitious Appropriation: Ren Bonian (1840–1895) and Japanese Culture in Shanghai, 1842–1895." PhD diss., Yale University, 2005.

Li Yifeng 李毅峰, ed. *Zhongguo zhuanke dacidian* 中国篆刻大辭典. Zhengzhou: Henan Meishu Chubanshe 河南美術出版社, 1997.

Lu Fusheng 盧輔聖, ed. *Jinxiandai shuhuajia kuanyin zonghui* 近現代書畫家款印綜匯. 2 vols. Shanghai: Shanghai Shuhua Chubanshe上海書畫出版社, 2002.

Mie Kenritsu Bijutsukan 三重県立美術館. *20 seiki Nihon bijutsu saiken [II]: 1920 nendai* 20世紀日本美術再見[II]：1920 年代. Exh. cat. Tsu, 1996.

Minomo Masao 蓑毛政雄. *Hikkei tenkoku inpu jiten* 必携篆書印譜辞典. Tokyo: Kashiwa Shobō 柏書房, 1991.

Miyagiken Bijutsukan 宮城県美術館. *Kindai no bunjinga* 近代の文人画. Exh. cat. Sendai, 1993.

Mizuta Norihisa 水田紀久, ed. *Nihon tenkokushi ronkō* 日本篆刻史論考. Musashimurayama: Aoshōdō Shoten 青裳堂書店, 1985.

Morioka, Michiyo, and Paul Berry. *Modern Masters of Kyoto: The Transformation of Japanese Painting Traditions, Nihonga from the Griffith and Patricia Way Collection*. Exh. cat. Seattle: Seattle Art Museum, 1999.

Motokata Masa 本方昌. "Shin bunjinga no sōzō" 新文人畫の創造. *Bi no kuni* 美之国 5, no. 7 (July 1929): 22–25.

Murase, Miyeko, et al. *The Written Image: Japanese Calligraphy and Painting from the Sylvan Barnet and William Burto Collection.* New York: Metropolitan Museum of Art, 2002.

Nakanishi Kōnan 中西庚南, ed. *Kindai tenkoku jiten.* 近代篆刻字典. Tokyo: Tōkyōdō Shuppan 東京堂出版, 1985.

Nakata Yūjirō 中田勇次郎, ed. *Nihon no tenkoku* 日本の篆刻. Tokyo: Nigensha 二玄社, 1966.

Nanga kanshō 南畫鑑賞 6, no. 1 [Shasei to shai tokushū 寫生と寫意特輯] (January 1937).

New Orleans Museum of Art. *An Enduring Vision: 17th- to 20th-Century Japanese Painting from the Gitter-Yelen Collection.* Exh. cat. New Orleans, 2002.

Nihon Bijutsusha 日本美術社. *Nihon shoga meika rakkan inpu shū* 日本書画名家落款印譜集. Tokyo: San'yō Shoin 三陽書院, 1935.

Nihon Chūō Nanshūgakai 日本中央南宗畫會. *Shitai ōsei* 姿態横生. Nagoya, 1911.

Oda Eiichi 小田栄一 and Koga Kenzō 古賀健蔵, eds. *Rakkan kaō daijiten* 落款花押大辞典. 2 vols. Tokyo: Tankōsha 淡交社, 1982.

Oka Jōji 丘襄二. *Tenkai jiten* 篆楷辞典. Tokyo: Kokusho Kankōkai 国書刊行会, 1976.

Ōnishi Seigai 大西西崖. *Bunjinga no fukkō* 文人畫の復興. Tokyo: Kōgeisha 巧藝社, 1921.

Rosenfield, John M. *Extraordinary Persons: Works by Eccentric, Nonconformist Japanese Artists of the Early Modern Era (1580–1868) in the Collection of Kimiko and John Powers.* 3 vols. Cambridge: Harvard University Art Museum, 1999.

Sakai Tetsurō 酒井哲朗. "Taishōki ni okeru nanga no saihyōka ni tsuite—Shin nanga o megutte" 大正期における南画の再評価について—新南画をめぐって. *Miyagiken Bijutsukan kenkyū kiyō* 宮城県美術館研究紀要 3 (1988): 1–20.

Shimada Shūjirō 島田修二郎 et al. *Zaigai Nihon no shihō 6: Bunjinga・shoha* 在外日本の至宝 6：文人画・諸派. Tokyo: Mainichi Shinbunsha 毎日新聞社, 1980.

Shimizu Yoshiaki and John Rosenfield. *Masters of Japanese Calligraphy, 8th–19th Century.* New York: Asia Society, 1984.

Soeda Tatsurei 添田達嶺. "Nanga no kanshō" 南畫の鑑賞. *Tōei* 搭影 9, no. 5 (June 1933): 7–16.

Takahashi Mitsuru 高橋満. *Hikkei rakkan jiten* 必携落款辞典. Tokyo: Kashiwa Shobō 柏書房, 1982.

Takahata Tsunenobu 高畑常信, ed. *Yūin kanshō daijiten* 遊印鑑賞大字典. Tokyo: Kashiwa Bijutsu Shuppansha 柏美術出版, 1992.

Takeda Kōichi 武田光一. "Nangaka no bunjin ishiki" 南画家の文人意識. *Edo bungaku 18: Tokushū bunjinga to kanshibun* 江戸文学18: 特集文人画と漢詩文 (July 1997): 80–113.

Takeuchi Umematsu 竹内梅松. "Meiji no nanshūgaka" 明治の南宗畫家. *Bi no kuni* 美之国 3, no. 6 (August 1927): 47–56.

———. "Meiji no nanshūgaka (shōzen)" 明治の南宗畫家 (承前). *Bi no kuni* 美之国 3, no. 7 (September 1927): 33–41.

Taki Seiichi 瀧精一. "Bunjinga no hongi" 文人畫の本義. *Shoga kottō zasshi* 書畫骨董雜誌 108 (June 1917): 1–6.

———. "Yamatoe oyobi nanga no fukkō" 大和繪及び南畫の復興. *Kokka* 国華 330 (November 1917): 151–56.

———. "Bunjinga to hyōgen shugi" 文人畫と表現主義. *Kokka* 国華 390 (November 1922): 160–65.

Tseng Yuho. *A History of Chinese Calligraphy.* 2d ed. Hong Kong: Chinese University Press, 1998.

Tsuji Nobuo 辻惟雄. "Nihon bunjiga kō—sono seiritsu made" 日本文人画考—その成立まで. *Bijutsushigaku* 美術史学 7 (March 1985): 1–28.

Tsuneishi Hideaki 常石英明. *Kaō daishūsei* 花押大集成. Tokyo: Kin'ensha 金園社, 1994.

Umezawa Seiichi 梅澤精一. *Nihon nangashi* 日本南畫史. Tokyo: Nanyōdō 南陽堂, 1919.

Umezawa Waken 梅澤和軒. "Hyōgen shugi no ryūkō to bunjinga no fukkō" 表現主義の流行と文人畫の復興. *Waseda bungaku* 早稲田文学 186 (May 1921): 23–31.

———. "Hyōgen shugi no ryūkō to bunjinga no bokkō (jō)" 表現主義の流行と文人畫の勃興 (上). *Kaiga seidan* 繪畫清談 9, no. 5 (May 1921): 1–8.

———. "Hyōgen shugi no ryūkō to bunjinga no bokkō (ge)" 表現主義の流行と文人畫の勃興 (下). *Kaiga seidan* 繪畫清談 9, no. 6 (June 1921): 1–5, 18.

Yamatane Bijutsukan 山種美術館. *Kindai no nanga—yūshin no sekai: Hyakusui・Hōan・Kōyū・Kōichiro* 近代の南画—遊心の世界：百穂・放菴・恒友・浩一路. Exh. cat. Tokyo, 1993.

Yamawaki Shintoku 山脇信徳. "Nangashū no ryūko" 南畫臭の流行. *Chūō bijutsu* 中央美術 3, no. 9 (September 1917): 22–24.

Yoshizawa Chū 吉澤忠. "Nanga to Bunjinga 1" 南畫と文人畫 (一). *Kokka* 国華 622 (September 1942): 257–62.

———. "Nanga to Bunjinga 2" 南畫と文人畫 (二). *Kokka* 国華 624 (November 1942): 345–50.

———. "Nanga to Bunjinga 3" 南畫と文人畫 (三). *Kokka* 国華 625 (December 1942): 376–81.

———. "Nanga to Bunjinga 4" 南畫と文人畫 (四). *Kokka* 国華 626 (January 1943): 27–32.

Uchiyama Takeo 内山武夫. *Genshoku gendai nihon no bijutsu 3: Kyōto gadan* 原色現代日本の美術 3：京都画壇. Tokyo: Shōgakukan 小学館, 1978.

Wong, Aida Yuen. *Parting the Mists: Discovering Japan and the Rise of National-Style Painting in Modern China.* Honolulu: University of Hawaii Press, 2006.

Yui Kazuto 油井一人. *Nijū seiiki bukko nihongaka jiten* 20世紀物故日本画家事典. Tokyo: Bijutsu Nenkansha 美術年鑑社, 1998.

Zhuanke zidian 篆刻字典. 2 vols. Taipei: Meishuwu 美術屋, n.d.

Index

Italicized page references indicate figures and photographs. Boldface page references indicate catalogue illustrations.